MICROSOFT C

Secrets, Shortcuts, and Solutions

MICROSOFT C

Secrets, Shortcuts, and Solutions

Microsoft
PRESS

K R I S   J A M S A

PUBLISHED BY
Microsoft Press
A Division of Microsoft Corporation
One Microsoft Way
Redmond, Washington 98052-6399

Library of Congress Cataloging in Publication Data
Jamsa, Kris A., 1960–
Microsoft C : secrets, shortcuts, and solutions.
        p.   cm.
Includes index.
1. C (Computer program language)   2. Microsoft C (Computer
program)   I. Title.
QA76.73.C15J355   1989   005.13'3--dc20   89-3430
ISBN 1-55615-203-5   CIP

Printed and bound in the United States of America.

3 4 5 6 7 8 9   FGFG   5 4 3 2 1

Distributed to the book trade in Canada by Macmillan of Canada,
a division of Canada Publishing Corporation

Distributed to the book trade outside the United States and Canada by Penguin Books Ltd.

Penguin Books Ltd., Harmondsworth, Middlesex, England
Penguin Books Australia Ltd., Ringwood, Victoria, Australia
Penguin Books N.Z. Ltd., 182–190 Wairau Road, Auckland 10, New Zealand

British Cataloging-in-Publication Data available

IBM®, PC/AT®, and PS/2® are registered trademarks
of International Business Machines Corporation.
Microsoft®, MS-DOS®, and QuickC® are registered trademarks
of Microsoft Corporation.

Acquisitions Editor: Dean Holmes   **Project Editor:** Eric Stroo
Technical Editor: Mike Halvorson

To Debbie

You are the wind that gives my sail direction

CONTENTS

PART II

GETTING PAST THE BASICS

PART III
UNLEASHING
THE POTENTIAL OF C

PART IV
TURNING PROFESSIONAL

Acknowledgments

The production of a book of this magnitude requires the tireless support of a dedicated team of professionals. Microsoft Press is dedicated to providing the C programmer with the best books on Microsoft C and QuickC. Its commitment starts with the acquisitions editors who bring the book in the door. Next, the copy and technical editors use their seemingly endless supply of red markers to ensure the book's technical correctness. In their turn, word processors, proofreaders, typographers, artists, and designers pore over the manuscript. All of them unselfishly contribute their expertise to the achievement of the Microsoft Press goal.

The list of contributors to this book is too long to permit me to express my gratitude to each individual. I hope the team at Microsoft Press feels my appreciation.

PART I

BUILDING A FOUNDATION

No two C programmers have the same level of expertise, so this book starts at square one. If you are new to C or to Microsoft C, don't worry. If you do the lessons in each chapter, you'll soon find yourself writing powerful C programs. C is easy when you know the secrets.

All the programs we examine are short. Type them in and experiment. This is the key to your success.

If you are already conversant in C, read the Facts, Tips, and Traps that appear in each chapter, keeping in mind the difficulty you had learning C. I think you'll agree that the format of this book simplifies the process significantly. Remember, the purpose of Parts I and II is to arm everyone with the fundamentals. If you find nothing new in these two sections, don't worry. Parts III and IV have something for programmers at every level of expertise!

## CHAPTER 1

Creating Your First Microsoft C Program

If you are new to C or to Microsoft C, this chapter will get you up and running. In fact, in this chapter you will create and execute several programs! If you have never programmed before, don't worry. Programming in C is quite straightforward. If you are familiar with C but new to Microsoft C, simply examine the tips and traps in this chapter. In most cases, doing this will get you started in the least amount of time.

WHAT IS A PROGRAM?

A *program* is simply a list of instructions for the computer to perform. C is a programming language that you will use to express your instructions to the computer. To understand the intent of the programs in this chapter, simply begin at the top of the program (list) and work your way toward the bottom.

As the programs in this book become more complex, don't let them intimidate you. Even the most sophisticated program is simply a list of instructions for the computer to perform.

CREATING A C PROGRAM

To create a C program you must use an editor or word processor. An *editor* is a program that lets you create and change (edit) files. EDLIN, for example, is the line editor provided with DOS. If you plan to program in C extensively, I strongly recommend that you acquire a full screen editor or word processor. Developing programs requires you to modify repeatedly the files that contain your program. A good editor simplifies this process considerably.

Programmers call the instructions that constitute a program *source code*. The file that contains your source code is the *source file*. (To help you master the sometimes confusing medley of programming terms, each chapter in this book concludes with a glossary of commonly used C terms. Among the terms at the end of this chapter, you will find the italicized terms defined above — *program, source code,* and *source file.*)

■ **TRAP:** *If you use a word processor to create your C programs, don't open or save the file in document (formatted) mode.*

Many word processors embed characters in your file when you open or save the file in document mode. These characters right justify paragraphs or perform other formatting functions when you create letters or reports. In most cases, these characters do not appear on your screen. Unfortunately, the C compiler regards these characters as part of your program; always create your source files in ASCII (unformatted) mode. If you don't know how to create ASCII files, refer to the documentation for your word processor.

The purpose of the program you will create in this section is simply to display the following message on your screen:

```
First C Program
```

■ **TIP:** *Give your C program files meaningful names. Files containing C programs should have the extension* C.

Just as you assign meaningful names to your other DOS files, you should assign meaningful and descriptive names to C program files. For example, if you write a C program that processes a payroll, name it PAYROLL.C. For our first C program, we create the file FIRST.C. As you can see, this program contains only four lines:

```
main()
{
    printf("First C Program");
}
```

Let's discuss the purpose of each line. Line 1 contains

```
main()
```

Every C program begins execution at the line containing *main().*

■ **FACT:** *Every C program must have a line containing* main(). *When your C program runs, execution begins at this line.*

For each of the simple programs we create in this chapter, a single source file is adequate; but even programs that occupy multiple source files have only one line with *main()*.

■ **TRAP:** *C distinguishes between UPPERCASE and lowercase letters.*

As you enter the sample programs from this book, keep in mind that C is case sensitive. For example, if you enter *main()* as *MAIN()*, the C compiler generates an error when it examines your program.

■ **TRAP:** *The parentheses following the word* main *are mandatory.*

Later in this book you will learn how to write programs that can process command line arguments, just as the DOS COPY command allows arguments:

```
C> COPY CONFIG.SYS B:CONFIG.BAK
```
Command   Command line arguments

When you reach that point in the book (Chapter 17), you will place specific names within the parentheses that follow *main* in the source file. For now, simply keep in mind that you must include the parentheses.

Line 2 of your program contains *{* (the left brace). This character, as well as *}* (the right brace) on line 4, is a *grouping symbol*. The braces group instructions within your program. Our next program will contain several lines of instructions that are grouped by *{* and *}*.

■ **TIP:** *Most C programmers indent the lines between the left and right grouping symbols. To do so, use the Spacebar or Tab key.*

Although C does not require indention, most programmers find that it makes their code more readable. Line 3 of your program contains the following statement:

```
printf("First C Program");
```

This statement displays a short message on your screen when you run the program:

```
First C Program
```

C provides numerous facilities called *functions* that you can use within programs. Each function performs a specific task. As you might guess from its use in line 3 of your program, *printf* is a function that sends output to the screen.

■ **FACT:** *The* printf *function lets C programs display information on the screen.*

In this example, the words that appear within quotation marks are the words *printf* is to display. Chapter 2 discusses *printf* in more detail.

■ **TRAP:** *You must place a semicolon after each statement in your C program.*

Not all the lines in your program are statements; for our purposes, only the executable lines, those that direct the compiler to perform a specific action (such as writing to the screen), are statements and must end with semicolons. Note the semicolon at the end of line 3:

```
printf("First C Program");
```

Remember, the line containing *main()* specifies the name or starting location of your program, and the symbols *{* and *}* are grouping symbols. The only statement in your program is line 3, the one containing *printf.*

ARE YOU READY TO RUN?

Before you run your first program, verify that the C compiler package has been successfully installed on your system. A typical installation has a directory for each of the following — utilities, include files, library files, and source files — plus modifications to a handful of DOS environment variables. Follow the installation instructions carefully, and if you have questions, consult the documentation for your C compiler and for DOS. This book provides information you need for developing programs with version 5.1 of the Microsoft C Compiler. If you have another version of the Microsoft C Compiler, Microsoft QuickC, or another C compiler, check your documentation for specific instructions.

If you're running the Microsoft C compiler under OS/2, all the programs in this book will compile and execute as described unless they are designed to manipulate specific components of DOS (programs that include routines from dos.h, signal.h, or bios.h). The programs in Chapters 30, 32, and 33 rely heavily on components of DOS and require significant revision for use under OS/2. While it is fairly easy to modify even these sample programs so that they run under OS/2, the challenge of developing applications that take advantage of the features of OS/2 involves differences in programming strategy that are beyond the scope of this book.

When you set up environment variables used by the compiler and linker under OS/2, specify any necessary OS/2 library files (OS2.LIB, API.LIB, and so on) with your LIB environment variable and define all your environment variables in CONFIG.SYS (not in AUTOEXEC.BAT as you would for DOS).

EXECUTING YOUR FIRST PROGRAM

After you create the source file FIRST.C, you are ready to compile and link it to produce an executable program. If the process is successful, the CL command creates a file named FIRST.EXE that you can execute.

To compile and link the source file FIRST.C with the Microsoft C Compiler, type the following command at the DOS prompt:

```
C> CL FIRST.C
```

The compiler now examines your source file for errors. If errors exist, the compiler displays them on the screen. If no errors exist, CL creates the executable program FIRST.EXE and displays the following information:

```
C> CL FIRST.C
Microsoft (R) C Optimizing Compiler Version 5.10
Copyright (c) Microsoft Corp 1984, 1985, 1986, 1987, 1988.
All rights reserved.

FIRST.C

Microsoft (R) Overlay Linker  Version 3.65
Copyright (C) Microsoft Corp 1983-1988.  All rights reserved.

Object Modules [.OBJ]: FIRST.OBJ
Run File [FIRST.EXE]: FIRST.EXE /NOI
List File [NUL.MAP]: NUL
Libraries [.LIB]:

C>
```

Assuming you have no errors, you can now execute your program. At the DOS prompt, type the following command:

```
C> FIRST
```

The following phrase appears on your screen:

```
First C Program
```

See how easy it is to create an executable program from a C source file? If the compiler found errors, your disk won't contain the executable file FIRST.EXE, and you will be unable to run your program. But do not despair. The next section of this book, which takes a close look at the program development process, explains what to do.

PROGRAM DEVELOPMENT PROCESS

The program development process involves four steps:

1. Creating or editing

2. Compiling

3. Linking

4. Executing

Thus far, you created a C source file called FIRST.C, and you compiled and executed it (if it contained no errors). When you issued the CL command, you invoked the compiler to check the source file for adherence to the rules of C.

■ **FACT:** *The C compiler is a software program that ensures that your source file has not violated any of the rules of C (such as forgetting a semicolon). If the file does not contain errors, the C compiler creates an intermediate file with the extension OBJ.*

C, like any language, has a specific set of rules. You have learned, for example, that in C each statement must end with a semicolon.

■ **TRAP:** *If your program violates one of the rules of C, the C compiler generates a syntax error.*

If the C compiler finds syntax errors in your source file, it displays messages describing those errors on your screen. When this occurs, simply edit the file to correct the error. Look, for example, at the source file FIRST.C, and assume that you inadvertently used a left parenthesis rather than a left brace as the first grouping symbol:

```
main()
(
printf("First C Program");
}
```

Because the compiler expects the character / to precede any program statements, you have violated a rule of C. When you issue the CL command, the compiler displays a syntax error, as shown here:

```
C> CL FIRST.C
Microsoft (R) C Optimizing Compiler Version 5.10
Copyright (c) Microsoft Corp 1984, 1985, 1986, 1987, 1988.
All rights reserved.

FIRST.C
FIRST.C(2) : error C2059: syntax error : '('

C>
```

Before you can successfully compile this source file, you must edit it to correct the error. After you correct the error, recompile the source file to generate the OBJ (object) file.

After compilation, the CL command proceeds to the next step in the program development process: linking. The Microsoft *linker*, LINK.EXE, creates an executable file from your OBJ file. The resulting program has an EXE extension and is ready to run.

■ **FACT:** *The linker combines one or more files having the OBJ extension with specific files having the LIB extension to create your executable program.*

Later, we will examine the linker in detail. For now, simply keep in mind that linking is the third step in the program development process.

■ **FACT:** *In Microsoft C, the CL command compiles your C source file and then links the OBJ file, assuming that no syntax errors exist.*

The last step in program development, executing the program, lets you verify that the program performs as you intended. When you execute FIRST.EXE, you expect its brief message to appear on your screen.

The process we used to develop FIRST.EXE included the four steps we have discussed:

1. Creating the source file FIRST.C

2. Compiling FIRST.C to create FIRST.OBJ

3. Linking FIRST.OBJ to create FIRST.EXE

4. Executing FIRST.EXE to verify its performance

In Microsoft C the CL command performs steps 2 and 3 — compiling and linking — as shown in Figure 1-1. The CL command first invokes the C compiler to check your program's syntax and create an object file. If the compiler finds no errors, CL invokes the linker.

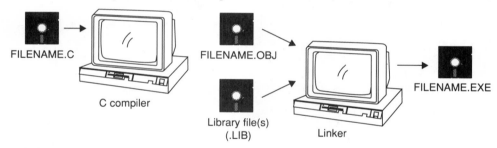

FIGURE 1-1.
Compiling and linking with Microsoft C.

```
C> CL FIRST.C
Microsoft (R) C Optimizing Compiler Version 5.10          Microsoft
Copyright (c) Microsoft Corp 1984, 1985, 1986, 1987, 1988.   C Compiler
All rights reserved.

FIRST.C

Microsoft (R) Overlay Linker   Version 3.65
Copyright (C) Microsoft Corp 1983-1988.  All rights reserved.
                                                            DOS
Object Modules [.OBJ]: FIRST.OBJ                            Linker
Run File [FIRST.EXE]: FIRST.EXE /NOI
List File [NUL.MAP]: NUL
Libraries [.LIB]:

C>
```

■ **TIP:** *To terminate the CL command, press Ctrl-C.*

If, for some reason, you need to terminate the C compilation and linking process before it finishes, simply hold down the Ctrl key and press C.

WHAT IF THE CL COMMAND FAILS?

If the CL command fails (and you are sure that your program is correct), your first step in troubleshooting should be to check the DOS *environment variables* used by the CL command. Environment variables contain system-wide aliases—definitions for often-used system values and directory locations. Common problems with environment variables used by the CL command are:

■ The *LIB=* and *INCLUDE=* environment variables are incorrect or incomplete.

■ The *TMP=* environment variable is set to an invalid drive or directory.

■ The CONFIG.SYS entry *FILES=* is set to a value less than 20.

To examine the current list of DOS environment variables, enter the DOS SET command:

```
C> SET
```

DOS will respond with a list of environment variables similar to the following:

```
COMSPEC=C:\DOS\COMMAND.COM
PATH=C:\DOS;C:\RBIN;C:\MSC;
LIB=C:\LIB;
INCLUDE=C:\INCLUDE;
INIT=C:\SOURCE\ME\INI;
TMP=C:\TEMP;
PROMPT=$P$G
```

Your DOS environment might contain more or fewer variables than those displayed, but it must contain *LIB=* and *INCLUDE=* for you to be able to compile and link C programs.

■ **TIP:** *After you determine the correct settings for your environment variables, place the corresponding SET commands in AUTOEXEC.BAT.*

To add or modify the *LIB, INCLUDE,* or *TMP* environment variable, include it in your AUTOEXEC.BAT file and restart your system. For example, to have the linker search the directories C:\LIB and C:\MYLIB for library files, include the line

```
SET LIB=C:\LIB;C:\MYLIB
```

in your AUTOEXEC.BAT file.

■ **TRAP:** *The CL command searches the DOS environment for the entries* LIB= *and* INCLUDE=. *If these entries do not exist, CL cannot complete its processing.*

The *LIB=* entry tells the CL command the location of the LIB (library) files. These files contain C functions (such as *printf*) that you need to use in your programs. The *INCLUDE=* entry specifies the location of files with the H extension—text files that the compiler uses during compilation. At a later point, each of these file types will be discussed in detail. For now, simply note that the CL command needs to know the location of both types to compile and link C programs.

The setup documentation that accompanies your C compiler tells you the correct values to assign to each of these entries.

The preceding list of environment variables includes a *TMP=* statement, which identifies a valid directory in which the compiler can create any temporary files it needs. If you omit this entry, the compiler uses the current directory.

■ **TIP:** *Many C programmers reduce compilation time by assigning* TMP= *to a directory on a RAM disk.*

As your source files get longer, you may find that setting *TMP=* to point to a RAM disk decreases the time required for compiling them. A RAM disk is a logical disk drive that resides in the computer's memory. Because the RAM disk is electronic rather than mechanical, it operates more rapidly than a floppy disk or fixed disk. Your DOS documentation explains how to create a RAM disk.

To add or modify the *FILES* environment variable, include it in your CONFIG.SYS file and restart your system. For example, to set the *FILES* environment variable to 20, include the line

```
FILES=20
```

in your CONFIG.SYS file.

■ **TRAP:** *The Microsoft C Compiler opens several files when it compiles your program. To ensure that the number of open files does not exceed the previously set (or the default) maximum, edit (or add) the* FILES= *entry in CONFIG.SYS to have a value of at least 20.*

The CONFIG.SYS entry *FILES=20* directs DOS to allow as many as 20 open files. Edit or add this entry as required—you can specify any number from 8 through 255. After you do so, restart DOS to effect the change.

Remember, each time your system starts, DOS executes the commands that reside in AUTOEXEC.BAT and CONFIG.SYS. If you define environment variables in AUTOEXEC.BAT or CONFIG.SYS, DOS recognizes the definitions each time you start your system.

LOCATING AND CORRECTING SYNTAX ERRORS

Throughout the early chapters, all the source files we examine are quite short. In most cases, locating a syntax error is straightforward. However, as the size of your files increases, so too does the difficulty of locating syntax errors.

As we discussed, if the C compiler locates syntax errors in your source file, it displays the errors on the screen.

```
C> CL FIRST.C
Microsoft (R) C Optimizing Compiler Version 5.10
Copyright (c) Microsoft Corp 1984, 1985, 1986, 1987, 1988.
All rights reserved.

FIRST.C
FIRST.C(2) : error C2059: syntax error : '('

C>
```

■ **TIP:** *To print the output of the CL command, use the DOS output redirection operator.*

When you invoke CL, you can use the DOS output redirection operator (>) to divert the output to your printer:

```
C> CL FIRST.C > PRN
```

Doing so gives you a hardcopy listing of your errors that you can read as you correct the source file.

■ **FACT:** *The /Fs switch directs CL to create a separate source listing that identifies syntax errors and provides additional program information.*

If you include the /Fs switch, as shown in the following command line, CL creates the list file FIRST.LST.

```
C> CL /Fs FIRST.C
```

If your source file contains syntax errors, FIRST.LST includes the corresponding error messages. You can print the contents of this file by using the DOS PRINT command:

```
C> PRINT FIRST.LST
```

The purpose of the list file is simply to help you locate and correct errors in your C source file. Using the list file as your guide, you can review the source code for your program, make changes to the source file, and then recompile it.

A FEW MORE EXAMPLES

To make you more comfortable with the Microsoft C Compiler, let's look at a few more C programs. Create the following file, SECOND.C:

```
main()
{
    printf("This is line one\n");
    printf("This is line two");
}
```

■ **FACT:** *The escape sequence \n directs* printf *to display a newline character (carriage return/linefeed).*

Notice the characters \n toward the end of the first *printf* statement. This series of characters is an escape sequence that causes the *printf* function to display subsequent output at the beginning of the next line on the screen. The combination of a carriage return and a linefeed is called a *newline character.*

When you compile and link the program SECOND.C, the screen shows:

```
C> CL SECOND.C
Microsoft (R) C Optimizing Compiler Version 5.10
Copyright (c) Microsoft Corp 1984, 1985, 1986, 1987, 1988.
All rights reserved.

SECOND.C

Microsoft (R) Overlay Linker  Version 3.65
Copyright (C) Microsoft Corp 1983-1988.  All rights reserved.

Object Modules [.OBJ]: SECOND.OBJ
Run File [SECOND.EXE]: SECOND.EXE /NOI
List File [NUL.MAP]: NUL
Libraries [.LIB]:

C>
```

To execute SECOND.EXE, enter the program name at the DOS prompt. The screen shows:

```
C> SECOND
This is line one
This is line two

C>
```

Had you not included the \n escape sequence, both lines of output would appear on the same line (despite the fact that the lines occur in separate *printf* statements):

```
This is line oneThis is line two
```

The escape sequence that produces a newline is one of several escape sequences that you can use with *printf.* Others are discussed in the next chapter.

For your last program, create the source file THREE.C, as follows:

```
main()
{
printf("This is line one\nThis is line two");
}
```

THIRD.C is functionally the same as SECOND.C. In this case, however, we have eliminated one *printf* statement. When the *printf* function encounters \n in the sequence of characters to display, it advances subsequent output to the beginning of the next line.

PROGRAM DEVELOPMENT PROCESS REVISITED

To simplify our discussion, we have viewed the program development cycle as a simple progression: editing, compiling, linking, and executing (as shown in Figure 1-1 on p. 9).

As you will discover, most of your time and effort will be spent testing and revising your C programs. Earlier we discussed syntax errors, which are the first type of error that your program can experience. After you remove any syntax errors in your program, you might also face *logical errors.* Logical errors are bugs. They prevent your program from executing as you intended. For example, your program might compile successfully but not display the output on two lines:

```
main()
{
printf("This is line oneThis is line two");
}
```

You must edit the file to include the \n control sequence. After you do so, you must recompile the program. Thus, extending the development process involves a repetition of the initial series of steps, as shown in Figure 1-2.

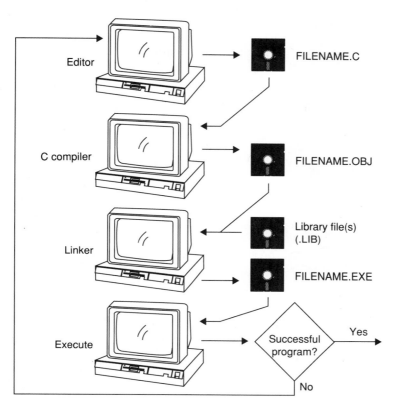

FIGURE 1-2.
The complete development process.

SUMMARY

Creating a C Program

■ **TRAP:** *If you use a word processor to create your C programs, don't open or save the file in document (formatted) mode.*

■ **TIP:** *Give your C program files meaningful names. Files containing C programs should have the extension* C.

■ **FACT:** *Every C program must have a line containing* main(). *When your C program runs, execution begins at this line.*

■ **TRAP:** *C distinguishes between UPPERCASE and lowercase letters.*

■ **TRAP:** *The parentheses following the word* main *are mandatory.*

■ **TIP:** *Most C programmers indent the lines between the left and right grouping symbols. To do so, use the Spacebar or Tab key.*

■ **FACT:** *The* printf *function lets C programs display information on the screen.*

■ **TRAP:** *You must place a semicolon after each statement in your C program.*

Program Development Process

■ **FACT:** *The C compiler is a software program that ensures that your source file has not violated any of the rules of C (such as forgetting a semicolon). If the file does not contain errors, the C compiler creates an intermediate file with the extension OBJ.*

■ **TRAP:** *If your program violates one of the rules of C, the C compiler generates a syntax error.*

■ **FACT:** *The linker combines one or more files having the OBJ extension with specific files having the LIB extension to create your executable program.*

■ **FACT:** *In Microsoft C, the CL command compiles your C source file and then links the OBJ file, assuming that no syntax errors exist.*

■ **TIP:** *To terminate the CL command, press Ctrl-C.*

What If the CL Command Fails?

■ **TIP:** *After you determine the correct settings for your environment variables, place the corresponding SET commands in AUTOEXEC.BAT.*

■ **TRAP:** *The CL command searches the DOS environment for the entries* LIB= *and* INCLUDE=. *If these entries do not exist, CL cannot complete its processing.*

■ **TIP:** *Many C programmers reduce compilation time by assigning* TMP= *to a directory on a RAM disk.*

■ **TRAP:** *The Microsoft C Compiler opens several files when it compiles your program. To ensure that the number of open files does not exceed the previously set (or the default) maximum, edit (or add) the* FILES= *entry in CONFIG.SYS to have a value of at least 20.*

Locating and Correcting Syntax Errors

■ **TIP:** *To print the output of the CL command, use the DOS output redirection operator.*

■ **FACT:** *The /Fs switch directs CL to create a separate source listing that identifies syntax errors and provides additional program information.*

A Few More Examples

■ **FACT:** *The escape sequence \n directs* printf *to display a newline character (carriage return/linefeed).*

GLOSSARY

C compiler A software program that examines your C program for syntax errors and, if successful, creates an object (OBJ) file.

editor A program that allows you to create or change a file.

environment variables Names defined system-wide that specify often-used values or directory locations.

function A block of code with a unique name that is called from within a program to carry out a specific task.

grouping symbols The characters { and } that let you group a related set of instructions.

linker A software program that combines object (OBJ) and library (LIB) files to create an executable program that has the extension EXE.

logical error An error that occurs when your program doesn't perform as you intended. Logical errors are also known as bugs.

newline character A combination of a carriage return and a linefeed that causes subsequent output to begin on the next line. The escape sequence for a newline character in the C programming language is \n.

object file A machine code file produced by compilation of source code.

program A list of instructions for the computer to perform. C programmers refer to these instructions as source code. Programs are also known as software.

source code The processing instructions that are written in a given computer language and that collectively constitute a source file.

source file A text file that contains a program. C source files have the extension C— for example, FILENAME.C.

syntax error An error that occurs when you violate one of the rules of C, such as forgetting a semicolon or a grouping symbol.

## CHAPTER 2

Getting Started with *printf*

In Chapter 1 you created several simple C programs that used *printf* to display messages on your screen. C provides the *printf* function to simplify the task of processing your program's output. So far, you have used *printf* only to display a string of alphabetic characters on the screen:

```
printf("First C Program");
```

In the preceding statement, the entire *control string,* the characters enclosed by quotation marks, consists of alphabetic characters that you want to appear in the displayed message. The same is true of all the *printf* examples in Chapter 1, with the exception in some control strings of the newline escape sequence, \n, which does not literally appear in your message.

The *printf* function also displays punctuation, whole numbers, numbers with decimal points, and even values in exponential notation (1.7e+02). C also supports escape sequences other than the \n (such as \t, which produces a horizontal tab).

To demonstrate the concepts explained in this book, the sample programs display results on the screen, and thus the presentation relies heavily on *printf.* This chapter provides a foundation for understanding and using *printf.* All the programs in this chapter are short. Execute them! The best way to understand *printf* is to experiment with it.

USING ESCAPE SEQUENCES

As you learned in Chapter 1, the \n escape sequence directs *printf* to "display" a newline, which causes subsequent output to begin at the first column of the next row.

C supports the following escape sequences:

Escape Sequence	Result
\a	Bell character
\b	Backspace character
\f	Formfeed character
\n	Newline character
\r	Carriage return character
\t	Horizontal tab character
\v	Vertical tab character
\\	Backslash character
\'	Single quote character
\"	Double quote character
\?	Question mark character
\nnn	Octal ASCII value
\xnnn	Hexadecimal ASCII value

The following program (NEWLINE.C) uses the newline character, produced by \n, to display the letters A, B, and C on three separate lines:

```
main()
{
    printf("A\nB\nC");
}
```

When you execute the program, your screen shows

```
A
B
C
```

■ **FACT:** *The \t escape sequence directs* printf *to resume output at the next tab stop.*

Now, modify NEWLINE.C slightly and name it TAB.C, using \t (horizontal tab) rather than a newline character to separate the letters, as follows:

```
main()
{
    printf("A\tB\tC");
}
```

When you compile and run the program again, your screen shows

```
A     B     C
```

■ **TRAP:** *Although C provides the vertical tab escape sequence, \v, few personal computer display devices support it.*

In addition to the horizontal tab, C provides a vertical tab escape sequence, \v. For the most part, this is a relic of earlier days of computing when output devices such as terminals and printers were mainstay display devices.

The popular personal computer display devices today (the IBM CGA, IBM EGA, and IBM VGA) display decimal ASCII character 11 (σ) when they encounter the \v escape sequence.

■ **FACT:** *The carriage return escape sequence, \r, directs* printf *to begin subsequent output at column 1 of the current line.*

Whereas the newline character directs *printf* to start subsequent output at the first column of the *next* line, the carriage return escape sequence, \r, causes output to resume at the first column of the *current* line. In the following program (CRTEST.C), for example, *printf* encounters the carriage return escape sequence, after which output resumes at column 1 of the current line. As a result, the third letter, *C*, overwrites the first letter, *A*.

```
main()
{
    printf("AB\rC");
}
```

When you execute the program, the display shows only the letters *CB*.

In a similar manner, the backspace escape sequence, \b, directs *printf* to continue subsequent output at the previous character position. The following program (BACK.C) also displays the letters *CB*:

```
main()
{
    printf("AB\b\bC");
}
```

When *printf* encounters the two backspace escape sequences, it writes subsequent output two character positions back. The backspace sequence does not erase the previous character.

■ **TIP:** *The carriage return and backspace escape sequences are convenient when you need to overwrite a portion of the current line based upon a user response.*

■ **FACT:** *The formfeed escape sequence, \f, directs the printer to resume output on the next sheet of paper.*

As a final escape sequence for positioning output, C provides the formfeed sequence, \f. Consider, for example, the program FORMFEED.C:

```
main()
{
    printf("Page 1\fPage 2\fPage 3");
}
```

After you run and compile the program, you can redirect its output to your printer with the following command:

```
C> FORMFEED > PRN
```

Your printer will then print three pages numbered *Page 1*, *Page 2*, and *Page 3*.

■ **FACT:** *The \a escape sequence directs* printf *to sound your computer's built-in bell.*

Many applications sound a bell or alarm to notify the user of a specific event. The following program (3BELL.C), for example, displays the word *Bell* three times and emits a tone from your computer's speaker each time.

```
main()
{
    printf("Bell\aBell\aBell\a");
}
```

■ **TIP:** *The C compiler allows you to place multiple escape sequences in the same control string.*

The following C program (3BELLTAB.C), for example, sounds the computer's bell three times and displays the word *Bell* at each of three tab stops.

```
main()
{
    printf("Bell\a\tBell\a\tBell\a");
}
```

Now try a few experiments with these escape sequences; place several in succession, such as \n\t\aBell. As you will find, the compiler lets you scatter escape sequences throughout the text to be displayed.

■ **TRAP:** *If the letter following a backslash does not form a valid escape sequence, the compiler ignores the slash and displays the letter that follows it.*

Each time the compiler encounters a backslash (\) in the sequence of characters, it tests for an escape sequence. In the following program (BACKONLY.C), *printf* ignores the backslash characters and simply displays the letters *ABC*.

```
main()
{
    printf("\A\B\C");
}
```

Notice C's case sensitivity. The compiler does not equate \A and \B in the control string with valid escape sequences \a and \b, so it ignores the backslash characters.

■ **FACT:** *To have* printf *display a backslash character (\), you must use the double backslash escape sequence, \\.*

Because *printf* treats a single backslash as the beginning of an escape sequence, a series of two backslashes is necessary to print a single backslash character. The following program (TWOBACK.C), for example, displays the name of a DOS subdirectory:

```
main()
{
    printf("DOS commands reside in C:\\DOS");
}
```

When you run the program, the screen displays

```
DOS commands reside in C:\DOS
```

The escape sequences \?, \', and \" work in the same manner. When *printf* encounters the backslash, it prints the character that follows. Of the three, the \" escape sequence deserves additional discussion.

As you have seen, *printf* displays the characters contained between opening and closing quotation marks. To distinguish quotation marks that are to be printed from those that open and close the control string, C provides the \" escape sequence. For example, the following program (QUOTE.C) displays the message *"Watch out!" yelled Bill*:

```
main()
{
    printf("\"Watch out!\" yelled Bill");
}
```

If you don't use the \" escape sequence, the compiler generates a syntax error:

```
error C2146: syntax error : missing ')' before identifier 'Watch'
```

■ **TIP:** *To print a string of characters that contains quotation marks, you must use \".*

■ **FACT:** *The escape sequences \nnn and \xnnn direct* printf *to display an octal or a hexa-decimal value.*

   Octal is the base 8 numbering system; hexadecimal is base 16. Computer programmers use octal and hexadecimal values to represent values not easily expressed in decimal. To compare octal, decimal, and hexadecimal values, examine the chart in Appendix A. Although these two escape sequences aren't as commonly used as many others, you will have some fun using them with the ANSI driver in the next section.

EXPERIMENTING WITH THE ANSI DRIVER

Under DOS, the ANSI.SYS *device driver* provides expanded screen and keyboard capabilities. To install the ANSI driver, you must place the following entry in the CONFIG.SYS file:

```
DEVICE=pathname\ANSI.SYS
```

where *pathname* specifies the location of the file ANSI.SYS. After you change CONFIG.SYS, you must restart DOS for the change to take effect.

■ **FACT:** *Once installed, the ANSI.SYS device driver increases your keyboard and screen capabilities.*

   To perform various tasks with the ANSI driver, you need to use specific escape sequences. Each ANSI escape sequence starts with the ASCII escape character (*Esc*), which is equivalent to decimal 27, octal 33, or hexadecimal 1B.
   To clear your screen, for example, use the following ANSI escape sequence:

```
Esc[2J
```

■ **TIP:** *The escape sequence \033 is equivalent to the escape character.*

   C compilers generally fail to provide a means of clearing the screen. The ANSI escape sequence for doing so is therefore often convenient to use. For example, create the program CLEAR.C, which clears your screen:

```
main()
{
    printf("\033[2J");
}
```

The program uses the escape sequence \033 to represent the escape character. When you execute CLEAR.EXE, your screen clears. If it does not, be sure that you have correctly installed the ANSI driver and that you typed an uppercase J rather than a lowercase j—case is significant in ANSI escape sequences.

■ **TIP:** *Case is significant in ANSI escape sequences.*

■ **TIP:** *Octal values are the default for an escape sequence composed of a backslash followed by an integer value. The escape sequences \033 and \33 are thus identical; both result in an octal 33.*

Try substituting the equivalent values \33 or \x1B (hexadecimal) for \033 in CLEAR.C. In either case, when you recompile and run the program, the result is the same as that of the original.

You can also use the ANSI driver to set the foreground and background colors of your screen. The following program (REDBACK.C), for example, sets your screen's background color to red (assuming that your system is capable of displaying color).

```
main()
{
    printf("\033[41m");
}
```

The lowercase *m* in the ANSI escape sequence tells the ANSI driver that the preceding number is a color choice for the video display; the number *41* selects red. To restore the screen background color to black, use the value 40 instead of 41.

The ANSI driver supports several foreground and background colors, as illustrated in the following tables:

Value	Foreground Color
30	Black
31	Red
32	Green
33	Orange
34	Blue
35	Magenta
36	Cyan
37	White

Value	Background Color
40	Black
41	Red
42	Green
43	Orange
44	Blue
45	Magenta
46	Cyan
47	White

You can have a great deal of fun with *printf* and the escape sequences. For example, the following program (FLAG.C) displays the words *RED*, *WHITE*, and *BLUE* in their corresponding foreground colors:

```
main()
{
    printf("\033[31mRED\033[37mWHITE\033[34mBLUE\033[37m");
}
```

The program simply selects the desired foreground color before displaying each word and then resets the foreground color to white.

In addition to clearing your screen and setting screen colors, the ANSI device driver provides the following capabilities:

Escape Sequence	Function	Example
Esc[#;#H	Set cursor row/column	printf("\033[1;2H");
Esc[#A	Move cursor up # rows	printf("\033[5A");
Esc[#B	Move cursor down # rows	printf("\033[5B");
Esc[#C	Move cursor right # columns	printf("\033[2C");
Esc[#D	Move cursor left # columns	printf("\033[4D");
Esc[s	Save current cursor position	printf("\033[s");
Esc[u	Restore previous cursor position	printf("\033[u");
Esc[2J	Clear screen display	printf("\033[2J");
Esc[K	Clear to end of current line	printf("\033[K");
Esc[#m	Set background/foreground color	printf("\033[41m");
Esc[#;#;"*text*";13p	Define key	printf("\033[0;68;\"DIR\";13p");

We cannot investigate the ANSI.SYS driver in detail; it was discussed here so that you would better understand the octal character escape sequence \ *nnn*. You can see, however, the considerable flexibility that ANSI.SYS provides.

USING FORMAT SPECIFIERS WITH *printf*

The *printf* function has many capabilities that you have not yet seen. These capabilities enable it to recognize another special type of sequence within the control string, *format specifiers*. These character sequences, which begin with a percent sign (%), give you considerable control over the appearance of text output with *printf.*

■ **FACT:** *The %d format specifier directs* printf *to display a decimal value.*

Consider the following C program DECIMAL.C:

```
main()
{
    printf("This is Chapter %d", 2);
}
```

This program displays the message

```
This is Chapter 2
```

The %d in the control string tells *printf* to display a whole number at the position currently occupied by the format specifier. When *printf* encounters %d, it displays as a decimal the first unused value to right of the quotation marks. In this case, that value is 2. Notice that the value 2 is separated from the control string by a comma.

The following program (EQUATION.C) displays the equation $3 + 4 = 7$:

```
main()
{
    printf("%d + %d = %d", 3, 4, 3 + 4);
}
```

When you run the program, the screen shows

```
3 + 4 = 7
```

Let's look at the program in detail. First, note that the plus sign and the equal sign in the control string are merely characters that *printf* is to display; they do not perform mathematical operations. They are present in the control string only to make the output meaningful.

Next, observe that *printf* can assign not only values but results of operations to the format specifier, as shown in Figure 2-1. Given a compound expression, the function first evaluates it and then displays the result.

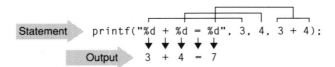

Figure 2-1.
The output of a printf *statement can include literal characters and replacements for format specifiers. The replacement might be a simple substitution or the result of a calculation.*

■ **TIP:** *Many C compilers support %d and %i interchangeably. For consistency, most programmers use %d. Both format specifiers equate a value with a decimal whole number.*

The following program (INTEGER.C) illustrates the use of %i as a format specifier for an integer:

```
main()
{
    printf("%d = %i", 3, 3);
}
```

A floating point value is one that contains a decimal point, for example, 5.1. You cannot use the %d (or %i) format specifier to display floating point values; use it only for integer (whole number) values.

■ **TRAP:** *If you use %d with a floating point value,* printf *displays an incorrect result.*

Using %d with a floating point value is a common error, yet a difficult one to detect. The following program (FLOATERR.C) illustrates this error:

```
main()
{
    printf("The value %d is a floating point number.", 3.3);
}
```

■ **FACT:** *The %f format specifier directs* printf *to display a floating point value.*

To correct this error, replace the format specifier %d with %f, which is appropriate for displaying a floating point value. Name the corrected program FLOAT.C.

```
main()
{
    printf("The value %f is a floating point number.", 3.3);
}
```

When you run FLOAT.C you get the following output:

```
The value 3.300000 is a floating point number.
```

The floating point value is displayed with 7 significant digits. The following program (FLOATSUM.C) displays the sum of two floating point values:

```
main()
{
    printf("%f + %f = %f", 3.3, 4.4, 3.3 + 4.4);
}
```

When you run the program, the screen shows

```
3.300000 + 4.400000 = 7.700000
```

Later in this chapter you will learn how to improve the format of your output by specifying the exact number of digits that you want *printf* to display.

■ **FACT:** *The %e and %E format specifiers direct* printf, *to display a value in exponential notation. The %e specifier displays the letter* e *in lowercase, for example, 5.273e+002. The %E specifier displays the letter* E *in uppercase, for example, 5.273E+002.*

The following program (EXPONENT.C) uses the format specifiers %e and %E to display numbers in exponential (scientific) notation:

```
main()
{
    printf("%e + %e = %E", 8.20e+002, 3.36e+005, 8.20e+002 + 3.36e+005);
}
```

When you run the program, the screen shows

```
8.200000e+002 + 3.360000e+005 = 3.368200E+005
```

The output of the program demonstrates the difference between the %e and %E format specifiers: If you use %e with *printf*, the resulting notation uses lowercase e, whereas %E yields notation with uppercase E.

The C compiler lets you express numbers in exponential notation in various ways. You can express the number 336,000 either as 3.36e+005 or as 3.36e005. The compiler assumes that the exponent is positive if you omit the sign. The compiler also lets you omit leading zeros from the exponent, 3.36e5.

■ **FACT:** *The %g and %G formats yield either floating point or exponential notation, based on the precision of the value to be displayed. When you use the %g format specifier, printf uses exponential notation (%e) if the exponent is less than −4 or if the precision of the value is greater than or equal to the floating point precision; otherwise, it uses floating point notation.*

Floating point precision specifies the accuracy with which a value is represented. Microsoft C provides about seven digits of accuracy for standard floating point values.

The following program (EXPTEST.C) displays the first value as a floating point value; it displays the second and third values in exponential notation:

```
main()
{
    printf("%g %g %G", 5.2e2, 0.00005, 5.01e-6);
}
```

When you run the program, the screen shows

```
520 5e-005 5.01E-006
```

In the first case, *printf* displays the value using %f. The second value (0.00005, or 5e−005), however, has an exponent that is less than −4; *printf* therefore uses the exponential notation format %e. The third value, like the second, has an exponent that is less than −4; *printf* uses the %E format in that case because the control string contains %G. The difference between %g and %G is simply the case of the letter *e* when the output uses exponential notation. Most programmers rarely use either %g or %G, however.

■ **FACT:** *The %o format specifier directs* printf *to display a value in octal.*

The following program (OCTAL.C) prints the value 10 twice, first in decimal, and then in octal:

```
main()
{
    printf("10 decimal appears as the number %d\n", 10);
    printf("10 decimal appears in octal as %o\n", 10);
}
```

When you run the program, the screen shows

```
10 decimal appears as the number 10
10 decimal appears in octal as 12
```

As mentioned earlier, the ASCII and IBM extended character sets in Appendix A show the different octal, decimal, and hexadecimal values.

■ **FACT:** *The %x and %X format specifiers direct* printf *to display a value in hexadecimal.*

Hexadecimal, the base 16 numbering system, uses as digits the numbers 0–9 and the letters A–F. The following program (HEX.C) uses the format specifiers %d, %x, and %X to display the value 255 in decimal and hexadecimal:

```
main()
{
    printf("%d %x %X", 255, 255, 255);
}
```

When you run the program, the screen shows

```
255 ff FF
```

The difference between using %x and %X is the case of the alphabetic digits in the output. If you use %x, *printf* displays the letters a through f in lowercase. If you use %X, these letters appear in uppercase.

■ **TRAP:** *When* printf *encounters a percent sign (%), it examines the character or characters that follow. If the sequence does not form a valid format specifier,* printf *ignores the percent sign and displays the letter.*

To display a percent sign, you must place double percent signs in your *printf* control string. The PERCENT.C sample program shows this in action:

```
main()
{
    printf("Use two percent signs to display a single %%");
}
```

Later in this book we will examine additional format specifiers. For now, the table in Figure 2-2 summarizes the *printf* specifiers.

Format Specifier	*Value Type*
%d	Integer value in decimal
%i	Integer value in decimal
%o	Integer value in octal
%x or %X	Integer value in hexadecimal
%f	Floating point value
%e or %E	Floating point value in exponential notation

FIGURE 2-2. *(continued)*
Format specifiers commonly used with printf.

FIGURE 2-2. *continued*

Format Specifier	Value Type
%g or %G	Floating point value in %f format or in exponential notation
%u	Unsigned integer in decimal
%c	Character in ASCII format
%s	Null-terminated string of characters
%p	Pointer value in implementation-dependent format
%n	Places into a variable the number of characters already written by *printf*
%%	Displays the percent sign character

USING WIDTH AND PRECISION SPECIFIERS

In many cases, you will want your programs to display output in a specific format. This might mean specifying a minimum field width for displaying a value. The following program (FIELD.C) illustrates a technique for doing so:

```
main()
{
    printf("%d%2d%3d", 7, 8, 9);
}
```

The values that appear between the percent sign and the letter *d* specify a minimum width of the output field. By default, *printf* uses the exact number of characters required to display the value. If you include a minimum width, *printf* precedes the value with a sufficient number of blank spaces to fill the field. When you run FIELD, the screen shows the value 8 preceded by one space and the value 9 preceded by two spaces (see Figure 2-3).

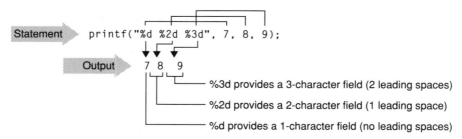

FIGURE 2-3.
When you specify a minimum width using %d, printf *displays spaces preceding the output value to fill the specified minimum.*

■ **TRAP:** *If* printf *requires more characters to display a value than are specified for the minimum width, the function uses the additional space.*

Remember, the minimum width specifies the least number of characters *printf* can use to display a value. The function exceeds the defined width if the output value contains more than the minimum number of characters. The *printf* function does not let you define a maximum width for the output field.

■ **TIP:** *Regardless of the type of value you are displaying,* printf *lets you specify a minimum width for the value.*

The minimum width field works for floating point values just as it does for integers. The following program (FIELD2.C), for example, directs *printf* to display two values consecutively, first as it would by default, and then with a minimum field width of 16 for each value.

```
main()
{
    printf("%f%f\n", 535.45, 73745.66);
    printf("%16f%16f", 535.45, 73745.66);
}
```

When you run the program, the screen shows

```
535.45000073745.660000
       535.450000       73745.660000
```

■ **FACT:** *For floating point values, the* printf *function recognizes an optional precision value, which specifies the number of digits to be displayed at the right of the decimal point. A period must separate the minimum field width from the precision value.*

The field width indicates the total number of character spaces the value will occupy (at a minimum). Another *printf* option lets you specify the precision of a floating point number—the number of digits displayed to the right of the decimal point. As the following program (FIELD3.C) demonstrates, you need to separate the field width from the precision field with a period (*width.precision*).

```
main()
{
    printf("%6.2f %6.4f %8.4f", 12.3456, 12.345, 12.3456);
}
```

When you run the program, the screen shows

```
 12.35 12.3450   12.3456
```

The *printf* function displays two digits after the decimal point for the first value, four digits after the decimal point for the second value, and four digits for the third. The function rounds the output value or adds trailing zeros as necessary. The following table compares the specifiers to the output:

Value	Specifier	Output	Notes
12.3456	%6.2f	12.35	Value rounded to leave two characters after the decimal. Leading space to achieve field width. (Decimal point is one character wide.)
12.345	%6.4f	12.3450	Zero appended to fulfill precision of 4. Minimum field width exceeded.
12.3456	%8.4f	12.3456	Leading space to achieve minimum field width.

When you use %d to display an integer, a precision specifier indicates the minimum number of digits the output will contain.

■ **TIP:** *If an integer has fewer digits than the precision value specified with %d,* printf *precedes the value with zeros as needed.*

The following program (FIELD4.C) illustrates the use of a precision value with a %d format specifier:

```
main()
{
    printf("%5.3d %5.5d", 2, 2);
}
```

When you run the program, the screen shows

```
002 00002
```

The following table illustrates the effect of indicating precision in the %d format specifier.

Value	Specifier	Output	Notes
5	%3.3d	005	Two leading zeros to indicate precision of at least three digits.
5	%3.2d	05	Leading space to fill field; leading zero to indicate precision of at least two digits.
555	%3.3d	555	Value contains minimum number of digits.
555	%7.5d	00555	Two leading spaces to attain field width; two leading zeros to indicate precision of at least five digits.

■ **FACT:** *By default,* printf *displays the sign of a value only when the value is negative.*

The following program (NEGVALS.C) displays two negative values; *printf* precedes each one with a minus sign:

```
main()
{
    printf("%d %f", -5, -63.32);
}
```

When you run the program, the screen shows

```
-5 -63.320000
```

■ **TIP:** *If you want* printf *to display the plus sign for positive values, use a plus sign in the format specifier.*

Placing a plus sign (+) in the format specifier directs *printf* to display the sign of the value, regardless of whether the value is positive or negative. The following program (SHOWSIGN.C) displays both a positive value and a negative value and indicates the sign of each value:

```
main()
{
    printf("%+d %+d", 3 + 4, 3 - 4);
}
```

When you run the program, the screen shows

```
+7 -1
```

■ **FACT:** *Placing a 0 in the format specifier directs* printf *to pad a value with zeros to achieve the minimum width.*

Rather than displaying the value 3 in a 4-character field with three blanks preceding it, you can cause *printf* to display *0003*. The following program (ZEROPAD.C) demonstrates the use of a 0 in the format specifier to pad a value with zeros:

```
main()
{
    printf("%04d %03d", 3, 23);
}
```

When you run the program, the screen shows

```
0003 023
```

■ **FACT:** *A minus sign (–) in the format specifier directs* printf *to display the value left justified.*

So far all the values you have displayed with *printf* have been right justified. This means that *printf* placed any "filler" spaces (or zeros) at the front of the value. As the following program (LEFTJUST.C) demonstrates, placing a minus sign in the format specifier causes *printf* to put the blanks at the end of the value:

```
main()
{
    printf("The total cost is $%-5.2f", 6.72);
}
```

When you run the program, the screen shows

```
The total cost is $6.72
```

■ **FACT:** *Using a # with either %x or %o directs* printf *to display a hexadecimal value with a leading* 0x *or an octal value with a leading* 0.

The *printf* function also lets you display octal values preceded by 0 and hexadecimal values preceded by 0x. To do so, insert a pound sign (#) in the appropriate format specifier. (The # is valid only for octal and hexadecimal numbers.)

The following program (POUND.C) demonstrates the use of # with hexadecimal (%x) and octal (%o) format specifiers:

```
main()
{
    printf("%#x %#o", 255, 10);
}
```

When you run the program, the screen shows

```
0xff 012
```

■ **TIP:** *The* printf *function lets you combine several of the format characters (–, +, 0, #) in the same format specifier.*

The following program (COMBO.C) displays three values. The first is a hexadecimal value padded on the left with zeros and preceded by the letters 0x. The second is a left justified hexadecimal value preceded by the letters 0x. The third value is a left justified integer, complete with its sign.

```
main()
{
    printf("%#04x\n%-#04x\n%+-4d", 255, 255, 3);
}
```

When you run the program, the screen shows

```
0x00ff
0xff
+3
```

The first example demonstrates what happens when you use # and 0 with a specific field width. The output value is padded with zeros to achieve the minimum field width, and the 0x lies outside the field. The second example shows what happens when you combine the – character with 0. The *printf* function left justifies the output, so no zeros are used as padding. Finally, the third example combines + with – to left justify a signed number.

The *printf* function is one of the most powerful functions you will use on a regular basis. You will continue to learn about the capabilities of *printf* as you proceed through this book.

SUMMARY

Using Escape Sequences

■ **FACT:** *The \t escape sequence directs* printf *to begin subsequent output at the next tab stop.*

■ **TRAP:** *Although C provides the vertical tab escape sequence, \v, few personal computer display devices support it.*

■ **FACT:** *The carriage return escape sequence, \r, directs* printf *to begin subsequent output at column 1 of the current line.*

■ **TIP:** *The carriage return and backspace escape sequences are convenient when you need to overwrite a portion of the current line based upon a user response.*

■ **FACT:** *The formfeed escape sequence, \f, directs the printer to resume output on the next sheet of paper.*

■ **FACT:** *The \a escape sequence directs* printf *to sound your computer's built-in bell.*

■ **TIP:** *The C compiler allows you to place multiple escape sequences in the same control string.*

■ **TRAP:** *If the letter following a backslash does not form a valid escape sequence, the compiler ignores the slash and displays the letter that follows it.*

■ **FACT:** *To have* printf *display a backslash character (\), you must use the double backslash escape sequence, \\.*

■ **TIP:** *To print a string of characters that contains embedded double quotes, you must use \".*

■ **FACT:** *The escape sequences \nnn and \xnnn direct* printf *to display an octal or a hexadecimal value.*

Experimenting with the ANSI Driver

■ **FACT:** *Once installed, the ANSI.SYS device driver increases your keyboard and screen capabilities.*

■ **TIP:** *The escape sequence \033 is equivalent to the escape character.*

■ **TIP:** *Case is significant in ANSI escape sequences.*

■ **TIP:** *Octal values are the default for an escape sequence composed of a backslash followed by an integer value. The escape sequences \033 and \33 are thus identical; both result in an octal 33.*

Using Format Specifiers with *printf*

■ **FACT:** *The %d format specifier directs* printf *to display a decimal value.*

■ **TIP:** *Many C compilers support %d and %i interchangeably. For consistency, most programmers use %d. Both format specifiers equate a value with a decimal whole number.*

■ **TRAP:** *If you use %d with a floating point value,* printf *displays an incorrect result.*

■ **FACT:** *The %f format specifier directs* printf *to display a floating point value.*

■ **FACT:** *The %e and %E format specifiers direct* printf *to display a value in exponential notation. The %e specifier displays the letter* e *in lowercase, for example, 5.273e+002. The %E specifier displays the letter* e *in uppercase, for example, 5.273E+002.*

■ **FACT:** *The %g and %G formats yield either floating point or exponential notation, based on the precision of the value to be displayed. When you use the %g format specifier,* printf *uses exponential notation (%e) if the exponent is less than −4 or if the precision of the value is greater than or equal to the floating point precision; otherwise, it uses floating point notation.*

■ **FACT:** *The %o format specifier directs* printf *to display a value in octal.*

■ **FACT:** *The %x and %X format specifiers direct* printf *to display a value in hexadecimal.*

■ **TRAP:** *When* printf *encounters a percent sign (%), it examines the character or characters that follow. If the sequence does not form a valid format specifier,* printf *ignores the percent sign and displays the letter.*

Using Width and Precision Specifiers

■ **TRAP:** *If* printf *requires more characters to display a value than are specified for the minimum width, the function uses the additional space.*

■ **TIP:** *Regardless of the type of value you are displaying,* printf *lets you specify a minimum width for the value.*

■ **FACT:** *For floating point values, the* printf *function recognizes an optional precision value, which specifies the number of digits to be displayed at the right of the decimal point. A period must separate the field width from the precision value.*

■ **TIP:** *If an integer has fewer digits than the precision specified with %d,* printf *precedes the value with zeros as needed.*

■ **FACT:** *By default,* printf *displays the sign of a value only when the value is negative.*

■ **TIP:** *If you want* printf *to display the plus sign for positive values, use a plus sign in the format specifier.*

■ **FACT:** *Placing a 0 in the format specifier directs* printf *to pad a value with zeros to achieve the minimum width.*

■ **FACT:** *A minus sign (–) in the format specifier directs* printf *to display the value left justified.*

■ **FACT:** *Using a # with either %x or %o directs* printf *to display a hexadecimal value with a leading 0x or an octal value with a leading 0.*

■ **TIP:** *The* printf *function lets you combine several of the format characters (–, +, 0, #) in the same format specifier.*

GLOSSARY

control string The series of characters in double quotation marks that follows the *printf* function name. The control string includes literal characters to write as well as characters that tell the function how to format your output. The characters "Find the sum of %d and %6f \n" are an example of a *printf* control sequence.

device driver A program that the operating system uses to communicate with a device. The ANSI.SYS device driver expands the capabilities of your screen and keyboard.

escape sequence A series of characters, beginning with the ASCII escape character (decimal 27), used to manipulate the display or keyboard. The *printf* function uses the escape sequence \t to indicate a tab. The ANSI.SYS device driver uses *Esc*[2J to clear your screen.

## CHAPTER 3

Variables, Types, and Operators

All the programs we examined in Chapters 1 and 2 used numeric constants, such as 5, 10, or 32.5. These values are called constants because they do not change. In addition to using constants, C programs must also store objects whose values can change during the execution of a program. The compiler places these values in memory as *variables*.

Variables enable a program to perform useful work. A variable is nothing more than a storage facility that holds values in a specific format, such as integer or floating point format. As your program executes, values can be stored as variables at particular locations in your computer's memory. Rather than referring to specific memory locations, your C programs can refer to the variable name. While the program executes, the value a variable contains may or may not change, as your programming needs require.

GETTING STARTED WITH C VARIABLES

The following C program (SUM.C) creates a variable called *sum* and assigns it the sum of the values 3 and 5. Because the variable contains only whole numbers, we declare an integer variable. C uses the type *int* to create an integer variable.

```
main()
{
    int sum;

    sum = 3 + 5;
    printf("Sum = %d", sum);
}
```

■ **FACT:** *A variable's type specifies the kind of values the variable can store, as well as the set of operations that can be applied to the variable.*

Integer variables store whole numbers. Floating point variables store values with decimal points. You can perform mathematical operations (addition, subtraction, and so on) on variables of both types.

■ **FACT:** *C supports four basic variable types* — int, float, char, *and* double.

The following table defines each C type:

Type	Value Stored
int	Integer values from −32,768 through 32,767[†]
float	Floating point values with 6 or 7 digits of precision
char	Character values (ASCII)
double	Floating point values with 13 or 14 digits of precision

[†] Range can vary with C compiler.

■ **TIP:** *Define your variables after the opening grouping symbol ({).*

Let's examine the previous C program listing. The following line declares, or creates, an integer variable called *sum*:

```
int sum;
```

To define a variable, use the form *type variable_name* followed by a semicolon.

■ **TRAP:** *You must define a variable before you can use it. If the C compiler encounters an undefined variable name in your program, the compiler generates a syntax error.*

In Microsoft C 5.1, variables of type *int* can store values in the range −32,768 through 32,767. The statement

```
sum = 3 + 5;
```

assigns the result of the addition to the variable *sum*.

■ **FACT:** *The equal sign (=) is the C assignment operator. When the C compiler encounters this operator, it assigns the result of the expression at the right of the equal sign to the variable at the left of the equal sign.*

Following the assignment operation, the variable *sum* contains the value 8. When you run the program, the screen shows

```
Sum = 8
```

The next program (HOURS.C) defines three variables — *hours*, *days*, and *total_hours*. The program calculates and displays the total number of hours in a year.

■ **TIP:** *Most C programmers use a blank line to separate variable declarations from program statements. Because the compiler requires you to declare all your variables before you use them in program statements, the blank line provides a distinction between the two.*

```
main()
{
    int hours, days, total_hours;

    hours = 24;
    days = 365;
    total_hours = hours * days;
    printf("Total hours in a year %d", total_hours);
}
```

■ **FACT:** *If several variables are the same type, the compiler lets you define all of them on one line, separated by commas.*

The following statement defines three variables of type *int*:

```
int hours, days, total_hours;
```

Because the variable types are the same, you can place them on one line. Of course, you could also put each on a separate line:

```
int hours;
int days;
int total_hours;
```

■ **TIP:** *Use meaningful variable names. Remember, C is case sensitive. The underscore character can improve the readability of longer variable names. For example, you might use* fiscal_year *as a variable name.*

In the past, many programmers got into the habit of using short, nondescriptive variable names, such as *A*, *B*, and *C*. Later, when they (or someone else) needed to change the programs, the purpose of each variable was difficult to determine. To avoid this problem, use meaningful variable names.

Every programming language reserves a set of predefined words that have special meaning. C, for example, uses the word *int* in variable declarations. Because these words have special meaning, they are called *keywords*.

■ **TRAP:** *Microsoft C defines 39 keywords that have specific meanings in your programs. You cannot use keywords as variable names.*

The following table lists the 32 standard C keywords (plus 7 shaded keywords specific to Microsoft C):

auto	default	float	register	struct	volatile	interrupt
break	do	for	return	switch	while	near
case	double	goto	short	typedef	cdecl	pascal
char	else	if	signed	union	far	
const	enum	int	sizeof	unsigned	fortran	
continue	extern	long	static	void	huge	

As you proceed through this book, you will use each keyword in the preceding list. Because each word serves a specific purpose, C does not allow you to use these words as variable names. Doing so would confuse readers and play havoc with the compiler. If you attempt to use a keyword as a variable name, the C compiler generates a syntax error.

■ **TIP:** *To generate a listing that lets you see all the variable names in your program, compile your source file with the /Fs qualifier, as discussed in Chapter 1. Knowing the name of each variable defined in your program is useful when you are searching for errors. The source listing is a very convenient tool. Use it!*

■ **FACT:** *C uses the basic mathematical operators +, −, ∗, and / for addition, subtraction, multiplication, and division.*

C uses the plus sign (+) to show addition and the minus sign, or hyphen, (−) to show subtraction. Like most programming languages, C uses the asterisk (∗) as its multiplication operator (*area = 5 ∗ 4*). Reserving the letter x to indicate multiplication would cause confusion and limit the range of valid variable names. Because the keyboard does not have a division symbol, the forward slash (/) is used to represent division (*width = 20 / 5*).

The following program (OPERATOR.C) illustrates the use of each of the basic C mathematical operators:

```
main()
{
    float div_result, mult_result, add_result, sub_result;

    div_result = 25.0 / 7.7;
    mult_result = 3.41 * 2.5;
    add_result = div_result + mult_result;
    sub_result = mult_result - div_result;

    printf("Division %f Multiplication %f\n", div_result, mult_result);

    printf("Addition %f Subtraction %f\n", add_result, sub_result);
}
```

When you run the program, your screen shows

```
Division 3.246753 Multiplication 8.525000
Addition 11.771753 Subtraction 5.278247
```

Note the use of the type *float* to create floating point variables.

■ **FACT:** *C provides the modulus operator, %, which returns the remainder of an integer division operation.*

The following C program (MOD.C) illustrates the use of the *modulus operator.* The first *printf* statement divides one integer by another. The second *printf* statement returns the remainder of the division.

```
main()
{
    printf("%d / %d = %d\n", 27, 5, 27 / 5);
    printf("%d %% %d = %d\n", 27, 5, 27 % 5);
}
```

When you run the program, your screen shows

```
27 / 5 = 5
27 % 5 = 2
```

In the second *printf* statement, note the use of consecutive percent signs in the control string to display a percent sign.

■ **TRAP:** *When using integer values, the C compiler performs integer division. As such, 27/5 is equal to 5, not 5.4.*

■ **FACT:** *C lets you assign initial values to variables when you declare them.*

In the following program (DECLARE.C), the first statement declares the variable *value* and "initializes" it to 5. The equal sign (=) is the assignment operator; it assigns the value on its right, 5, to the variable on the left, *value.*

```
main()
{
    int value = 5; ◂

    printf("%d", value);
}
```

■ **FACT:** *C uses the type* char *to store ASCII characters, which include punctuation characters and the letters of the alphabet.*

The type *char* is used to declare a variable that contains a single ASCII character. The following program (CHAR.C), for example, defines a variable called *letter* and assigns it the ASCII letter 'A'.

```
main()
{
    char letter = 'A';

    printf("The letter is %c", letter);
}
```

When you run the program, your screen shows

```
The letter is A
```

If you examine the ASCII chart in Appendix A, you will find that the uppercase letter A corresponds to the decimal value 65. The following program (CHAR2.C) assigns the value 65 (rather than the letter 'A') to *letter*. The result, however, is the same.

```
main()
{
    char letter = 65;

    printf("The letter is %c", letter);
}
```

■ **FACT:** *C allows you to assign the values −127 through 128 to variables of type* char.

Microsoft C restricts variables of type *char* to values in the range −128 through 127. The chart in Appendix A shows that the ASCII characters range from 0 through 127.

USING TYPE QUALIFIERS

Beyond declaring its basic C data type, you can further qualify a variable to meet the needs of specific applications. For example, variables of type *int* can normally store only those values in the range −32,768 through 32,767. The program on the following page (OVERFLOW.C) illustrates what happens when values exceed the limits.

```
main()
{
    int maxint = 32767;
    int minint = -32768;

    printf("maxint = %d\t", maxint);
    printf("maxint + 2 = %d\n", maxint + 2);
    printf("minint = %d\t", minint);
    printf("minint - 2 = %d\n", minint - 2);
}
```

When you run the program, your screen shows

```
maxint = 32767   maxint + 2 = -32767
minint = -32768  minint - 2 = 32766
```

Note that when you exceed the range of a positive value, the value becomes negative. When you exceed the range of a negative value, the value becomes positive.

■ **FACT:** *The* unsigned *qualifier creates an integer value capable of storing values in the range 0 through 65,535. Unsigned values can never be negative.*

As you have seen, variables of the type *char* can store numbers in the range −128 through 127. The *unsigned* qualifier allows variables of type *char* to store values in the range 0 through 255.

■ **TRAP:** *If you use the %d format specifier for unsigned integer values, you might get incorrect results. The %d specifier expects values in the range −32,768 through 32,767.*

■ **FACT:** *The %u format specifier directs* printf *to display an* unsigned *integer value.*

The following program (LARGE.C) declares and initializes the variable *large* and displays the contents of the variable using the %d and %u format specifiers:

```
main()
{
    unsigned int large = 35000;

    printf("%d %u", large, large);
}
```

When you run the program, your screen shows

```
-30536 35000
```

Notice that the first output value is incorrect, whereas the second value, which is displayed using %u, is correct.

As we have seen, values of type *int* are restricted to the range −32,768 through 32,767, and unsigned variables cannot exceed 65,535. In some cases, however, your programs may need to use the *long* qualifier to store very large integer values.

■ **FACT:** *The* long *qualifier directs the compiler to reserve storage space for an integer variable capable of storing values in the range −2,147,483,648 through 2,147,483,647.*

For most applications, a variable of type *long int* provides sufficient storage capacity.

■ **FACT:** *The %ld format specifier directs* printf *to display a* long *integer value.*

The following program (LONG.C) illustrates the use of *long int* variables:

```
main()
{
    long int distance = 93000000;

    printf("The distance to the sun is %ld miles", distance);
}
```

■ **TRAP:** *The compiler does not let you place commas within large numbers. For example, it would not recognize 93,000,000 as 93000000.*

When you run the program, the screen shows

```
The distance to the sun is 93000000 miles
```

■ **FACT:** *C allows you to use the* unsigned *qualifier with* long int *to create a variable capable of storing values in the range 0 through 4,294,967,295.*

Some applications need to work with extremely large integer values. As long as the value can never be negative, you can use the *unsigned long int* type, which gives you the largest possible integer value.

Most C compilers use 16 binary digits to represent values of type *int*. Likewise, most use 32 binary digits to represent values of type *long int*. Microsoft C conforms to this standard.

■ **TRAP:** *In Microsoft C 5.1, variables of type* int *can range from −32,768 through 32,767. If you are using a different C compiler, this range might be different.*

The range of integer values that can be stored in a variable of type *int* is not determined by the C language. Some C compilers set aside 32 bits of storage for variables of type *int*, which affords them the same range of values as *long int*. To insulate your code from such variations, you can use the *short* qualifier, which restricts *int* values to the 16-bit range.

■ **FACT:** *The* short *qualifier directs the C compiler to create an integer variable capable of storing values only in the range −32,768 through 32,767.*

Although Microsoft C does not require the *short* qualifier, you might find it useful if you foresee moving your C programs to a different system.

Some C compilers represent values of type *char* as positive (unsigned) by default.

■ **FACT:** *The* signed *qualifier directs the compiler to create a variable of type* char *capable of storing values in the range −128 through 127.*

Again, Microsoft C supports the *signed* qualifier but does not require it.

■ **FACT:** *C supports the* register *qualifier, which directs the compiler to store a variable in a register whenever possible to improve performance.*

Most C variables reside in memory. When your program uses a variable, the computer must access the corresponding memory location. Computers also have a set of fast temporary storage locations called registers that reside within the microprocessor itself. Because the computer can access values in registers without accessing memory, your programs might run slightly faster if you place values in registers. The C *register* qualifier directs the compiler to store a variable in a register whenever possible. The following statement uses the *register* qualifier to declare a variable of type *int*.

```
register int count;
```

Because each microprocessor has a fixed number of registers, and because the registers are used for many other purposes, there is no guarantee that the variable will always reside in a register. You are simply assured that the compiler makes every effort to see that variables are stored in registers. In Chapter 4 we will examine the *for* statement. Variables used by *for* loops are often good candidates for register variables.

MAKING YOUR PROGRAMS MORE READABLE

All the programs thus far in this book have been quite straightforward. As the complexity of your programs increases, however, you will need to place explanatory comments within them. Comments help you remember the purpose of a specific section of code so that you (or someone else) can make changes later. Frequently, they are the only tool available to another programmer who is trying to understand your code.

■ **FACT:** *For processing purposes, the C compiler ignores any text that lies between the character combinations /* and */ in your source file.*

The first program on the following page (SQUARE.C) has no comments; the one following (SQUARE2.C) contains comments. You can see that comments make the program listing more immediately understandable.

```
main()
{
    int side = 5;

    printf("P = %d\n", side * 4);
    printf("A = %d\n", side * side);
}
```

```
/* Display the perimeter and area of a square */

main()
{
    int side = 5; /* each side is 5 feet */

    /* compute and display perimeter s + s + s + s */
    printf("P = %d\n", side * 4);

    /* compute and display area s * s */
    printf("A = %d\n", side * side);
}
```

■ **TIP:** *Make comments meaningful. Most programs should have a heading, or a leading comment, which tells the purpose of the program, its writer, and when it was written.*

Consider, for example, the following program heading:

```
/*
 * PAYROLL.C
 *
 * Generate and print weekly
 * employee paychecks.
 *
 * Written 5/8/89 by K. Jamsa
 *
 */
```

As you can see, comments can span several lines within your programs. Once the C compiler encounters the characters /*, which start a comment, it ignores all text that follows until it encounters the characters */, which close the comment.

■ **TRAP:** *Be sure you close your comments with the characters */.*

In some cases, programmers forget to place the closing characters */ or inadvertently place a blank character between the asterisk and the slash. When this occurs, the compiler continues to ignore the source file's contents, including program statements, until it encounters */. This may result in syntax errors that are difficult to detect.

USING THE C INCREMENT AND DECREMENT OPERATORS

In many of your programs, you will need to increment or decrement a variable by 1. Using the C assignment operator, you can easily add or subtract the value 1 from a variable, as shown here:

```
variable = variable + 1;
```

or

```
variable = variable - 1;
```

When the variable name to which you want to assign a value also appears in the expression to the right of the equal sign, the compiler uses the current value of the variable to perform the mathematical operation (on the right). After it evaluates the expression, the compiler assigns the result to the variable (on the left). The following program (COUNT.C), for example, initializes the variable *count* to 1 and later adds 1 to the variable.

```
main()
{
    int count = 1;

    count = count + 1;    /* add 1 to count */

    printf("The final count is %d", count);
}
```

When you run the program, your screen shows

```
The final count is 2
```

■ **TIP:** *As a shorthand notation, C provides the ++ and -- operators, which increment or decrement a variable by 1.*

Valid formats for the increment and decrement operators are as follows:

```
++variable
```

```
variable++
```

```
--variable
```

```
variable--
```

The following program (INCR.C) shows how to use these operators:

```
main()
{
    int value = 0;

    printf("Starting value %d\n", value);
    ++value;
    printf("Value after increment %d\n", value);
    --value;
    printf("Value after decrement %d\n", value);
}
```

When you run the program, your screen shows

```
Starting value 0
Value after increment 1
Value after decrement 0
```

■ **FACT:** *If you place the ++ or −− operator before a variable, the compiler first increments or decrements the variable, and then it uses the variable's contents. If the operator comes at the end of the variable, the compiler first uses the value of the variable, and then it increments or decrements the variable.*

The following program (INCR2.C) uses the increment and decrement operators:

```
main()
{
    int value = 0;

    printf("Starting value %d\n", value);
    printf("Prefix increment value %d\n", ++value);
    printf("Postfix decrement value %d\n", value--);
    printf("Ending value %d\n", value);
}
```

When you run the program, your screen shows

```
Starting value 0
Prefix increment value 1
Postfix decrement value 1
Ending value 0
```

When the compiler encounters the increment operator in the line

```
printf("Prefix increment value %d\n", ++value);
```

it first increments the value and then displays it. That is, because the operator is prefixed to the variable name, *printf* displays the value 1. The following line, however, uses the postfix decrement operator:

```
printf("Postfix decrement value %d\n", value--);
```

In this case, the compiler first uses the value of the variable in the *printf* statement, and then it decrements the value. When the final statement of the program executes, you can see that the decrement operator in the preceding statement did decrement the value as desired.

The increment and decrement operators are quite convenient. Experiment with them to ensure that you understand them fully.

DOING MORE WITH THE ASSIGNMENT OPERATOR

Earlier in this chapter you learned that = is the C assignment operator. You also learned that you can assign a value to a variable when you declare it, or you can do so in a statement within your program.

The following program (COUNT2.C) declares and initializes the variable *count* in a single statement; the variable *score* is declared first and then assigned a value in a subsequent statement:

```
main()
{
    int count = 0;  /* value assigned at declaration */
    int score;

    score = 0;      /* value assigned in a statement */
}
```

C also supports an alternate form of assignment within a statement.

■ **FACT:** *C allows a mathematical operator to precede the assignment operator. When the compiler encounters a statement in the form* variable += expression, *it reads the statement as* variable = variable + expression.

You can use this shorthand form of assignment with all C operators.

Shorthand Notation	*Equivalent*
a += 5;	a = a + 5;
a -= 2;	a = a - 2;
a *= 7;	a = a * 7;
a /= 3;	a = a / 3;

The following program (ASSIGN.C) illustrates the use of this form of the assignment operator:

```
main()
{
    int value = 100;

    printf("Starting value %d\n", value);

    value /= 10;   /* value = value / 10 */
    printf("After division %d\n", value);

    value -= 5;    /* value = value - 5 */
    printf("after subtraction %d\n", value);

    value *=   5; /* value = value * 5 */
    printf("After multiplication %d\n", value);
}
```

When you run the program, the screen shows

```
Starting value 100
After division 10
After subtraction 5
After multiplication 25
```

UNDERSTANDING OPERATOR PRECEDENCE

As your C programs become more complex, your statements will contain multiple C operators. The following statement uses the plus and multiplication operators. The result depends on whether the C compiler performs the addition or the multiplication first.

```
value = 3 + 2 * 5;
```

Addition First	*Multiplication First*
value = 3 + 2 * 5	value = 3 + 2 * 5
= 5 * 5	= 3 + 10
= 25	= 13

The table in Figure 3-1 shows the order in which mathematical operations occur in C.

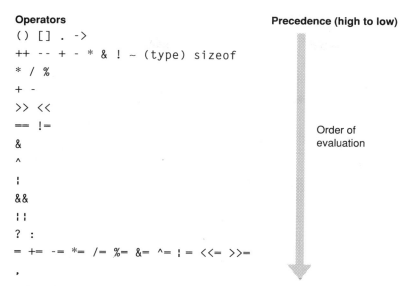

Operators

```
() [] . ->
++ -- + - * & ! ~ (type) sizeof
* / %
+ -
>> <<
== !=
&
^
|
&&
||
? :
= += -= *= /= %= &= ^= |= <<= >>=
,
```

Precedence (high to low)

Order of
evaluation

FIGURE 3-1.

If operators at different levels of precedence occur in the same statement, the operations are evaluated in order of precedence (high to low).

If two operators have the same level of precedence, the compiler performs the associated operations from left to right. Let's look at some examples.

Statement	Order of Operations	Result
a = 15 − 2 * 3;	*, −	9
a = (15 − 2) * 3;	(−), *	39
a = 5 * 9 / 15;	*, / (left to right)	3
a = (5 + 2) * 5;	(+), *	35
a = 5 + 2 * 5;	*, +	15
a = (3 + 5 + 2) * 2;	(+, +), *	20
a = (3 + 5) + 2 * 2;	(+), *, +	12
a = (3 + 5 * 2) * 2;	(*, +), *	26

We will discuss each operator in the precedence table as we proceed through the remainder of this book. For now, be sure to notice that parentheses have the highest order of precedence. You can use parentheses to override the default order of evaluation.

USING C BITWISE OPERATORS

Many programmers turn to C because it lets them manipulate binary digits, or bits. Several C operators, called bitwise operators, manipulate values at the bit level. C provides the following bitwise operators:

Operator	Function	Example
>>	Right shift operator	a = a >> 5;
<<	Left shift operator	a = a << 3;
~	Ones complement operator	a = ~ b;
^	Bitwise exclusive OR operator	a = a ^ b;
&	Bitwise AND operator	a = b & c;
¦	Bitwise OR operator	a = b ¦ c;

To understand how these operators work, you must view values as binary digits.

■ **FACT:** *The right and left shift operators, >> and <<, direct the compiler to shift the bits in a value the number of positions specified. The compiler places 0s in the locations left vacant by the shift.*

The decimal value 255 is represented in binary as 0000 0000 1111 1111. The C right shift operator, >>, directs C to shift bits to the right. In the following example, note that the compiler supplies zeros for bit locations left vacant by the shift operation:

```
value      = 0000 0000 1111 1111
value >> 3 = 0000 0000 0001 1111
```

The left shift operator, <<, works in the opposite manner:

```
value      = 0000 0000 1111 1111
value << 4 = 0000 1111 1111 0000
```

■ **FACT:** *The ones complement operator, ~, changes each binary digit with the value 1 to a 0 and changes each 0 to a 1.*

Again, using the value 255, the ones complement operator yields

```
value  = 0000 0000 1111 1111
~value = 1111 1111 0000 0000
```

■ **FACT:** *The exclusive OR operator, ^, works with two values. The operator compares corresponding bits in each value. The result has a 1 in each bit position where the binary digits of the two values differ, and it has a 0 where the digits are the same.*

Given the following binary values, the exclusive OR operator, ∧, returns a 1 for the bits that differ and a 0 for the bits that are the same, as shown here:

```
    0000 0101 0101 0000
  ∧ 1100 1100 1100 1100
    1100 1001 1001 1100   ——————— Result
```

■ **FACT:** *The bitwise OR operator, ¦, compares corresponding bits in each of two values. The result has a 1 in the bit position that contains a 1 in either or both values.*

Given the following binary values, the bitwise OR operator, ¦, places a 1 at the bit positions that contain a 1 in either or both values, as shown here:

```
    0000 0101 0101 0000
  ¦ 1100 1100 1100 1100
    1100 1101 1101 1100   ——————— Result
```

■ **FACT:** *The bitwise AND operator, &, compares the corresponding bits of each of two values. The result has a 1 only in the bit locations that contain a 1 in both values.*

Given the following binary values, the C bitwise operator places a 1 only in those locations that contain 1 in both values, as shown here:

```
    0000 0101 0101 0000
  & 1100 1100 1100 1100
    0000 0100 0100 0000   ——————— Result
```

TYPE STORAGE REQUIREMENTS

Many advanced programmers are curious about how the compiler stores values for each data type. For example, earlier in this chapter you learned that values of type *int* generated by the Microsoft C Compiler can store numbers −32,768 through 32,767. Knowing how the values are stored helps explain why these limits exist. The Microsoft C compiler stores integer values as 16-bit values. The most significant (leftmost) bit specifies the sign of the value. The remaining 15 binary digits represent the value.

Fifteen binary digits can represent 32,768 values. Because these values can be positive or negative, the range of values becomes −32,768 through 32,767. (Zero is included in the positive half of the range.)

■ **FACT:** *The C* sizeof *operator returns the number of bytes used to store a value in a specified variable or data type.*

In Microsoft C, the type *int* uses 16 bits (2 bytes) to store its values. The following program (INTSIZE.C) verifies this fact using the *sizeof* operator with a variable *value* declared as an *int*:

```
main()
{
    printf("C uses %d bytes to store an int in memory", sizeof(int));
}
```

When you run the program, your screen shows

```
C uses 2 bytes to store an int in memory
```

In a similar way, you can use the C *sizeof* operator with the data type keywords to determine the number of bytes used to store each type, as shown in the following program (TYPESIZE.C):

```
main()
{
    printf("int %d unsigned int %d long int %d\n",
        sizeof(int), sizeof(unsigned int), sizeof(long int));

    printf("float %d double %d char %d",
        sizeof(float), sizeof(double), sizeof(char));
}
```

When you run this program, your screen shows

```
int 2 unsigned int 2 long int 4
float 4 double 8 char 1
```

The diagrams in Figure 3-2 illustrate the storage formats for Microsoft C types. Notice that C stores floating point values in two parts: the mantissa, which stores the decimal portion of the value, and the exponent. For example, given the value 538.664, the mantissa stores 5.38664, and the exponent stores the value 2. Combining them, your value becomes 5.38664e2 or 538.664

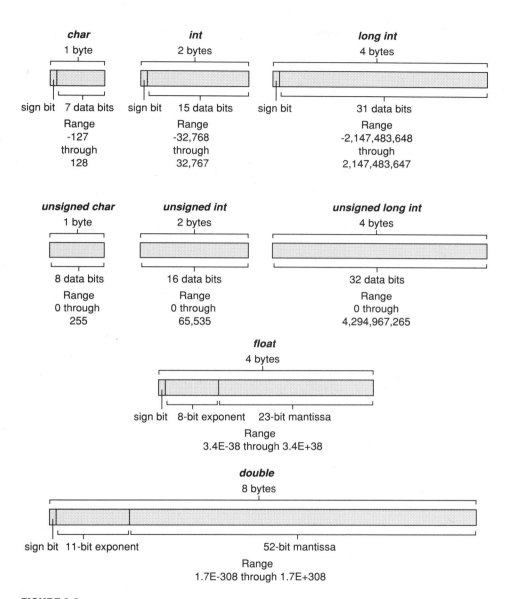

FIGURE 3-2.

Depiction of storage reserved for various data types by Microsoft C Compiler.

SUMMARY

Getting Started with C Variables

■ **FACT:** *A variable's type specifies the kind of values the variable can store, as well as the set of operations that can be applied to the variable.*

■ **FACT:** *C supports four basic variable types —* int, float, char, *and* double.

■ **TIP:** *Define your variables after the opening grouping symbol ({).*

■ **TRAP:** *You must define a variable before you can use it. If the C compiler encounters an undefined variable name in your program, the compiler generates a syntax error.*

■ **FACT:** *The equal sign (=) is the C assignment operator. When the compiler encounters this operator, it assigns the result of the expression at the right of the equal sign to the variable at the left of the equal sign.*

■ **TIP:** *Most C programmers use a blank line to separate variable declarations from program statements. Because the compiler requires you to declare all your variables before you use them in program statements, the blank line provides a distinction between the two.*

■ **FACT:** *If several variables are the same type, the compiler lets you define all of them on one line, separated by commas.*

■ **TIP:** *Use meaningful variable names. Remember, C is case sensitive. The underscore character can improve the readability of longer variable names. For example, you might use* fiscal_year *as a variable name.*

■ **TRAP:** *Microsoft C defines 39 keywords that have specific meanings in your programs. You cannot use keywords as variable names.*

■ **TIP:** *To generate a listing that lets you see all the variable names in your program, compile your source file with the /Fs qualifier, as discussed in Chapter 1. Knowing the name of each variable defined in your program is useful when you are searching for errors. The source listing is a very convenient tool. Use it!*

■ **FACT:** *C uses the basic mathematical operators +, −, ∗, and / for addition, subtraction, multiplication, and division.*

■ **FACT:** *C provides the modulus operator, %, which returns the remainder of an integer division operation.*

■ **TRAP:** *When using integer values, the C compiler performs integer division. As such, 27 / 5 is equal to 5, not 5.4.*

■ **FACT:** *C lets you assign initial values to variables when you declare them.*

■ **FACT:** *C uses the type* char *to store ASCII characters, which include punctuation characters and the letters of the alphabet.*

■ **FACT:** *C allows you to assign the values −127 through 128 to variables of type* char.

Using Type Qualifiers

■ **FACT:** *The* unsigned *qualifier creates an integer value capable of storing values in the range 0 through 65,535. Unsigned values can never be negative.*

■ **TRAP:** *If you use the %d format specifier for unsigned integer values, you might get incorrect results. The %d specifier expects values in the range −32,768 through 32,767.*

■ **FACT:** *The %u format specifier directs* printf *to display an* unsigned *integer value.*

■ **FACT:** *The* long *qualifier directs the compiler to reserve storage space for an integer variable capable of storing values in the range −2,147,483,648 through 2,147,483,647.*

■ **FACT:** *The %ld format specifier directs* printf *to display a* long *integer value.*

■ **TRAP:** *The compiler does not let you place commas within large numbers. For example, it would not recognize 93,000,000 as 93000000.*

■ **FACT:** *C allows you to use the* unsigned *qualifier with* long int *to create a variable capable of storing values in the range 0 through 4,294,967,295.*

■ **TRAP:** *In Microsoft C 5.1, variables of type* int *can range from −32,768 through 32,767. If you are using a different C compiler, this range might be different.*

■ **FACT:** *The* short *qualifier directs the C compiler to create an integer variable capable of storing values only in the range −32,768 through 32,767.*

■ **FACT:** *The* signed *qualifier directs the compiler to create a variable of type* char *capable of storing values in the range −128 through 127.*

■ **FACT:** *C supports the* register *qualifier, which directs the compiler to store a variable in a register whenever possible to improve performance.*

Making Your Programs More Readable

■ **FACT:** *For processing purposes, the C compiler ignores any text that lies between the character combinations /* and */ in your source file.*

■ **TIP:** *Make comments meaningful. Most programs should have a heading, or a leading comment, which tells the purpose of the program, its writer, and when it was written.*

■ **TRAP:** *Be sure you close your comments with the characters */.*

Using the C Increment and Decrement Operators

■ **TIP:** *As a shorthand notation, C provides the ++ and -- operators, which increment or decrement a variable by 1.*

■ **FACT:** *If you place the ++ or -- operator before a variable, the compiler first increments or decrements the variable, and then it uses the variable's contents. If the operator comes at the end of the variable, the compiler first uses the value of the variable, and then it increments or decrements the variable.*

Doing More with the Assignment Operator

■ **FACT:** *C allows a mathematical operator to precede the assignment operator. When the compiler encounters a statement in the form* variable += expression, *it reads the statement as* variable = variable + expression.

Using C Bitwise Operators

■ **FACT:** *The right and left shift operators, >> and <<, direct the compiler to shift the bits in a value the number of positions specified. The compiler places 0s in the locations left vacant by the shift.*

■ **FACT:** *The ones complement operator, ~, changes each binary digit with the value 1 to a 0 and changes each 0 to a 1.*

■ **FACT:** *The exclusive OR operator, ^, works with two values. The operator compares corresponding bits in each value. The result has a 1 in each bit position where the binary digits differ, and it has a 0 where the digits are the same.*

■ **FACT:** *The bitwise OR operator, ¦, compares corresponding bits in each of two values. The result has a 1 in the bit position that contains a 1 in either or both values.*

■ **FACT:** *The bitwise AND operator, &, compares the corresponding bits in each of two values. The result has a 1 only in the bit locations that contain a 1 in both values.*

Type Storage Requirements

■ **FACT:** *The C* sizeof *operator returns the number of bytes used to store a value in a specified variable or data type.*

GLOSSARY

bitwise operator A C operator that lets you manipulate values in their binary representations.

floating point value A value that contains a decimal point. In C, the type *float* defines a floating point value.

integer value A whole number. In C, the type *int* defines an integer value.

keyword A word that has special meaning within the C language. The compiler does not allow you to use keywords as variable names in your programs.

modulus operator A mathematical operator that returns the remainder of an integer division. The modulus operator in C is the percent sign (%). Read the expression *15 % 4* as "the remainder of 15 divided by four."

operator precedence The order in which C evaluates the operations that constitute an expression. Because multiplication has a higher operator precedence than addition, C finds the product of 2 and 3 before it adds 4 in the expression *a = 4 + 2 * 3.*

type A C keyword that defines the kind of values a variable can store, as well as the set of operations that can be performed on the variable. C provides the basic types *int, float, char,* and *double.*

type qualifier A C keyword that modifies the way C stores values within a specific type. C supports the type qualifiers *signed, unsigned, short,* and *long.*

variable A name that C assigns to a memory location. Rather than referring directly to memory locations when they store and retrieve values, your C programs can instead refer to variable names.

CHAPTER 4

Basic C Control Structures

In Chapter 1 you learned that a program is simply a list of instructions. Unless told to do otherwise, a program executes from the top of the list to the bottom. As a program becomes more complex, however, so does its flow of execution. Most programs must make decisions and alter processing accordingly, and many programs need to repeat a specific set of instructions until a given condition is met.

In this chapter you learn to use C's control structures (constructs) to change a program's flow of execution. You will first use the *if* construct to execute a series of statements when a specific condition exists. Next, you will learn how to repeat a set of instructions using the *while* and *for* statements. These constructs—*if*, *while*, and *for*—are the building blocks for all C programs.

USING RELATIONAL OPERATORS

In Chapter 3 you examined C's mathematical operators. C also provides a set of *relational* operators that your programs can use to compare two values.

■ **FACT:** *The C relational operators test whether a value is greater than, less than, equal to, or not equal to another value.*

In this chapter we use each of C's relational operators, summarized in the table on the following page, as we examine the basic C constructs.

Operator	Function	Example
>	Greater than	a > b
<	Less than	a + b < c
>=	Greater than or equal to	a >= b
<=	Less than or equal to	a <= 0
==	Equal	a == b
!=	Not equal	a != 0

■ **TRAP:** *Accidentally using the C assignment operator (=) in a test for equality produces an error that is difficult to detect.*

Remember, the expression $a = b$ assigns the value of b to the variable a. The expression $a == b$ tests whether the variables a and b are equal.

DECISION MAKING WITH *if*

The C *if* statement alters the sequential execution of program instructions.

■ **FACT:** *The C* if *statement examines a specific condition. If the condition is true, the program executes the statement that follows. If the condition is false, the statement that follows the condition is not executed.*

The following program (IFTEST.C) illustrates the use of an *if* statement:

```
main()
{
    int value = 5;

    if (value >= 0)
        printf("Value is positive\n");

    printf("Value is %d", value);
}
```

When the program executes, the statement

```
if (value >= 0)
```

examines the variable *value*. If *value* is greater than or equal to 0, the following statement executes:

```
printf("Value is positive\n");
```

Experiment with the program by having it assign other integers to *value*. If *value* is less than 0, the program displays only the second *printf* statement. In other words, if the condition is true (met), the subsequent statement executes; if the condition is false (not met), the subsequent statement does not execute.

Note that a semicolon does not conclude the line containing

```
if (value >= 0)
```

An *if* statement actually contains two parts. The first part specifies the condition, and the second contains the statement that executes if the condition is true. As you can see, the second part of the *if* statement (the indented *printf*) does end with a semicolon.

Also note that the statement associated with the *if* is indented. Although the C compiler does not require this indentation, programmers indent the statements associated with C constructs to make them easier to recognize.

In this case, the indentation shows that the first *printf* is associated with the *if*, while the second *printf* is not. Remember, the indentation does not influence the processing. It is simply a visual aid to programmers.

■ **FACT:** *To execute several statements when a condition is true, you must group the statements with the C grouping symbols, { and }.*

The following program (IFTEST2.C) uses the C grouping symbols to display two lines of output when the condition is true:

```
main()
{
    int value = 3;

    if (value >= 0)
        {
        printf("Value is positive\n");
        printf("Current value is %d\n", value);
        }
}
```

All C constructs support compound statements as well as simple statements. A compound statement is a series of instructions that appear between the grouping symbols. The statement that follows an *if* condition can be a single line, as follows:

```
if (value >= 0)
    printf("Value is positive"); ——————— Simple statement
```

Or it can be a compound statement, enclosed by the grouping symbols { and }, as it is in IFTEST2.C:

```
if (value >= 0)
    {
    printf("Value is positive\n");
        printf("Current value is %d\n", value);
    }
```
— Compound statement

The complete program actually uses two sets of grouping symbols as shown in Figure 4-1. The first set groups all the program instructions. The second set groups the instructions that execute when the *if* statement's condition is met.

```
        main()
        {
            int value = 3;

            if (value >= 0)
                {
                printf("Value is positive\n");
                printf("Current value is %d\n", value);
                }
        }
```

Program statements

Conditional statements

FIGURE 4-1.
The C grouping symbols define blocks of instructions within your source code.

■ **FACT:** *C evaluates any nonzero value as true.*

The result of a condition is either true or false. C uses the value 0 to represent a false outcome and considers any nonzero value—positive or negative—to be true. In the following program (IFTEST3.C), the *if* statement simply examines the value 2. Because 2 is a nonzero value, the condition is true.

```
main()
{
    if (2)
        printf("Any nonzero value is true");
}
```

■ **FACT:** *The C* else *statement lets you specify a set of instructions that execute when the condition in an* if *statement is false.*

Just as you use the *if* statement to specify a set of instructions that execute when a condition is true, you can attach the *else* statement to specify instructions that execute only when the condition is not met.

The following program (ELSETEST.C) examines the variable *value* and displays a message stating whether the value is positive or negative:

```
main()
{
    int value = 1;

    if (value >= 0)
        printf("Value is positive");
    else
        printf("Value is negative");
}
```

When you run the program, the screen shows

```
Value is positive
```

Experiment with this program by assigning −5 to the variable. When the revised program executes, the condition fails. The program then executes the statement associated with the *else*. In other words, if the condition is true, the compiler executes the statement associated with the *if*. Then it bypasses the statement associated with the *else* and continues execution after the *else* statement. If the condition is false, the compiler bypasses the statements associated with the *if* and executes only the statement related to the *else*. Afterward, execution continues at the first line following the *else* statement.

USING LOGICAL OPERATORS

So far, we have examined conditions in which only one criterion must be met. In many cases, however, you will want statements to execute under more complex conditions—when two or more criteria are met, when a condition is not true, or when one or more of several conditions are met. To express such complex conditions in C, use the three logical operators.

■ **FACT:** *The logical operators in C are AND (&&), OR (¦ ¦), and NOT (!).*

The following table presents the C logical operators:

Operator	*Function*	*Example*
&&	Logical AND	if (letter >= 'a' && letter <= 'z')
¦¦	Logical OR	if (letter == 'y' ¦¦ letter == 'Y')
!	Logical NOT	if (!(letter == 'y' ¦¦ letter == 'n'))

If you examine the operator precedence table on p. 55 in Chapter 3, you'll find that the precedence of the logical operators is quite low. Therefore, when the C compiler encounters an expression such as

```
if (a < b && b < c || a > d)
```

the compiler first tests the relational operators, < and >, and then it tests the logical operators, && and ||, from left to right.

USING *while* TO REPEAT
A SET OF INSTRUCTIONS

Many C programs repeat a set of instructions until a given condition is met. C has three looping, or iterative, constructs that provide this capability: *while*, *for*, and *do-while*. In this chapter we discuss *while* and *for*; we discuss *do-while* in Chapter 5.

■ **FACT:** *The* while *statement examines a specific condition. As long as the condition is true, the statement that follows executes repeatedly. When the condition fails, execution passes to the first statement that follows the* while *loop.*

The following program (WHILE.C) displays the numbers 1 through 100. It begins by initializing the variable *count* to 1. As long as the value of *count* is less than or equal to 100, the *while* loop continues: It displays *count*'s value and then increments it. When the value of *count* exceeds 100, the *while* loop completes and the program ends.

```
main()
{
    int count = 1;

    while (count <= 100)
        {
        printf("%d\n", count);
        count++;
        }
}
```

As before, note that the *while* statement does not have a semicolon after the condition. Like the *if* statement, a *while* statement can be viewed as two parts. The first contains the condition to test. The second part contains the statement to execute when the condition is true. If the statement is a compound statement, it must be enclosed by the C grouping symbols. Again, note the customary indentation of statements associated with the *while* loop.

The preceding program illustrates the use of a compound statement with a *while* loop. As long as the condition is true, all the statements grouped in the compound statement continue to execute. Each time the statements complete, execution loops back to the condition.

```
main()
{
    int count = 1;

    while (count <= 100)        ◄─────┐
        {                             │  Loops until
        printf("%d\n", count);        │  condition
        count++;                      │  is false
        } ───────────────────────────┘
}
```

If the condition remains true, the corresponding statements again execute. If the condition fails, execution continues at the statement that follows the *while* loop. Now change the point at which the variable *count* increments, as follows, to create the following simplified version of the program (WHILE2.C):

```
main()
{
    int count = 1;

    while (count <= 100)
        printf("%d\n", count++);
}
```

As discussed in Chapter 3, the postfix operator does not affect the value of *count* until *printf* has displayed the current value.

■ **TRAP:** *If the* while *loop never meets its ending condition, the associated statement repeats forever. This situation is called an infinite loop. In some cases, you can end an infinite loop by pressing the Ctrl-C keyboard combination.*

The program on the following page (WHILE3.C) is similar to the previous one. Its goal is to display the numbers from 1 through 100. Unfortunately, the program fails to increment the variable *count*. As a result, the ending condition, which occurs when *count* exceeds 100, is never met.

```
main()
{
    int count = 1;

    while (count <= 100)
        printf("%d\n", count);
}
```

If you execute this program, use Ctrl-C to terminate it.

■ **TIP:** *To analyze the cause of an infinite loop, review the way it achieves these four steps: initialization of a variable, testing the variable, execution of the desired instructions, and modification of the value of the control variable.*

The program with the infinite loop fails to modify the test variable's value. Our successful program, however, performs all four steps, as shown in Figure 4-2. If your programs correctly perform these four steps, you will prevent an infinite loop from happening.

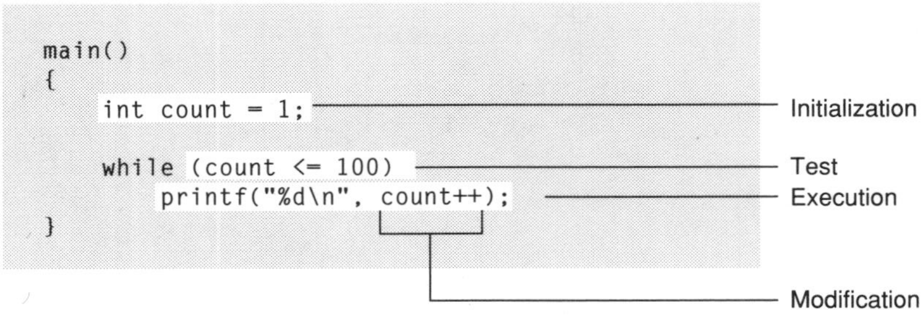

FIGURE 4-2.
A while *loop performs four basic steps.*

■ **TRAP:** *Do not assume that the compiler initializes variables to 0 by default. You must initialize any variables you test in your loops.*

The following program (WHILE4.C) modifies the previous program slightly. It displays only the odd values of *count* by applying the modulus operator, discussed in Chapter 3.

```
main()
{
    int count = 1;

    while (count <= 100)
        {
        if (count % 2 == 1)
            printf("%d\n", count);
        count++;
        }
}
```

The *if* condition, *count % 2 == 1*, compares the remainder of *count* divided by 2 with the value 1. As the following table demonstrates, the value of *count* is odd whenever the condition is met:

Value	Value % 2	Modulus
1	1 % 2	1
2	2 % 2	0
3	3 % 2	1
4	4 % 2	0
5	5 % 2	1
⋮	⋮	⋮

Remember, C does not restrict you to incrementing a value by 1. By incrementing the variable *count* by 2, the following program (WHILE5.C) also displays the odd numbers from 1 through 100.

```
main()
{
    int count = 1;

    while (count <= 100)
        {
        printf("%d\n", count);
        count += 2;
        }
}
```

The C compiler does not restrict you to incrementing the value of a variable within a *while* loop. Just as the previous program added the value 2 to the variable *count* with each iteration of the loop, you might choose to perform any other mathematical operation.

The following program (WHILE6.C), for example, uses subtraction to count down and display the values from 100 to 1.

```
main()
{
    int count = 100;

    while (count >= 0)
        printf("%d\n", count--);
}
```

Keep in mind the four steps in an iterative process:

1. Initialize of one or more variables

2. Test a control variable

3. Execute desired code

4. Modify a control variable

USING THE *for* STATEMENT

You can use the *for* statement to combine these four steps into one statement.

■ **FACT:** *The C* for *statement allows you to repeat a set of one or more instructions, initialize one or more variables, test a control variable, and increment one or more variables with each iteration.*

The following program (FOR.C) displays the values 1 through 100. The *for* statement initializes the variable *count* to 1, tests the value, and later increments *count* after the *printf* statement executes.

```
main()
{
    int count;

    for (count = 1; count <= 100; count++)
        printf("%d\n", count);
}
```

The four iterative steps of the *for* statement are identified in Figure 4-3.

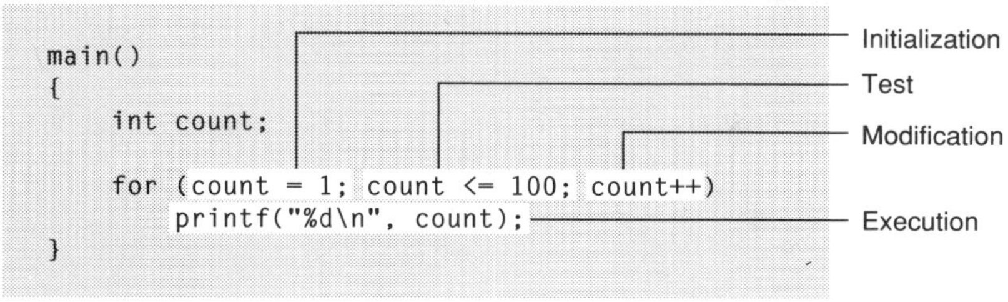

FIGURE 4-3.
A for *loop presents the four iterative steps compactly.*

The *for* statement initializes the variable *count* and then tests the condition specified. If the condition is true, the statement that follows executes. After the statement exeutes, *for* increments the variable *count* and again tests the condition. If the condition is still true, the execution and increment steps repeat. Note that *for* does not reinitialize *count* to 1; instead, the value of *count* increases with each iteration of the loop.

Again, note that the *for* loop does not have a semicolon at the end of the line containing the initialization, test, and increment. The initialization, condition, and modification comprise the first part of the statement; the second part contains the statement to execute. The statement can be simple or compound.

The following program (FOR2.C) resembles the one preceding but counts down from 100 to 0 by 5s.

```
main()
{
    int count;

    for (count = 100; count >= 0; count -= 5)
        printf("%d\n", count);
}
```

In Chapter 3 we stated that values can be expressed in decimal, octal, and hexadecimal notation. The following program (FOR3.C) displays a table of values in each format. It uses a *for* loop to show the values 0 through 255 in decimal, octal, and hexadecimal notation.

```
main()
{
    int count;

    printf("Decimal\t\tOctal\t\tHexadecimal\n");
    for (count = 0; count <= 255; count++)
        printf("%d\t\t%o\t\t%x\n", count, count, count);
}
```

■ **FACT:** *The C comma operator (,) lets you initialize or modify two or more variables in a* for *statement.*

In some programs, you need to use several variables within a *for* statement. In such cases, the C comma operator may provide a solution. The following program (FOR4.C) displays the uppercase and lowercase letters A through F. It initializes and increments two variables within the *for* loop.

```
main()
{
    char upper, lower;

    printf("Upper\tLower\n");
    for (lower = 'a', upper = 'A'; upper <= 'F'; upper++, lower++)
        printf("%c\t%c\n", upper, lower);
}
```

■ **TIP:** *You can use the* while *and* for *statements to repeat a series of commands. Many programmers prefer the* for *statement when they want the initialization and modification of the control variable to be conspicuous.*

USING A SERIES OF *if-else* STATEMENTS

Earlier in this chapter we examined the *if* and *else* statements. At that time, our programs were quite simple. Recall ELSETEST.C, for example. It executes the statements associated with the *else* statement if the condition fails.

```
main()
{
    int value = 1;

    if (value >= 0)
        printf("Value is positive");
    else
        printf("Value is negative");
}
```

By placing a series of related *if-else* statements in succession, your program can execute along any of several paths. The C compiler lets you combine the *if* and *else* statements to create a list of successive tests. For example, the following statements test the value of *a* against a series of constants.

```
if(a == 1)
    printf("ONE");
else if (a == 2)
    printf("TWO");
else if (a == 3)
    printf("THREE");
else
    printf("Not ONE, TWO, or THREE");
```

If *a* equals 1, the program displays the message *ONE* and continues at the statement following the *if-else* statements. If the value is not 1, the program tests to see whether the value is 2. If so, the program displays the message *TWO* and continues at the statement following the *if-else* statements. If *a* matches neither 1 nor 2, the process repeats for the value 3. If the value of *a* is not 1, 2, or 3, the program executes the statement that corresponds with the last *else* statement. The following program (VOWELS.C), for example, displays the uppercase vowels:

```
main()
{
    char letter;

    for (letter = 'A'; letter <= 'Z'; letter++)
        if (letter == 'A')
            printf("%c\n", letter);
        else if (letter == 'E')
            printf("%c\n", letter);
        else if (letter == 'I')
            printf("%c\n", letter);
        else if (letter == 'O')
            printf("%c\n", letter);
        else if (letter == 'U')
            printf("%c\n", letter);
}
```

In this case, the statement that executes with each iteration of the loop is an *if-else* statement, the many lines of which actually compose one continuous statement. Because the *if-else* statements are nested in this manner, you are not *required* to group them under the *for* condition as a compound statement.

■ **TRAP:** *The C compiler associates the* else *statement with the first* else-less *if.*

When the compiler encounters an *else* statement within your program, it associates the *else* statement with the first *if* statement above the *else* that does not have a corresponding *else*. C programmers refer to the *if* that lacks an *else* as an "*else*-less *if.*"

The following program (IFELSE.C) illustrates the importance of recognizing the way *else* and *if* statements are paired:

```
main()
{
    int value = 50;

    if (value <= 100)
        if (value < 10)
            printf("The value is less than 10");
    else
        printf("The value is greater than 100");
}
```

C associates the *else* statement with the first *else*-less *if.* Therefore, the processing does not correspond to the indentation of the source file. Although the variable *value* is equal to 50, the program displays the following message:

```
The value is greater than 100
```

The correct version of this program (IFELSE2.C) would be:

```
main()
{
    int value = 50;

    if (value <= 100)
        {
        if (value < 10)
            printf("Value is less than 10");
        }
    else
        printf("Value is greater than 100");
}
```

Because the nested *if* statement appears within grouping symbols, the compiler does not associate the *else* statement with it.

Associating an *else* with the incorrect *if* statement can result in an error that is very difficult to detect. Be careful to ensure that your code actually executes the way you intend it to execute.

SUMMARY

Using Relational Operators

■ **FACT:** *The C relational operators test whether a value is greater than, less than, equal to, or not equal to another value.*

■ **TRAP:** *Accidentally using the C assignment operator (=) in a test for equality produces an error that is difficult to detect.*

Decision Making with *if*

■ **FACT:** *The C* if *statement examines a specific condition. If the condition is true, the program executes the statement that follows. If the condition is false, the statement that follows the condition is not executed.*

■ **FACT:** *To execute several statements when a condition is true, you must group the statements with the C grouping symbols, { and }.*

■ **FACT:** *C evaluates any nonzero value as true.*

■ **FACT:** *The C* else *statement lets you specify a set of instructions that execute when the condition in an* if *statement is false.*

Using Logical Operators

■ **FACT:** *The logical operators in C are the AND (&&), OR (¦ ¦), and NOT (!).*

Using *while* to Repeat a Set of Instructions

■ **FACT:** *The* while *statement examines a specific condition. As long as the condition is true, the statement that follows executes repeatedly. When the condition fails, execution passes to the first statement that follows the* while *loop.*

■ **TRAP:** *If the* while *loop never meets its ending condition, the statements repeats forever. This situation is called an infinite loop. In some cases, you can end an infinite loop by pressing the Ctrl-C keyboard combination.*

■ **TIP:** *To analyze the cause of an infinite loop, review the way it achieves these four steps: initialization of a variable, testing the variable, execution of the desired instructions, and modification of the value of the control variable.*

■ **TRAP:** *Do not assume that the compiler initializes variables to 0 by default. You must initialize any variables you test in your loops.*

Using the *for* Statement

■ **FACT:** *The C* for *statement allows you to repeat a set of one or more instructions, initialize one or more variables, test a control variable, and increment one or more variables with each iteration.*

■ **FACT:** *The C comma operator lets you initialize or modify two or more variables in a* for *statement.*

■ **TIP:** *You can use the* while *and* for *statements to repeat a series of commands. Many programmers prefer the* for *statement when they want the initialization and modification of the control variable to be conspicuous.*

Using a Series of *if-else* Statements

■ **TRAP:** *The C compiler associates the* else *statement with the first* else-*less* if.

GLOSSARY

compound statement A series of instructions enclosed by a pair of grouping symbols, the left and right braces { and }.

conditional statement A statement that executes only when a given condition is true. The *if* statement provides conditional processing.

iterative process A series of one or more instructions that repeat until an ending condition is met. The three iterative constructs in C are the *while, for,* and *do-while* statements.

logical operator Any of a set of C operators, (&&, ¦¦, !) that yield a true or false (nonzero or zero) result. The result depends on the truth or falsity of the expression or expressions to which the operator is applied.

relational operator Any of a set of C operators (>, <, ==, >=, <=, !=) that let you compare two values. The result is either true or false (nonzero or zero).

## CHAPTER 5

Advanced C Constructs

In Chapter 4 you learned the three most common C constructs—*if, while*, and *for*. In this chapter we examine several additional statements that alter the execution flow of your C programs. Each statement we discuss is well suited to a particular programming situation. Therefore, we will discuss not only how a construct works but also the circumstances in which you might want to use it.

USING THE *do-while* STATEMENT

You have already used two iterative constructs—the *while* and *for* statements. The third iterative construct in C is the *do-while* statement.

■ **FACT:** *Unlike the* while *and* for *statements, which test a condition and execute corresponding statements if the condition is true, the C* do-while *statement first executes a set of statements and then tests a condition. If the condition is true, the statements execute again, and this cycle repeats until the condition is no longer true.*

The following program (DOWHILE.C) uses the *do-while* statement to display the letters A through G on your screen:

```
main()
{
    char letter = 'A';

    do
        printf("%c\n", letter++);
    while (letter <= 'G');   /* note semicolon */
}
```

81

When you run the program, your screen shows

```
A
B
C
D
E
F
G
```

Although *do-while* is similar to the *while* and *for* statements in that it lets you repeat a set of instructions until a condition is met, it has one syntactic difference. The *do-while* statement requires a semicolon after the condition that is associated with *while*. If you do not include the semicolon, the C compiler generates a syntax error.

As you can see, this program first displays a letter and then tests a condition. If the condition is true, the statement within the *do-while* loop repeats. In this case, the *do-while* statement is a simple statement; to use a compound statement, you must enclose the instructions with braces.

■ **TIP:** *Use the* do-while *statement for application programs in which a set of instructions must execute at least once and then repeat conditionally.*

The *while* loop is best suited for applications that need to repeat until a specific condition is met but that do not necessarily rely upon the repeated modification of a specific variable. Later in the book you will write C programs that read the contents of a file character by character until the end of file occurs. As you will find, the *while* loop is well suited to this type of processing.

The *for* loop is best suited for applications that initialize, test, and then modify a control variable. For such applications, a *for* loop makes all the control information easily visible to a reader of the program.

The *do-while* loop is best suited for applications in which instructions execute at least once and then repeat as long as a given condition is met. For example, an application might display a menu once and then redisplay the menu based on the user's selection. We will use all these statements in programs throughout this book.

USING THE *continue* STATEMENT

As the complexity of the processing within your loops increases, you might encounter situations in which you need to proceed to the evaluation portion of the loop without executing the remaining statements in the loop. In such cases you can use the *continue* statement to direct your program to skip the remaining statements in the loop and continue processing at the condition evaluation portion of the *while* or *do-while* loop or at the increment portion of the *for* loop.

■ **FACT:** *The C* continue *statement immediately directs the flow of execution to the condition portion of the* while *or* do-while *loop or to the increment portion of the* for *loop.*

The following program (CONTINUE.C) uses the *continue* statement to skip every third value between 1 and 100:

```
main()
{
    int count;

    for (count = 1; count <= 100; count++)
        {
        if (count % 3 == 0)
            continue;
        printf("%d\n", count);
        }
}
```

This program uses the *for* loop to assign the variable *count* the values 1 through 100. Within the loop, the conditional expression uses the modulus operator to test the remainder of *count* divided by 3:

```
if (count % 3 == 0)
```

If the remainder is 0, the *continue* statement directs the program to skip the *printf* statement and to continue at the increment portion of the *for* loop. In so doing, the program does not display the values of *count* that, when divided by 3, have a remainder of 0 (3, 6, 9, and so on).

■ **TRAP:** *Using the C* continue *statement can adversely affect the readability of your code. Be selective when you use the* continue *statement. In most cases you can rewrite code to eliminate it.*

The C *continue* statement suffers from the dilemma "convenience at a cost." Although it provides a convenient method of continuing execution at the next iteration of a loop, it often diminishes a program's readability. Eventually, every program needs to be updated, and when that time comes, you will discover that the understandability of a program is as important as its functionality. If the program is hard to read or understand, the possibility of introducing errors increases. If you must use the *continue* statement, include comments within your program that thoroughly explain the processing.

The previous C program used the *continue* statement to display every third value from 1 to 100. The following program (NOCONT.C) performs the same task but does not use *continue*.

```
main()
{
    int count;

    for (count = 0; count <= 100; count++)
        if (count % 3 != 0)
            printf("%d\n", count);
}
```

In some cases the *continue* statement can simplify a difficult programming task, but most programs won't require *continue*.

A LOOK AT THE *break* STATEMENT

As you have seen, the *continue* statement directs the compiler to continue with the next iteration of a loop. The *break* statement ends the processing of a loop.

■ **FACT:** *The C* break *statement terminates the processing of a loop and continues execution at the first statement that follows the loop.*

In Chapter 4 we examined a program that displayed each vowel in the alphabet. When that program displays the last vowel, the program need not continue examining the letters V through Z. The following program (BKVOWELS.C) ends the *for* loop with the *break* statement to reduce needless iterations.

```
main()
{
    char letter;

    for (letter = 'A'; letter <= 'Z'; letter++)
        if (letter == 'A')
            printf("%c\n", letter);
        else if (letter == 'E')
            printf("%c\n", letter);
        else if (letter == 'I')
            printf("%c\n", letter);
        else if (letter == 'O')
            printf("%c\n", letter);
        else if (letter == 'U')
            {
            printf("%c\n", letter);
            break;
            }
}
```

This program has the same output if you remove the *break* statement. The *break* statement in this case simply eliminates the testing of the letters V through Z.

Most C programs won't need the *break* statement with *while, for,* or *do-while* loops. They will, however, need *break* with the *switch* statement (discussed later in this chapter).

EXECUTING A LOOP WITHIN ANOTHER LOOP

All the loops we have examined so far have been quite simple. However, in the same manner that we nested *if-else* statements, we can construct a loop that executes within another loop.

■ **FACT:** *C lets you place a looping construct in the set of instructions that execute for another loop. The inner loop is called a nested loop.*

The following program (NESTFOR.C) uses a nested *for* loop to display the letters of the alphabet five times.

```
main()
{
    int count;
    char letter;

    for (count = 1; count <= 5; count++)
        {
        for (letter = 'A'; letter <= 'Z'; letter++)  /* nested loop */
            printf("%c", letter);
        printf("\n");
        }
}
```

When you run the program, the screen shows

```
ABCDEFGHIJKLMNOPQRSTUVWXYZ
ABCDEFGHIJKLMNOPQRSTUVWXYZ
ABCDEFGHIJKLMNOPQRSTUVWXYZ
ABCDEFGHIJKLMNOPQRSTUVWXYZ
ABCDEFGHIJKLMNOPQRSTUVWXYZ
```

As you can see, this program contains two *for* loops. It performs the statements in the outer loop five times. Because these statements include a *for* loop, the inner *for* loop executes each time, displaying the letters of the alphabet. After the inner loop displays the last letter of the alphabet, the program uses the newline character to start the next set of letters on the following line.

To better understand this processing, modify the program slightly and name it NESTFOR2.C, as follows:

```
main()
{
    int count;
    char letter;

    for (count = 1; count <= 5; count++)
        {
        printf("\n%-2d", count);  /* left justified iteration count */
        for (letter = 'A'; letter <= 'Z'; letter++)
            printf("%c", letter);
        }
}
```

When you compile and run the program again, the screen shows

```
1 ABCDEFGHIJKLMNOPQRSTUVWXYZ
2 ABCDEFGHIJKLMNOPQRSTUVWXYZ
3 ABCDEFGHIJKLMNOPQRSTUVWXYZ
4 ABCDEFGHIJKLMNOPQRSTUVWXYZ
5 ABCDEFGHIJKLMNOPQRSTUVWXYZ
```

Each time the program displays the alphabet, it precedes the first letter with a number (left justified in a 2-character field) indicating the current value of *count*.

■ **FACT:** *For nested loops, the* break *and* continue *statements affect only the currently executing loop.*

If a nested loop executes a *continue* statement, processing continues with the next iteration of that loop. If a nested loop executes a *break* statement, processing continues at the first statement in the outer loop that follows the nested loop.

USING THE *switch* STATEMENT

In addition to the *if-else* statement, C programs can use the *switch* statement for conditional processing.

■ **FACT:** *The C* switch *statement evaluates an expression and then tries to locate a match in the associated list of values. If the list contains a match,* switch *executes the statements associated with the matching value. If* switch *fails to find a match, execution continues at the first statement following the switch.*

■ **TRAP:** *Once your program locates a matching value in the list, it executes the statements associated with the value. However, unless those statements are followed by a* break *statement, your program continues executing the instructions associated with the remaining values in the list.*

To construct a *switch* statement, follow the keyword *switch* with an expression in parentheses. Then introduce each prospective matching value with the word *case*, and conclude it with a colon. The statements that execute when a match occurs appear after the colon.

The following program (SWITCH.C) demonstrates the way a *switch* statement behaves:

```
main()
{
    char letter;

    for (letter = 'A'; letter <= 'Z'; letter++)
        switch (letter)
            {
            case 'A': printf("%c", letter);
            case 'E': printf("%c", letter);
            case 'I': printf("%c", letter);
            case 'O': printf("%c", letter);
            case 'U': printf("%c", letter);
            }
}
```

When you run the program, the output, shown here, might not be what you expected:

AAAAAEEEEIIIOOU

The program begins by comparing the letter *A* with the list of possible values. Because a match exists for the initial value of *letter*, the program executes the line associated with the matching case. However, once the program finds a matching value, it continues to execute instructions until a *break* statement occurs or until it exhausts all the instructions. When *letter* is equal to *A*, the program displays the letter *A* five times (one time for each of the identical *printf* statements in the switch. The next match occurs when *letter* is equal to *E*, so the program executes the *printf* associated with the matching *case* and each of the three subsequent *printf* statements. The program continues in this manner, displaying the letter *I* three times, the letter *O* twice, and the letter *U* once. Assuming that you actually want the program to display each vowel only once, you need to place a *break* after each *printf* statement. The revised program, SWITCH2.C, appears on the following page.

```
main()
{
    char letter;

    for (letter = 'A'; letter <= 'Z'; letter++)
        switch (letter)
            {
            case 'A': printf("%c", letter);
                    break;
            case 'E': printf("%c", letter);
                    break;
            case 'I': printf("%c", letter);
                    break;
            case 'O': printf("%c", letter);
                    break;
            case 'U': printf("%c", letter);
                    break;
            }
}
```

When you compile and run the program again, the screen shows

```
AEIOU
```

■ **FACT:** *The C* break *statement ends the execution of instructions within a* switch *statement. Execution resumes at the first instruction that follows the* switch *statement.*

By default, a program executes all *case* statements in a *switch* statement once a match occurs, beginning with the statement that is associated with the matching case. The following program (SWITCH3.C) executes the statement associated with the last *case* when it encounters any letter in the list. When you execute the program, your screen displays each vowel one time.

```
main()
{
    char letter;

    for (letter = 'A'; letter <= 'Z'; letter++)
        switch (letter)
            {
            case 'A':
            case 'E':
            case 'I':
            case 'O':
            case 'U': printf("%c", letter);
            }
}
```

Programmers refer to this process of allowing cases within a switch to execute the same set of statements as *fall-through*. Sometimes, as in the previous program, using this fall-through technique can be convenient. At other times, forgetting a *break* statement to prevent fall-through can result in an error that is difficult to detect.

■ **TRAP:** *The value that follows the keyword* case *in the* switch *statement must be a constant. You cannot use a variable.*

Although the expression that *switch* evaluates can be a variable or a mathematical expression, the values in the switch list must be constants. If you specify a variable in this list, the C compiler generates a syntax error.

■ **FACT:** *The* default *label in a* switch *statement lets you specify one or more statements that execute if* switch *fails to find a matching value.*

To specify default entries in your *switch* statement, place an entry labeled *default* in the list of values. For example, the following program (SWITCH4.C) counts the number of vowels and consonants in the alphabet.

```c
main()
{
    char letter;
    int vowels = 0;
    int consonants = 0;

    for (letter = 'A'; letter <= 'Z'; letter++)
        switch (letter)
            {
            case 'A':
            case 'E':
            case 'I':
            case 'O':
            case 'U': vowels++;
                      break;
            default: consonants++;
            }

        printf("Vowels: %d  Consonants: %d", vowels, consonants);
}
```

When you run the program, the screen shows

```
Vowels: 5   Consonants: 21
```

The *default* entry is a useful alternative when processing complexity increases.

USING THE C *goto* STATEMENT

All programming languages provide a means to branch from one area of a program to another. In most languages, this construct is the *goto* statement, and C is no exception.

■ **FACT:** *The C* goto *statement lets you branch from one location in your program to another. The* goto *statement specifies a label that identifies the location at which execution continues.*

When the compiler encounters a *goto* statement, execution continues at the first statement that follows the label specified by the *goto*. A C label is one or more characters followed by a colon. If you reference a nonexistent label, the C compiler generates a syntax error.

■ **TIP:** *You can write most programs without using the* goto *statement.*

Misusing *goto* can make your program far less readable, so most programmers avoid using it. However, so that you can see how the *goto* statement works, the following program (GOTO.C) uses *goto* to display the letters A through Z.

```
main()
{
    char letter = 'A';

    loop:
        printf("%c\n", letter++);

        if (letter <= 'Z')
            goto loop;
}
```

USING THE CONDITIONAL OPERATOR

In Chapter 4 we discussed conditional processing by means of *if-else* statements. In this chapter you learned that you can use the *switch* statement to provide conditional processing. Both *if-else* and *switch* are C control structures. In addition, C provides a unique operator called the conditional operator.

■ **FACT:** *The C conditional operator takes the form*

```
(expression) ? true_expression : false_expression
```

If expression *is true, the result of the operation is* true_expression. *If* expression *is false, the result is* false_expression.

When the C compiler encounters the conditional operator, it evaluates the first of its three expressions. If the first result is true, the compiler evaluates the second expression, which is then the result of the operation. If the first expression is false, then the third expression is evaluated, and its result is the outcome of the operation.

The following program (CONDOP.C) uses the conditional operator to compare two values and then displays the maximum and minimum.

```
main()
{
    int max, min, a = 10, b = 5;

    max = (a > b) ? a : b;
    min = (a < b) ? a : b;

    printf("Max = %d   Min = %d", max, min);
}
```

When you run the program, the screen shows

```
Max = 10   Min = 5
```

When the compiler encounters the statement

```
max = (a > b) ? a : b;
```

it first evaluates the expression $a > b$. Given the values assigned to a and b, the expression is true, so the program assigns *max* the value contained in a. To determine the minimum value, the program evaluates $a < b$. In this case, the expression is false, so the statement assigns *min* the value contained in b.

The following program also displays the minimum and maximum of two values. Unlike the previous program, which used the variables *min* and *max*, this program (CONDOP2.C) simply determines the correct values within the *printf* statement.

```
main()
{
    int a = 10, b = 5;

    printf("Max = %d   Min = %d", (a > b) ? a : b, (a < b) ? a : b);
}
```

You will find the conditional operator in many programs, but don't let it intimidate you. As you can see, its processing is quite straightforward.

HANDLING LONG CONTROL STRINGS

Later in this book, we use long *printf* statements to display the results of several calculations. The C compiler lets you break such statements after a comma or an arithmetic operator. The following program (LINEBRK.C) displays two values and their sum using *printf*:

```
main()
{
    printf("First value %d  Second value %d  Sum %d",
            5, 10, 10 + 5);
}
```

The compiler lets you wrap the *printf* statement following the comma. You cannot simply break a long control string, however; you must use the backslash character to interrupt a control string.

■ **FACT:** *To wrap a* printf *control string to the next line, place the backslash character (\ ) at the end of the interrupted line.*

The following program (LINEBRK2.C) uses a backslash to break the control string:

```
main()
{
    printf("First value %d  Second value %d\
Sum %d", 5, 10, 10 + 5);
}
```

■ **TRAP:** *If you break a* printf *control string, don't use extra spaces before the continuation. Remember, the control string tells the function how to display the output. If the control string contains extra spaces, they will appear in the output.*

The following program (LINEBRK3.C) illustrates the effect of embedding extra spaces in the control sequence:

```
main()
{
    printf("First value %d  Second value %d\
        Sum %d", 5, 10, 10 + 5);  /* leading blank spaces */
}
```

When you run the program, your screen shows

```
First value 5  Second value 10        Sum 15
```

As you can see, the extra spaces in the control string are apparent in the output.

SUMMARY

Using the *do-while* Statement

■ **FACT:** *Unlike the* while *and* for *statements, which test a condition and execute corresponding statements if the condition is true, the C* do-while *statement first executes a set of statements and then tests a condition. If the condition is true, the statements execute again and this cycle repeats until the condition is no longer true.*

■ **TIP:** *Use the* do-while *statement for application programs in which a set of instructions must execute at least once and then repeat conditionally.*

Using the *continue* Statement

■ **FACT:** *The C* continue *statement immediately directs the flow of execution to the condition portion of the* while *or* do-while *loop or to the increment portion of the* for *loop.*

■ **TRAP:** *Using the C* continue *statement can adversely affect the readability of your code. Be selective when you use the* continue *statement. In most cases you can rewrite code to eliminate it.*

A Look at the *break* Statement

■ **FACT:** *The C* break *statement terminates the processing of a loop and continues execution at the first statement that follows the loop.*

Executing a Loop Within Another Loop

■ **FACT:** *C lets you place a looping construct in the set of instructions that execute for another loop. The inner loop is called a nested loop.*

■ **FACT:** *For nested loops, the* break *and* continue *statements affect only the currently executing loop.*

Using the *switch* Statement

■ **FACT:** *The C* switch *statement evaluates an expression and then tries to locate a match in the associated list of values. If the list contains a match,* switch *executes the statements associated with the matching value. If* switch *fails to find a match, execution resumes at the first statement following the switch.*

■ **TRAP:** *Once your program locates a matching value in the list, it executes the statements associated with the value. However, unless those statements are followed by a* break *statement, your program continues executing the instructions associated with the remaining values in the list.*

■ **FACT:** *The C* break *statement ends the execution of instructions within a* switch *statement. Execution resumes at the first instruction that follows the* switch *statement.*

■ **TRAP:** *The value that follows the keyword* case *in the* switch *statement must be a constant. You cannot use a variable.*

■ **FACT:** *The* default *label in a* switch *statement lets you specify one or more statements that execute if* switch *fails to find a matching value.*

Using the C *goto* Statement

■ **FACT:** *The C* goto *statement lets you branch from one location in your program to another. The* goto *statement specifies a label that identifies the location at which execution continues.*

■ **TIP:** *You can write most applications without using the* goto *statement.*

Using the Conditional Operator

■ **FACT:** *The C conditional operator takes the form*

```
(expression) ? true_expression : false_expression
```

If expression *is true, the result of the operation is* true_expression. *If* expression *is false, the result is* false_expression.

Handling Long Control Strings

■ **FACT:** *To wrap a* printf *control string to the next line, place the backward slash character (\ ) at the end of the interrupted line.*

■ **TRAP:** *If you break a* printf *control string, don't use extra spaces before the continuation. Remember, the control string tells the function how to display the output. If the control string contains extra spaces, they will appear in the output.*

GLOSSARY

nested loop A loop that is embedded within another loop.

## CHAPTER 6

Getting Started with C Constants and Macros

As you learned in Chapter 3, you can specify meaningful names for variables in C. You can also define names for constants—values that don't change during program execution. In this chapter you learn to define constants, and you learn the advantages of doing do. You also learn about include files, which we briefly discussed in Chapter 1, and about the C macros *putchar* and *getchar*, which perform input or output a character at a time.

WHAT IS THE C PREPROCESSOR?

Each time you compile a C source file, a program called the C preprocessor runs to include other necessary files or to make specific substitutions you have defined in your source file.

■ **FACT:** *Before the C compiler examines the syntax of your source code, the preprocessor executes directives that result in insertions or substitutions of text in the file.*

This chapter examines the C preprocessor directives and the advantages they provide to your programs.

GETTING STARTED WITH *#define*

The processing that a program accomplishes often relies on the manipulation of numeric constants. For example, the following program (WEEKDAY.C) performs specific processing based on the indicated day of the week:

```
main()
{
    int week_day = 1;

    if (week_day == 0)
        printf("Day of the week is Monday");

    else if (week_day == 1)
        printf("Day of the week is Tuesday");

    else if (week_day == 2)
        printf("Day of the week is Wednesday");

    else if (week_day == 3)
        printf("Day of the week is Thursday");

    else if (week_day == 4)
        printf("Day of the week is Friday");
}
```

This program bases its processing on the value of the variable *week_day*. The valid replacements for the variable—the values 0, 1, 2, 3, and 4—are themselves constants.

■ **FACT:** *C lets you assign meaningful names to constants by using the* #define *preprocessor directive.*

You use the *#define* preprocessor directive to assign meaningful names to constants. For example, rather than referring to Monday as the value 0, you can associate the name *MONDAY* with the value 0, as shown here:

```
#define MONDAY 0
```

■ **TIP:** *To distinguish constants from variables, most C programmers use lowercase letters for variable names and uppercase letters for constants.*

Although you can define constants throughout your program, for consistency, place your definitions at the start of your code. Most programmers follow this practice. Grouping *#define* directives at the beginning of the file helps you locate quickly the value associated with a specific constant.

The following program (WEEKDAY2.C) enhances the preceding program by using meaningful constant names:

```
#define MONDAY      0
#define TUESDAY     1
#define WEDNESDAY   2
#define THURSDAY    3
#define FRIDAY      4

main()
{
    int week_day = TUESDAY;

    if (week_day == MONDAY)
        printf("Day of the week is Monday");

    else if (week_day == TUESDAY)
        printf("Day of the week is Tuesday");

    else if (week_day == WEDNESDAY)
        printf("Day of the week is Wednesday");

    else if (week_day == THURSDAY)
        printf("Day of the week is Thursday");

    else if (week_day == FRIDAY)
        printf("Day of the week is Friday");
}
```

Using meaningful constant names, like choosing intelligible names for variables, makes your program more readable. In addition, constant names simplify the process of changing a program. Assume, for example, that your program uses constant values instead of defined constant names and tests multiple times to see whether the weekday equals 1 (for Tuesday, in our example). If you later want to associate a different value with Tuesday, you have to locate and change each occurrence of the following condition:

```
if (week_day == 1)
```

Had you instead written each expression as

```
if (week_day == TUESDAY)
```

the only line you have to change is the initial *#define* directive in which you associate the constant name with its value:

```
#define TUESDAY 1
```

When you recompile the program, the preprocessor substitutes the values for you.

■ **FACT:** *The preprocessor substitutes the values associated with each constant into the correct location in the program.*

When the preprocessor completes its substitutions, the C compiler examines and compiles your program.

■ **FACT:** *Just as you can define numeric constants, you can use the* #define *directive to define character string constants.*

The following program (STRNGDEF.C) defines the constant *CHAPTER*, which contains the characters *"This is Chapter 6"*. This program demonstrates the fact that a *#define* directive can replace a constant name with a string. (The replacement need not be a numeric value.) The program uses the %s format specifier with *printf* to display the characters.

```
#define CHAPTER "This is Chapter 6"

main()
{
    printf("%s", CHAPTER);
}
```

When you run the program, the screen shows

```
This is Chapter 6
```

■ **FACT:** *The %s format specifier directs* printf *to display a string of characters.*

In Chapter 2 you examined most of the *printf* format specifiers. We will use %s extensively in the next chapter as we discuss character strings in C.

■ **FACT:** *The /E and /P options direct CL to let you view the intermediate, preprocessed file. The /E option directs CL to display the file on your screen. The /P option directs CL to create a file with the extension I. The options must precede the filename on the command line.*

Suppose you compile the source file WEEKDAY2.C (on the preceding page) with the following command:

```
C> CL /P WEEKDAY2.C
```

This command creates a file called WEEKDAY2.I that contains the file after preprocessing. Remember, you must specify the /P option in uppercase as shown. The file WEEKDAY2.I now contains the text on the following page. Use the DOS or OS/2 TYPE command to display the contents of the file on your screen.

```
main()
{
    int week_day = 1;

    if (week_day == 0)
        printf("Day of the week is Monday");

    else if (week_day == 1)
        printf("Day of the week is Tuesday");

    else if (week_day == 2)
        printf("Day of the week is Wednesday");

    else if (week_day == 3)
        printf("Day of the week is Thursday");

    else if (week_day == 4)
        printf("Day of the week is Friday");
}
```

■ **TRAP:** *If you specify /E or /P, CL only preprocesses the file. It does not compile and link.*

The purpose of the /E and /P qualifiers is to let you examine the intermediate preprocessor file. To compile and link your code, you must invoke CL without these qualifiers.

CREATING SIMPLE MACROS USING *#define*

A macro is simply a shorthand notation that you can use to assign meaningful names to specific expressions. In Chapter 5 you used the following statement to assign the maximum of two values to the variable *max*:

```
max = (a > b) ? a : b;
```

When you want to find a maximum in your program, you must type the conditional expression in its entirety. However, if you use a macro, you simply give the expression in shorthand at the start of your program with a *#define* directive and then use the macro name whenever you want to refer to the expression. You could treat the conditional expression above as a macro by defining it as follows at the start of your program:

```
#define MAX(a,b) (a > b) ? a : b
```

■ **TRAP:** *If a macro requires values, be sure that you type no spaces between the macro name and the left parenthesis that follows it.*

The parenthesis next to the macro name in the *#define* directive indicates that the name is a macro, not a constant. If a space appears between the macro name and the parenthesis, the preprocessor assumes that the parenthesized characters are part of the replacement for a constant. With this exception, you are free to use spaces within your macro as you require.

When the preprocessor encounters a reference to a macro in a program, it replaces the reference with the associated expression. This process is called macro expansion.

The following program (MAX.C) demonstrates the use of the MAX macro:

```
#define MAX(a,b) (a > b) ? a : b

main()
{
    int a = 10, b = 5;

    printf("The maximum value is %d", MAX(a,b));
}
```

Compile the program with the /E option. When you do so, the screen shows

```
C> CL /E MAX.C
Microsoft (R) C Optimizing Compiler Version 5.10
Copyright (c) Microsoft Corp 1984, 1985, 1986, 1987, 1988. All rights reserved.

#line 1 "MAX.C"

main()
{
    int a = 10, b = 5;

    printf("The maximum value is %d", (a > b) ? a : b);
}

C>
```

■ **TRAP:** *The preprocessor replaces each macro reference in your source file with the substitute text exactly as it is written in the macro definition. In most cases, you don't want a semicolon in the substituted text.*

The C preprocessor performs a one-for-one substitution. If your macro definition contains a semicolon,

```
#define MAX(a,b) (a > b) ? a : b;
```

the preprocessor includes the semicolon in each substitution. Given the sample statement

```
printf("%d", MAX(a,b));
```

the C preprocessor expands the macro, including the semicolon as shown here:

```
printf("%d", (a > b) ? a : b ;);
```

Because the expansion includes a semicolon in the *printf* statement, the C compiler will generate a syntax error.

The following directive defines a macro that returns the minimum of two values:

```
#define MIN(x,y) (x < y) ? x : y
```

As you can see, you can use any letters within the parentheses that follow the macro. These letters need not be declared variables because they are essentially placeholders. When you compile your source file, the preprocessor substitutes the first value within the parentheses for each occurrence of x and the second value for each occurrence of y, as shown in the following example:

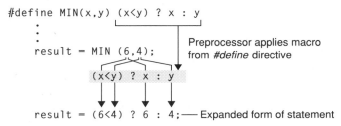

```
#define MIN(x,y) (x<y) ? x : y
      .
      .
      .
   result = MIN (6,4);
```

Preprocessor applies macro from *#define* directive

```
   (x<y) ? x : y
```

```
   result = (6<4) ? 6 : 4;
```
—— Expanded form of statement

■ **TIP:** *Place parentheses around each component in a macro definition. Doing so ensures that the preprocessor expands a macro correctly.*

The following macro, SQUARE, returns the square of a value. Let's examine SQUARE closely to see why programmers usually isolate each component of a macro definition with parentheses:

```
#define SQUARE(x) x * x
```

If your program invokes SQUARE with an integer, as in the following statement:

```
value = SQUARE(5);
```

the preprocessor substitution becomes

```
value = 5 * 5;
```

However, if the program invokes SQUARE with an expression, as in the following statement:

```
value = SQUARE(5 + 2);
```

the preprocessor expands the macro as

```
value = 5 + 2 * 5 + 2;
```

Because of C's operator precedence (multiplication before addition), the result is 17 rather than 49 (the correct square of 7). However, by grouping the macro elements in parentheses, as follows:

```
#define SQUARE(x) ((x) * (x))
```

you ensure that the preprocessor expands the macro correctly. For example, the following statement

```
value = SQUARE(2 + 5);
```

would be expanded by the preprocessor to

```
value = ((2 + 5) * (2 + 5));
```

Because the compiler evaluates expressions in parentheses first, the addition occurs before the multiplication, and the program assigns the variable the correct value, 49. Also note that we grouped not only each *x* but the entire macro text within parentheses:

```
((x) * (x))
```

Suppose you write a program that uses the macro in a statement such as the following:

```
amount = 25 / SQUARE(5);
```

If the macro lacks the outer pair of parentheses:

```
#define SQUARE(x) (x) * (x)
```

then expansion of the preceding statement results in

```
amount = 25 / (5) * (5);
```

This statement assigns *amount* the value 25, which is not the correct result. If you enclose the entire macro definition within parentheses, as follows:

```
#define SQUARE(x) ((x) * (x))
```

the statement in your program

```
amount = 25 / SQUARE(5);
```

expands to

```
amount = 25 / ((5) * (5))
```

In this form, the statement correctly assigns *amount* the value 1.

■ **TIP:** *If your macro or constant does not fit on one line, place the backslash character (\ ) at the end of the line to be continued.*

The macro TO_UPPERCASE returns the uppercase character that corresponds to the letter it receives. By ending the first line of the macro with a backslash, we can continue the macro on a second line, as shown on the following page.

```
#define TO_UPPERCASE(letter) (letter >= 'a' && letter <= 'z')\
    ? 'A' + letter - 'a' : letter
```

This macro works by examining the value of *letter*. If the variable represents a lowercase letter, the macro converts it to uppercase. If *letter* lies outside the range of lowercase letters, the macro leaves the letter unchanged.

The following program (MACROTST.C) demonstrates the TO_UPPERCASE macro:

```
#define to_uppercase(letter) (letter >= 'a' && letter <= 'z')\
    ? 'A' + letter - 'a' : letter

main()
{
    char testchar = 'a';

    printf("The letter is %c", to_uppercase(testchar));
}
```

When you compile the program, the preprocessor expands the TO_UPPERCASE macro. When you execute the program, the value of *testchar* is changed from 'a' to 'A' and displayed by a *printf* statement.

USING THE /D OPTION

Just as you must define variables before you reference them, you must define constants and macros before you reference them. The CL option /D lets you define a constant on the command line when you compile a program. This option is useful if, for some reason, you left a constant undefined in your source file.

■ **FACT:** *The /D option directs CL to define a constant or macro for use in the program.*

The following program (CONSTDEF.C) uses the constant MONDAY but does not define it:

```
main()
{
    printf("%d", MONDAY);
}
```

When you compile the program, the compiler generates a syntax error because MONDAY is undefined. As a temporary solution, use the /D option with CL to define the macro, as shown here:

```
C> CL /D MONDAY=0 CONSTDEF.C
```

The C compiler treats MONDAY as if the source file defined it with a *#define* directive. Be sure that you later edit the file to include the *#define* directive.

GETTING STARTED WITH INCLUDE FILES

In Chapter 1 we noted that the C compiler examines your C source code and, optionally, any include files (those with the extension H) that your program requires.

■ **FACT:** *An include file is a file containing C source code that the preprocessor reads into your program for use during compilation.*

Normally, include files contain constant and macro definitions. By placing commonly used constants and macros into a separate file, you can include that file in several programs to ensure that all the programs use the same set of constants and that the macros are expressed consistently.

■ **FACT:** *The #include directive tells the C preprocessor to include the specified file.*

The C compiler actually lets you reference the file you want to include in two ways. First, you can place the filename within angle brackets, as shown here:

```
#include <stdio.h>
```

Second, you can place the filename in quotation marks:

```
#include "mydef.h"
```

The difference between the two methods lies in the directories the preprocessor searches for the file.

■ **FACT:** *If you place the filename in angle brackets, the preprocessor first searches the directory associated with the* INCLUDE= *environment setting, and then it searches the current directory. If you place the filename in quotation marks, the preprocessor searches only the current directory (or the specified pathname).*

If you include a file whose name appears within brackets, *<stdio.h>*, for example, the preprocessor first searches the directory associated with the *INCLUDE=* environment setting. If the preprocessor fails to locate the file in that directory, it searches the current directory.

The Microsoft C compiler places its own include files in the directory that corresponds to the default *INCLUDE=* environment entry. (As you will recall, the Microsoft C installation process creates three environment entries: *LIB=*, *TMP=*, and *INCLUDE=*. The *INCLUDE=* entry specifies the location of the Microsoft C include files.) When you need to access an include file that resides in that directory, place the filename within angle brackets.

If you include a file whose name appears within quotation marks, *"mydef.h"*, for example, the preprocessor searches for the file only in the specified directory, or in the current directory if none is specified.

■ **TIP:** *Place user-defined include files in a directory other than the compiler's include directory. This prevents your inadvertently overwriting an essential compiler file.*

Most C programmers use angle brackets to refer to the include files that came with the compiler. By placing quotation marks around user-defined include files, you ensure that another programmer can easily distinguish whether the file is compiler specific or user defined.

■ **TRAP:** *If the preprocessor cannot find the file specified in an #include directive, the compiler generates a syntax error.*

If the C compiler cannot find the specified file, it generates a syntax error. Be sure you spelled the filename correctly and included a subdirectory path if necessary.

■ **TIP:** *Print or display the include files provided with your compiler.*

Most C compilers provide several include files. Those provided with Microsoft C are described in the following table. Take time to examine each. Not only will you gain a better understanding of their contents, but you can also learn good C programming techniques.

File	*Function*
assert.h	Defines the assert macro
bios.h	Defines structures, constants, and functions used to interact with the PC BIOS
conio.h	Defines the functions used for console and port I/O
ctype.h	Defines the macros used for character classification
direct.h	Defines the functions used for directory manipulation
dos.h	Defines the structures, macros, and functions used to interact with DOS
errno.h	Defines the system-wide error numbers
fcntl.h	Defines the constants used for file control in the open function
float.h	Defines compiler-specific floating point values
graph.h	Defines the functions and constants used for graphics operations
io.h	Contains function declarations for low-level file I/O operations
limits.h	Defines compiler-specific type limit values
malloc.h	Defines the functions and constants used for memory allocation

(continued)

continued

File	Function
math.h	Defines the functions and constants used for C mathematical operations
memory.h	Defines the functions used for buffer (memory) manipulation
process.h	Defines the functions and constants used in process control (*spawn*)
search.h	Defines the functions used for sorting and searching operations
setjmp.h	Defines the buffer used to store the machine state prior to a *setjmp* operation
share.h	Defines the file-sharing modes for the routine *sopen*
signal.h	Defines the functions used in signal processing operations
stdarg.h	Defines macros for accessing arguments when a function uses a variable number of arguments
stddef.h	Defines the commonly used constants, types, and variables
stdlib.h	Defines functions that are standard to C compilers but that don't fit in another category
stdio.h	Defines the functions, constants, macros, and structures used for standard I/O operations
string.h	Defines functions used in string manipulation routines
time.h	Defines functions and structures used for date and time manipulation
varargs.h	Defines the XENIX-style macros used to access function arguments when a variable number of arguments are used

USING *putchar* FOR CHARACTER OUTPUT

So far, all the programs we have examined have used *printf* for character output. C also provides the *putchar* macro that allows you to write a character at a time.

■ **FACT:** *C provides the* putchar *macro, which outputs a single character at a time.*

To use *putchar*, a program must include the file stdio.h. The following program (PUTCHTST.C) uses *putchar* to display the letters of the alphabet:

```
#include <stdio.h>  /* needed for putchar */

main()
{
    char letter;

    for (letter = 'A'; letter <= 'Z'; letter++)
        putchar(letter);
}
```

■ **TRAP:** *If you use the* putchar *macro in your program but fail to include the file stdio.h, the macro is undefined, and your program will not link.*

In the preceding program, notice that we used angle brackets around the filename stdio.h in the *#include* directive. The brackets tell the compiler to locate the file in the subdirectory associated with the *INCLUDE=* environment entry.

■ **FACT:** *The* putchar *macro displays the ASCII representation of a value.*

The chart in Appendix A shows the ASCII values that correspond to the decimal values 0 through 127. You can use these values with *putchar* to display characters on the screen. For example, to display the uppercase letter A on the screen, use the ASCII equivalent with *putchar*:

```
putchar(65);
```

USING *getchar* FOR CHARACTER INPUT

Just as the *putchar* macro directs the compiler to display an ASCII character, the *getchar* macro directs it to get a character of input from the user.

■ **FACT:** *The* getchar *macro accepts a single character of input at a time. To use* getchar, *a program must include the file stdio.h.*

The following program (GETCHTST.C) prompts the user to type a letter and then to press Enter. The program then displays the letter.

```
#include <stdio.h>   /* needed for getchar */

main()
{
    char letter;

    printf("Type a letter and press Enter\n");

    letter = getchar();

    printf("The letter entered was %c", letter);
}
```

As you can see, *getchar* also requires that you include stdio.h. When *getchar* gets a character, it assigns it to the specified variable:

```
letter = getchar();
```

The following program (LINEOUT.C) uses *getchar* and *putchar* to display an entire line of text:

```
#include <stdio.h>   /* needed for getchar and putchar */

main()
{
    char letter;

    printf("Type a line of text\n");
    do
        {
        letter = getchar();
        putchar(letter);
        }
    while (letter != '\n');
}
```

Remember that the C newline character is equivalent to a carriage return and linefeed. When the user presses the Enter key, *getchar* assigns *letter* the newline character, which causes the condition in the *while* statement to be false and the loop to end.

■ **FACT:** *The* getchar *macro uses a technique called buffered input. The characters the user types are not available to* getchar *until the user presses Enter.*

Although *getchar* gets a single character at a time, the entire string of input characters is held in a memory buffer and is not available for processing until the user presses Enter. In the preceding program, this attribute of *getchar* lets the user make changes with the Backspace key before pressing Enter. Later in this book we will examine C routines that allow your programs to access keystrokes as they are pressed.

SUMMARY

What Is the C Preprocessor?

■ **FACT:** *Before the C compiler examines the syntax of your source code, the pre-processor executes directives that result in insertions or substitutions of text in the file.*

Getting Started with *#define*

■ **FACT:** *C lets you assign meaningful names to constants by using the* #define *pre-processor directive.*

■ **TIP:** *To distinguish constants from variables, most C programmers use lowercase letters for variable names and uppercase letters for constants.*

■ **FACT:** *The preprocessor substitutes the values associated with each constant into the correct location in the program.*

■ **FACT:** *Just as you can define numeric constants, you can use the* #define *directive to define character string constants.*

■ **FACT:** *The %s format specifier directs* printf *to display a string of characters.*

■ **FACT:** *The /E and /P options direct CL to let you view the intermediate, pre-processed file. The /E option directs CL to display the file on your screen. The /P option directs CL to create a file with the extension I. The options must precede the filename on the command line.*

■ **TRAP:** *If you specify /E or /P, CL only preprocesses the file. It does not compile and link.*

Creating Simple Macros Using *#define*

■ **TRAP:** *If a macro requires values, be sure that you type no spaces between the macro name and the left parenthesis that follows it.*

■ **TRAP:** *The preprocessor replaces each macro reference in your source file with the substitute text exactly as it is written in the macro definition. In most cases, you don't want a semicolon in the substituted text.*

■ **TIP:** *Place parentheses around each component in a macro definition. Doing so ensures that the preprocessor expands a macro correctly.*

■ **TIP:** *If your macro or constant does not fit on one line, place the backslash character (\ ) at the end of the line to be continued.*

Using the /D Qualifier

■ **FACT:** *The /D option directs CL to define a constant or macro for use in the program.*

Getting Started with Include Files

■ **FACT:** *An include file is a file containing C source code that the preprocessor reads into your program for use during compilation.*

■ **FACT:** *The #include directive tells the C preprocessor to include the specified file.*

■ **FACT:** *If you place the filename in angle brackets, the preprocessor first searches the directory associated with the* INCLUDE= *environment setting, and then it searches the current directory. If you place the filename in quotation marks, the preprocessor searches only the current directory (or the specified pathname).*

■ **TIP:** *Place user-defined include files in a directory other than the compiler's include directory. This prevents your inadvertently overwriting an essential compiler file.*

■ **TRAP:** *If the preprocessor cannot find the file specified in an #include directive, the compiler generates a syntax error.*

■ **TIP:** *Print or display the include files provided with your compiler.*

Using *putchar* for Character Output

■ **FACT:** *C provides the* putchar *macro, which outputs a single character at a time.*

■ **TRAP:** *If you use the* putchar *macro in your program but fail to include the file stdio.h, the macro is undefined, and your program will not link.*

■ **FACT:** *The* putchar *macro displays the ASCII representation of a value.*

Using *getchar* for Character Input

■ **FACT:** *The* getchar *macro accepts a single character of input at a time. To use* getchar, *a program must include the file stdio.h.*

■ **FACT:** *The* getchar *macro uses a technique called buffered input. The characters the user types are not available to* getchar *until the user presses Enter.*

GLOSSARY

constant A value that does not change during the execution of a program. The C *#define* directive lets you assign meaningful names to constants.

macro A shorthand notation for an expression or a group of instructions. The *#define* directive lets you define a C macro.

preprocessor A program that runs before C compiles your program. The C preprocessor replaces the constants and macros with their corresponding values and inserts any include files you specify with *#include*.

CHAPTER 7

Getting Started with Character Strings

Several programs that we have examined so far have stored values in variables of types *char*, *int*, and *float*. Most application programs, however, need to store and manipulate a set of related characters, such as a name or an address. To store characters in this manner, you need to define character strings. In this chapter you learn how to create and manipulate character strings in C.

DEFINING A CHARACTER STRING

The C data type *char* stores one character of information. To store multiple characters, you need to tell the C compiler the number of characters to store.

■ **FACT:** *To define a character string, create a variable of type* char *that specifies within left and right brackets the number of characters to store.*

The following definitions create character strings named *small*, *medium*, and *large*. Each string is capable of storing the number of characters that appears in brackets after the variable name.

```
char small[64], medium[128], large[256];
```

■ **FACT:** *The compiler stores each character of a string in a unique storage location. The first character of a string resides in element 0.*

■ **TRAP:** *Both the size of a character string and the specific elements of the string are iden-*
tified by the string name followed by a number in brackets. However, because the first char-
acter resides in element 0, the number of the last element is always 1 less than the string size.

Given the definition

```
char name[10];
```

the compiler creates a character string called *name* that is capable of storing 10 characters.
The letters in the string reside in elements 0–9, as shown in Figure 7-1.

```
name [0]
name [1]
name [2]
name [3]
name [4]
name [5]
name [6]
name [7]
name [8]
name [9]
```

FIGURE 7-1.
The characters of a string reside in separate memory locations and can be
individually identified.

■ **TIP:** *A null character (ASCII 0) must be the last character in your string. Represent the*
null character in C with the escape sequence '\0'.

You can set aside space for character strings of any length. The number of characters
you assign to a string may be fewer than the number that were set aside; you can terminate
the string at any point using the null character, '\0'. In fact, the compiler requires the null
character at the end of every string.

The following program (AZSTRING.C) creates a character string called *alphabet* with
storage for 27 characters (26 letters plus the null character). It then assigns the letters of the
alphabet to the string. To specify the end of the string, the program assigns the last character
the constant '\0'. Finally, the program uses *printf* to display the contents of the string.

```
main()
{
    char alphabet[27];   /* 26 letters plus null */
    char letter;
    int index;

    for (letter = 'A', index = 0; letter <= 'Z'; letter++, index++)
```

(continued)

continued

```
        alphabet[index] = letter;

    alphabet[index] = '\0';  /* add null byte to end string */

    printf("%s", alphabet);
}
```

The program uses the variable *letter* to store a letter of the alphabet. The integer variable *index* reflects the position of each letter within the string. The program initializes *index* to 0, which is the first storage position in the string, *string[0]*. Each iteration of the loop increments both *letter* and *index*. As a result, the program stores letters in the string as shown in Figure 7-2.

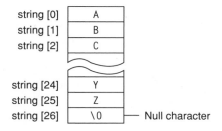

FIGURE 7-2.
The AZSTRING program stores 27 consecutive items in memory to fill the string alphabet.

When the *printf* function displays the string, it examines the string a character at a time until it encounters '\0'. Because *printf* displays the entire string of characters, as opposed to displaying a specific character, the *printf* statement refers to the string name *alphabet* without brackets.

The following program (NULLTEST.C) demonstrates the use of the null character in a loop. To display the contents of the string, it uses the *putchar* macro instead of *printf.*

```
#include <stdio.h>  /* needed for putchar macro */

main()
{
    char alphabet[27], letter;
    int index;

    for (letter = 'A', index = 0; letter <= 'Z'; letter++, index++)
        alphabet[index] = letter;
```

(continued)

continued

```
    alphabet[index] = '\0';

    for (index = 0; alphabet[index] != '\0'; index++)
        putchar(alphabet[index]);
}
```

The first *for* loop assigns each letter of the alphabet to an element of the string. The statement after that loop assigns the null character to the string element that follows 'Z'. The second *for* loop repeatedly tests whether the value of the current string element is the null character. If the element is not '\0', the *putchar* macro displays the character. When *alphabet[index]* does contain the null character, the loop ends.

The following program (INSTRING.C) prompts the user to enter a string. The program redisplays the input string as well as the number of characters it contains.

```
#include <stdio.h>   /* needed for getchar macro */
#define END '\0'

main()
{
    char string[128];
    int index = 0;

    printf("Type a string of characters and press Enter\n");
    while ((string[index] = getchar()) != '\n')
        index++;
    string[index] = END;
    printf("%s\n(string contains %d characters)", string, index);
}
```

The program uses the preprocessor directive *#define* to assign the name END to the ASCII null character '\0', which marks the end of a character string.

Now let's look closely at the *while* loop:

```
while ((string[index] = getchar()) != '\n')
    index++;
```

The compiler first evaluates the instruction in the inner pair of parentheses, *string[index] = getchar()*. That instruction assigns the character returned by *getchar* to the current element of *string*. After that assignment is made, the compiler tests whether the element is equal to the newline character. If the current character is '\n', the loop ends; if that condition is not met, *getchar* retrieves the next character.

The following program (STRCOMP.C) compares the contents of two strings. The program prompts the user to enter the strings, and then it displays the first difference between the strings.

```
#include <stdio.h>   /* needed for getchar macro */
#define END '\0'

main()
{
    char first[128], second[128];
    int i;

    printf("Enter first string to compare\n");
    for (i = 0; (first[i] = getchar()) != '\n'; ++i)
        { ; }
    first[i] = END;

    printf ("Enter second string to compare\n");
    for (i = 0; (second[i] = getchar()) != '\n'; ++i)
        { ; }
    second[i] = END;

    /* compare the strings character by character */

    for (i = 0; first[i] == second[i]; ++i)
        if (first[i] == END)
            break;

    /* If the characters in the two strings are identical,
     * the current elements of both are null characters.
     * Otherwise, i is the index to the first character
     * at which the strings differ. Because the first position
     * in the string is zero, the characters that differ are i + 1
     */ characters from the left.

    if (first[i] == END && second[i] == END)
        printf("Strings are identical");
    else
        printf("Strings first differ %d character(s) from the left", i + 1);
}
```

Most C programs work extensively with character strings, so you need to become familiar with the large set of string manipulation routines that C provides. We will examine many of these routines in the remaining chapters of this book.

UNDERSTANDING STRING CONSTANTS

In Chapter 6 you learned that C lets you define character string constants, such as

```
#define CHAPTER "This is Chapter 7"
```

■ **FACT:** *When you specify a string constant within quotation marks, the compiler appends the null character to the string.*

When the compiler stores the character string *This is Chapter 7* in memory, it appends an ASCII 0, or null character. As Figure 7-3 shows, the compiler places the null escape sequence '\0' in the last character location of the string.

T	h	i	s		i	s		C	h	a	p	t	e	r		7	\0

FIGURE 7-3.
When stored in memory, a string constant is terminated with a null character.

Escape sequences occupy only one character location. If, for example, we change the string constant to

```
#define CHAPTER "This is Chapter 7\n"
```

the compiler stores the characters in memory as shown in Figure 7-4.

T	h	i	s		i	s		C	h	a	p	t	e	r		7	\n	\0

FIGURE 7-4.
The newline and null escape sequences each reside in one character position.

■ **FACT:** *C programmers often refer to character strings as ASCII zero strings or null-terminated strings, because of the null character in the last position.*

INITIALIZING CHARACTER STRINGS

As you have learned, C lets you initialize variables at the same time that you declare them:

```
int index = 0;
```

C character strings are a slight exception. If you attempt to initialize a string as shown at the top of the next page (BADINIT.C), many C compilers (including Microsoft 5.1) generate a syntax error.

```
main()
{
    char string[128] = "This is Chapter 7";

    printf("%s", string);
}
```

Later in this book we will discuss global variables, which provide a solution to this problem. As an alternative, the following program (GOODINIT.C) precedes the string declaration with the keyword *static*.

```
main()
{
    static char string[128] = "This is Chapter 7";

    printf("%s", string);
}
```

Your C compiler supports two types of variables, automatic and static. By default, C variables are automatic. Unlike the four basic data types, complex data types, such as character strings, cannot be initialized as automatic variables. To initialize a character string, you must declare it using the *static* qualifier. In Chapter 16 we will examine the characteristics of static variables.

USING *gets* AND *puts* FOR STRING I/O

The *gets* function obtains a character string from the user; the *puts* function displays a character string.

■ **FACT:** *The built-in function* gets *obtains a character string from the user. The* puts *function displays a character string.*

The following program (GETSPUTS.C) prompts the user to enter a string and uses the *gets* function to retrieve it. The program then uses the *puts* function to display the string.

```
main()
{
    char string[128];

    puts("Type a string and press Enter");
    gets(string);
    puts(string);
}
```

■ **FACT:** *The* gets *function places a null character at the end of your string.*

The *gets* function works much like our previous programs. The function itself uses *getchar* to get characters until it locates a carriage return. As with *getchar*, *gets* lets the user edit the line of text using the Backspace key. Once the user presses Enter, *gets* retrieves only the characters that appear on the screen.

■ **TRAP:** *If the user types more characters than your string has space for,* gets *overwrites other values in memory. This can cause your program to fail and can even lock up your computer.*

Be sure to define character strings that are large enough to store the required number of characters. Functions such as *gets* test for '\0' to find the end of a string. They assume that you have provided sufficient character storage space.

■ **FACT:** *The* puts *function displays a newline character at the end of each string.*

When *puts* encounters a null character, which terminates the string, the function displays the newline character. This characteristic of *puts* enables us to use the statement

```
puts("Type a string and press Enter");
```

to display a string and return the cursor to the beginning of the next line.

COMPARING "A" TO 'A'

C defines characters contained within double quotation marks as a character string and terminates each character string with the null character. For example, the compiler stores the string "A" as a null-terminated string.

The compiler does not place the null character after a character constant enclosed by single quotation marks. For example, it stores the character constant 'A' in memory without the null character. The following illustration shows the difference between "A" and 'A' in storage:

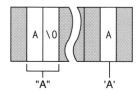

SUMMARY

Defining a Character String

■ **FACT:** *To define a character string, create a variable of type* char *that specifies within left and right brackets the number of characters to store.*

■ **FACT:** *The compiler stores each character of a string in a unique storage location. The first character of a string resides in element 0.*

■ **TRAP:** *Both the size of a character string and the specific elements of the string are identified by the string name followed by a number in brackets. However, because the first character resides in element 0, the number of the last element is always 1 less than the string size.*

■ **TIP:** *A null character (ASCII 0) must be the last character in your string. Represent the null character in C with the escape sequence '\0'.*

Understanding String Constants

■ **FACT:** *When you specify a string constant within quotation marks, the compiler appends the null character to the string.*

■ **FACT:** *C programmers often refer to character strings as ASCII zero strings, or null-terminated strings, because of the null character in the last position.*

Using *gets* and *puts* for String I/O

■ **FACT:** *The built-in function* gets *obtains a character string from the user. The* puts *function displays a character string.*

■ **FACT:** *The* gets *function places a null character at the end of your string.*

■ **TRAP:** *If the user types more characters than your string has space for,* gets *overwrites other values in memory. This can cause your program to fail and can even lock up your computer.*

■ **FACT:** *The* puts *function displays a newline character at the end of each string.*

GLOSSARY

character string A collection of one or more related characters. C programmers also call character strings ASCII zero strings or null-terminated strings.

null character An undisplayed character with ASCII code 0. The compiler terminates character strings with the null character. To represent the null character, type the sequence '\0'.

## CHAPTER 8

Building Simple
C Functions

The C programs we have examined so far are quite simple—short, uncomplicated source files with limited usefulness. But as the complexity of your programs increases, so does the number of statements they employ. To simplify your programming tasks, the C compiler lets you break a large program into logically related collections of statements called functions.

This chapter shows you how to write C functions. In addition to simplifying difficult programming tasks, functions improve the readability of your programs. You'll also find that you can use many functions in more than one program, which saves you development and testing time. After all, if you have a function that works well, why reinvent it every time you need it? And in a programming shop, the division of a task into separate functions permits work on a program to be distributed by function among several people.

GETTING STARTED WITH C FUNCTIONS

Using C functions is quite straightforward. You've already used four: *main, printf, puts,* and *gets.* In this section you will create your first C functions. As you create functions, simply think of them as subprograms that perform specific tasks.

■ **FACT:** *C programs contain one or more functions. The first function that executes is always* main. *The function* main *can invoke other functions to perform its processing.*

The following program (GETSPUTS.C), which we created in Chapter 7, uses three functions. It begins execution at *main*, which in turn calls the functions *puts* and *gets*.

```
main()
{
    char string[128];

    puts("Type a string and press Enter");
    gets(string);
    puts(string);
}
```

■ **TIP:** *Treat your own C functions as you treat* main. *Each function has a name followed by parentheses, grouping symbols, and statements.*

The following program (GIMME5.C) creates and uses the function *show_digit* to display the number 5 on your screen:

```
main()
{
    show_digit();
}

show_digit()
{
    printf("5\n");
}
```

The program begins execution at *main*. Within *main*, the program refers to the function *show_digit*. The program then passes control to the function *show_digit*, which displays the number 5. When *show_digit* finishes processing, it returns control to *main*, and the program completes execution.

■ **TRAP:** *The parentheses following a function name must be present. If you omit them, the C compiler generates a syntax error.*

In your source code, the parentheses following a function name inform the C compiler that the name refers to a function rather than to a variable. Later in this chapter you will learn how to pass values to your functions. To do so, you must place the values within the parentheses, as you do when you pass a control string to *printf*.

The program at the top of the next page (GIMME5_2.C) expands GIMME5.C to demonstrate the flow of control more clearly.

```
main()
{
    printf("About to call show_digit\n");
    show_digit();
    printf("Back from the function");
}

show_digit()
{
    printf("5\n");
}
```

When you run the program, the screen shows

```
About to call show_digit
5
Back from the function
```

The program begins by calling the *printf* function. After *printf* executes, the program calls the function *show_digit*, which displays the value 5 on the screen. When execution returns from *show_digit*, it continues in *main*, which again calls *printf*.

■ **TRAP:** *If you misspell a function name in the program, CL compiles the program but does not link it.*

If the DOS linker displays the following message:

```
LINK : error L2029: Unresolved externals:
```

function_name in file(s):
  `FILENAME.OBJ(filename.c)`

```
There was 1 error detected
```

be sure that you correctly spelled the name of each function in your program.

The following program (ALPHAFN.C) uses the function *show_alphabet* to display the letters of the alphabet five times.

```
#include <stdio.h>  /* needed for putchar */

main()
{
    int i;
```

(continued)

continued

```
    for (i = 1; i <= 5; ++i)
        show_alphabet();  /* invoke function inside loop */
}

show_alphabet()
{
    int i;

    for (i = 'A'; i <= 'Z'; ++i)
        putchar(i);

    putchar('\n');
}
```

Although the processing in the program is still quite straightforward, the use of a variable *i* in both *main* and *show_alphabet* illustrates an important point.

■ **FACT:** *Variables defined within a given function's grouping symbols pertain only to the given function. If two or more functions define a variable of the same name, the compiler keeps the variables distinct.*

Variables defined within a function's grouping symbols are called local variables. Their values and existence are known only to the function that declares them. Global variables, on the other hand, are known to every function in your program.

■ **FACT:** *To define a global variable, you need to declare it outside a function.*

The following program (GLOBAL.C) modifies the function *show_digit* to display the value of the global variable *digit*. Note that the program defines the variable globally— outside any function (including *main*):

```
int digit = 5;  /* global variable */

main()
{
    printf("Value of digit in main is %d\n", digit);
    show_digit();
}

show_digit()
{
    /* display global variable */
    printf("Value of digit in show_digit is %d", digit);
}
```

Because *digit* is a global variable, every function in the program can change or use the value of *digit*. Although at first this appears convenient, in actuality it often leads to problems.

As your programs increase in size, remembering the processing each routine performs is often difficult, as is remembering the variables that each function uses. Therefore, you can often avoid unexpected changes to a variable by passing values to functions via arguments rather than using global variables.

USING ARGUMENTS TO PASS VALUES TO FUNCTIONS

Earlier we examined two versions of the function *show_digit*. The first version (GIMME5.C) simply displayed the value 5. The second version (GIMME5_2.C) used the global variable *digit* to specify the value to display. The following program (PASS5.C) uses a third method to indicate the value for *show_digit* to display.

```
main()
{
    show_digit(5);      /* call the function with 5 as argument */
}

show_digit(int digit)  /* declare type of argument */
{
    printf("%d\n", digit);
}
```

In the preceding example, the statement

```
show_digit(5);
```

calls the function *show_digit* with the value 5 as an *argument*. An argument, or parameter, is a value enclosed by parentheses that is passed to a function.

■ **FACT:** *If a function uses arguments, it must specify a type and a name for each argument.*

Because our program passes an argument to *show_digit*, the function must declare an appropriate type for the variable that receives the argument:

```
show_digit(int digit)
```

In this case, *int* states that the argument *digit* is an integer value. The argument is declared as a local variable, one that exists only in the function *show_digit*.

The function *show_digit* has only one argument. If it used a second argument, a value of type *float*, for example, the type and name of each would have to be declared. The type and name pairs are separated by a comma, as follows:

```
show_digit(int digit, float value)
```

■ **TRAP:** *Older C compilers require that the types of arguments be defined outside the parenthesized argument list.*

Another technique for defining argument types is to declare them after the parenthesized list and before the opening grouping symbol. Only the variable name appears within the parentheses, as the following example shows:

```
show_digit(digit)
    int digit;
{
    printf("%d\n", digit);
}
```

Although C lets you define function arguments in either manner, the currently preferred method (not supported by older compilers) is to specify the type and name within the parentheses.

The following program (PASS1-10.C) adds a loop to *main* that calls the *show_digit* function to display the numbers 1 through 10.

```
main()
{
    int i;

    for (i = 1; i <= 10; ++i)
        show_digit(i);
}

show_digit(int digit)
{
    printf("%d\n", digit);
}
```

The program invokes *show_digit* with a different value during each iteration of the *for* loop. The *show_digit* function simply assigns the argument value it receives to the variable *digit* and then displays the value.

At this point in your investigation of C functions, you will need to keep any functions you create in the same source file as *main*. Later in this book you will learn how to separate functions into separate source files, and you will come to see the advantage of doing so.

USING MULTIPLE ARGUMENTS

The *show_digit* function we created used only one argument. The following program (2ARGS.C) invokes the *display_sum* function with two values. The function adds the values and then displays the sum.

```
main()
{
    display_sum(100, 57);
}

display_sum(int a, int b)
{
    printf("%d + %d = %d\n", a, b, a + b);
}
```

■ **TRAP:** *You must specify the name and type for each argument. If you omit a type, the compiler generates a syntax error.*

The *display_sum* function receives two arguments, which it assigns to the variables *a* and *b*. When a function call passes two or more arguments, the C compiler matches arguments to the function's variables from left to right.

```
display_sum(100, 57); /* function call */
   ⋮
display_sum(int a, int b) /* function definition */
```

■ **TRAP:** *Be sure that the values you pass to a function match the types of the arguments the function expects. In some cases the C compiler does not detect such errors during compilation, and they are therefore difficult to locate and correct.*

If a function expects to be passed an integer value, don't pass the function a floating point value. If you do so, an error will normally result. Essentially, C will assign a meaningless value to the variable.

By now you should be feeling a little more comfortable with functions, so let's move on to the true capability of functions—performing calculations and returning a result to the statement that called the function.

USING THE *return* STATEMENT

So far, you have used functions only to display information. In this section you will learn how to return a value to the statement that called the function. This value might be a number indicating a particular error status, or it might be the result of a calculation.

■ **FACT:** *The C* return *statement directs a function to return control to the calling function. The* return *statement optionally lets your functions return a value.*

The following program (RETURN.C) invokes the function *sum_values* to add two values and return their sum to *main.*

```
main()
{
    int result;

    result = sum_values(10, 53);
    printf("Result is %d\n", result);
}

sum_values(int a, int b)
{
    return(a + b);
}
```

The program uses *sum_values* as part of an assignment statement. First, the function call passes the integer values 10 and 53 to *sum_values.* Within *sum_values,* the *return* statement tells the function to return the sum of the variables *a* and *b* to the calling routine. The program then assigns the value returned by *sum_values* to the variable *result.*

■ **FACT:** *If your program invokes a function that returns a value, but the program does not use the return value, the compiler ignores the unused value.*

Earlier in this book you used the *puts* function to display text on the screen. As it turns out, the *puts* function not only performs output, it also returns a status value to the function that called it. When successful, *puts* returns the value 0. If an error occurs, *puts* returns a status code associated with the error.

Because your previous programs that used *gets* and *puts* didn't process the return values, the compiler simply ignored them. However, writing a program that examines the return code is not difficult, as demonstrated by the program (ERRCHECK.C) at the top of the following page.

```
main()
{
    int status;

    status = puts("Message sent to display...");

    if (status == 0)
        printf("Output is successful");
    else
        printf("Error status from puts is %d\n", status);
}
```

In this case, the program assigns the return value from *puts* to the variable *status*. Our error processing is then quite simple. If *puts* returns 0, the function was successful. If it returns any other value, an error occurred.

In Chapter 9 we will examine functions that create and remove directories. In those cases, error status values might indicate that the directory already exists or cannot be deleted because it contains files. Checking the status might let us give the user specific advice for correcting the error.

■ **TIP:** *C lets you display a function's return value with* printf *without assigning the return value to an intermediate variable.*

The RETURN.C program used the variable *result* to store the return value from the function *sum_values*. Change *main* in that program slightly and name it RETURN2.C to eliminate the need for the variable *result*.

```
main()
{
    printf("Result is %d\n", sum_values(10, 53));
}

sum_values(int a, int b)
{
    return(a + b);
}
```

The program begins execution in *main*, which in turn calls the *printf* function. As *printf* examines the values it is to display, it encounters a call to the *sum_values* function. Therefore, the *printf* function actually calls the function that will return the value for it to display.

As you proceed through this book, you will frequently see a function's return value used in this manner. For example, the following code fragment tests to see whether the sum of two variables exceeds 1000:

```
if (sum_values(a, b) > 1000)
    printf("Error in processing");
```

When the compiler encounters the function call within the *if* statement, it invokes *sum_values* and then compares the function's return value to 1000.

■ **FACT:** *By default, the C compiler assumes that a function returns a value of type* int. *If you want a function to return a value of a type other than* int, *you must precede the function name with the correct type and define the function within the calling routine.*

For example, the following program (FLOATFN.C) creates the function *average*, which returns the average of two floating point values. Because the function returns a value of type *float*, you must precede the function declaration with the keyword *float*, and you must precede the function definition in *main* with the type *float* to identify it as a function that returns a floating point value.

```
main()
{
    float average(float, float); /* defines the function */

    printf("The average value is %f", average(7.88, 8.37));
}

float average(float a, float b)  /* declares return type */
{
    return((a + b) / 2.0);
}
```

Note the statement in *main* that defines the *average* function:

```
float average(float, float);
```

The function definition indicates not only the type of value the function returns, but also the types of each argument. The list of argument types doesn't include variable names; it includes only types. By specifying *float* as the function's return type, you enable the program to execute successfully. If you fail to specify type *float*, the compiler assumes type *int*, and the program will give errant results.

■ **TIP:** *Although the compiler allows a function to use multiple* return *statements, most C programmers create their functions with only one.*

USING THE TYPE *void*

As discussed, the compiler assumes that your function returns an integer value unless you specify otherwise. Not all functions, however, need to return a value. For such cases, C provides the type *void*.

■ **FACT:** *When placed before a function name, the type* void *tells the C compiler that the function does not return a value.*

Earlier we examined the function *show_digit* that displayed a value on the screen. The function did not return a value to the calling routine. Unless your program specifies otherwise, the compiler assumes that *show_digit* returns a value of type *int*. The following program (VOIDFN.C) uses the type *void* with *show_digit*:

```
main()
{
    void show_digit(int);   /* define function */

    show_digit(5);
}

void show_digit(int digit)  /* declare function */
{
    printf("%d\n", digit);
}
```

■ **TIP:** *Get into the habit of declaring as type* void *functions that do not return a value. Following this practice establishes clearly for the compiler (and another programmer who is reading your program) which functions return a value and which do not.*

GETTING BACK TO INCLUDE FILES

In Chapter 9 we will examine many of the built-in C functions and discuss related include files. If you examine the include files that your compiler provides, you will find that many of them simply contain function type and argument definitions. As you examine the routines in Chapter 9, feel free to print and study these files. In addition to helping you understand C functions, these files might provide you with additional C insights.

PASSING CHARACTER STRINGS TO FUNCTIONS

Passing strings to C functions is a straightforward process. You have already passed character string arguments to the *printf, puts,* and *gets* functions. In this section we will write the function *display_string,* which displays a string on your screen. The following program (STRINGFN.C) passes a string to the function *display_string,* which simply displays characters one at a time until it encounters the null character.

```c
#include <stdio.h>   /* needed for putchar */
#define END '\0'

main()
{
    void display_string(char *);

    display_string("Message to display");
}

void display_string(char string[])
{
    int index;

    for(index = 0; string[index] != END; index++)
        putchar(string[index]);
}
```

Note the function declaration for *display_string*:

```c
void display_string(char string[])
```

As discussed, *void* tells the compiler that the function does not return a value. Next, notice that the character string declaration does not specify the number of characters in the string.

■ **FACT:** *Within a function's argument declarations, the compiler does not require you to specify the size of a character string. Instead, you can simply use the left and right brackets to identify the argument as a string. For example:* char string[].

Because C routines recognize the null character as the end of a string, the number of characters in the string need not be declared. The string-handling routines simply loop until they encounter the null character. Most of the functions in this book take advantage of this fact to define character strings without explicit lengths.

Notice also the definition of the *display_string* function in *main.* The argument type is shown as *char *,* which means that the argument is the memory address of a *char* value. For now, don't worry about this detail. You will learn about such types in Chapter 10, which explains the use of pointers.

■ **TIP:** *Remember that in C the value 0 represents a false condition and any nonzero value represents true. Because the null character ('\0') has an ASCII value of 0, you can reduce the condition* while (string[i] != '\0') *to* while (string[i]). *As long as the character in* string[i] *is not the null character, the* while *loop continues processing.*

The following program (NEWGETS.C) implements a simplified version of the built-in function *gets*. In this case, the function is called *newgets*.

```
#include <stdio.h>   /* needed for puts */
#define END '\0'

main()
{
    char string[128];
    void newgets();

    puts("Type a string and press Enter");
    newgets(string);
    puts(string);
}

void newgets(char string[])
{
    int i = 0;

    while ((string[i] = getchar()) != '\n')
        i++;
    string[i] = END;
}
```

■ **TIP:** *If you create a function with the same name as a built-in C function, such as* gets, *the compiler ignores the built-in function and uses the user-defined function instead.*

To reduce the chance for confusion, we have avoided the name *gets* for our string-reading function. As briefly discussed earlier, the built-in function *gets* performs error checking and returns an appropriate error status value. Our *newgets* function, a simplified implementation of *gets*, does not.

UNDERSTANDING CALL BY VALUE

Each time you call a function, the compiler copies the value of each argument. Rather than allowing a function to access the value of an argument directly, the compiler lets the function change only the copy of the value.

■ **FACT:** *The C compiler passes arguments using call by value. This means that functions access a copy of an argument's value rather than the argument itself.*

The following program (VALUEFN.C) demonstrates the independence of a variable from the manipulation of its value in another function:

```
main()
{
    int amount = 10;
    void change_value(int);

    printf("Before function %d\n", amount);
    change_value(amount);
    printf("After function %d\n", amount);
}

void change_value(int a)
{
    a = 5;
    printf("Value in function %d\n", a);
}
```

When you run the program, the screen shows

```
Before function 10
Value in function 5
After function 10
```

The VALUEFN program prints the value of the variable *amount* and then calls the function *change_value* with *amount* as its argument. When *change_value* assigns the value 5 to the variable *a*, it is manipulating a copy of the argument's value, not the argument itself. Within *main*, the value of the variable amount remains unchanged, as the final output message illustrates.

■ **FACT:** *When you pass the value of a variable to a function, the manipulation of that value in the function does not affect the variable in the calling function.*

In Chapter 10 you will learn how to use C pointers to change the value of an argument within a function. For now, keep in mind that a function cannot change an argument's value unless your program uses pointers.

RECURSION—A FUNCTION CALLING ITSELF

As you have seen, C functions can invoke one another to perform specific tasks. A special case of this function-calling process occurs when a function calls itself. This process is called *recursion*.

The following program (RECURSE.C) uses a simple function that calls itself recursively to display the characters in a string. The *display_rec* function makes use of pointers for passing strings.

```
#include <stdio.h>  /* needed for putchar */

main()
{
    void display_rec(char *, int);

    display_rec("Recursion test", 0);
}

void display_rec(char str[], int i)
{
    if (str[i])
        {
        putchar(str[i]);         /* display character */
        display_rec(str, ++i);  /* recursive call */
        }
}
```

■ **FACT:** *Recursive functions continue to call themselves until an ending condition is met.*

In this case, the function *display_rec* invokes itself until *str[i]* is '\0' (the last character in the string). As long as the character in *str[i]* is not '\0', the *if* condition is true (nonzero), and the function displays the character and invokes itself again with the string and an index to the next character in the string.

When *str[i]* reaches '\0' (ASCII value 0), the *if* condition is false, so the function returns control to the previous invocation, which does the same, and so on. Using the string "TRAP", we might visualize the processing as shown in Figure 8-1 on the following page. Notice the way a recursive function creates a chain of function invocations, each of which must later return control to the previous invocation.

Output   **Recursion**

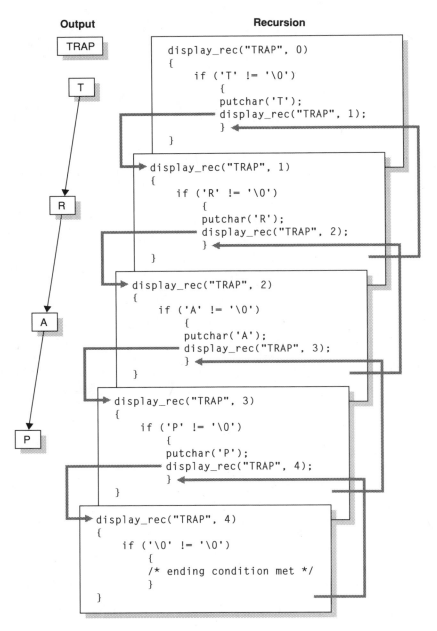

FIGURE 8-1.
The display_rec *function displays a character and then calls itself to display the next character until it reaches the end of the string.*

To better understand this processing, let's look at the function *display_reverse* in the following program (REVERSE.C), which also displays the characters in a string, but this time in reverse order:

```
#include <stdio.h>  /* needed for putchar */

main()
{
    void display_reverse(char *, int);

    display_reverse("Recursion test", 0);
}

void display_reverse(char str[], int i)
{
    if (str[i])
        {
        display_reverse(str, i + 1)
        putchar(str[i]);
        }
}
```

As before, as long as *str[i]* is not at the end of the string, *display_reverse* invokes itself recursively, including as arguments the string and an index to the next character in the string. Again using the string "TRAP", the functions build an invocation chain identical to the one in Figure 8-1 except that the recursive function calls occur before rather than after the calls to *putchar*. When *str[i]* reaches '\0', the function displays the current character and then returns to the previous invocation, which displays the preceding character, and so on. Ultimately, the function displays the string in reverse, as shown in Figure 8-2 on the following page.

■ **TIP:** *Recursive functions are slow because they incur significant overhead each time one invocation is interrupted to launch another. Whenever possible, design functions to be nonrecursive. In so doing, you will decrease the execution time for your programs.*

Admittedly, you could easily rewrite these string display functions to avoid recursion. We used recursion here to demonstrate the flow of recursive functions.

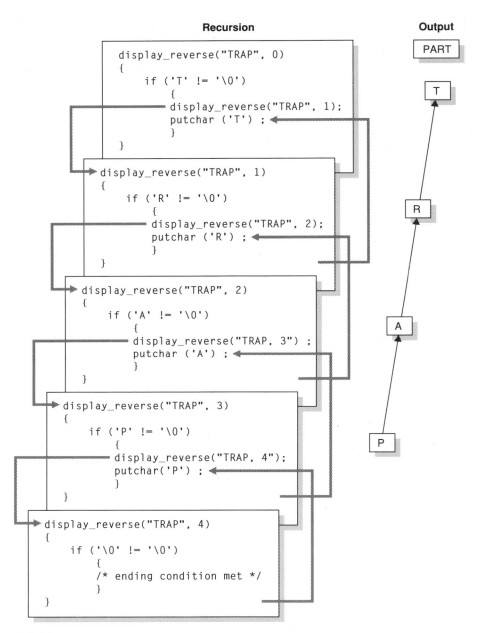

FIGURE 8-2.

The display_reverse *function reverses the order of the characters in a string because the call to* putchar *occurs after the function invokes itself.*

SUMMARY

Getting Started with C Functions

■ **FACT:** *C programs contain one or more functions. The first function that executes is always* main. *The function* main *can invoke other functions to perform its processing.*

■ **TIP:** *Treat your own C functions as you treat* main. *Each function has a name followed by parentheses, grouping symbols, and statements.*

■ **TRAP:** *The parentheses following a function name must be present. If you omit them, the C compiler generates a syntax error.*

■ **TRAP:** *If you misspell a function name in the program, CL compiles the program but does not link it.*

■ **FACT:** *Variables defined within a given function's grouping symbols pertain only to the given function. If two or more functions define a variable of the same name, the compiler keeps the variables distinct.*

■ **FACT:** *To define a global variable, you need to declare it outside a function.*

Using Arguments to Pass Values to Functions

■ **FACT:** *If a function uses arguments, it must specify a type and a name for each argument.*

■ **TRAP:** *Older C compilers require that the types of arguments be defined outside the parenthesized argument list.*

Using Multiple Arguments

■ **TRAP:** *You must specify the name and type for each argument. If you omit a type, the compiler generates a syntax error.*

■ **TRAP:** *Be sure that the values you pass to a function match the types of the arguments the function expects. In some cases the C compiler does not detect such errors during compilation, and they are therefore difficult to locate and correct.*

Using the *return* Statement

■ **FACT:** *The C* return *statement directs a function to return control to the calling function. The* return *statement optionally lets your functions return a value.*

■ **FACT:** *If your program invokes a function that returns a value, but the program does not use the return value, the compiler ignores the unused value.*

■ **TIP:** *C lets you display a function's return value with* printf *without assigning the return value to an intermediate variable.*

■ **FACT:** *By default, the C compiler assumes that a function returns a value of type* int. *If you want a function to return a value of a type other than* int, *you must precede the function name with the correct type and define the function within the calling routine.*

■ **TIP:** *Although the compiler allows a function to use multiple* return *statements, most C programmers create their functions with only one.*

Using the Type *void*

■ **FACT:** *When placed before a function name, the type* void *tells the C compiler that the function does not return a value.*

■ **TIP:** *Get into the habit of declaring as type* void *functions that do not return a value. Following this practice establishes clearly for the compiler (and another programmer who is reading your program) which functions return a value and which do not.*

Passing Character Strings to Functions

■ **FACT:** *Within a function's argument declarations, the compiler does not require you to specify the size of a character string. Instead, you can simply use the left and right brackets to identify the argument as a string. For example:* char string[].

■ **TIP:** *Remember that in C the value 0 represents a false condition and any nonzero value represents true. Because the null character ('\0') has an ASCII value of 0, you can reduce the condition* while (string[i] != '\0') *to* while (string[i]). *As long as the character in* string[i] *is not the null character, the* while *loop continues processing.*

■ **TIP:** *If you create a function with the same name as a built-in C function such as* gets, *the compiler ignores the built-in function and uses the user-defined function instead.*

Understanding Call by Value

■ **FACT:** *The C compiler passes arguments using call by value. This means that functions access a copy of an argument's value rather than the argument itself.*

■ **FACT:** *When you pass the value of a variable of a function, the manipulation of that value in the function does not affect the variable in the calling function.*

Recursion—A Function Calling Itself

■ **FACT:** *Recursive functions continue to call themselves until an ending condition is met.*

■ **TIP:** *Recursive functions are slow because they incur significant overhead each time one invocation is interrupted to launch another. Whenever possible, design functions to be nonrecursive. In so doing, you will decrease the execution time for your programs.*

GLOSSARY

argument A value passed to a function. The C compiler passes arguments by value, which means that functions receive a copy of the value stored in a variable rather than accessing the value itself.

recursion The process by which a function calls itself successively until an ending condition is met.

CHAPTER 9

Using Predefined Functions

Every C compiler provides a collection of useful routines, called its *run-time library*. You have used three run-time library functions already: *printf, puts,* and *gets.* In Chapter 8 you learned that one advantage in creating functions is that you can reuse them from one application to the next. Obviously, reusing an existing routine can save you a considerable amount of development and testing time.

The C run-time library is a collection of several hundred routines—the tools you will need to use regularly in your programs. Successful C programmers are thoroughly conversant with the run-time library and the routines that it contains.

This chapter introduces several categories of run-time library routines. By the end of the chapter, you will have the secret to developing C programs with impressive processing capabilities. Like any tool, the C run-time library can't help you if you don't use it.

DIRECTORY MANIPULATION ROUTINES

You are, of course, familiar with the DOS directory manipulation commands MKDIR, CHDIR, and RMDIR. The C run-time library gives you access to the same directory manipulation capabilities.

■ **FACT:** *The C run-time library function* getcwd *returns the current working directory.*

The following program (GETDIR.C) uses the *getcwd* function to display the current working directory. The program defines a character string called *directory* that it passes as an argument to *getcwd*. The function *getcwd* in turn places the disk drive letter and the name of the current directory into the character string.

```
#include <direct.h>   /* defines getcwd function */

main()
{
    char directory[67];

    if (getcwd(directory, sizeof(directory)))
        printf("Current directory is %s", directory);
    else
        printf("Error in call to getcwd");
}
```

The program includes the file direct.h, which defines the directory manipulation routines in the run-time library. The first statement in *main* defines the character string *directory*. The program uses a 67-character string, which allows 2 characters for the drive letter and colon, 64 characters for the maximum directory name length, and 1 character for the null character. If the *getcwd* function encounters an error, it returns a value of zero.

■ **FACT:** *The C run-time library function* chdir *changes the current working directory for the current disk drive or the specified disk drive.*

The run-time library function *chdir* selects the current working directory; that is, you call *chdir* with the name of a directory, and it makes that directory the new working directory. The following program (CDTEST.C) uses *chdir* to change the current directory on the disk in drive A to TOOLS:

```
#include <direct.h>   /* needed for chdir */

main()
{
    if (chdir("A:\\TOOLS"))
        printf("Error in call to chdir");
    else
        printf("Call to chdir successful");
}
```

If successful, the *chdir* function returns a value of zero. If it encounters an error (such as an invalid directory name), *chdir* returns the value –1. Note that the call to *chdir* uses two backslash characters in the directory name, A:\\TOOLS. Remember, a single backslash character starts a C escape sequence. To specify a backslash within a character string, you must use two consecutive backslashes.

■ **TIP:** *C provides an alternative to using double backslashes in character strings — the forward slash (/) character. For example, the strings "A:\\TOOLS" and "A:/TOOLS" are equal.*

■ **FACT:** *The C run-time library function* mkdir *creates a directory on the specified disk drive. If* mkdir *is successful, it returns the value 0; if* mkdir *encounters an error, it returns the value −1.*

The following program (MDTEST.C) uses *mkdir* to create the subdirectory TOOLS on the disk in drive A. The *mkdir* function creates a directory using the specified pathname and optional drive letter.

```
#include <direct.h>  /* needed for mkdir */

main()
{
    if (mkdir("A:/TOOLS"))
        printf("Error in call to mkdir");
    else
        printf("Directory successfully created");
}
```

If the specified directory already exists, *mkdir* returns the value −1, and the program displays its error message.

■ **FACT:** *The C run-time library function* rmdir *removes a directory from the specified disk. If* rmdir *is successful, it returns the value 0; if unsuccessful,* rmdir *returns the value −1.*

The following program (RDTEST.C) uses another run-time library function, *rmdir*, to remove the directory TOOLS from the disk in drive A.

■ **TRAP:** *The* rmdir *function cannot remove the current directory or a directory that contains files.*

```
#include <direct.h>  /* needed for rmdir */

main()
{
    if (rmdir("A:/TOOLS"))
        printf("Error in call to rmdir");
    else
        printf("Directory successfully removed");
}
```

The *rmdir* run-time library routine is identical in function to the DOS RMDIR command. If you do not specify a complete pathname, *rmdir* searches for the directory within the current directory. Also, like the DOS RMDIR command, *rmdir* is unsuccessful if you call it to remove the current working directory or a directory that still contains files or directories.

By now you should be getting a good feel for the flexibility and convenience of the C run-time library, so let's pick up the pace a little and discuss some other categories of run-time library routines, but in less detail. Remember, the documentation that accompanies your C compiler contains specific information about each run-time library routine.

USING MATHEMATICAL FUNCTIONS

Many programmers aren't aware of the powerful math tools that C provides. The fastest way to become familiar with C's math functions is to print the file math.h (located in your INCLUDE directory). The table in Figure 9-1 summarizes many of C's run-time library math functions.

■ **FACT:** *The file math.h contains the function definitions for the C math routines. By examining math.h you can learn the return types as well as the argument types for each math function.*

The following program (TRIG.C) uses the math run-time library to display the sine, cosine, and tangent for the constant PI, which has the approximate value of π.

```
#include <math.h>  /* needed for sin, cos, and tan */

main()
{
    /* define PI as double precision constant */
    const double PI = 3.1415926535;

    printf("pi = %f\n", PI);
    printf("sine(pi) = %f\n", sin(PI));
    printf("cosine(pi) = %f\n", cos(PI));
    printf("tangent(pi) = %f\n", tan(PI));
}
```

When you run the program, the screen shows

```
pi = 3.141593
sine(pi) = 0.000000
cosine(pi) = -1.000000
tangent(pi) = -0.000000
```

Because the program includes the file math.h, which defines each function's return type, the compiler knows that each routine returns a value of type *double*. You are relieved of the obligation to declare explicitly the return type of each function.

Name of Routine	Description	Calling Sequence
abs	Absolute value of an *int*	`int abs(int);`
acos	Arccosine function	`double acos(double);`
asin	Arcsine function	`double asin(double);`
atan	Arctangent -π/2 to π/2	`double atan(double);`
atan2	Arctangent -π to π	`double atan2(double, double);`
atof	ASCII to *float*	`double atof(const char *);`
cabs	Absolute value of complex number	`double cabs(struct complex);`
ceil	Smallest integer >= argument	`double ceil(double);`
cos	Cosine function	`double cos(double);`
cosh	Hyperbolic cosine function	`double cosh(double);`
dieeetomsbin	IEEE *double* to MSC *double*	`int dieeetomsbin(double *, double *);`
dmsbintoieee	MSC *double* to IEEE *double*	`int dmsbintoieee(double *, double *);`
exp	Exponential function	`double exp(double);`
fabs	Absolute value of *float*	`double fabs(double);`
fieeetomsbin	IEEE *float* to MSC *float*	`int fieeetomsbin(float *, float *);`
floor	Largest integer <= argument	`double floor(double);`
fmod	Floating point modulus	`double fmod(double, double);`
fmsbintoieee	MSC *float* to IEEE *float*	`int fmsbintoieee(float *, float *);`
frexp	Return exponent and mantissa	`double frexp(double, int *);`
hypot	Return hypotenuse given *x* and *y*	`double hypot(double, double);`
labs	Absolute value on a *long*	`long labs(long);`
ldexp	Exponential function	`double ldexp(double, int);`
log	Natural logarithm	`double log(double);`
log10	Log to the base 10	`double log10(double);`
matherr	Handle math error exceptions	`int matherr(struct exception *);`
modf	Return integer and fraction	`double modf(double, double *);`
pow	Return *x* to *y* power	`double pow(double, double);`
sin	Sine function	`double sin(double);`
sinh	Hyperbolic sine function	`double sinh(double);`
sqrt	Square root	`double sqrt(double);`
tan	Tangent function	`double tan(double);`
tanh	Hyperbolic tangent function	`double tanh(double);`

FIGURE 9-1.
Summary of run-time library routines for mathematical operations.

TESTING CHARACTER ATTRIBUTES

As we have seen, the ASCII character set consists of 128 distinct values, most of which correspond to letters of the alphabet, numbers, and punctuation marks. Several of the values are used for special purposes, such as data communication. By testing the range of character values, we can determine their use.

Earlier in this book we used the condition

```
if (letter >= 'a' && letter <= 'z')
```

to determine whether a letter was lowercase. As it turns out, C provides a complete set of macros that examine character attributes. In this case, we could simplify our condition to

```
if (islower(letter))
```

Using macros not only reduces the size of your code, it also makes your code more readable. The table in Figure 9-2 summarizes many of the macros found in ctype.h.

■ **FACT:** *The include file ctype.h contains macros that return specific information about character values.*

Macro Name	*Description*
isalpha(c)	True if *c* is a letter 'A'–'Z' or 'a'–'z'
isupper(c)	True if *c* is an uppercase letter 'A'–'Z'
islower(c)	True if *c* is a lowercase letter 'a'–'z'
isdigit(c)	True if *c* is a digit '0'–'9'
isxdigit(c)	True if *c* is a hexadecimal digit '0'–'9', 'a'–'f', or 'A'–'F'
isspace(c)	True if *c* is an ASCII white space character 9–13 or 32
ispunct(c)	True if *c* is a punctuation character
isalnum(c)	True if *c* is alphanumeric 'A'–'Z', 'a'–'z', or '0'–'9'
isprint(c)	True if *c* is printable ASCII 32–126
isgraph(c)	True if *c* is printable and not a space ASCII 33–127
iscntrl(c)	True if *c* is an ASCII control character 0–31 or 127
isascii(c)	True if *c* is an ASCII character 0–127

FIGURE 9-2.
Summary of run-time library routines for determining character attributes.

The following program (CHARTEST.C) examines the attributes associated with character values 0 through 127.

```
#include <ctype.h>  /* needed for character attribute functions */

main()
{
    int i;

    for (i = 0; i <= 127; i++)
        {
        printf("\n%d", i);

        if (isalpha(i))
            printf(" Alpha");

        if (isupper(i))
            printf(" Upper");

        if (islower(i))
            printf(" Lower");

        if (isdigit(i))
            printf(" Digit");

        if (isxdigit(i))
            printf(" Hex Digit");

        if (isspace(i))
            printf(" Space");

        if (ispunct(i))
            printf(" Punctuation");

        if (isalnum(i))
            printf(" Alphanumeric");

        if (isprint(i))
            printf(" Print");

        if (isgraph(i))
            printf(" Graph");

        if (iscntrl(i))
            printf(" Ctrl");

        if (isascii(i))
            printf(" ASCII");
        }
}
```

After you compile this program, run it while redirecting output to the DOS MORE filter, which lets you look at the output a screenful at a time:

```
C> CHARTYPE : MORE
```

The program examines each ASCII character using the macros in ctype.h and displays the specific categories to which each character belongs.

If you examine the include file ctype.h, you will learn how C actually implements several of these macros. Keep these routines in mind. We will use them throughout the remainder of this book.

CHARACTER CONVERSION ROUTINES

The include file ctype.h provides not only routines that test a character's attributes but also a set of routines that convert a character from one format to another. The following table defines the C character conversion routines.

Name of Routine	Type	Description
tolower(*c*)	Function	Converts *c* to lowercase if uppercase
toupper(*c*)	Function	Converts *c* to uppercase if lowercase
toascii(*c*)	Function	Clears all but lower 7 bits of *c*
_tolower(*c*)	Macro	Converts *c* to lowercase without checking case
_toupper(*c*)	Macro	Converts *c* to uppercase without checking case

■ **TIP:** *C provides both macro and function implementations for the routines* tolower *and* toupper. *If program speed is more important than program size, use the macro. Macros are faster than functions but result in a larger executable file.*

The *_tolower* and *_toupper* routines are simply macro implementations of the functions *tolower* and *toupper*. Unlike the function *toupper*, which ensures that a character is lowercase before converting it, the macro *_toupper* converts a character regardless of whether it is lowercase. Likewise, the macro *_tolower* does not verify (as its function counterpart does) that it is converting an uppercase character.

As you have learned, using macros results in more executable code than using functions because each occurrence of the macro is expanded by the preprocessor, whereas multiple calls to a function reference the same block of executable code. Later in this book you will learn why functions execute more slowly than macros. For now, simply keep this fact in mind.

■ **TIP:** *Microsoft C compilers use the initial underscore character to identify routines that are not fully compatible with ANSI standards.*

The following program (UPPER.C) uses the *toupper* function to display a user-entered string in uppercase.

```c
#include <ctype.h>   /* needed for toupper */
#include <stdio.h>   /* needed for putchar and gets */

main()
{
    char string[128];
    int i;

    puts("Enter a string");
    gets(string);

    for (i = 0; string[i]; i++)
        putchar(toupper(string[i]));
}
```

PERFORMING NUMERIC CONVERSIONS

So far, the only input operations that you've learned to perform are character-based operations that employ *getchar* and *gets*. Many C programs need to get a number (not an ASCII code) from the user. To obtain a number, let's use *gets* to get an ASCII character string and then use functions in the C run-time library to convert the string representation of a value to the actual value.

■ **TRAP:** *Don't neglect the fact that a digit's ASCII value is different from its numeric value. The digit 6, for example, is stored in a character string as ASCII code 54 (decimal).*

■ **FACT:** *The C run-time library provides three functions — atoi, atol, and atof — that convert a character string representation of a value to its numeric representation.*

The numeric conversion functions derive their names from the types they convert: The *atoi* function converts an ASCII value to *int*, *atol* converts ASCII to *long*, and *atof* converts ASCII to *float*. The include file stdlib.h defines these functions.

■ **TRAP:** *If the run-time library functions cannot convert a character string to a value, they return the value 0. When this occurs, your program cannot determine whether 0 was returned because the user entered a 0 or because an error occurred.*

The following program (CONVERT.C) demonstrates each of the C conversion functions. It prompts the user to enter positive or negative values, and then it converts the ASCII representation of each value to its numeric representation.

```c
#include <stdlib.h>  /* needed for puts, gets, atoi, atol, and atof */

main()
{
    char string[128];

    puts("Enter an integer value");
    gets(string);
    printf("Value entered was %d\n", atoi(string));

    puts("Enter a long integer value");
    gets(string);
    printf("Value entered was %ld\n", atol(string));

    puts("Enter a floating point value");
    gets(string);
    printf("Value entered was %f\n", atof(string));
}
```

■ **FACT:** *The functions* itoa, ltoa, *and* ultoa *convert numeric values of types* int, long, *and* unsigned long *to character string equivalents.*

Just as the run-time library provides functions that convert ASCII values to *int, float,* and *long*, it provides the *itoa, ltoa,* and *ultoa* functions to convert *int, long int,* and *unsigned long int* values to their ASCII representations. In addition, each function lets you select the base in which you want to represent the result, such as binary, octal, decimal, or hexadecimal. Include stdlib.h whenever you use one of these functions. The following program (BASES.C) displays the binary, octal, decimal, and hexadecimal representations of the values 0 through 255.

```c
#include <stdlib.h>  /* needed for itoa */

main()
{
    char string[128];
    int i;

    printf("Binary\t\tOctal\tDecimal\tHexadecimal\n\n");
    for (i = 0; i <= 255; i++)
```

(continued)

continued

```
        {
        itoa(i, string, 2);  /* get binary representation */
        printf("%-10s\t%o\t%d\t%x\n", string, i, i, i);
        }
    }
```

Look closely at the statement that calls *itoa*. The variable *i* contains the value to convert. The variable string is assigned the ASCII representation of the value. The program specifies a base of 2. Valid bases are 2 through 36. As a result of this call, *itoa* places the binary representation of *i*.

STRING MANIPULATION ROUTINES

As we noted in Chapter 7, string manipulation is the principal activity of many C programs. For example, programs often need to compare two strings for equality, search a string for a key word, or append the contents of one string to another. Because these needs are common to any applications, the C run-time library provides an extensive collection of string manipulation routines.

■ **FACT:** *The include file string.h contains the function declarations for the C string manipulation functions.*

The following table defines many of the C run-time library string manipulation functions. We will use these functions frequently throughout the remainder of this book. Taken together, they implement virtually every string manipulation routine you need.

Name of Routine	Description
strcat	Appends one string to another
strchr	Searches a string for the first occurrence of a letter
strcmp	Compares two strings
strcmpi	Compares two strings, ignoring uppercase *vs* lowercase
strcpy	Copies contents of one string to another
strcspn	Returns first letter in one string that is in a second string
strdup	Allocates memory and copies a string
strerror	Returns error message associated with the last run-time library routine call that produced an error
stricmp	Compares two strings, ignoring uppercase *vs* lowercase

(continued)

continued

Name of Routine	Description
strlen	Returns the number of characters in the string
strlwr	Converts a string to lowercase
strncat	Appends *n* characters to a string
strncmp	Compares the first *n* characters of two strings
strncpy	Copies the first *n* characters of one string to another
strnicmp	Compares the first *n* characters of two strings, ignoring uppercase *vs* lowercase
strnset	Initializes the first *n* characters of a string to the specified character
strpbrk	Locates the first character in the first string that is also in the second
strrchr	Locates the last occurrence of a letter in a string
strrev	Reverses the order of the letters in a string
strset	Sets all the characters in a string to a specified letter
strspn	Returns the first character in the first string that is not in the set of characters in the second string
strstr	Returns a pointer to the location of the second string within the first, or NULL if the string does not exist
strtod	Converts a string to a decimal value
strtol	Converts a string to a *long* value
strtoul	Converts a string to an *unsigned long* value
strupr	Converts a string to uppercase

IMPORTANCE OF THE RUN-TIME LIBRARY

Although this chapter has provided only a brief look at the C run-time library, keep in mind the library's importance. The run-time library simplifies your programming tasks. It will save you programming effort time and time again.

The goal of this book is to present C secrets that make you a more productive C programmer. The most successful C programmers exploit the run-time library extensively.

SUMMARY

Directory Manipulation Routines

■ **FACT:** *The C run-time library function* getcwd *returns the current working directory.*

■ **FACT:** *The C run-time library function* chdir *changes the current working directory for the current disk drive or specified disk drive.*

■ **TIP:** *C provides an alternative to using double backslashes in character strings — the forward slash (/) character. For example, the strings "A:\\TOOLS" and "A:/TOOLS" are equal.*

■ **FACT:** *The C run-time library function* mkdir *creates a directory on the specified disk drive. If* mkdir *is successful, it returns the value 0; if* mkdir *encounters an error, it returns the value −1.*

■ **FACT:** *The C run-time library routine* rmdir *removes a directory from the specified disk. If* rmdir *is successful, it returns the value 0; if unsuccessful,* rmdir *returns the value −1.*

■ **TRAP:** *The* rmdir *function cannot remove the current directory or a directory that contains files.*

Using Mathematical Functions

■ **FACT:** *The file math.h contains the function definitions for the C math routines. By examining math.h you can learn the return types as well as the argument types for each math function.*

Testing Character Attributes

■ **FACT:** *The include file ctype.h contains macros that return specific information about character values.*

Character Conversion Routines

■ **TIP:** *C provides both macro and function implementations for the routines* tolower *and* toupper. *If program speed is more important than program size, use the macro. Macros are faster than functions but result in a larger executable file.*

■ **TIP:** *Microsoft C compilers use the initial underscore character to identify routines that are not fully compatible with ANSI standards.*

Performing Numeric Conversions

■ **TRAP:** *Don't neglect the fact that a digit's ASCII value is different from its numeric value. The digit 6, for example, is stored in a character string as ASCII code 54 (decimal).*

■ **FACT:** *The C run-time library provides three functions —atoi, atol, and atof —that convert a character string representation of a value to its numeric representation.*

■ **TRAP:** *If the run-time library functions cannot convert a character string to a value, they return the value 0. When this occurs, your program cannot determine whether the user entered a 0 or whether an error occurred.*

■ **FACT:** *The functions* itoa, ltoa, *and* ultoa *convert numeric values of types* int, long, *and* unsigned long *to character string equivalents.*

String Manipulation Routines

■ **FACT:** *The include file string.h contains the function declarations for the C string manipulation functions.*

GLOSSARY

run-time library A collection of existing routines that your programs can access. The run-time library contains functions and macros that perform memory allocation, string manipulation, math functions, and file and screen I/O. The run-time library is the C programmer's tool set. The Microsoft C run-time library is the collection of functions and macros supplied with the Microsoft C Compiler.

PART II

GETTING PAST THE BASICS

CONGRATULATIONS! BY WORKING YOUR WAY THROUGH PART I OF THIS BOOK, you have built a solid foundation in C programming concepts. In this part of the book we will round out your knowledge of C. You will learn about C pointers, arrays, files, and structures. In fact, by the end of Part II, your knowledge of C will be nearly complete. Once you finish Part II, Parts III and IV simply put your knowledge to use.

As before, the programs in each lesson are short. Execute them. You can't learn C simply by reading a book; you have to experiment. Part II picks up the pace a little. I think you'll have fun!

CHAPTER 10

Getting Started with C Pointers

During program execution, a C program stores certain values in variables. A variable is a name that is associated with a memory location. Depending upon the variable's type, the amount of memory associated with the variable is different. To keep track of variables in memory, the compiler assigns each variable a unique memory location.

In this chapter you learn how to determine the address of a variable and how to assign an address to a variable type called a pointer. You also learn how to use pointers as arguments, a practice that lets you manipulate variables in calling functions. This use of pointers is one of the major advantages they offer.

Last, this chapter discusses the *scanf* function and shows you how to use it to perform formatted input operations. As you will see, once you learn the secrets of pointers, *scanf* can be a powerful function.

DISPLAYING MEMORY ADDRESSES AND THEIR CONTENTS

Before we examine C pointer types, let's discuss the C address operator (&). The address operator obtains the memory address of a variable (the sort of value that we want a pointer to contain).

■ **FACT:** *In C the ampersand character (&) is the address operator. The address operator returns the* address *of a variable in memory, not the* value *of the variable.*

163

The following program (ADDRESS.C) defines a variable called *count*, assigns it the value 1, and displays the value and memory address of *count*. It uses the %X format specifier with *printf* to display the memory address.

```
main()
{
    int count = 1;

    printf("Value  = %d  Address = %04X", count, &count);
}
```

When you run the program, your screen shows

```
Value = 1  Address = 0DD6
```

The address operator (&) returns the location of *count* in memory. Note that the memory location your screen displays may vary from the above output. The address of a variable depends on the memory location at which the operating system loads the program.

Memory locations or *addresses* are expressed as a hexadecimal *segment* and a hexadecimal *offset* into the segment. The %X format specifier lets you display only the offset portion of the address. The segment value is not critical for the facts we are illustrating in this chapter—all the offsets we display apply to the same segment. (In Chapter 12 we will begin to examine complete segmented addresses.)

The following program (ADDRESS2.C) declares a variable of type *int* and a variable of type *float* and displays the value and address of both variables.

```
main()
{
    int count = 1;
    float value = 3.3;

    printf("int value = %d\t\tint address = %04X\n", count, &count);
    printf("float value = %f\tfloat address = %04X\n", value, &value);
}
```

When you run the program, your screen shows

```
int value = 1          int address = 10D4
float value 3.300000   float address = 10D0
```

As you can see, *printf* displays the address of a value of type *int* in the same format as the address of a value of type *float*. It should. Remember, an address is simply a memory location—the starting point of the "space" that a value occupies in the computer's memory. Whether the storage space contains a value of type *int, float,* or *double* or even a character string, the format of the memory address is the same, as illustrated in Figure 10-1.

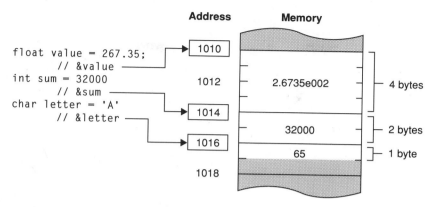

FIGURE 10-1.
The address of a variable is its starting location in storage.

In the next section you will learn how to define and use pointer variables. A pointer is simply a variable that contains a memory address.

DECLARING A POINTER VARIABLE

In Chapter 3 you learned how to declare variables of type *int*, *float*, *double*, and *char*. As you will learn in this section, you declare a pointer in much the same way.

A pointer declaration must specify the name of the pointer variable and the type of the value to which it points. In addition, you must precede the variable name with an asterisk (∗).

■ **FACT:** *To declare a pointer, precede the variable name with an asterisk (∗). The compiler creates a pointer variable to the type specified. For example:* int ∗ptr; *declares a pointer named* ptr *to a value of type* int.

The following program (INTPTR.C) declares a variable of type *int* and declares a pointer to a value of type *int*. It assigns the address of the variable *count* to the pointer *ptr* and then displays the value and the address of *count*, followed by the value of the pointer.

```
main()
{
    int count = 1;
    int *ptr;      /* declare pointer */

    ptr = &count;  /* assign count's address */

    printf("Value of count = %d   Address of count = %04X\n",
           count, &count);
    printf("Value of ptr = %04X", ptr);
}
```

When you run the program, your screen shows

```
Value of count = 1  Address of count = 0DF6
Value of ptr = 0DF6
```

Figure 10-2 shows that the pointer variable *ptr* contains the address of the variable *count*.

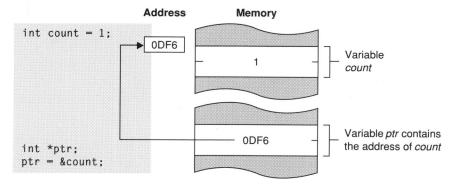

FIGURE 10-2.
The statement ptr = &count *sets the pointer* ptr *to the address of* count.

■ **FACT:** *In C the asterisk (*) serves as the indirection operator. The indirection operator tells the compiler to change or access the value contained in the memory location referenced by a pointer.*

In the preceding program, the statement

```
ptr = &count;
```

assigns to the pointer variable *ptr* the address of the variable *count*. Using the indirection operator, the following statement displays the value of *count*, that is, the value contained at the memory location to which *ptr* is pointing:

```
printf("%d", *ptr);
```

■ **TIP:** *Read the expression* *ptr *as "the value in the memory location specified by the pointer variable* ptr.*" In contrast,* ptr *without the asterisk refers to an address, not to the value stored at that address.*

The following program (INTPTR2.C) displays the value and address of *count* on the first line. On the next line, it displays not only the value of the pointer variable *ptr* but also the value stored at the memory location that *ptr* references.

```
main()
{
    int count = 1;
    int *ptr;

    ptr = &count;

    printf("Value of count = %d  Address of count = %04X\n",
           count, &count);
    printf("Value of ptr = %04X  Value of *ptr = %d", ptr, *ptr);
}
```

When you run the program, your screen shows

```
Value of count = 1  Address of count = 1492
Value of ptr = 1492  Value of *ptr = 1
```

■ **FACT:** *Using the C indirection operator, you can view and change the value contained in a memory location.*

The following program (MODPTR.C) shows how to use the indirection operator to change the value that a pointer references. The program uses the statement

```
*ptr = 2;
```

to change the value in the memory location referenced by *ptr*. Because this memory location refers to the storage location associated with *count*, the value of *count* becomes 2.

```
main()
{
    int count = 1;
    int *ptr = &count;  /* declare and initialize pointer */

    printf("count's starting value = %d\n", count);

    *ptr = 2;  /* change value of count by indirection */

    printf("count's ending value = %d", count);
}
```

When you run the program, your screen shows

```
count's starting value = 1
count's ending value = 2
```

In the next section we discuss using pointers with function arguments. Before we turn to that topic, let's review what we have learned.

- The C address operator (&) returns the address in memory of a variable of any type. To use the address operator, simply precede the variable name with the ampersand.

- A pointer is a variable that contains a memory address. You can define a pointer to any variable type.

- The %x format specifier directs *printf* to display in hexadecimal form the offset portion of an address (pointer) value.

- To declare a pointer variable, specify the pointer type (*int, char, double, float*) followed by the pointer variable name. Precede the variable name with an asterisk to indicate that the variable is a pointer. For example: *float *ptr;*

- The indirection operator (*) tells the compiler to manipulate the value contained in the memory location referenced by a pointer. For example, the statement *ptr = 3;* places the value 3 in the memory location referenced by the pointer variable *ptr.*

With these fundamentals in hand, you are ready to move on to a common pointer operation—argument modification.

USING POINTERS WITH FUNCTIONS

In Chapter 8 you learned that the compiler passes arguments by value, which means that a calling function can manipulate the value it receives but cannot affect the argument itself. The following program (VALCALL.C) demonstrates call by value:

```
main()
{
    int count = 5;
    void change_value(int);

    printf("Initial value = %d\n", count);
    change_value(count);
    printf("Ending value = %d", count);
}

void change_value(int a)
{
    a += 4;
    printf("Value within function = %d\n", a);
}
```

When you run the program, the screen shows

```
Initial value = 5
Value within function = 9
Ending value = 5
```

As the output shows, the value of *count* is passed to *change_value*, but changes to the value in the function are not reflected in *count*.

■ **FACT:** *To change a variable's value within a function, you must pass the address of the variable to the function. Within the function, you must use a pointer.*

The following program (PTRCALL.C) is similar to the previous program but uses pointers:

```
main()
{
    int count = 5;
    void change_value(int *);  /* pointer to int */

    printf("Initial value = %d\n", count);
    change_value(&count);        /* pass address */
    printf("Ending value = %d", count);
}

void change_value(int *a)       /* receive address */
{
    *a += 4;                     /* add 4 to value at address a */
    printf("Value within function = %d\n", *a);
}
```

Let's look at the differences between this program and the one preceding. First, notice that *main* now calls the function *change_value* with the address of the variable *count*:

```
change_value(&count);  /* pass address */
```

Correspondingly, the argument for *change_value* is declared as a pointer to a variable of type *int*:

```
void change_value(int *a)
```

When you run the program (which uses pointers), the screen shows

```
Initial value = 5
Value within function = 9
Ending value = 9
```

The function *change_value* changed the argument *count* as you intended. To see why this occurred, modify the program slightly and name it PTRCALL2.C. The modified program displays both the address of the variable *count* and the memory location referenced by the pointer *a* in the function *change_value*.

```
main()
{
    int count = 5;
    void change_value(int *);

    printf("Initial value = %d\nAddress of value = %04X\n",
            count, &count);
    change_value(&count);
    printf("Ending value = %d", count);
}

void change_value(int *a)
{
    printf("Address of value within function = %04X\n", a);
    *a += 4;
    printf("Value within function = %d\n", *a);
}
```

When you compile and run the program again, the output on your screen is as follows (where the exact address of *value* can vary):

```
Initial value = 5
Address of value = 11B0
Address of value within function = 11B0
Value within function = 9
Ending value = 9
```

As you can see, the pointer *a* in the function *change_value* references the memory location associated with the variable *count* in *main*. The following statement adds 4 to the value that resides in memory location allocated for the variable *count* (as shown in Figure 10-3):

```
*a += 4;
```

As you can see, when functions receive and pass pointers, the functions increase dramatically in capability. Before we turn to another example, let's take a look at the function definition of *change_value* within *main*.

```
void change_value(int *);
```

As discussed in Chapter 8, the type *void* tells the compiler that the function does not return a value. Next, the definition *int **, which falls within the parentheses, tells the compiler that the argument to *change_value* is a pointer to a value of type *int*.

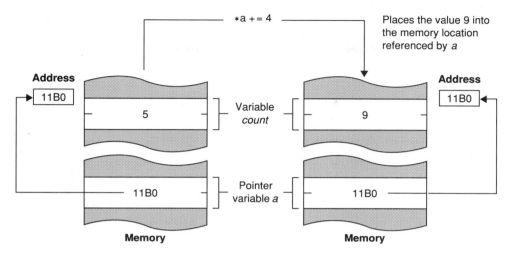

FIGURE 10-3.
The indirection operator (∗) lets you alter the value in the location referenced by a pointer.

The following program (SWITCH.C) uses the function *exchange_values* to exchange the values of two variables that are declared and initialized in *main*. The *exchange_values* function receives pointers to two variables.

```
main()
{
    int first = 1, second = 2;
    void exchange_values(int *, int *);

    printf("Before exchange:  first = %d  second = %d\n", first, second);
    exchange_values(&first, &second);
    printf("After exchange:  first = %d  second = %d\n", first, second);
}

void exchange_values(int *a, int *b)
{
    int temp;

    temp = *a;
    *a = *b;
    *b = temp;
}
```

When you run the program, your screen shows

```
Before exchange:  first = 1  second = 2
After exchange:  first = 2  second = 1
```

Within *exchange_values*, the function exchanges the values of the arguments as shown in Figure 10-4. If you change the program so that it does not use pointers, the call to *exchange_values* leaves the arguments unchanged.

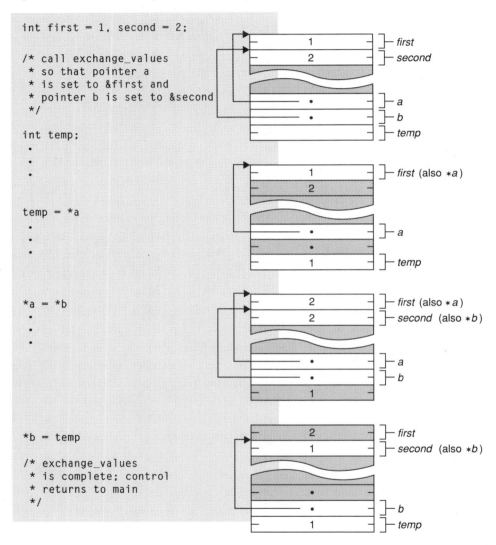

FIGURE10-4.
The exchange_values *function swaps the values referenced by the pointers it receives as arguments.*

■ **TIP:** *If you are confused about whether you need to use pointers, ask yourself, "Does the function change the argument?" If the answer is yes, pass a pointer. If the answer is no, pass the variable by value.*

With these basics in mind, let's examine the input function *scanf.*

GETTING STARTED WITH *scanf*

The *scanf* function is the counterpart of *printf* for input operations.

■ **FACT:** *The* scanf *function lets C programs perform formatted input operations.*

The syntax of the *scanf* function is similar to that of *printf*:

```
scanf("control_string", argumentpointer(s));
```

Both *printf* and *scanf* use the % character to begin a format specifier. The table in Figure 10-5 summarizes the *scanf* format specifiers. We will discuss the use of these format specifiers in detail.

Format Specifier	*Description*
%d	Obtains a decimal integer value
%i	Obtains an integer value (The value can be entered in decimal, in octal with a leading 0, or in hexadecimal with a leading 0x.)
%u	Obtains an unsigned decimal integer value
%o	Obtains an octal integer value
%x	Obtains a hexadecimal integer value
%c	Obtains a character value
%f	Obtains a floating point value
%e,%E	Obtains a floating point value in exponential notation
%g,%G	Obtains a floating point value in standard or exponential form
%p	Obtains a pointer value
%n	Writes the number of characters read so far to an integer variable associated with the pointer argument specified
%%	Reads a % sign (No assignment is made to a corresponding variable.)
%[]	Used for string input
%[^]	Used for string input (Read ends when the character specified is entered.)
%s	Obtains a character string (Input stops at the first whitespace character.)

FIGURE 10-5.
Many format specifiers for scanf *parallel those for* printf.

■ **FACT:** *The %d specifier directs* scanf *to obtain an integer value. The function acts upon characters entered by the user until it encounters a character that is not a digit.*

The following program (SCANF.C) uses the %d format specifier to get an integer value from the user and then displays that value in decimal, octal, and hexadecimal notation:

```
main()
{
    int value;

    printf("Type an integer value and press Enter:  ");
    scanf("%d", &value);
    printf("Value in decimal is %d\n", value);
    printf("Value in octal is %o\n", value);
    printf("Value in hexadecimal is %x\n", value);
}
```

Experiment with this program. Enter an integer value, a negative value, and then a value outside the range −32,768 through 32,767. Notice the way *scanf* handles each.

■ **FACT:** *For numeric data input,* scanf *skips leading whitespace.*

The difficulty in formatting input is that users don't always enter data consistently. The *scanf* function takes into account many common input occurrences, such as whitespace preceding numeric values. In C *whitespace* characters are unprinted characters, such as blank spaces, tabs, or formfeeds. The *scanf* function skips leading whitespace characters in search of user input.

■ **TRAP:** *If* scanf *cannot convert the characters that the user enters into the specified format, it assigns as much of the value as it has converted.*

Execute the previous program (SCANF.C). When the program prompts you to enter an integer character, type a sequence of keys that includes nonnumeric characters. As you will see, *scanf* assigns as many of the valid digits as possible to the variable *value*. If *scanf* cannot convert the input characters into a meaningful value, it assigns the value 0 to the corresponding variable.

The *scanf* function returns the number of variables to which it successfully assigns user-entered values. This return value can be useful if you want to know whether a variable that receives a value of 0 from *scanf* did so because the user entered 0 or because *scanf* encountered invalid characters. We will discuss this procedure in a later section, "Using *printf* and *scanf* Return Values."

■ **FACT:** *If blank spaces occur within the control string,* scanf *regards a space in the user's input as a separator between the values that correspond to each variable.*

The following program (SCANF2.C) is similar to the previous one in that it uses *scanf* to read integer values; however, SCANF2.C adds the two values that the user enters and displays the result.

```
main( )
{
    int a, b;

    puts("Type two values (separated by a space) to be added together.");
    scanf("%d %d", &a, &b);
    printf("%d + %d = %d", a, b, a + b);
}
```

To enter two values, simply separate the values with a space and press Enter after the second value. Remember, if the sum of the values you enter exceeds 32,767, the program yields incorrect results.

The %ld format specifier allows *scanf* to obtain a long *int*. The following program (SCANF3.C) illustrates the use of %ld:

```
main( )
{
    long int large_value;

    printf("Type a long integer value and press Enter:  ");
    scanf("%ld", &large_value);
    printf("The value entered was %ld", large_value);
}
```

■ **FACT:** *The* scanf *function lets you use the long qualifier l in the %i, %o, and %x format specifiers.*

Like the %d specifier, the %i, %o, and %x format specifiers direct *scanf* to obtain an integer value. In each of these cases, however, the function expects the input in a unique format. Let's take a detailed look at each one.

■ **FACT:** *The %o format specifier directs* scanf *to obtain an integer value that the user enters in octal notation (with or without a leading zero).*

The following program (SCANFOCT.C), for example, uses the %o format specifier to get an octal value and then displays that value in octal, decimal, and hexadecimal notation.

```
main()
{
    int value;

    printf("Type an octal value and press Enter:  ");
    scanf("%o", &value);
    printf("Value in octal is %o\n", value);
    printf("Value in decimal is %d\n", value);
    printf("Value in hexadecimal is %x\n", value);
}
```

When you run the program, enter a value at the prompt. In the following example, the input value is shown in italics:

```
Type an octal value and press Enter:   17
Value in octal is 17
Value in decimal is 15
Value in hexadecimal is f
```

■ **TRAP:** *If* scanf *expects an octal value and the user enters a nonoctal value, the function assigns as many of the valid octal digits as possible to the variable. When the function encounters a nonoctal digit,* scanf *regards the value as complete.*

■ **FACT:** *The %x format specifier directs* scanf *to obtain a hexadecimal value (with or without the leading 0x).*

The following program (SCANFHEX.C) prompts the user to enter a hexadecimal value. It uses the C run-time library routine *itoa* to convert the value to its binary representation. The program then displays the value in binary, octal, decimal, and hexadecimal.

```
#include <stdlib.h>  /* needed for itoa */

main()
{
    int value;
    char binary[12];  /* character array for binary string */

    printf("Type a hex value (3 digits or fewer) and press Enter:  ");
    scanf("%x", &value);
    itoa(value, binary, 2);  /* convert hex value to binary string */
    printf("Value in binary is %s\n", binary);
    printf("Value in octal is %o\n", value);
    printf("Value in decimal is %d\n", value);
    printf("Value in hexadecimal is %x\n", value);
}
```

When you run the program, enter a hexadecimal value at the prompt. Your output will resemble the following:

```
Type a hex value (3 digits or less) and press Enter:   fff
Value in binary is 111111111111
Value in octal is 7777
Value in decimal is 4095
Value in hexadecimal is fff
```

■ **TRAP:** *If* scanf *expects a hexadecimal value and the user enters a value other than hexadecimal, the function truncates the input value at the first nonhexadecimal digit.*

■ **FACT:** *The %i format specifier directs* scanf *to obtain an integer value. The user can enter the value in decimal or, with the appropriate prefix, in octal or hexadecimal.*

The %i format specifier lets the user enter a value in decimal, octal, or hexadecimal notation. If the user precedes the value with a 0, *scanf* interprets the value in octal format. If the user precedes the value with 0x, *scanf* interprets the value in hexadecimal format.

The following program (SCANFINT.C) demonstrates the use of the %i format specifier:

```
main()
{
    int value;

    printf("Type an integer value and press Enter:  ");
    scanf("%i", &value);
    printf("Value in octal is %o\n", value);
    printf("Value in decimal is %d\n", value);
    printf("Value in hexadecimal is %x\n", value);
}
```

Now experiment with this program by entering decimal, octal, and hexadecimal values. If you type in the hexadecimal value *0xfff,* your screen will show

```
Type an integer value and press Enter:   0xfff
Value in octal is 7777
Value in decimal is 4095
Value in hexadecimal is fff
```

■ **FACT:** *The Microsoft C Compiler supports the use of %D, %I, %O, and %U with* scanf *to obtain long integers.*

The following table summarizes five additional format specifiers that the Microsoft C Compiler provides for integer input. The effect of using each is parallel to that of using the l qualifier with %d, %o, %x, or %u.

Format Specifier	Description
%D	Obtains a decimal *long int*
%I	Obtains a *long int* value (The value can be entered in decimal, in octal with a leading 0, or in hexadecimal with a leading 0x.)
%O	Obtains a *long int* octal value
%X	Obtains a *long int* hexadecimal value
%U	Obtains an *unsigned long int* value

The following program (SCANLONG.C) illustrates the use of the %I format specifier to obtain a *long int* value:

```
main()
{
    long int value;

    printf("Type a long integer and press Enter:  ");
    scanf("%I", &value);
    printf("The long integer entered was %ld", value);
}
```

When you run the program, enter a long integer at the prompt. Use a prefix if necessary. The output on your screen will resemble the following sample:

```
Type a long integer and press Enter:  1000000
The long integer entered was 1000000
```

■ **FACT:** *The %c format specifier directs* scanf *to obtain a single character.*

Most programmers use the *getchar* macro and the *gets* function to perform character-based input. The *scanf* %c format specifier lets the user enter a nonnumeric character in a line that contains other types, such as *int* or *float*.

The following program (PARSE.C) prompts the user to enter a simple expression, such as *5 * 4* or *255 / 7*. It uses *scanf* to read the expression and defines the values as the floating point variables *a* and *b*. In the same statement, the program directs *scanf* to read the mathematical operator into the variable *operator*. As before, the user must separate each entry with a blank character. After you enter the expression, the program uses a *switch* statement to perform the correct operation.

```
main()
{
    float a, b;
    char operator;

    puts("Type an expression such as 7 * 5 and press Enter.");

    /* use %g rather than %f for readability */
    scanf("%g %c %g", &a, &operator, &b);

    switch (operator)
        {
        case '*':  printf("Result is %g", a * b);
                   break;
        case '+':  printf("Result is %g", a + b);
                   break;
        case '-':  printf("Result is %g", a - b);
                   break;
        case '/':  printf("Result is %g", a / b);
                   break;
        default:   printf("Invalid operator");
        }
}
```

■ **TRAP:** *If the* scanf *control string includes several format specifiers and the user enters too few values,* scanf *assigns 0 to each remaining variable. The function ignores any superfluous values you enter.*

■ **FACT:** *The %% format specifier directs* scanf *to read a percent sign. The function simply ignores the percent sign once it is read.*

Programs need to accept input in the format the user expects. For example, if the user enters a value such as 80%, the %% format specifier directs *scanf* to read through the percent sign character without assigning it to a variable.

■ **TRAP:** *When the control string contains multiple format specifiers,* scanf *completes the input operation at the first invalid character and leaves remaining values unchanged.*

Although the %f, %e, and %g format qualifiers all permit *scanf* to obtain a floating point value, each expects the user to enter the data in a specific format. Let's look at each in detail.

■ **FACT:** *The %f format specifier directs* scanf *to obtain a floating point value.*

The following program (SCANFLT.C) illustrates the use of the %f format specifier:

```
main()
{
    float value;

    printf("Type a floating point value and press Enter:  ");
    scanf("%f", &value);
    printf("Floating point value entered is %f", value);
}
```

When you run the program, enter a floating point value at the prompt. Your screen output will resemble the following sample:

```
Type a floating point value and press Enter:  3.45e-04
Floating point value entered is 0.000345
```

■ **FACT:** *The %e specifier directs* scanf *to obtain a floating point value entered in exponential notation by the user.*

The following program (SCANFLT2.C) illustrates use of the %e format specifier to obtain a floating point value entered in exponential notation by the user:

```
main()
{
    float value;

    puts("Type a floating point value (n.nEn) and press Enter");
    scanf("%e", &value);
    printf("Value entered is %e", value);
}
```

When you run the program, enter a floating point value below the prompt. Use exponential notation with either an uppercase E or a lowercase e. Your screen output will resemble the following sample:

```
Type a floating point value (n.nEn) and press Enter
7.543E7
Value entered is 7.543000e+007
```

■ **FACT:** *The %g format specifier directs* scanf *to obtain a floating point value. The user can enter the value in decimal or exponential format.*

The following program (SCANFLT3.C) illustrates use of the %g format specifier to obtain a floating point value:

```
main()
{
    float value;

    puts("Type a floating point value and press Enter");
    scanf("%g", &value);
    printf("Value entered is %g (%%g format)\n", value);
    printf("Value entered is %f (%%f format)\n", value);
    printf("Value entered is %e (%%e format)\n", value);
}
```

When you run the program, enter a floating point value at the prompt. The %g format specifier lets you enter a value in either decimal or exponential format. The output on your screen will resemble the following sample:

```
Type a floating point value and press Enter
7.43e04
Value entered is 74300 (g% format)
Value entered is 74300.000000 (%f format)
Value entered is 7.430000e+004 (%e format)
```

All three of these format specifiers—%f, %e, and %g—direct *scanf* to obtain a floating point value within the range of a *float* variable. To read a value of type *double*, use the l qualifier with the appropriate floating point format specifier.

■ **TIP:** *Specifying the lowercase l in the* scanf *%f, %e, or %g format specifier directs* scanf *to obtain a value of type* double.

The following program (SCANFLT4.C) shows how to use the l qualifier to obtain values of type *double*:

```
main()
{
    double value;

    puts("Type a value of type double and press Enter");
    scanf("%lf", &value);
    printf("Value entered is %lf", value);
}
```

Your screen output will resemble the following:

```
Type a value of type double and press Enter
12345678.12345678
Value entered is 12345678.123457
```

Notice how the decimal portion of the number has been rounded. Variables of type *double* can store a maximum of 14 digits, 13 of which are significant.

Next let's look quickly at the %p and %n format specifiers.

■ **FACT:** *The %p format specifier directs* scanf *to obtain an address, or pointer value.*

Most users will not need the %p format specifier, which obtains a memory address. An application that might use %p is a utility that dumps the contents of memory starting at the memory location the user enters.

■ **FACT:** *The %n format specifier directs* scanf *to assign the number of characters it has read so far.*

The following program (CHARREAD.C) prompts the user to enter an integer value. After the program reads the value, *printf* displays the value entered and uses the %n format specifier to display the number of characters *scanf* read:

```
main()
{
    int value, count;

    puts("Type an integer value and press Enter");
    scanf("%d%n", &value, &count);
    printf("Value entered is %d  Character count is %d", value, count);
}
```

Notice that the *scanf* control string contains no space between the two format specifiers. An intervening space would cause *scanf* to wait for a second value separated from the first by whitespace.

When you run the program, enter an integer at the prompt. Your screen output will resemble the following sample:

```
Type an integer value and press Enter
8876
Value entered is 8876  Character count is 4
```

REVISITING *printf*

In Chapter 2 we briefly discussed the *printf* %n format specifier, which directs *printf* to assign the number of characters it has written so far to a variable associated with the specified pointer. Because we had not yet discussed pointers, we postponed further exploration of this format specifier. Let's take a look now at how *printf* uses %n.

■ **FACT:** *The %n format specifier directs* printf *to assign the number of characters it has written so far to the variable associated with the specified pointer.*

The following program (CHAROUT.C) shows how to use the *printf* %n qualifier to display intermediate counts of the number of characters it has displayed.

```
main()
{
    int count1, count2;

    printf("ABCDE%nFGH%n", &count1, &count2);
    printf("\nFirst count = %d  Second count = %d\n", count1, count2);
}
```

When you run the program, your screen shows

```
ABCDEFGH
First count = 5  Second count = 8
```

USING *printf* AND *scanf* RETURN VALUES

As you know, *printf* and *scanf* are functions. Because C does not define them with the keyword *void*, each will return a value.

■ **FACT:** *The* printf *function returns the number of characters it displayed on the screen. The* scanf *function returns the number of values it assigned to variables before an error occurred or before the input was completed.*

Although most programmers don't test the value returned by *printf*, testing the value that *scanf* returns is often the only indicator of whether an input conversion error occurred. For example, the following *scanf* statement is designed to read three integer values.

```
scanf("%d %d %d", &a, &b, &c);
```

Suppose that a user enters the values 1 and 2 and then inadvertently types a letter instead of a number for the third value. When *scanf* returns, it assigns 1 to *a*, 2 to *b*, and 0 to *c*. It returns the value 2, which indicates that it assigned input values to only two variables.

■ **TIP:** *For critical applications, test the value* scanf *returns. In most cases this is the only way to trap input errors.*

In some situations, identifying input errors is crucial to the success of the program. The following program (SCANTEST.C) assigns the value returned by *scanf* to the variable *result* within an *if* statement to verify that all three variables are assigned user input:

```
main()
{
    int result, a, b, c;

    puts("Type three integers separated by a space and press Enter");
    if ((result = scanf("%d %d %d", &a, &b, &c)) != 3)
        printf("INPUT ERROR:  Only %d value(s) read by scanf", result);
}
```

Because *scanf* stops assigning values when it encounters the first invalid entry, the return value identifies the last valid input value that was obtained from the user. Your screen output will resemble the following sample:

```
Type three integers separated by a space and press Enter
777 888 aaa
INPUT ERROR:  Only 2 value(s) read by scanf
```

USING *scanf* WITH CHARACTER STRINGS

As previously discussed, the %s format specifier directs *scanf* to read a character string.

■ **FACT:** *The %s format specifier directs* scanf *to obtain a character string. Using %s,* scanf *continues to assign characters to the string until it encounters a whitespace character.*

When you pass a character string to a function, the compiler actually passes the address of the first character in the string. Implicitly, the name of a string variable *is* a pointer. Specifying the address operator in front of a string is therefore redundant.

■ **TIP:** *When you call* scanf *with the name of a string, omit the address operator.*

The following program (SCANCHAR.C) passes a character string to *scanf.* As you can see, the program does not use the C address operator with the name of the string.

```
main()
{
    char string[128];

    puts("Type a string and press Enter");
    scanf("%s", string);
    puts(string);
}
```

When you run the program, enter the string *This is a test.* Your screen shows

```
Type a string and press Enter
This is a test
This
```

■ **TRAP:** *Remember, when* scanf *reads characters for %s, it uses the first whitespace character as the ending point. Although the user may type several words (separated by spaces),* scanf *assigns only the first word to the string.*

Most programs use the *gets* routine to get a character string from the user. The *scanf* %s format specifier exists primarily to allow users to input a string in the same line that contains values of type *int, float,* and so on. To help programs obtain character strings with *scanf,* C provides the %[] and %[^] format specifiers.

■ **FACT:** *The %[] format specifier directs* scanf *to place characters into a string until it encounters a character that is not in the set specified within the brackets.*

The *scanf* function compares each input character with the characters listed between the brackets of the %[] format specifier. When *scanf* encounters a character that does not appear in the bracketed set, it continues with the next format specifier. The following program (SCANSTR.C) uses the %[] format specifier with *scanf* to read characters into a string until the function reads a character that is not an uppercase letter:

```
main()
{
    char string[128];

    puts("Type a string and press Enter");
    scanf("%[ABCDEFGHIJKLMNOPQRSTUVWXYZ]", string);
    puts(string);
}
```

When you run the program, *scanf* completes the read operation when you enter a value outside the range A through Z.

■ **FACT:** *The %[^] format specifier directs* scanf *to place characters into a string until the user enters one of the characters in the set.*

The %[^] format specifier lets you identify particular characters that break the input string. If the space character is not in the exclusion set, *scanf* can read multiple words into a string.

■ **TIP:** *By using the %[^] format specifier, you can invoke* scanf *to read a character string that contains blanks.*

The following program (SCANSTR2.C) uses the %[^] format specifier to continue the input operation until the user enters a horizontal tab or a newline character.

```
main()
{
    char string[128];

    puts("Type a string and press Enter");
    scanf("%[^\t\n]", string);
    puts(string);
}
```

GAINING ADDITIONAL CONTROL WITH *scanf*

So far, the examples we've seen have used whitespace characters to separate input values. In some instances, however, you might need more control: By specifying a width within *scanf* control strings, you can specify the number of input characters to assign to each variable.

For example, the following program (SCNFIELD.C) directs *scanf* to assign the first digit entered to the variable *one_digit*, the next two digits to the variable *two_digit*, and the last three digits to the variable *three_digit*. As before, the value that *scanf* returns specifies the number of arguments filled.

```
main()
{
    int one_digit, two_digit, three_digit;

    puts("Type a 6-digit value and press Enter");
    scanf("%1d%2d%3d", &one_digit, &two_digit, &three_digit);
    printf("Individual values are %d %d %d", one_digit, two_digit,
            three_digit);
}
```

When you run the program, enter a 6-digit value at the prompt. Your screen output will resemble the following sample:

```
Type a 6-digit value and press Enter
123456
Individual values are 1 23 456
```

■ **TIP:** *If you place a specific character between format specifiers in the* scanf *control string, such as the hyphen that divides parts of a date or social security number,* scanf *ignores the character and goes on to the next format specifier.*

To perform input operations in a format convenient to the end user, you might find it useful to separate format specifiers in the *scanf* control string with characters other than spaces. For example, the following program (SHOWDATE.C) prompts the user to enter a date in the form mm-dd-yyyy and then displays the date entered:

```
main()
{
    int month, day, year;

    puts("Enter today's date in the form mm-dd-yyyy");
    scanf("%d-%d-%d", &month, &day, &year);
    printf("Date:  %d-%d-%d", month, day, year);
}
```

When you run the program, enter the date in the format shown. Your screen output will resemble the following sample:

```
Enter today's date in the form mm-dd-yyyy
2-6-1989
Date: 2-6-1989
```

■ **FACT:** *If you place an asterisk (∗) in a* scanf *format specifier,* scanf *ignores the value entered for that field and continues with the next format specifier.*

The following program (SKIPVAL.C) directs the user to enter a value of type *float* followed by a value of type *int*:

```
main()
{
    int value;

    puts("Enter a floating point value and an integer value");
    scanf("%*f %d", &value);
    printf("Integer value is %d", value);
}
```

When you run the program, type two values as requested, and press Enter. Your screen output will resemble the following sample:

```
Enter a floating point and an integer value
78.95 11
Integer value is 11
```

Because the control sequence contains an asterisk in the %*f format specifier, *scanf* ignores the characters the user enters for the floating point value and continues with the integer value. Although the user types a floating point value, 78.95, *scanf* ignores it.

Most programmers fail to use *scanf* because they are uncomfortable controlling its capabilities. This chapter has provided the secrets to doing so. One of those secrets lies in using pointers correctly. The sample programs we have examined should put you at ease with pointers. We will discuss them further in Chapter 12.

SUMMARY

Displaying Memory Addresses and Their Contents

■ **FACT:** *In C the ampersand character (&) is the address operator. The address operator returns the* address *of a variable in memory, not the* value *of the variable.*

Declaring a Pointer Variable

■ **FACT:** *To declare a pointer, precede the variable name with an asterisk (*). The compiler creates a pointer variable to the type specified. For example:* int *ptr; *declares a pointer named* ptr *to a value of type* int.

■ **FACT:** *In C the asterisk (*) serves as the indirection operator. The indirection operator tells the compiler to change or access the value contained in the memory location referenced by a pointer.*

■ **TIP:** *Read the expression* *ptr *as "the value in the memory location specified by the pointer variable* ptr*." In contrast,* ptr *without the asterisk refers to an address, not to the value stored at that address.*

■ **FACT:** *Using the C indirection operator, you can view and change the value contained in a memory location.*

Using Pointers with Functions

■ **FACT:** *To change a variable's value within a function, you must pass the address of the variable to the function. Within the function, you must use a pointer.*

■ **TIP:** *If you are confused about whether you need to use pointers, ask yourself, "Does the function change the argument?" If the answer is yes, pass a pointer. If the answer is no, pass the variable by value.*

Getting Started with *scanf*

■ **FACT:** *The* scanf *function lets C programs perform formatted input operations.*

■ **FACT:** *The %d specifier directs* scanf *to obtain an integer value. The function acts upon characters entered by the user until it encounters a character that is not a digit.*

■ **FACT:** *For numeric data input,* scanf *skips leading whitespace.*

■ **TRAP:** *If* scanf *cannot convert the characters that the user enters into the specified format, it assigns as much of the value as it has converted.*

■ **FACT:** *If blank spaces occur within the control string,* scanf *regards a space in the user's input as a separator between the values that correspond to each variable.*

■ **FACT:** *The* scanf *function lets you use the long qualifier l in the %i, %o, and %x format specifiers.*

■ **FACT:** *The %o format specifier directs* scanf *to obtain an integer value that the user enters in octal notation (with or without a leading zero).*

■ **TRAP:** *If* scanf *expects an octal value and the user enters a nonoctal value, the function assigns as many of the valid octal digits as possible to the variable. When it encounters a nonoctal digit,* scanf *regards the value as complete.*

■ **FACT:** *The %x format specifier directs* scanf *to obtain a hexadecimal value (with or without the leading 0x).*

■ **TRAP:** *If* scanf *expects a hexadecimal value and the user enters a value other than hexadecimal, the function truncates the input value at the first nonhexadecimal digit.*

■ **FACT:** *The %i format specifier directs* scanf *to obtain an integer value. The user can enter the value in decimal or, with the appropriate prefix, in octal or hexadecimal.*

■ **FACT:** *The Microsoft C Compiler supports %D, %I, %O, and %U with* scanf *to obtain long integers.*

■ **FACT:** *The %c format specifier directs* scanf *to obtain a single character.*

■ **TRAP:** *If the* scanf *control string includes several format specifiers and the user enters too few values,* scanf *assigns 0 to each remaining variable. The function ignores any superfluous values you enter.*

■ **FACT:** *The %% format specifier directs* scanf *to read a percent sign. The function simply ignores the percent sign once it is read.*

■ **TRAP:** *When the control string contains multiple format specifiers,* scanf *completes the input operation at the first invalid character and leaves remaining values unchanged.*

■ **FACT:** *The %f format specifier directs* scanf *to obtain a floating point value.*

■ **FACT:** *The %e specifier directs* scanf *to obtain a floating point value entered in exponential notation by the user.*

■ **FACT:** *The %g format specifier directs* scanf *to obtain a floating point value. The user can enter the value in decimal or exponential format.*

■ **TIP:** *Specifying the lowercase l in the scanf %f, %e, or %g format specifier directs* scanf *to obtain a value of type* double.

■ **FACT:** *The %p format specifier directs* scanf *to obtain an address, or pointer value.*

■ **FACT:** *The %n format specifier directs* scanf *to assign the number of characters it has read so far.*

Revisiting *printf*

■ **FACT:** *The %n format specifier directs* printf *to assign the number of characters it has written so far to the variable associated with the specified pointer.*

Using *printf* and *scanf* Return Values

■ **FACT:** *The* printf *function returns the number of characters it displayed on the screen. The* scanf *function returns the number of values it assigned to variables made before an error occurred or before the input was completed.*

■ **TIP:** *For critical applications, test the value* scanf *returns. In most cases this is the only way to trap input errors.*

Using *scanf* with Character Strings

■ **FACT:** *The %s format specifier directs* scanf *to obtain a character string. Using %s,* scanf *continues to assign characters to the string until it encounters a whitespace character.*

■ **TIP:** *When you call* scanf *with the name of a string, omit the address operator.*

■ **TRAP:** *Remember, when* scanf *reads characters for %s, it uses the first whitespace character as the ending point. Although the user may type several words (separated by spaces),* scanf *assigns only the first word to the string.*

■ **FACT:** *The %[] format specifier directs* scanf *to place characters into a string until it encounters a character that is not in the set specified within the brackets.*

■ **FACT:** *The %[^] format specifier directs* scanf *to place characters into a string until the user enters one of the characters in the set.*

■ **TIP:** *By using the %[^] format specifier, you can invoke* scanf *to read a character string that contains blanks.*

Gaining Additional Control with *scanf*

■ **TIP:** *If you place a specific character between format specifiers in the* scanf *control string, such as the hyphen that divides parts of a date or social security number,* scanf *ignores the character and goes on to the next format specifier.*

■ **FACT:** *If you place an asterisk (∗) in a* scanf *format specifier,* scanf *ignores the value entered for that field and continues with the next format specifier.*

GLOSSARY

address operator An operator that returns the memory location of a variable. Its symbol is the ampersand (&).

indirection operator An operator that lets you access the value in the memory location referenced by a pointer. Its symbol is the asterisk (∗). For example: *value = ∗ptr;*

pointer A variable type that contains a memory address. To declare a pointer in C, specify a type and immediately precede the variable name with an asterisk. For example, the statement *int ∗ptr;* declares the pointer *ptr,* which references an *int* value.

whitespace Unprinted characters such as blank spaces, tabs, or formfeeds.

## CHAPTER 11

Using C Arrays

In earlier chapters you learned how to define variables of type *int*, *float*, *char*, and *double*. In many cases your programs will need to manipulate a group of related variables such as a set of test scores, weekly sales information, or the monthly prices for a stock.

In this chapter you learn how to group multiple related values into a single variable called an array. You learn how to access specific entries in an array and how to pass an array to functions. You also learn how to create and use multidimensional arrays.

CREATING ARRAYS IN C

Let's assume that you need a program that tracks and displays unit sales for each weekday and the deviation from the previous day's sales. This program will prompt the user to enter the number of daily sales and will then display a report in the following format:

```
              Sales        Plus/Minus
Monday        35           --
Tuesday       42           7
Wednesday     39           -3
Thursday      40           1
Friday        43           3

Total sales   199
```

Column 1 of the report shows the days of the week, Column 2 shows the number of daily sales, and Column 3 reveals the change in unit sales from the previous day. The bottom line lists the total number of sales for the week.

The first task in writing this program is to declare the variables that will store the number of sales for each weekday:

```
int Monday, Tuesday, Wednesday, Thursday, Friday;
```

The program (SALES.C) can then prompt the user to enter the number of sales for each day and produce the report from the individual variables.

```
main()
{
    int Monday, Tuesday, Wednesday, Thursday, Friday;

    printf("Enter the number of sales for each weekday (Mon-Fri):  ");
    scanf("%d %d %d %d %d", &Monday, &Tuesday, &Wednesday,
          &Thursday, &Friday);

    printf("\n\t\tSales\t\tPlus/Minus\n");
    printf("Monday\t\t%d\t\t--\n", Monday);
    printf("Tuesday\t\t%d\t\t%d\n", Tuesday, Tuesday - Monday);
    printf("Wednesday\t%d\t\t%d\n", Wednesday, Wednesday - Tuesday);
    printf("Thursday\t%d\t\t%d\n", Thursday, Thursday - Wednesday);
    printf("Friday\t\t%d\t\t%d\n", Friday, Friday - Thursday);

    printf("\nTotal sales\t%d", Monday + Tuesday + Wednesday + Thursday +
           Friday);
}
```

Although this program eventually displays the report, declaring and manipulating five variables makes the code cumbersome. If you later wanted to track unit sales for an entire month, you would need more than 20 individual variables.

When a set of values are all of the same type, you can simplify the process of data storage by using an array.

■ **FACT:** *An array can store one or more values of the same type. To create an array in C, declare an array variable in the general form* type name[num_elements].

You have already worked with one type of C array, the character string. In Chapter 7 we used the following declaration to create an array capable of storing 128 characters:

```
char string[128];
```

The following declaration creates an array of type *int* capable of storing five integer values:

```
int sales[5];
```

When you create an array in C, the value between the left and right brackets specifies the number of elements in the array. As with strings, the compiler uses 0 as the index for the first elements of other arrays beginning with 0. As such, the declaration of the array *sales* creates a series of five elements indexed *sales[0]*, *sales[1]*, *sales[2]*, *sales[3]*, and *sales[4]*. By defining other arrays in the same manner, you can create arrays of any type.

Definition	Storage	Index
int sales[5];	5 integer values	*sales[0]* through *sales[4]*
float price[30];	30 floating point values	*price[0]* through *price[29]*
long int distance[10];	10 long integer values	*distance[0]* through *distance[9]*
char name[80];	80 characters	*name[0]* through *name[79]*

Let's return to our program for reporting unit sales and replace the five variables with a single five-element array. Each element of the array *sales* can store the unit sales figure for a given weekday, as shown in Figure 11-1.

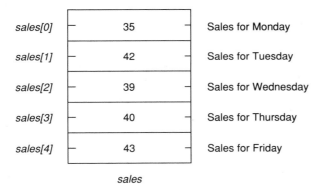

FIGURE 11-1.
The array sales *has five elements, which are indexed 0 through 4. Each element can store an* int *value.*

The following program (SALES2.C) uses the *sales* array to store sales information for each workday in a week:

```
main()
{
    int sales[5];
    int i, total_sales = 0;

    for (i = 0; i <= 4; ++i)
        {
        printf("Enter the number of sales for day %d: ", i + 1);
        scanf("%d", &sales[i]);  /* pass the address of an element */
        total_sales += sales[i];
        }
```

(continued)

continued

```
    printf("\nDay\t\tSales\t\tPlus/Minus\n");
    printf("1\t\t%d\t\t--\n", sales[0]);

    for (i = 1; i <= 4; ++i)
        printf("%d\t\t%d\t\t%+d\n", i+1, sales[i], sales[i] - sales[i-1]);

    printf("\nTotal sales \t%d\n", total_sales);
}
```

■ **FACT:** *To change individual array elements in a function, you must pass the elements by address using the C address operator.*

In Chapter 10 you learned that when you pass a character string (array of characters) to a function, the compiler passes the starting address of the array. When you pass individual array elements, however, it passes a copy of the actual value. If the function is to change the value of an element, your program must pass the address of the element. For this reason, the preceding program passes the address of each array element to *scanf,* which assigns an input value to the referenced elements.

The program compares the sales of the current day with the sales of the previous day by comparing the array elements *sales[i]* and *sales[i-1],* as shown in Figure 11-2.

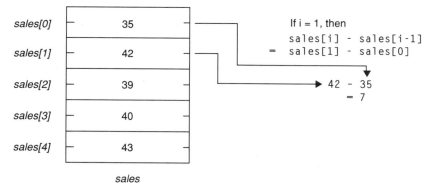

FIGURE 11-2.
The SALES2.C program compares consecutive array elements. Notice that the compiler lets you use an expression to specify an array index.

The compiler appends the null character only at the end of character strings. Arrays of other types do not use the null character to indicate the last element. Remember, the null character has a value of 0. Nonstring arrays commonly have elements with values of 0 and thus cannot reserve the value 0 to indicate the last array element.

■ **TRAP:** *If your program assigns a value to an array index outside the range of array elements, errors will occur.*

If your program defines an array of type *int* as

```
int array[10];
```

and later tries to assign a value to an element outside the range 0 through 9, such as *array[10]*, your program will overwrite a memory location that corresponds to another variable or that contains program information. In either case, an error will occur—which could possibly lock up your system.

PASSING ARRAYS TO FUNCTIONS

In Chapter 7 you learned how to pass a string to a function. The general procedure for passing an array to a function is similar.

The following program (PASARRAY.C) declares two arrays of type *int*. The first stores the integer values 0 through 4; the second stores the values 0 through 9. The program calls the function *display_values* twice, each time passing one of the arrays as an argument. The function *display_values* displays the contents of each array.

```
main()
{
    int small[5], large[10];
    int i;
    void display_values();

    for (i = 0; i <= 4; ++i)
        small[i] = i;

    for (i = 0; i <= 9; ++i)
        large[i] = i;

    printf("small array:  ");
    display_values(small, 5);  /* pass array name and number of elements */

    printf("\nlarge array:  ");
    display_values(large, 10);
}

void display_values(int array[], int num_elements)
{
    int i;

    for (i = 0; i < num_elements; ++i)
        printf("%d ", array[i]);
}
```

■ **FACT:** *To declare an array within the argument list of a function, specify the array type followed by a name and the left and right brackets. For example:* int array[];

Just as you need not specify the size of a character string in the argument list of a function, you need not specify the size of arrays of other types. Here's why.

Each time your program passes an array to a function, whether the array is of type *int* or of type *char* (a string), it passes the address of the first element of the array. For example, when the preceding program passes the array *small* to the function *display_values*, the variable *array* within the function references the elements of the array *small* as shown in Figure 11-3.

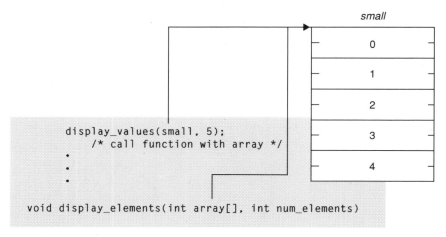

FIGURE 11-3.
An array argument is passed by reference, which gives the function access to the memory location at which the elements are stored.

■ **FACT:** *When you pass an entire array to a function, the compiler passes the function an address that references the first element of the array. This method of relaying an argument is known as call by reference. It lets the function change the array's contents directly because the function knows where the array resides in memory.*

Earlier you learned that, by default, the compiler passes a copy of an argument's value to a function. Using this method, known as call by value, the compiler prevents a function from changing the value of an argument. In Chapter 10 you learned that the compiler lets you use pointers to achieve call by reference. You also learned that strings are an exception. So are arrays of other types. The compiler always passes arrays by reference. Note, however, that if a program passes a specific element of an array, such as *sales[2]*, it uses call by value.

The following program (RANDOM.C) uses the C run-time library routine *rand*, which returns a random integer in the range 0 through 32,767. The program generates 10 random integers and assigns each to the array *random*. Next the program uses the function *average* to determine the average value. Then it displays in a column each value stored in the array.

```
#include <stdlib.h>   /* needed for rand */

main()
{
    int random[10];
    int i;

    for (i = 0; i < 10; ++i)
        random[i] = rand();

    printf("The average value generated was %d\n\n", average(random, 10));

    for (i = 0; i < 10; ++i)
        printf("%d\n", random[i]);
}

average(int values[], int count)
{
    long int sum = 0;
    int i;

    for (i = 0; i < count; ++i)
        sum += values[i];

    return (sum / count);
}
```

Note that the function *average* uses the type *long int* for the variable *sum*. Because *rand* can return integers in the range 0 through 32,767, the sum of 10 such values could quickly exceed the range of values a variable of type *int* can store. By using the type *long int*, you avoid this problem.

■ **TIP:** *Using constant definitions to declare the dimensions of your arrays makes your code easier to maintain.*

The preceding program computes the average of 10 random integers. To perform the same processing for 25 values, you would have to change your array declarations and each of the loops in the program to use the value 25. A simple shortcut is to define a constant that contains your array size. In the program on the following page (RANDOM2.C), the *main* function uses a constant called SIZE.

```
#include <stdlib.h> /* needed for rand */
#define SIZE 10

main()
{
    int random[SIZE];
    int i;

    for (i = 0; i < SIZE; ++i)
        random[i] = rand();
    printf("The average value generated was %d\n\n",
            average(random, SIZE));
    for (i = 0; i < SIZE; ++i)
        printf("%d\n", random[i]);
}

average(int values[], int count)
{
    long int sum = 0;
    int i;

    for (i = 0; i < count; ++i)
        sum += values[i];
    return (sum / count);
}
```

Now, to change RANDOM2.C to generate 25 random numbers, simply change the constant definition of SIZE as follows and then recompile the program:

```
#define SIZE 25
```

As you learned in Chapter 6, constants improve your program's readability and simplify the process of changing a program.

INITIALIZING ARRAY ELEMENTS

In Chapter 7 you learned how to initialize character strings within a program. For example, the following program (INIT.C) initializes and prints the contents of the *string* array:

```
main()
{
    static char string[128] = "This is a test";

    printf("%s", string);
}
```

The keyword *static* lets us initialize a local array—one that is declared inside a function. In this case, the initialization assigns characters to the first 15 elements of the string (14 for the string and one for the null character). The compiler does not assign characters to the remaining 113 elements.

The following program (STRINIT.C) initializes a string to the same source text (*"This is a test"*) but does not specifically define the size of the string:

```
main()
{
    static char string[] = "This is a test";

    printf("%s\n%d elements", string, sizeof(string));
}
```

When a program initializes an array in this manner, the compiler creates an array large enough to store only the number of characters in the string, including the null byte character. You can verify this by compiling and executing the preceding program. When you do so, your screen shows

```
This is a test
15 elements
```

The *sizeof* operator, used here with the name of an array, returns the number of bytes the array occupies. For character arrays, that number matches the number of elements.

The following program (INTARAY.C) declares an array of fixed size and initializes the array at declaration:

```
main()
{
    static int array[10] = { 0, 1, 2, 3, 4, 5, 6, 7, 8, 9 };
    int i;

    for (i = 0; i < 10; ++i)
        printf("%d ", array[i]);
}
```

If the program does not specify the size of the array, the compiler creates an array large enough to store the number of values specified, as shown in the program on the following page (INTARAY2.C).

```
main()
{
    static int array[] = { 0, 1, 2, 3, 4, 5, 6, 7, 8, 9 };
    int i;

    for (i = 0; i < 10; ++i)
        printf("%d ", array[i]);

    printf("\n%d elements", sizeof(array) / sizeof(int));
}
```

When you run the program, your screen shows

```
0 1 2 3 4 5 6 7 8 9
10 elements
```

Notice in the second *printf* statement that *sizeof(array)* results in the number of bytes in the array; when you divide that number by the number of bytes in each *int* value, the result is the number of elements in the array.

USING MULTIDIMENSIONAL ARRAYS IN C

In addition to manipulating values stored in an array, many programs need to work with a table of values. However, before a program can work with tabular data, you must define a multidimensional array that specifies the number of rows and the number of columns.

■ **FACT:** *The C compiler lets you declare multidimensional arrays for each C type. To do so, specify the type followed by the name and the dimensions within pairs of brackets.*

The first value in a two-dimensional array specifies the number of rows in an array; the second value specifies the number of columns. For example, the array definition in Figure 11-4 creates an array with two rows and three columns. To access an array element, use the corresponding index values.

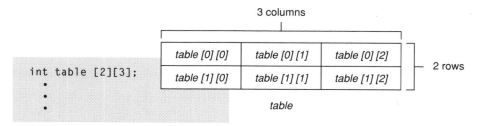

FIGURE 11-4.
Each element of a two-dimensional array has a unique pair of index values.

The following program (MULTIDIM.C) assigns the integer values 1 through 100 to a multidimensional array with 10 rows and 10 columns. The program uses two variables named *row* and *column* to access individual elements of the array.

```c
main()
{
    int table[10][10], row, column, i = 0;
    void display_array();

    for (row = 0; row < 10; row++)
        for (column = 0; column < 10; column++)
            table[row][column] = ++i;

    display_array(table, 10);
}


void display_array(int a[][10], int size)
{
    int i, j;

    for (i = 0; i < size; ++i)
        {
        for (j = 0; j < size; ++j)
            printf("%4d", a[i][j]);
        printf("\n");
        }
}
```

When you run the program, your screen shows

```
 1   2   3   4   5   6   7   8   9  10
11  12  13  14  15  16  17  18  19  20
21  22  23  24  25  26  27  28  29  30
31  32  33  34  35  36  37  38  39  40
41  42  43  44  45  46  47  48  49  50
51  52  53  54  55  56  57  58  59  60
61  62  63  64  65  66  67  68  69  70
71  72  73  74  75  76  77  78  79  80
81  82  83  84  85  86  87  88  89  90
91  92  93  94  95  96  97  98  99 100
```

The preceding program points out several key concepts. First, the elements of the array are accessed as *table[row][column]* and *a[i][j]*, with brackets around each index value.

■ **TRAP:** *To access elements in a C multidimensional array, you must bracket the index for each dimension. In most programming languages, a single set of brackets encloses the index values for all dimensions. This is not the case with C.*

Second, the multidimensional array is defined within the function *display_array*:

```
void display_value (int a[][10], int size)
```

■ **FACT:** *When you pass a two-dimensional array to a C function, you can omit the number of rows; however, you must, at a minimum, specify the number of columns in the array when you declare the array argument.*

Later in this chapter you will learn how C stores the values of a two-dimensional array in memory and why the compiler requires a declaration to specify at least the number of columns in the array.

■ **FACT:** *For each dimension an array contains, the declaration must include a size within brackets.*

When you create multidimensional arrays, you need to add a bracketed size for each dimension. The following declaration, for example, declares a three-dimensional array:

```
int tables[5][10][3];
```

In this case, view the array *tables* as shown in Figure 11-5: 5 rows of 10 columns, 3 levels deep.

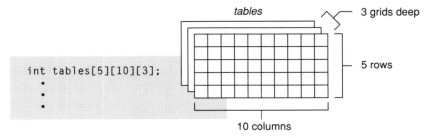

FIGURE 11-5.
You can view a three-dimensional array as an array of two-dimensional arrays.

You can similarly process arrays of an essentially unlimited number of dimensions. For example, the following array declarations are valid:

```
int sales [5][10][3][2];
```

```
float expenses [10][3][5][2][3];
```

```
long int distances [3][3][3][3][5];
```

Admittedly, most arrays will have no more than two or three dimensions. However, you should recognize the format if you see it.

INITIALIZING MULTIDIMENSIONAL ARRAYS

Just as you can initialize a one-dimensional array, you can assign values to the elements of a multidimensional array in the statement that declares it.

■ **FACT:** *To initialize a multidimensional array at declaration, specify the values for each row grouped within braces {}. Separate each row of braces with a comma, and enclose the entire initialization within a set of braces.*

The following declaration initializes the elements of an array called *box*:

```
static int box[3][3] = {
    {1, 2, 3},
    {4, 5, 6},
    {7, 8, 9},
};
```

As before, if you don't specify both dimensions, the compiler creates an array large enough to store the initialization values.

SIMPLIFYING ARRAY MANIPULATION FUNCTIONS

In Chapter 8 you learned that a major advantage of functions is that you can often use a function in more than one program. By knowing a single secret about how the compiler stores multidimensional arrays, you can reuse many of the functions you wrote for one-dimensional arrays when you work with multidimensional arrays.

The following program (AVERAGE.C) uses the function *average* to calculate the average value of the elements in each of two arrays. The first statement defines an integer array called *values* that contains 10 elements, and it defines an integer array called *table* that contains 3 rows of 3 columns each. The program uses the *rand* function to assign random numbers to each array, and then it passes both arrays (one at a time) to the function *average*, which returns the average value in each array. The *average* function takes advantage of the sequential arrangement of elements in memory (Figure 11-6 on the following page) to access both *values* and *table* as one-dimensional arrays.

```
#include <stdlib.h>   /* needed for rand */

main()
{
    int values[10], table[3][3];
    int i, j;

    for (i = 0; i < 10; ++i)
        values[i] = rand();
```

(continued)

continued

```
    for (i = 0; i < 3; i++)
        for (j = 0; j < 3; j++)
            table[i][j] = rand();

    printf("Average value in first array is %d\n", average(values, 10));
    printf("Average value in table is %d", average(table, 9));
}

int average(int a[], int size)
{
    int i;
    long int sum = 0;

    for (i = 0; i < size; ++i)
        sum += a[i];

    return (sum / size);
}
```

■ **FACT:** *The Microsoft C Compiler, like most compilers, stores multidimensional arrays as a single list of values.*

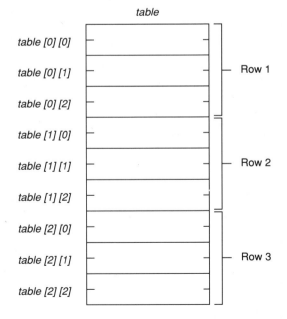

FIGURE 11-6.
The Microsoft C Compiler stores array elements sequentially in memory.

Because the C compiler stores multidimensional arrays as shown in Figure 11-6, the function *average* simply treats *table* as a one-dimensional, 9-element array. Therefore, although your application uses multidimensional arrays, you can still use many of the routines you developed for one-dimensional arrays.

In the next chapter we will take another look at C arrays, in the context both of pointers as array elements and of built-in C run-time library routines for sorting and searching.

SUMMARY

Creating Arrays in C

■ **FACT:** *An array can store one or more values of the same type. To create an array in C, declare an array variable in the general form* type name[num_elements].

■ **FACT:** *To change individual array elements in a function, you must pass the elements by address using the C address operator.*

■ **TRAP:** *If your program assigns a value to an array index outside the range of array elements, errors will occur.*

Passing Arrays to Functions

■ **FACT:** *To declare an array within the argument list of a function, specify the array type followed by a name and the left and right brackets. For example:* int array[];

■ **FACT:** *When you pass an entire array to a function, the compiler passes the function an address that references the first element of the array. This method of relaying an argument is known as call by reference. It lets the function change the array's contents directly because the function knows where the array resides in memory.*

■ **TIP:** *Using constant definitions to declare the dimensions of your arrays makes your code easier to maintain.*

Using Multidimensional Arrays in C

■ **FACT:** *The C compiler lets you declare multidimensional arrays for each C type. To do so, specify the type followed by the name and the dimensions within pairs of brackets.*

■ **TRAP:** *To access elements in a C multidimensional array, you must bracket the index for each dimension. In most programming languages, a single set of brackets encloses the index values for all dimensions. This is not the case with C.*

■ **FACT:** *When you pass a two-dimensional array to a C function, you must, at a minimum, specify the number of columns in the array when you declare the array argument.*

■ **FACT:** *For each dimension an array contains, the declaration must include a size within brackets.*

Initializing Multidimensional Arrays

■ **FACT:** *To initialize a multidimensional array at declaration, specify the values for each row grouped within braces {}. Separate each row of braces with a comma, and enclose the entire initialization within a set of braces.*

Simplifying Array Manipulation Functions

■ **FACT:** *The Microsoft C Compiler, like most C compilers, stores C multidimensional arrays as a single list of values.*

GLOSSARY

array A compound data type that lets you group logically related values of the same type in a single variable.

array index The means of accessing a specific element in an array. Using an index value of 0, *sales[0]* accesses the first element in the *sales* array. Similarly, with an index value of 1, *sales[1]* accesses the second element.

call by reference A method of passing function arguments. The function receives the address of a variable and thereby the ability to manipulate the value of the variable itself.

call by value The default method of passing an argument to a function. The function receives a copy of the argument's value but no means of manipulating the argument itself.

multidimensional array An array that specifies columns of values as well as rows. The declaration *int box[3][5];* creates an integer array named *box* with 3 rows of 5 columns each.

## CHAPTER 12

Advanced Pointer Manipulation

In Chapter 10 you learned how to create and manipulate pointer variables. At that time you found that the C address operator (&) returns the address of an object in memory and that the indirection operator (*) lets you access the value referenced by a pointer. Chapter 10 also taught you how to modify an argument's value within a function by using pointers. In general, Chapter 10 laid the foundation for the topics in this chapter.

As you will learn, you can use C pointers to do much more than change the value of an argument. You can use pointers to reduce the amount of code required to manipulate strings, to reduce the processing time associated with array manipulation operations, and to increase the flexibility of functions by allowing them to support multiple operations.

USING POINTERS TO ACCESS A CHARACTER STRING

As you have seen, each time your program passes a character string (or any array) to a function, it passes the address of the first element in the array.

■ **FACT:** *Any C function that manipulates an array of elements can use pointers instead. Pointers often simplify the code and reduce the processing time.*

The function *str_display* in the following program (SHOWSTR.C) displays the characters in a string.

```
#include <stdio.h>   /* needed for putchar */

main()
{
    str_display("Message to display");
}

str_display(char string[])
{
    int i;

    for (i = 0; string[i] != '\0'; ++i)
        putchar(string[i]);
}
```

The function *str_display* examines the characters in the array one character at a time until it finds the null character. When you execute this program, your screen shows

```
Message to display
```

Now change the *for* loop within *str_display* as follows:

```
for (i = 0; string[i] != '\0'; ++i)
    printf("%04X %c\n", &string[i], string[i],);
```

When you compile and run the program again, your screen shows

```
0282 M
0283 e
0284 s
0285 s
0286 a
0287 g
0288 e
0289
028A t
028B o
028C
028D d
028E i
028F s
0290 p
0291 l
0292 a
0293 y
```

As you can see, the characters in the array reside in successive memory locations. Figure 12-1 depicts this arrangement of elements. Note that the exact memory locations in your computer might be different from those shown here.

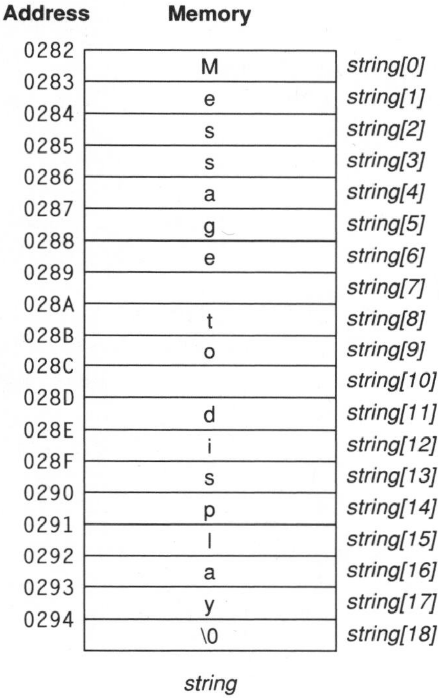

Address	Memory	
0282	M	string[0]
0283	e	string[1]
0284	s	string[2]
0285	s	string[3]
0286	a	string[4]
0287	g	string[5]
0288	e	string[6]
0289		string[7]
028A	t	string[8]
028B	o	string[9]
028C		string[10]
028D	d	string[11]
028E	i	string[12]
028F	s	string[13]
0290	p	string[14]
0291	l	string[15]
0292	a	string[16]
0293	y	string[17]
0294	\0	string[18]

string

FIGURE 12-1.
String elements are stored at successive memory locations.

Because the function knows the starting address of the array, it can use a pointer to display the string. The following program (SHOWSTR2.C) also displays *Message to display*, but in it the function *str_display* uses a pointer rather than an array.

```c
#include <stdio.h>  /* needed for putchar */

main()
{
    str_display("Message to display");
}

str_display(char *string)  /* pointer to string */
{
    while (*string != '\0')
        putchar(*string++);
}
```

First, the function declares *string* as a pointer to a variable of type *char* rather than declaring it as an array variable. The pointer might reference a single character or a long string—the length is not indicated.

```
str_display(char *string)   /* pointer to string */
```

■ **TIP:** *A pointer to a string does not specify the number of characters in the string. Therefore, the string must end with the null character so that string-handling routines can identify the last character in the string.*

The *str_display* function in the preceding program displays successive characters of *string*. The expression

```
while (*string != '\0')
```

uses the indirection operator (∗) to examine the character pointed to by *string*. As long as that character is not null, the loop continues. Remember, the C compiler equates the '\0' character to the value 0, which also indicates a false result. Therefore, an expression such as *while (∗string != '\0')* is equivalent to *while (∗string)*.

Next, look at the statement

```
putchar(*string++);
```

The *putchar* statement first displays the character pointed to by *string*. Next it uses the postfix increment operator to increment the pointer *string* to point to the next character in the string. To better understand this processing, let's change the *while* loop in the preceding program as follows:

```
while (*string)
{
    printf("%04X %c\n", string, *string);
    string++;
}
```

When you compile and run the program again, your screen shows the same columns of addresses and characters as those produced by SHOWSTR.C (on p. 212).

In a similar manner, the following program (SCOPY.C) uses the function *str_copy* to copy the contents of one string to another:

```
main()
{
    char target[128];
    void str_copy(char *, char *);

    str_copy("String to copy", target);
    puts(target);
}
```

You can implement *str_copy* in two ways. You can use arrays (ARYCOPY.C), or you can use pointers (PTRCOPY.C):

```
void str_copy(char source[], char target[]) /* array implementation */
{
    int i = 0;

    while (target[i] = source[i])
        ++i;
}
```

```
void str_copy(char *source, char *target) /* pointer implementation */
{
    while (*target++ = *source++)
        { ; }
}
```

Let's first examine the *while* loop used in the array method:

```
while (target[i] = source[i])
    ++i;
```

The while statement first assigns the letter in *string[i]* to *target[i]* and then tests the value assigned. As long as the value is not the null character (false), the loop continues. (Remember that the condition following *while* does not test whether the elements in two strings are equal—that would require the == operator.)

Note the way in which the function *str_copy* is defined in *main*:

```
void str_copy(char *, char *);
```

Not only does this declaration indicate that *str_copy* does not return a value, but it also specifies the type of each argument. The identical declarations of type *char ** state that the arguments are pointers to character strings.

■ **TIP:** *Whenever possible, use pointers instead of arrays. In most cases, your program will execute faster.*

As a rule, pointers are more efficient than arrays. To understand why this is so, we must look at the assembly language code that the C compiler generates for each implementation of *str_copy*.

Use the /Fa option with the CL command to create assembly language code that corresponds to the array and pointer versions of the function, which are contrasted in Figure 12-2. For example, the following command directs the compiler to generate an assembly language equivalent to ARYCOPY.C:

```
C> CL /c /Fa ARYCOPY.C
```

The resulting assembly language listing is stored in the file ARYCOPY.ASM.

```
_str_copy         PROC NEAR
①        push     bp
②        mov      bp,sp
③        mov      ax,2
④        call     __chkstk
⑤        push     si
;        source  = 4
;        target  = 6
;        i = -2
; Line 3
⑥        mov      WORD PTR [bp-2],0    ;i
; Line 5
⑦        jmp      SHORT $L20001
⑧        nop
$FC106:
; Line 6
⑨        inc      WORD PTR [bp-2]      ;i
$L20001:
⑩        mov      bx,WORD PTR [bp-2]   ;i
⑪        mov      si,WORD PTR [bp+4]   ;source
⑫        mov      al,[bx][si]
⑬        mov      si,WORD PTR [bp+6]   ;target
⑭        mov      [bx][si],al
⑮        or       al,al
⑯        jne      $FC106
; Line 7
⑰        pop      si
⑱        mov      sp,bp
⑲        pop      bp
⑳        ret
㉑        nop

_str_copy         ENDP
```

FIGURE 12-2.   *(continued)*
The array implementation of our string-copying function, shown above, requires more lines of code than the pointer implementation on the right-hand page.

FIGURE 12-2. *continued*

```
_str_copy          PROC NEAR
①        push     bp
②        mov      bp,sp
③        xor      ax,ax
④        call     __chkstk
⑤        push     si
;        source   = 4
;        target   = 6
; Line 3
$FC105:
⑥        mov      bx,WORD PTR [bp+6]    ;target
⑦        inc      WORD PTR [bp+6]       ;target
⑧        mov      si,WORD PTR [bp+4]    ;source
⑨        inc      WORD PTR [bp+4]       ;source
⑩        mov      al,BYTE PTR [si]
⑪        mov      BYTE PTR [bx],al
⑫        or       al,al
⑬        jne      $FC105
; Line 4
; Line 5
⑭        pop      si
⑮        pop      bp
⑯        ret

_str_copy          ENDP
```

■ **FACT:** *The CL /Fa option directs the C compiler to generate an assembly language listing of a C program. CL creates a file with the extension ASM that contains the assembly language listing. (The Microsoft QuickC Compiler does not support the /Fa switch.)*

By examining the respective assembly language listings, you can see that pointer implementation requires five fewer instructions, which reduces the function's execution time. Most of the additional processing results from the array indexing and the creation and manipulation of the variable *i*. Depending on the number of times the program calls the function, even a small decrease in the amount of processing can become significant.

UNDERSTANDING POINTER ARITHMETIC

In the previous section you learned that by incrementing the pointer to a character string the pointer references the next character location in memory.

■ **FACT:** *When a program increments a pointer variable, it examines the pointer's type and increments the pointer by the number of bytes required to store a variable of that type.*

The C compiler stores characters in a string in consecutive byte locations. Therefore, when your program increments a pointer to a character string, it increments the pointer by 1, as shown in Figure 12-3.

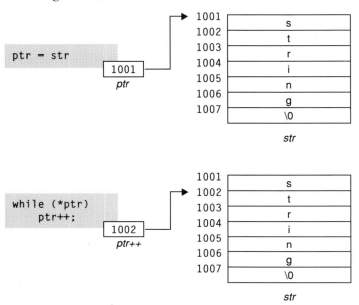

FIGURE 12-3.

Incrementing a pointer to a string advances the pointer to the address of the next character.

A value of type *int*, however, requires 2 bytes of storage for each element. When your program increments a pointer to an array of type *int*, it increments the pointer by 2 bytes, as shown in Figure 12-4.

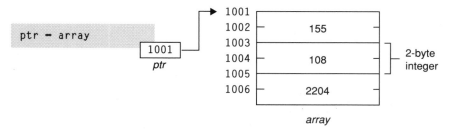

FIGURE 12-4. *(continued)*

Incrementing a pointer to an array of int *values advances the pointer 2 bytes to the address of the next element, as shown on the following page.*

FIGURE 12-4. *continued*

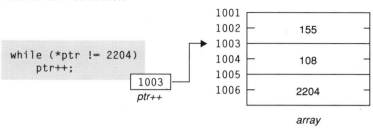

The following program (PASSFLT.C) passes an array containing five floating point values to the function *show_values*, which uses a pointer to display the values:

```
main()
{
    static float values[5] = { 1.1, 2.2, 3.3, 4.4, 5.5 };
    void show_values(float *, int);

    show_values(values, 5);
}

void show_values(float *value, int size)
{
    int i = 1;

    while (i++ <= size)
        printf("%f\n", *value++);
}
```

When you execute the program, your screen shows:

```
1.100000
2.200000
3.300000
4.400000
5.500000
```

When a program performs arithmetic operations on a pointer, the results aren't always what you would expect. For example, if your program adds 1 to a pointer of type *float*, it does not simply add the value 1 to the address. Instead, it changes the value of the pointer to reference the next *float* value. Adding 2 to a pointer of type *float* directs the compiler to change the value of the pointer so that it points to the second *float* value that follows the current pointer location.

■ **FACT:** *Adding or subtracting a value* n *from a pointer directs the compiler to access the* n*th value that corresponds to the type.*

The following program (PASSFLT2.C) uses a modified version of *show_values* to display the floating point values by adding 1 to the pointer with each iteration:

```
main()
{
    static float values[5] = { 1.1, 2.2, 3.3, 4.4, 5.5 };
    void show_values(float *, int);

    show_values(values, 5);
}

void show_values(float *value, int size)
{
    int i = 1;

    while (i++ <= size)
    {
        printf("Value %f Address %04X\n", *value, value);
        value = value + 1;
    }
}
```

When you run the program, your screen shows

```
Value 1.100000   Address 0042
Value 2.200000   Address 0046
Value 3.300000   Address 004A
Value 4.400000   Address 004E
Value 5.500000   Address 0052
```

As you can see, adding 1 to a pointer changes the address to point to the next element.

USING AN ARRAY OF POINTERS

You can create arrays of pointers for each C data type. For example, the following declaration creates an array of pointers to 10 integer values. A sample of such an array is illustrated in Figure 12-5. Note that the pointers are arranged sequentially in memory, although the *int* values are not.

```
int *int_values[10];
```

■ **FACT:** *An array of pointers is an array of memory addresses that reference values of a specific type.*

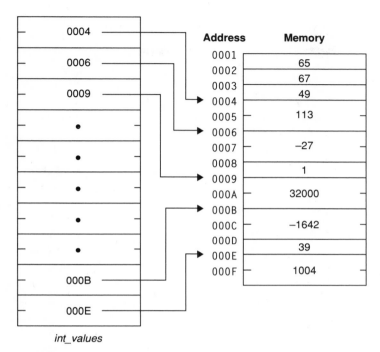

int_values

FIGURE 12-5.
An array of pointers initialized to int *values at nonconsecutive memory locations.*

■ **TIP:** *An array of pointers is commonly used to reference a series of character strings.*

The following declaration creates an array of pointers to seven character strings:

```
char *lines[7];
```

In this case, *lines[0]* contains the starting address of the first string, and *lines[6]* contains the starting address of the last string.

In the following program (PTRARRAY.C), an array of pointers is initialized to a series of character strings:

```
main()
{
    static char *steps[4] =
        {
        "Editing",
        "Compiling",
```

(continued)

continued

```
        "Linking",
        "Executing"
        };
    int i;

    printf("The program development steps are:\n");

    for (i = 0; i < 4; ++i)
        printf("%d %s\n", i + 1, steps[i]);
}
```

When you run the program, your screen shows

```
The program development steps are:
1 Editing
2 Compiling
3 Linking
4 Executing
```

In this case each element of the array contains the address of the first character in a string, as shown in Figure 12-6.

The following program (MONTHS.C) uses an array of pointers to character strings that contain the months of the year. It prompts the user to enter a date in the form *mm-dd-yy* and then displays the date using the corresponding month name.

```
main()
{
    int month, day, year;

    static char *calendar[12] =
        {
        "January", "February", "March", "April",
        "May", "June", "July", "August",
        "September", "October", "November", "December"
        };

    printf("Enter a date in the form mm-dd-yy\n");
    scanf("%d-%d-%d", &month, &day, &year);

    if (month < 1 || month > 12)  /* Is month value out of range? */
        printf("Invalid month entered\n");
    else
        printf("%s %d, %d\n", calendar[month-1], day, year);
}
```

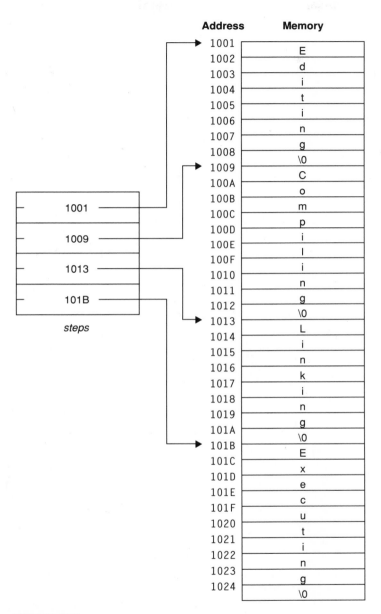

FIGURE 12-6.
Each element in the array contains the address of the first character of a string.

When you run the program, enter a date in the requested format. In the following sample output, the input is shown in italics:

```
Enter a date in the form mm-dd-yy
10-15-89
October 15, 89
```

Because the array *calendar* contains the address of the first character in each month, the program uses the *printf* %s format specifier to display the name of the month. Notice that the program actually displays the string pointed to by *calendar [month-1]*. Remember, C uses the elements 0 to 11. The program subtracts 1 from the input value for the month so that *printf* will index the correct string.

FUNCTIONS THAT RETURN POINTERS

As you know, functions can return values of type *int*, *float*, *char*, and *double*; functions can also return pointers. In fact several functions in the C run-time library return pointers. In this section you will learn to write your own functions that do so.

The following program (GETMONTH.C) uses the function *get_month*, which returns a pointer to the string containing a month's name:

```c
main()
{
    int day, month, year;
    char *get_month(int);

    puts("Enter a date in the form mm-dd-yy");
    scanf("%d-%d-%d", &month, &day, &year);

    if (month < 1 || month > 12)
        printf("Invalid month");
    else
        printf("%s %d, %d", get_month(month), day, year);
}

char *get_month(int month)
{
    static char *calendar[12] =
        {
        "January", "February", "March", "April",
        "May", "June", "July", "August",
        "September", "October", "November", "December"
        };

    return ((month > 0 && month < 13) ? calendar[month-1] : '\0');
}
```

Note that the program declares the function *get_month* as follows:

```
char *get_month(int);
```

Remember, if a function returns a type other than *int*, you must explicitly declare the function's return type. The return type of *get_month* is *char**, a pointer to a string. Also take a look at the use of the conditional operator in the function's return statement. If the month is valid, the function returns a pointer to the corresponding name. If the month is invalid, the function returns the null character.

USING POINTERS TO FUNCTIONS

As we have discussed, a goal in writing functions is that they can be used in a range of unrelated programs. In some cases, passing pointers to functions makes this possible. Your functions can satisfy more applications.

■ **FACT:** *In C you can pass the address of a function as an argument. The program can then call the function by referencing the pointer's value.*

The following program (GETMAX.C) uses a function called *get_max*, which returns the largest value in an integer array:

```
main()
{
    static int values[5] = { 20, 40, 10, 80, 30 };

    printf("The largest value is %d", get_max(values, 5));
}

get_max(int *value, int size)
{
    int i = 1;
    int max;

    max = *value++;

    while (i++ < size)
        {
        if (max < *value)
            max = *value;
        value++;
        }

    return (max);
}
```

In a similar manner, a program (GETMIN.C) might create a function that returns the minimum value:

```
main()
{
    static int values[5] = { 20, 40, 10, 80, 30 };

    printf("The smallest value is %d", get_min(values, 5));
}
get_min(int *value, int size)
{
    int i = 1;
    int min;

    min = *value++;

    while (i++ < size)
        {
        if (min > *value)
            min = *value;
        value++;
        }

    return (min);
}
```

As you can see, the processing in *get_max* and *get_min* is almost identical. In fact, the only difference is the line that performs the comparison:

```
        get_max comparison          get_min comparison
             |                           |
   ┌─────────┴─────────┐       ┌─────────┴─────────┐
   if (max < *value)           if (min > *value)
```

To avoid the repetition of code in *get_max* and *get_min*, let's define two simple functions, *min_compare* and *max_compare*:

```
min_compare(int a, int b)
{
    return ((a > b) ? 1 : 0);
}

max_compare(int a, int b)
{
    return (( a < b) ? 1 : 0);
}
```

We can now create a versatile function called *get_min_max* that returns either the minimum or the maximum value in an array, based on the function pointer it receives as an argument. The following program (MIN_MAX.C) uses such a function to calculate the maximum and minimum values of an array:

```
main()
{
    int max_compare(int, int), min_compare(int, int);
    static int values[5] = { 10, 20, 15, 80, 25 };

    printf("Max value %d\n", get_min_max(values, 5, max_compare));
    printf("Min value %d", get_min_max(values, 5, min_compare));
}

get_min_max(int *value, int size, int (*comp)(int, int))
{
    int i = 1;
    int result;

    result = *value++;
    while (i++ < size)
        {
        if ((*comp)(result, *value))
            result = *value;
        ++value;
        }

    return (result);
}
min_compare(int a, int b)
{
    return ((a > b) ? 1 : 0);
}

max_compare(int a, int b)
{
    return (( a < b) ? 1 : 0);
}
```

When you run the program, your screen shows

```
Max value 80
Min value 10
```

In this case the argument *comp* contains the address of the function passed by *main* to *get_min_max*. The statement

```
if ((*comp) (result, *value))
```

directs the routine to call the function referenced by the pointer *comp*, passing the variables *result* and *value*. The first time the program calls *get_min_max*, it passes the address of the function *max_compare*. The second invocation passes *min_compare*. By using a pointer to a function, *get_min_max* can call the appropriate function.

Admittedly, this program could have been written so that it didn't need to use pointers to functions. However, the program shows their use. C provides several built-in searching and sorting routines that rely on pointers to functions.

C TYPE CONVERSION

Several functions that we discuss in this chapter expect pointers to types other than the types we will be using. In those instances, C provides the cast operator, which changes the type of a value.

■ **FACT:** *The cast operator converts an expression to the type specified within parentheses. For example, the statement* a = (int) (a + b); *uses a cast to convert the sum of* a *and* b *to an* int *value.*

To better understand how the cast operator works, let's look at a few examples. In Chapter 2 you learned that if you attempt to display a floating point value using the *printf* %d format specifier, you get incorrect results. The %d format specifier does not truncate a floating point value. The following program (CAST.C), however, uses the cast operator to convert a value from type *float* to type *int*:

```
main()
{
    printf("Errant result %d\n", 5.5);
    printf("Cast value %d", (int) 5.5);
}
```

When you run the program, your screen shows

```
Errant result 0
Cast value 5
```

■ **TRAP:** *When you cast a value from type* float *to type* int, *the compiler truncates the integer value. A cast operation does not round.*

As the preceding program shows, the *(int)* cast truncates the floating point expression that follows it.

■ **TIP:** *To round an expression of type* float *to one of type* int, *either add the value 0.5 to the expression or use the run-time library function* ceil *before you cast.*

The following program (CAST2.C) illustrates two methods of rounding a floating point value:

```
#include <math.h>   /* needed for ceil */

main()
{
    printf("Cast without rounding %d\n", (int) 5.5);
    printf("Cast after rounding %d\n", (int) (5.5 + 0.5));
    printf("Cast result of ceil %d", (int) ceil(5.5));
}
```

When you run the program, your screen shows

```
Cast without rounding 5
Cast after rounding 6
Cast result of ceil 6
```

A common use of the cast operator is to convert a pointer value that references one type to a pointer value that references another type. Later in this chapter we use the cast operator to display 32-bit far pointer values using the *printf* %p format specifier.

■ **TIP:** *To determine whether you need to use a cast, compare the argument types you are passing to the function definitions that appear in the C run-time library documentation or in the include files.*

The C compiler displays the following message to indicate a conflict between expected and received data types:

```
FILENAME.C(5) : warning C4047: '=' : different levels of indirection
```

When this occurs, first be sure you are passing values to the functions in the correct order. Second, if your type declarations are correct, use a cast to resolve the conflict.

USING BUILT-IN SEARCHING AND SORTING FUNCTIONS

In Chapter 11 you learned how to manipulate arrays. As you work with arrays, your programs will often require the array values to be in order from lowest to highest (ascending order) or from highest to lowest (descending).

■ **FACT:** *The* qsort *function sorts the values in an array by using a quick sort algorithm. The* qsort *function requires a pointer to a comparison function.*

The C library function *qsort* uses a quick sort, one of the fastest sorting techniques. Like most other run-time functions, *qsort* is a highly efficient routine that can save you considerable effort and development time.

■ **TRAP:** *Many programmers write their own sorting routines. The C* qsort *function lets you sort values of any array type in any order. In most cases,* qsort *is more efficient than a routine you might write.*

The following program (SORT.C) uses the *qsort* function to sort and display the values of an integer and a floating point array. As you will see, the program defines the functions *int_comp* and *float_comp.* The values that these functions return have the following important similarities:

- If *a is less than *b, the return value is an integer less than 0.

- If *a equals *b, the return value is 0.

- If *a is greater than *b, the return value is an integer greater than 0.

The *qsort* function passes pointers to two values to the user-defined comparison functions. We have therefore defined our comparison functions, *int_comp* and *float_comp*, so that they use pointer variables.

```c
#include <search.h>  /* needed for qsort */

main()
{
    int i;
    static int int_values[5] = { 3, 2, 1, 5, 4 };
    static float float_values[3] = { 33.3, 44.4, 22.2 };
    int int_comp(int *, int *), float_comp(float *, float *);

    qsort(int_values, 5, sizeof(int), int_comp);
    qsort(float_values, 3, sizeof(float), float_comp);

    printf("Sorted Results\n");

    for (i = 0; i < 5; ++i)
        printf("%d\n", int_values[i]);

    printf("\n");
    for (i = 0; i < 3; ++i)
        printf("%4.1f\n", float_values[i]);
}
```

(continued)

continued

```
int_comp(int *a, int *b)
{
    return (*a - *b);
}

float_comp(float *a, float *b)
{
    int result;

    if (*a == *b)
        result = 0;
    else if (*a > *b)
        result = 1;
    else
        result = -1;

    return (result);
}
```

When you run the program, your screen shows

```
Sorted Results
1
2
3
4
5

22.2
33.3
44.4
```

To change the order of the sort, simply change the *qsort* comparison functions to yield the following results:

- If *a is less than *b, the return value is greater than 0.
- If *a equals *b, the return value is 0.
- If *a is greater than *b, the return value is less than 0.

Also available from the run-time library are searching routines, which help your programs locate the index value of a specific element in an array. A searching routine finds a given value in an array and returns either the index of the value or a pointer to it.

■ **FACT:** *The C run-time library provides three searching routines —* lsearch, lfind, *and* bsearch. *Each supports arrays of any type.*

■ **FACT:** *The C run-time library function* lfind *examines an array for a specific value. If* lfind *locates the value, it returns a pointer to it; if it fails to locate the value,* lfind *returns a NULL pointer.*

The following program (LFIND.C) uses *lfind* to search an array of integer values for the value 50. The *lfind* function searches the contents of an array in a linear manner, beginning with element 0 and proceeding toward the last element. If *lfind* locates the value, it returns a pointer to the value in memory. If the value is not in the array, *lfind* returns the NULL pointer, a predefined constant that points to the value 0. Notice that the call to *lfind* uses the cast operator to pass a pointer of the types that the function expects.

```
#include <search.h>   /* needed for lfind */

main()
{
    static int array[5] = { 10, 20, 50, 35, 40 };

    int *ptr, value = 50, size = 5;
    int int_comp(int *, int *);
    int i;

    ptr = (int *) lfind((char *) &value, (char *) array,
           &size, sizeof(int), int_comp);

    if (ptr)
        printf("Value found at offset %04X is %d\n", ptr, *ptr);
    else
        printf("Value not found\n");
}

int_comp (int *a, int *b)
{
    return (*a - *b);
}
```

The function *lfind* relies on a user-defined function that returns the value 0 if the two values compared are equal; it returns a nonzero value if they differ. As before, the program must cast several arguments to *lfind*. When you run the program, your screen shows

```
Value found at offset 0070 is 50
```

■ **FACT:** *Like* lfind, *the* lsearch *function returns a pointer to a value in an array. Unlike* lfind, *however, if* lsearch *fails to locate the specified value in the array, it appends the value to the end of the array.*

The following program (LSEARCH.C) shows the use of the *lsearch* function, which also performs a linear search of an array. If the array does not hold the value you specify, *lsearch* appends it.

```c
#include <search.h>  /* needed for lsearch */

main()
{
    int int_comp(int *, int *);
    static int array[10] = { 10, 50, 40, 30, 20 };
    int *ptr, i, value = 55, size = 5;

    ptr = (int *) lsearch((char *) &value, (char *) array,
            &size, sizeof(int), int_comp);

    printf("Address returned by lsearch = %04X\n", ptr);
    printf("Array contents:\n");

    for (i = 0; i < size; ++i)
        printf("%d\n", array[i]);
}

int_comp(int *a, int *b)
{
    return ((*a == *b) ? 0 : 1);
}
```

When you run the program, your screen shows

```
Address returned by lsearch = 0074
Array contents:
10
50
40
30
20
55
```

As you can see, *lsearch* did not locate 55, so it placed the value at the end of the array.

■ **TRAP:** *When you use* lsearch, *be sure that the array contains empty elements to append additional values. If* lsearch *stores the value at a memory location outside the region set aside for your array, your program will give errant results.*

The *lfind* and *lsearch* functions don't require that the array contents be in any particular order. The cost of this convenience is that both functions are slower than *bsearch*, the third built-in searching routine.

■ **FACT:** *The C run-time library function* bsearch *returns a pointer to a specific value in an array or the NULL pointer if the value is not in the array. The* bsearch *function uses a binary search and requires the values to be in ascending order (lowest to highest).*

Conceptually, a binary search, such as the one *bsearch* performs, works much like a typical search for a name in the phone book. As often as not, you open the book in the middle. Then if the name you want to find precedes the names on the page, you search the pages to the left; otherwise, you search the pages to the right. You repeat this process until you either find the name or realize that the name is not in the phone book.

Like the other two search functions, the *bsearch* function relies on a function that you must supply. In this case the user-defined function must return one of the following values:

- If *a is less than *b, the return value is less than 0.

- If *a equals *b, the return value is 0.

- If *a is greater than *b, the return value is greater than 0.

■ **TRAP:** *If your program passes to* bsearch *an array that is not sorted into ascending order, the function is likely to enter an infinite loop, and your program will hang.*

The following program (BSEARCH.C) uses *bsearch* to locate the value 80 in an array:

```
#include <search.h>   /* needed for bsearch */

main()
{
    int value = 80, *ptr, size = 10;
    static int array[10] = { 10, 20, 30, 40, 50, 60, 70, 80, 90, 100 };
    int int_comp(int *, int *);

    ptr = (int *) bsearch(&value, array, size, sizeof(int), int_comp);
    if (ptr)
        printf("Value at offset %04X is %d", ptr, *ptr);
    else
        printf("Value not found");
}

int_comp(int *a, int *b)
{
    return (*a - *b);
}
```

When you run the program, your screen shows

```
Value at offset 0050 is 80
```

Given the array of *int* values shown in Figure 12-7, *bsearch* locates the value 80 by examining different ranges of the array. The array is already in ascending order—as the index value increases, the value of the element increases. The binary search is fast but requires that your array elements be in ascending order. Use a linear search function with unsorted arrays.

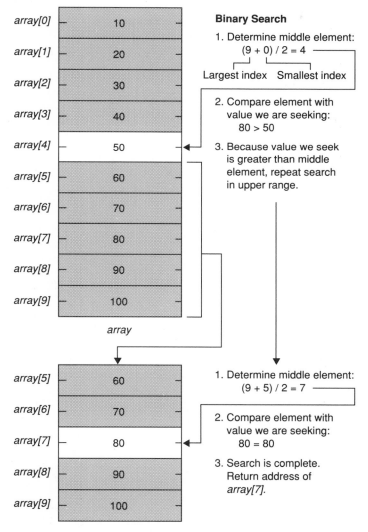

FIGURE 12-7.
The bsearch *function works with an array whose elements are in ascending order. The function isolates a value by confining the search to successively smaller portions of the array.*

SEARCHING AND SORTING AN ARRAY OF CHARACTER STRINGS

So far, we have examined the functions *qsort*, *lfind*, *lsearch*, and *bsearch* only with numeric arrays. Each function fully supports character string arrays as well. As we did for numeric arrays, we need to supply a function that compares the values of array elements.

Let's examine such a function, *str_comp*, which we can use with each of the searching and sorting routines. This function uses *strncmp* and *strlen*, two of the string manipulation routines discussed in Chapter 9.

```
str_comp(char **a, **b)
{
    return (strncmp(*a, *b, strlen(*a)));
}
```

This function compares two strings and returns one of the following values:

- If *a is less than *b, the return value is less than 0.

- If *a equals *b, the return value is 0.

- If *a is greater than *b, the return value is greater than 0.

■ **FACT:** *The declaration* char **a *defines the variable* a *as a pointer to a pointer to a character string*.

Remember, each sorting and searching function passes two pointers to the user-defined comparison function—one to each of the objects to be compared. Because the objects in this array are themselves pointers to character strings, each argument of *str_comp* must be a pointer to a pointer to a string. Figure 12-8 shows the contents of the variables.

The following program (ARAYSORT.C) uses *qsort* to sort an array of character strings. After the sort, the program passes the array to *bsearch* to locate the string *"ccccc"*.

```
#include <search.h>  /* needed for qsort and bsearch */
#include <string.h>  /* needed for strncmp and strlen */

main()
{
    static char *array[5] = { "aaaaa", "eeeee", "ccccc", "bbbbb", "ddddd" };
    int size = 5, str_comp(char **, char **);
    char *value = "ccccc";
    char **ptr;

    qsort(array, size, sizeof(char *), str_comp);
```

(continued)

continued

```
    ptr = (char **) bsearch((char *) &value, (char *) array, size,
            sizeof(char *), str_comp);

    if (ptr)
        printf("Value found at offset %04X is %s", ptr, *ptr);
    else
        printf("Value not found");
}

str_comp(char **a, char **b)
{
    return (strncmp(*a, *b, strlen(*a)));
}
```

The *lfind* and *lsearch* functions work in this same manner. The important thing to note is the use of a pointer to a pointer to declare the strings in the user-defined function.

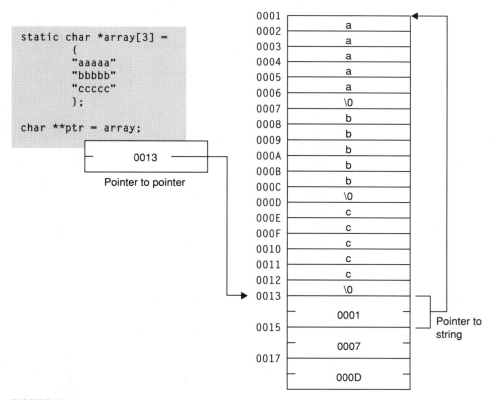

FIGURE 12-8.
A pointer to an element in an array of strings is a pointer to a pointer.

NEAR vs FAR POINTERS

Each time you create a C program under DOS or OS/2, the C compiler assigns your program code to a region called the code segment and assigns your data to a region called the data segment. By default, both regions are 64 kilobytes in size. Later in this book you learn how to use the C memory models in your programs to exceed these values.

■ **FACT:** *Using 16-bit pointers, you can access any location in a 64 KB region called the data segment.*

So far, all the pointers we have examined were 16-bit pointers, or *near pointers*. A 16-bit address can represent as many as 65,536 distinct values—the full range of values in a 64 KB memory region. Because all the programs we have examined so far used a 64 KB data segment, 16-bit (near) pointers were sufficient.

■ **FACT:** *C supports 32-bit (far) pointers that let you access values outside the 64 KB data segment.*

To specify a memory location that lies outside your program's data segment, you can use a 32-bit pointer, called a *far pointer*. Let's examine the memory layout of the IBM PC and compatibles to get an understanding of the way far pointers work.

■ **FACT:** *The IBM PC addresses each memory location using a 16-bit segment and a 16-bit offset address.*

A segment address specifies the starting location of a 64 KB memory region. Within each memory region, the PC can use the offset value to address each of the 65,536 storage locations. An individual storage location is thus a combination of the 16-bit segment and offset addresses, as shown in Figure 12-9.

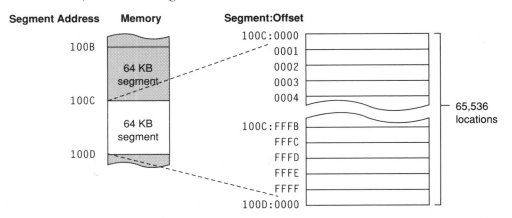

FIGURE 12-9.
In PC memory, each unique address identifies a 64 KB segment and an offset from the beginning of the segment.

To view the use of segment and offset addresses, let's modify the function *str_display* presented earlier in this chapter so that it uses far pointers. Name the new program SHOWSTR3.C.

```
main()
{
    char far *str = "Message to display";   /* declare far pointer */
                                             /* to character string */

    str_display(str);
}

str_display(char far string [])              /* display far pointer */
{                                            /* address and string */
    int i;

    for (i=0; string [i] != '\0'; ++i)
        printf("%p %c\n", &string[i], string[i]);
}
```

When you run this program, your screen shows

```
6CB2:0282 M
6CB2:0283 e
6CB2:0284 s
6CB2:0285 s
6CB2:0286 a
6CB2:0287 g
6CB2:0288 e
6CB2:0289
6CB2:028A t
6CB2:028B o
6CB2:028C
6CB2:028D d
6CB2:028E i
6CB2:028F s
6CB2:0290 p
6CB2:0291 l
6CB2:0292 a
6CB2:0293 y
```

Note the segment and offset combinations, such as the following:

```
6CB2:0282 M
```

As you will recall from Chapter 3, the %p format specifier directs *printf* to display a far pointer address. The *printf* routine always displays far pointers in this segment:offset address.

The preceding program uses a far pointer to a character string to simplify the use of the %p format specifier. As discussed earlier in this chapter, we can also use the cast operator to convert a pointer from one type to another. The following program (SHOWSTR4.C) uses the cast operator to display the segment (far address) and offset of each character of a string:

```
main()
{
    char *str = "Message to display";
    int i;

    for (i = 0; str[i] != '\0'; ++i)
        printf("%p %04X %c\n", (char far *) &str[i], &str[i], str[i]);
}
```

When you run this program, your screen shows

```
3B19:0282 0282 M
3B19:0283 0283 e
3B19:0284 0284 s
3B19:0285 0285 s
3B19:0286 0286 a
3B19:0287 0287 g
3B19:0288 0288 e
3B19:0289 0289
3B19:028A 028A t
3B19:028B 028B o
3B19:028C 028C
3B19:028D 028D d
3B19:028E 028E i
3B19:028F 028F s
3B19:0290 0290 p
3B19:0291 0291 l
3B19:0292 0292 a
3B19:0293 0293 y
```

Note the cast of the array element address:

```
(char far *) &str[i]
```

In this case the compiler converts the 16-bit offset address into a 32-bit far pointer. The program thereby ensures that *printf* displays the correct segment and offset address.

The best way to understand the PC addressing scheme is to look at video memory. Before your computer displays a character on your screen, the character must reside in the PC's video memory. For color graphics systems, it starts at segment B800, as shown in Figure 12-10. (For monochrome display systems, this memory region starts at location B000.)

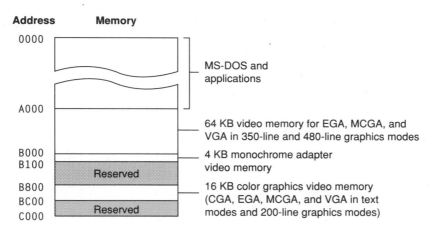

FIGURE 12-10.
Video memory occupies fixed regions of RAM in the IBM PC.

The PC uses two adjacent bytes to store information about each character. The first contains the ASCII value that corresponds to the character. The second value specifies the display attribute (color, bold, blinking, and so on). For a color graphics system, the PC stores the character that corresponds to the upper left corner of your screen display at segment B800, offset 0 (B800:0000). The character's display attribute is at offset 1 (B800:0001).

■ **FACT:** *To create a far pointer, simply precede your pointer name with the keyword* far. *For example, the statement* char far *letter; *creates a far pointer* letter *to a string.*

The following program (FARTEST.C) uses the keyword *far* to declare far pointers to two *char* variables. The program displays the letter C in the upper left corner of your screen. Because it writes values directly to the video memory region for color/graphics display, the program works only if your display adapter is currently running in CGA mode.

```
main()
{
    char far *letter = 0xB8000000;    /* offset 0 */
    char far *attribute = 0xB8000001; /* offset 1 */

    *letter = 'C';
    *attribute = 7;                   /* normal attribute */
}
```

Because the video memory segment resides outside the data segment, we must use a far pointer to access it. The program on the following page (FARTEST2.C) uses a similar technique to display the message *Chapter 12* in the upper left corner of a CGA display.

```
main()
{
    char far *letter = 0xB8000000;
    char far *attribute = 0xB8000001;
    char *message = "Chapter 12";

    while (*message)
    {
        *letter = *message++;    /* display the letter */
        *attribute = 7;          /* specify the attribute */
        letter += 2;             /* move to the next character location */
        attribute += 2;          /* move to the next attribute location */
    }
}
```

Remember, the PC stores characters and attributes in every other storage location. Therefore, the program increments both pointers by 2 after it assigns each element in the string.

These examples of far pointer manipulation are quite straightforward. In many cases, however, you will need to create a far pointer from a 16-bit segment and offset combination or convert a far pointer into a corresponding segment and offset value. Two C macros let you do just that.

■ **FACT:** *The macros* FP_SEG *and* FP_OFF *return the segment and offset address associated with a far pointer. These two macros reside in the include file dos.h.*

The following program (SHOWFAR.C) calls the function *show_far* to display the segment and offset address of a far pointer. The function uses the macros *FP_SEG* and *FP_OFF* to isolate the segment and offset values. SHOWFAR.C is designed for the DOS environment only and should not be run under OS/2.

```
#include <dos.h>   /* needed for FP_SEG and FP_OFF */

main()
{
    char far *letter = 0xB8000000;
    void show_far(char far *);

    show_far(letter);
}

void show_far(char far *ptr)
{
    printf("Segment %04X Offset %04X\n", FP_SEG(ptr), FP_OFF(ptr));
}
```

At times you will need to break a far pointer into its segment and offset addresses, and at times you will need to build a far pointer.

■ **TIP:** *Many C compilers provide the macro MK_FP, which builds a far pointer from a segment and offset addresses. If your compiler does not provide this macro, simply define MK_FP as follows:*

```
#define MK_FP(seg, ofs) ((void far *) (((long) (seg) << 16) ¦ (ofs)))
```

The following program (BUILDFAR.C) uses the *MK_FP* macro to display the letter C in the upper left corner of your screen.

```
#define MK_FP(seg, ofs) ((void far *) (((long) (seg) << 16) ¦ (ofs)))

main()
{
    unsigned int seg = 0xB800;
    unsigned int ofs = 0;
    char far *letter;
    char far *attribute;

    letter = MK_FP(seg, ofs);
    attribute = MK_FP(seg, ofs + 1);

    *letter = 'C';
    *attribute = 7;
}
```

This has been a quick look at far pointers. We will examine other uses of far pointers when we discuss memory models later in this book. For now, keep in mind that most C pointers are near pointers and are restricted to a 64 KB region. A far pointer uses a 32-bit value that contains a segment and an offset address.

SUMMARY

Using Pointers to Access a Character String

■ **FACT:** *Any C function that manipulates an array of elements can use pointers instead. Pointers often simplify the code and reduce the processing time.*

■ **TIP:** *A pointer to a string does not specify the number of characters in the string. Therefore, the string must end with the null character so that string-handling routines can identify the last character in the string.*

■ **TIP:** *Whenever possible, use pointers instead of arrays. In most cases, your program will execute faster.*

■ **FACT:** *The CL /Fa option directs the C compiler to generate an assembly language listing of a C program. CL creates a file with the extension ASM that contains the assembly language listing. (The Microsoft QuickC Compiler does not support the /Fa switch.)*

Understanding Pointer Arithmetic

■ **FACT:** *When a program increments a pointer variable, it examines the pointer's type and increments the pointer by the number of bytes required to store a variable of that type.*

■ **FACT:** *Adding or subtracting a value n from a pointer directs the compiler to access the nth value that corresponds to the type.*

Using an Array of Pointers

■ **FACT:** *An array of pointers is an array of addresses that reference values of a specific type.*

■ **TIP:** *An array of pointers is commonly used to reference a series of character strings.*

Using Pointers to Functions

■ **FACT:** *In C you can pass the address of a function as an argument. The program can then call the function by referencing the pointer's value.*

C Type Conversion

■ **FACT:** *The cast operator converts an expression to the type specified within paren-theses. For example, the statement* a = (int) (a + b); *uses a cast to convert the sum of* a *and* b *to an* int *value.*

■ **TRAP:** *When you cast a value from type* int *to type* float, *the compiler truncates the integer value. A cast operation does not round.*

■ **TIP:** *To round an expression of type* float *to one of type* int, *either add the value 0.5 to the expression or use the run-time library function* ceil *before you cast.*

■ **TIP:** *To determine whether you need to use a cast, compare the argument types you are passing to the function definitions that appear in the C run-time library documen-tation or in the include files.*

Using Built-in Searching and Sorting Functions

■ **FACT:** *The* qsort *function sorts the values in an array by using a quick sort algorithm. The* qsort *function requires a pointer to a comparison function.*

■ **TRAP:** *Many programmers write their own sorting routines. The C* qsort *routine lets you sort values of any array type in any order. In most cases,* qsort *is more efficient than a routine you might write.*

■ **FACT:** *The C run-time library provides three searching routines —* lsearch, lfind, *and* bsearch. *Each supports arrays of any type.*

■ **FACT:** *The C run-time library function* lfind *examines an array for a specific value. If* lfind *locates the value, it returns a pointer to it; if it fails to locate the value,* lfind *returns a NULL pointer.*

■ **FACT:** *Like* lfind, *the* lsearch *function returns the pointer to a value in an array. Unlike* lfind, *however, if* lsearch *fails to locate the specified value in the array, it ap-pends the value to the end of the array.*

■ **TRAP:** *When you use* lsearch, *be sure that the array contains enough empty ele-ments to append additional values. If* lsearch *stores the value at a memory location outside the region set aside for your array, your program will give errant results.*

■ **FACT:** *The C run-time library function* bsearch *returns a pointer to a specific value in an array or the NULL pointer if the value is not in the array. The* bsearch *function uses a binary search and requires the values to be in ascending order (lowest to highest).*

■ **TRAP:** *If your program passes to* bsearch *an array that is not sorted into ascending order, the function is likely to enter an infinite loop, and your program will hang.*

Searching and Sorting an Array of Character Strings

■ **FACT:** *The declaration* char **a *defines the variable* a *as a pointer to a pointer to a character string.*

Near vs Far Pointers

■ **FACT:** *Using 16-bit pointers, you can access any location in a 64 KB region called the data segment.*

■ **FACT:** *C supports 32-bit (far) pointers that let you access values outside the 64 KB data segment.*

■ **FACT:** *The IBM PC addresses each memory location using a 16-bit segment and a 16-bit offset address.*

■ **FACT:** *To create a far pointer, simply precede your pointer name with the keyword* far. *For example, the statement* char far *letter; *creates a far pointer* letter *to a string.*

■ **FACT:** *The macros* FP_SEG *and* FP_OFF *return the segment and offset address associated with a far pointer. These two macros reside in the include file dos.h.*

■ **TIP:** *Many C compilers provide the macro* MK_FP, *which builds a far pointer from a segment and offset addresses. If your compiler does not provide the macro, simply define* MK_FP *as follows:*

```
#define MK_FP(seg, ofs) ((void far *) (((long) (seg) << 16) : (ofs)))
```

GLOSSARY

cast operator Directs the compiler to convert an expression of one type to the type contained in parentheses before the expression. For example: *a = (float) b;*

far pointer A 32-bit pointer that contains a 16-bit segment and a 16-bit offset value. Far pointers let your programs access memory locations outside the 64 KB data segment.

near pointer A 16-bit pointer that can reference values contained in the 64 KB data segment. Unless a pointer declaration contains the keyword *far*, the variable is a near pointer.

CHAPTER 13

Getting Started with File Manipulation

As your programs become more complex, they will need to access information that resides on disk. In this chapter we discuss functions that manipulate files. Many of these functions are similar to functions you have encountered already. For example, the run-time library provides the functions *fputs* and *fgets*, which write or read a character string to a file. We also discuss *fprintf* and *fscanf*, which perform formatted file input and output operations.

As you will see, to use the information that resides in a file, you must first open the file. After you do so, you can use the C run-time library functions that read information from or write information to the file. After your file manipulation is complete, you must close the file. Once you know the secrets, file manipulation in C is quite straightforward.

UNDERSTANDING FILE POINTERS

To access a file, your program must use a file pointer, which is conceptually similar to a placemarker. As you read from or write to a file, the file pointer keeps track of your current position in the file. You must use a unique file pointer for each file you open.

■ **FACT:** *To declare a file pointer, you must include stdio.h and create a pointer variable of the type* FILE. *For example, the statement* FILE *fp; *declares the file pointer* fp.

The file stdio.h defines a special data type to hold the information in a file pointer. Use this data type, called *FILE*, when you declare a pointer to a file. To assign a value to a file pointer, you must first open or create the file.

■ **FACT:** *The* fopen *function opens or creates a file and returns a file pointer to the file. If* fopen *cannot open or create the file as specified,* fopen *returns the NULL pointer.*

The general format of a call to *fopen* is as follows:

```
file_pointer = fopen("filename", "mode");
```

where *file_pointer* is a variable of type *FILE* to which the statement assigns a pointer to the open file. The *filename* argument specifies the name of the file to open and can contain a disk drive specifier as well as a pathname. The second argument, *mode*, specifies the way in which the program needs to access the file.

■ **FACT:** *You can open a file for read, write, or append operations. The* fopen *mode argument determines the way in which the program opens a file.*

Microsoft C supports the following mode options:

Mode	*Type of Access*
r	Read-only operations. If the file does not exist, *fopen* returns NULL.
w	Write operations. If the file exists, it is overwritten. If it does not exist, *fopen* creates it.
a	Open for appending. If the file exists, it is opened for appending. If it does not exist, *fopen* creates it.
r+	Read or write operations. The file must already exist.
w+	Read or write operations. If the file exists, it is overwritten. If it does not exist, *fopen* creates it.
a+	Open for appending. The file can also be read. If the file does not exist, *fopen* creates it.

The following program (OPENFILE.C) creates a sample file called DEMO.DAT:

```
#include <stdio.h>  /* needed for file operations */

main()
{
    FILE *fp;        /* declare file pointer using type FILE */

    if ((fp = fopen("DEMO.DAT", "w")) == NULL)
        printf("Error creating DEMO.DAT");
```

(continued)

continued

```
    else
        {
        printf("File successfully created");
        fclose(fp);
        }
    }
```

Notice the test for a successful file opening:

```
if ((fp = fopen("DEMO.DAT", "w")) == NULL)
```

As you can see, the call to *fopen* specifies the filename and the write access mode. Because of the parentheses, the *if* statement first assigns the file pointer returned by *fopen* to the variable *fp*, and then it compares the value of *fp* with NULL. If *fopen* cannot open a file as specified, *fopen* returns NULL.

Next, note the last statement in the program:

```
fclose(fp);
```

Your programs must not only open files but they should close files when they are no longer needed.

■ **FACT:** *The* fclose *function closes the file associated with the specified file pointer. When you close a file, the operating system updates the directory entry for that file.*

When your program terminates, the operating system closes all open files. However, good programming practice is to close a file using *fclose* as soon as your program no longer requires it.

■ **TIP:** *Assign meaningful names to the files that you create with* fopen. *By examining the file's name and extension, you should be able to determine its contents.*

Once a program successfully opens or creates a file, the program can read data from or write data to the file as specified by the access mode.

■ **FACT:** *The* putc *macro writes a character to the file associated with the specified file pointer. For example, the statement* putc('a', fp); *writes the character* a *to the file associated with pointer* fp.

The program on the following page (MAKEFILE.C) writes information to a file. It first creates the file ALPHABET.DAT and then writes the letters of the alphabet to it five times. The program uses the macro *putc* to write each character.

```
#include <stdio.h>  /* needed for file operations */

main()
{
    FILE *fp;
    int i;
    char letter;

    if ((fp = fopen("ALPHABET.DAT", "w")) == NULL)
        printf("Error creating ALPHABET.DAT");
    else
        {
        for (i = 1; i <= 5; ++i)
            {
            for (letter = 'A'; letter <= 'Z'; ++letter)
                putc(letter, fp);

            putc('\n', fp);  /* write newline character */
            }

        fclose(fp);
        }
}
```

When you run the program, the file ALPHABET.DAT is created. You can use the DOS TYPE command to display the contents of ALPHABET.DAT:

```
C> TYPE ALPHABET.DAT
ABCDEFGHIJKLMNOPQRSTUVWXYZ
ABCDEFGHIJKLMNOPQRSTUVWXYZ
ABCDEFGHIJKLMNOPQRSTUVWXYZ
ABCDEFGHIJKLMNOPQRSTUVWXYZ
ABCDEFGHIJKLMNOPQRSTUVWXYZ

C>
```

Now that ALPHABET.DAT exists on disk, let's write a program that displays its contents on your screen.

■ **FACT:** *The getc macro returns the next character in the file associated with the specified file pointer. If no characters remain in the file,* getc *returns the constant EOF. For example, the statement* letter = getc(fp); *assigns to* letter *the next character in the file associated with file pointer* fp.

The following program (SHOWFILE.C) opens the file ALPHABET.DAT that you just created and uses the *getc* macro to read the contents of the file. It calls *putchar* to display each character in the file.

```
#include <stdio.h>    /* needed for file operations */

main()
{
    FILE *fp;
    char letter;

    if ((fp = fopen("ALPHABET.DAT", "r")) == NULL)
        puts("Unable to open file ALPHABET.DAT");
    else
        {
        while ((letter = getc(fp)) != EOF)
            putchar(letter);

        fclose(fp);
        }
}
```

Notice that the *for* loops that use *putc* in MAKEFILE.C and the *while* loop that uses *getc* in SHOWFILE.C do not increment the file pointer *fp*. Execution of the *putc* and *getc* macros includes an increase in the file pointer so that it points to the next character.

■ **FACT:** *The functions* fgetc *and* fputc *perform character input from and output to a file.*

Both the *putc* and *getc* macros are also implemented as functions—*fputc* and *fgetc*—in the run-time library. Most programmers use the macros because of the improved program performance. Remember, macros execute faster than functions but increase the size of an executable program.

Just as the C run-time library provides functions (*gets* and *puts*) that read and write character strings, it also provides the functions *fgets* and *fputs*, which read and write characters from and to files.

■ **FACT:** *The* fgets *function reads a character string from the file associated with the specified file pointer. If* fgets *encounters an error or reaches the end of file, it returns the NULL pointer.*

The *fgets* function takes three arguments. The first argument is the name of a string into which *fgets* places the characters of the file. The second argument specifies the maximum number of characters the string can store. The third argument is the file pointer associated with the file from which *fgets* is to read.

The program on the following page (READFILE.C) uses *fgets* to read the contents of the file ALPHABET.DAT and then uses *puts* to display the contents of the file on the screen.

```
#include <stdio.h>      /* needed for file operations */

main()
{
    FILE *fp;
    char string[128];   /* buffer to hold string read by fgets */

    if ((fp = fopen("ALPHABET.DAT", "r")) == NULL)
        puts("Error opening ALPHABET.DAT");
    else
        {
        while (fgets(string, sizeof(string), fp))
            puts(string);

        fclose(fp);
        }
}
```

When you execute the program, your screen shows

```
ABCDEFGHIJKLMNOPQRSTUVWXYZ
ABCDEFGHIJKLMNOPQRSTUVWXYZ
ABCDEFGHIJKLMNOPQRSTUVWXYZ
ABCDEFGHIJKLMNOPQRSTUVWXYZ
ABCDEFGHIJKLMNOPQRSTUVWXYZ
```

Remember, the *puts* function displays a newline character at the end of each line it writes to the screen. Because the file ALPHABET.DAT already contains a newline character at the end of each line, two line spaces follow each line of output. If you don't want the extra newline character, replace *puts(string);* with *printf("%s", string);*.

■ **FACT:** *The* fputs *function writes a null-terminated character string to the file associated with the specified file pointer. If successful,* fputs *returns the value zero. If unsuccessful,* fputs *returns a nonzero error code. For example, the statement* fputs(string, fp); *writes the string referenced by* string *to the file associated with pointer* fp.

The following program (LOWER.C) demonstrates the use of *fputs* to write a string to a specified file. The program opens the file ALPHABET.DAT and reads its contents. It then uses the *strlwr* and *fputs* functions to convert each string to lowercase and write each converted string to the file ALPHABET.LWR. The program uses two file pointers—one for input and one for output.

```
#include <stdio.h>   /* needed for file operations */
#include <string.h>  /* needed for strlwr */

main()
{
    FILE *input, *output;
    char string[128];

    if (!(input = fopen("ALPHABET.DAT", "r")))
        puts("Error opening ALPHABET.DAT");
    else if (!(output = fopen("ALPHABET.LWR", "w")))
        puts("Error opening ALPHABET.LWR");
    else
        {
        while (fgets(string, sizeof(string), input))
            fputs(strlwr(string), output);

        fclose(input);
        fclose(output);
        }
}
```

The LOWER.C program is quite similar to the previous programs. Note, however, the condition

```
if (!(input = fopen("ALPHABET.DAT", "r")))
```

Remember, if *fopen* cannot open the file as specified, the function returns NULL. The NOT operator (!) makes the condition read "if *fopen* was not successful." As discussed, the NOT operator makes a nonzero value logically equivalent to 0 (or false), and it makes a zero value logically equivalent to a nonzero value (or true).

Also notice the statement

```
fputs(strlwr(string), output);
```

If you examine the file string.h, you will find that the *strlwr* function converts the characters in a string to lowercase and then returns a pointer to the first character in the string. The program can use the return value from *strlwr* in the function call to *fputs* because the *fputs* function expects as its first argument the address of the string to display.

■ **TRAP:** *If the macro getc encounters an end of file or an error, it returns the value EOF. If fgets encounters an end of file or an error, it returns the NULL pointer. In either case, you have no way of knowing whether the return value resulted from reaching the end of file or from an error.*

So far, all the programs we have written have assumed that a NULL pointer from *fgets* or the EOF value from *fgetc* indicates an end of file. If an error occurs, the functions also return NULL; the programs assume that an end of file occurred, and they end.

■ **FACT:** *The macro* ferror *returns a nonzero (true) value when an error occurs in an attempted file read or write operation. If no error occurs,* ferror *returns the value zero.*

■ **FACT:** *The macro* feof *returns a nonzero (true) value when the file associated with the specified file pointer has encountered an end of file. If the pointer has not reached the end of file,* feof *returns the value zero.*

The following program (LOWER2.C) contains several changes to the previous program. It uses the *ferror* function to test for an error, and it uses *feof* to test for an end of file condition. Both functions return a nonzero value when they encounter the condition they are designed to detect. The program displays an error message each time a read or write error occurs.

```c
#include <stdio.h>   /* needed for file operations */
#include <string.h>  /* needed for strlwr */

main()
{
    FILE *input, *output;
    char string[128];

    if (!(input = fopen("ALPHABET.DAT", "r")))
        puts("Error opening ALPHABET.DAT");
    else if (!(output = fopen("ALPHABET.LWR", "w")))
        puts("Error opening ALPHABET.LWR");
    else
        {
        while (!feof(input))
            {
            fgets(string, sizeof(string), input);
            if (!feof(input))
                {
                fputs(strlwr(string), output);
                if (ferror(input))
                    {
                    puts("Error reading file\a");
                    clearerr(input);
                    }
                if (ferror(output))
                    {
                    puts("Error writing file\a");
                    clearerr(output);
                    }
                }
            }

        fclose(input);
        fclose(output);
        }
}
```

■ **TIP:** *Most programs should end whenever an error or an end of file occurs.*

In most programs, simply looping until *fgets* returns NULL or until *fgetc* returns EOF is sufficient. If an error occurs, the program will end. Although you can test more thoroughly, many programs do not need to continue if a file error occurs.

■ **FACT:** *The function* clearerr *resets the error or end of file flag for the file associated with the specified file pointer.*

If a file error does occur, the program displays an error message and then calls the function *clearerr.*

When a C file manipulation function encounters a read or write file error, it sets an error status flag for the file, which allows the macro *ferror* to test whether a file error has occurred. The flag remains set until the program closes the file or uses the function *clearerr* to clear the error.

The following program (LOWER3.C) takes a middle-of-the-road approach. It ends if either an error or an end of file is encountered. Before it terminates, however, the program performs error checking, which notifies the user if a file error occurs.

```c
#include <stdio.h>    /* needed for file operations */
#include <string.h>   /* needed for strlwr */

main()
{
    FILE *input, *output;
    char string[128];

    if (!(input = fopen("ALPHABET.DAT", "r")))
        puts("Error opening ALPHABET.DAT");
    else if (!(output = fopen("ALPHABET.LWR", "w")))
        puts("Error opening ALPHABET.LWR");
    else
        {
        while (fgets(string, sizeof(string), input))
            fputs(strlwr (string), output);

        if (ferror(input))
            puts("\a\aError reading ALPHABET.DAT");
        else if (ferror(output))
            puts("\a\aError writing ALPHABET.LWR");

        fclose(input);
        fclose(output);
        }
}
```

PERFORMING FORMATTED FILE I/O

Just as you can perform formatted I/O to your screen or from your keyboard (in terms of spacing, output precision, and so on), you can perform formatted I/O from or to a file.

■ **FACT:** *The* fprintf *function directs the compiler to write formatted output to the file associated with the specified file pointer. For example, the statement* fprintf(fp, "This is Chapter %d", 13); *tells the C compiler to write the string* This is Chapter 13 *to the file associated with pointer* fp.

The *fprintf* function is almost identical to the *printf* function. The only essential difference is that *fprintf* specifies a file pointer before the control string. All the format specifiers and escape sequences valid for *printf* are valid for *fprintf*.

The following program (FPRINTF.C) uses *fprintf* to create a file called VALUES.DAT, which contains a listing of the octal, decimal, and hexadecimal values in the range 0 through 16.

```
#include <stdio.h>   /* needed for file operations */

main()
{
    FILE *fp;
    int i;

    if (!(fp = fopen("VALUES.DAT", "w")))
        puts("Error opening file VALUES.DAT");
    else
        {
        for (i = 0; i <= 16; ++i)
            fprintf(fp, "%o\t%d\t%x\n", i, i, i);

        fclose(fp);
        }
}
```

■ **FACT:** *The* fscanf *function directs the compiler to perform formatted input from the file associated with the specified file pointer. If successful,* fscanf *returns the number of values assigned to variables. When the pointer reaches the end of file,* fscanf *returns the value EOF.*

The *fscanf* function provides formatted file input from a file. It takes as its first argument a file pointer to the file to be scanned. The remaining arguments are identical to those you use for *scanf* operations.

The following program (FSCANF.C) uses *fscanf* to read the contents of VALUES.DAT, the file created by the previous program. It displays each set of values using *printf*.

```
#include <stdio.h>   /* needed for file operations */

main()
{
    FILE *fp;
    int octal, decimal, hex;

    if (!(fp = fopen("VALUES.DAT", "r")))
        puts("Error opening file VALUES.DAT");
    else
        {
        while (!feof(fp))
            {
            fscanf(fp, "%o\t%d\t%x\n", &octal, &decimal, &hex);
            printf("%o\t%d\t%x\n", octal, decimal, hex);
            }

        fclose(fp);
        }
}
```

SPECIFYING CHARACTER TRANSLATION

All the file operations we have discussed in this chapter have dealt with standard DOS text files. Files of this type contain ASCII characters and use the Ctrl-Z character to indicate the end of file.

By default, when you open a file for reading, its contents are interpreted in *text mode*, which means that the *fgets* function or the macro *getc* reads until it encounters the Ctrl-Z character. Although this technique works well for reading text files, you must use an alternate method to read EXE or COM files. Here's why.

The Ctrl-Z character is represented in decimal as the value 26. An executable file cannot reserve this value to signify the end of file; the value might occur frequently in such a file. In text mode, a program using *fgets* or *getc* to read data will end when it encounters the first Ctrl-Z character, even though the entire file has probably not been read.

To resolve this difficulty in interpreting Ctrl-Z, the *fopen* function has a second access mode, *binary mode*. When you access a file in binary mode, the file manipulation functions do not interpret the value 26 as the end of file; instead, they locate the end of file using the file size specified in the directory entry for the file.

■ **FACT:** *To open a file in binary access mode, simply include the letter* b *within the access mode specifier to* fopen. *In binary mode,* fopen *does not perform character translation, nor does it acknowledge a decimal 26 as an end of file character. For example, the statement* fp = fopen("DISPLAY.EXE", "rb"); *directs the compiler to open DISPLAY.EXE in read-only binary access mode and to assign the file pointer to* fp.

Text and binary files require different handling in another respect. For text files, the C file manipulation functions translate a carriage return–linefeed combination into a single linefeed character for input. For output operations, the file manipulation routines translate a linefeed character into a carriage return–linefeed combination. In binary access mode, the functions do not perform these translations.

Later in this book you will write C programs that implement the DOS COPY command. So that the programs can copy all types of files, you will open them in binary access mode.

The Microsoft C compiler uses the value associated with *_fmode*, as defined in the include file fcntl.h, to determine the default mode. Unless you change this file, the default setting for *_fmode* is text. For most applications you won't need to be concerned with whether your file is in text or binary mode; text, the default, will suffice.

■ **FACT:** *In addition to the binary access mode, Microsoft C lets you open a file explicitly in text mode using the access specifier* t. *Text mode forces the translation of linefeeds to carriage return –linefeeds, as well as the interpretation of the Ctrl-Z character as the end of file. For example, the statement* fp = fopen("FILENAME.EXT", "rt"); *directs the compiler to open FILENAME.EXT in read-only text access mode and to assign the file pointer to* fp.

If you need to open a file explicitly in text mode (because the default was changed to binary mode, for example), you can specify text mode in the call to *fopen* by including the letter *t* in the access mode argument.

■ **TRAP:** *The translated text access specifier* t *is available only in Microsoft C.*

If you are writing programs that need to be compatible with ANSI C, do not use the *t* access specifier. It is available only in Microsoft C.

LOOKING AT ONE LAST FUNCTION: *ungetc*

As you have seen, the *getc* and *fgetc* functions read a character from a file and increment the file pointer. In some cases, a program needs to "push back" a character and pretend that the character was never read.

■ **FACT:** *The* ungetc *function places the last character read back into a file's input buffer. The next* getc *call returns the character that was pushed back.*

The general format of a call to *ungetc* is as follows:

```
ungetc(letter, fp)
```

The function places the character specified by *letter* back into the input buffer at the position indicated by *fp*. The file pointer *fp* is unchanged, which means that *letter* is the next character to be read from the file.

■ **TRAP:** *For most applications, use of the* ungetc *function adds unnecessary complexity. Most applications can be rewritten to remove the need for* ungetc.

Later in this book we will take a detailed look at additional file manipulation operations.

SUMMARY

Understanding File Pointers

■ **FACT:** *To declare a file pointer, you must include stdio.h and create a pointer variable of the type* FILE. *For example, the statement* FILE *fp; *declares the file pointer* fp.

■ **FACT:** *The* fopen *function opens or creates a file and returns a file pointer to the file. If* fopen *cannot open or create the file as specified,* fopen *returns the NULL pointer.*

■ **FACT:** *You can open a file for read, write, or append operations. The* fopen *mode argument determines the way in which the program opens a file.*

■ **FACT:** *The* fclose *function closes the file associated with the specified file pointer. When you close a file, the operating system updates the directory entry for that file.*

■ **TIP:** *Assign meaningful names to the files that you create with* fopen. *By examining the file's name and extension, you should be able to determine its contents.*

■ **FACT:** *The* putc *macro writes a character to the file associated with the specified file pointer. For example, the statement* putc('a', fp); *writes the character* a *to the file associated with pointer* fp.

■ **FACT:** *The* getc *macro returns the next character in the file associated with the specified file pointer. If no characters remain in the file,* getc *returns the constant EOF. For example, the statement* letter = getc(fp); *assigns to* letter *the next character in the file associated with file pointer* fp.

■ **FACT:** *The functions* fgetc *and* fputc *perform character input from and output to a file.*

■ **FACT:** *The* fgets *function reads a character string from the file associated with the specified file pointer. If* fgets *encounters an error or reaches the end of file, it returns the NULL pointer.*

■ **FACT:** *The* fputs *function writes a null-terminated character string to the file associated with the specified file pointer. If successful,* fputs *returns the value zero. If unsuccessful,* fputs *returns a nonzero error code. For example, the statement* fputs(string, fp); *writes the string referenced by* string *to the file associated with pointer* fp.

■ **TRAP:** *If the macro* getc *encounters an end of file or an error, it returns the value* EOF. *If* fgets *encounters an end of file or an error, it returns the NULL pointer. In either case, you have no way of knowing whether the return value resulted from reaching the end of file or from an error.*

■ **FACT:** *The macro* ferror *returns a nonzero (true) value when an error occurs in an attempted file read or write operation. If no error occurs,* ferror *returns the value zero.*

■ **FACT:** *The macro* feof *returns a nonzero (true) value when the file associated with the specified file pointer has encountered an end of file. If the pointer has not reached the end of file,* feof *returns the value zero.*

■ **TIP:** *Most programs should end whenever an error or an end of file occurs.*

■ **FACT:** *The function* clearerr *resets the error or end of file flag for the file associated with the specified file pointer.*

Performing Formatted File I/O

■ **FACT:** *The* fprintf *function directs the compiler to write formatted output to the file associated with the specified file pointer. For example, the statement* fprintf(fp, "This is Chapter %d", 13); *tells the compiler to write the string* This is Chapter 13 *to the file associated with pointer* fp.

■ **FACT:** *The* fscanf *function directs the compiler to perform formatted input from the file associated with the specified file pointer. If successful,* fscanf *returns the number of values assigned to variables. When the pointer reaches the end of file,* fscanf *returns the value EOF.*

Specifying Character Translation

■ **FACT:** *To open a file in binary access mode, simply include the letter* b *within the access mode specifier to* fopen. *In binary mode,* fopen *does not perform character translation, nor does it acknowledge a decimal 26 as an end of file character. For example, the statement* fp = fopen("DISPLAY.EXE", "rb"); *directs the compiler to open DISPLAY.EXE in read-only binary access mode and to assign the file pointer to* fp.

■ **FACT:** *In addition to the binary access mode, Microsoft C lets you open a file explicitly in text mode using the access specifier* t. *Text mode forces the translation of linefeeds to carriage return–linefeeds, as well as the interpretation of the Ctrl-Z character as the end of file. For example, the statement* fp = fopen("FILENAME.EXT", "rt"); *directs the compiler to open FILENAME.EXT in read-only text access mode and to assign the file pointer to* fp.

■ **TRAP:** *The translated text access specifier* t *is available only in Microsoft C.*

Looking at One Last Function: *ungetc*

■ **FACT:** *The* ungetc *function places the last character read back into a file's input buffer. The next* getc *call returns the character that was pushed back.*

■ **TRAP:** *For most applications, use of the* ungetc *function adds unnecessary complexity. Most applications can be rewritten to remove the need for* ungetc.

GLOSSARY

access mode An argument that specifies the way in which a program can access a file. C supports read, write, append, and read/write modes. Your program must specify an access mode when it opens a file using *fopen.*

binary mode A file access mode in which C file manipulation functions do not translate the file contents when they read or write information. In binary mode, the file manipulation functions locate the end of file using the file size specified in the directory entry for the file.

file pointer A variable that points to a memory location containing information specific to an open file. To declare a file pointer, your program must include the file stdio.h and then declare the pointer in the form *FILE *fp;*.

text mode The default file access mode. C file manipulation functions translate carriage return–linefeed characters and interpret Ctrl-Z as an end of file indicator.

## CHAPTER 14

Advanced Preprocessing

In Chapter 6 we examined C constant and macro definitions that used the *#define* directive, and we looked at the inclusion of header files using the *#include* directive. At that time, you learned that the CL command executes a program called the preprocessor before it compiles your code. The preprocessor expands macros and includes specified files. In this chapter we examine C preprocessor directives that let you perform conditional preprocessing. Also, we look again at include files. This time we place C functions into include files (with the extension C) so that other C programs can access them easily.

USING CONDITIONAL PREPROCESSING DIRECTIVES

Just as your programs can perform conditional processing using the *if* statement, they can also direct the preprocessor to respond to specific conditions. To control the operations that the preprocessor performs during compilation of your program, C provides several conditional preprocessor directives.

In Chapter 6 you learned how to define a constant or macro using *#define*. Simply using *#define* can sometimes cause a problem: You have no way of knowing whether an include file has defined a constant or a macro of the same name, and you could be overwriting its value. By using the directive *#ifdef*, you can instruct the preprocessor to perform specific processing only when a constant or a macro that you specify is already defined.

■ **FACT:** *The* #ifdef *directive instructs the preprocessor to process the subsequent state-ments only if the specified identifier is defined. The* #ifndef *directive instructs the pre-processor to perform the processing only if the identifier is not defined.*

The following code fragment uses *#ifndef*, which is the converse of *#ifdef*. The frag-ment tests whether the value NULL is not defined. If it is not, the preprocessor executes the associated directive, which defines NULL as 0.

```
#ifndef NULL
#define NULL 0
#endif
```

■ **FACT:** *The* #endif *directive indicates the last statement in a list of conditional pre-processor directives.*

Just as the C compiler recognizes the left and right braces as grouping symbols, the precompiler recognizes the *#endif* directive as the concluding statement in a list of pre-processor directives. The precompiler lets you place multiple statements before *#endif*, as shown here:

```
#ifdef 8087
#define MATH_COPROCESSOR TRUE
#include <math.h>
#include <limits.h>
#endif
```

■ **FACT:** *To enhance conditional preprocessing, C provides the* #elif *and* #else *pre-processor directives. The* #elif *directive works as an* else if *statement, enabling you to test another condition. The* #else *directive simply specifies a set of directives to be processed when the preceding condition fails.*

The following code fragment illustrates the use of the *#elif* and *#else* directives, which add flexibility to your *#ifdef* directives, as the *else* keyword enhances *if* statements.

```
#ifdef MSDOS
#define TARGET "Microsoft MS-DOS"
#elif PCDOS
#define TARGET "IBM PC-DOS"
#else
#define TARGET "Operating System/2"
#endif
```

■ **FACT:** *You can place preprocessor directives throughout your program.*

All the examples we have examined so far have used the conditional preprocessor directives only to define additional constants. Perhaps the greatest benefit of these direc-tives is their use within a program to enable or disable processing of specific statements. For example, the following program (AVERAGE.C) uses the routine *average_value* to return the average value in an array of integer values. To help the programmer debug the program, the code contains two *printf* statements that display intermediate results.

```
main()
{
    static int array[5] = { 10, 20, 30, 40, 50 };

    printf("The average value in the array is %d\n",
            average_value(array, 5));
}

average_value(int *values, int size)
{
    int i = 0;
    long int sum = 0;

    while (i++ < size)
        {
        printf("sum = %3ld   value = %d   i = %d\n",
                sum, *values, i);
        sum += *values++;
        }

    printf("Final sum = %ld\n", sum);
    return (sum / size);
}
```

When you run the program, your screen shows

```
sum =    0   value = 10   i = 1
sum =   10   value = 20   i = 2
sum =   30   value = 30   i = 3
sum =   60   value = 40   i = 4
sum =  100   value = 50   i = 5
Final sum = 150
The average value in the array is 30
```

As you can see, the additional *printf* statements make it easy to examine the processing that *average_value* performs. Statements of this type, called *debug write* statements, help you locate bugs in your program. Inserting debug write statements is normally the first step programmers take to find errors.

Unfortunately, programmers often remove debug write statements too soon, thinking that the program is working correctly. By using conditional preprocessor directives, however, you can disable or enable these statements without removing them from your source file. For example, the following directive sets up an identifier called DEBUGGING to tell the preprocessor to include the debug write statements listed later in the program:

```
#define DEBUGGING "ON"
```

In the program, simply group each debug write statement within *#ifdef* and *#endif* preprocessor directives, as shown here:

```
#ifdef DEBUGGING
printf("Sum = %3ld  Value = %d  i = %d\n", sum, value, i);
#endif
```

If the identifier DEBUGGING is defined, the preprocessor includes the associated *printf* statement; if the identifier DEBUGGING is not defined, the preprocessor does not include the *printf* statement in your code. In essence, you have an on/off switch for debug write statements.

USING *#undef*

Whereas the preprocessor directive *#define* creates a constant or macro, the *#undef* directive undefines a macro.

■ **FACT:** *The* #undef *directive instructs the preprocessor to undefine the identifier specified. Any references to the identifier that follow the* #undef *statement will be undefined.*

Let's revisit the preceding scenario, in which we used *#ifdef* directives to enable and disable debug write statements. Suppose you want to enable debugging for some functions and disable it for others. The *#undef* statement allows you to do just that. The following program (DEBUGAVE.C) defines the constant DEBUGGING in specific locations and later uses *#undef* to undefine the constant. In so doing, the program is able to turn on and off the processing of debug write statements for specific functions.

```
main()
{
    long int total_value(int *, int);
    static int values[5] = { 10, 20, 30, 40, 50 };

    printf("Total value = %ld    Average value = %d\n",
           total_value(values, 5), average_value(values, 5));
}

#define DEBUGGING "ON"

long int total_value(int *value, int size)
{
    int i = 0;
    long int sum = 0;
```

(continued)

268

continued

```
    while (i++ < size)
        {
#ifdef DEBUGGING
        printf("In total_value sum = %3ld  value = %d  i = %d\n",
            sum, *value, i);
#endif

    sum += *value++;
        }
    return (sum);
}

#undef DEBUGGING  /* turn debug write statements off */

average_value(int *value, int size)
{
    long int sum;

    sum = total_value(value, size);

#ifdef DEBUGGING
    printf("In average_value sum = %ld\n", sum);
#endif

    return (sum / size);
}
```

When you run the program, your screen shows

```
In total_value sum =   0  value = 10  i = 1
In total_value sum =  10  value = 20  i = 2
In total_value sum =  30  value = 30  i = 3
In total_value sum =  60  value = 40  i = 4
In total_value sum = 100  value = 50  i = 5
In total_value sum =   0  value = 10  i = 1
In total_value sum =  10  value = 20  i = 2
In total_value sum =  30  value = 30  i = 3
In total_value sum =  60  value = 40  i = 4
In total_value sum = 100  value = 50  i = 5
Total value = 150  Average value = 30
```

As you can see, the program does not display the debug write statements in the *average_value* function. Because the *#undef* directive undefines DEBUGGING before the call to *average_value*, the preprocessor does not include the *printf* statement in the executable program. To enable debugging in the *average_value* function, simply remove the *#undef* statement.

USING THE *#error* DIRECTIVE

In some instances you might want to generate an immediate compiler error if an identifier is not defined. The *#error* preprocessor directive lets your programs do that.

■ **FACT:** *The* #error *directive instructs to the preprocessor to generate a compiler error and display the text specified in the* #error *directive. For example, the directive* #error Define the identifier SIZE to be at least 275 *tells the precompiler to generate a compiler error and display the message* Define the identifier SIZE to be at least 275.

The following conditional preprocessing tests whether the program has failed to define the identifier MSDOS:

```
#ifndef MSDOS
#error This program requires MS-DOS services.
#endif
```

If the identifier is not defined, the *#error* directive results in the following message:

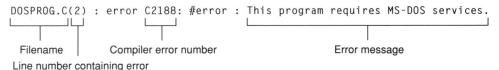

The *#error* directive prevents the compiler from compiling the program until you edit the file to correct the cause of the error. As you can see, the compiler displays the filename and the line number of the instruction responsible for the error. Next the error number C2188 is displayed, which indicates that the error was induced by *#error.* Last, the compiler displays the message that accompanied the *#error* directive.

Most programs won't require the *#error* directive. However, if you are working on a large project with several other programmers, *#error* can help you relay critical messages to another programmer who is compiling the source file.

USING PREDEFINED PREPROCESSOR CONSTANTS

During compilation, the preprocessor defines several constants that help with program development. For example, you can display at run-time the date and time of the last compilation by accessing the character strings stored in the constants __DATE__ and __TIME__.

■ **FACT:** *During preprocessing, the current system date and time are stored in the constants __DATE__ and __TIME__.*

The following program (SHOWDATE.C) displays its compilation date and time when it begins execution. Remember, __DATE__ and __TIME__ contain the date and time you last *compiled* your program, not the current (run-time) system time.

```
main()
{
    printf("Last compilation %s %s\n", __DATE__, __TIME__);
}
```

■ TIP: *By displaying the compilation date and time in your programs as you develop them, you can verify that you are executing the latest compiled version of the program.*

As your programs increase in size and complexity, you will spend more time testing and editing them. In some instances, a compiler error or a linker error can prevent a new executable file from being created. If you don't notice the error, you will be executing the previous version of the program, but you will think that it corresponds to an updated source file. However, if you examine the compilation date and time displayed by __DATE__ and __TIME__, you can detect the error.

■ FACT: *C provides the constant __TIMESTAMP__, which contains the date and time the source file was last modified.*

The following program (LASTMOD.C) uses __TIMESTAMP__ to display the date and time that the source file was created or last changed.

```
main()
{
    printf("Last modification %s\n", __TIMESTAMP__);
}
```

Remember, the only time this value changes is when you edit and recompile your program. This constant can help you match the compiled version of a program with the corresponding source file.

■ FACT: *During compilation, the current line number is stored in the constant __LINE__, and the current filename is stored as __FILE__.*

As the compiler examines a source file, it assigns the name of the current file to __FILE__ and the current line number to __LINE__. As the compiler advances to the next line of the source file, it increments the value of __LINE__. Likewise, if the compiler examines the contents of an include file, it assigns the name of the include file to __FILE__. If your program displays a message using *printf*, as is the case in the following statement:

```
printf("File %s Line %d\n", __FILE__, __LINE__);
```

the compiler assigns the current filename and line number to the constants.

The following program (FILENAME.C) uses the constant __FILE__ to display the program filename.

```
main()
{
    printf("Current source file is %s\n", __FILE__);
}
```

Programmers use __LINE__ as a debugging tool. Assume, for example, that you have a function named *some_function* that repeatedly updates the value of a variable named *count*. The following program (SHOWLINE.C) uses debug write statements to display the value of *count*.

```
main()
{
    int count = 2;
    void some_function();

    printf("Line %2d -- Value of count is %d\n", __LINE__, count);

    some_function();
}

void some_function()
{
    int count = 4;

    printf("Line %2d -- Value of count is %d\n", __LINE__, count);

    count += 2;

    printf("Line %2d -- Value of count is %d\n", __LINE__, count);
}
```

By using __LINE__ with your debug write statements, you can associate the messages to specific line numbers within your source file. When you compile and execute SHOWLINE.C, you get the following output:

```
Line   6 -- Value of count is 2
Line  15 -- Value of count is 4
Line  19 -- Value of count is 6
```

The output tells you exactly where within your source file the debug write statements are being executed.

The following table shows several additional constants supported by Microsoft C that you might want to use for conditional processing. The table contains only a partial list of the remaining constants.

Constant	*Meaning*
_CHAR_UNSIGNED	Defined when the default for type *char* is changed from signed to unsigned (The CL /J compiler option defines this constant.)
M_I86	Defined when code is generated for a machine in the Intel 8086 family
M_I86SM	Defined for Intel small memory model
M_I86CM	Defined for Intel compact memory model
M_I86MM	Defined for Intel medium memory model
M_I86LM	Defined for Intel large memory model
M_I86HM	Defined for Intel huge memory model
MSDOS	Defined for MS-DOS
_NO_EXT_KEYS	Defined when Microsoft C extensions are disabled (The CL /Za option disables language extensions.)

■ **FACT:** *The C #line directive lets you set the line counter C uses as it displays error messages during compilation.*

As your programs increase in length, you might have trouble locating syntax errors in a function. By using the *#line* preprocessor directive, you can set the line counter to any number you want. For example, you could reset the line counter to 0 at the start of a function:

```
#line 0
```

When the compiler later displays a syntax error for line 5, the error is easier to locate.

■ **FACT:** *In addition to setting the compiler's line counter, the #line directive lets you specify the name of the file you want the compiler to display when it generates a syntax error. For example, the directive #line 0 "MAINPRG.C" resets the line counter to 0 and directs the compiler to display MAINPRG.C if a syntax error occurs.*

Although most programmers never require this form of the *#line* directive, it can be useful in locating syntax errors. If a program contains many C functions, you might begin each function with a *#line* directive that specifies a portion of the function name instead of a filename:

```
#line 0 "average"
```

If the function *average* contains syntax errors, the directive results in a compiler error message in the following form:

```
average(1) : error C2059: syntax error : '{'
```

In this case you can determine not only the line containing the error, but also the function.

INCLUDING C SOURCE FILES

So far you have used the *#include* directive only to include files with the extension H. As you will see in this section, you can place functions into separate source files that you can later include in your programs.

■ **FACT:** *You can use the #include directive to include not only the header files (those with the extension H) provided with the C compiler, but also your own files of constants and macros and even C source code.*

As you develop more programs, you will probably find that you are using the same collection of constants and macros in numerous programs. Consider grouping all the constants into an include file with the extension H. Within your programs, simply include the file within quotation marks, as follows:

```
#include "filename.h"
```

A major advantage of including all your definitions in a single file is consistency. If you need to change a macro or constant definition, you have only one change to make. This also ensures that all programs use the same set of values.

■ **TRAP:** *Do not change the include files provided with your compiler.*

Many of the include files are interdependent. Rather than changing a constant or a macro in an include file, simply redefine it for your specific application using *#define* within your source file. Doing so prevents your change from inadvertently affecting future applications.

Another discovery you will make as you continue to program in C is that you are developing similar functions for many of your programs. Many programmers maintain source files that contain groups of related functions; such files can be included in a program that requires one or more of the functions.

■ **TIP:** *Group related functions into a single source file, and include that file in your programs whenever you need the functions. Because this include file contains C source code, it should have the extension C.*

Assume, for example, that the file STRINGS.C contains the functions *str_copy* and *str_length*, as shown here:

```
void str_copy(char *source, char *target)
{
    while (*target++ = *source++)
        { ; }

}
```

(continued)

continued

```
str_length(char *str)
{
    int size = 0;

    while (*str++)
        size++;

    return (size);
}
```

Within a different file, you can create a program that includes the file STRINGS.C, as shown here in the program CALLFILE.C:

```
#include "strings.c"

main()
{
    char target[128];

    str_copy("MESSAGE TO COPY", target);
    printf("The string %s contains %d characters",
           target, str_length(target));
}
```

When the C preprocessor encounters the *#include* directive, it reads the contents of the file into your program. Remember, you can verify this by generating a preprocessor file using the /P option with CL.

If you are not sure whether your file should have a C or an H extension, follow this rule: Files containing only macros and constants have the H extension, whereas files containing functions are better described using the C extension.

Later in this book you will learn how libraries simplify the sharing of functions among applications. For now, including C source files enables you to share functions and to reduce the amount of code in your primary source file.

SUMMARY

Using Conditional Preprocessing Directives

■ **FACT:** *The* #ifdef *directive instructs the preprocessor to process the subsequent statements only if the specified identifier is defined. The* #ifndef *directive directs the preprocessor to perform the processing only if the identifier is not defined.*

■ **FACT:** *The* #endif *directive indicates the last statement in a list of conditional preprocessor directives.*

■ **FACT:** *To enhance conditional preprocessing, C provides the* #elif *and* #else *preprocessor directives. The* #elif *directive works as an* else if *statement, enabling you to test another condition. The* #else *directive simply specifies a set of directives to be processed when the preceding condition fails.*

■ **FACT:** *You can place preprocessor directives throughout your program.*

Using *#undef*

■ **FACT:** *The* #undef *directive directs the preprocessor to undefine the identifier specified. Any references to the identifier that follow the* #undef *statement will be undefined.*

Using the *#error* Directive

■ **FACT:** *The* #error *directive instructs the preprocessor to generate a compiler error and display the text specified in the* #error *directive. For example, the directive* #error Define the identifier SIZE to be at least 275 *tells the precompiler to generate a compiler error and display the message* Define the identifier SIZE to be at least 275.

Using Predefined Preprocessor Constants

■ **FACT:** *During preprocessing, the current system date and time are stored in the constants* __DATE__ *and* __TIME__.

■ **TIP:** *By displaying the compilation date and time in your programs as you develop them, you can verify that you are executing the latest compiled version of the program.*

■ **FACT:** *C provides the constant* __TIMESTAMP__, *which contains the date and time the source file was last modified.*

■ **FACT:** *During compilation, the current line number is stored in the constant __LINE__, and the current filename is stored as __FILE__.*

■ **FACT:** *The C #line directive lets you set the line counter C uses as it displays error messages during compilation.*

■ **FACT:** *In addition to setting the compiler's line counter, the #line directive lets you specify the name of the file you want the compiler to display when it generates a syntax error. For example, the directive #line 0 "MAINPRG.C" resets the line counter to 0 and directs the compiler to display MAINPRG.C if a syntax error occurs.*

Including C Source Files

■ **FACT:** *You can use the #include directive to include not only the header files (those with the extension H) provided with the C compiler, but also your own files of constants and macros and even C source code.*

■ **TRAP:** *Do not change the include files provided with your compiler.*

■ **TIP:** *Group related functions into a single source file, and include that file in your programs whenever you need the functions. Because this include file contains C source code, it should have the extension C.*

GLOSSARY

conditional preprocessor directive A preprocessor directive that controls the inclusion of subsequent instructions, depending on the truth value of the condition it presents. For example, *#ifdef NAME* includes the instructions that follow if the identifier NAME is defined.

debug write statement An output statement that displays an intermediate result or a message that you can use to track down logic errors in your program.

## CHAPTER 15

Working with C Structures

In Chapter 11 you learned that C lets you group related values of the same data type into arrays. Another storage facility, called a *structure*, lets you group related values of different types. A structure might, for example, contain both character strings and *int* values.

Structures are essential to several concepts we will discuss later in this book. Many of C's more powerful run-time library routines use structures because of their convenience. Take time to enter and execute the programs in this chapter; you will find structure manipulation quite straightforward.

UNDERSTANDING THE NEED FOR STRUCTURES

So that you can better understand the advantages of structures, let's examine an application well suited for a structure. Assume you are writing a program that tracks and displays employee records, as shown in Figure 15-1 on the next page.

Name	Age	Paygrade	Salary	SSN	Dependents	Phone	Office
Anderson	35	2	35000	217-66-8819	1	555-1572	14
Baker	47	3	50000	111-22-3333	4	555-2019	15
Smith	29	1	27500	382-11-5217	2	555-1841	16

FIGURE 15-1.
The structure data type is well suited to representation of employee records.

To display employee information, you could create a function called *show_employee*, as shown here:

```
void show_employee(char *name, int age, int paygrade, float salary,
    char *SSN, int dependents, char *phone, int office)

{
    printf("%20s  %2d  %2d  %9.2f  %10s  %2d  %-14s  %2d\n",
           name, age, paygrade, salary, SSN, dependents, phone, office);
}
```

Within your main program, you need to track eight distinct variables and pass them to the function in the correct order. For example:

```
show_employee(emp_name, emp_age, emp_paygrade, emp_salary, emp_SSN,
              emp_dependents, emp_phone, emp_office);
```

■ **TRAP:** *As the number of arguments to a function increases, so does the potential for confusion.*

Keep in mind that a program for maintaining employee records will probably need the following additional routines: *get_employee, file_employee, print_employee, add_employee, delete_employee,* and *change_employee.*

Each of these functions will require the same eight parameters. The difficulty really begins when the company decides that it needs to track additional employee information, such as a home address or a tax grade. In such a case you would need to add the extra arguments to every function in the program. As the number of changes to a program increases, so does the likelihood of introducing an error. C structures provide a clean alternative.

■ **FACT:** *A C structure is a named collection of related variables. To create a structure, you must first define the structure and then declare variables of that type.*

For convenience, you can create a composite data type that comprises all the related values you want to store for each employee. To create a structure called *employee_record*, for example, you first define the following structure:

```
struct employee_record
    {
    char name[20];
    int age;
    int paygrade;
    float salary;
    char SSN[10];
    int dependents;
    char phone[14];
    int office;
    };
```

A structure definition has three parts: the keyword *struct*, which tells the compiler that you are defining a structure; the structure name, which is optional; and the structure members, which are enclosed by the left and right braces. Note that the definition associates the series of members with the structure name but does not direct the compiler to create a variable.

■ **FACT:** *C programmers refer to the structure name as a tag.*

The optional structure name is referred to as a *tag*. In the previous structure definition, the name *employee_record* is the structure tag. The following statement defines a structure but does not assign it a tag. After listing the members, the statement declares three variables of the specified structure type.

```
struct
    {
    char name[20];
    int age;
    int payroll;
    float salary;
    char SSN[10];
    int dependents;
    char phone[14];
    int office;
    } emp, new_emp, old_emp;
```

As you can see, the variable names *emp*, *new_emp*, and *old_emp* follow the closing grouping symbol.

■ **FACT:** *If you don't specify variable names with a structure definition, the compiler does not create any variables of the type defined. Instead, the definition provides a template for future variable declarations.*

A structure tag is important because you can use the tag to declare variables of the structure type. As stated earlier, the *employee_record* structure definition does not create any variables. Instead, it provides a template you can use for variable declarations. The following program (EMPREC.C), for example, defines the structure *employee_record* and later declares variables of that structure type in *main*:

```
struct employee_record
    {
    char name[20];
    int age;
    int paygrade;
    float salary;
    char SSN[10];
    int dependents;
    char phone[14];
    int office;
    };

main()
{
    struct employee_record emp, new_emp;

    /* remainder of program code */
}
```

In most cases you will want to specify a structure tag. Using tags can simplify variable declarations throughout the program.

The elements that constitute a structure are known as members. The following statement defines a structure with the name *payroll* and declares two variables of the specified type:

```
struct payroll                          Keyword for defining
    {                                   a structure
    float salary;                       Structure tag
    int    deductions;
    char   state_residence[20];         Structure members
    } emp_payroll, new_payroll;

                                        Variable declarations
```

■ **FACT:** *To access specific members of a structure, you must use the dot operator. For example, the statement* emp.age = 27; *assigns the value 27 to member* age *of the structure* emp.

Earlier in this chapter we examined the routine *show_employee*, which used eight parameters to display the fields of an employee record. In the following version of *show_employee*, a structure replaces the series of separate variables. The function thus gets one argument, a structure; it then uses the dot (.) operator to display each field of the employee record.

```
void show_employee(struct employee_record emp)
{
    printf("%-20s  %2d  %2d  %9.2f  %10s  %2d  %-14s  %2d\n",
           emp.name, emp.age, emp.paygrade, emp.salary,
           emp.SSN, emp.dependents, emp.phone, emp.office);
}
```

If requirements later change and you need to add members to the structure, you won't need to change the calls to each function. Regardless of the number of members in the structure, you still pass the single structure argument to your functions. The use of a structure therefore reduces the number of changes and the chance for errors.

USING STRUCTURES

As we noted earlier, the C run-time library provides several structure-based routines. Let's examine a program that uses two such routines, *_dos_gettime* and *_dos_getdate*, to display the current system time and date. First, however, we need to look at two structures upon which these functions rely.

■ **FACT:** *The Microsoft C run-time library routine* _dos_gettime *returns the current system time. The routine uses a structure called* dostime_t *defined in dos.h.*

The include file dos.h defines the structure *dostime_t* as follows:

```
struct dostime_t {
    unsigned char hour;      /* 0-23 */
    unsigned char minute;    /* 0-59 */
    unsigned char second;    /* 0-59 */
    unsigned char hsecond;   /* 0-99 */
    };
```

■ **FACT:** *The Microsoft C run-time library function* _dos_getdate *returns the current system date. The function uses a structure called* dosdate_t *defined in dos.h.*

The include file dos.h defines the structure *dosdate_t* as follows:

```
struct dosdate_t {
    unsigned char day;       /* 1-31 */
    unsigned char month;     /* 1-12 */
    unsigned char year;      /* 1980-2099 */
    unsigned char dayofweek; /* 0-6, 0=Sunday */
    };
```

The following program (DATETIME.C) creates variables of type *dostime_t* and *dosdate_t* and passes them by address to the functions *_dos_gettime* and *_dos_getdate*.

■ **FACT:** *A function can assign or modify a structure member only if you pass the function a pointer to the structure.*

The functions *_get_dosdate* and *_get_dostime* assign values to the members of their associated structures. DATETIME.C accommodates the functions by passing both structures by address.

```
#include <dos.h> /* needed for _dos_getdate, _dos_gettime, and structs */

main()
{
    struct dosdate_t date;
    struct dostime_t time;

    _dos_getdate(&date);
    _dos_gettime(&time);

    printf("%d-%d-%d %d:%d:%d.%d",
           date.month, date.day, date.year,
           time.hour, time.minute, time.second, time.hsecond);
}
```

In a similar manner, the following program (FILEINFO.C) uses the run-time library functions *_dos_findfirst* and *_dos_findnext* to display all the files in the current directory. First, *_dos_findfirst* locates the first file that matches the filename argument; *_dos_findnext* then locates subsequent matching files (because DOS wildcard characters occur in the call to *_dos_findfirst*).

■ **FACT:** *The Microsoft C run-time library function* _dos_findfirst *examines the file specification that you provide and places file-specific information for the first matching file into a structure. The function uses a structure called* find_t *defined in dos.h.*

```
#include <dos.h> /* needed for _dos_findfirst and _dos_findnext */

main()
{
    struct find_t fileinfo;

    int result;

    result = _dos_findfirst("*.*", 0, &fileinfo);

    while (!result)
        {
        printf("%s\n", fileinfo.name);
        result = _dos_findnext(&fileinfo);
        }
}
```

■ **FACT:** *If you pass wildcard characters to* dos_findfirst, *the function lets you locate subsequent matching files. The function returns directory information for the next file in a structure of type* find_t. *As long as* _dos_findnext *locates another matching file, it returns the value 0.*

Both _dos_findfirst and _dos_findnext use a structure of type *find_t* to hold specific file information. The file dos.h defines the structure *find_t* as follows:

```
struct find_t {
    char reserved[21];
    char attib;             /* file attribute */
    unsigned wr_time;       /* time last written */
    unsigned wr_date;       /* date last written */
    long size;              /* in bytes */
    char name[13];          /* FILENAME.EXT */
    };
```

■ **TIP:** *Using the routines* _dos_findfirst *and* _dos_findnext, *you can create powerful utility programs that support the DOS wildcard characters.*

In later chapters we will create utility programs in C. As you will see, the Microsoft C run-time library routines *_dos_findfirst* and *_dos_findnext* greatly improve the functionality of those programs.

ACCESSING STRUCTURES IN FUNCTIONS

We have noted that a function that assigns or modifies the members of a structure must receive the address of the structure. Within the function, you simply work with a pointer to the structure.

■ **TRAP:** *Recall that the dot operator has a higher precedence than the indirection operator. Therefore, if the compiler is to evaluate your pointers correctly, you must use the format* (*ptr).member.

The following program (TRIANGLE.C) assigns three values to a structure called *isosceles*. It then invokes the function *get_perimeter*, which assigns the sum of those three values to the structure member *perimeter*.

```c
struct triangle
    {
    int side1;
    int side2;
    int side3;
    int perimeter;
    };

main()
{
    struct triangle isosceles;
    void get_perimeter(struct triangle *);

    isosceles.side1 = 6;
    isosceles.side2 = 6;
    isosceles.side3 = 6;
    get_perimeter(&isosceles);
    printf("Perimeter = %d", isosceles.perimeter);
}

void get_perimeter(struct triangle *tri)
{
    (*tri).perimeter = (*tri).side1 + (*tri).side2 + (*tri).side3;
}
```

Notice the technique in *get_perimeter* for accessing structure members indirectly. The parentheses are required because indirection is otherwise preceded by the dot operation. (To confirm this, review the operator precedence table in Chapter 3 on page 55.)

■ **FACT:** *An alternative to referencing structure members indirectly as* (*ptr).member *is to use the format* ptr–>member.

The following modification of *get_perimeter* uses the *ptr–>member* notation. This notation uses the characters –> to indicate that *perimeter* is a member of a structure at the address held in the pointer variable *tri*.

```
void get_perimeter(struct triangle *tri)
{
    tri->perimeter = tri->side1 + tri->side2 + tri->side3;
}
```

■ **TIP:** *Although the notations* (*ptr).member *and* ptr–>member *are functionally identical, the second,* ptr–>member, *is more frequently used.*

Later in this book we will write several routines that work with pointers to structures. At that time we will use the notation *ptr–>member* extensively.

STRUCTURES AND ARRAYS

In C you can create arrays of any data type—including structures. For example, the following statement declares an array of structures:

```
struct employee_record employees[100];
```

The array *employees* can store 100 employee records. To access a member of a specific employee record, identify the array element and the member of the associated structure:

```
employees[1].age = 30;
```

You can also include arrays in structures. The following statement creates a structure that can store 50 student names and test scores; the statement also declares two variables, *test1* and *test2*, of the specified type:

```
struct test_results
    {
    char *name[50];
    int score[50];
    } test1, test2;
```

To access an individual score, you must identify the member array of a particular structure and specify the element of the array. For example, the following statement assigns the value 88 to element 30 of array *score*, which is itself a member of structure *test1*:

```
test1.score[30] = 88;
```

INITIALIZING STRUCTURES

The C compiler lets you initialize structures at declaration. Earlier we examined a structure that stored the three sides of a triangle. That program, TRIANGLE.C, declared a variable named *isosceles* of the *triangle* structure type and then used three statements to initialize the values of members. Instead, the program could have simply used the following statement:

```
static struct triangle tri = { 6, 6, 6 };
```

The compiler assigns the initialization values to the members of the structure in the order the values and members appear.

UNIONS—SPECIAL C STRUCTURES

All the structures we have examined in this chapter have stored multiple values of different types. Another variable type, called a *union*, allows a variable to store values of several types, but only one value can occupy the variable at any given time. Unions are defined and declared like structures; however, the members that can occupy a union cannot do so simultaneously.

■ **FACT:** *A union is a variable that can store one of several types of variables. You manipulate a union using dot notation.*

The following program (UNIONTST.C) defines a union called *keys* that can store a value of type *int, float,* or *char*. The program creates a union variable called *key*; then it assigns and displays each member of the union, one member at a time. Notice the use of the dot operator to specify the union member.

```
main()
{
    union keys
        {
        int ikey;
        float fkey;
        char ckey;
        } key;

    key.ikey = 7;
    printf("Current union value = %d\n", key.ikey);

    key.fkey = 88.2;
    printf("Current union value = %f\n", key.fkey);

    key.ckey = 'A';
    printf("Current union value = %c\n", key.ckey);
}
```

When you run the program, your screen shows

```
Current union value = 7
Current union value = 88.200000
Current union value = A
```

■ **TRAP:** *A program that uses a union must keep track of the type that currently occupies the union's memory space. If you reference a union member that does not currently occupy the union's memory space, you are likely to get erroneous results.*

■ **FACT:** *The compiler allocates only enough space to store the largest member of the union.*

Because a union can store only one value at a time, the compiler does not allocate storage space for each entry. Instead, it provides space for the largest element. The following program (DATASIZE.C) illustrates this by displaying the number of bytes used to store a structure versus the amount of storage required for a similar union.

```
main()
{
    struct s_entry
        {
        int ivalue;     /* 2 bytes */
        float fvalue;   /* 4 bytes */
        char cvalue;    /* 1 byte  */
        };

    union u_entry
        {
        int ivalue;
        float fvalue;   /* largest member (4 bytes) */
        char cvalue;
        };

    printf("Size of structure = %d bytes\n", sizeof(struct s_entry));
    printf("Size of union = %d bytes\n", sizeof(union u_entry));
}
```

When you run the program, your screen shows

```
Size of structure = 8 bytes
Size of union = 4 bytes
```

The members of structure *s_entry* require only 7 bytes of memory; the compiler, however, aligns the members on word boundaries (by default), which results in the eighth padding byte. As you can see, although unions and structures are similar in format, they behave differently. Most programs won't require unions; they are presented here because of their similarity to C structures.

USING NESTED STRUCTURES

In Chapter 4 you learned that a nested *if* statement is an *if* statement that appears within another *if* construct. For example:

```
if (value < max)
    if (value >= min)  /* nested if */
        printf("%d", value);
```

■ **FACT:** *The C compiler lets you nest one structure as a member within another structure.*

Assume, for example, that you want to track specifics about each employee's office within the employee record. One approach is to include the additional members within the structure:

```
struct employee_record
    {
    char name[20];
    int age;
    int paygrade;
    float salary;
    char SSN[10];
    int dependents;
    char phone[14];
    int office_number;        /* structure    */
    int extension;            /* members      */
    char office_mate[20];     /* to provide   */
    int building_number;      /* office       */
    int computer_type;        /* information */
    } emp;
```

A second approach is to define first a structure containing the office information, such as the *office_info* structure shown here:

```
struct office_info
    {
    int office_number;
    int extension;
    char office_mate[20];
    int building_number;
    int computer_type;
    };
```

Next, within the *employee_record* structure you can simply include a member that is a structure of type *office_info*.

```
struct employee_record
    {
    char name[20];
    int age;
    int paygrade;
    float salary;
    char SSN[10];
    int dependents;
    char phone[14];
    struct office_info office;   /* nested structure */
    } emp;
```

To access the members of the nested structure, simply use dot notation. The following statement, for example, assigns the value 15 to the member *office_number* in the structure *office*, which is itself a member of structure *emp*.

```
emp.office.office_number = 15;
```

Grouping related members into nested structures reduces much of the clutter in your structure definitions.

USING BIT FIELDS

In addition to unions, C provides another special structure type that programmers call a *bit field*—a structure that holds each member in a specific number of bits.

■ **FACT:** *A bit field structure is one in which each member resides in a specific number of bits.*

Assume that you have an application that tracks students' membership in the following clubs: Archery, Band, Cheerleading, Art, Computer, or Scuba. If the school has 1000 students, you can create 6 arrays, as shown here:

```
int archery[1000], band[1000], cheerleading[1000],
    art[1000], computer[1000], scuba[1000];
```

For each student, you can set the corresponding array value to 1 if the student is a club member or to 0 if the student is not a member. For example, the statement

```
art[44] = 0;
```

indicates that student 44 is not in the Art Club. Although this method works, it consumes considerable memory. With 1000 entries in each array, the 6 arrays have 6000 entries. And with 2 bytes for each entry, the information will occupy 12,000 bytes of memory.

A more memory-efficient method is to declare a bit field structure. The number of bits allotted to each member is indicated by a value that follows the name of the member. Use a colon to separate the name of the bit field member from the size. For example, the following structure contains six 1-bit fields:

```
struct clubs
    {
    unsigned int archery:1;
    unsigned int band:1;
    unsigned int cheerleading:1;
    unsigned int art:1;
    unsigned int computer:1;
    unsigned int scuba:1;
    };
```

■ **FACT:** *The value following each member in a bit field structure specifies the number of bits required to store the value.*

We can use the value 0 to indicate that the student is not in the club and the value 1 to indicate that the student is in the club. A single binary digit is sufficient to represent a 0 or a 1. Figure 15-2 shows how compactly the bit field structure stores its members. Note, however, that exact bit assignments can vary with the compiler.

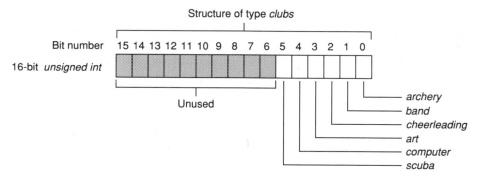

FIGURE 15-2.
By creating a bit field structure, you can use a single unsigned int *value to represent all the club affiliations for a given student.*

To store club membership data for all the students, the program can declare a single array of these bit field structures.

```
struct clubs students[1000];
```

To indicate (as we did previously) that student 44 is not in the Art Club, use the dot operator as you would with any other structure:

```
student[44].art = 0;
```

Note that we reduced the number of arrays required to store the club membership data from 6 to 1; likewise, we reduced the memory requirement from 12,000 bytes to 2000 bytes!

A bit field can contain several bits. As the size of a field changes, so does the range of values the field can store. The following table shows this simple correlation:

Size of Field	Range of Values
1	0 through 1
2	0 through 3
3	0 through 7
4	0 through 15
5	0 through 31
6	0 through 63
7	0 through 127
8	0 through 255

■ **FACT:** *The members of a bit field must be of the type* unsigned int.

You must define each member of a bit field as the type *unsigned int*. Thus the greatest number of bits any field can reference is 16.

Applications that use bit fields aren't common, but as you can see, bit fields can reduce considerably the amount of memory your program consumes.

SUMMARY

Understanding the Need for Structures

■ **TRAP:** *As the number of arguments to a function increases, so does the potential for confusion.*

■ **FACT:** *A C structure is a named collection of related variables. To create a structure, you must first define the structure and then declare variables of that type.*

■ **FACT:** *C programmers refer to the structure name as a tag.*

■ **FACT:** *If you don't specify variable names with a structure definition, the compiler does not create any variables of the type defined. Instead, the definition provides a template for future variable declarations.*

■ **FACT:** *To access specific members of a structure, you must use the dot operator. For example, the statement* emp.age = 27; *assigns the value 27 to member* age *of the structure* emp.

Using Structures

■ **FACT:** *The Microsoft C run-time library function* _dos_gettime *returns the current system time. The function uses a structure called* dostime_t *defined in dos.h.*

■ **FACT:** *The Microsoft C run-time library function* _dos_getdate *returns the current system date. The function uses a structure called* dosdate_t *defined in dos.h.*

■ **FACT:** *A function can assign or modify a structure member only if you pass the function a pointer to the structure.*

■ **FACT:** *The Microsoft C run-time library function* _dos_findfirst *examines the file specification that you provide and places file-specific information for first matching file into a structure. The function uses a structure called* find_t *defined in dos.h.*

■ **FACT:** *If you pass wildcard characters to* dos_findfirst, *the function lets you locate subsequent matching files. The function returns directory information for the next file in a structure of type* find_t. *As long as* _dos_findnext *locates another matching file, it returns the value 0.*

■ **TIP:** *Using the functions* _dos_findfirst *and* _dos_findnext, *you can create powerful utility programs that support the DOS wildcard characters.*

Accessing Structures in Functions

■ **TRAP:** *Recall that the dot operator has a higher precedence than the indirection operator. Therefore, if the compiler is to evaluate your pointers correctly, you must use the format* (*ptr).member.

■ **FACT:** *An alternative to referencing structure members indirectly, using the format* (*ptr).member, *is to use the format* ptr–>member.

■ **TIP:** *Although the notations* (*ptr).member *and* ptr–>member *are functionally identical, the second,* ptr–>member, *is more frequently used.*

Unions—Special C Structures

■ **FACT:** *A union is a variable that can store one of several types of variables. You manipulate a union using dot notation.*

■ **TRAP:** *A program that uses a union must keep track of the type that currently occupies the union's memory space. If you reference a union member that does not currently occupy the union's memory space, you are likely to get erroneous results.*

■ **FACT:** *The compiler allocates only enough space to store the largest member of the union.*

Using Nested Structures

■ **FACT:** *The C compiler lets you nest one structure as a member within another structure.*

Using Bit Fields

■ **FACT:** *A bit field structure is one in which each member resides in a specific number of bits.*

■ **FACT:** *The value following each member in a bit field structure specifies the number of bits required to store the value.*

■ **FACT:** *The members of a bit field must be of the type* unsigned int.

GLOSSARY

bit field structure A structure in which each member resides in a specific number of bits. Each member is declared as an *unsigned int*, and a value that follows the name of the member specifies the number of bits allotted to that member.

member One of the entries in a structure. To refer to a structure member, use the dot operator between the variable name and the name of the member.

structure A user-defined C type that lets programs group variables of different types into one named type. The C keyword *struct* declares a C structure.

tag The optional name of a structure type. After you define a structure and assign it a tag, you can use the tag when you declare structure variables of the defined type.

union A data type that lets you store one of several types of values. Unlike a structure, which can contain many values at the same time, a union can store only one value at any time.

## CHAPTER 16

Filling the Gaps

You have now worked with almost every aspect of the C programming language, but before we go on to Part III, we need to fill some gaps.

First, this chapter shows how you can save time in development by editing functions in separate source files, compiling them independently, and later using the linker to create an executable file. Next, we examine C enumerated types, the *typedef* statement, and the *const* and *volatile* qualifiers. We also try to build a better understanding of several complex C declarations. Finally, we conclude with a look at an optional way to designate comments in your source code.

CREATING SEPARATELY COMPILED OBJECT MODULES

In Chapter 14 you learned that you can include files that contain other C functions by using the preprocessor *#include* directive. For example, the directive *#include "string.c"* includes the source file string.c.

Used in this way, the *#include* directive does let you share functions among programs, but compilation time can increase significantly.

■ **TRAP:** *When you include a file containing C source code, the C compiler has to compile not only your main program but also the source file that you have included. If you include a large file or several files, the compilation time can increase significantly.*

As we have discussed, the process of testing, changing, and recompiling occupies the majority of program development time. If you can reduce compilation time, you will become more productive.

In Chapter 1 you learned that the linker combines object files (those produced by the C compiler) with library files to create an executable program. If you compile source files separately rather than combining the code using *#include* directives, you can later use the linker to create an executable program.

The advantage of combining object files in this manner is that you don't have to recompile the include file each time you change your program. Because the compiler has fewer lines of code to examine, it completes its work faster.

■ **FACT:** *The /c option directs CL to create an object file but not to execute the linker.*

Let's use the file STRINGS.C, which we created in Chapter 14, to demonstrate linking with precompiled object files. Recall that STRINGS.C implemented two string-handling functions, *str_copy* and *str_length*:

```c
void str_copy(char *source, char *target)
{
    while (*target++ = *source++)
        { ; }
}

str_length(char *str)
{
    int size = 0;

    while (*str++)
        size++;

    return (size);
}
```

Use the /c option with CL to create an object file:

```
C> CL /c STRINGS.C
```

The /c option directs CL to compile STRINGS.C to create STRINGS.OBJ but prevents CL from invoking the linker. Next, enter the following program (TESTOBJ.C):

```c
main()
{
    char target[128];

    str_copy("MESSAGE TO COPY", target);

    printf("The string %s contains %d characters", target,
            str_length(target));
}
```

■ **FACT:** *To direct CL to link another object file to your program, you must specify the name of the object file in the CL command line with the extension OBJ. The basename of the resulting executable file will be the same as that of the first file on the command line.*

In the command line for compiling TESTOBJ.C, specify the object file that CL must link with the compiled source file:

```
C> CL TESTOBJ.C STRING.OBJ
```

When CL encounters the file with the OBJ extension, CL uses the object during linking, as shown here:

```
C> CL TESTOBJ.C STRING.OBJ

Microsoft (R) C Optimizing Compiler Version 5.10
Copyright (c) Microsoft Corp 1984, 1985, 1986, 1987, 1988. All rights reserved.

TESTOBJ.C

Microsoft (R) Overlay Linker  Version 3.65
Copyright (C) Microsoft Corp 1983-1988.  All rights reserved.

Object Modules [.OBJ]: TESTOBJ.OBJ +
Object Modules [.OBJ]: STRINGS.OBJ
Run File [TESTOBJ.EXE]: TESTOBJ.EXE /NOI
List File [NUL.MAP]: NUL
Libraries [.LIB]:
```

The resulting executable file (TESTOBJ.EXE) has the same basename as the first file specified (TESTOBJ.C). When you run TESTOBJ.EXE, your screen shows

```
The string MESSAGE TO COPY contains 15 characters
```

As you can see, the linker combined the two files. When you separate routines into distinct object files, overall compilation time is reduced, and often-used routines can be reused easily. The only difference between programs that reside in one object module and programs that reside in multiple object modules is the manner in which global variables are used. We'll discuss this topic later in the chapter.

ENUMERATED TYPES

In Chapter 3 you learned that a variable's type determines the set of values that the variable can store and specifies a set of operations that you can perform on the variable. You have worked with values of type *int*, *char*, *float*, and *double*; with arrays, structures, and unions; and with pointers, which can reference any of the preceding types. In this section we examine one last C data type, the enumerated type.

■ **FACT:** *The C type* enum *lets you create your own data type; a variable of your type can be assigned only a value that appears in the list you specify. For example, the statement* enum suits { clubs, diamonds, hearts, spades }; *defines an enumerated type called* suits, *whose permissible values are those listed between the braces.*

Many programs use meaningless constant values to represent specific categories or choices. For example, a program might use the values 0 through 4 to represent the workdays, where Monday = 0, Tuesday = 1, Wednesday = 2, and so on. Within the program the code to determine the processing for a particular day might appear as follows:

```
if (day == 0)
    schedule_meeting();
else if (day == 4)
    schedule_dinner();
```

C enumerated types provide an alternative. For example, you could declare an enumerated type called *workdays* and specify within the type a set of possible values, as follows:

```
enum workdays { Monday, Tuesday, Wednesday, Thursday, Friday };
```

■ **FACT:** *The name you assign to an enumerated type works much like a structure tag. You can declare variables when you define the type, or you can declare variables later using the name you specified in the definition.*

You can declare *day* as a variable of the enumerated type *workdays* in the same statement in which you define *workdays*:

```
enum workdays { Monday, Tuesday, Wednesday, Thursday, Friday } day;
```

You can also declare *day* after you define the type, as shown here:

```
enum workdays { Monday, Tuesday, Wednesday, Thursday, Friday };
main()
{
    enum workdays day;

    /* remainder of program code */
}
```

Once *day* is defined, you can use the replacement strings in your program code:

```
if (day == Monday)
    schedule_meetings();
else if (day == Friday)
    schedule_dinner();
```

Why not simply define constants? You could enter a series of directives, as follows:

```
#define Monday 0
#define Tuesday 1
#define Wednesday 2
#define Thursday 3
#define Friday 4
```

In so doing, you could still work with meaningful names as opposed to the values 0 through 4. Enumerated types, however, provide one advantage constants don't—the ability to specify the set of values a variable can store.

■ **FACT:** *Most compilers generate a syntax error if you attempt to assign a value outside the set of values associated with the type.*

By default, the compiler assigns consecutive integer values, beginning with 0, to the series of values in the enumerated type. In the following declaration, for example, the compiler represents clubs as 0, diamonds as 1, hearts as 2, and spades as 3:

```
enum suits { clubs, diamonds, hearts, spades };
```

■ **FACT:** *The compiler lets you assign integer values to each entry of an enumerated type when you define the type.*

As discussed, by default C assigns the value 0 to the first entry in an enumerated type. To override this assignment, specify values for each entry when you define the type, as shown here:

```
enum suits { clubs = 10, diamonds = 20, hearts = 30, spades = 40 };
```

The values you assign must be integer values. If you don't specify values for each entry, the compiler assigns to successive entries the value of the previous entry plus 1. For example, in the following case, diamonds will be 11, hearts 12, and spades 13:

```
enum suits { clubs = 10, diamonds, hearts, spades };
```

■ **TRAP:** *The member names in an enumerated type must not duplicate any of your variable or constant names.*

If an entry name in your enumerated type has the same name as a variable or constant name, the compiler generates a syntax error. Each name must be unique. Enumerated types are a fairly recent addition to C, and you will probably see them used increasingly as time goes on.

CREATING VARIABLE TYPES WITH *typedef*

Program portability determines how easily a program can be moved from one operating system to another. When you recompile the program using a different C compiler, you are said to be "porting" the program to a new environment.

In Chapter 3 we discussed one of the common compiler differences that impede portability: Some compilers represent values of type *int* as 32-bit values, whereas others use 16-bit values. If you plan to create a program with one compiler and then move it to a different C compiler, you need to declare integer values explicitly as either *long int* or *short int*.

The following declarations, for example, ensure that the variables are consistently defined in environments with either *int* size:

```
long int count;
short int discount;
```

An alternative is to use the C *typedef* statement, which enables you to associate a name with a specific data type.

■ **FACT:** *The* typedef *statement directs the C compiler to associate a user-defined name with a specific type.*

Once you define a type using *typedef,* you can reference the new type throughout your program. The following program (DEFINT.C) defines and uses the type *integer*:

```
typedef long int integer;

main()
{
    integer value = 55555;
    void display_value(integer);

    display_value(value);

}

void display_value(integer a)
{
    printf("%ld\n", a);
}
```

During compilation, the compiler associates the type *long int* with the variables declared as *integer* values. If you later change the program to use *short int*, simply change the *typedef* statement:

```
typedef short int integer;
```

You will also need to modify any values and formatting characters that are designed for long integers only. For example, change *%ld* to *%d*. When you recompile the program, the compiler assigns the correct types.

■ **TIP:** *You can simplify repetitive complex declarations by using* typedef *statements.*

If your program frequently uses a complex declaration, such as a pointer to a function or pointers to an array, you might consider defining a simpler type using *typedef.* After you define the new type, you can reference it throughout your program. For example, the statement on the following page associates an array of structures with the name *emp_data*.

```
typedef struct employee_records emp_data[100];
```

You can then declare a pointer to such an object in the following form:

```
emp_data *ptr;
```

STATIC *vs* AUTOMATIC VARIABLES

In preceding chapters we have used the keyword *static* to initialize locally declared arrays or structures, as demonstrated here in the program STATIC.C:

```
main()
{
    static char string[128] = "Test string";

    puts(string);
}
```

■ **FACT:** *By default, the variables you declare within your functions are automatic variables. The compiler automatically creates the variable each time the function is called and automatically deletes the variable when the function ends.*

The following program (AUTOVAR.C) invokes the function *show_value*, which displays its local variable *a* and then assigns *a* the value 6. By default, a local variable such as *a* is an automatic variable; it ceases to exist when the function that created it ends. When the program invokes *show_value* a second time, therefore, the function is not aware that the variable *a* ever contained the value 6.

```
main()
{
    void show_value(void);

    show_value();
    show_value();
}

void show_value(void)
{
    int a;

    printf("%d\n", a);
    a = 6;
}
```

When you run the program, your screen shows

37
37

Your output might not match the output above. The variable *a* is not initialized and does not, therefore, contain a meaningful value. Because the compiler creates the local variable each time the function is called, the value 6 assigned to the variable is lost when the function returns.

■ **TIP:** *If a function does not use arguments, point this out explicitly to the compiler by placing the keyword* void *in the argument list for the function.*

Incidentally, you might note the use of the keyword *void* in the argument list for the function *show_value*:

```
void show_value(void)
```

Explicitly declaring an argument list *void* helps the compiler detect inconsistencies in your use of a function.

In some cases, functions need to remember the last value assigned to a local variable. Use the *static* qualifier in such instances to ensure that the value of a local variable is stored from one invocation of the function to the next.

■ **FACT:** *The* static *qualifier directs the compiler to store the value of a local variable from one invocation of the function to the next. If the variable is initialized at declaration, the compiler performs the initialization one time.*

In the following program (STATIC2.C), the function *show_value* has been changed so that it uses a static variable. The compiler initializes the static variable *a* only once.

```
main()
{
    int i;
    void show_value(void);

    for (i = 0; i < 10; ++i)
        show_value();
}

void show_value(void)
{
    static int a = 0;

    printf("%d\n", a++);
}
```

When you run the program, your screen shows

```
0
1
2
3
4
5
6
7
8
9
```

Because *show_value* declares the variable *a* as *static*, the function retains the value of *a* from one invocation to the next.

■ **FACT:** *The* auto *keyword directs the compiler to classify a variable as automatic.*

You can explicitly declare a variable automatic with the *auto* keyword. Uses for this keyword are limited: You cannot use the *auto* keyword with variables declared outside functions, and those declared internally are automatic by default. In some situations, *auto* can make your code more readable.

TAKING A SECOND LOOK AT GLOBAL VARIABLES

In Chapter 8 you learned that a global variable is a variable defined outside any function. As you recall from that discussion, all the functions in a program have direct access to global variables. Because global access to a variable can make detecting errors difficult, we discourage the use of global variables. Nevertheless, as you examine C programs, you will eventually encounter global variables, so let's examine a few more of their characteristics.

■ **FACT:** *Global variables are not automatic variables. They exist throughout the life of the program. Therefore, the compiler lets you initialize global arrays or structures without the need for the* static *qualifier.*

The following program (GLOBAL.C) initializes and displays a global character string:

```
char string[255] = "Global string";

main()
{
    void display(void);

    puts(string);
    display();
}
```

(continued)

continued

```
void display(void)
{
    puts(string);
}
```

When you run the program, your screen shows

```
Global string
Global string
```

Because *string* is a global variable, its existence is known both in *main* and in *display*.

As we discussed, you can link separately compiled object files to produce an executable file. In some instances, a function contained in one object file might need to reference a global variable defined in another. In such cases, you must use the *extern* qualifier.

■ **FACT:** *The* extern *qualifier informs the compiler that the specified variable is declared in an object file that is external to the current file.*

If you qualify a variable with the keyword *extern*, the compiler defers until link time the task of locating the variable. For example, the statement *extern int julian_date;* informs the compiler that references to the variable *julian_date* must be resolved by the linker based on global instructions in a separate object file.

To demonstrate the use of the *extern* qualifier, let's create a file that contains a function as well as a global variable called *score*. Next we will create a separate file that defines a *main* function that references the global variable *score*. Because *score* is defined as a global variable outside the file, you must use *extern* to access it.

Place the following code in the file INIT.C:

```
int score;  /* global variable */

void init_score(void)
{
    score = 1;
}
```

Next, place the following code in SCORE.C:

```
main()
{
    extern int score;  /* reference global variable */
    void init_score(void);
```

(continued)

continued

```
    init_score();
    printf("Starting value of score = %d", score);
}
```

Then compile INIT.C to create the object file INIT.OBJ, as shown here:

```
C> CL /c INIT.C
```

Last, compile SCORE.C, and specify INIT.OBJ as an additional object file to be linked:

```
C> CL SCORE.C INIT.OBJ
```

When you run SCORE.EXE, your screen shows

```
Starting value of score = 1
```

As you can see, placing the *extern* qualifier before the variable *score* ensures that *main* references the global variable. If you omit the *extern* qualifier, the compiler assumes that *score* is a local variable for the function *main*.

■ **FACT:** *If you precede a global variable declaration with the* static *qualifier, the compiler restricts knowledge of the global variable to routines that reside in that specific object file.*

In some cases a program defines a global variable in a source file containing a specific set of routines that should not be accessed by routines in a different source file. If you precede a global variable declaration with the *static* qualifier, the compiler hides the variable from routines outside the source file.

■ **FACT:** *By default, function names are global. If you declare a function as* static*, the compiler restricts knowledge of the function to other functions in the same object file.*

The *static* qualifier likewise directs the compiler to restrict knowledge of a function to other functions in the same object file. Suppose, for example, you write a function that is critical to other functions in the same file, but you anticipate problems if routines in other modules have knowledge of or invoke the function. In such cases, declaring the function as *static* hides it from routines in other object files.

LOOKING BEHIND THE SCENES AT TYPE CONVERSION

Most of the mathematical expressions you have seen in this book have not mixed types. (An expression that mixes types might, for example, add an *int* value and a *float* value.) In many cases, however, a program needs to manipulate mixed type expressions. In such cases, the compiler performs temporary type conversions on the values to ensure that the expression is evaluated correctly. Because the compiler performs these type conversions, you need not use the cast operator. Using a cast would not be incorrect; it would simply be redundant.

■ **FACT:** *The C compiler follows a specific set of rules that dictate when and how automatic type conversions occur.*

The following table summarizes the type conversions the compiler performs, based on the operand types. As you can see, the compiler always promotes a value's type to a type with greater precision. As a consequence, mathematical expressions maintain their accuracy.

Operand Types	Conversion
double, any type	The second type is promoted to *double*.
float, any type	The second type is promoted to *float*.
char, any type	The *char* is promoted to *int*.
short int, any type	The *short int* is promoted to *int*.
bit field, any type	The bit field is converted to *int*, or to *unsigned int* if the value is large.
unsigned long int, any type	The second type is promoted to *unsigned long int*.
long int, any type	The second type is promoted to *long int*, with one exception. If a *long int* cannot store values in the range of an *unsigned int*, both types become *unsigned long int* values.
unsigned int, any type	The second type is promoted to *unsigned int*.
int, any type	The second type is promoted to *int*.
enum, any type	The *enum* type is converted to *int* or *unsigned int*.

USING THE *const* AND *volatile* SPECIFIERS

So far, you have defined all your program constants using the preprocessor *#define* directive. The preprocessor substitutes the value of the constant for each occurrence of the constant in your program. In addition to defining constants using *#define*, you can use the *const* specifier with "variables" whose values don't change. For example, the statement *const int size = 80;* creates an *int* constant named *size* whose value is fixed at 80.

■ **FACT:** *The* const *specifier informs the compiler that the value of a variable does not change during execution.*

Once you create a variable using the *const* specifier, the compiler generates a syntax error if your program attempts to change it. To prevent a program from using a pointer to modify the value, the compiler places the constant in a segment outside the data segment.

The following program (CONSTANT.C) creates a constant called *key* and assigns it the value 255:

```
main()
{
    const int key = 255;
    int a, b, c;

    printf("%d", key);
}
```

If you generate an assembly language listing of the program using the /Fa option with CL, you can see that the compiler has placed the constant in a segment other than the data segment. Figure 16-1 shows such a listing. (Note that the Microsoft QuickC Compiler does not support the /Fa option.)

```
;       Static Name Aliases
;
        TITLE   CONSTANT.C
        NAME    CONSTANT

        .8087
_TEXT   SEGMENT WORD PUBLIC 'CODE'
_TEXT   ENDS
_DATA   SEGMENT WORD PUBLIC 'DATA'
_DATA   ENDS
CONST   SEGMENT WORD PUBLIC 'CONST'┐── Separate segment
CONST   ENDS                       ┘   for constants
_BSS    SEGMENT WORD PUBLIC 'BSS'
_BSS    ENDS
DGROUP  GROUP   CONST, _BSS, _DATA
        ASSUME  CS: _TEXT, DS: DGROUP, SS: DGROUP
EXTRN   __acrtused:ABS
EXTRN   __chkstk:NEAR
EXTRN   _printf:NEAR
_DATA   SEGMENT
$SG107  DB      '%d', 00H
_DATA   ENDS
_TEXT   SEGMENT
        ASSUME  CS: _TEXT
```

FIGURE 16-1.   *(continued)*
The compiler stores the values of const *variables in a segment separate from the data segment.*

FIGURE 16-1. *continued*

```
; Line 2
        PUBLIC  _main
_main   PROC NEAR
        push    bp
        mov     bp,sp
        mov     ax,8
        call    __chkstk
;       key = -8
;       a = -2
;       b = -4
;       c = -6
; Line 3
        mov     WORD PTR [bp-8],255     ;key
; Line 6
        mov     ax,255
        push    ax
        mov     ax,OFFSET DGROUP:$SG107
        push    ax
        call    _printf
; Line 7
        mov     sp,bp
        pop     bp
        ret
        nop

_main   ENDP
_TEXT   ENDS
END
```

Whereas the *const* specifier ensures that the program cannot modify a variable's value, the *volatile* specifier informs the C compiler that the variable must be allowed to change.

■ **FACT:** *The* volatile *specifier ensures that the C compiler does not disregard the variability of an object, despite its being specified as a constant within the program.*

In some cases a compiler attempts to optimize your program by removing any reference to the variable and using instead the constant value of the variable. The *volatile* specifier tells the compiler that a source external to the program *can* change the value of the constant, although the program cannot change it.

Most programs do not require the *const* and *volatile* specifiers; however, they are presented here to "fill the gaps."

UNDERSTANDING COMPLEX DECLARATIONS

As your programs increase in complexity, you will eventually work with pointers to various types, arrays, and functions. Although pointers provide you with this vast flexibility, they often result in complicated variable declarations. In this section we examine a few tips for making sense of complex declarations.

■ **TIP:** *Read pointer declarations from right to left.*

Pointer declarations are better understood if read from right to left. For example, read the following declaration as "a pointer to a value of type *int*":

```
int *ptr;
```

Likewise, you can read the following declaration as "an array of five pointers to *int* values":

```
int *values[5];
```

And the following declaration is a function that returns a pointer to a value of type *int*:

```
int *result();
```

■ **TIP:** *If a declaration contains specific information within parentheses, interpret the parentheses first from left to right.*

When you examine parenthesized information, it helps to read that part of the declaration from left to right. The following declaration, for example,

```
int (*array[5])();
```

becomes "an array of five pointers to functions that return values of type *int*." And the following declaration is "an array of five pointers to functions that return pointers to values of type *int*":

```
int *(*array[5])();
```

Use this method to verify the types in the following table. By using the simple rules contained in the two preceding tips, you should be able to master complicated declarations.

Declaration	*Type*
`char *str[5];`	Array of five pointers to *char* values
`char *str();`	Function that returns a pointer to a *char* value
`float (*sum)();`	Pointer to a function that returns a *float* value
`float (*values[5])();`	Array of five pointers to functions that return *float* values
`int *(*y[3]);`	Array of three pointers to pointers to *int* values
`int *(*y[3])();`	Array of three pointers to functions that return pointers to *int* values
`int (*(*y[3])())();`	Array of three pointers to functions that return pointers to functions that return *int* values

COMMENTS REINTRODUCED

Earlier you learned that the compiler regards all the text contained between the characters /* and */ as a comment. At that time you found that a comment can appear on the same lines with or even within a program statement; a comment can even span several lines.

The ANSI C standard also allows you to introduce a comment with a pair of forward slashes (//). When the compiler encounters the pair of slashes, it ignores all the remaining text on the line.

■ **FACT:** *The C compiler recognizes a pair of slashes (//) as the beginning of a comment and ignores the subsequent text on that line.*

The following program (SAMPLE.C) illustrates the use of comments in this form.

```
// SAMPLE.C
// Written by KAJ 5-1-89
// Demonstrates ANSI comment style

#include <stdio.h>       // needed for gets

main()
{
    char string [81];  // character array for string
    char *result;      // location for string

    // get string from user and echo it to the display

    printf("Enter a string:  ");   // prompt user for string
    result = gets(string);
    printf("The string entered was:  %s", result);
}
```

Regardless of which comment format you choose, use comments extensively throughout your programs.

SUMMARY

Creating Separately Compiled Object Modules

■ **TRAP:** *When you include a file containing C source code, the C compiler has to compile not only your main program but also the source file that you have included. If you include a large file or several files, the compilation time can increase significantly.*

■ **FACT:** *The /c option directs CL to create an object file but not to execute the linker.*

■ **FACT:** *To direct CL to link another object file to your program, you must specify the name of the object file in the CL command line with the extension OBJ. The basename of the resulting executable file will be the same as that of the first file on the command line.*

Enumerated Types

■ **FACT:** *The C type* enum *lets you create your own data type; a variable of your type can be assigned only a value that appears in the list you specify. For example, the statement* enum suits { clubs, diamonds, hearts, spades }; *defines an enumerated type called* suits, *whose permissible values are those listed between the braces.*

■ **FACT:** *The name you assign to an enumerated type works much like a structure tag. You can declare variables when you define the type, or you can declare variables later using the name you specified in the definition.*

■ **FACT:** *Most compilers generate a syntax error if you attempt to assign a value outside the set of values associated with the type.*

■ **FACT:** *The compiler lets you assign integer values to each entry of an enumerated type when you define the type.*

■ **TRAP:** *The member names in an enumerated type must not duplicate any of your variable or constant names.*

Creating Variable Types with *typedef*

■ **FACT:** *The* typedef *statement directs the C compiler to associate a user-defined name with a specific type.*

■ **TIP:** *You can simplify repetitive complex declarations by using* typedef *statements.*

Static *vs* Automatic Variables

■ **FACT:** *By default, the variables you declare within your functions are automatic variables. The compiler automatically creates the variable each time the function is called and automatically deletes the variable when the function ends.*

■ **TIP:** *If a function does not use arguments, point this out explicitly to the compiler by placing the keyword* void *in the argument list for the function.*

■ **FACT:** *The* static *qualifier directs the compiler to store the value of a local variable from one invocation of the function to the next. If the variable is initialized at declaration, the compiler performs the initialization one time.*

■ **FACT:** *The* auto *keyword directs the compiler to classify a variable as automatic.*

Taking a Second Look at Global Variables

■ **FACT:** *Global variables are not automatic variables. They exist throughout the life of the program. Therefore, the compiler lets you initialize global arrays or structures without the need for the* static *qualifier.*

■ **FACT:** *The* extern *qualifier informs the compiler that the specified variable is declared in an object file that is external to the current file.*

■ **FACT:** *If you precede a global variable declaration with the* static *qualifier, the compiler restricts knowledge of the global variable to routines that reside in that specific object file.*

■ **FACT:** *By default, function names are global. If you declare a function as* static, *the compiler restricts knowledge of the function to other functions in the same object file.*

Looking Behind the Scenes at Type Conversion

■ **FACT:** *The C compiler follows a specific set of rules that dictate when and how automatic type conversions occur.*

Using the *const* and *volatile* Specifiers

■ **FACT:** *The* const *specifier informs the compiler that the value of a variable does not change during execution.*

■ **FACT:** *The* volatile *specifier ensures that the C compiler does not disregard the variability of an object, despite its being specified as a constant within the program.*

Understanding Complex Declarations

■ **TIP:** *Read pointer declarations from right to left.*

■ **TIP:** *If a declaration contains specific information within parentheses, interpret the parentheses first from left to right.*

Comments Reintroduced

■ **FACT:** *The C compiler recognizes a pair of slashes (//) as the beginning of a comment and ignores the subsequent text on that line.*

GLOSSARY

enumerated type A user-defined type that identifies the specific values a variable of that type can store. The declaration *enum suits { spades, hearts, diamonds, clubs };*, for example, creates a type called *suits*, which can store one of four possible values.

external variable A global variable defined in a different object file. To access an external variable, you must precede the variable declarations with the *extern* specifier.

static variable A variable that retains its value from one invocation of a function to the next. To create a static variable, include the *static* specifier in the declaration.

PART III

UNLEASHING THE POTENTIAL OF C

BELIEVE IT OR NOT, YOU'VE MADE IT THROUGH THE DIFFICULT CHAPTERS OF the book! In the next two sections the fun begins. Using the foundation you built in Chapters 1 through 16, Part III teaches you how to write programs that access the command line, how to access entries in the environment, and how to expand wildcard characters into matching filenames. You will also learn how to write programs that return exit status values that your batch files can test using IF ERRORLEVEL directives, and how to write programs that support I/O redirection.

Part III also examines low-level file manipulation functions appropriate for database applications, dynamic memory allocation for use in linked lists, and predefined global variables provided by Microsoft C. Finally, you will learn how to write functions, such as *printf* and *scanf*, that support a variable number of arguments.

## CHAPTER 17

Command Line
Processing

Each time you type a command at the DOS prompt, the line you enter becomes the command line. When you compile a source file, for example, the command line might include the CL command, a series of command line options, the name of your source file, and an additional object file to be incorporated at link time. To this point, the only item that you have typed to execute your C programs has been the program name.

In this chapter you learn how to access the command line from within a C program. By using command line entries, you can quickly create utility routines that copy one file to another or that set the background color of your screen. As you proceed through the chapter, you will evolve a program that displays the contents of multiple files and lets you specify filenames on the command line using DOS wildcard characters.

GETTING STARTED
WITH COMMAND LINE PROCESSING

Each time you run a C program, it executes a built-in routine called _setargv that gathers the command line entries. To make the command line arguments available to your program, the compiler passes two arguments to *main*. The first argument, *argc*, is an integer value that specifies the number of entries in the command line. The second argument, *argv*, is an array of pointers to character strings. Each element of *argv* points to a command line argument.

■ **FACT:** *A compiled C program passes two arguments to* main. *The first is an integer value named* argc, *which contains the number of entries in the command line. The second is an array of character string pointers named* argv, *which contains pointers to each entry in the command line.*

For the following command line, the value of *argc* is 3 because the command line contains three entries:

```
C> COPY TEST.C TEST.BAK
```

The elements of *argv* have the following references:

- *argv[0]* points to "COPY"
- *argv[1]* points to "TEST.C"
- *argv[2]* points to "TEST.BAK"
- *argv[3]* points to null

As you can see, *argv* has a pointer to null to signify its last entry.

■ **FACT:** *To access the arguments that the compiler passes to* main, *declare* main *as* main(int argc, char *argv[]) *in your program.*

The following program (COMLINE.C) displays the command line arguments:

```
main(int argc, char *argv[])
{
    int i;

    printf("There are %d arguments on the command line:\n\n", argc);

    for (i = 0; i < argc; ++i)
        puts(argv[i]);
}
```

If you run the program with the command line

```
C> COMLINE ONE TWO THREE
```

your screen displays the information shown below. Note that the program name is provided as a fully qualified pathname, which includes drive, directory, and extension.

```
There are 4 arguments on the command line:

C:\CH17\COMLINE.EXE
ONE
TWO
THREE
```

In some cases you might want your program to receive a single argument that contains embedded blank characters. As you have seen, the compiler uses spaces to separate arguments in the command line. If you enclose a phrase with quotation marks, however, _setargv_ assigns the phrase to one entry in *argv*. For example, the command

```
C> COMLINE FIRST "SECOND THIRD" FOURTH
```

results in the output

```
There are 4 arguments on the command line:
```

```
C:\CH12\COMLINE.EXE
FIRST
SECOND THIRD
FOURTH
```

Now let's look at a way command line processing can add power and flexibility to your programs. In Chapter 13 you wrote several programs that opened the file ALPHABET.DAT and displayed its contents on the screen. Although the programs work well for that specific file, they are unable to display a file other than ALPHABET.DAT. You must edit and recompile the programs to have them display a different file.

■ **TIP:** *Using command line arguments, you can write a program that opens and displays the contents of the file associated with a given command line entry, such as* argv[1].

If you use *argv[1]* to identify the file to open, you can create a program (DISPLAY.C) that displays the contents of any file the user specifies in the command line. The effect of such a program is similar to that of the DOS TYPE command.

DISPLAY.C begins by testing the value of *argc*. If the user fails to specify a file in the command line, *argc* equals 1 because only the program name is present; in that case the program displays the following error message and then ends:

```
DISPLAY: must specify filename
```

If *argc* is greater than 1, the program tries to open the file specified by *argv[1]*. If it opens the specified file, the program displays the contents of the file; if it fails to open the file (presumably because the file does not exist in the current directory), the program displays an error message and ends.

```
#include <stdio.h>  /* needed for file-related functions */

main(int argc, char *argv[])
{
    FILE *fp;
    char string[128];
```

(continued)

continued

```
    if (argc == 1)
        puts("DISPLAY:  must specify filename");
    else if (!(fp = fopen(argv[1], "r")))
        printf("DISPLAY:  error opening file %s\n", argv[1]);
    else
        {
        while (fgets(string, sizeof(string), fp))
            printf("%s", string);

        fclose(fp);
        }
}
```

If you run the program with the file ALPHABET.DAT you created in Chapter 13,

`C> DISPLAY ALPHABET.DAT`

DISPLAY shows the contents of the file.

The following program (MYCOPY.C) lets you copy the contents of the first text file specified in the command line to the file named in the next argument:

```
#include <stdio.h>  /* needed for file-related functions */

main(int argc, char *argv[])
{
    FILE *source, *target;
    char string[256];

    if (argc < 3)
        printf("MYCOPY:  must specify source and target file");
    else if (!(source = fopen(argv[1], "r")))
        printf("MYCOPY:  error opening %s", argv[1]);
    else if (!(target = fopen(argv[2], "w")))
        printf("MYCOPY:  error opening %s", argv[2]);
    else
        {
        while (fgets(string, sizeof(string), source))
            fputs(string, target);

        fclose(source);
        fclose(target);
        }
}
```

To run this program, use a command line in the following form:

C> MYCOPY *SOURCE.EXT TARGET.EXT*

Remember, this program copies only ASCII text files. Later in this book you will learn to copy executable files.

In Chapter 2 you learned how to use the ANSI driver to set the background colors of your screen. If the ANSI driver is still installed (and if you have a color monitor), you can execute the following program (SETCOLOR.C) to set the background color:

```
main(int argc, char *argv[])
{
    int background;

    if (argc < 2)
        printf("SETCOLOR:  must specify color");
    else if ((background = getcolor(strupr(argv[1]))) != -1)
        printf("\033[%dm", background);
    else
        printf("SETCOLOR:  invalid color %s", argv[1]);
}

getcolor(char *color)
{
    static struct
        {
        char *background;
        int color_value;
        } colors[8] = {{"BLACK", 40}, {"RED", 41}, {"GREEN", 42},
                        {"ORANGE", 43}, {"BLUE", 44}, {"MAGENTA", 45},
                        {"CYAN", 46}, {"WHITE", 47}};

    int i = 0;

    while (strcmpi(color, colors[i].background) && i < 8)
        i++;

    return ((i < 8) ? colors[i].color_value : -1);
}
```

The program passes *argv[1]* (in uppercase characters) to the *getcolor* function; *getcolor* compares the argument with the background colors defined by the array of structures *colors*. If the color is valid, the function returns the corresponding color value; if the color is not valid, the function returns the value –1. If *getcolor* returns a value other than –1, the program uses the ANSI escape sequence to set the background color.

Suppose, for example, you enter the command line

```
C> SETCOLOR BLUE
```

The program passes the second command line entry, *BLUE*, to *getcolor*, which compares it with the first member of each structure. After *getcolor* finds a match for the argument string, it returns the associated value, 44, to *main*, which inserts that value into the ANSI escape sequence and sets the background color to blue.

USING *argv* AS A POINTER

In Chapter 12 you learned that you can use a pointer to access all the values in an array. The declaration of the second argument to *main*

```
char *argv[]
```

tells us that *argv* is an array of pointers to the type *char*. Because *argv* is an array variable, you can treat it as a pointer.

■ **FACT:** *Many C programmers treat* argv *as a pointer to a pointer to a value of type* char *and declare* argv *as* char **argv *in the argument list for* main.

In the following declaration, the argument list shows *argv* as a pointer to a pointer to a value of type *char*:

```
main(int argc, char **argv)
```

Initially, *argv* points to the first command line entry. If you increment the value of *argv*, *argv* points to the second entry, and so on.

The following program (COMLINE2.C) changes COMLINE.C to use *argv* as a pointer:

```
main(int argc, char **argv)
{
    printf("There are %d arguments on the command line:\n\n", argc);

    while (*argv)
        puts(*argv++);
}
```

The program loops as long as the string pointed to by *argv* is not null. Remember, the compiled program terminates the list of command line entries with a null value.

In a similar manner, the program on the following page (DISPLAY2.C) opens and displays the contents of a text file using *argv* as a pointer.

```
#include <stdio.h>   /* needed for file-related functions */

main(int argc, char **argv)
{
    FILE *fp;
    char string[128];

    if (!(fp = fopen(*(++argv), "r")))
        printf("DISPLAY:  error opening %s", *argv);
    else
        {
        while (fgets(string, sizeof(string), fp))
            printf("%s", string);

        fclose(fp);
        }
}
```

Take a look at the statement that opens the file:

```
if (!(fp = fopen(*(++argv), "r")))
```

When the program begins, *argv* points to the program name. Therefore, the *if* statement first increments *argv* and then calls *fopen* with the string to which it points. If the user doesn't specify a second command line argument, *argv* points to null. If a filename is the second argument in the command line, the program tries to open the file. If *fopen* receives a null argument or is unable to open the specified file, it assigns *fp* a value of zero, and the program displays an error message and ends.

Whether you use *argv* as an array or as a pointer is a matter of personal preference. Most programmers declare *argv* as an array to increase the readability of their programs.

EXPANDING WILDCARD CHARACTERS

Everyone who works frequently with DOS appreciates the convenience of the wildcard characters for manipulating files. Consider a program that lets you display a single file:

```
C> SHOW FILENAME.EXT
```

or all the files with a specific extension:

```
C> SHOW *.DAT
```

or even all the files in the current directory:

```
C> SHOW *.*
```

By default, when the user places wildcard characters in the command line of a C program, the compiled program treats the wildcard characters in the same manner as all command arguments. If you run the DISPLAY program to display all the files in the current directory, as in the last example above, *argv[0]* points to the program name, and *argv[1]* points to "*.*".

As discussed briefly at the beginning of this chapter, each time your compiled program runs, it invokes a function called *_setargv* that groups the command line arguments. A version of *_setargv* (provided with Microsoft C compilers) expands wildcard characters into the appropriate list of filenames. If you examine the directory containing the Microsoft C library files, you will find the corresponding object file, SETARGV.OBJ.

■ **FACT:** *The object file SETARGV.OBJ contains a version of _setargv that expands DOS wildcard characters into a corresponding list of filenames and then assigns the filenames to* argv.

Assume that the DOS DIR command shows the following DAT files in the root directory:

```
C> DIR *.DAT

 Volume in drive C is DOSDISK
 Volume Serial Number is 413E-11EB
 Directory of  C:\

BUFFER   DAT      2194 11-04-88    3:42p
SALES    DAT      2194 11-04-88    3:42p
TEST     DAT      2195 11-07-88    5:20p
ALPHABET DAT      2195 11-07-88    5:20p
        4 File(s)      1342016 bytes free

C>
```

The version of *_setargv* contained in SETARGV.OBJ expands the wildcard in the command

```
C> SHOW *.DAT
```

so that the command lists all the matching filenames. The function assigns *argv* the following values:

- *argv[0]* points to "DISPLAY"

- *argv[1]* points to "BUFFER.DAT"

- *argv[2]* points to "SALES.DAT"

- *argv[3]* points to "TEST.DAT"

- *argv[4]* points to "ALPHABET.DAT"

- *argv[5]* points to null

The following program (SHOW.C) supports not only wildcard processing via _setargv but also multiple files in the command line. For example, the following command displays the files SHOW.C, TEST.C, and STDIO.H in the order specified:

```
C> SHOW SHOW.C TEST.C \INCLUDE\STDIO.H
```

The user can combine the new capability with the support for wildcards:

```
C> SHOW *.H *.C
```

In this case the program displays each file with the extension H and then displays each file with the extension C.

```c
#include <stdio.h>  /* needed for file-related functions */

main(int argc, char *argv[])
{
    FILE *fp;
    char string[256];
    int i;

    for (i = 1; argv[i] != NULL; ++i)
        if (!(fp = fopen(argv[i], "r")))
            printf("SHOW:  error opening %s\n", argv[i]);
        else
            {
            printf("\n-------- %s --------\n\n", argv[i]);
            while (fgets(string, sizeof(string), fp))
                puts(string);
            fclose(fp);
            }
}
```

Assuming that the file SETARGV.OBJ resides in drive C: in the directory \LIB, compile and link SHOW.C as follows:

```
C> CL /c SHOW.C
C> LINK /NOE SHOW.OBJ C:\LIB\SETARGV.OBJ;
```

If you link with the file SETARGV.OBJ, your compiled program will expand filenames for you. In some cases, however, you might want to expand the command line arguments yourself. The final section of this chapter shows you how to do that.

REVISITING _dos_findfirst AND _dos_findnext

In Chapter 15 we examined a program that displayed the filename of each file in your directory using the routines _dos_findfirst and _dos_findnext.

■ **FACT:** *Rather than rely on SETARGV.OBJ, you can use the run-time library functions* _dos_findfirst *and* _dos_findnext *to expand DOS wildcard characters.*

Let's create another program to display files—this time using *_dos_findfirst* and *_dos_findnext* rather than SETARGV.OBJ to expand the wildcard characters. When you compile the following program (SHOW2.C), you need not specify SETARGV.OBJ for linking:

```
#include <stdio.h>   /* needed for fopen, fgets, and fclose */
#include <dos.h>     /* needed for dos functions and find_t struct */

main(int argc, char *argv[])
{
    FILE *fp;
    struct find_t fileinfo;
    int result;
    int i;
    char string[256];

    for (i = 1; argv[i] != NULL; ++i)
        {
        result = _dos_findfirst(argv[i], 0, &fileinfo);

        if (result)
            printf("SHOW:  no such file %s\n", argv[i]);
        else
            while (!result)
                {
                if (!(fp = fopen(fileinfo.name, "r")))
                    printf("SHOW:  error opening %s\n", fileinfo.name);
                else
                    {
                    printf("\n-------- %s --------\n\n", fileinfo.name);
                    while (fgets(string, sizeof(string), fp))
                        printf("%s", string);
                    fclose(fp);
                    }
                result = _dos_findnext(&fileinfo);
                }
        }
}
```

SUMMARY

Getting Started with Command Line Processing

■ **FACT:** *A compiled C program passes two arguments to* main. *The first is an integer value named* argc, *which contains the number of entries in the command line. The second is an array of character string pointers named* argv, *which contains pointers to each entry in the command line.*

■ **FACT:** *To access the arguments that the compiler passes to* main, *declare* main *as* main(int argc, char *argv[]) *in your program.*

■ **TIP:** *Using command line arguments, you can write a program that opens and displays the contents of the file associated with a given command line entry, such as* argv[1].

Using *argv* as a Pointer

■ **FACT:** *Many C programmers treat* argv *as a pointer to a pointer to a value of type* char *and declare* argv *as* char **argv *in the argument list for* main.

Expanding Wildcard Characters

■ **FACT:** *The object file SETARGV.OBJ contains a version of* _setargv *that expands DOS wildcard characters into a corresponding list of filenames and then assigns the filenames to* argv.

Revisiting *_dos_findfirst* and *_dos_findnext*

■ **FACT:** *Rather than rely on SETARGV.OBJ, you can use the run-time library functions* _dos_findfirst *and* _dos_findnext *to expand DOS wildcard characters.*

GLOSSARY

command line The characters you enter at the system prompt. Command line processing is the use of information contained in the command line within a program.

wildcard expansion The process of converting DOS wildcard characters to the corresponding filenames. Microsoft C provides a routine in the object file SETARGV.OBJ that performs wildcard expansion of your command line and assigns the corresponding files to *argv*.

## CHAPTER 18

Accessing the Environment

When you start DOS, it sets aside a region of memory called the environment. In Chapter 1 we briefly examined components of the environment—the *LIB=*, *INCLUDE=*, and *TMP=* entries that the C compiler uses to locate resources and to create temporary files. At that time you learned that you can invoke the DOS SET command to add or display environment entries. In this chapter you learn how to access the environment entries from within a C program.

The programs in this chapter are designed to compile and run under both DOS and OS/2. If you are running your C compiler under OS/2, you can use C to read and write OS/2 environment entries in the same manner that you do under DOS. Bear in mind, however, that some variables differ between the systems, so porting programs from DOS to OS/2 may require some changes in the way environment variables are used. For more information about OS/2 environment variables and about programming specifically for OS/2, see your OS/2 documentation.

DISPLAYING THE CURRENT ENVIRONMENT

If you type the SET command at the DOS prompt, the operating system displays the current environment contents. The series of entries you see on your screen will resemble the one on the following page.

```
COMSPEC=C:\DOS\COMMAND.COM
PATH=C:\DOS;C:\RBIN;C:\MSC;
LIB=C:\LIB;
INCLUDE=C:\INCLUDE;
INIT=C:\SOURCE\ME\INI;
TMP=D:\
PROMPT=$P$G
```

In this section you create a C program that displays the DOS environment entries.

■ **FACT:** *A compiled C program passes a pointer to the list of environment entries. To access these entries, declare* main *as* main(int argc, char *argv[], char *envp[]) *in your programs.*

The startup function that executes when you run your compiled program always sends the three arguments *argc*, *argv*, and *envp* to *main* from DOS, whether you use them or not. When you're specifying arguments to be received by *main*, always declare them in this order.

In the same way that the variable *argv* is an array of pointers to the command line arguments, the variable *envp* is an array of pointers to the environment entries. If, for example, the environment contains the entries shown in the preceding list, the elements of *envp* point to those entries in the following sequence:

- envp[0] points to "COMSPEC=C:\DOS\COMMAND.COM"

- envp[1] points to "PATH=C:\DOS;C:\RBIN;C:\MSC;"

- envp[2] points to "LIB=C:\LIB;"

- envp[3] points to "INCLUDE=C:\INCLUDE;"

- envp[4] points to "INIT=C:\SOURCE\ME\INI;"

- envp[5] points to "TMP=D:\"

- envp[6] points to "PROMPT=PG"

- envp[7] points to null

The following program (SHOWENV.C) uses *envp* to display the current contents of the environment:

```
#include <stdio.h>   /* needed for NULL */

main(int argc, char *argv[], char *envp[])
{
    int i;

    for (i = 0; envp[i] != NULL; ++i)
        puts(envp[i]);
}
```

As with the array of command line arguments, the compiler indicates the last entry in the environment with a NULL pointer. The program simply loops until *envp[i]* is equal to NULL.

■ **FACT:** *Because* envp *is an array of pointers to character strings, some programmers treat* envp *as a pointer to a pointer to a value of type* char. *In such cases, programmers declare* envp *as* char **envp.

The following program (SHOWENV2.C) treats *envp* as a pointer to display the current contents of the environment:

```
main(int argc, char **argv, char **envp)
{
    while (*envp)
        puts(*envp++);
}
```

Declaring *envp* as a pointer rather than as an array decreases the lines of code in a program by eliminating the need for an array index. Achieving this slight advantage does, however, forfeit some readability of your code.

ACCESSING ENVIRONMENT ENTRIES
WITH *getenv*

In addition to providing access to the environment entries with *envp*, C provides the run-time library function *getenv*, which returns environment information.

■ **TIP:** *Entries in the environment are best viewed as variable names and their associated values. For example, the entry* LIB=C:\LIB *associates the variable* LIB *with the value* C:\LIB.

The *getenv* function takes as an argument the name of an environment variable. It returns a pointer to the value associated with an environment entry.

■ **FACT:** *The* getenv *function returns a pointer to a string that contains the value of the specified variable. If no such environment entry exists,* getenv *returns NULL. For example, the statement* puts(getenv("PATH")); *returns a pointer to the string associated with* PATH *in the program's environment.*

The program on the following page (GETENTRY.C) combines command line processing and the use of *getenv* to access the DOS environment.

```
#include <stdlib.h>   /* needed for getenv */
#include <string.h>   /* needed for strupr */

main(int argc, char *argv[])
{
    char *result;

    if (argv[1])
        {
        if (result = getenv(strupr(argv[1])))
            printf("%s = %s", argv[1], result);
        else
            printf("No such entry:  %s", argv[1]);
        }
    else
        printf("You must specify an environment variable");
}
```

To execute the program, type the program name followed by the name of an environment variable:

```
C> GETENTRY TMP
```

If the environment entry exists, the program displays its value, for example,

```
TMP = D:\
```

If the entry does not exist, the program displays the following message:

```
No such entry:  TMP
```

■ **TRAP:** *The* getenv *function is case sensitive: It does not match a lowercase argument string to an uppercase environment variable.*

Because *getenv* is case sensitive, the program GETENTRY.C uses the run-time library routine *strupr* to convert the string pointed to by *argv[1]* to uppercase. Thus, the user need not use uppercase to enter environment variable names. Accommodations, such as this use of *strupr*, that reduce the burden on the user improve the likelihood your program will be well received.

PLACING ENTRIES INTO THE ENVIRONMENT WITH *putenv*

Just as the C run-time library provides a function that returns the value of environment entries, it provides another function, *putenv*, that lets you place entries into the environment.

■ **FACT:** *The* putenv *function lets a program place entries into its copy of the environment. If successful,* putenv *returns the value 0; if an error occurs,* putenv *returns the value −1.*

The following program (PUTDATA.C) uses *putenv* to define *DATA* with the entry *DATA=C:\DATA* and then uses *getenv* to display the value of *DATA*:

```
#include <stdlib.h>  /* needed for getenv and putenv */

main()
{
    if (putenv("DATA=C:\\DATA") == -1)
        puts("Error writing environment variable DATA");
    else
        puts(getenv("DATA"));
}
```

When you run the program, your screen shows

```
C:\DATA
```

As you can see, the run-time library routine *getenv* located the newly inserted entry *DATA* within the environment. However, if you issue the DOS SET command after you run PUTDATA, the entry *DATA* does not exist in the environment.

■ **TRAP:** *Each time DOS executes a program, it gives the program a copy of the current environment contents rather than access to the actual environment. When a program changes the environment with* putenv, *it is changing only its copy of the environment.*

Because the program changes only its copy of the environment, the routine *getenv* finds the new environment entry, but when the program is complete, the DOS environment is unchanged. The only way to change the contents of the DOS environment is to use the DOS SET command.

USING THE ENVIRONMENT

Most users organize a disk into subdirectories. If you write a program for a user, you cannot always assume that the program or data files reside in the current directory. For this reason, the DOS environment provides the *PATH* variable to store directories that contain executable files, and it provides the *APPEND* variable (DOS versions 3.2 and later) to store directories that contain data files. In your C programs, you can get access to these variables with the *getenv* function. As you'll see, the benefit in doing so is the flexibility your programs achieve.

Suppose you want to create a focused environment variable of your own. Such a variable, named *DATA*, for example, might allow the user to select the directory in which data files will reside. Once the user selects the directory and places the files into it, he or she can create an environment entry such as *DATA=C:\DATA* that tells the program where to look for the files.

The following program (DATACAT.C) needs to locate and open the file DATA.DAT. It first searches the environment for the user-defined entry *DATA*. If the program locates the entry, it tries to open the file DATA.DAT in the specified directory. If the program finds no environment entry for *DATA*, it tries to open the file in the root directory.

```
#include <stdlib.h>   /* needed for getenv */
#include <stdio.h>    /* needed for strcat and fopen */

main()
{
    FILE *fp;
    char pathname[64];

    pathname[0] = '\0';

    strcat(pathname, getenv("DATA"));
    strcat(pathname, "\\DATA.DAT");
    if (!(fp = fopen(pathname, "r")))
        printf("Error opening %s", pathname);
}
```

If you execute the program without an environment entry called *DATA*, your screen shows the following message:

```
Error opening \DATA.DAT
```

Now create the environment entry using the DOS SET command:

```
C> SET DATA = C:\LIB
```

When you run the program a second time, your screen shows

```
Error opening C:\LIB\DATA.DAT
```

As you can see, giving your programs access to the DOS environment relieves them of the requirement that they reside in a specific directory.

SUMMARY

Displaying the Current Environment

■ **FACT:** *A compiled C program passes a pointer to the list of environment entries. To access these entries, declare* main *as* main(int argc, char *argv[], char *envp[]) *in your programs.*

■ **FACT:** *Because* envp *is an array of pointers to character strings, some programmers treat* envp *as a pointer to a pointer to a value of type* char. *In such cases, programmers declare* envp *as* char **envp.

Accessing Environment Entries with *getenv*

■ **TIP:** *Entries in the environment are best viewed as variable names and their associated values. For example, the entry* LIB=C:\LIB *associates the variable* LIB *with the value* C:\LIB.

■ **FACT:** *The* getenv *function returns a pointer to a string that contains the value of the specified variable. If no such environment entry exists,* getenv *returns NULL. For example, the statement* puts(getenv("PATH")); *returns a pointer to the string associated with* PATH *in the program's environment.*

■ **TRAP:** *The* getenv *function is case sensitive. It does not match a lowercase argument string to an uppercase environment variable.*

Placing Entries into the Environment with *putenv*

■ **FACT:** *The* putenv *function lets a program place entries into its copy of the environment. If successful,* putenv *returns the value 0; if an error occurs,* putenv *returns the value −1.*

■ **TRAP:** *Each time DOS executes a program, it gives the program a copy of the current environment contents rather than access to the actual environment. When a program changes the environment with* putenv, *it is changing only its copy of the environment.*

GLOSSARY

environment A region in memory that DOS and OS/2 set aside each time your system starts. The environment is used to store information such as the system prompt, command path, and other information your programs can access, such as the location of specific files.

## CHAPTER 19

Program Termination Considerations

So far, all the programs we have examined begin execution at the first statement in *main* and end with the last statement in *main*. In some cases, however, processing requires a program to end immediately. In this chapter we investigate several run-time library functions that let a program end prematurely and several functions that influence the behavior of a program when it ends.

TERMINATING A PROGRAM WITH *exit*

Suppose that a user turns off an input device in the middle of a program's processing and that, as a result, the program needs to end abruptly. In such a case the *exit* function lets you terminate the program and return control to the operating system.

■ **FACT:** *The* exit *function terminates the current program and returns an exit status to the operating system.*

The following program (EXITTST.C) shows the use of the *exit* function. The program tries to open and display the file associated with *argv[1]*. If successful, the program displays the contents of the file; if unsuccessful, the program uses the *exit* function to end.

```
#include <stdlib.h>  /* needed for exit */
#include <stdio.h>   /* needed for file-related functions */

main(int argc, char *argv[])
{
    FILE *fp;
    char string[128];

    if (!(fp = fopen(argv[1], "r")))
        {
        printf("Error opening %s\n", argv[1]);
        exit(1);
        }

    while (fgets(string, sizeof(string), fp))
        printf("%s", string);
    fclose(fp);
}
```

If EXITTST cannot open the specified file, the program displays the error message, and the call to *exit* ends the program and returns the status value 1. If the program opens the file, execution continues at the *while* statement.

■ **TIP:** *To improve readability, construct your programs so that they have only one entry point and one exit point.*

Excessive use of the *exit* function can make a program's flow of control difficult to follow. You can rewrite most programs to perform the same processing without the need to use *exit*. For example, the following program (NOEXIT.C) performs the same processing as the previous program but without recourse to the *exit* function:

```
#include <stdio.h>  /* needed for file-related functions */

main(int argc, char *argv[])
{
    FILE *fp;
    char string[128];

    if (!(fp = fopen(argv[1], "r")))
        printf("Error opening %s\n", argv[1]);
    else
        {
        while (fgets(string, sizeof(string), fp))
            printf("%s", string);
        fclose(fp);
        }
}
```

In this case another programmer can easily locate the only possible point at which the program can end. So when is it acceptable to use *exit?* The answer relates to batch processing.

■ **FACT:** *The DOS batch command IF ERRORLEVEL tests the exit status of the previous program. If the exit value is greater than or equal to the specified value, the DOS batch processor evaluates the condition as true.*

The following batch file (ERRORCHK.BAT) executes the EXITTST program shown above and checks to see if it terminated with an error:

```
@ECHO OFF
IF NOT EXIST EXITTST.EXE GOTO ERROR
EXITTST %1
IF ERRORLEVEL 1 GOTO ERROR
ECHO EXITTST HAS EXECUTED SUCCESSFULLY
GOTO END
:ERROR
ECHO EXITTST HAS NOT EXECUTED SUCCESSFULLY
:END
```

The batch file first checks to see if the file EXITTST.EXE exists in the current directory. If it does not exist, the batch file jumps to the :ERROR label and prints the message *EXITTST HAS NOT EXECUTED SUCCESSFULLY.* If EXITTST.EXE does exist, the batch file runs EXITTST with the first argument specified on the command line. If EXITTST terminates with an exit status of 1 or greater, the batch file jumps to the :ERROR label and displays an error message. If EXITTST terminates with an exit status of less than 1, the batch file displays the message *EXITTST HAS EXECUTED SUCCESSFULLY* and jumps to the label :END. (If you're trying these examples on an OS/2 system, change the extension of your batch files from BAT to CMD.)

■ **FACT:** *By default, C programs exit with a status of 0. The* exit *function lets you specify an exit status for your program.*

The first program in this chapter, EXITTST, used the *exit* function to terminate when it could not open the file specified on the command line. In that case the critical processing was as follows:

```
if (!(fp = fopen(argv[1], "r")))
    {
    printf("Error opening %s\n", argv[1]);
    exit(1);
    }
```

As you can see, the call to *exit* passes the value 1 as an argument. The program's exit status is thus 1. If the program successfully opens and displays the contents of the file, the program exits with the default status of 0. By using *exit* in this manner, you increase your program's batch processing capabilities; the trade-off, however, is a possible decrease in the program's readability.

■ **TIP:** *If you use the* exit *function to end the processing of your program, try to restrict the use of* exit *to* main *so that the program does not mysteriously end during a function invocation.*

When you invoke the *exit* function, the compiler closes all open files. Later in this chapter you will learn that you can specify a list of functions, called an exit list, that executes as your program terminates.

■ **FACT:** *In addition to* exit, *C provides the run-time library function* _exit, *which ends your program without closing files or invoking the exit list routines.*

The *_exit* function lets you end a program without closing files or invoking the exit list routines. Most programs use the *exit* function instead of *_exit* because *exit* ensures that files are closed.

TERMINATING A PROGRAM WITH *abort*

The run-time library function *abort* ends the program and displays the following message:

```
Abnormal program termination
```

■ **FACT:** *The* abort *function ends the program with an exit status of 3 and displays a termination message.*

The following program (ABORTIT.C) uses *abort* to terminate when the *fopen* function cannot open the file associated with *argv[1]*:

```
#include <stdlib.h>   /* needed for abort */
#include <stdio.h>    /* needed for file-related functions */

main(int argc, char *argv[])
{
    FILE *fp;
    char string[128];
```

(continued)

continued

```
    if (!(fp = fopen(argv[1], "r")))
        {
        printf("Error opening %s\n", argv[1]);
        abort();
        }

    while (fgets(string, sizeof(string), fp))
        printf("%s", string);

    fclose(fp);
}
```

If ABORTIT cannot open the file you specify on the command line, it displays the following error message:

```
Error opening FILENAME.EXT
```

```
Abnormal program termination
```

Likewise, if you call the program from within a DOS batch file, the following condition yields a true result if the program terminates with *abort*:

```
IF ERRORLEVEL 3 GOTO ERROR
```

Programmers use *abort* to guarantee that the termination message is visible—the DOS I/O redirection operators cannot redirect the error message away from the screen to a file or device. In the next chapter you will learn how to develop programs that support I/O redirection and how to implement a function, such as *abort*, whose output DOS cannot redirect from the screen.

As we noted with regard to the *exit* function, you can rewrite most programs to remove the need for the *abort* function. Once again, you trade some functionality for improved readability.

DEBUGGING PROGRAMS WITH *assert*

Chapter 14 introduced the use of *printf* for debug write statements. At that time you found that by using preprocessor directives you can easily enable or disable debug write statements. The run-time library function *assert* is another handy debugging tool.

■ **FACT:** *The* assert *function tests a specific condition. If the condition fails,* assert *ends the program and displays an error message that identifies the filename and line number of the failed assertion.*

The *assert* function tests for a specific condition. If a routine is giving incorrect results, place several assertions that you believe to be true within the routine. If an assertion proves to be false, the program ends and *assert* displays an error message in the following format:

```
Assertion failed: file FILENAME.C line nnnn
```

The following program (ASSERT.C) is a candidate for debugging. It uses the function *str_copy* to copy the contents of the first string specified to the second.

```
main()
{
    static char source[128] = "source string";
    static char target[128] = "original target string";
    void str_copy(char *, char *);

    str_copy(source, target);

    puts(target);
}

void str_copy(char *source, char *target)
{
    while (*source)
        *target++ = *source++;
}
```

By examining the output of the program, you can see that the target string appears to lack a critical null character:

```
source stringet string
```

To isolate the problem, you can change *str_copy* to use *assert*, as shown here in ASSERT2.C:

```
#include <assert.h>  /* needed for assert */

main()
{
    static char source[128] = "source string";
    static char target[128] = "original target string";
    void str_copy(char *, char *);

    str_copy(source, target);

    puts(target);
}
```

(continued)

continued

```
void str_copy(char *source, char *target)
{
    while (*source)
        *target++ = *source++;

    assert(*source == '\0');   /* source string terminated? */
    assert(*target == '\0');   /* target string terminated? */
}
```

When you run the program, your screen shows

```
Assertion failed: *target == '\0', file ASSERT2.C, line 21
```

```
Abnormal program termination
```

As you can see, one of the assertions failed. If you edit your program, you'll find that it never appends to the null character the string *target*. Therefore, you need to either append the null character to *target* or change the loop to make the assignment a side effect of the *while* condition:

```
while (*target++ = *string++)
    { ; }
```

■ **FACT:** *You can enable and disable assertion processing based on the constant NDEBUG (for "no debug"). If NDEBUG is defined, the compiler does not include calls to* assert.

Rather than removing all calls to *assert* after your program is working, Microsoft C lets you direct the preprocessor not to include calls to *assert*. Simply define the identifier NDEBUG with a *#define* directive or use the /D compiler directive.

USING C EXIT LISTS

As the complexity of your programs increases, you might need to perform several housekeeping tasks when a program ends, such as closing files, restoring video attributes, or releasing shared resources in the OS/2 environment. The C run-time library function *atexit* lets you specify as many as 32 functions that C executes before your program ends.

■ **FACT:** *The* atexit *function lets you specify a function that executes when your program ends. The compiler supports the inclusion of as many as 32 functions in this exit list.*

The compiler executes the functions you specify in the exit list in the opposite order from that in which you invoke *atexit* to include them. In other words, the last function you specify is the first function to be executed.

The following program (EXITLIST.C) shows the use of *atexit*. The program places the functions *one*, *two*, and *three* in the exit list.

```c
#include <stdlib.h>  /* needed for atexit */

main()
{
    void one(void), two(void), three(void);

    atexit(one);
    atexit(two);
    atexit(three);
    puts("Program complete");
}

void one(void)
{
    puts("ONE");
}

void two(void)
{
    puts("TWO");
}

void three(void)
{
    puts("THREE");
}
```

When you run the program, your screen shows

```
Program complete
THREE
TWO
ONE
```

As you can see, the program executed the functions in the exit list in a last-in-first-out manner. Although this example of *atexit* is trivial, it offers a model for using the function to build complex applications. Remember, by using the _*exit* routine, your program can bypass the exit list when it terminates.

USING THE *return* STATEMENT FROM *main*

As you know, *main* is a function, and as with any other C function, you can use the *return* statement in *main* to terminate its processing.

■ **FACT:** *If the compiler encounters a* return *statement in* main, *it ends the program and returns an optional exit status.*

The following program (EXITMAIN.C) tries to open the file ALPHABET.DAT. If it opens the file successfully, the program then writes the letters of the alphabet to it five times. If the file-opening operation fails, a *return* statement ends the program with an exit status of 1. Remember, if you do not explicitly specify an exit status for *return*, the default value is 0.

```
#include <stdio.h>  /* needed for file-related functions */

main(int argc, char *argv[])
{
    FILE *fp;
    char string[128];

    if (!(fp = fopen(argv[1], "r")))
        {
        printf("Error opening %s\n", argv[1]);
        return (1);
        }

    while (fgets(string, sizeof(string), fp))
        printf("%s", string);

    fclose(fp);
}
```

As previously discussed, most programs can be written to have only one entry point and one exit point. To improve the readability of your programs, you should generally try to avoid using *return* as describe above (prior to the end of *main*).

SUMMARY

Terminating a Program with *exit*

■ **FACT:** *The* exit *function terminates the current program and returns an exit status to the operating system.*

■ **TIP:** *To improve readability, construct your programs so that they have only one entry point and one exit point.*

■ **FACT:** *The DOS batch command IF ERRORLEVEL tests the exit status of the previous program. If the exit value is greater than or equal to the specified value, the DOS batch processor evaluates the condition as true.*

■ **FACT:** *By default, C programs exit with a status of 0. The* exit *function lets you specify an exit status for your program.*

■ **TIP:** *If you use the* exit *function to end the processing of your program, try to restrict the use of* exit *to* main *so that the program does not mysteriously end during a function invocation.*

■ **FACT:** *In addition to* exit, *C provides the run-time library function* _exit, *which ends your program without closing files or invoking the exit list routines.*

Terminating a Program with *abort*

■ **FACT:** *The* abort *function ends the program with an exit status of 3 and displays a termination message.*

Debugging Programs with *assert*

■ **FACT:** *The* assert *function tests a specific condition. If the condition fails,* assert *ends the program and displays an error message that identifies the filename and line number of the failed assertion.*

■ **FACT:** *You can enable and disable assertion processing based on the constant NDEBUG (for "no debug"). If NDEBUG is defined, the compiler does not include calls to* assert.

Using C Exit Lists

■ **FACT:** *The* atexit *function lets you specify a function that executes when your program ends. The compiler supports the inclusion of as many as 32 functions in this exit list.*

Using the *return* Statement from *main*

■ **FACT:** *If the compiler encounters a* return *statement in* main, *it ends the program and returns an optional exit status.*

GLOSSARY

exit list A list of functions that a program executes when your program terminates. The C run-time library routine *atexit* lets you define the functions contained in the exit list.

exit status A value that a terminating program returns to the operating system. The DOS batch command IF ERRORLEVEL lets you test a program's exit status.

## CHAPTER 20

Writing Programs That Support I/O Redirection

If you have worked closely with DOS, OS/2, or UNIX, you know that each operating system supports redirection operators that you can use on the command line to change the destination of a program's output or to change the source of a program's input.

In this chapter we examine the I/O redirection operators and their function. I/O redirection gives your programs tremendous flexibility, and as you will learn, writing C programs that support it is not difficult.

REVIEWING THE REDIRECTION OPERATORS

By default, each time you issue a DOS or OS/2 command, the system writes the output on your screen. For example, at the system prompt, issue the following command:

```
C> LINK /HELP
```

Your screen displays a summary of the Linker options. Now, with your printer turned on and on line, issue the following command at the DOS prompt:

```
C> LINK /HELP > PRN
```

In this case the output redirection operator, >, tells DOS to write the output to your printer.

■ **FACT:** *The output redirection operator, >, tells the system to route the output of the com-mand to the specified file or device.*

Now create a file called OPTIONS.LNK that contains the valid options for the LINK command. At the DOS prompt, type:

```
C> LINK /HELP > OPTIONS.LNK
```

The redirection operator tells DOS to redirect output from your screen to the filename. If a file exists with the same name, the system overwrites its contents.

To create a similar file that contains the valid options for the CL command, type the following command:

```
C> CL /HELP > OPTIONS.CL
```

The CL /HELP command requires you to press Enter several times to see successive screens of information. Because we have redirected the output of the command, the system also re-directs the prompt

```
(press <return> to continue)
```

As a result your system might appear to hang after you issue the command; simply press the Enter key several times to complete the command. You might find it convenient to print a copy of OPTIONS.CL for future reference.

When you run the program, notice that the compiler's copyright information appears on your screen despite the redirection of the command output. As you will see later in this chapter, C provides a way to circumvent redirection of output.

■ **FACT:** *The input redirection operator, <, tells the system to route a command's source of input away from the keyboard to a file.*

By default, programs expect input to come from the keyboard. In some cases, how-ever, you might want to sort an existing file or display it a screenful at a time. The input redi-rection operator lets you specify a file as the source of input for a program.

The DOS and OS/2 MORE command displays redirected input a screenful at a time. At the *--More--* prompt, the user presses any key to display the next screenful of information.

Let's use the MORE command to display the file you just created, OPTIONS.CL. At the system prompt, type the following command:

```
C> MORE < OPTIONS.CL
```

Your screen displays the first screenful of information, which is shown on the following page.

```
                       C COMPILER OPTIONS

                        -MEMORY MODEL-
/AS small model (default)           /AC compact model
/AM medium model                    /AL large model
/AH huge model
                        -OPTIMIZATION-
/O enable optimization (same as /Ot)  /Oa ignore aliasing
/Od disable optimizations           /Oi enable intrinsic functions
/Ol enable loop optimizations       /On disable "unsafe" optimizations
/Op enable precision optimizations  /Or disable in_line return
/Os optimize for space              /Ot optimize for speed (default)
/Ox max. optimization (/Oailt /Gs)
                        -CODE GENERATION-
/G0 8086 instructions (default)     /G1  186 instructions
/G2  286 instructions               /Gm put strings in constant segment
/Gc Pascal style function calls     /Gs no stack checking
/Gt[number] data size threshold
                        -OUTPUT FILES-
/Fa[assembly listing file]          /Fb[bound executable file]
/Fc[mixed source/object listing file]  /Fe<executable file>
/Fl[object listing file]            /Fm[map file]
/Fo<object file>                    /Fs[source listing file]
                        -PREPROCESSOR-
-- More --
```

To display the next screenful of information, press any key. If you type the Ctrl-C combination, the system ends the command and displays the system prompt.

■ **FACT:** *The append redirection operator, >>, tells the system to append the contents of the redirected output to an existing file. If the file does not exist, the system creates it.*

The append redirection operator, >>, tells DOS to append the output of a DOS or OS/2 command to an existing file. Suppose the files DEFN.H and TEST.C exist as follows:

```
/* defn.h -- macro definitions */

#define SQUARE(x) ((x) * (x))
#define MIN(x, y) ((x) < (y) ? x : y)
```

```
/* test.c */

main()
{
    printf("Square of 5 is %d\n", SQUARE(5));
    printf("Minimum value is %d\n", MIN(2 * 6, 2 + 6));
}
```

To create the file TESTFILE.C, which contains a copy of DEFN.H, enter the following command:

```
C> TYPE DEFN.H > TESTFILE.C
```

Then enter the following command, which uses redirection to append the contents of TEST.C to the file TESTFILE.C:

```
C> TYPE TEST.C >> TESTFILE.C
```

TESTFILE.C now contains the following:

```
/* defn.h -- macro definitions */

#define SQUARE(x) ((x) * (x))
#define MIN(x, y) ((x) < (y) ? x : y)

/* test.c */

main()
{
    printf("Square of the value 5 is %d\n", SQUARE(5));
    printf("Minimum value is %d\n", MIN(2 * 6, 2 + 6));
}
```

■ **FACT:** *The pipe redirection operator,* ¦*, tells the system to make the output of one program the input to another.*

The pipe operator, ¦, is the most powerful redirection operator. It changes the output destination for one command and makes it the input source for another command. For example, the following command directs DOS or OS/2 to route the output of the TYPE command to become the input to the MORE command:

```
C> TYPE OPTIONS.CL ¦ MORE
```

The system then displays the contents of the file a screenful at a time.

The DOS commands SORT and FIND also support I/O redirection. The SORT command rearranges the contents of a file. For example, use the output redirection operator to create the file FILES.DIR, which contains the files in the current directory:

```
C> DIR > FILES.DIR
```

Next, use the input redirection operator to sort the contents of the file FILES.DIR:

```
C> SORT < FILES.DIR
```

The FIND command searches redirected input for a key word or phrase. The following command, for example, displays the name of each subdirectory in the current directory. Input is redirected to FIND from the file you sorted, FILES.DIR.

```
C> FIND "<DIR>" < FILES.DIR
```

When you execute this command, the screen shows the subdirectories of the current directory, arranged alphabetically.

You can use more than one redirection operator in a command line. The following command, for example, sends a sorted directory listing to your printer:

```
C> DIR : SORT > PRN
```

The following command displays all the directory entries for your C source files, a screenful at a time:

```
C> DIR *.C : MORE
```

Using the pipe operator twice, you can even display a sorted listing of your C files a screenful at a time:

```
C> DIR *.C : FIND " C  " : SORT : MORE
```

As you can see, I/O redirection gives you considerable command line flexibility. By developing a collection of C utility programs that support I/O redirection, you can increase your productivity considerably.

SUPPORTING I/O REDIRECTION

Before we examine a C program that supports I/O redirection, you need to understand the terms *stdin* and *stdout*.

■ **FACT:** *Each time a program executes, DOS defines the program's source of input as stdin and defines the source of output as stdout. If I/O redirection is not used, stdin points to the keyboard, and stdout points to your screen.*

The standard input source, stdin, is defined by DOS and OS/2 to be your keyboard, unless you redirect it, and the standard output destination, stdout, is normally your screen. When you issue a command that redirects I/O, such as the following,

```
C> MORE < FILENAME.EXT
```

or

```
C> DIR > PRN
```

the system changes the standard input source or the output destination to reference the specified file or device.

■ **FACT:** *C provides two predefined file pointers,* stdin *and* stdout, *which reference the source of input and the destination of output as defined by DOS and OS/2.*

The include file stdio.h defines *stdin* and *stdout* as file pointers to standard input and standard output. A C program that gets its input from *stdin* and writes its output to *stdout* is ready to support I/O redirection.

■ **FACT:** *The macro* getchar *is defined in terms of* stdin, *and the macro* putchar *is defined in terms of* stdout.

In Chapter 13 you learned that the routine *getc* returns the next character in the specified file, for example:

```
letter = getc(fp);
```

In the file stdio.h, C defines *getchar* in terms of *stdin*, as follows:

```
#define getchar() getc(stdin)
```

By default, *stdin* points to the keyboard. If you redirect I/O, *stdin* points to the new input source. Therefore, a program written to use *getchar* for input already supports input redirection.

In Chapter 13 you also learned that the *putc* routine writes the specified character to a file, for example:

```
putc(letter, fp);
```

Again, stdio.h defines *putchar* in terms of *stdout*, as follows:

```
#define putchar(c) putc((c), stdout)
```

By default, *stdout* points to the screen. If the command line redirects the output of the program, the file pointer *stdout* points to the correct location. Therefore, a program written to perform its output using *putchar* is ready to perform output redirection.

The following program (ALPHA.C) uses *putchar* to write the letters of the alphabet on your screen five times:

```
#include <stdio.h>  /* needed for putchar */

main()
{
    char letter;
    int count;

    for (count = 0; count < 5; count++)
```

(continued)

continued

```
        {
        for (letter = 'A'; letter <= 'Z'; letter++)
            putchar(letter);
        putchar('\n');
        }
    }
```

When you run the program, your screen shows

```
ABCDEFGHIJKLMNOPQRSTUVWXYZ
ABCDEFGHIJKLMNOPQRSTUVWXYZ
ABCDEFGHIJKLMNOPQRSTUVWXYZ
ABCDEFGHIJKLMNOPQRSTUVWXYZ
ABCDEFGHIJKLMNOPQRSTUVWXYZ
```

You can redirect the output of this program to a file named ALPHABET.DAT by typing the following command at the system prompt:

```
C> ALPHA > ALPHABET.DAT
```

The program now sends its output to the specified file. Use the TYPE command to verify the contents of ALPHABET.DAT, as follows:

```
C> TYPE ALPHABET.DAT
ABCDEFGHIJKLMNOPQRSTUVWXYZ
ABCDEFGHIJKLMNOPQRSTUVWXYZ
ABCDEFGHIJKLMNOPQRSTUVWXYZ
ABCDEFGHIJKLMNOPQRSTUVWXYZ
ABCDEFGHIJKLMNOPQRSTUVWXYZ

C>
```

C defines *putchar* in terms of *stdout*; therefore, the program supports I/O redirection with no changes. The following program (LOWER.C) uses *getchar* to read letters and convert them to lowercase until it encounters an end of file:

```
#include <stdio.h>   /* needed for getchar, putchar, and EOF */
#include <ctype.h>   /* needed for tolower */

main()
{
    char letter;

    while ((letter = getchar()) != EOF)
        putchar(tolower(letter));
}
```

If you run this program from the DOS prompt, as follows:

```
A> LOWER
```

it echoes in lowercase each line that you enter. To end the program, send an end of file character, Ctrl-Z (^Z). To type Ctrl-Z, hold down Ctrl and press Z. When you press Enter, the program ends.

If you run LOWER from the system prompt, as follows:

```
C> LOWER < ALPHABET.DAT
```

DOS redirects the program's input from the keyboard to the file ALPHABET.DAT, and your screen shows

```
abcdefghijklmnopqrstuvwxyz
abcdefghijklmnopqrstuvwxyz
abcdefghijklmnopqrstuvwxyz
abcdefghijklmnopqrstuvwxyz
abcdefghijklmnopqrstuvwxyz
```

You can also use the pipe symbol to redirect the output of the program ALPHA to become the input to the program LOWER, as follows:

```
C> ALPHA | LOWER
```

When the program ALPHA ends, DOS sends a Ctrl-Z character to LOWER, which ends its processing.

The following program (SHOWWORD.C) searches for the word or phrase specified by the first command line argument. If SHOWWORD locates the word or phrase, it displays the line that contains the phrase, as well as the line number.

```c
#include <string.h>   /* needed for strstr */
#include <stdio.h>    /* needed for fgets and stdin */

main(int argc, char *argv[])
{
    char string[128];
    int line = 0;

    while (fgets(string, sizeof(string), stdin))
        {
        ++line;
        if (strstr(string, argv[1]))
            printf("%02d %s", line, string);
        }
}
```

The SHOWWORD program uses *stdin* as the file pointer to the *fgets* routine. If you run the program as follows:

```
C> SHOWWORD argv < SHOWWORD.C
```

your screen shows

```
04 main(int argc, char *argv[])
12         if (strstr(string, argv[1]))
```

(SHOWWORD does not expand tab characters; if you use them in your input file, the SHOWWORD output might not match precisely.) A command such as

```
C:\MSC> DIR *.* ; SHOWWORD "<DIR>"
```

results in output such as the following:

```
06 .              <DIR>     01-10-89    9:36a
07 ..             <DIR>     01-10-89    9:36a
09 INCLUDE        <DIR>     01-10-89    9:39a
10 BIN            <DIR>     01-10-89    9:40a
11 LIB            <DIR>     01-10-89    9:42a
12 SOURCE         <DIR>     01-10-89    9:45a
```

USING *stderr* FOR ERROR MESSAGES

In Chapter 19 you examined the *abort* function, which ends the current program and displays the following message:

```
Abnormal program termination
```

At that time we noted that the advantage to using *abort* is that DOS and OS/2 cannot redirect the output of the function. The following program (MAKEIT.C) tries to open the file ALPHABET.DAT to write the letters of the alphabet to the file five times:

```c
#include <stdio.h>  /* needed for fopen, puts, putc, and fclose */

main()
{
    FILE *fp;
    char letter;
    int count;

    if (!(fp = fopen("ALPHABET.DAT", "w")))
        puts("Error opening ALPHABET.DAT");
    else
        {
        for (count = 0; count < 5; count++)
```

(continued)

continued

```
            {
            for (letter = 'A'; letter <= 'Z'; letter++)
                putc(letter, fp);
            putc(letter, fp);
            }
        fclose(fp);
        }
}
```

If this program fails to open the file ALPHABET.DAT (if ALPHABET.DAT is read-only, for example), the program displays the following message:

```
Error opening ALPHABET.DAT
```

If you redirect the output of this program to a file or to another program, you will not see a message if an error occurs. To prevent redirection of your error messages, write them to the predefined file pointer *stderr*.

■ **FACT:** *The file stdio.h defines the file pointer* stderr, *which points to your screen. The system cannot redirect output that is written to* stderr.

If your programs write their error messages to the file pointer *stderr*, the compiler ensures that the error message appears on the screen. The following program (MAKEIT2.C) uses *stderr* to display the file-opening error message:

```
#include <stdio.h>  /* needed for fopen, fputs, stderr, putc, and fclose */

main()
{
    FILE *fp;
    int count;
    char letter;

    if (!(fp = fopen("ALPHABET.DAT", "w")))
        fputs("Error opening ALPHABET.DAT", stderr);
    else
        {
        for (count = 0; count < 5; count++)
            {
            for (letter = 'A'; letter <= 'Z'; ++letter)
                putc(letter, fp);
            putc('\n', fp);
            }
        fclose(fp);
        }
}
```

The program uses *fputs* rather than *puts* to display the error message, and it specifies *stderr* as the destination of the message.

■ **TIP:** *Get in the habit of writing error messages to* stderr. *Most DOS commands do so to prevent the user from redirecting critical error messages.*

Now let's write a function named EXITLIST.C (as promised in Chapter 19) that is similar to the *abort* function. The *abort_program* function lets you pass an error message that will be written to *stderr* and a status value with which the program will exit.

```
void abort_program(char *message, int status)
{
    fputs(message, stderr);
    exit(status);
}
```

By letting the calling program pass an error message and exit status to the function, you can use your *abort_program* function for many applications and error types.

WHAT ARE *stdprn* AND *stdaux*?

The file stdio.h defines two additional file pointers, *stdprn* and *stdaux*, that your programs can access. The first, *stdprn*, points to your printer; and the second, *stdaux*, points to your first serial communications port, COM1.

■ **FACT:** *C defines the file pointer* stdprn *as a file pointer to the standard printer device, and it defines* stdaux *as a file pointer to the serial port COM1.*

The following program (STDPRN.C) writes each redirected input character it receives to the printer using *stdprn*:

```
#include <stdio.h>   /* needed for getchar, EOF, putc, and stdprn */

main()
{
    char letter;

    while ((letter = getchar()) != EOF)
        putc(letter, stdprn);
}
```

If you redirect input to this program, as in either of the following cases:

```
C> STDPRN < ALPHABET.DAT
```

or

```
C> DIR ¦ STDPRN
```

the program writes its output to your system printer.

REVISITING THE
DOS *FILES=* ENTRY IN CONFIG.SYS

Each time DOS starts, it searches the root directory of the boot disk for the file CONFIG.SYS. If DOS locates this file, it uses the entries in the file to help configure the operating system. The *FILES=* entry specifies the number of files a program can open at one time. If CONFIG.SYS does not contain a *FILES=* entry, DOS uses the default value 8. As we have discussed, however, DOS predefines five file pointers that the C compiler references with *stdin*, *stdout*, *stderr*, *stdprn*, and *stdaux*. Thus, only three additional file pointers remain for the program. As discussed in Chapter 1, the C compiler needs to open several files during compilation. If DOS supports only three files, the compiler cannot execute. You can now better appreciate the reason you were told in Chapter 1 to change CONFIG.SYS to include an entry such as *FILES=20*. (If you are running OS/2, you do not need the *FILES=* entry in your CONFIG.SYS file.)

SUMMARY

Reviewing the Redirection Operators

■ **FACT:** *The output redirection operator, >, tells the system to route the output of the command to the specified file or device.*

■ **FACT:** *The input redirection operator, <, tells the system to route a command's source of input away from the keyboard to a file.*

■ **FACT:** *The append redirection operator, >>, tells the system to append the contents of the redirected output to an existing file. If the file does not exist, the system creates it.*

■ **FACT:** *The pipe redirection operator, |, tells the system to make the output of one program the input to another.*

Supporting I/O Redirection

■ **FACT:** *Each time a program executes, DOS defines the program's source of input as stdin and defines the source of output as stdout. If I/O redirection is not used, stdin points to the keyboard, and stdout points to your screen.*

■ **FACT:** *C provides two predefined file pointers,* stdin *and* stdout, *which reference the source of input and the destination of output as defined by DOS and OS/2.*

■ **FACT:** *The macro* getchar *is defined in terms of* stdin, *and the macro* putchar *is defined in terms of* stdout.

Using *stderr* for Error Messages

■ **FACT:** *The file stdio.h defines the file pointer* stderr, *which points to your screen. The system cannot redirect output that is written to* stderr.

■ **TIP:** *Get in the habit of writing error messages to* stderr. *Most DOS commands do so to prevent the user from redirecting critical error messages.*

What Are *stdprn* and *stdaux*?

■ **FACT:** *C defines the file pointer* stdprn *as a file pointer to the standard printer device, and it defines* stdaux *as a file pointer to the serial port COM1.*

GLOSSARY

I/O redirection The process of using either the system input redirection operator or the system output redirection operator to route input to a command from a source other than the keyboard, or to write output from a command to a destination other than the screen.

stdaux The location of the standard auxiliary device. By default, DOS and OS/2 associate stdaux with COM1.

stderr The standard error destination for programs. Stderr always points to the screen. The DOS and OS/2 redirection operators cannot redirect error messages written to stderr away from the screen.

stdin The standard input source for programs. By default, DOS and OS/2 associate stdin with the keyboard. By using the input redirection operator, <, you can redirect stdin from the keyboard to an existing file.

stdout The standard output destination for programs. By default, DOS and OS/2 associate stdout with the screen. By using the output (>) or append (>>) redirection operator, you can redirect stdout from the screen to a file or a different device.

stdprn The location of the standard printer device. By default, DOS and OS/2 associate stdprn with LPT1.

CHAPTER 21

Revisiting File Operations

In Chapter 13 you learned how to perform basic file manipulation operations in C. In subsequent chapters you have written programs that display the contents of one or more files, expand wildcard characters during file manipulation operations, and copy the contents of one ASCII file to another.

In this chapter we examine several convenient file manipulation capabilities built into the C run-time library. We develop programs that enable you to rename files, delete files, and change the attributes of a file. In addition, we look at ways to create and manipulate temporary files and at several ways to traverse your files by changing the current file position.

Like many of the chapters to follow, this chapter is packed with information. The best way to absorb all the material is to execute the sample programs.

MANIPULATING EXISTING FILES

As your programs' processing requirements increase, so does the need to manipulate files quickly. The run-time library functions we examine in this section simplify the manipulation of existing files. You learn how to delete and rename files and how to see whether a given file exists on disk. You also learn how to set a file to read, write, or read/write access, and you look at the advantages to doing so.

To determine whether a file exists, many programs try to open the file for read operations. An unsuccessful attempt indicates that the file does not exist or that the file cannot be opened in the specified mode. The C run-time library function *access* provides a less crude method of file interrogation.

■ **FACT:** *The* access *function lets you determine whether a file exists on disk and whether your program can access the file in a specified mode. If the file does not exist or cannot be accessed in the specified mode,* access *returns −1; if the file does exist and can be accessed in the specified mode,* access *returns 0.*

The format for a call to the *access* function is as follows:

```
result = access("filename", access_mode);
```

The *filename* argument is a character string containing either the name of a file in the current directory or a complete pathname. The *access_mode* argument contains one of the values shown in the following table:

Mode	Meaning
0	Does the file exist on disk?
2	Does the file have write permission?
4	Does the file have read permission?
6	Does the file have read and write permission?

Many programs simply attempt to open a file using *fopen*. If the file cannot be opened, the programs display a general error message. By using *access*, a program can provide more specific information to the user as to why the file could not be opened.

In Chapter 17 you wrote a program called MYCOPY.C that copies the contents of one ASCII file to another, for example,

```
C> MYCOPY SOURCE.TXT TARGET.TXT
```

If the target file specified in the command line exists on disk, the program overwrites it. The following revision of MYCOPY.C (MYCOPY2.C) uses *access* to test whether the specified target file already exists. If it exists, the program displays the following prompt:

```
TARGET.TXT already exists. Overwrite (Y/N)?
```

If the user enters Y, the program overwrites the existing file. If the user enters N, the program ends without copying the file.

```
#include <io.h>      /* needed for access */
#include <stdio.h>   /* needed for getchar, toupper, and file functions */

main(int argc, char *argv[])
{
    FILE *source, *target;
    char string[256], response = 'Y';
    int result;

    if (argc < 3)
        printf("MYCOPY:  must specify source and target file");
    else
        {
        if (access(argv[2], 0) == 0)  /* does target exist? */
            do
                {
                printf("\n%s already exists - Overwrite (Y/N)?", argv[2]);
                response = getchar();
                while (getchar() != '\n')
                    { ; }
                response = toupper(response);
                } /* loop until Y or N */
            while (response != 'Y' && response != 'N');

        if (response == 'Y')  /* overwrite the file */
            {
            if (!(source = fopen(argv[1], "r")))
                printf("MYCOPY:  error opening %s", argv[1]);

            else if (!(target = fopen(argv[2], "w")))
                printf("MYCOPY:  error opening %s", argv[2]);

            else
                {
                while (fgets(string, sizeof(string), source))
                    fputs(string, target);
                fclose(source);
                fclose(target);
                }
            }
        }
}
```

Although this program helps prevent you from overwriting an existing file, it does have one shortcoming. If the existing file is a read-only file, the program tries to open it in write access mode and fails. Using an additional call to *access*,

```
result = access(argv[2], 2);
```

the following program (MYCOPY3.C) examines the existing target file to see whether it can be overwritten. If you cannot write to the file, the program displays the following message and ends:

```
MYCOPY:  target file FILENAME.EXT is read-only
```

```c
#include <io.h>     /* needed for access */
#include <stdio.h>  /* needed for getchar, toupper, and file functions */

main(int argc, char *argv[])
{
    FILE *source, *target;
    char string[256], response = 'Y';
    int result;

    if (argc < 3)
        printf("MYCOPY:  must specify source and target file");
    else
        {
        if (access(argv[2], 0) == 0)  /* does target exist? */
            {
            if (access(argv[2], 2) == 0)  /* is it writable? */
                {
                do
                    {
                    printf("\n%s already exists - Overwrite (Y/N)?",
                            argv[2]);
                    response = getchar();
                    while (getchar() != '\n')
                        { ; }
                    response = toupper(response);
                    } /* loop until Y or N */
                while (response != 'Y' && response != 'N');
                }
            else
                {
                printf("MYCOPY:  target file %s is read-only", argv[2]);
                response = 'N';
                }
            }
        if (response == 'Y')  /* overwrite the file */
            {
            if (!(source = fopen(argv[1], "r")))
                printf("MYCOPY:  error opening %s", argv[1]);
```

(continued)

continued

```
        else if (!(target = fopen(argv[2], "w")))
            printf("MYCOPY:  error opening %s", argv[2]);

        else
            {
            while (fgets(string, sizeof(string), source))
                fputs(string, target);
            fclose(source);
            fclose(target);
            }
        }
    }
}
```

You have probably used the DOS (or OS/2) ATTRIB command, which lets you set or display the attribute of a file.

For example, the following command sets the file ALPHABET.DAT to read-only:

```
C> ATTRIB +R ALPHABET.DAT
```

You cannot change or delete the contents of a read-only file. If you attempt to delete a read-only file, the system displays the message *Access denied*.

Of course, you can still access the file in a read-only mode, using, for example, the TYPE or PRINT command. By setting a file to read-only, you prevent an errant command from deleting or overwriting the file. All files on your disk that don't change on a regular basis are good candidates for read-only status.

By using the C run-time library routine *chmod*, your programs can set a file to read-only or to read/write access.

■ **FACT:** *The* chmod *function lets you set a file's access modes. If successful,* chmod *returns the value 0. If an error occurs,* chmod *returns −1.*

The following program (CHMOD.C) is similar to the ATTRIB command. It uses a command line option to specify the access mode to set, read-only or read/write.

```
#include <dos.h>          /* needed for _dos_findfirst and _dos_findnext */
#include <sys\types.h>    /* needed for chmod */
#include <sys\stat.h>     /* needed for S_IWRITE and S_IREAD */
#include <stdio.h>        /* needed for file-related functions */
#include <string.h>       /* needed for stricmp */
```

(continued)

continued

```
main(int argc, char *argv[])
{
    int chmod_result;
    int result;
    struct find_t fileinfo;
    enum operation {readonly, readwrite, invalid} setting;

    if (argc < 3)
        puts("CHMOD:  must specify +R or -R FILENAME.EXT");

    else
        {
        if (stricmp(argv[1], "+R") == 0)
            setting = readonly;
        else if (stricmp(argv[1], "-R") == 0)
            setting = readwrite;
        else
            {
            setting = invalid;
            puts("CHMOD:  invalid option - use +R or -R");
            }

        if (setting != invalid)
            {
            result = _dos_findfirst(argv[2], 0, &fileinfo);

            if (result != 0)
                printf("CHMOD:  error accessing %s", argv[2]);

            while (result == 0)
                {
                if (setting == readonly)
                    chmod_result = chmod(fileinfo.name, S_IREAD);
                else
                    chmod_result = chmod(fileinfo.name, S_IREAD | S_IWRITE);
                if (chmod_result)
                    printf("Error modifying %s\n", fileinfo.name);
                else
                    printf("File %s modified\n", fileinfo.name);

                result = _dos_findnext(&fileinfo);
                }
            }
        }
}
```

If you execute the program as follows, the program sets ALPHABET.DAT to read-only:

C> CHMOD +R ALPHABET.DAT

If you execute the program with the –R option, it sets the file to read/write access:

C> CHMOD -R ALPHABET.DAT

CHMOD.C uses the run-time library routines *_dos_findfirst* and *_dos_findnext*, so it supports the DOS wildcard characters. Because it uses routines in dos.h, however, it will not run under OS/2. Notice that CHMOD.C uses the constants S_IWRITE and S_IREAD to specify write access and read access. The include file sys\stat.h defines these constants. The expression

S_IWRITE ¦ S_IREAD

uses the bitwise OR operator to specify write or read access. CHMOD.C gives you a feel for how easy developing utility programs in C can be.

■ **TIP:** *Many programmers use the* chmod *function to set critical data files to read-only before the program ends. Doing so protects the files from being deleted or overwritten by a misguided user command.*

The *chmod* function is convenient for protecting files from the end user. A program can use *chmod* to set a file to write access when the program begins and then to set the file to read-only when the program ends.

In some cases a program needs to delete a file from the disk when the file is no longer needed. The C run-time library function *remove* lets you delete the specified file.

■ **FACT:** *The* remove *function deletes the specified file. If the file is deleted,* remove *returns the value 0; if the file is not deleted,* remove *returns the value –1.*

The following program (DELETE.C) enhances the DOS (or OS/2) DEL command by displaying the following prompt for each file specified:

Delete FILENAME.EXT (Y/N)?

If the user types Y and presses Enter, the program deletes the file; if the user types N and presses Enter, the program continues processing the next file specified, assuming the command line contains wildcard characters.

```
#include <dos.h>      /* needed for _dos functions */
#include <stdio.h>    /* needed for remove and file-related functions */

main(int argc, char *argv[])
{
    int result;
```

(continued)

continued

```
    struct find_t fileinfo;
    char response;

    if (argc < 2)
        puts("DELETE:  must specify filename");
    else
        {
        result = _dos_findfirst(argv[1], 0, &fileinfo);
        if (result != 0)
            printf("DELETE:  no such file %s", argv[1]);
        else
            while (!result)  /* expand wildcards */
                {
                do
                    {
                    printf("Delete %s (Y/N)?", fileinfo.name);
                    response = getchar();
                    while (getchar() != '\n')
                        { ; }
                    response = toupper(response);
                    }  /* loop until Y or N */
                while (response != 'N' && response != 'Y');

                if (response == 'Y')  /* delete the file */
                    {
                    if (remove(fileinfo.name))
                        printf("DELETE:  cannot delete %s\n",
                                fileinfo.name);
                    }

                result = _dos_findnext(&fileinfo);
                }
        }
}
```

■ **TIP:** *By using the* remove *function, your programs can easily create and later delete temporary files without user intervention.*

When you need to rename a file, you use the C run-time library routine *rename.*

■ **FACT:** *The* rename *function lets you rename a file. If the file is renamed,* rename *returns the value 0; if the file is not renamed,* rename *returns an error status.*

The following program (RNM.C) uses *rename* to rename the file specified by the second command line entry to the name specified by the third command line entry. For example, the following command,

```
C> RNM ALPHABET.DAT ALPHABET.BAK
```

renames the file ALPHABET.DAT as ALPHABET.BAK. The two filenames on the command line are used via *argv[1]* and *argv[2]* as arguments to the *rename* function.

```
#include <io.h>  /* needed for access and rename */

main(int argc, char *argv[])
{
    int status;

    if (argc < 3)
        puts("RNM:  must specify source and target");
    else
        {
        if (access(argv[2], 0) == 0)  /* does target exist? */
            printf("%s already exists", argv[2]);
        else if (rename(argv[1], argv[2]) != 0)
            puts("RNM:  error renaming files");
        }
}
```

Although you cannot use the DOS REN command to rename a file from one subdirectory to another, you can do so with RNM.C. For example, the following command moves ALPHA.C to the DOS directory:

```
C> RNM ALPHA.C \DOS\ALPHA.C
```

As you can see, the C run-time library routines enable you to develop routines with capabilities similar to those of the DOS commands.

BUILDING AND PARSING PATHNAMES

A DOS pathname can consist of a disk drive letter, a subdirectory name, an 8-character filename, and a 3-character extension. DOS allows you to process filenames of a maximum of 64 characters. Because DOS pathnames are commonly required, the C run-time library provides a function that builds a complete path from its composite parts, and another function that breaks a pathname into a disk drive letter, a directory, a filename, and an extension.

■ **FACT:** *The* _makepath *function returns a character string containing a complete DOS pathname based on four component parts: drive letter, directory name, filename, and 3-character extension.*

The following program (MKPATH.C) uses the _*makepath* function to build a complete pathname. The _*makepath* function assigns to the string variable named in its first argument a pathname built from the elements specified in the four subsequent arguments.

```
#include <stdlib.h>   /* needed for _makepath */

main()
{
    char pathname[_MAX_PATH];

    _makepath(pathname, "C", "\\DOS", "FILENAME", "EXT");

    printf("The complete pathname is %s", pathname);
}
```

When you run the program, your screen shows

```
The complete pathname is C:\DOS\FILENAME.EXT
```

The program uses the constant _MAX_PATH defined in stdlib.h to create a string large enough to store a complete pathname.

In the opposite manner, the C run-time library function _splitpath parses a pathname, or breaks the complete pathname into its component parts.

■ **FACT:** *The* _splitpath *function breaks a complete DOS pathname into its components: disk drive letter, directory name, filename, and extension.*

The following program (PARSE.C) uses _splitpath to parse a pathname. The program uses the constants _MAX_DRIVE, _MAX_DIR, _MAX_FNAME, and _MAX_EXT defined in stdlib.h.

```
#include <stdlib.h>   /* needed for _splitpath and pathname constants */

main()
{
    char drive[_MAX_DRIVE], directory[_MAX_DIR];
    char filename[_MAX_FNAME], extension[_MAX_EXT];
    static char pathname[_MAX_PATH] = "C:\\DOS\\FILENAME.EXT";

    _splitpath(pathname, drive, directory, filename, extension);

    printf("Complete path is \%s\n", pathname);
    printf("Drive is %s\nDirectory is %s\nFile is %s\nExtension is %s",
           drive, directory, filename, extension);
}
```

When you run the program, your screen shows

```
Complete path is C:\DOS\FILENAME.EXT
Drive is C:
Directory is \DOS\
File is FILENAME
Extension is .EXT
```

TRAVERSING YOUR FILE

So far, any file-reading routines we have developed have read a file from start to finish sequentially, one line after another. In this section we will examine several run-time library functions that let you move to specific positions in a file without reading the contents. The first such function is *rewind*, a run-time library routine that sets a file pointer back to the beginning of a file.

■ **FACT:** *The* rewind *function resets a file pointer to the beginning of the file and clears the end of file flag if it is set.*

The following program (LAST.C) displays the last *n* lines of a file. For example, the command

```
C> LAST 3 ALPHABET.DAT
```

displays the last three lines in the file ALPHABET.DAT.

```c
#include <stdio.h>   /* needed for rewind and file-related functions */
#include <math.h>    /* needed for atoi */

main(int argc, char *argv[])
{
    int start_line, display_count;
    int linecount = 0;  /* number of lines in file */
    char string[128];
    FILE *fp;

    if (argc < 3)
        fputs("LAST:  must specify LAST <lines> <filename>", stderr);
    else if (!(fp = fopen(argv[2], "r")))
        fputs("LAST:  cannot open file specified", stderr);
    else
        {
        /* count the number of lines in the file */
        while (fgets(string, sizeof(string), fp))
            linecount++;
```

(continued)

continued

```
        rewind(fp);  /* start at beginning of file */

        display_count = atoi(argv[1]);

        start_line = linecount - display_count;

        linecount = 0;

        /* the line after start_line is the first to be displayed */
        while (linecount++ < start_line && !feof(fp))
            fgets(string, sizeof(string), fp);

        /* display desired lines */
        while (fgets(string, sizeof(string), fp))
            fputs(string, stdout);
        fclose(fp);
        }
}
```

The program begins by counting the number of lines in the file. Then the program determines the first line to display. For example, if the user wants to display the last 20 lines and the file contains 200 lines, the following formula calculates the last line to be skipped.

```
start_line = linecount - display_count;
           = 200        - 20
           = 180
```

Next, the program rewinds the file and begins reading (but ignoring) lines until the starting line is found. The program then displays the last *n* lines of the file beginning with the line after *start_line*.

In addition to the *rewind* function, the C run-time library provides *fseek*, which allows a program to move to specific byte offsets from the start, from the current position, or from the end of the file.

■ **FACT:** *The* fseek *function lets a program move to various offset locations throughout a file. The offset can be specified from the beginning, from the end, or from the current position in the file. If* fseek *sets the file pointer to the specified location, it returns the value 0. If it is unable to set the pointer as requested,* fseek *returns an error status.*

In LAST.C, we used the *rewind* function to move the file pointer back to the start of the file. We could have used *fseek* instead of *rewind*:

```
fseek(fp, 0L, SEEK_SET);
```

The second argument is a long integer that specifies the offset, which is 0 in this case. Recall that the letter *L* following the constant 0 informs the compiler that the value is to be treated as a *long int*. Unlike *rewind*, which can move the file pointer only to the beginning of a file, *fseek* can move the file pointer to any position in the file.

The third argument, SEEK_SET, is a constant that identifies the beginning of the file as the point from which the offset is to be applied. The file stdio.h defines three constants— SEEK_SET, SEEK_CUR, and SEEK_END—for this purpose.

Constant	Meaning
SEEK_SET	Offset from the beginning of the file
SEEK_CUR	Offset from the current file position
SEEK_END	Offset from the end of the file

As you begin moving from one location in the file to another, you might need to determine your current position in the file. The run-time library routine *ftell* enables you to do that.

■ **FACT:** *The* ftell *function returns a* long int *value that contains the current location of the file pointer. The return value is an offset from the beginning of the file.*

The following program (SHOWLINE.C) uses *ftell* to display the starting location of each line in a file. Remember, in text mode the output values might not match the byte offsets you would expect because of carriage-return/linefeed translation. Therefore, this program opens the file in binary mode.

```c
#include <stdio.h>  /* needed for file-related functions */

main(int argc, char *argv[])
{
    FILE *fp;
    char string[128];

    long int offset = 0;

    if (!(fp = fopen(argv[1], "rb")))
        fputs("SHOWLINE:  error opening file", stderr);
    else
        {
        while (fgets(string, sizeof(string), fp))
            {
            printf("%03ld - %s", offset, string);
            offset = ftell(fp);
            }
        fclose(fp);
        }
}
```

When you run the program, your screen displays output of the following form:

```
000 - ABCDEFGHIJKLMNOPQRSTUVWXYZ
028 - ABCDEFGHIJKLMNOPQRSTUVWXYZ
056 - ABCDEFGHIJKLMNOPQRSTUVWXYZ
084 - ABCDEFGHIJKLMNOPQRSTUVWXYZ
112 - ABCDEFGHIJKLMNOPQRSTUVWXYZ
140 -
```

Last, the C run-time library provides two routines that work in conjunction to save and restore the current file position.

■ **FACT:** *The* fgetpos *function obtains the current file position and stores it in a variable of type* fpos_t. *The include file stdio.h defines* fpos_t *as the data type* long.

After you store the current file position using *fgetpos*, you can later restore it using *fsetpos*.

■ **FACT:** *The* fsetpos *function restores the current file position to the position previously saved by a call to* fgetpos. *If successful,* fsetpos *returns 0; if* fsetpos *cannot restore the saved pointer value, it returns an error status.*

The following revision of LAST.C (LAST2.C) improves its performance by using *ftell* to save the position of the first 1000 lines in the file. In so doing, the program eliminates the requirement to reread the file to get to *start_line*. If the file exceeds 1000 lines, however, the program must reread the file to locate the correct starting line.

```c
#include <stdio.h>   /* needed for rewind and file-related functions */
#include <math.h>    /* needed for atoi */

main(int argc, char *argv[])
{
    FILE *fp;
    char string[128];
    int linecount = 0;  /* number of lines in file */
    int start_line;     /* first line to be displayed */
    int display_count;  /* number of lines to display */
    fpos_t positions[1000];

    if (argc < 3)
        fputs("LAST:  must specify LAST <lines> <filename>", stderr);
    else if ((display_count = atoi(argv[1])) <= 0)
        fputs("LAST:  invalid number of lines specified", stderr);
    else if (!(fp = fopen(argv[2], "rb")))
        fputs("LAST:  cannot open source file", stderr);
    else
```

(continued)

continued

```
    {
    positions[linecount] = ftell(fp);

    /* save the starting position of each line in the file */
    while (fgets(string, sizeof(string), fp))
        if (linecount < 1000)
            positions[++linecount] = ftell(fp);
        else
            linecount++;   /* more than 1000 lines */

    start_line = linecount - display_count+1;

    if (start_line < 1000)
        {
        if (start_line < 1)   /* first line is in element 0, */
            start_line = 1;   /* so subtract one for index */
        fseek(fp, positions[start_line - 1], SEEK_SET);
        }
    else
        {
        fseek(fp, 0L, SEEK_SET);   /* rewind the file */
        linecount = 0;

        while (linecount++ < start_line && !feof(fp))
            fgets(string, sizeof(string), fp);
        }

    /* display desired lines */
    while (fgets(string, sizeof(string), fp))
        fputs(string, stdout);

    fclose(fp);
    }
}
```

In Chapter 25 we discuss memory utilization in detail. At that time you will find that, by default, the small memory model creates a 2000-byte stack. Unfortunately, this stack is not large enough to support the program LAST.C. Therefore, when you compile LAST2.C, increase the stack size to 5000 bytes. To specify a stack size, use the /stack linker option, as follows:

```
C> CL LAST2.C /link /stack:5000
```

If you do not increase the stack size, the system displays a stack overflow message and the program fails.

MANIPULATING TEMPORARY FILES

In Chapter 1 we noted briefly that the C compiler periodically creates temporary files. When a program creates a temporary file, it must first ensure that the file does not have the same name as an existing file. Second, the program must remove the temporary file from the disk when it is no longer needed. The C run-time library provides a powerful set of functions that deal specifically with temporary files.

■ **FACT:** *The* tmpnam *function returns a filename that is unique in the root directory. If successful,* tmpnam *returns a pointer to a unique filename. If* tmpnam *is unable to generate an appropriate filename, it returns NULL.*

The following program (MAKETMP.C) uses *tmpnam* to create a unique filename in the root directory. Remember, *tmpnam* does not create a file; it simply generates a unique filename.

```
#include <io.h>   /* needed for tmpnam */

main()
{
    char filename[64];

    tmpnam(filename);
    printf("Filename returned is %s", filename);
}
```

When you run the program, your screen displays a message, such as the following, that identifies the temporary filename:

```
Filename returned is \2
```

As discussed, *tmpnam* assumes that the file resides in the root directory. To create unique filenames in a specific directory, use the function *tempnam*.

■ **FACT:** *The* tempnam *function lets you generate a unique filename for a specific directory. The function lets you specify a target directory for the file as well as a prefix for the filename. The prefix can contain a maximum of eight characters. For example, the statement* unique_name = tempnam("\\DATA", "MAY"); *assigns* unique_name *a temporary filename with the prefix* MAY *in the* \DATA *directory.*

If the program passes a prefix to *tempnam*, the routine uses the prefix as the starting characters in the filename and appends the digits 0 through 9 to the prefix to create the unique filename. The prefix and the digits together cannot exceed eight characters.

The following program (MAKETMP2.C) uses *tempnam* to create a unique file in the directory DOS that uses the prefix *TEXT.*

```
#include <io.h>  /* needed for tempnam */

main()
{
    char *filename;

    filename = tempnam("\\DOS", "TEXT");
    printf("Unique filename is %s", filename);
}
```

When you run the program, your screen shows

```
Unique filename is \DOS\TEXT2
```

Remember, the routine does not create a file; it simply returns a unique filename that you can later use to create a file with *fopen.*

■ **FACT:** *The* tempnam *function examines the DOS environment* TMP= *entry. If the entry exists,* tempnam *uses the specified directory as the target for the filename.*

If you define the environment variable *TMP*, *tempnam* generates a filename for the drive and directory associated with *TMP*. For example, MAKETMP2 has the following output if *TMP* is set to E:\DATA (and that directory exists):

```
Unique filename is E:\DATA\TEXT2
```

Finally, C provides the run-time library function *mktemp* that creates a unique filename based on a user-defined template.

■ **FACT:** *The* mktemp *function creates a unique filename in the current directory based on a user-specified template. The template takes the form* AAAXXXXX, *where the letters* A *are the prefix to the filename, and the Xs are the character locations that* mktemp *fills with the characters '0' through 'z' to create the unique name.*

As before, *mktemp* does not create a file; instead, it returns a pointer to a unique filename, using the template supplied in the function argument. For example, the statement *ptr = mktemp("TPXXXXXX")* assigns to *ptr* a pointer to a unique string of characters beginning with *TP.*

The program on the following page (MAKETMP3.C) demonstrates a call to the *mktemp* function.

```
#include <io.h>  /* needed for mktemp */

main()
{
    char *result;

    result = mktemp ("TPXXXXXX");
    printf("Temp filename is %s\n", result);
}
```

When you run the program, your screen displays output in the following form:

```
Temp filename is TP014698
```

Two additional C run-time library routines work in conjunction with each other to create and later remove a unique file from the disk. The first routine, *tmpfile*, creates a unique file and returns a file pointer to it.

■ **FACT:** *The* tmpfile *function opens a unique temporary file in read/write binary access mode. If successful,* tmpfile *returns a file pointer that you can use for file I/O. If an error occurs,* tmpfile *returns NULL.*

After a program creates temporary files, it can remove them with the run-time library function *rmtmp* when it is no longer needed.

■ **FACT:** *The* rmtmp *function closes all the temporary files created by* tmpfile *and deletes them from the current directory.*

The following program (USETMP.C) uses *tmpfile* to return a file pointer to a temporary file. The program then writes the letters of the alphabet to the file five times. Next, the program resets the file pointer to the beginning of the file and reads and displays the contents of the file. After it displays the data, the program closes and deletes the file using *rmtmp*. When the program ends, no temporary files remain on the disk.

```
#include <io.h>     /* needed for tmpfile and rmtmp */
#include <stdio.h>  /* needed for file-related functions */

main()
{
    FILE *fp;
    int count;
    char letter;
    int i;
```

(continued)

continued

```
    if ((fp = tmpfile()) == NULL)
        fputs("USETMP:  error creating temporary file", stderr);
    else
        {
        for (i = 0; i < 5; ++i)
            {
            for (letter = 'A'; letter <= 'Z'; letter++)
                putc(letter, fp);
            putc('\n', fp);
            }

        rewind(fp);

        while ((letter = getc(fp)) != EOF)
            putchar(letter);

        rmtmp();
        }
}
```

The C run-time library provides a powerful collection of file manipulation routines. As we proceed to other topics in this book, we will use many of these routines introduced in this chapter, and we will introduce several more.

SUMMARY

Manipulating Existing Files

■ **FACT:** *The* access *function lets you determine whether a file exists on disk and whether your program can access the file in a specified mode. If the file does not exist or cannot be accessed in the specified mode,* access *returns −1; if the file does exist and can be accessed in the specified mode,* access *returns 0.*

■ **FACT:** *The* chmod *function lets you set a file's access modes. If successful,* chmod *returns the value 0. If an error occurs,* chmod *returns −1.*

■ **TIP:** *Many programmers use the* chmod *function to set critical data files to read-only before the program ends. Doing so protects the files from being deleted or over-written by a misguided user command.*

■ **FACT:** *The* remove *function deletes the specified file. If the file is deleted,* remove *returns the value 0; if the file is not deleted,* remove *returns the value −1.*

■ **TIP:** *By using the* remove *function, your programs can easily create and later delete temporary files without user intervention.*

■ **FACT:** *The* rename *function lets you rename a file. If the file is renamed,* rename *returns the value 0; if the file is not renamed,* rename *returns an error status.*

Building and Parsing Pathnames

■ **FACT:** *The* _makepath *function returns a character string containing a complete DOS pathname based on four component parts: drive letter, directory name, filename, and 3-character extension.*

■ **FACT:** *The* _splitpath *function breaks a complete DOS pathname into its components: disk drive letter, directory name, filename, and extension.*

Traversing Your File

■ **FACT:** *The* rewind *function resets a file pointer to the beginning of the file and clears the end of file flag if it is set.*

■ **FACT:** *The* fseek *function lets a program move to various offset locations throughout a file. The offset can be specified from the beginning, from the end, or from the current position in the file. If* fseek *sets the file pointer to the specified location, it returns the value 0. If it is unable to set the pointer as requested,* fseek *returns an error status.*

■ **FACT:** *The* ftell *function returns a* long int *value that contains the current location of the file pointer. The return value is an offset from the beginning of the file.*

■ **FACT:** *The* fgetpos *function obtains the current file position and stores it in a variable of type* fpos_t. *The include file stdio.h defines* fpos_t *as the data type* long.

■ **FACT:** *The* fsetpos *function restores the current file position to the position previously saved by a call to* fgetpos. *If successful,* fsetpos *returns 0; if* fsetpos *cannot restore the saved pointer value, it returns an error status.*

Manipulating Temporary Files

■ **FACT:** *The* tmpnam *function returns a filename that is unique in the root directory. If successful,* tmpnam *returns a pointer to a unique filename. If* tmpnam *is unable to generate an appropriate filename, it returns NULL.*

■ **FACT:** *The* tempnam *function lets you generate a unique filename for a specific directory. The function lets you specify a target directory for the file as well as a prefix for the filename. The filename can contain a maximum of eight characters. For example, the statement* unique_name = tempnam("\\DATA", "MAY"); *assigns* unique_name *a temporary filename with the prefix* MAY *in the* \DATA *directory.*

■ **FACT:** *The* tempnam *function examines the DOS environment* TMP= *entry. If the entry exists,* tempnam *uses the specified directory as the target for the filename.*

■ **FACT:** *The* mktemp *function creates a unique filename in the current directory based on a user-specified template. The template takes the form AAAXXXXX, where the letters A are the prefix to the filename, and the Xs are the character locations that* mktemp *fills with the characters '0' through 'z' to create the unique name.*

■ **FACT:** *The* tmpfile *function opens a unique temporary file in read/write binary access mode. If successful,* tmpfile *returns a file pointer that you can use for file I/O. If an error occurs,* tmpfile *returns NULL.*

■ **FACT:** *The* rmtmp *function closes all the temporary files created by* tmpfile *and deletes them from the current directory.*

GLOSSARY

parse To examine the contents of a string and break the string into distinct fields. For example, the C run-time library function _splitpath_ parses a pathname into its components: disk drive, path, filename, and extension.

read-only file A file whose contents a program can read but cannot modify. When you set the mode of a file to read-only, the system lets you read the file with commands such as TYPE and PRINT. However, the system does not let you modify the file or delete it from disk. The C run-time library function _chmod_ lets you set a file to read-only access.

## CHAPTER 22

Using Predefined Global Variables

The include files provided with your C compiler contain structure type declarations, macros, constants, function declarations, and global variable declarations. In this chapter we examine several global variables that Microsoft C defines for use in your programs, and we discuss the advantages of using them.

The global variables we examine are defined in specific include files. Pay particular attention to the *#include* directives at the beginning of each program.

GETTING SPECIFICS ABOUT THE OPERATING SYSTEM

Part IV of this book describes methods for accessing specific capabilities of the operating system, some of which are available only under particular versions of the operating system. Microsoft C provides specific information about the operating system version number in three global variables defined in stdlib.h.

■ **FACT:** *The global variables* _osmajor *and* _osminor *contain the major and the minor version numbers of the operating system.*

Operating system version numbers have two parts, a major version number and a minor version number. For example, in DOS version 3.2 the major version number is 3, and the minor version number is 2. When developers release a new version of the operating system, they increment the version number. If the new operating system contains significant enhancements, the increment affects the major number. For example, a new menu-driven shell was added to DOS 3.3, so the major version number was incremented, and the system was released as DOS 4.0. If the new operating system contains only bug fixes or performance enhancements, the developers increment the minor version number; such was the case, for example, when DOS 3.2 became DOS 3.3. You can use the global variables _osmajor_ and _osminor_ in your programs to determine from within the program the current version of the operating system.

The following program (GETVER.C) uses the global variables _osmajor_ and _osminor_ to display the version number of the current operating system:

```
#include <stdlib.h>  /* needed for global variables */

main()
{
    printf("Operating System Version %d.%d", _osmajor, _osminor);
}
```

When you execute the program under DOS version 3.3, the screen shows

```
Operating System Version 3.30
```

When you execute the program under OS/2 1.1, the screen shows

```
Operating System Version 10.10
```

Note that the _osmajor_ variable contains a value of 10 in OS/2 to avoid confusion with DOS version 1.

As mentioned above, you will learn later in this book to access operating system services from within your programs. If a specific capability exists only in a specific version of the operating system, testing the version number using these global variables lets you determine whether the program should continue.

TAKING ANOTHER LOOK AT THE ENVIRONMENT

In Chapter 18 you learned how to retrieve and display entries from within the operating system environment using the _env_ array or the run-time library routine _getenv_. You learned that each time your C program executes, the operating system provides the program with a copy of the current environment entries. Any changes you make to the environment entries using _putenv_ affect only your copy of the environment. When your program ends, the environment contains only the settings that were in effect before the program was executed.

■ **FACT:** *Each time you execute a compiled program, its start-up routine copies the contents of its working copy of the environment into an array of pointers called* environ, *which is declared in stdlib.h. If the program uses* putenv *to add an environment entry or uses* getenv *to return the value of an entry, the program manipulates the array* environ.

The file stdlib.h contains the declaration of the array *environ*. Each time your program executes, it invokes a routine called *_setenvp* that lets your programs access the environment entries. Part of this processing includes assigning environment entries to the *environ* array. When your program uses *getenv* or *putenv* to manipulate the environment entries, it actually updates *environ*.

The following program (ENVIRON.C) displays the strings referenced by the arrays *env* and *environ*. Next it uses the run-time library routine *putenv* to place the entry *TEST= Testing environ* into the environment. The program then redisplays the contents of *env* and *environ*. As the program output reflects, only the array *environ* contains the new entry.

```c
#include <stdlib.h>  /* needed for environ */

main(int argc, char *argv[], char *env[])
{
    int i;

    puts("Original contents of env");
    for (i = 0; env[i]; ++i)
        puts(env[i]);

    puts("\nOriginal contents of environ");
    for (i = 0; environ[i]; ++i)
        puts(environ[i]);

    putenv("TEST=Testing environ");

    puts("\nContents of env after call to putenv");
    for (i = 0; env[i]; ++i)
        puts(env[i]);

    puts("\nContents of environ after call to putenv");
    for (i = 0; environ[i]; ++i)
        puts(environ[i]);
}
```

When you run the program, your screen shows

```
Original contents of env
COMSPEC=C:\DOS\COMMAND.COM
PATH=C:\DOS;C:\RBIN;C:\MSC;
LIB=C:\LIB;
INCLUDE=C:\INCLUDE;
INIT=C:\SOURCE\ME\INI;
PROMPT=$P$G

Original contents of environ
COMSPEC=C:\DOS\COMMAND.COM
PATH=C:\DOS;C:\RBIN;C:\MSC;
LIB=C:\LIB;
INCLUDE=C:\INCLUDE;
INIT=C:\SOURCE\ME\INI;
PROMPT=$P$G

Contents of env after call to putenv
COMSPEC=C:\DOS\COMMAND.COM
PATH=C:\DOS;C:\RBIN;C:\MSC;
LIB=C:\LIB;
INCLUDE=C:\INCLUDE;
INIT=C:\SOURCE\ME\INI;
PROMPT=$P$G

Contents of environ after call to putenv
COMSPEC=C:\DOS\COMMAND.COM
PATH=C:\DOS;C:\RBIN;C:\MSC;
LIB=C:\LIB;
INCLUDE=C:\INCLUDE;
INIT=C:\SOURCE\ME\INI;
PROMPT=$P$G
TEST=Testing environ ──────  Entry placed into environment by putenv
```

We have examined the arrays *env* and *environ* to increase your understanding of how *getenv* and *putenv* work. You should not access the entries of *environ* directly; instead, use *putenv* and *getenv*. In some cases, adding an entry requires that execution move to the location at which the array *environ* resides in memory. The *getenv* and *putenv* functions perform this processing, and it is invisible to your programs.

DETERMINING THE DEFAULT FILE TRANSLATION

In Chapter 13 you learned that you can open files in binary mode or in text mode. You learned that specifying "b" in the access mode causes *fopen* to open a file in binary mode:

```
fp = fopen("FILENAME.EXT", "rb");
```

If you specify neither "b" nor "t", *fopen* examines the global variable *_fmode* to determine whether text mode or binary mode is the default.

■ **FACT:** *The C compiler provides the global variable* _fmode, *which specifies the default file translation mode for* fopen *operations. By default, Microsoft C sets* _fmode *to text mode.*

The *_fmode* variable is declared in the file stdlib.h. The declaration does not initialize the variable; as a consequence, the compiler uses the mode value 0, which results in text mode translation.

DETERMINING THE EXECUTION MODE: REAL OR PROTECTED

If you are writing applications under OS/2, you know that OS/2 supports two modes of program execution. In OS/2 protected mode you can execute several programs simultaneously and switch from one application to another. To provide compatibility for DOS applications, OS/2 also provides a real mode of operation. Only one program can run in real mode at any given time. To help an OS/2 program determine its mode of execution, the C run-time library provides the global variable *_osmode*.

■ **FACT:** *The global variable* _osmode *contains the value 0 when the program is running in real mode; it contains the value 1 when the program is running in protected mode.*

The following program (SHOWMODE.C) uses *_osmode*, declared in stdlib.h, to display the mode of operation. It takes advantage of the fact that the variable contains the value 0, equivalent to a false condition, when the program is running in real mode. Note that the program must be compiled by a compiler capable of producing executable OS/2 programs if the program is to be run in protected mode.

```c
#include <stdlib.h> /* needed for _osmode */

main()
{
    printf("Current mode is %s", (_osmode) ? "Protected" : "Real");
}
```

If you run SHOWMODE under DOS or OS/2 real mode, your screen shows

```
Current mode is Real
```

Under OS/2 protected mode, your screen shows

```
Current mode is Protected
```

CHECKING STRICT ANSI C COMPLIANCE

To standardize C across compilers and operating systems, the American National Standards Institute (ANSI) has written a document that specifies how a C compiler should handle specific conditions. Most C compilers try to meet the ANSI standards. The global variable __STDC__ contains the value 1 when the compiler is enforcing strict ANSI standards and will accept any strictly conforming program, and it contains the value 0 when the compiler does not meet all ANSI standards.

■ **FACT:** *The global variable __STDC__ contains the value 1 when the compiler supports strict ANSI standards; it contains 0 if the compiler does not.*

The following program (ANSISUPP.C) displays a message that states whether the compiler supports ANSI standards:

```
main()
{
    if (__STDC__)
        puts("Strict ANSI support");
    else
        puts("Strict ANSI support disabled");
}
```

Many compilers provide extensions to the ANSI standards that you can enable or disable. For example, if you compile the preceding program with Microsoft C, your screen shows

```
Strict ANSI support disabled
```

The Microsoft C language extensions are enabled by default. Disabling the extensions does not, however, alter the value of __STDC__ because version 5.1 of the compiler does not accept *all* strictly conforming programs.

LOOKING AT THE PROGRAM SEGMENT PREFIX

Each time DOS executes a program, it places a block of data at the front of the program that contains information such as the command line, a pointer to the environment, and the addresses of the program's Ctrl-Break and critical error handlers. This block is commonly called the program segment prefix (PSP), which is depicted in Figure 22-1.

As you have learned, each time you run a compiled C program, it executes the functions _setargv and _setenvp to create the arrays *argv* and *envp*. These functions examine the command line and the environment referenced in the program segment prefix.

Offset

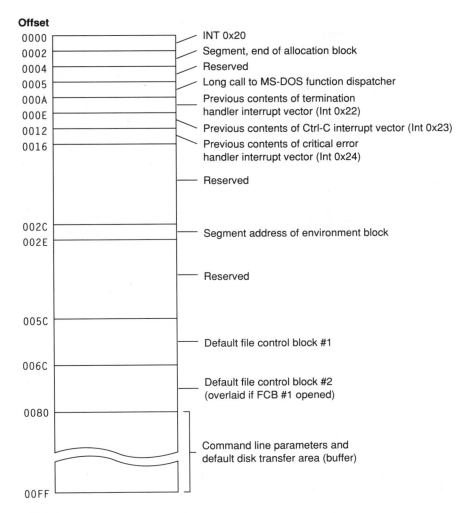

0000	INT 0x20
0002	Segment, end of allocation block
0004	Reserved
0005	Long call to MS-DOS function dispatcher
000A	Previous contents of termination
000E	handler interrupt vector (Int 0x22)
0012	Previous contents of Ctrl-C interrupt vector (Int 0x23)
0016	Previous contents of critical error
	handler interrupt vector (Int 0x24)

Reserved

002C
002E — Segment address of environment block

Reserved

005C

Default file control block #1

006C

Default file control block #2
(overlaid if FCB #1 opened)

0080

Command line parameters and
default disk transfer area (buffer)

00FF

FIGURE 22-1.
DOS makes information available to your program in the program segment prefix.

■ **FACT:** *The global variable* _psp *points to the start of the program segment prefix.*

The following program (COMMLINE.C) uses the global variable *_psp*, declared in stdlib.h, to display the program's command line. The command begins at offset 0x80 in the program segment prefix. The first byte at this location contains the number of characters in the command line.

```
#include <stdlib.h>  /* needed for _psp */
#include <stdio.h>   /* needed for putchar */

main()
{
    /* ptr is a far pointer to offset 0x80 of the PSP */
    char far *ptr = (char far *) (((long) _psp << 16) | 0x80);

    int num_characters, count;

    num_characters = *ptr++; /* number of characters in the command line */

    printf("Number of characters in the command line is %d\n",
            num_characters);

    for (count = 0; count < num_characters; count++)
        putchar(*(ptr + count));
}
```

For example, DOS stores the command line

```
C> COPY SOURCE.DAT TARGET.DAT
```

as the following null-terminated string:

When you execute the program using the command line

```
C> COMMLINE THIS IS A TEST
```

your screen shows

```
Number of characters in the command line is 15
THIS IS A TEST
```

Remember, DOS includes the leading blank (before the word *THIS*) in the command line. The program begins by using the value of _psp_ as a far pointer to the program segment prefix. Therefore, the program begins to access the contents of the PSP at offset 0x80—the start of the command line.

Most programs won't need to examine the PSP. However, the _psp_ global variable is a convenient way to access the command line and the environment when your program begins.

USING THE TIME MANIPULATION FUNCTIONS

The C run-time library contains several time manipulation functions that are based on seconds since midnight in Greenwich, England, which is the site of the prime meridian (0° longitude). Because the functions are based on Greenwich mean time, a program can add or subtract an offset in seconds to determine the time for any specific time zone.

■ **FACT:** *The* time *function assigns a value of type* long *that contains the number of seconds since midnight, January 1, 1980, Greenwich mean time (GMT). For example, the statement* time(&seconds); *assigns the time in seconds (relative to 1/1/89 GMT) to the variable* seconds.

After you use the *time* function to get the number of seconds since midnight, January 1, 1980, Greenwich mean time, you can calculate the current time in Greenwich and in your local time zone by writing time manipulation routines or by using those built into the C run-time library.

■ **FACT:** *The run-time library functions that compute local times based on Greenwich time use the environment variable* TZ, *which specifies the time zone, the number of hours from Greenwich, and the daylight saving status.*

Using the environment variable *TZ*, you can express the time at various locations relative to Greenwich time. For example, the setting *TZ=EST5EDT* specifies eastern standard time, five hours from Greenwich, and indicates that when daylight saving time is in effect, the time zone is called EDT. Let's look at the function *gmtime*, which uses the *TZ* environment setting to return the current local time.

■ **FACT:** *The* gmtime *function examines the number of seconds since January 1, 1980, Greenwich time, and determines the current local time. The function searches the environment for the* TZ *entry to determine the local time zone. If* TZ *is undefined,* gmtime *uses the default value PST8PDT.*

The following program (SHOWTIME.C) uses *gmtime* to display the local time.

```
#include <time.h>  /* needed for gmtime and tm structure */

main()
{
    struct tm *local_time;
    long seconds;
```

(continued)

continued

```
    time(&seconds);  /* get seconds since 01/01/88 */

    local_time = gmtime(&seconds);  /* get local time */

    /* display time */
    printf("Current time is %d:%02d:%02d\n", local_time->tm_hour,
           local_time->tm_min, local_time->tm_sec);

    /* display date -- add one to month to get current month */
    printf("Current date is %d/%d/%d", local_time->tm_mon + 1,
           local_time->tm_mday, local_time->tm_year);
}
```

The program uses a pointer to a structure of type *tm*, which is defined in time.h to contain the following members:

```
struct tm {
    int tm_sec;         /* seconds after the minute - [0,59] */
    int tm_min;         /* minutes after the hour - [0,59] */
    int tm_hour;        /* hours since midnight - [0,23] */
    int tm_mday;        /* day of the month - [1,31] */
    int tm_mon;         /* months since January - [0,11] */
    int tm_year;        /* years since 1900 */
    int tm_wday;        /* days since Sunday - [0,6] */
    int tm_yday;        /* days since January 1 - [0,365] */
    int tm_isdst;       /* daylight savings time flag */
};
```

When you call *gmtime*, the function searches the environment for the *TZ* entry. If it does not locate the entry, it uses the default PST8PDT setting. Suppose you run the program using the default value of *TZ*; your screen shows

```
Current time is 12:09:59
Current date is 6/11/89
```

Now issue the following command:

```
C> SET TZ=EST5EDT
```

When you execute the program again, your screen shows the time for the East Coast three hours later.

To assist you in the calculation of local times, the C compiler provides three global variables—*daylight*, *timezone*, and *tzname*, all of which are declared in time.h.

■ **FACT:** *The global variable* daylight *contains the value 1 when the* TZ *environment setting indicates daylight saving time, and it contains 0 if* TZ *indicates standard time.*

The following program (SHOWDSAV.C) uses *daylight* to determine whether daylight saving is in effect.

```
#include <time.h>  /* needed for tzset */

main()
{
    tzset();  /* get settings from environment */

    if (daylight)
        puts("Daylight saving active");
    else
        puts("No daylight saving");
}
```

The program begins by invoking the *tzset* function, which examines the environment for the *TZ* variable and sets the time-related global variables accordingly.

■ **FACT:** *The* tzset *function examines the environment for the* TZ *entry. If* TZ *is found,* tzset *assigns corresponding values to the global variables* daylight, timezone, *and* tzname; *if* TZ *is not found,* tzset *uses the default setting PST8PDT.*

If you run this program without defining the environment entry *TZ*, your screen shows

```
Daylight saving active
```

Daylight saving is assumed to be active because PST8PDT is the default setting. Next, issue the following command:

```
C> SET TZ=EST
```

Now execute the program again; your screen shows

```
No daylight saving
```

The global variable *timezone* contains the number of seconds by which the current time zone differs from Greenwich time.

■ **FACT:** *The global variable* timezone *contains the number of seconds by which the current time zone differs from Greenwich time.*

The program on the following page (ZONE.C) displays the current value of *timezone*. By dividing the number of seconds by 3600, the program also displays the number of hours by which local time differs from Greenwich time.

```
#include <time.h>   /* needed for tzset */

main()
{
    tzset();
    printf("Offset in seconds %ld\n", timezone);
    printf("Offset in hours %d", timezone / 3600);
}
```

To demonstrate the correlation between the value of *timezone* and the value of *TZ*, experiment with this program by changing the *TZ* environment setting. If you issue the following command,

SET TZ = EST5EDT

the ZONE program will display the following output:

Offset in seconds 18000
Offset in hours 5

The global variable *tzname* contains the abbreviated names of the current time zone and the daylight saving zone, if present.

■ **FACT:** *The global variable* tzname *is an array of pointers to character strings. The first element (*tzname[0]*) points to the name of the time zone, and the second element (*tzname[1]*) points to the daylight saving zone or has the value NULL.*

The following program (ZONE2.C) uses the global variable *tzname* to display the current time zones.

```
#include <time.h>   /* needed for tzset */

main()
{
    tzset();
    printf("Current time zone is %s\n", tzname[0]);
    printf("Daylight saving zone is %s", (tzname[1]) ? tzname[1] :
            "undefined");
}
```

As you can see, Greenwich time provides a standard for time operations; the global variables and run-time library functions supplied with the C compiler use this standard to enhance the flexibility of your programs.

UNDERSTANDING AND HANDLING
ERROR STATUS VALUES

Many run-time library functions return the value 0 when they are successful or −1 when an error occurs. To help you determine the cause of the error, stdlib.h defines the global variable *errno*, which a function can set to the corresponding error number.

■ **FACT:** *The global variable* errno *receives error numbers from run-time library functions. By examining the value of* errno*, your programs can often determine the cause of an error.*

The following program (MAKEDIR.C) creates a directory called TEST using the run-time library routine *mkdir*. If *mkdir* is successful, the program ends; if *mkdir* is not successful, the program displays a message that corresponds to the cause of the error. To display the correct message, the program uses *errno* as an index to a second global variable, an array called *sys_errlist*.

■ **FACT:** *The global variable* sys_errlist *contains an array of pointers to error messages. By accessing* sys_errlist *as* sys_errlist[errno]*, your programs can display the error messages that correspond to particular errors.*

```
#include <direct.h>   /* needed for mkdir */
#include <stdlib.h>   /* needed for global variables */

main()
{
    if (mkdir("TEST") == -1)
        puts(sys_errlist[errno]);
}
```

When you run this program the first time, it successfully creates the directory. When you run the program a second time, the directory TEST already exists, so *mkdir* fails, and your screen shows

```
Permission denied
```

The compiler provides a third global variable related to error message processing, *sys_nerr*, which contains the number of elements in the array *sys_errlist*.

■ **FACT:** *The global variable* sys_nerr *contains the number of error message strings that reside in the array* sys_errlist.

The following program (MESSAGES.C) displays the error messages contained in *sys_errlist*. It relies on *sys_nerr* to specify the number of elements to display:

```
#include <stdlib.h>  /* needed for global variables */

main()
{
    int i;

    for (i = 0; i < sys_nerr; ++i)
        if (sys_errlist[i])
            printf("%2d %s\n", i, sys_errlist[i]);
}
```

When you run the program, your screen shows the list of error messages that *sys_errlist* makes available to your program.

SUMMARY

Getting Specifics About the Operating System

■ **FACT:** *The global variables* _osmajor *and* _osminor *contain the major and the minor version numbers of the operating system.*

Taking Another Look at the Environment

■ **FACT:** *Each time you execute a compiled program, its start-up routine copies the contents of its working copy of the environment into an array of pointers called* environ, *which is declared in stdlib.h. If the program uses* putenv *to add an environment entry or uses* getenv *to return the value of an entry, the program manipulates the array* environ.

Determining the Default File Translation

■ **FACT:** *The C compiler provides the global variable* _fmode, *which specifies the default file translation mode for* fopen *operations. By default, Microsoft C sets* _fmode *to text mode.*

Determining the Execution Mode: Real or Protected

■ **FACT:** *The global variable* _osmode *contains the value 0 when the program is running in real mode; it contains the value 1 when the program is running in protected mode.*

Checking Strict ANSI C Compliance

■ **FACT:** *The global variable* __STDC__ *contains the value 1 when the compiler supports strict ANSI standards; it contains 0 if the compiler does not.*

Looking at the Program Segment Prefix

■ **FACT:** *The global variable* _psp *points to the start of the program segment prefix.*

Using the Time Manipulation Functions

■ **FACT:** *The* time *function assigns a value of type* long *that contains the number of seconds since midnight, January 1, 1980, Greenwich mean time (GMT). For example, the statement* time(&seconds); *assigns the time in seconds (relative to 1/1/89 GMT) to the variable* seconds.

■ **FACT:** *The run-time library functions that compute local times based on Green-wich time use the environment variable* TZ, *which specifies the time zone, the number of hours from Greenwich, and the daylight saving status.*

■ **FACT:** *The* gmtime *function examines the number of seconds since January 1, 1980, Greenwich time, and determines the current local time. The function searches the environment for the TZ entry to determine the local time zone. If* TZ *is undefined,* gmtime *uses the default value PST8PDT.*

■ **FACT:** *The global variable* daylight *contains the value 1 when the TZ environment setting indicates daylight saving time, and it contains 0 if* TZ *indicates standard time.*

■ **FACT:** *The* tzset *function examines the environment for the TZ entry. If TZ is found,* tzset *assigns corresponding values to the global variables* daylight, timezone, *and* tzname; *if TZ is not found,* tzset *uses the default setting PST8PDT.*

■ **FACT:** *The global variable* timezone *contains the number of seconds by which the current time zone differs from Greenwich time.*

■ **FACT:** *The global variable* tzname *is an array of pointers to character strings. The first element points to the name of the time zone (*tzname[0]*), and the second element (*tzname[1]*) points to the daylight savings zone or has the value NULL.*

Understanding and Handling Error Status Values

■ **FACT:** *The global variable* errno *receives error numbers from run-time library functions. By examining the value of* errno, *your programs can often determine the cause of an error.*

■ **FACT:** *The global variable* sys_errlist *contains an array of pointers to error messages. By accessing* sys_errlist *as* sys_errlist[errno], *your programs can display the error messages that correspond to particular errors.*

■ **FACT:** *The global variable* sys_nerr *contains the number of error message strings that reside in the array* sys_errlist.

GLOSSARY

ANSI C The standards for implementing C in compliance with the specifications written by the American National Standards Institute (ANSI). By conforming to ANSI standards, programs written in C under one compiler or operating system will compile and run using another compliant compiler or operating system.

Greenwich mean time (GMT) The time in Greenwich, England, through which the prime meridian (0° longitude) passes. The C run-time library provides several functions based on Greenwich mean time.

program segment prefix (PSP) A 256-byte data block that contains information, such as the program's environment entries and its Ctrl-Break handling routine. DOS places this information at the beginning of your program at run time.

protected mode Execution mode supported under OS/2 that lets you execute several programs at the same time, sharing files and other information among them.

real mode Execution mode in which DOS programs run. Under OS/2 real mode, only one program can execute in real mode at any given time. Real mode is often called DOS mode.

## CHAPTER 23

Handling a Variable Number of Arguments

So far, every time you invoked a function you wrote yourself, you had to match the number of arguments in the function call to the number of arguments in the function declaration. If your program passed too few or too many arguments, an error occurred. In this chapter you learn to write functions that, like *printf* and *scanf*, support a variable number of arguments. As you will see, the processing that makes such functions work relies on two easy-to-master C macros.

UNDERSTANDING THE BASICS

Each time your program passes arguments to a function, the compiler places the arguments and a return address to the program into a memory region called the stack. As the stack is normally depicted, the arguments appear on top of one another, corresponding to the items in the list from right to left. For example, the stack shown in Figure 23-1A results from the following function call:

```
display(1, 2, 3);
```

When the compiler encounters the function declaration

```
void display(int a, int b, int c)
```

the compiler maps the function's local variables to the values on the stack, as shown in Figure 23-1B.

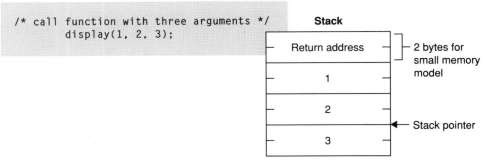

(A)

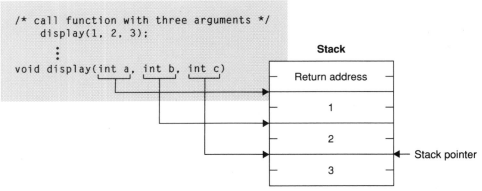

(B)

FIGURE 23-1.
(A) The call to display *places three arguments on the stack. Values are taken from the argument list consecutively, beginning at the right side of the list, with each new value pushed on the top of the stack. (B) The values are mapped to local variables when* display *is executed.*

If your program passes five arguments to the *display* function, as follows,

```
display(1, 2, 3, 4, 5);
```

the compiler pushes them on the stack as shown in Figure 23-2A. In turn, the *display* function maps its local variables to the entries on the stack as shown in Figure 23-2B.

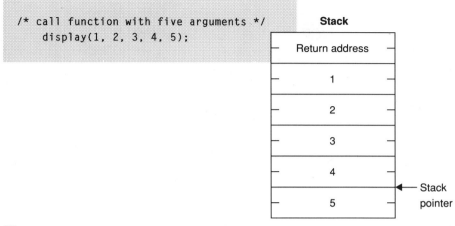

(A)

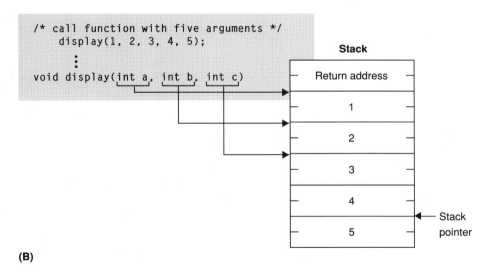

(B)

FIGURE 23-2.
(A) The call to display *places five arguments on the stack. (B) The first three arguments placed on the stack are mapped to local variables when* display *is executed.*

As you can see, the additional arguments are placed on the stack, but the *display* function simply ignores them. Now let's examine a way to access these additional arguments on the stack.

ACCESSING ARGUMENTS ON THE STACK

Routines that support a variable number of arguments must declare at least one local variable. To demonstrate the necessary steps, let's write a function called *display* that displays integer values on your screen until it receives an argument whose value is −1. You can call *display* from within your program as follows:

```
#include <stdarg.h>   /* needed for va_list, va_start, and va_arg */

main()
{
    void display();

    display(1, 2, 3, 4, 5, -1);
    display(6, 7, 8, 9, -1);
    display(10, 11, 12, -1);
    display(13, 14, -1);
    display(15, -1);
    display(-1);
}
```

To begin, simply declare *display* as follows:

```
void display(int a)
```

■ **FACT:** *Functions that support a variable number of arguments must declare at least one argument.*

As you can see, the function declaration for *display* declares the argument *a*. This variable marks the starting location of the arguments on the stack.

■ **FACT:** *To work with a variable number of arguments on the stack, a function must declare a variable of type* va_list *that serves as a placeholder.*

After you tell the compiler the starting location of the first argument in the stack, you can access the subsequent arguments. To do so, you must use a variable of type *va_list*, which is defined in the header file stdarg.h. Within our *display* function, we can declare the variable *marker*, as shown here:

```
void display(int a)
{
    va_list marker;

    /* remaining code */
}
```

■ **FACT:** *The* va_start *macro sets the placeholder to the variable on the stack that follows the specified argument. For example, the statement* va_start(marker, a); *sets* marker *to the variable that follows the variable* a *on the stack.*

Suppose we call the *display* function as follows:

```
display(1, 2, 3, 4, -1);
```

The compiler maps the value 1 to the argument *a*. The additional arguments start immediately after *a* on the stack. The *va_start* macro assigns this position to the variable *marker*, as shown in Figure 23-3.

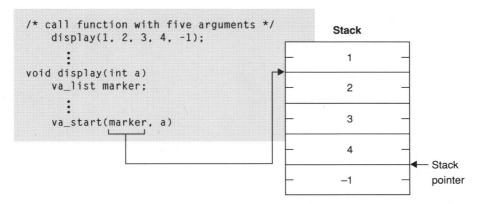

FIGURE 23-3.
The va_start *macro has two arguments; it assigns to the first argument the location of the item that follows the second argument on the stack.*

Let's use the *va_start* macro to locate the first additional argument so that our *display* function becomes

```
void display(int a)
{
    va_list marker;
    int value;  /* value to display */

    va_start(marker, a);

    /* remainder of code */
}
```

Now we need to access the next argument. To do so, we can use the macro *va_arg*.

■ **FACT:** *The* va_arg *macro returns the value in the stack to which the current placeholder points and then increments the placeholder to point to the next value.*

To use the macro *va_arg* in the *display* function, we supply the name of the placeholder variable, *marker*, and the type of the next argument. Because all the arguments are *int* values, we can complete the *display* function and combine it with *main*, as shown in the following program (VARARGS.C):

```
#include <stdarg.h>  /* needed for va_list, va_start, and va_arg */

main()
{
    void display();

    display(1, 2, 3, 4, 5, -1);
    display(6, 7, 8, 9, -1);
    display(10, 11, 12, -1);
    display(13, 14, -1);
    display(15, -1);
    display(-1);
}

void display(int a)
{
    va_list marker;
    int value;

    va_start(marker, a);
    value = a;

    while (value != -1)
        {
        printf("%d\n", value);
        value = va_arg(marker, int);
        }
}
```

The *display* function simply loops, displaying and retrieving *int* values from the stack until it encounters a −1. It reserves the value −1 as the end-of-list indicator. The *display_float* function takes a slightly different approach; it receives an argument that tells it the number of additional arguments on the stack:

```
void display_float(int count)
{
    va_list marker;
    int i;

    va_start(marker, count);

    for (i = 0; i < count; ++i)
        printf("%f\n", va_arg(marker, double));
}
```

As you can see, this function loops until it has displayed the number of arguments specified by the first argument, *count*. Now you can invoke *display_float* from *main* to print float values on your screen, as demonstrated by the following program (VARARGS2.C):

```
#include <stdarg.h>  /* needed for va_list, va_start, and va_arg */

main()
{
    void display_float();

    display_float(3, 42.7, 55.6, 77.3);
    display_float(2, 88.1, 92.7);
    display_float(1, 77.6);
    display_float(0);
}

void display_float(int count)
{
    va_list marker;
    int i;

    va_start(marker, count);

    for (i = 0; i < count; ++i)
        printf("%f\n", va_arg(marker, double));
}
```

HANDLING ARGUMENTS OF DIFFERENT TYPES

The *display* and *display_float* functions we created dealt with only one type of argument, either *int* or *float*. Functions such as *printf* and *scanf*, however, must handle a variable number of arguments *and* arguments of various types. Let's see how they do it.

As we have seen, functions that use a variable number of arguments must declare at least one argument. In the case of *printf* and *scanf*, this argument is the control string, which specifies the type of each successive argument. For example, given the control string

`"%d %f %c"`

printf knows that the subsequent items on the stack are values of types *int*, *float*, and *char*. Consequently, *printf* can specify the correct types in the macro *va_arg*.

The following program (MYPRINTF.C) implements a "poor man's *printf*" function named *poormans_printf*. The function is similar to *printf* in that it uses a control string to determine the correct types to display. It supports six format specifiers, as described in the table on the following page.

Specifier	Result
%d	Decimal integer output
%b	Binary output
%o	Octal output
%x	Hexadecimal output
%f	Floating point output
%c	ASCII character output

The function also supports the *printf* escape sequences, such as \n, \t, and \a.

```
#include <stdarg.h>  /* needed for va_list, va_start, and va_arg */
#include <stdio.h>   /* needed for putchar, itoa, and sprintf */

main()
{
    void poormans_printf();

    poormans_printf("%b \t %o \n %d %x %c %f %d DONE", 255, 255,
                    255, 255, 65, 3.43, 5);
    poormans_printf("\n%f + %f = %f", -3.4, 343.22, -3.4 + 343.22);
}

void poormans_printf(char *str)
{
    va_list marker;
    char buffer[128];

    va_start(marker, str);  /* mark first additional argument */

    while (*str)            /* examine each character in the string */
        {
        if (*str != '%')    /* if not a %_ format specifier, print it */
            putchar(*str);
        else                /* print value that corresponds to specifier */
            {
            switch (*(++str))
                {
                case 'd': itoa(va_arg(marker, int), buffer, 10);
                        poormans_printf(buffer);
                        break;
                case 'b': itoa(va_arg(marker, int), buffer, 2);
                        poormans_printf(buffer);
                        break;
                case 'o': itoa(va_arg(marker, int), buffer, 8);
                        poormans_printf(buffer);
                        break;
```

(continued)

continued

```
                case 'x': itoa(va_arg(marker, int), buffer, 16);
                          poormans_printf(buffer);
                          break;
                case 'f': sprintf(buffer, "%f", va_arg(marker, double));
                          poormans_printf(buffer);
                          break;
                case 'c': putchar(va_arg(marker, int));
                          break;
                default:  putchar(*str);
                }
        }
    str++;
    }
}
```

The function begins by setting the marker to the additional arguments on the stack. Next it examines a letter in the control string. As long as that letter is not the signal for a format specifier (%), the function displays it. If the letter is a %, however, the function uses a *switch* statement to determine the type of the value to be displayed. If, for example, the specifier is %d, the function converts the first additional argument in the stack to a string representation of the *int* value using the run-time library function *itoa*.

When *itoa* returns, *poormans_printf* passes the string representation of the value to itself recursively. After the recursive call displays the string, it returns control to the function, which examines the next character in the control sequence. The function uses this technique for each of the integer format specifiers.

In the case of %f, the function uses *sprintf* to convert the floating point value on the stack to a string.

■ **FACT:** *The* sprintf *function writes a* printf *control string not to the screen but rather to a character string. For example,* sprintf(string, "This is Chapter %d", 23); *writes to the variable* string *the result of processing subsequent arguments, which produces* This is Chapter 23.

The capabilities of the *sprintf* function are similar to those of *printf*. But whereas *printf* displays its output on the screen, *sprintf* writes the output to a character string. The *sprintf* function is convenient for formatting output or converting a value of one type to another.

■ **TRAP:** *When you use* va_arg *to retrieve arguments passed on the stack, specify* double *for* float *values and* int *for* char *values; otherwise, you will get incorrect results.*

If you add additional format specifier support to *poormans_printf*, keep in mind the way the compiler passes values of different types to functions. If you examine the %f and %c processing in *poormans_printf*, you find that the compiler promotes values of type *float* to type *double* when it puts them on the stack, and it passes characters as *int* values. Specify these types correctly when you use *va_arg* to ensure that the macro returns the correct value and increments the placeholder appropriately.

HANDLING A VARIABLE NUMBER OF STRINGS

So far, we have learned to handle a variable number of arguments of types *int*, *float*, and *char*. In this section we learn a technique for working with character strings. Remember, when your program passes a character string to a function, the compiler actually passes the starting address of the string. Figure 23-4 shows an example of a stack in which a character string is passed as a pointer to its first element.

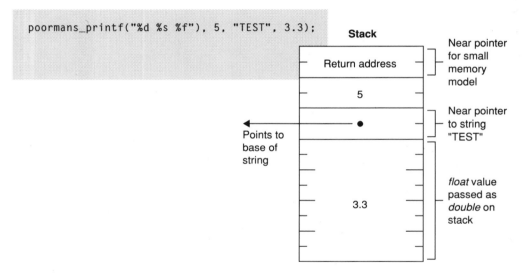

FIGURE 23-4.
A character string argument is placed on the stack as a pointer to the base of the string.

To support the %s format specifier in *poormans_printf*, simply include code for *case 's'* to display the string and adjust the placeholder on the stack. Name the new version PRINTF2.C.

```
#include <stdarg.h>   /* needed for va_list, va_start, and va_arg */
#include <stdio.h>    /* needed for putchar, itoa, and sprintf */
#include <string.h>   /* needed for strcpy */
```

(continued)

continued

```
main()
{
    void poormans_printf();
    poormans_printf("%s", "The Microsoft C Compiler");
}

void poormans_printf(char *str)
{
    va_list marker;
    char buffer[128];
    int i;

    va_start(marker, str);   /* mark first additional argument */
    while (*str)             /* examine each character in the string */
        {
        if (*str != '%')     /* if not a %_ format specifier, print it */
            putchar(*str);
        else                 /* print value that corresponds to specifier */
            {
            switch(*(++str))
                {
                case 'd': itoa(va_arg(marker, int), buffer, 10);
                          poormans_printf(buffer);
                          break;
                case 's': strcpy(buffer, va_arg(marker, char *));
                          for (i = 0; buffer[i]; i++)
                              putchar(buffer[i]);
                          break;
                case 'b': itoa(va_arg(marker, int), buffer, 2);
                          poormans_printf(buffer);
                          break;
                case 'o': itoa(va_arg(marker, int), buffer, 8);
                          poormans_printf(buffer);
                          break;
                case 'x': itoa(va_arg(marker, int), buffer, 16);
                          poormans_printf(buffer);
                          break;
                case 'f': sprintf(buffer, "%f", va_arg(marker, double));
                          poormans_printf(buffer);
                          break;
                case 'c': putchar(va_arg(marker, int));
                          break;
                default:  putchar(*str);
                }
            }
        str++;
        }
}
```

USING *vprintf* AND *vfprintf*

The run-time library provides two routines that resemble *poormans_printf*: *vprintf* and *vfprintf*.

■ **FACT:** *The* vprintf *function writes formatted output to the standard output device using a control sequence and a variable number of arguments.*

Suppose you are writing a critical error handling function (CRITERR.C) that receives an exit status value and one or more possible error messages:

```
void critical_error(int status, char *format)
{
    va_list marker;

    va_start(marker, format);
    vprintf(format, marker);

    exit(status);
}
```

A program can call the function in any of the following ways:

■ `critical-error(1, "Error in file open");`

■ `critical-error(1, "Error opening %s", argv[0]);`

■ `critical-error(3, "Error %d in routine %s", error-status, "average");`

As you can see, the *critical_error* function receives a variable number of arguments. Using *va_start* and *vprintf*, *critical_error* displays the correct error message and then terminates the calling program with the specified exit status value.

The function begins by marking the start of the optional parameters using *va_start*. Next it passes the control string contained in *format* to *vprintf* along with the argument *marker*. After *vprintf* displays the error information, it terminates the program and returns the appropriate exit status.

In Chapter 20 you learned that you should route error messages to *stderr* to prevent the user from redirecting them at the operating system level. In this case we can use the run-time library routine *vfprintf* to exercise greater control over the output location.

■ **FACT:** *Like* vprintf, *the* vfprintf *function supports a variable number of arguments. The* vfprintf *function writes its output to a file (rather than to standard output).*

In the following revision (CRITERR2.C) the *critical_error* function is modified to support output to *stderr*. Because *vfprintf* writes output to a file rather than to standard output, we can direct the output to *stderr* and prevent its being redirected.

```
void critical_error(int status, char *format)
{
    va_list marker;

    va_start(marker, format);
    vfprintf(stderr, format, marker);
    exit(status);
}
```

DECLARING FUNCTIONS THAT SUPPORT A VARIABLE NUMBER OF ARGUMENTS

The file stdio.h declares the *printf* function as follows:

```
int _CDECL printf(const char *, ...);
```

The three periods (...) tell you that the function supports a variable number of arguments.

■ **TIP:** *To declare a function that supports a variable number of arguments, use the three periods after the last mandatory argument.*

If we apply this technique to the *display* function that we created at the beginning of this chapter (DISPLAY.C), the function declaration takes the following form:

```
#include <stdarg.h>  /* needed for va_list, va_start, and va_arg */

main()
{
    void display(int, ...);

    display(1, 2, 3, 4, 5, -1);
    display(6, 7, 8, 9, -1);
}

void display(int a, ...)
{
    va_list marker;
    int value;

    va_start(marker, a);
    value = a;
    while (value != -1)
        {
        printf("%d\n", value);
        value = va_arg(marker, int);
        }
}
```

SUMMARY

Accessing Arguments on the Stack

■ **FACT:** *Functions that support a variable number of arguments must declare at least one argument.*

■ **FACT:** *To work with a variable number of arguments on the stack, a function must declare a variable of type* va_list *that serves as a placeholder.*

■ **FACT:** *The* va_start *macro sets the placeholder to the variable on the stack that follows the specified argument. For example, the statement* va_start(marker, a); *sets* marker *to the variable that follows the variable* a *on the stack.*

■ **FACT:** *The* va_arg *macro returns the value in the stack to which the current placeholder points and then increments the placeholder to point to the next value.*

Handling Arguments of Different Types

■ **FACT:** *The* sprintf *function writes a* printf *control string not to the screen but rather to a character string. For example,* sprintf(string, "This is Chapter %d", 23); *writes to the variable* string *the result of processing subsequent arguments, which produces* This is Chapter 23.

■ **TRAP:** *When you use* va_arg *to retrieve arguments passed on the stack, specify* double *for* float *values and* int *for* char *values; otherwise, you will get incorrect results.*

Using *vprintf* and *vfprintf*

■ **FACT:** *The* vprintf *function writes formatted output to the standard output device using a control sequence and a variable number of arguments.*

■ **FACT:** *Like* vprintf, *the* vfprintf *function supports a variable number of arguments. The* vfprintf *function writes its output to a file (rather than to standard output).*

Declaring Functions That Support a Variable Number of Arguments

■ **TIP:** *To declare a function that supports a variable number of arguments, use the three periods after the last mandatory argument.*

GLOSSARY

stack A region of memory that the compiler uses for temporary storage of arguments passed to a function. When the function ends, the compiler removes the arguments from the stack.

## CHAPTER 24

Low-Level File I/O

In Chapter 13 you learned how to manipulate files using file pointers with the routines *fopen*, *fgets*, *fputs*, and *fclose*. At that time you learned how to open a file and read its contents one character or one line at a time. File manipulation of this type is called *stream I/O*. Essentially you are reading a stream of characters from the file, one after another, and testing for the end of file character, which indicates the end of the file stream.

C offers you a second way to manipulate files: *low-level I/O*. This method relies on a collection of "low-level routines," so called because they bypass many of the operating system's buffering capabilities. In this chapter we examine the low-level routines in the C run-time library. You learn how to use them to copy one file to another, regardless of whether the file contains ASCII characters or compiled, executable code.

COMPARING STREAM AND LOW-LEVEL FILE I/O

In Chapter 13 we were strictly concerned with file manipulation functions that use a file pointer, a variable of type *FILE*, declared as follows:

```
FILE *fp;
```

The low-level file manipulation functions don't use a file pointer; instead, they use an integer value called a file *handle*, or descriptor.

■ **FACT:** *Low-level file manipulation functions use an integer value called a file handle, or descriptor. The C run-time library routines* creat *and* open *return a file handle to a specific file.*

The C run-time library provides a low-level counterpart for each of the stream I/O functions. The following table summarizes several of the functions we examine in this chapter and relates each one to a comparable stream I/O function:

Stream	Low-Level	Description
fopen	open creat	Opens or creates a file on disk
fgets	read	Reads data from a file into a buffer
fputs	write	Writes data from a buffer to a file on disk
fclose	close	Closes a file and updates the file's directory entry
fseek	lseek	Branches to a specific offset in a file
ftell	tell	Determines the current position in a file
feof	eof	Tests for end of file

Low-level file I/O functions are particularly useful for manipulating binary files. Applications well suited for binary file operations include file-copying programs and database applications. Low-level file I/O functions serve equally well for reading and writing large amounts of data to and from the disk in a single operation.

USING LOW-LEVEL FUNCTIONS: A FIRST EXAMPLE

In this section we use low-level file I/O functions to implement a file-copying routine that copies the contents of one file to another. Unlike the file-copying programs we wrote earlier in this book, LCOPY is not restricted to supporting ASCII files—it can copy both ASCII files and executable files.

Before we examine the low-level file I/O functions in detail, let's look at the following program (LCOPY.C):

```
#include <io.h>          /* needed for open, close, read, write, and eof */
#include <fcntl.h>       /* needed for open mode arguments */
#include <sys\types.h>   /* needed for file types */
#include <sys\stat.h>    /* needed for file status flags */
#include <stdio.h>       /* needed for fprintf and constants */

main(int argc, char *argv[])
{
    int source, target;  /* file handles */
    char buffer[1024];    /* buffer for file I/O operations */
    int bytes_read;       /* number of bytes read */
```

(continued)

continued

```
    if (argc < 3)
        fprintf(stderr, "LCOPY:  must specify source and target files\n");
    else if ((source = open(argv[1], O_BINARY : O_RDONLY)) == -1)
        fprintf(stderr, "LCOPY:  error opening %s\n", argv[1]);
    else if ((target = open(argv[2], O_WRONLY : O_BINARY : O_TRUNC :
            O_CREAT, S_IWRITE)) == -1)
        fprintf(stderr, "LCOPY:  error opening %s\n", argv[2]);
    else
        {
        while (!eof(source))
            {
            if ((bytes_read = read(source, buffer, sizeof(buffer))) <= 0)
                fprintf(stderr, "LCOPY:  error reading from source file");
            else if (write(target, buffer, bytes_read) != bytes_read)
                fprintf(stderr, "LCOPY:  error writing to target file");
            }
        close(source);
        close(target);
        }
    }
```

The program begins by ensuring that the user has specified at least three command line arguments. If the command line contains too few arguments, the program writes an error message to *stderr* and ends. If the user has specified at least three command line arguments, the program tries to open the source file for the file-copying operation, using the run-time library function *open*.

■ **FACT:** *The* open *function opens an existing file on disk for read, write, or read/write operations. If it opens the file in the specified mode,* open *returns a file handle; if* open *cannot open the file as requested, it returns an error status of −1.*

The most common format for a call to the *open* function is the following:

```
handle = open(filename, mode);
```

The *open* function returns a file handle, which you can assign to an *int* variable. The *filename* argument is the name of the file to open. It can contain a complete DOS (or OS/2) pathname and disk drive specifier. The *mode* argument states how the file is to be opened. The table on the following page shows the valid modes.

Access Mode	Description
O_APPEND	Opens the file and places the file pointer at the end of the file for append operations
O_CREAT	Opens a file for write operations and creates the file on disk if it doesn't exist
O_EXCL	Returns an error status if the O_CREAT mode is used and the file currently exists on disk
O_RDONLY	Opens the file for read-only operations
O_RDWR	Opens the file for read/write operations
O_TRUNC	Opens a file for write operations and truncates it (In other words, the first write operation overwrites the file's contents.)
O_WRONLY	Opens the file for write-only operations
O_BINARY	Opens the file in binary mode with no character translation
O_TEXT	Opens the file in text mode with character translation

By using the bitwise OR operator, you can specify several access modes in one call. For example, the following condition directs the compiler to open the file in binary mode with read-only access:

```
if ((source = open(argv[1], O_BINARY | O_RDONLY)) == -1)
```

■ **TRAP:** *If the file specified in the call to* open *does not exist,* open *does not create the file unless you also specified the O_CREAT mode.*

By default, *open* does not create a file on disk, but if you include O_CREAT in the open mode, the function does create the file. However, if you specify O_CREAT mode, you must also include a permission mode with which the file is to be created. The following table lists the permission modes:

Permission Mode	Meaning
S_IREAD	Read-only operations
S_IWRITE	Write-only operations

You can group the permission modes using the bitwise OR operator:

```
fd = open("TEST", O_CREAT | O_RDWR, S_IREAD | S_IWRITE);
```

The preceding statement opens the file TEST for read/write operations if the file exists. If necessary, *open* creates the file with permission for both read and write operations.

The LCOPY program opens the target file as a binary file with write-only access; it creates a file if necessary or truncates an existing file. Most older C programs use the *creat* function to create a file on disk if it does not exist.

■ **FACT:** *The* creat *function creates a file on disk using the specified permission mode. If it creates the file with the requested permission setting,* creat *returns an integer file handle. If an error occurs,* creat *returns −1.*

A call to the *creat* function takes the following form:

```
handle = creat(filename, mode);
```

If *creat* opens the file as requested, it returns a file handle, which you can assign to an *int* variable. The *filename* argument specifies the name of the file to create on disk. It can contain a disk drive letter and a pathname. The *mode* argument specifies the way the file can be accessed. The valid modes are the same as those for *open*, which are listed in the preceding table. If *filename* already exists on disk, *creat* truncates the existing file.

■ **TIP:** *To create files, use the* open *function with the O_CREAT value in the access mode. Use of the* creat *function is discouraged.*

In the past, *open* did not support the O_CREAT mode value; therefore, older C programs use *creat* to create a file on disk. Microsoft documentation recommends that programmers use O_CREAT in the *open* function, rather than calling *creat*, to create files.

If the LCOPY program opens the specified files, it begins to read the contents of the source file and to write the contents to the target file. The program uses the *eof* function to test for end of file. The *eof* function takes a single argument, the handle of the file to be tested.

■ **FACT:** *The* eof *function tests for an end of file condition in the file associated with the specified handle. If the file pointer is at the end of the file,* eof *returns 1; if it is not at the end of the file,* eof *returns 0.*

LCOPY uses the run-time library function *read* to read data from the source file and uses the *write* function to write data to the target file.

■ **FACT:** *The* read *function reads a specified number of bytes from a file into a buffer. If it reads into the buffer as requested,* read *returns the number of bytes read. If an error occurs,* read *returns −1. If it immediately encounters the end of file,* read *returns 0.*

In the following example, the *read* function obtains data from the file associated with the handle *source*:

```
result = read(source, buffer, sizeof(buffer));
```

The function places data into *buffer*; the maximum number of bytes *read* obtains is expressed here by *sizeof(buffer)*. The statement assigns to *result* the value returned by the *read* function.

In LCOPY.C *read* places data from the source file into the variable *buffer.* If *read* returns a value less than or equal to 0, LCOPY displays the following error message:

```
LCOPY:  error reading from source file
```

If *read* obtains the requested data, it assigns to the variable *bytes_read* the actual number of bytes read from the file. The program then uses this value to tell the run-time library function *write* how many bytes to write to *target.*

■ **FACT:** *The* write *function writes a specified number of bytes from a buffer to a file. Upon completion,* write *returns the number of bytes actually written to a file; if an error occurs,* write *returns −1.*

In LCOPY.C the return value matches the number of bytes *write* was directed to write, unless an error has occurred. The program uses the following test for a write error:

```
if (write(target, buffer, bytes_read) != bytes_read)
```

If the return value and *bytes_read* are unequal, the program displays an error message.

Once the file-copying operation completes, LCOPY.C uses the run-time library function *close* to close the file on disk.

■ **FACT:** *The* close *function closes the file associated with the specified file handle and updates the directory on disk.*

The functions *open, read, write,* and *close* are clearly similar to their stream I/O counterparts. In the next section we examine several additional capabilities that file handles give your programs.

GETTING FILE INFORMATION

As you know, the DOS and OS/2 directory command DIR displays a file's name and extension as well as its size and the date and time it was last modified. In this section we create a program called STAT that displays a file listing similar to that provided by the DIR command. To list a specific file, such as LCOPY.C, enter the following command:

```
C> STAT LCOPY.C
```

To list several files, enter a command such as the following:

```
C> STAT LCOPY.C LCOPY.OBJ LCOPY.EXE
```

STAT does not support the DOS wildcard characters. If you want the program to support wildcard characters, link it with the object file SETARGV.OBJ, as discussed in Chapter 17.

STAT uses the C run-time library function *fstat* to get specific information about a file.

■ **FACT:** *The* fstat *function returns a structure that contains specific information about the file associated with the specified file handle. If* fstat *obtains the file information, it returns 0; if it cannot obtain the information,* fstat *returns −1.*

The *fstat* function uses a structure of type *stat* defined in the include file sys\stat.h. The *stat* structure contains the following members:

```
struct stat {
    dev_t st_dev; ————————————— Drive number for a file, or handle for a device
    ino_t st_ino;
    unsigned short st_mode; ————— Permission mode for the file
    short st_nlink; —————————————— Always 1
    short st_uid;
    short st_gid;
    dev_t st_rdev; ——————————————— Same as st_dev
    off_t st_size; ——————————————— File size in bytes
    time_t st_atime; ————————————— Time file was last modified
    time_t st_mtime; ————————————— Same as st_atime
    time_t st_ctime; ————————————— Same as st_atime
    };
```

The following program (STAT.C) tries to open the file specified on the command line. If it does so, the program uses the file handle returned by *open* as an argument to *fstat* and displays the file information.

```
#include <io.h>          /* needed for open and close */
#include <sys\types.h>  /* needed for file types */
#include <sys\stat.h>   /* needed for fstat and stat structure */
#include <fcntl.h>       /* needed for open mode arguments */
#include <stdio.h>       /* needed for fprintf and constants */

main(int argc, char *argv[])
{
    int fd;                 /* file handle */
    struct stat file_info;

    if (argv < 2)
        printf("STAT:  must specify a filename");
    else
        {
        while (*(++argv))
            {
            if ((fd = open(*argv, O_RDONLY)) == -1)
                fprintf(stderr, "STAT:  error accessing %s\n", *argv);
            else if (fstat(fd, &file_info) == -1)
                fprintf(stderr, "STAT:  error accessing %s\n", *argv);
            else
```

(continued)

continued

```
            {
            printf("NAME:  %s\nSIZE:  %ld bytes\nDATE:  %s\n", *argv,
                    file_info.st_size, ctime(&file_info.st_atime));
            close(fd);
            }
        }
    }
}
```

The program uses the run-time library function *ctime* to convert a time in seconds since midnight 01-01-1980 to a time and date in the following form:

```
Wed May 03 02:03:14 1989
```

■ **FACT:** *The* ctime *function converts a time stored as seconds since midnight 01-01-1980 to a 26-character ASCII string in the form* Wed May 03 02:03:14 1989.

Suppose the TEMP directory contains the following:

```
.            <DIR>      09-27-88    1:25p
..           <DIR>      09-27-88    1:25p
TMPNAM   C         384 03-03-89    3:23p
QUOTE    C          55 10-15-88    9:25p
MYFILE   TXT      1792 04-10-89   11:26a
         5 File(s)   41922560 bytes free
```

If you execute STAT to display information about your C source files, your screen shows

```
C> STAT \TEMP\TMPNAM.C \TEMP\QUOTE.C
NAME:  \TEMP\TMPNAM.C
SIZE:  384 bytes
DATE:  Fri Mar 03 15:23:06 1989

NAME:  \TEMP\QUOTE.C
SIZE:  55 bytes
DATE:  Sat Oct 15 21:25:00 1988
```

As you can see, *fstat* lets your program determine the size of a file and its modification date and time. In some cases, however, you might want to know only the length of a file. The run-time library function *filelength* returns the number of bytes a file contains.

■ **FACT:** *The* filelength *function returns a long integer value that represents the size (in bytes) of the file associated with a specified file handle.*

The following program (SIZE.C) displays the size of the file specified on the command line:

```
#include <fcntl.h>      /* needed for open mode arguments */
#include <io.h>         /* needed for open, close, and filelength */
#include <stdio.h>      /* needed for fprintf and constants */

main(int argc, char *argv[])
{
    int fd;  /* file handle */

    if (*(++argv))
        {
        if ((fd = open(*argv, O_RDONLY)) == -1)
            fprintf(stderr, "SIZE:  error accessing %s\n", *argv);
        else
            {
            printf("%s contains %ld bytes\n", *argv, filelength(fd));
            close(fd);
            }
        }
    else
        printf("SIZE:  must specify a filename");
}
```

To run the program, type the program name followed by a filename, as in the following example:

```
C> SIZE MYFILE.TXT
```

DETERMINING A FILE HANDLE TYPE

The return value of the *open* function is a handle to either a file or a device. The following revision of LCOPY.C (PRNCOPY.C) uses low-level I/O functions to copy the contents of an ASCII file to the printer.

```
#include <io.h>          /* needed for open, close, read, write, and eof */
#include <fcntl.h>       /* needed for open mode arguments */
#include <sys\types.h>   /* needed for file types */
#include <sys\stat.h>    /* needed for file status flags */
#include <stdio.h>       /* needed for fprintf and constants */
```

(continued)

429

continued

```
main(int argc, char *argv[])
{
    int source, target;    /* file handles */
    char buffer[1024];     /* buffer for file I/O operations */
    int bytes_read;        /* number of bytes read */

    if (argc < 2)
        fprintf(stderr, "PRNCOPY:  must specify source file\n");
    else if ((source = open(argv[1], O_BINARY : O_RDONLY)) == -1)
        fprintf(stderr, "PRNCOPY:  error opening %s\n", argv[1]);
    else if ((target = open("PRN", O_BINARY : O_WRONLY)) == -1)
        fprintf(stderr, "PRNCOPY:  error accessing PRN");
    else
        {
        while (!eof(source))
            {
            if ((bytes_read = read(source, buffer, sizeof(buffer))) <= 0)
                fprintf(stderr, "PRNCOPY:  error reading from source file");
            else
                if (write(target, buffer, bytes_read) != bytes_read)
                    fprintf(stderr, "PRNCOPY:  error writing to PRN");
            }

        close(source);
        close(target);
        }
}
```

The PRNCOPY program returns a handle to the device PRN. In some cases an operation, such as branching to a specific location in the file or returning the current file position, makes sense only when the handle references a file rather than a device. The C run-time library function *isatty* lets you determine whether a handle references a file or a device.

■ **FACT:** *The* isatty *function examines a file handle. If the handle references a device,* isatty *returns 1; if the handle references a file,* isatty *returns 0.*

The following program (DEVICE.C) opens the file or device specified by the first command line argument.

```
#include <io.h>          /* needed for open, close, and isatty */
#include <fcntl.h>       /* needed for open mode arguments */
#include <sys\types.h>   /* needed for file types */
#include <sys\stat.h>    /* needed for file status flags */
#include <stdio.h>       /* needed for fprintf and constants */
```

(continued)

continued

```
main(int argc, char *argv[])
{
    int fd;

    if ((fd = open(argv[1], O_RDONLY)) == -1)
        fprintf(stderr, "DEVICE:  error accessing %s\n", argv[1]);
    else
        if (isatty(fd))
            printf("%s is a device name\n", argv[1]);
        else
            printf("%s is a filename\n", argv[1]);
}
```

If the user specifies a device, such as CON, the screen shows

```
CON is a device name
```

If the user enters an existing filename, the screen displays a message like the following:

```
FILENAME.EXT is a filename
```

In Chapter 20 you learned how to write C programs that support I/O redirection. If you do not want the operating system to redirect your program's input or output to a file, *isatty* gives you partial control.

■ **FACT:** *C assigns the values 0, 1, 2, 3, and 4 to the file handles for stdin, stdout, stderr, stdprn, and stdaux.*

The following program (REDIR.C) uses *isatty* to test whether the handles associated with stdin and stdout reference a file or a device. If a given handle does not reference a device, it has been redirected by the operating system.

```
#include <io.h>  /* needed for isatty */

main()
{
    if (isatty(0))
        puts("stdin points to device");
    else
        puts("stdin redirected to file");

    if (isatty(1))
        puts("stdout points to device");
    else
        puts("stdout redirected to file");
}
```

If you run the program without redirection, your screen shows

```
C> REDIR
stdin points to device
stdout points to device
```

If you run the program with redirected input, as follows, your screen shows

```
C> DIR ¦ REDIR
stdin redirected to file
stdout points to device
```

By including this simple test for redirection at the start of your programs, you can detect most redirections. However, if the user issues the following command:

```
C> REDIR > PRN
```

the handle to stdout still references a device, and the user is unable to determine whether the device is the screen or another device. Later in this chapter you learn how to ensure that your program output is always written to the screen.

USING *lseek* AND *tell*

In Chapter 21 you learned that the C run-time library function *fseek* lets you move a file pointer to a new offset in the file. The *ftell* function returns the current position in the file. The run-time library routines *lseek* and *tell* work in similar ways, but you can call them with file handles returned by *open* or *creat* rather than with file pointers.

■ **FACT:** *The* lseek *function moves the file pointer associated with a given file handle to the specified offset. If* lseek *repositions the file pointer, it returns the new offset. If an error occurs,* lseek *returns −1.*

The format of a call to the *lseek* function is as follows:

```
new_offset = lseek(handle, long_offset, origin);
```

The variable *new_offset* represents a long integer value to which the statement assigns the new offset returned by *lseek*. The return value is always an offset from the beginning of the file. The *handle* argument is the file handle returned by *open* or *creat*. The *long_offset* argument is a long integer value that specifies the requested offset in bytes. The *origin* argument specifies the location in the file from which you want to apply the offset. The table on the following page lists valid constants for identifying the offset location.

Constant	Meaning
SEEK_SET	Offset from the beginning of the file
SEEK_CUR	Offset from the current position
SEEK_END	Offset from the end of the file

■ **FACT:** *The* tell *function returns the current position of the file pointer associated with a given file handle. If* tell *retrieves the current position, it returns a long value containing the current file position. If an error occurs,* tell *returns −1.*

The *tell* function takes one argument, a file handle provided by *open* or *creat*. It returns the current position in the file. The return value is an offset from the beginning of the file.

DUPLICATING A FILE HANDLE

As you develop more programs that support I/O redirection, you might eventually want to save or duplicate a file handle to stdin, stdout, stderr, stdprn, or stdaux. Two run-time library functions let you do that.

■ **FACT:** *The* dup *function lets you copy the value of a file handle. If* dup *copies the specified handle, it returns a copy of the file handle. If an error occurs,* dup *returns −1. For example, the statement* output = dup(1); *assigns to the variable* output *the value of the handle associated with stdout.*

The run-time library function *dup* is useful for copying a file handle. The sample program in this section uses *dup* to save the current value of a file handle.

■ **FACT:** *The* dup2 *function forces a second file handle to contain the value of the handle associated with an open file. If* dup2 *duplicates the handle, it returns 0; if it cannot duplicate the handle,* dup2 *returns −1. For example,* status = dup2(handle, duplicate); *copies the value of* handle *to* duplicate *and assigns a return value to* status.

As you learned in Chapter 20, the operating system cannot redirect output written to the standard error device. If you have a program whose output you don't want redirected, you can rewrite the entire program to write output to *stderr*, or you can use the run-time library function *dup2* to assign stdout to point to stderr. Regardless of any redirection on the command line, the program writes its output to the screen.

The program on the following page (NOREDIR.C) uses *dup* and *dup2* to prevent output from being redirected from the screen.

```
#include <io.h>      /* needed for dup and dup2 */
#include <stdio.h>   /* needed for putchar */

main()
{
    int count, save_handle;
    char letter;

    save_handle = dup(1);   /* save stdout */
    dup2(2, 1);             /* point stdout (1) to stderr (2) */

    for (count = 0; count < 5; count++)
        {
        for (letter = 'A'; letter <= 'Z'; letter++)
            putchar(letter);
        putchar('\n');
        }

    dup2(save_handle, 1);   /* restore stdout */
}
```

Regardless of any redirection of output on the command line, the program output appears on the screen. The program begins by saving the current value of the handle associated with stdout. Next the program uses *dup2* to copy the handle associated with stderr to stdout. The *dup2* function has as arguments a pair of file handles; it duplicates the value of the first argument in the second. After the program completes its output, it restores the handle associated with stdout to its original value.

As this chapter has shown, the file manipulation functions in the C run-time library can contribute tremendous flexibility to your programs.

SUMMARY

Comparing Stream and Low-Level File I/O

■ **FACT:** *Low-level file manipulation functions use an integer value called a file handle, or descriptor. The C run-time library routines* creat *and* open *return a file handle to a specific file.*

Using Low-Level Functions: A First Example

■ **FACT:** *The* open *function opens an existing file on disk for read, write, or read/write operations. If it opens the file in the specified mode,* open *returns a file handle; if* open *cannot open the file as requested, it returns an error status of −1.*

■ **TRAP:** *If the file specified in the call to* open *does not exist,* open *does not create the file unless you also specified the O_CREAT mode.*

■ **FACT:** *The* creat *function creates a file on disk using the specified permission mode. If it creates the file with the requested permission setting,* creat *returns an integer file handle. If an error occurs,* creat *returns −1.*

■ **TIP:** *To create files, use the* open *function with the O_CREAT value in the access mode. Use of the* creat *function is discouraged.*

■ **FACT:** *The* eof *function tests for an end of file condition in the file associated with the specified handle. If the file pointer is at the end of the file,* eof *returns 1; if it is not at the end of the file,* eof *returns 0.*

■ **FACT:** *The* read *function reads a specified number of bytes from a file into a buffer. If it reads into the buffer as requested,* read *returns the number of bytes read. If an error occurs,* read *returns −1. If it immediately encounters the end of file,* read *returns 0.*

■ **FACT:** *The* write *function writes a specified number of bytes from a buffer to a file. Upon completion,* write *returns the number of bytes actually written to a file; if an error occurs,* write *returns −1.*

■ **FACT:** *The* close *function closes the file associated with the specified file handle and updates the directory on disk.*

Getting File Information

■ **FACT:** *The* fstat *function returns a structure that contains specific information about the file associated with the specified file handle. If* fstat *obtains the file information, it returns 0; if it cannot obtain the information,* fstat *returns −1.*

■ **FACT:** *The* ctime *function converts a time stored as seconds since midnight 01-01-1980 to a 26-character ASCII string in the form* Wed May 03 02:03:14 1989.

■ **FACT:** *The* filelength *function returns a long integer value that represents the size (in bytes) of the file associated with a specified file handle.*

Determining a File Handle Type

■ **FACT:** *The* isatty *function examines a file handle. If the handle references a device,* isatty *returns 1; if the handle references a file,* isatty *returns 0.*

■ **FACT:** *C assigns the values 0, 1, 2, 3, and 4 to the file handles for stdin, stdout, stderr, stdprn, and stdaux.*

Using *lseek* and *tell*

■ **FACT:** *The* lseek *function moves the file pointer associated with a given file handle to the specified offset. If* lseek *repositions the file pointer, it returns the new offset. If an error occurs,* lseek *returns −1.*

■ **FACT:** *The* tell *function returns the current position of the file pointer associated with a given file handle. If* tell *retrieves the current position, it returns a long value containing the current file position. If an error occurs,* tell *returns −1.*

Duplicating a File Handle

■ **FACT:** *The* dup *function lets you copy the value of a file handle. If* dup *copies the specified handle, it returns a copy of the file handle. If an error occurs,* dup *returns −1. For example, the statement* output = dup(1); *assigns to the variable* output *the value of the handle associated with stdout.*

■ **FACT:** *The* dup2 *function forces a second file handle to contain the value of the handle associated with an open file. If* dup2 *duplicates the handle, it returns 0; if it cannot duplicate the handle,* dup2 *returns −1. For example, the statement* status = dup2(handle, duplicate); *copies the value of* handle *to* duplicate *and assigns a return value to* status.

GLOSSARY

handle An integer value used by the C low-level file I/O routines to access a file or device. The run-time library routines *open* and *creat* return a file handle. Some C programmers refer to file handles as file descriptors.

low-level I/O File input or output that relies on a set of run-time library functions that bypass the buffering capacities of the operating system. Low-level functions use integer file handles rather than file pointers to identify files.

stream I/O Character-based input or output in which the input or output is handled one character at a time in a continuous stream until the end of file occurs. The C functions *fopen*, *fgets*, *fputs*, and so forth are commonly used stream I/O routines.

## CHAPTER 25

Dynamic Memory Allocation

All the programs we have worked with so far have used arrays and character strings of fixed length. To change the size of these arrays and character strings, you must edit the source file and recompile your program. For example, assume that you create an array to store 100 directory entries that your program later sorts and displays in alphabetic order. As long as the directory contains fewer than 100 files, the program works successfully. However, if the number of files exceeds 100, you must change the program and recompile.

One solution is to make your array large enough to store 1000 file entries. A user's directory is very unlikely to contain 1000 entries. Unfortunately, when you create an array this large, you waste a considerable amount of memory. An ideal solution is to allocate memory storage as the program requires. This process of allocating memory "on the fly" is called dynamic memory allocation. As you will see, the C run-time library contains several routines that support the use of dynamic memory allocation.

LAYING A FOUNDATION

By default, each time you execute a program, DOS sets aside a 64 KB segment, called the code segment, that contains your program code. DOS also sets aside a 64 KB segment called the data segment. If you use a memory model other than the default small memory model, the program can have multiple code and data segments. The discussion in this chapter, however, assumes the small memory model. We look at other memory models in Part IV.

The C compiler uses the data segment to store your program's global and static variables. It also allocates, by default, 2000 bytes within the data segment for the stack. As discussed in Chapter 23, the compiler passes arguments on the stack when you call a function. The compiler also allocates memory from the stack for the function's local variables. After allocating portions to global and static variables and to the stack, the compiler devotes the remainder of the data segment to the *heap*, as shown in Figure 25-1.

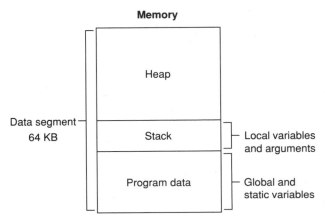

FIGURE 25-1.
The data segment is divided into three regions.

Most of the run-time library routines that we examine in this chapter allocate memory from the heap. To better understand use of the data segment, let's look at the C run-time library functions *stackavail* and *_memavl*.

■ **FACT:** *The* stackavail *function returns the number of bytes currently available in the stack. The value returned is an unsigned integer.*

The following program (SEESTACK.C) uses the *stackavail* function to display the size of the stack at different points in the execution of the program:

```
#include <malloc.h>   /* needed for stackavail */

main()
{
    void some_function(void);

    printf("Starting stack size %u\n", stackavail());
    some_function();
    printf("Ending stack size %u\n", stackavail());
}
```

(continued)

continued

```
void some_function(void)
{
    int array[100];

    printf("Stack size in function %u\n", stackavail());
}
```

When you run the program, your screen shows

```
Starting stack size 1764
Stack size in function 1560
Ending stack size 1764
```

As you can see, the amount of space available in the stack changes as your program invokes different functions. Note, for example, that *some_function* allocates 200 bytes from the stack for its local variable *array*. In Chapter 26 you will learn how to increase the size of the stack using switches on the CL command line.

■ **FACT:** *The* _memavl *function returns an unsigned integer that represents the number of bytes available for allocation in the heap.*

The following program (SEEHEAP.C) uses *_memavl* to obtain the current heap size:

```
#include <malloc.h>   /* needed for _memavl */

main()
{
    printf("Current heap size is %u", _memavl());
}
```

Later in this chapter we create programs that allocate memory from the heap. Those programs can use *_memavl* to determine the amount of heap space available for allocation.

Many programs allocate space from the heap, use the space, and then give it back to the heap. Assume, for example, that a program allocates 100 bytes of space on three separate occasions, as shown in Figure 25-2A on the following page. Next, assume that the program allocates a 500-byte section from the heap, as shown in Figure 25-2B. If the program later returns the three 100-byte segments to the heap, as shown in Figure 25-2C, the available heap space becomes divided.

Once the heap is divided, the largest available block is smaller than the total available heap space. The C run-time library function *_memmax* returns the largest block of available memory in the heap.

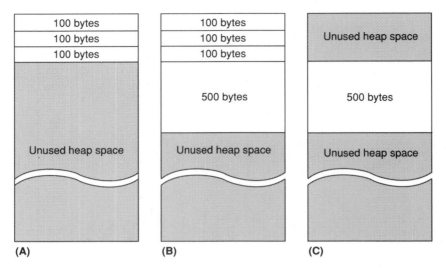

| 100 bytes |
| 100 bytes |
| 100 bytes |

Unused heap space

(A)

| 100 bytes |
| 100 bytes |
| 100 bytes |

500 bytes

Unused heap space

(B)

Unused heap space

500 bytes

Unused heap space

(C)

FIGURE 25-2.
(A) A program allocates three 100-byte blocks. (B) It then allocates an additional 500 bytes. (C) The heap is divided when the first three entries are released.

■ **FACT:** *The _memmax function returns an unsigned integer that represents the largest block of space available in the heap.*

Most programs that need to allocate space from the heap need to obtain the space as a single block. Such programs can use *_memmax* to determine the largest block of available heap space.

FASTCOPY: A FIRST EXAMPLE

In Chapter 24 we wrote a program called LCOPY that copied the contents of one file to another. The program used a buffer of 1024 bytes for each file I/O operation. In this section we examine a program (FASTCOPY.C) that dynamically allocates as large a buffer as needed to copy the file (or the largest available block, whichever is smaller). As a rule, the larger the copy buffer, the fewer the disk I/O operations required.

To begin, FASTCOPY uses the run-time library function *filelength* to determine the size of the file in bytes. Next the program calls *_memmax* to obtain the size of the largest block of available heap space. The program then dynamically allocates memory for the buffer using the C run-time library function *malloc*.

```c
#include <io.h>           /* needed for open, close, read, write, */
                          /* filelength, and eof */
#include <fcntl.h>        /* needed for open mode arguments */
#include <sys\types.h>    /* needed for file types */
#include <sys\stat.h>     /* needed for status flags */
#include <stdio.h>        /* needed for fprintf and constants */
#include <malloc.h>       /* needed for _memmax, malloc, and free */

main(int argc, char *argv[])
{
    int source, target;        /* file handles */
    char *buffer;              /* buffer for file I/O operations */
    unsigned int bytes_read;   /* number of bytes read */
    unsigned int heap_size;    /* largest block in the heap */
    unsigned int file_size;    /* size of the file to copy in bytes */
    unsigned int buffer_size;  /* size of buffer to allocate */

    if (argc < 3)
        fprintf(stderr, "FASTCOPY:  must specify source and target\n");
    else if ((source = open(argv[1], O_BINARY : O_RDONLY)) == -1)
        fprintf(stderr, "FASTCOPY:  error opening %s\n", argv[1]);
    else if ((target = open(argv[2], O_WRONLY : O_BINARY :
            O_TRUNC : O_CREAT, S_IWRITE)) == -1)
        fprintf(stderr, "FASTCOPY:  error opening %s\n", argv[2]);
    else
        {
        file_size = filelength(source);
        heap_size = _memmax();
        buffer_size = (file_size < heap_size) ? file_size : heap_size;

        if ((buffer = malloc(buffer_size)) == NULL)
            fprintf(stderr, "FASTCOPY:  unable to allocate memory\n");
        else
            while (!eof(source))
                {
                if ((bytes_read = read(source, buffer, buffer_size)) <= 0)
                    fprintf(stderr, "FASTCOPY:  error reading source\n");
                else
                    if (write(target, buffer, bytes_read) != bytes_read)
                        fprintf(stderr, "FASTCOPY:  error writing target\n");
                }

        free(buffer);
        close(source);
        close(target);
        }
}
```

■ **FACT:** *The* malloc *function allocates a specified number of bytes from the heap. The largest block* malloc *can allocate is 64 KB. If* malloc *allocates the requested block, it returns a pointer to the first byte of the allocated memory. If an error occurs,* malloc *returns NULL.*

After FASTCOPY completes the file-copying operation, it uses the run-time library function *free* to return the allocated memory to the heap.

■ **FACT:** *The* free *function returns to the heap the memory associated with a specified pointer. The function does not return a value.*

As discussed, once a program finishes using allocated memory, it should return the memory to the heap so that it can be allocated for another purpose. The run-time library function *free* returns memory to the heap.

After it opens the two required files, FASTCOPY compares the size of the source file with the available heap size and allocates memory based on the smaller of the two. If the file is smaller than the available heap, allocating more bytes of memory than the file contains is unneccessary. If, on the other hand, the file is larger than the available memory, you are constrained by the available heap space.

As you can see, dynamic memory allocation gives your programs considerable flexibility. Simply remember to follow these steps:

1. Determine the amount of memory required.

2. Determine whether the heap has enough memory available.

3. Allocate the memory.

4. Release the memory to the heap when it is no longer needed.

OTHER WAYS TO DYNAMICALLY ALLOCATE MEMORY

The FASTCOPY program used the *malloc* function to allocate memory from the heap. Another run-time library routine, *calloc*, also allocates memory from the heap. Unlike *malloc*, it initializes each byte in the allocated memory to 0.

■ **FACT:** *The* calloc *function allocates memory from the heap. A call to* calloc *has two arguments, the number of items and the length of each (in bytes). The function initializes each element to 0. If* calloc *allocates the heap space as requested, it returns a pointer to the first byte in the dynamic memory. If an error occurs,* calloc *returns NULL.*

Unlike the call to *malloc*, in which you specify only the number of bytes for which to allocate space, invoking the *calloc* function requires you to specify the number of items of a specified size. For example, the statement *ptr = calloc(1, 80);* allocates one 80-byte block of memory.

The following program (AMEM.C) uses *calloc* to allocate memory for an array of 10 integer values. The program then assigns 10 random numbers to the array and invokes the function *show_values* to display them.

```c
#include <stdlib.h>   /* needed for rand */
#include <malloc.h>   /* needed for calloc and free */
#include <stdio.h>    /* needed for fprintf and constants */

main()
{
    void show_values(int *, int);
    int *ptr, i;

    if ((ptr = (int *) calloc(10, sizeof(int))) == NULL)
        fprintf(stderr, "AMEM:  error allocating memory\n");
    else
        {
        for (i = 0; i < 10; ++i)
            ptr[i] = rand();   /* assign random number*/

        show_values(ptr, 10);  /* display values */
        free(ptr);             /* release memory */
        }
}

void show_values(int *array, int size)
{
    int i = 0;

    while (i++ < size)
        printf("%d\n", *array++);
}
```

As you can see, once the program allocates memory with *calloc*, the compiler lets you use either pointers or arrays to access the contents of the allocated space.

■ **TRAP:** *By default,* calloc *returns a pointer to a value of type* char. *To obtain a pointer to a different type, you must use a cast.*

Notice in AMEM.C that we cast the value that *calloc* returns to a pointer to a value of type *int*. The cast is necessary because we want to access *ptr* as an array of values of *sizeof(int)* bytes each. The default type returned by *calloc* is a pointer to a *char* value.

Because *calloc* requires that the first argument specify the number of entries for which to allocate space, you might need to precede a call to *calloc* with a call to *_freect*. The runtime library function *_freect* lets you determine the maximum number of objects of a specific size for which you can allocate space.

■ **FACT:** *The _freect function determines the maximum number of elements a program can allocate from the heap using* calloc. *The function takes one argument — the size of each element (in bytes) — and returns the maximum number of elements as an unsigned integer.*

The following program (FREEHEAP.C) uses *_freect* to display the number of items of different types that can fit in the available heap space.

```
#include <malloc.h>  /* needed for _memavl and _freect */

main()
{
    printf("Available heap space %u bytes\n", _memavl());
    printf("Space for %u items of type char\n", _freect(sizeof(char)));
    printf("Space for %u items of type int\n", _freect(sizeof(int)));
    printf("Space for %u items of type float\n", _freect(sizeof(float)));
    printf("Space for %u items of type double\n", _freect(sizeof(double)));
}
```

When you run the program, your screen shows output similar to the following:

```
Available heap space 60752 bytes
Space for 15188 items of type char
Space for 15188 items of type int
Space for 10124 items of type float
Space for 6075 items of type double
```

As you can see, the *_freect* routine gives you a quick means to determine how many entries of a specific type you can allocate with *calloc*.

Both *calloc* and *malloc* allocate memory from the heap, but *calloc* initializes the memory to 0, whereas *malloc* does not. Depending on your processing requirements, the initialization might simply consume processing time unnecessarily.

The C run-time library function *alloca* enables a function to allocate memory from the stack.

■ **FACT:** *The* alloca *function allocates a specified number of bytes from the stack. When the function that allocated the memory ends, the compiler releases the allocated space to the stack. If* alloca *allocates the requested space, it returns a pointer to the allocated memory. If* alloca *cannot reserve the space, it returns NULL.*

The following program (ASTACK.C) displays the current available stack space. Next the program invokes the function *alloc_stack*, which allocates 100 bytes of stack space and then displays the available stack. Remember, the compiler stores the function's local variables in the stack, too. When the function ends, the compiler returns the allocated space to the stack, and the program displays the available stack space before it terminates.

```
#include <malloc.h>   /* needed for stackavail and alloca */
#include <stdio.h>    /* needed for fprintf and constants */

main()
{
    void alloc_stack(void);

    printf("Starting stack space %u\n", stackavail());
    alloc_stack();
    printf("Ending stack space %u", stackavail());
}

void alloc_stack(void)
{
    int *ptr;

    if ((ptr = alloca(10 * sizeof(int))) == NULL)
        fprintf(stderr, "ASTACK:  error allocating stack\n");
    else
        printf("In function, available stack space %u\n", stackavail());
}
```

When you run the program, your screen shows

```
Starting stack space 1764
In function, available stack space 1732
Ending stack space 1764
```

As you can see, the compiler releases the stack space when the function that allocated the space ends. Like *calloc*, the *alloca* function returns a pointer to type *char*. To obtain a pointer to a different type, you must use a cast.

■ **TRAP:** *Do not pass the pointer returned by* alloca *to the* free *function. The* free *function releases memory from the heap, not from the stack. If you pass the pointer from* alloca *to* free*, your program is likely to fail, and your computer might hang.*

Keep in mind that, by default, the compiler provides a stack space of only 2000 bytes. If you exceed this amount, you will overwrite program data, and your program will get incorrect results or fail. Because of the limited stack size, most programs allocate memory from the heap rather than from the stack. Allocating memory from the stack becomes practical when you learn (in the next chapter) to increase the stack size for your program.

CREATING AND ALLOCATING HUGE ARRAYS

As we noted earlier, the default small memory model provides your program with one 64 KB data segment. All your variables must reside in this segment. If, however, you need to declare an array that exceeds 64 KB, specify the keyword *huge* in the array declaration.

■ **FACT:** *The keyword* huge *tells the compiler that the size of the array exceeds 64 KB. The compiler is then able to place the array in memory outside your data segment. For example, the statement* int huge voters[100000]; *declares a huge array.*

If you need to allocate more than 64 KB, use the C run-time library function *halloc.*

■ **FACT:** *The* halloc *function lets your program allocate a huge block of memory (greater than 64 KB). Like* calloc, *the* halloc *function initializes each element to 0. If successful,* halloc *returns a pointer to the memory; if it cannot allocate the requested memory,* halloc *returns NULL.*

The following program (AHUGE.C) uses *halloc* to allocate a block of memory for a huge array of 100,000 *long int* values. The program assigns the values 0 through 99,999 to the array and then calls the function *display_values* to display every thousandth element of the array on the screen. (Displaying every element of the array would take about 30 minutes.)

```
#include <malloc.h>  /* needed for halloc and hfree */
#include <stdio.h>   /* needed for fprintf and constants */

main()
{
    long int huge *array;  /* pointer to allocated memory */
    long int i;            /* index into the array */

    if ((array = (long int huge *) halloc(100000,
                                 sizeof(long int))) == NULL)
        fprintf(stderr, "AHUGE:  can't allocate memory\n");
    else
        {
        for (i = 0; i < 100000; i++)
            array[i] = i;

        display_array(array, i);  /* display array values */

        hfree(array);             /* release memory */
        }
}
```

(continued)

continued

```
display_array(long int huge array[], long int size)
{
    long int i;

    for (i = 0; i < size; i += 1000)   /* display every 1000th element */
        printf("%ld\n", array[i]);
}
```

When the program no longer needs the memory, it invokes the run-time library function *hfree* to release it. For example, the statement *hfree(huge_array);* frees the memory allocated to *huge_array*.

■ **FACT:** *The* hfree *function releases huge memory blocks allocated previously with* halloc.

The *malloc, calloc, alloca*, and *halloc* functions provide you with a variety of ways to allocate memory as your needs require.

CHANGING AN ALLOCATION

Dynamic allocation lets you match the amount of memory you use to the amount you actually need. If you find that you have dynamically allocated and even assigned values to a block of memory that is too large or too small, the C run-time library can help. The *realloc* and *_expand* functions enable you to change the size of an allocated block of memory.

■ **FACT:** *The* realloc *function adjusts the size of a previously allocated block of memory. To adjust the size,* realloc *might need to move the block within the heap. Any previously assigned values remain unchanged. If* realloc *makes the adjustment, it returns a pointer to the new memory block; if it cannot adjust the size as requested,* realloc *returns NULL.*

A call to *realloc* must contain the pointer to the existing block and the number of bytes by which the block size is to be adjusted. For example, the following statement,

```
new_ptr = realloc(old_ptr, 10000);
```

requests an increase in the size of the block associated with *old_ptr*. The statement assigns the location of the new block to *new_ptr*.

In a similar manner, C provides the run-time library function *_expand*, which changes the size of a previously allocated block of memory. Unlike *realloc*, which can move allocated memory within the heap to satisfy the request, *_expand* adjusts the size of a block without changing its location.

■ **FACT:** *The* _expand *function expands or shrinks an allocated block of memory without moving the block within the heap. If* _expand *changes the size of the block, it returns the pointer to the original block of memory; if it cannot adjust the size of the block without changing the location of the block,* _expand *returns NULL.*

Suppose you have several pointers assigned to key elements within the allocated memory. If you need to increase the size of the memory block, you don't want the block to move. Under those circumstances, you need to use *_expand*. If you don't care whether the block moves in memory, use *realloc*.

■ **FACT:** *The* _msize *function returns an unsigned integer value that specifies the number of bytes in a block of allocated memory.*

The run-time library function *_msize* can tell you the size of a block of allocated memory. The function takes one argument, a pointer to the block in question.

The following program (MEMMOD.C) demonstrates the functions *realloc*, *_expand*, and *_msize*. The program first uses *malloc* to allocate 100 bytes of memory. Next, using *realloc*, it increases the size of the allocated block to 1000 bytes. Last, the program uses *_expand* to shrink the block to 500 bytes. At each stage, the program calls *_msize* within a *printf* statement to display the current size of the block.

```
#include <malloc.h>  /* needed for realloc, _expand, _msize, and free */
#include <stdio.h>   /* needed for fprintf and constants */

main()
{
    char *ptr;

    if ((ptr = malloc(100)) == NULL)
        fprintf(stderr, "MEMMOD:  error in call to malloc\n");
    else
        {
        printf("Size after malloc %u\n", _msize(ptr));
        if ((ptr = realloc(ptr, 1000)) == NULL)
            fprintf(stderr, "MEMMOD:  error in call to realloc\n");
        else
            {
            printf("Size after realloc %u\n", _msize(ptr));

            if ((ptr = _expand(ptr, 500)) == NULL)
                fprintf(stderr, "MEMMOD:  error in call to _expand\n");
            else
                printf("Ending size %u\n", _msize(ptr));
            }
        free(ptr);
        }
}
```

When you run the program, your screen shows

```
Size after malloc 100
Size after realloc 1000
Ending size 500
```

As you can see, the run-time library not only gives you the ability to allocate memory dynamically but also lets you change your previous allocations as your needs require.

USING LINKED LISTS

So far, each program in this chapter has allocated memory in one large section. However, one of the powerful uses of dynamic memory manipulation is to create a chain of values called a *linked list*. For example, at the beginning of this chapter we discussed a program that displays a sorted directory listing of your files. We noted that one (nondynamic) way to accommodate large directories is to create an array large enough to store 1000 directory entries, as shown here:

```
struct find_t directory[1000];
```

As *_dos_findfirst* and *_dos_findnext* return directory entries, the program simply adds each one to the array. An alternative method is to allocate memory for each directory entry as needed by creating a *linked list*, in which each entry is part of a structure that includes a pointer to the next entry in the list. Figure 25-3A shows such a linked list of directory entries.

When *_dos_findnext* returns the next file in the directory, the program simply adds another entry to the end of the list, as shown in Figure 25-3B.

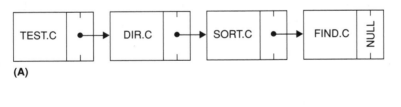

(A)

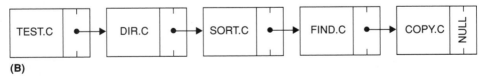

(B)

FIGURE 25-3.
(A) In a linked list, each entry includes a pointer to the next entry. (B) To add an entry, set the pointer in the preceding entry so that it references the new entry.

The linked list is declared as a self-referential structure, one which has a member that points to a structure of the same type.

The following program (MYDIR.C) uses *_dos_findfirst* and *_dos_findnext* to create a linked list of the files in the directory. In MYDIR.C the *directory* structure contains a pointer to another structure of type *directory*:

```
struct directory
    {
    struct find_t file_info;
    struct directory *next;  /* next entry in list */
    };
```

As you can see, the other member of the *directory* structure is itself a structure of type *find_t*, which is defined in stdio.h.

```
#include <dos.h>      /* needed for _dos_findfirst and _dos_findnext */
#include <malloc.h>   /* needed for malloc */
#include <stdio.h>    /* needed for find_t structure */
#include <memory.h>   /* needed for memcpy */

main()
{
    struct directory
        {
        struct find_t file_info;  /* directory information */
        struct directory *next;   /* pointer to next entry */
        } *first, *node;

    struct find_t file_info;      /* passed to _dos_findfirst/next */

    int result;                   /* result of _dos_findfirst/next */

    /* allocate memory for first entry in the list */

    if ((first = malloc(sizeof(struct directory))) == NULL)
        fprintf(stderr, "MYDIR:  error allocating first entry\n");
    else
        {
        node = first;             /* current node */
        node->next = NULL;        /* no other nodes in the list */
        node->file_info.name[0] = NULL;

        /* find all files in the current directory */
        result = _dos_findfirst("*.*", 0, &file_info);

        while (!result)
            {
            /* copy the file information into the list */
            memcpy(&(node->file_info), &file_info, sizeof(struct find_t));
```

(continued)

continued

```
                    /* allocate memory for the next entry in the list */
            if ((node->next = malloc(sizeof(struct directory))) == NULL)
                {
                fprintf(stderr, "MYDIR:  error allocating memory\n");
                break;
                }
            else
                {
                result = _dos_findnext(&file_info);

                if (result)
                    node->next = NULL;  /* no files remain - end list */
                else
                    node = node->next;
                }
            }

        /* display the entries in the list */
        node = first;           /* start at front of list */
        while (node)            /* while entries exist */
            {
            printf("%s\n", node->file_info.name);
            node = node->next;      /* get next entry in the list */
            }
        }
    }
```

MYDIR.C uses two structure variables, *first* and *node*, called *headers*, that track the entries in the list. The *first* header always points to the first entry in the list. The *node* header points to the current entry. Remember, because we are using pointers to structures, we can use the notation *structure–>member* to access particular structure members.

Let's walk through the processing that occurs in MYDIR.C. We'll assume that our directory contains three files, as follows:

```
MYDIR   C       1792 11-10-88  11:26a
MYDIR   OBJ       660 11-11-88   4:00p
MYDIR   EXE      7619 11-11-88   4:00p
```

First, the program allocates memory for the first directory entry. If the call to *malloc* succeeds, *first* contains the address of a structure capable of storing the directory information for a file (Figure 25-4A on the following page). Next, the program assigns the address held in *first* to the pointer *node*, which always contains the current entry (Figure 25-4B).

Using *_dos_findfirst*, the program gets specific information about the file MYDIR.C. The program then enters the *while* loop, in which the run-time library function *memcpy* copies the file information to the memory location referenced by *node* (Figure 25-4C).

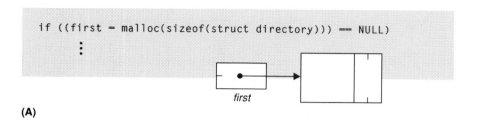

```
if ((first = malloc(sizeof(struct directory))) == NULL)
     ⋮
```

(A)

```
if ((first = malloc(sizeof(struct directory))) == NULL)
     ⋮
   node = first
```

(B)

```
if ((first = malloc(sizeof(struct directory))) == NULL)
      ⋮
   node = first
   node->next = NULL;
         ⋮
      memcpy(&(node->file_info),
             &file_info, sizeof(struct find_t));
```

(C)

FIGURE 25-4.

(A) The MYDIR program dynamically allocates space for each entry. (B) The pointer to the current structure is initially set to first. *(C) After a call to* _dos_findfirst, *the program assigns file information with* memcpy.

■ **FACT:** *The* memcpy *function copies the number of bytes specified from a source location to a target. For example,* memcpy(target, source, sizeof(source)); *uses* sizeof *to specify that all of* source *be copied to* target.

Next the program calls *malloc* again to allocate space for the second entry. This time the address returned by *malloc* is assigned to the pointer member of the first entry. The pointer becomes a link between the first entry and the second.

The program then calls *_dos_findnext*, which retrieves information for the file MYDIR.OBJ. The program again uses *memcpy* to copy file information to the current entry, as shown in Figure 25-5A. This process is repeated for the third entry: Structure space is allocated, the new entry is linked to the one preceding, and file information is copied to the *file_info* member (Figure 25-5B). When *_dos_findnext* looks for a fourth file, no files remain; accordingly, the program ends the list by assigning the pointer *next* in the third entry to NULL.

After the list is complete, MYDIR starts at the beginning of the list with *first* and displays each value. The final *while* loop uses the links in the list to locate successive members until it encounters NULL. The program then ends, and its heap memory is released.

■ **FACT:** *When a program ends, memory allocated by the program from the heap is automatically released.*

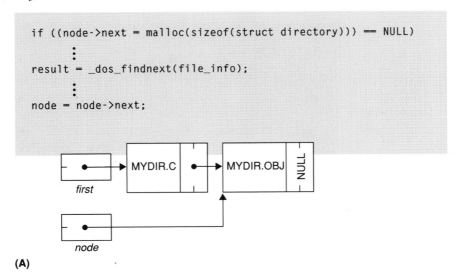

```
if ((node->next = malloc(sizeof(struct directory))) == NULL)
     ⋮
result = _dos_findnext(file_info);
     ⋮
node = node->next;
```

(A)

FIGURE 25-5. *(continued)*
(A) The address of the second list entry is assigned to node, *and file information is copied for MYDIR.OBJ. (B) The program repeats the process for MYDIR.EXE.*

FIGURE 25-5. *continued*

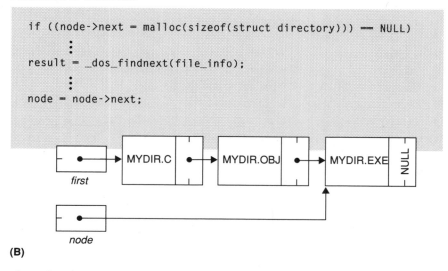

```
if ((node->next = malloc(sizeof(struct directory))) == NULL)
    ⋮
result = _dos_findnext(file_info);
    ⋮
node = node->next;
```

(B)

If you finish using allocated memory before your program is ready to end, release the memory using *free*. You need not release the memory if your program uses it throughout the program; it is released when the program ends.

LINKED LIST *vs* ARRAY

You have seen two methods for handling large amounts of data: arrays declared with the *huge* qualifier, and linked lists that allocate memory dynamically. As you begin an application that processes a large amount of data, you must determine whether your storage needs are better met by an array or by a linked list. As a general rule, linked lists offer flexibility but sacrifice speed.

If you expect considerable fluctuation in the amount of data your program manipulates, you might prefer the flexibility of linked lists. As the MYDIR program illustrates, linked lists can grow dynamically to match your needs. Linked lists are also quite convenient when you need to sort large amounts of data. Inserting and deleting items is much easier in a linked list than it is in an array.

If your data size is fixed, you would probably benefit from the speed of array manipulation. The run-time library functions that allocate memory from the heap are time consuming. A program that dynamically allocates space for 100 entries executes more slowly than an application that uses a predefined array of 100 elements.

USING DOUBLY LINKED LISTS

The linked list that we examined in the preceding example was a singly linked list: It contained a pointer from one entry to the next. To simplify the insertion and deletion of entries in a linked list, many programs use a doubly linked list, in which each entry contains a pointer not only to the subsequent entry but also to the preceding entry in the list, as shown in Figure 25-6.

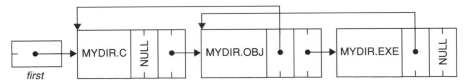

FIGURE 25-6.
Entries in a doubly linked list have pointers to both the subsequent entry and the preceding entry in the list.

The following program (MYDIR2.C) displays the directory listing sorted by filename. The program uses a doubly linked list to insert a file into the correct location in the list.

```
#include <dos.h>     /* needed for _dos_findfirst and _dos_findnext */
#include <malloc.h>  /* needed for malloc */
#include <stdio.h>   /* needed for fprintf and find_t structure */
#include <memory.h>  /* needed for memcpy */
#include <string.h>  /* needed for strcmp */


main()
{
    struct directory
        {
        struct find_t file_info;  /* directory information */
        struct directory *prev;   /* pointer to previous entry */
        struct directory *next;   /* pointer to next entry */
        } *first, *node, *new;

    struct find_t file_info;      /* passed to _dos_findfirst/next */

    int result;                   /* result of _dos_findfirst/next */

    /* allocate memory for first entry in the list */

    if ((first = malloc(sizeof(struct directory))) == NULL)
        fprintf(stderr, "MYDIR2:  error allocating first entry\n");
```

(continued)

continued

```
    else
        {
        new = first;              /* current node */
        new->prev = NULL;         /* no preceding nodes */
        new->next = NULL;         /* no succeeding nodes */
        new->file_info.name[0] = NULL;

        /* find all files in the current directory */
        result = _dos_findfirst("*.*", 0, &file_info);

        if (!result)  /* copy the file information into the list */
            memcpy(&(new->file_info), &file_info, sizeof(struct find_t));

        while (!result)
            {
            result = _dos_findnext(&file_info);

            if (!result)
                {
                /* allocate memory for the next entry in the list */
                if ((new = malloc(sizeof(struct directory))) == NULL)
                    {
                    fprintf(stderr, "MYDIR:  error allocating memory\n");
                    break;
                    }

                /* copy the file information into the list */
                memcpy(&(new->file_info), &file_info,
                        sizeof(struct find_t));

                /* put the new entry in the list in alphabetic order */
                node = first;
                while (node)
                    {
                    if (strcmp(new->file_info.name,
                        node->file_info.name) <= 0)
                        {
                        if (node != first)
                            {
                            node->prev->next = new;
                            new->prev = node->prev;
                            new->next = node;
                            node->prev = new;
                            }
```

(continued)

continued

```
                        else
                            {
                            new->prev = NULL;
                            new->next = first;
                            first->prev = new;
                            first = new;
                            }
                        break;
                        }
                    else if (node->next == NULL)
                        {
                        node->next = new;
                        new->prev = node;
                        new->next = NULL;
                        break;
                        }
                    else
                        node = node->next;

                    }                       /* while loop */
                }                           /* if !result */
            }                               /* while !result */

        /* display the entries in the list */
        node = first;                   /* start at front of list */
        while (node)                    /* while entries exist */
            {
            printf("%s\n", node->file_info.name);
            node = node->next;          /* get next entry in the list */
            }
        }
    }
```

Let's examine each step of the program. We'll assume that our current directory contains three files, as follows:

```
BBB     C           660 04-11-88    4:00p
AAA     C          1792 04-10-88   11:26a
MYDIR2  C          2759 04-11-88    4:00p
```

To begin, MYDIR2 allocates space for the first entry in the list, BBB.C. If *_dos_findfirst* locates a file, the program copies the file information to the first entry (Figure 25-7A on the following page). Next, *_dos_findnext* encounters the file AAA.C, allocates space for the new entry, and copies file information to it (Figure 25-7B).

Then the program determines where the new entry belongs in the list. It assigns the pointer *node* to the first entry in the list and then compares the filename of the first entry to that of the new entry. The *strcmp* function returns –1, which indicates that the new file-name, AAA.C, should precede the entry referenced by *node*, BBB.C. Because the entry referenced by *node* is the first entry, the program places the file BBB.C at the start of the list and changes the variable *first* to point to it (Figure 25-7C).

The next call to *_dos_findnext* locates the file MYDIR2.C. As before, the program allocates memory for the new entry and then determines the correct location for the entry. MYDIR2.C follows the two preceding filenames, so the program appends the entry to the list (Figure 25-7D).

When *_dos_findnext* fails to locate another file, the loop ends, and the program displays the entries in the list. Because the program placed each entry in the correct location, the directory listing is sorted.

If you choose to use linked lists in your programs, a doubly linked list simplifies insertions and deletions.

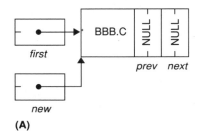

(A)

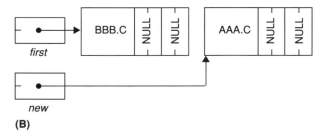

(B)

FIGURE 25-7. (continued)

(A) MYDIR2 uses _dos_findfirst to locate the first entry, and then it copies file information to the entry. (B) The program locates the next entry with_dos_findnext and assigns information to it. (C) After comparing the filenames for the two entries, the program resets pointers to change the order of the entries. (D) MYDIR2 obtains the third entry and appends it to the list.

FIGURE 25-7. *continued*

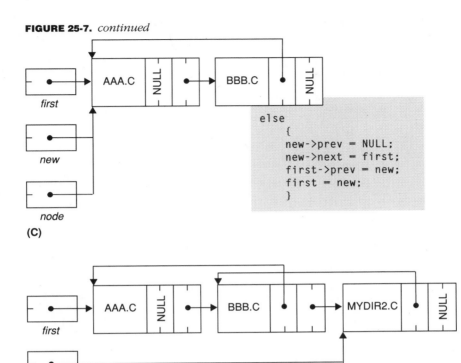

```
else
    {
    new->prev = NULL;
    new->next = first;
    first->prev = new;
    first = new;
    }
```

(C)

(D)

EXAMINING THE CONTENTS OF THE HEAP

The C compiler actually implements the heap as a linked list of memory blocks available for allocation. This list stores information about each block of memory in the heap. To help you debug applications that allocate memory using *malloc* or *calloc*, the run-time library provides several functions that examine the heap for consistency.

■ **FACT:** *The _heapchk function examines the current status of the heap and returns a status value.*

In some cases a program dynamically allocates a block of memory from the heap and then writes past the boundary of that block. The _heapchk_ function can help you pinpoint the error. A call to _heapchk_ returns one of the following constants, which are defined in malloc.h.

Constant	Meaning
_HEAPOK	Heap pointers reference valid nodes.
_HEAPEMPTY	Heap currently not in use.
_HEAPBADBEGIN	Heap header information missing.
_HEAPBADNODE	Heap contains at least one bad node.

The following program (CHKHEAP.C) displays the status of the heap and then allocates an array of 100 integer storage locations. The program then assigns values beyond the bounds of the array by looping through index values from 0 to 150. When the program calls _heapchk_ a second time, the error becomes apparent.

```c
#include <malloc.h>   /* needed for _heapchk and malloc */
#include <stdio.h>    /* needed for fprintf and constants */

main()
{
    char *ptr;
    int i, result;

    result = _heapchk();

    if (result == _HEAPOK)
        printf("Heap is OK\n:);
    else if (result == _HEAPEMPTY)
        printf("No memory allocated from the heap\n");
    else
        printf("Heap contains an inconsistency\n");

    if ((ptr = malloc(100)) == NULL)
        fprintf(stderr, "CHKHEAP:  error allocating memory\n");
    else
        {
        for (i = 0; i < 150; i++)
            ptr[i] = 'A';

        result = _heapchk();
```

(continued)

continued

```
        if (result == _HEAPOK)
            printf("Heap is OK\n");
        else if (result == _HEAPEMPTY)
            printf("No memory allocated from the heap\n");
        else
            printf("Heap contains an inconsistency\n");
    }
}
```

The run-time library function *_heapset* lets you perform the same consistency check on the heap as *_heapchk*. In addition, *_heapset* assigns all the unused blocks of memory a value that you specify. For example, the following statement,

```
_result = _heapset('A');
```

returns the heap's status and assigns all available locations the value 'A'.

■ **FACT:** *The* _heapset *function checks the consistency of the heap and returns the same values as* _heapchk. *In addition,* _heapset *assigns a specified value to all the available memory locations in the heap.*

Remember, if you allocate memory using *malloc*, the function does not initialize the memory locations. Therefore, if you set the locations in the heap to a specific value using *_heapset*, the memory you subsequently allocate using *malloc* contains that initial value (if the heap is consistent).

The following program (HEAPTOA.C) uses *_heapset* to set all available heap locations to the letter 'A'. Next the program allocates 1000 bytes from the heap. HEAPTOA.C then displays the value of each character allocated. If the heap is consistent, the program displays the letter *A* 1000 times.

```
#include <malloc.h>   /* needed for malloc, _heapset, and free */
#include <stdio.h>    /* needed for fprintf and constants */

main()
{
    char *ptr1, *ptr2;
    int i, j, result;

    /* allocate memory to make heap active */
    if ((ptr2 = malloc(50)) == NULL)
        fprintf (stderr, "HEAPTOA:  error allocating initial heap\n");
```

(continued)

continued

```
    else
        {
        result = _heapset(65);

        if ((ptr1 = malloc(1000)) == NULL)
            fprintf(stderr, "HEAPTOA:  error allocating memory\n");
        else  /* dump 1000 (20 * 50) bytes of memory */
            for (i = 0; i < 20; i++)
                {
                for (j = 0; j < 50; j++)
                    printf("%c", ptr1[j]);
                printf("\n");
                }

        free(ptr1);
        free(ptr2);
        }
}
```

Using another run-time library function, *_heapwalk*, you can traverse the linked list of heap entries and check the status of each entry.

■ **FACT:** *The* _heapwalk *function is a debugging tool that your programs can use to traverse the linked list of heap entries. Each call to the function returns information about an entry in the heap.*

A call to *_heapwalk* has one argument, a pointer to a structure of type *_heapinfo*. The function places information in the structure about the *next* heap entry. The include file malloc.h contains the following structure definition for *_heapinfo*:

```
type struct _heapinfo {
    int far * _pentry;
    size_t _size;
    int _useflag;
    };
```

The first member of the structure is a pointer to a block of memory in the heap. The second member tells the size of the block. The third entry, *useflag*, indicates true if the block is in use or false if the block is free.

The following program (HEAPWALK.C) allocates two blocks of memory. The program then uses *_heapwalk* to obtain current heap information. The program assigns to NULL the member *_pentry* of the structure it passes to *_heapwalk*; as a result, *_heapwalk* begins with the first entry in the heap.

```c
#include <malloc.h>  /* needed for malloc, _memavl, _memmax, _heapwalk, */
                      /* and _heapinfo structure */
#include <stdio.h>    /* needed for fprintf and constants */

main()
{
    struct _heapinfo entry;

    char *ptr1, *ptr2;

    int result;

    if ((ptr1 = malloc(100)) == NULL)
        fprintf(stderr, "HEAPWALK:  error allocating memory\n");
    else if ((ptr2 = malloc(200)) == NULL)
        fprintf(stderr, "HEAPWALK:  error allocating memory\n");
    else
        {
        printf("Available heap space %u bytes\n", _memavl());
        printf("Largest block size %u bytes\n\n", _memmax());

        entry._pentry = NULL;

        while ((result = _heapwalk(&entry)) != _HEAPEND)
            {
            printf("Entry Address %p Entry Status %d Entry Size %u bytes ",
                    entry._pentry, entry._useflag, entry._size);

            if (result == _HEAPOK)
                printf("Status OK\n");
            else if (result == _HEAPBADBEGIN)
                {
                printf("Heap header damaged\n");
                break;
                }
            else if (result == _HEAPBADPTR)
                {
                printf("_pentry is invalid\n");
                break;
                }
            else if (result == _HEAPBADNODE)
                {
                printf("Node is corrupted\n");
                break;
                }
            else if (result = _HEAPEND)
                printf("Last heap entry\n");
            }
        }
}
```

When you run the program, the output resembles the following:

```
Available heap space 60352 bytes
Largest block size 60352 bytes

Entry Address 1CC0:130A Entry Status 1 Entry Size 100 bytes Status OK
Entry Address 1CC0:1370 Entry Status 1 Entry Size 200 bytes Status OK
Entry Address 1CC0:143A Entry Status 0 Entry Size 3012 bytes Status OK
```

Each call to _heapwalk_ returns an integer associated with one of the following constants:

Constant	Meaning
_HEAPOK	Heap is consistent through this entry.
_HEAPBADBEGIN	Heap header information does not exist.
_HEAPBADNODE	Current node is bad.
_HEAPBADPTR	The _pentry_ member contains an invalid pointer.
_HEAPEND	No more nodes in the heap.

If you change the program slightly (BADHEAP.C) to overwrite the contents of the second buffer, the output reveals that the heap contains an error.

```c
#include <malloc.h>   /* needed for malloc, _memavl, _memmax, _heapwalk, */
                      /* and _heapinfo structure */
#include <stdio.h>    /* needed for fprintf and constants */

main()
{
    struct _heapinfo entry;

    char *ptr1, *ptr2;
    int i, result;

    if ((ptr1 = malloc(100)) == NULL)
        fprintf(stderr, "BADHEAP:  error allocating memory\n");
    else if ((ptr2 = malloc(200)) == NULL)
        fprintf(stderr, "BADHEAP:  error allocating memory\n";
    else
        {
        printf("Available heap space %u bytes\n", _memavl());
        printf("Largest block size %u bytes\n\n", _memmax());

        for (i = 0; i < 1000; i++)
            ptr2[i] = 'A';

        entry._pentry = NULL;
```

(continued)

continued

```
        while ((result = _heapwalk(&entry)) != _HEAPEND)
            {
            printf("Entry Address %p Entry Status %d Entry Size %u bytes ",
                    entry._pentry, entry._useflag, entry._size);

            if (result == _HEAPOK)
                printf("Status OK\n");
            else if (result == _HEAPBADBEGIN)
                {
                printf("Heap header damaged\n");
                break;
                }
            else if (result == _HEAPBADPTR)
                {
                printf("_pentry is invalid\n");
                break;
                }
            else if (result == _HEAPBADNODE)
                {
                printf("Node is corrupted\n");
                break;
                }
            else if (result = _HEAPEND)
                printf("Last heap entry\n");
            }
        }
    }
```

Each function presented in this section is useful for debugging. In many cases these functions can help you locate your programming bugs rapidly.

MEMORY MODEL CONSIDERATIONS

If you are using a memory model other than the default small memory model, you might need a memory allocation function that specifically supports use of the near or far heap. In the run-time library, function names preceded by _f or _n, such as _fmalloc or _nmalloc, are intended for far or near heap access.

We will discuss memory allocation again when we examine the C memory models later in this book.

SUMMARY

Laying a Foundation

■ **FACT:** *The* stackavail *function returns the number of bytes currently available in the stack. The value returned is an unsigned integer.*

■ **FACT:** *The* _memavl *function returns an unsigned integer that represents the number of bytes available for allocation in the heap.*

■ **FACT:** *The* _memmax *function returns an unsigned integer that represents the largest block of space available in the heap.*

FASTCOPY: A First Example

■ **FACT:** *The* malloc *function allocates a specified number of bytes from the heap. The largest block* malloc *can allocate is 64 KB. If* malloc *allocates the requested block, it returns a pointer to the first byte of the allocated memory. If an error occurs,* malloc *returns NULL.*

■ **FACT:** *The* free *function returns to the heap the memory associated with a specified pointer. The function does not return a value.*

Other Ways to Dynamically Allocate Memory

■ **FACT:** *The* calloc *function allocates memory from the heap. A call to* calloc *has two arguments, the number of items and the length of each (in bytes). The function initializes each element to 0. If* calloc *allocates the heap space as requested, it returns a pointer to the first byte in the dynamic memory. If an error occurs,* calloc *returns NULL.*

■ **TRAP:** *By default,* calloc *returns a pointer to a value of the type* char. *To obtain a pointer to a different type, you must use a cast.*

■ **FACT:** *The* _freect *function determines the maximum number of elements a program can allocate from the heap using* calloc. *The function takes one argument — the size of each element (in bytes) — and returns the maximum number of elements as an unsigned integer.*

■ **FACT:** *The* alloca *function allocates a specified number of bytes from the stack. When the function that allocated the memory ends, the compiler releases the allocated space to the stack. If* alloca *allocates the requested space, it returns a pointer to the allocated memory. If* alloca *cannot reserve the space, it returns NULL.*

■ **TRAP:** *Do not pass the pointer returned by* alloca *to the* free *function. The* free *function releases memory from the heap, not from the stack. If you pass the pointer from* alloca *to* free, *your program is likely to fail, and your computer might hang.*

Creating and Allocating Huge Arrays

■ **FACT:** *The keyword* huge *tells the compiler that the size of the array exceeds 64 KB. The compiler is then able to place the array in memory outside your data segment. For example, the statement* int huge voters[100000]; *declares a huge array.*

■ **FACT:** *The* halloc *function lets your program allocate a huge block of memory (greater than 64 KB). Like* calloc, *the* halloc *function initializes each element to 0. If successful,* halloc *returns a pointer to the memory; if it cannot allocate the requested memory,* halloc *returns NULL.*

■ **FACT:** *The* hfree *function releases huge memory blocks allocated previously with* halloc.

Changing an Allocation

■ **FACT:** *The* realloc *function adjusts the size of a previously allocated block of memory. To adjust the size,* realloc *might need to move the block within the heap. Any previously assigned values remain unchanged. If* realloc *makes the adjustment, it returns a pointer to the new memory block; if it cannot adjust the size as requested,* realloc *returns NULL.*

■ **FACT:** *The* _expand *function expands or shrinks an allocated block of memory without moving the block within the heap. If* _expand *changes the size of the block, it returns the pointer to the original block of memory; if it cannot adjust the size of the block without changing the location of the block,* _expand *returns NULL.*

■ **FACT:** *The* _msize *function returns an unsigned integer value that specifies the number of bytes in a block of allocated memory.*

Using Linked Lists

■ **FACT:** *The* memcpy *function copies the number of bytes specified from a source location to a target. For example,* memcpy(target, source, sizeof(source)); *uses sizeof to specify that all of* source *be copied to* target.

■ **FACT:** *When a program ends, memory allocated by the program from the heap is automatically released.*

Examining the Contents of the Heap

■ **FACT:** *The _heapchk function examines the current status of the heap and returns a status value.*

■ **FACT:** *The _heapset function checks the consistency of the heap and returns the same values as _heapchk. In addition, _heapset assigns a specified value to all the available memory locations in the heap.*

■ **FACT:** *The _heapwalk function is a debugging tool that your programs can use to traverse the linked list of heap entries. Each call to the function returns information about an entry in the heap.*

GLOSSARY

heap The unused portion of the data segment that is available for dynamic memory allocation. The C run-time library routines *calloc* and *malloc* allocate memory from the heap.

huge array An array that exceeds 64 KB. The compiler lets you create a huge array by specifying the keyword *huge* in your array declaration.

linked list A storage facility that contains a list of entries connected by pointers. In a singly linked list, each entry contains a single pointer to the next entry. A doubly linked list contains two pointers per entry—one to the previous entry and one to the next entry.

P A R T   I V

TURNING PROFESSIONAL

In PART III WE TOOK A LOOK AT SEVERAL WAYS C ALLOWS YOUR PROGRAMS TO gain tremendous flexibility. We examined methods for accessing the command line and environment entries, supporting I/O redirection, manipulating a variable number of function arguments, and allocating memory dynamically. As you saw, each of these techniques was easy to use once you learned the secrets.

Part IV continues in this same manner, presenting concepts critical to programmers who want to know the compiler well enough to develop applications professionally. Specifically, you learn how to optimize your programs for increased speed, how to access facilities built into the operating system, how to enhance the video appearance of your program, and how to decrease your development time by using the LIB and MAKE programming tools. The chapters in Part IV are each designed to help your programs acquire a professional flair!

## CHAPTER 26

Getting the Most from Compiler Options

In the previous chapters of this book, you have used several of the Microsoft C Compiler options, such as /Fa to generate an assembly language output of the program and /D to define a macro or constant. In this chapter we examine the compiler options supported by the Microsoft compilers. You learn how each option influences the C compiler and how certain options can improve the performance of your program. The following table lists all the available options for the Microsoft C 5.1 Compiler and the Microsoft QuickC 2.0 Compiler. Options that are not available for Microsoft QuickC are marked with a dagger (†).

Option	*Meaning*	*Example*
/AC	Selects compact memory model	CL /AC FILE.C
/AS	Selects small memory model (default)	CL /AS FILE.C
/AM	Selects medium memory model	CL /AM FILE.C
/AL	Selects large memory model	CL /AL FILE.C
/AH	Selects huge memory model	CL /AH FILE.C
/c	Compiles only, does not run linker	CL /c FILE.C
/C	Does not strip comments	CL /EP /C FILE.C

(continued)

continued

Option	Meaning	Example
/D<*def*>	Defines macro or constant used in source file	CL /DTOTAL=5 FILE.C
/E	Sends preprocessor output to stdout	CL /E FILE.C
/EP	Same as /E, but no line numbers	CL /EP FILE.C
/F<*num*>	Sets stack size (in hex bytes)	CL /F:2000 FILE.C
/Fa†	Generates assembly listing (ASM file)	CL /Fa FILE.C
/Fb	Runs LINK and BIND to create dual mode executable program	CL /Fb FILE.C
/Fc†	Generates mixed source/object listing (COD file)	CL /Fc FILE.C
/Fe<*file*>	Forces executable filename	CL /FeNEW.EXE FILE.C
/Fl†	Generates object listing (COD file)	CL /Fl FILE.C
/Fm	Generates map (MAP file)	CL /Fm FILE.C
/Fo<*file*>	Forces object module filename	CL /FoFILE6.OBJ FILE.C
/FPa†	Resolves floating point calculations with alternative math library	CL /FPa FILE.C
/FPc†	Resolves floating point calculations with emulator library	CL /FPc FILE.C
/FPc87†	Resolves floating point calculations with 8087 library	CL /FPc87 FILE.C
/FPi	Resolves floating point calculations with in-line emulator code	CL /FPi FILE.C
/FPi87	Resolves floating point calculations with in-line 8087 code	CL /FPi87 FILE.C
/Fs†	Generates source listing (LST file)	CL /Fs FILE.C
/G0	Generates 8086 instructions	CL /G0 FILE.C
/G1	Generates 80186 instructions	CL /G1 FILE.C
/G2	Generates 80286 instructions	CL /G2 FILE.C
/Gc	Generates Pascal-style function calls	CL /Gc FILE.C
/Gm†	Places strings in constant segment	CL /Gm FILE.C
/Gs	Disables stack checking	CL /Gs FILE.C
/H<*num*>†	Specifies external identifier length	CL /H8 OLDFILE.C
/HELP	Displays CL syntax and available options	CL /HELP
/I<*path*>	Specifies additional #*include* path	CL /I \TEST FILE.C
/J	Sets default char type to unsigned	CL /J FILE.C
/Lc	Links for execution under MS-DOS	CL /Lc FILE.C
/link<*opt*>	Passes LINK options to linker	CL FILE.C /link /stack:4096
/Lp	Links for execution under OS/2	CL /Lp FILE.C
/Lr	Same as /Lc	CL /Lr FILE.C
/Oa	Disables alias checking	CL /Oa FILE.C

(continued)

continued

Option	Meaning	Example
/Od	Disables optimizations	CL /Od FILE.C
/Oi	Generates fast in-line functions	CL /Oi FILE.C
/Ol	Enables loop optimizations	CL /Ola FILE.C
/Op	Enables precision optimizations	CL /Op FILE.C
/Os	Optimizes for size	CL /Os FILE.C
/Ot	Optimizes for speed (default)	CL /Ot FILE.C
/Ox	Maximizes optimization (/Oailt /Gs)	CL /Ox FILE.C
/P	Sends preprocessor output to file	CL /P FILE.C
/Sl<*cols*>†	Sets line width in source listing file	CL /Fs /Sl132 FILE.C
/Sp<*lines*>†	Sets page length in source listing file	CL /Fs /Sp55 FILE.C
/Ss<*str*>†	Sets subtitle string in source listing file	CL /Fs /Ss"FILE.C" FILE.C
/St<*str*>†	Sets title string in source listing file	CL /Fs /St"FILE Program" FILE.C
/Tc<*file*>	Compiles file without C extension	CL /Tc FILE.MSC
/u	Removes all predefined macros	CL /u FILE.C
/U<*name*>	Removes specified predefined macros	CL /UMSDOS FILE.C
/V<*string*>	Includes string in object file	CL /V"FILE V2.1" FILE.C
/W<*num*>	Sets warning level (0–3)	CL /W3 FILE.C
/X	Ignores *INCLUDE* environment variable when searching for *#include* files	CL /X /I \TEST FILE.C
/Za	Disables Microsoft C extensions (compile with strict ANSI compatibility)	CL /Za FILE.C
/Zd	Includes SYMDEB debugging information	CL /Zd FILE.C
/Ze	Enables Microsoft C extensions (default)	CL /Ze FILE.C
/Zg	Generates function declarations	CL /Zg FILE.C
/Zi	Includes CodeView debugging information	CL /Zi FILE.C
/Zl	Removes default library information	CL /Zl FILE.C
/Zp<*num*>	Packs structures on *num*-byte boundary (1, 2, or 4)	CL /Zp2 FILE.C
/Zs	Checks C syntax only	CL /Zs FILE.C

† Not available with Microsoft QuickC Compiler

If you want to print a copy of the available options, type the following command:

```
C> CL /HELP > PRN
```

Press the Enter key several times in response to the redirected prompt *(press <return> to continue)*.

LOOKING AT PREPROCESSOR DIRECTIVES

In Chapter 6 you learned that you could define a constant or macro outside your source code with the /D compiler option.

■ **FACT:** *The CL option /D lets you define a macro or constant in the CL command line for use in the program.*

The following program (TOTAL.C) references the constant TOTAL, which is not defined in the source file:

```
main()
{
    int i = 0;

    while (i < TOTAL)
        printf("%d\n", i++);
}
```

To define TOTAL when you compile the source file, use the following command line:

```
C> CL /DTOTAL=5 TOTAL.C
```

The /D option has the same effect as the following statement at the beginning of your program:

```
#define TOTAL 5
```

Later in the development process, after you test various values for a constant, you can define it within the program itself.

■ **FACT:** *If you are using the Microsoft QuickC Compiler, you can compile programs from the command line with the QCL command.*

If you are using Microsoft QuickC, you can compile your programs at the system prompt with the QCL command. The QCL command reads command-line options and compiles and links a program just as the CL command does. Be sure to enter options exactly as shown—the QCL command, like the CL command, is case sensitive when it processes command line options. Note, however, that some options available for the CL command are not available in the QCL command. For details, see the table of compiler options on the preceding pages.

The Microsoft C Compiler predefines the constants MSDOS, M_I86, M_I86xM, NO_EXT_KEYS, and _CHAR_UNSIGNED. The CL option /U lets you undefine these constants.

■ **FACT:** *The /U option directs CL to undefine one of the constants that are predefined by the Microsoft C Compiler.*

The following program (CHKDOS.C) uses the preprocessor directive *#ifdef* to determine whether to include statements specific to MS-DOS:

```
main()
{
#ifdef MSDOS
    printf("MS-DOS statements active\n");

#else
    printf("MS-DOS statements disabled\n");
#endif
}
```

If you compile the program without the /U option, the constant MSDOS remains defined. However, if you compile the program as follows:

```
C> CL /UMSDOS CHKDOS.C
```

CL undefines the constant, and the following output results:

```
MS-DOS statements disabled
```

The /U option has the same effect as the statement

```
#undef MSDOS
```

at the beginning of your program.

■ **FACT:** *The /u option directs CL to undefine each of its predefined constants.*

The /u compiler option directs the compiler to undefine all its predefined constants. If you compile the previous program as follows, CL undefines the constant MSDOS:

```
C> CL /u CHKDOS.C
```

By default, the C compiler first looks for bracketed include files, such as <stdio.h>, in the directory specified by the *INCLUDE* environment variable. The CL command provides two compiler directives that change this processing.

■ **FACT:** *The CL option /I changes the search order that the preprocessor uses to locate include files. The preprocessor first searches the specified directories and then searches the default location if the include files have not been found.*

The following command directs CL to search the directory \TEST for include files before it searches the default location:

```
C> CL /I \TEST ALPHA.C
```

Using the /I option, you can place multiple paths in the include file search list:

```
C> CL /I \TEST /I \DEBUG ALPHA.C
```

■ **FACT:** *The /X option directs CL not to examine the default include directory.*

By excluding the default include file directory using /X, the user can ensure that only the user-defined include files are accessed. For example, the following command line directs the compiler to search for bracketed include files in \MYINC but not in the default include file directory:

```
CL /X /I \MYINC TEST.C
```

In Chapter 6 you learned that you can generate an intermediate file that contains the preprocessor output. Using compiler options, you can send this intermediate file to your screen or to a file.

■ **FACT:** *The /E option directs CL to send the output of the preprocessor to the screen. CL does not compile and link the file; it generates only the preprocessor output.*

Suppose you create the source file MINMAX.C that contains the following code:

```
#define MAX(a, b) ((a) > (b) ? (a) : (b))
#define MIN(a, b) ((a) < (b) ? (a) : (b))

main()
{
    printf("%d MAX\n", MAX(7 * 2, 7 + 2));
    printf("%d MIN\n", MIN(3 * 7, 7 * 4));
}
```

If you execute CL with /E in the command line, your screen shows

```
C> CL /E MINMAX.C
Microsoft (R) C Optimizing Compiler Version 5.10
Copyright (c) Microsoft Corp 1984, 1985, 1986, 1987, 1988. All rights reserved.

#line 1 "MINMAX.C"


main()
{
    printf("%d MAX\n", ((7 * 2) > (7 + 2) ? (7 * 2) : (7 + 2)));
    printf("%d MIN\n", ((3 * 7) < (7 * 4) ? (3 * 7) : (7 * 4)));
}
```

In a similar manner, the /P option directs CL to write the preprocessor output to a file.

■ **FACT:** *The /P option directs CL to write the preprocessor output to a file with the exten-sion I. CL does not compile and link the program; it generates only the preprocessor output.*

The following command line directs CL to create the file MINMAX.I, which contains the preprocessor output:

```
C> CL /P MINMAX.C
```

■ **FACT:** *The /EP option directs CL to write the preprocessor output to the screen but to sup-press the #*line *information normally displayed with /E. CL does not compile and link the file; it generates only the preprocessor output.*

If you execute CL with the following command line,

```
C> CL /EP MINMAX.C
```

the output is identical to that for the preceding command, which used the /E option, except that CL suppresses the *#line* information.

Comments within your program exist to help you or another programmer understand the code; the C compiler ignores them. One job of the preprocessor is therefore to remove comments from your code. If you are studying the output of the preprocessor, however, you might encounter situations in which the comments would be useful.

■ **FACT:** *The /C option directs CL to leave comments in the preprocessor output if the com-mand line also contains the /E, /P, or /EP option. The command line CL /EP /C MINMAX.C, for example, performs preprocessing on MINMAX.C and writes the output to the screen with comments but without #*line *information.*

Suppose you create the source file MINMAX2.C, which contains the following code:

```
/*
 * Define MAX and MIN constants
 *
 * MAX returns the larger of two expressions
 *
 */

#define MAX(a, b) ((a) > (b) ? (a) : (b))

/*
 * MIN returns the smaller of two expressions
 */

#define MIN(a, b) ((a) < (b) ? (a) : (b))
```

(continued)

continued

```
main()
{
    /* use MAX and MIN to compare expressions */
    printf("%d MAX\n", MAX(7 * 2, 7 + 2));
    printf("%d MIN\n", MIN(3 * 7, 7 * 4));
}
```

If you execute CL with both /EP and /C in the command line, your screen shows

```
C> CL /EP /C MINMAX2.C
Microsoft (R) C Optimizing Compiler Version 5.10
Copyright (c) Microsoft Corp 1984, 1985, 1986, 1987, 1988. All rights reserved.

/*
 * Define MAX and MIN constants
 *
 * MAX returns the larger of two expressions
 *
 */

/*
 * MIN returns the smaller of two expressions
 */

main()
{
    /* use MAX and MIN to compare expressions */
    printf("%d MAX\n", ((7 * 2) > (7 + 2) ? (7 * 2) : (7 + 2)));
    printf("%d MIN\n", ((3 * 7) < (7 * 4) ? (3 * 7) : (7 * 4)));
}
```

In the displayed output, preprocessor directives are performed, macros are expanded, and *#line* information is omitted; but the comments are preserved.

GENERATING VARIOUS OUTPUT FILES

As you know, CL not only compiles your C source file but also links the resulting object file to produce an executable file. Because CL performs each of these steps, it is capable of producing several different output files. We have already seen that the /P option writes the preprocessor output to a file with the extension I. The options we examine in this section, unlike /P, allow CL to continue with compilation and linking. To demonstrate these options, let's use the program DISPLAY.C, which calls the function *display* to write the numbers 1 through 100 on your screen.

```
main()
{
    void display(int);
    int i;

    for (i = 1; i <= 100; ++i)
        display(i);
}

void display(int a)
{
    printf("%d\n", a);
}
```

To begin, let's examine a line-numbered listing of the source file that contains a summary of variables and functions.

■ **FACT:** *The /Fs option directs CL to produce a listing of the source file. By default, CL uses the basename of the source file and adds the extension LST.*

If you compile the file DISPLAY.C with the following command line,

```
C> CL /Fs DISPLAY.C
```

CL produces the file DISPLAY.LST, which contains the following:

```
                                                    PAGE    1
                                                    05-01-89
                                                    12:00:00

Line#  Source Line                      Microsoft C Compiler Version 5.10

    1  main()
    2  {
    3      void display (int);
    4      int i;
    5
    6      for (i = 1; i <= 100; i++)
    7          display(i);
    8  }

main   Local Symbols

Name                      Class   Type        Size   Offset  Register

i . . . . . . . . . . . . auto                       -0002
```

(continued)

continued

```
     9
    10   void display(int a)
    11   {
    12       printf("%d\n", a);
    13   }

display   Local Symbols

Name                          Class   Type            Size   Offset   Register

a . . . . . . . . . . . . param                              0004

Global Symbols

Name                          Class   Type            Size   Offset

display . . . . . . . . . global  near function    ***     0024
main. . . . . . . . . . . global  near function    ***     0000
printf. . . . . . . . . . extern  near function    ***     ***

Code size = 003c (60)
Data size = 0004 (4)
Bss size  = 0000 (0)
No errors detected
```

Later in this chapter we examine compiler optimization. The best way to appreciate optimization is to generate assembly language listings of the program.

■ **FACT:** *The /Fa option directs CL to produce an assembly language listing of the program. By default, CL uses the basename of the source file and adds the extension ASM.*

If you recompile DISPLAY.C with the following command line,

```
C> CL /Fa DISPLAY.C
```

CL produces the file DISPLAY.ASM, which contains the following:

```
;       Static Name Aliases
;
        TITLE   DISPLAY.C
        NAME    DISPLAY
```

(continued)

continued

```
        .8087
_TEXT   SEGMENT  WORD PUBLIC 'CODE'
_TEXT   ENDS
_DATA   SEGMENT  WORD PUBLIC 'DATA'
_DATA   ENDS
CONST   SEGMENT  WORD PUBLIC 'CONST'
CONST   ENDS
_BSS    SEGMENT  WORD PUBLIC 'BSS'
_BSS    ENDS
DGROUP  GROUP    CONST, _BSS, _DATA
        ASSUME   CS: _TEXT, DS: DGROUP, SS: DGROUP
EXTRN   __acrtused:ABS
EXTRN   __chkstk:NEAR
EXTRN   _printf:NEAR
_DATA       SEGMENT
$SG110  DB          '%d',  0aH,  00H
_DATA       ENDS
_TEXT       SEGMENT
        ASSUME   CS: _TEXT
; Line 2
        PUBLIC      _main
_main   PROC NEAR
        push    bp
        mov     bp,sp
        mov     ax,2
        call    __chkstk
;           i = -2
; Line 6
        mov     WORD PTR [bp-2],1       ;i
$FC105:
; Line 7
        push    WORD PTR [bp-2] ;i
        call    _display
        add     sp,2
        inc     WORD PTR [bp-2] ;i
        cmp     WORD PTR [bp-2],100     ;i
        jle     $FC105
; Line 8
        mov     sp,bp
        pop     bp
        ret

_main   ENDP
; Line 11
        PUBLIC  _display
_display        PROC NEAR
        push    bp
        mov     bp,sp
```

(continued)

continued

```
            xor     ax,ax
            call    __chkstk
        ;       a = 4
        ; Line 12
            push    WORD PTR [bp+4] ;a
            mov     ax,OFFSET DGROUP:$SG110
            push    ax
            call    _printf
            add     sp,4
        ; Line 13
            pop     bp
            ret
            nop

_display          ENDP
_TEXT     ENDS
END
```

Don't let the assembly language intimidate you. When we use the preceding listing later in this chapter, all the items of interest are quite straightforward.

Some programmers are interested in examining the object code the compiler generates. The CL option /Fl lets you create a listing of an object file. The file contains not only the assembly language output of the compiler but also the hexadecimal machine code. A second option, /FC, creates a similar object code listing but also includes source code intermixed with the object code. By examining the resulting file, you can compare the compiler output to your original source.

■ **FACT:** *The /Fl option directs CL to create an object code listing of your source code. By default, CL uses the basename of the source file and adds the extension COD.*

If you compile the file DISPLAY.C with the following command line,

```
C> CL /Fl DISPLAY.C
```

CL creates the file DISPLAY.COD, which contains the following:

```
;       Static Name Aliases
;
        TITLE     DISPLAY.C
        NAME      DISPLAY

        .8087
_TEXT   SEGMENT   WORD PUBLIC 'CODE'
_TEXT   ENDS
```

(continued)

continued

```
_DATA    SEGMENT   WORD PUBLIC 'DATA'
_DATA    ENDS
CONST    SEGMENT   WORD PUBLIC 'CONST'
CONST    ENDS
_BSS     SEGMENT   WORD PUBLIC 'BSS'
_BSS     ENDS
DGROUP   GROUP    CONST, _BSS, _DATA
         ASSUME  CS: _TEXT, DS: DGROUP, SS: DGROUP
EXTRN    __acrtused:ABS
EXTRN    __chkstk:NEAR
EXTRN    _printf:NEAR
_DATA      SEGMENT
$SG110   DB       '%d', 0aH,  00H
_DATA      ENDS
_TEXT      SEGMENT
         ASSUME  CS: _TEXT
; Line 2
         PUBLIC_main
_main    PROC NEAR
         *** 000000    55                          push    bp
         *** 000001    8b ec                       mov     bp,sp
         *** 000003    b8 02 00                    mov     ax,2
         *** 000006    e8 00 00                    call    __chkstk
;            i = -2
; Line 6
         *** 000009    c7 46 fe 01 00              mov     WORD PTR [bp-2],1
                                      $FC105:
; Line 7
         *** 00000e    ff 76 fe                    push    WORD PTR [bp-2] ;i
         *** 000011    e8 00 00                    call    _display
         *** 000014    83 c4 02                    add     sp,2
         *** 000017    ff 46 fe                    inc     WORD PTR [bp-2] ;i
         *** 00001a    83 7e fe 64                 cmp     WORD PTR [bp-2],100
         *** 00001e    7e ee                       jle     $FC105
; Line 8
         *** 000020    8b e5                       mov     sp,bp
         *** 000022    5d                          pop     bp
         *** 000023    c3                          ret
_main    ENDP
; Line 11
         PUBLIC _display
_display       PROC NEAR
         *** 000024    55                          push    bp
         *** 000025    8b ec                       mov     bp,sp
         *** 000027    33 c0                       xor     ax,ax
         *** 000029    e8 00 00                    call    __chkstk
;            a = 4
```

(continued)

continued

```
; Line 12
      *** 00002c      ff 76 04           push    WORD PTR [bp+4] ;a
      *** 00002f      b8 00 00           mov     ax,OFFSET DGROUP:$SG110
      *** 000032      50                 push    ax
      *** 000033      e8 00 00           call    _printf
      *** 000036      83 c4 04           add     sp,4
; Line 13
      *** 000039      5d                 pop     bp
      *** 00003a      c3                 ret
      *** 00003b      90                 nop


_display           ENDP
_TEXT   ENDS
END
```

■ **FACT:** *The /Fc option directs CL to create an object code listing that contains not only the assembly language output and equivalent hexadecimal machine code but also the C source code. By default, CL uses the basename of the source file and adds the extension COD.*

If you compile DISPLAY.C with the following command line,

`C> CL /Fc DISPLAY.C`

CL creates the file DISPLAY.COD, which contains the following:

```
;         Static Name Aliases
;
          TITLE    DISPLAY.C
          NAME     DISPLAY

          .8087
_TEXT   SEGMENT  WORD PUBLIC 'CODE'
_TEXT   ENDS
_DATA   SEGMENT  WORD PUBLIC 'DATA'
_DATA   ENDS
CONST   SEGMENT  WORD PUBLIC 'CONST'
CONST   ENDS
_BSS    SEGMENT  WORD PUBLIC 'BSS'
_BSS    ENDS
DGROUP  GROUP CONST, _BSS, _DATA
        ASSUME  CS: _TEXT, DS: DGROUP, SS: DGROUP
EXTRN   __acrtused:ABS
EXTRN   __chkstk:NEAR
```

(continued)

continued

```
EXTRN    _printf:NEAR
_DATA        SEGMENT
$SG110   DB        '%d', 0aH,  00H
_DATA        ENDS
_TEXT        SEGMENT
        ASSUME   CS: _TEXT
;!*** main()
;!*** {
; Line 2
        PUBLIC  _main
_main    PROC NEAR
        *** 000000    55                          push    bp
        *** 000001    8b ec                       mov     bp,sp
        *** 000003    b8 02 00                    mov     ax,2
        *** 000006    e8 00 00                    call    __chkstk
;       i = -2
;!***   void display(int);
;!***   int i;
;!***
;!***   for (i = 1; i <= 100; i++)
; Line 6
        *** 000009    c7 46 fe 01 00              mov     WORD PTR [bp-2],1     ;i
                                    $FC105:
;!***     display(i);
; Line 7
        *** 00000e    ff 76 fe                    push    WORD PTR [bp-2] ;i
        *** 000011    e8 00 00                    call    _display
        *** 000014    83 c4 02                    add     sp,2
        *** 000017    ff 46 fe                    inc     WORD PTR [bp-2] ;i
        *** 00001a    83 7e fe 64                 cmp     WORD PTR [bp-2],100 ;i
        *** 00001e    7e ee                       jle     $FC105
;!*** }
; Line 8
        *** 000020    8b e5                       mov     sp,bp
        *** 000022    5d                          pop     bp
        *** 000023    c3                          ret

_main    ENDP
;!***
;!*** void display(int a)
;!*** {
; Line 11
        PUBLIC  _display
_display        PROC NEAR
        *** 000024    55                          push    bp
        *** 000025    8b ec                       mov     bp,sp
        *** 000027    33 c0                       xor     ax,ax
        *** 000029    e8 00 00                    call    __chkstk
```

(continued)

continued

```
;         a = 4
;!***    printf("%d\n", a);
; Line 12
        *** 00002c      ff 76 04                push    WORD PTR [bp+4] ;a
        *** 00002f      b8 00 00                mov     ax,OFFSET DGROUP:$SG110
        *** 000032      50                      push    ax
        *** 000033      e8 00 00                call    _printf
        *** 000036      83 c4 04                add     sp,4
;!*** }
; Line 13
        *** 000039      5d                      pop     bp
        *** 00003a      c3                      ret
        *** 00003b      90                      nop

_display        ENDP
_TEXT   ENDS
END
```

The linker produces another output file called a map file, which contains a list of entry points for the functions used by or available to the program.

■ **FACT:** *The /Fm option directs CL to create a file containing the link map. By default, CL uses the basename of the source file and adds the extension MAP.*

Using the /Fm switch, create the link map for DISPLAY.C with the following command:

```
C> CL /Fm DISPLAY.C
```

To display the file DISPLAY.MAP, use the DOS or OS/2 TYPE command. You might be surprised at the length of the map file that our tiny DISPLAY.C file generates.

CHANGING OBJECT OR EXECUTABLE FILENAMES

All the programs we have compiled so far have used the same basename for the source, object, and executable files; only the extensions have changed. If you want to use a different name for either your object or your executable file, you can include CL command options that let you do so.

■ **FACT:** *The CL option /Fo lets you specify the name of the object file.*

The following command compiles the file DISPLAY.C and creates the object file DISP.OBJ:

```
C> CL /FoDISP.OBJ DISPLAY.C
```

Notice that the /Fo option affects the name of the object file only; the executable file still receives the default name, DISPLAY.EXE.

■ **FACT:** *The CL option /Fe lets you change the name of an executable file.*

If you compile DISPLAY.C with the following command line,

```
C> CL /FeCOUNT.EXE DISPLAY.C
```

CL creates the executable file COUNT.EXE. You can include both the /Fo and /Fe compiler directives in the same command, as in the following:

```
C> CL /FoDISP.OBJ /FeCOUNT.EXE DISPLAY.C
```

In this case CL generates the object file DISP.OBJ and the executable file COUNT.EXE.

CUSTOMIZING SOURCE LISTINGS

Earlier you learned that the CL option /Fs lets you produce a list file that contains a line-numbered source listing and specific information about each variable and function. The CL command supports four other options that enable you to customize your source listing.

■ **FACT:** *The /Sl option directs CL to use a specified number of columns when it creates the source listing. By default, CL creates an 80-column source listing.*

If your printer is capable of displaying 132 columns of information, you might want to increase the line length in your list file to 132 columns, as in the following command:

```
C> CL /Fs /Sl132 DISPLAY.C
```

In a similar manner, you can specify the number of lines to display on each page of the source listing.

■ **FACT:** *The /Sp option directs CL to place only the specified number of lines on each page of the source listing. By default, CL places 65 lines on each page.*

If you compile DISPLAY.C with the following command line, CL creates a source listing, DISPLAY.LST, that contains 55 lines per page.

```
C> CL /Fs /Sp55 DISPLAY.C
```

■ **FACT:** *The CL option /St lets you assign a title that appears on each page of the source listing.*

The following command line directs CL to include the title *Display Program* on each page of the source listing:

```
C> CL /Fs /St"Display Program" DISPLAY.C
```

If you have several different source file listings, placing a title on each page helps you organize the listings.

You can place several files with the extension C in the CL command line, as follows:

```
C> CL MAIN.C DISPLAY.C
```

CL compiles and links the specified files and creates an executable file using the basename of the first file. If you place several source files in the CL command line, you can subtitle the pages in the source listing to distinguish the two source files.

■ **FACT:** *The CL option /Ss lets you assign a subtitle within the source listing. The subtitle appears below the main title on each page.*

If you compile DISPLAY.C with the following CL command line,

```
C> CL /Fs /St"DISPLAY PROGRAM" /Ss"DISPLAY.C" DISPLAY.C
```

CL creates a source listing that contains the following text:

```
DISPLAY PROGRAM                                               PAGE   1
DISPLAY.C                                                     05-01-89
                                                             12:00:00

  Line#  Source Line                      Microsoft C Compiler Version 5.10

      1  main()
      2  {
      3      void display(int);
      4      int i;
      5
      6      for (i = 1; i <= 100; i++)
      7          display(i);
      8  }


main   Local Symbols

Name                     Class   Type          Size    Offset  Register

i . . . . . . . . . . . . auto                         -0002


      9
     10  void display(int a)
     11  {
     12      printf("%d\n", a);
     13  }


display  Local Symbols
```

(continued)

continued

```
Name                      Class   Type            Size   Offset  Register

a . . . . . . . . . . . . param                          0004


Global Symbols

Name                      Class   Type            Size   Offset

display . . . . . . . . . global  near function   ***    0024
main. . . . . . . . . . . global  near function   ***    0000
printf. . . . . . . . . . extern  near function   ***    ***

Code size = 003c (60)
Data size = 0004 (4)
Bss size  = 0000 (0)
No errors detected
```

If you print the list file, the title and subtitle of the program appear in the upper left corner of the page.

SPECIFYING THE MEMORY MODEL

Later in this book we discuss in detail the C memory models—small, compact, medium, large, and huge. For now, simply note that CL supports options that let you specify a particular model.

■ **FACT:** *The /AS, /AC, /AM, /AL, or /AH option directs CL to use the small, compact, medium, large, or huge memory model. The default memory model is the small model.*

The CL command uses one of five memory models, based on the following options:

Option	Meaning
/AS	Small memory model (default)
/AC	Compact memory model
/AM	Medium memory model
/AL	Large memory model
/AH	Huge memory model

FLOATING POINT PROCESSING

The Microsoft C Compiler provides several different floating point math libraries. First, for systems that rely on a math coprocessor chip, 8087 or 80287, the compiler provides a library that uses the coprocessor. Second, for systems that don't have the coprocessor, the compiler provides a math library that emulates the work done by the coprocessor. This emulation provides the same functionality as the coprocessor, but it performs more slowly. Last, for applications that can exchange precision for speed, the compiler provides an alternative math library. To help you select a specific floating point library, CL supports five command options.

■ **FACT:** *The /FPc option directs CL to use calls to the floating point emulator. If the system has a math coprocessor, the library uses it.*

The floating point emulator is the most flexible library. If the system contains a math coprocessor, the routines use the coprocessor; if no coprocessor exists, the routines use software to perform the same calculations.

■ **FACT:** *The /FPi option directs CL to generate in-line code to support a math coprocessor if one exists. If the system has no math coprocessor, calls to the emulator library are used. This option specifies the default method for floating point processing.*

By default, C places in-line calls to the math coprocessor within the object file. If the system has no math coprocessor, the program calls go to the emulator library. If the system has a math coprocessor, the in-line code results in faster execution than the calls to the math coprocessor library that result from compilation with the /FPc option.

■ **TIP:** *A program compiled with the /FPc or /FPi option offers the advantage of running on a system with or without a math coprocessor.*

■ **FACT:** *The /FPc87 option directs CL to generate calls to the math coprocessor library. A computer must have a math coprocessor to execute programs compiled with /FPc87.*

A program that can use the floating point emulator libraries can be executed regardless of whether the system has a math coprocessor; however, a program compiled with the /FPc87 or /FPi87 option specifically relies on the math coprocessor libraries. Such a program can execute only on a system that has a math coprocessor.

■ **FACT:** *The /FPi87 option directs CL to generate in-line code that references the math coprocessor libraries.*

The in-line code resulting from compilation with /FPi87 executes faster than the calls to the math coprocessor libraries, but in-line code results in a larger executable file. Compactness is sacrificed for the sake of speed.

■ **FACT:** *The /FPa option directs CL to use the alternative math library, which trades precision for speed.*

The alternative math library provides less precision but greater speed than the other floating point libraries. To use it, compile your program with the /FPa option.

MISCELLANEOUS OPTIONS

Earlier in the book we noted the advantage, in certain situations, of compiling to produce an object file, but not linking. The CL option /c enables you to do that.

■ **FACT:** *The /c option directs CL to compile the specified source file to create an object file but not to link the file.*

Later in this book we examine the creation and manipulation of object file libraries. At that time the ability to compile a source file without linking becomes quite important.

■ **FACT:** *The CL option /V lets you place in your object file a string that specifies the version number.*

If you compile DISPLAY.C with the following command line,

```
C> CL /V"DISPLAY V2.1" DISPLAY.C
```

CL places the string *DISPLAY V2.1* in the object file DISPLAY.OBJ. The primary use of /V is to include version or copyright information in an object file.

By default, the C compiler treats the type *char* as a signed integer, capable of storing values in the range −128 through 127. To create an unsigned *char* variable, you can use the *unsigned* qualifier or the /J compiler option.

■ **FACT:** *The /J option directs CL to treat the type* char *as* unsigned *and thus capable of storing the values 0 through 255.*

The following program (COUNT.C) assigns the values 0 through 255 to a variable of type *char*.

```
main()
{
    char count;

    for (count = 0; count < 255; ++count)
        printf("%d\n", count);

    printf("%d\n", count);
}
```

Compile COUNT.C as follows:

```
C> CL COUNT.C
```

When you run the program, it displays the values 0 through 127, followed by the values −128 through −1. The process repeats in an infinite loop. To end the program, press Ctrl-Break. The infinite loop occurs because the type *char* is signed by default; it cannot store a value greater than 127. Therefore, the test expression

```
count < 255
```

is always true. Now recompile the program using /J, as follows:

```
C> CL /J COUNT.C
```

When you execute the program, it displays the values 0 through 255 and then ends.

Older C compilers differentiated only the first eight characters of an identifier. To these compilers, the following function names are not distinct:

```
sort_values_ascending
sort_values_descending
```

The function names are identical within the first eight characters, *sort_val.* To give you greater flexibility, the Microsoft C Compiler differentiates the first 31 characters of an identifier name. As a carryover, CL supports the /H option, which restricts external names to a specified length.

■ **FACT:** *The CL option /H lets you restrict the number of characters the compiler distinguishes in external names.*

All the source files we have compiled have had the extension C. In some cases, however, you might need to compile a C source file with a different filename extension.

■ **FACT:** *The /Tc option informs CL that the filename that follows identifies a C source file.*

By default, CL assumes that files with the extension C contain C source code, that files with the extension LIB are library files, and that files with no extension are object files. The /Tc option lets you compile C source files that don't conform to this naming convention.

As the compiler examines your source files, it displays error messages as well as warning messages. Warning messages do not indicate errors; they indicate rather the potential for errors. The CL option /W lets you enable or disable the display of compiler warning messages.

■ **FACT:** *The CL options /W0, /W1, /W2, and /W3 indicate levels of warning messages the C compiler displays on your screen. Warning level 1, which you specify with /W1, is the default level.*

The following table lists the four warning levels. The higher the warning level, the more exhaustive the list of warning messages.

Level	Option	Meaning
0	/W0	Displays no warning messages
1	/W1	Displays most warning messages (the default)
2	/W2	Displays messages that indicate a return statement in type *void* functions or data conversions
3	/W3	Displays all warning messages

By default, CL uses /W1 to display warning messages. If you are developing an application for commercial use, you need the most exhaustive list of warnings you can obtain.

■ **TIP:** *Use /W3 for production programs. In so doing, you might catch errors during compilation that would be difficult to debug.*

LOOKING AT CODE GENERATION

Every microprocessor has its own collection of instructions, called an instruction set. As microprocessors have increased in capability, so too have their instruction sets. The Intel 80286 microprocessor (found in the IBM PC AT) uses the 80286 instruction set, which is a superset of the 8086 instruction set used by the Intel 8086 microprocessor found in the IBM PC. This relationship permits the IBM PC AT to be compatible with the IBM PC. By default, the Microsoft C Compiler generates object code based on the 8086 instruction set. Compiled programs can therefore run on the 8086, 80186, 80286, and 80386 processors. If you are writing a program for an 80286 that does not need to run on an 8086, you can direct the C compiler to produce object code that maximizes performance by using the 80286 instruction set.

■ **FACT:** *The /G0, /G1, or /G2 option directs CL to generate code for the 8086, 80186, or 80286 instruction set. The default compiler output is restricted to the 8086 instruction set, which you can specify explicitly with /G0.*

Remember, once you generate code for the 80286, you decrease the portability of the executable file. In other words, you can no longer assume that the resulting EXE file can execute on a computer that uses an 8086 processor. The Microsoft C Compiler version 5.1 does not support code generation specifically for the 80386 instruction set.

■ **FACT:** *The /Gc option directs CL to handle a function's arguments from left to right.*

As discussed in Chapter 23, the C compiler passes arguments on the stack from right to left. Other programming languages, such as Pascal and FORTRAN, pass arguments on the stack from left to right. If you are writing a function to be called by other programming languages, you can use the /Gc option to direct CL to handle arguments from left to right.

Later in this book we look in detail at the interface between C and other high-level languages. For now, simply be aware that the default order in which C places arguments on the stack is the opposite of the order used in Pascal or FORTRAN.

By default, each time you use a character string constant, as in the following program (STR.C), the compiler places the string in the data segment:

```
main()
{
    printf("Character string constant");
}
```

Using the /Fa compiler directive, you can generate an assembly language listing that shows this use of the data segment, _DATA.

Because these strings do not change, you might prefer to conserve space in the data segment by having the compiler place them in the constant segment, CONST.

■ **FACT:** *The /Gm option directs CL to place string constants in the constant segment.*

Recompile the STR.C program with the following command line:

```
C> CL /Fa /Gm STR.C
```

This time, the assembly language listing reveals that the compiler has placed the string constant into the segment CONST.

LOOKING AT LANGUAGE SPECIFICS

As we have noted, the ANSI Committee has produced a set of standards for the implementation of a C compiler. Microsoft C provides several capabilities that extend beyond those defined by the ANSI Committee. These capabilities, called *extensions,* include the *far, near,* and *huge* qualifiers, as well as the interlanguage calling features we examine later in this book. The CL command provides two options that enable and disable the compiler extensions.

■ **FACT:** *The /Ze option directs CL to enable extensions to the ANSI specification. The extensions are enabled by default.*

If you are developing a program with Microsoft C that you might want to port to a different operating system or compiler, you will probably want to disable the extensions.

■ **FACT:** *The /Za option directs CL to disable extensions to the ANSI specification.*

Create the following program (NEARFAR.C), which uses the *far* keyword:

```
main()
{
    char far *ptr;
    char near *ptrz;
}
```

If you compile the program with extensions enabled, CL creates NEARFAR.EXE successfully:

C> CL NEARFAR.C

However, if you disable extensions with the /Za option,

C> CL /Za NEARFAR.C

the compiler generates a syntax error. With the extensions disabled, CL does not recognize *far* as a keyword.

By default, the compiler stores structure members as follows:

Type	*Alignment*
char	Byte aligned
unsigned char	Byte aligned
All other types	Word aligned
Nested structures	Padded to reside in an even number of bytes

Depending on your memory requirements, you might want the compiler to align each member of a structure on 1-byte, 2-byte, or 4-byte boundaries. CL supports a (rarely used) option, /Zp, that lets you do so.

■ **FACT:** *The /Zp option directs CL to align members of a structure on 1-byte, 2-byte, or 4-byte boundaries.*

When CL creates an object file, it includes the name of the default library that supports the memory model and the floating point library. Eliminating this library name leaves the object file slightly smaller.

■ **FACT:** *The /Zl option directs CL not to place the name of the default library into object files.*

The amount of space saved by removing the library name from one object file is negligible, but if you are building a large library of object files, the total amount you save becomes significant. If the library name for a number of object files is the same, and you plan to link all the object files to produce one executable file, you can avoid repeating the library filename by using the /Zl option to remove the library names from all but one of the object files.

To assist in debugging your programs, CL supports two options that direct the compiler to include information that is used by the SYMDEB and CodeView debuggers.

■ **FACT:** *The /Zi option directs CL to include in the object file information used by the CodeView debugger, such as symbol tables and line numbers.*

To debug your program with CodeView, you must use the /Zi option when you compile the source file.

■ **FACT:** *The /Zd option directs CL to include in the object file line number information used by the SYMDEB debugger.*

Compiling with the /Zd option lets you debug with SYMDEB. This option directs the C compiler to include line number information in the object file.

As you begin to build object libraries later in this book, you will discover the value of the /Zg option. It extracts a list of function declarations from a source file.

■ **FACT:** *The /Zg option directs CL to display the functions declared in the specified source file. You can redirect the list of function declarations to a file. CL does not compile the source file.*

A function declaration contains the function's return type, name, and argument types. If you examine the contents of the include file stdio.h, for example, you find declarations for the I/O functions. If you have a large file of related functions, the Cl option /Zg lets you generate a function declaration list that you can redirect to a file to create an include file.

Suppose you create the file STRINGS.C, which contains the following functions:

```
void str_copy(char *source, char *target)
{
    while (*target++ = *source++)
        { ; }
}

str_length(char *str)
{
    int size = 0;

    while (*str++)
        size++;

    return (size);
}
```

(continued)

continued

```
#include <stdio.h> /* needed for putchar */

void str_display(char *str)
{
    while (*str)
        putchar(*str++);
}
```

If you execute CL with the following command line:

```
C> CL /Zg STRINGS.C
```

your screen shows the following output:

```
Microsoft (R) C Optimizing Compiler Version 5.10
Copyright (c) Microsoft Corp 1984, 1985, 1986, 1987, 1988. All rights reserved.

STRINGS.C
extern  void str_copy(char *source,char *target);
extern  int str_length(char *str);
extern  void str_display(char *str);
```

As you know, the CL command compiles and links your files. If CL encounters syntax errors during compilation, it displays the errors. CL then invokes the linker to link the file. Because the file contains syntax errors, invoking the linker is a waste of time. As an alternative, you can execute CL only to examine the syntax of a file; CL does not go on to create an object file or invoke the linker.

■ **FACT:** *The /Zs option directs CL to examine the syntax of a file but not to generate an object file or invoke the linker.*

By restricting CL to an examination of a file's syntax, you avoid unnecessary invocation of the linker each time you compile a file.

LOOKING AT LINKER OPTIONS

Just as the CL command supports numerous options that influence the C compiler, CL also supports several options that affect the linker.

As discussed in the last chapter, CL reserves, by default, 2000 bytes of stack space for your program. If you attempt to run a program and receive the following message:

```
run-time error R6000
- stack overflow
```

you need to increase the size of the stack. One method for increasing stack size is to use the /F switch.

■ **FACT:** *The CL option /F directs the linker to allocate a specified number of bytes for the stack. The number of bytes must be expressed as a hexadecimal value.*

The following command uses the /F option to allocate more than the default amount of stack space:

```
C> CL /F:1000 PROG.C
```

The linker allocates 1000H, or 4096, bytes of stack space for execution of PROG.C.

CL supports three linker directives that deal with OS/2 executable files. The /Lp option directs CL to produce an executable file that runs in protected mode. In OS/2 protected mode, you can run several programs simultaneously.

■ **FACT:** *The CL option /Lp directs the linker to produce a protected mode executable file.*

OS/2 protected mode applications do not run under DOS. To use the /Lp option, you must link with OS/2 protected mode libraries.

■ **FACT:** *The CL option /Lc directs the linker to produce a real mode executable file.*

If your compiler produces OS/2 protected mode programs by default, you can create programs that run only in real mode (the OS/2 compatibility box or the MS-DOS environment) by using the /Lc option. To use the /Lc option, you must have the OS/2 real mode libraries. The CL option /Lr is identical to /Lc and can also be used to create real mode programs.

If your system has been properly configured, you can use the /Fb switch to create a dual mode application that can execute in either OS/2 protected mode or DOS real mode.

■ **FACT:** *The /Fb option directs the CL command to execute the linker and the Bind utility to produce a bound dual mode executable program.*

Not all OS/2 programs can be compiled and linked as dual mode programs. To use this option you must have the OS/2 libraries and the BIND.EXE program.

Some of the options that affect the linker are provided as qualifiers to the LINK command rather than as direct qualifiers to CL.

■ **FACT:** *The LINK option /HELP directs the linker to display a summary of its command line switches.*

To display a list of options that apply to the linker, type the following command at the system prompt:

```
C> LINK /HELP
```

The screen then shows a list of linker options. You can use them with the LINK command, or you can apply them on the CL command line by preceding them with the option /link.

```
Microsoft (R) Overlay Linker  Version 3.65
Copyright (C) Microsoft Corp 1983-1988.  All rights reserved.

Valid options are:
  /BATCH                      /CODEVIEW
  /CPARMAXALLOC               /DOSSEG
  /DSALLOCATE                 /EXEPACK
  /FARCALLTRANSLATION         /HELP
  /HIGH                       /INFORMATION
  /LINENUMBERS                /MAP
  /NODEFAULTLIBRARYSEARCH     /NOEXTDICTIONARY
  /NOFARCALLTRANSLATION       /NOGROUPASSOCIATION
  /NOIGNORECASE               /NOPACKCODE
  /OVERLAYINTERRUPT           /PACKCODE
  /PAUSE                      /QUICKLIBRARY
  /SEGMENTS                   /STACK
```

■ **FACT:** *The CL option /link lets you include linker options in the CL command line.*

For example, the following command compiles DISPLAY.C and increases the stack size from 2000 to 4096 bytes:

```
C> CL DISPLAY.C /link /stack:4096
```

The linker option /stack is equivalent to the CL option /F, except that stack size is specified in decimal rather than hexadecimal notation. Place the linker switches at the end of your command line, as shown above.

OPTIMIZING FOR PERFORMANCE

The CL options in this section let you optimize your programs for speed and size. These options can substantially improve the performance of your programs.

The /O option is discussed in this section with its various optimizing arguments (the letters a, d, i, l, p, s, t, and x). Note that you can combine optimizing arguments after the /O option in any order and that each letter applies to all source files on the command line. For example, /Oatl is a valid combination of optimizing letters that relaxes alias checking, favors execution speed, and enables loop optimization.

To begin, let's examine the influence of stack checking. Each time you invoke a function, the compiler invokes a function called _chkstk to ensure that sufficient space exists on the stack. If the stack space is insufficient, the program fails.

The program on the following page (GETSUM.C) uses the function *get_sum*, which adds two values and returns their sum.

```
main()
{
    int result;

    result = get_sum(3, 5);
}

get_sum(int a, int b)
{
    return (a + b);
}
```

If you compile GETSUM.C with the /Fa option,

```
C> CL /Fa GETSUM.C
```

you can see the calls to _chkstk in the resulting assembly language listing:

```
;          Static Name Aliases
;
           TITLE    GETSUM.C
           NAME     GETSUM

           .8087
_TEXT    SEGMENT    WORD PUBLIC 'CODE'
_TEXT    ENDS
_DATA    SEGMENT    WORD PUBLIC 'DATA'
_DATA    ENDS
CONST    SEGMENT    WORD PUBLIC 'CONST'
CONST    ENDS
_BSS     SEGMENT    WORD PUBLIC 'BSS'
_BSS     ENDS
DGROUP   GROUP    CONST, _BSS, _DATA
           ASSUME   CS: _TEXT, DS: DGROUP, SS: DGROUP
EXTRN    __acrtused:ABS
EXTRN    __chkstk:NEAR
_TEXT       SEGMENT
           ASSUME CS: _TEXT
; Line 4
           PUBLIC   _main
_main    PROC NEAR
           push     bp
           mov      bp,sp
           mov      ax,2
           call     __chkstk ─────────────── Stack checking
;          result = -2
```

(continued)

continued

```
; Line 7
        mov     ax,5
        push    ax
        mov     ax,3
        push    ax
        call    _get_sum
        mov     WORD PTR [bp-2],ax          ;result
; Line 8
        mov     sp,bp
        pop     bp
        ret
        nop

_main   ENDP
; Line 11
        PUBLIC  _get_sum
_get_sum        PROC NEAR
        push    bp
        mov     bp,sp
        xor     ax,ax
        call    __chkstk ————————————— Stack checking
;       a = 4
;       b = 6
; Line 13
        mov     ax,WORD PTR [bp+4]          ;a
        add     ax,WORD PTR [bp+6]          ;b
        pop     bp
        ret

_get_sum        ENDP
_TEXT   ENDS
END
```

■ **FACT:** *The /Gs option directs CL to disable stack checking.*

If you recompile the program with the /Gs option, the compiler suppresses stack checking. To see the result, enter the following command:

```
C> CL /Fa /Gs GETSUM.C
```

The calls to *_chkstk* that appeared in the preceding assembly language listing are absent from the listing on the following pages.

```
;        Static Name Aliases
;
         TITLE    GETSUM.C
         NAME     GETSUM


         .8087
_TEXT    SEGMENT  WORD PUBLIC 'CODE'
_TEXT    ENDS
_DATA    SEGMENT  WORD PUBLIC 'DATA'
_DATA    ENDS
CONST    SEGMENT  WORD PUBLIC 'CONST'
CONST    ENDS
_BSS     SEGMENT  WORD PUBLIC 'BSS'
_BSS     ENDS
DGROUP   GROUP    CONST, _BSS, _DATA
         ASSUME   CS: _TEXT, DS: DGROUP, SS: DGROUP
EXTRN    __acrtused:ABS
_TEXT        SEGMENT
         ASSUME   CS: _TEXT
; Line 4
         PUBLIC   _main
_main    PROC NEAR
         push    bp
         mov     bp,sp
         sub     sp,2 ─────────────────────── Stack checking removed
;        result = -2
; Line 7
         mov     ax,5
         push    ax
         mov     ax,3
         push    ax
         call    _get_sum
         mov     WORD PTR [bp-2],ax        ;result
; Line 8
         mov     sp,bp
         pop     bp
         ret


_main    ENDP
; Line 11
         PUBLIC   _get_sum
_get_sum         PROC NEAR
         push    bp
         mov     bp,sp ───────────────────── Stack checking removed
;        a = 4
;        b = 6
```

(continued)

continued

```
; Line 13
        mov     ax,WORD PTR [bp+4]      ;a
        add     ax,WORD PTR [bp+6]      ;b
        pop     bp
        ret
        nop

_get_sum         ENDP
_TEXT    ENDS
END
```

By disabling stack checking, you permit your program to execute faster because it makes fewer function calls.

To understand the impact stack checking can have on the performance of your program, change GETSUM.C as follows (GETSUM2.C):

```c
#include <time.h>  /* needed for ctime */

main()
    {
    long int seconds;
    long int i;
    int result;

    time(&seconds);
    printf("Start time:  %s\n", ctime(&seconds));
    for (i = 0; i < 300000L; i++)
        result = get_sum(3, 5);
    time(&seconds);
    printf("End time:  %s\n", ctime(&seconds));
    }

get_sum(int a, int b)
{
    return (a + b);
}
```

Compile the program without any options so that stack checking is introduced. Then run the program, and record the start time and end time it displays.

Next, recompile the program and disable stack checking using /Gs:

```
C> CL /Gs GETSUM2.C
```

When you run the recompiled program, the time elapsed between start and end times demonstrates that removing stack checking improves performance.

■ **TIP:** *After you finish testing your program, recompile it with stack checking disabled to improve its performance.*

■ **FACT:** *The /Oi option directs CL to generate in-line code for a set of run-time library functions. The in-line code executes faster than a function call.*

If your program uses any of the following functions, compiling with the /Oi option results in the use of in-line code and special argument-passing conventions:

- *memset, memcpy, memcmp*

- *strset, strcpy, strcmp, strcat*

- *inp, outp*

- *_rotl, _rotr, _lrotl, _lrotr*

- *min, max, abs*

- *pow, log, loglo, exp*

- *sin, cos, tan*

- *asin, acos, atan, atan2*

- *sinh, cosh, tanh*

- *sqrt, floor, ceil, fabs, fmod*

The following program (SQRT.C) uses the *sqrt* function to calculate the square root of 100. The calculation occurs in a loop that repeats 30,000 times.

```
#include <time.h>  /* needed for ctime */
#include <math.h>  /* needed for sqrt */

main()
    {
    long int seconds;
    long int i;
    float result;

    time(&seconds);
    printf("Start time:  %s\n", ctime(&seconds));

    for (i = 0; i < 30000L; i++)
        result = sqrt(100);

    time(&seconds);
    printf("End time:  %s\n", ctime(&seconds));
    }
```

First, compile the program with the /Fa option, as follows:

```
C> CL /Fa SQRT.C
```

Then run the program and record the start and stop times. If you examine the resulting assembly language file, you can see the call to _sqrt. Figure 26-1A shows the assembly code for line 14, which contains the function call. Because the compiler places arguments onto the stack with each function call, function calls are slow. If you recompile the program with the additional option /Oi,

```
C> CL /Oi /Fa SQRT.C
```

the compiler actually places the code that _sqrt performs in line at each reference. Figure 26-1B on the following page shows the code for line 14 in the new assembly language listing. By removing the function calls from the executable program, the compiler produces a program that executes considerably faster.

```
; Line 14
        fld     QWORD PTR $T20002
        sub     sp,8
        mov     bx,sp
        fstp    QWORD PTR [bx]
        fwait
        call    _sqrt ─────────────────── Function call to sqrt
        add     sp,8
        lea     di,WORD PTR [bp-20]
        mov     si,ax
        push    ss
        pop     es
        movsw
        movsw
        movsw
        movsw
        fld     QWORD PTR [bp-20]
        fstp    DWORD PTR [bp-8]         ;result
        fwait
        jmp     SHORT $FC182
        nop
```

FIGURE 26-1A.
The assembly language code for line 14 of SQRT.C contains a call to _sqrt.

```
; Line 14
        fld     QWORD PTR $T20003
        call    _CIsqrt
        fstp    DWORD PTR [bp-8]          ;result
        fwait
        jmp     SHORT $FC200
        nop
```

FIGURE 26-1B.
When SQRT.C is compiled with the /Oi option, in-line code replaces the function call in line 14.

By default, CL uses the /Ot option, which directs the compiler to optimize for speed.

■ **FACT:** *The /Ot option directs CL to optimize for execution time. The /Ot option is exercised by default.*

As we have noted in previous chapters, program size almost invariably conflicts with execution time. We cut execution time at the cost of compactness. Most programmers are more concerned with speed than size, so /Ot is the default optimization setting. For those programmers concerned with program size, CL supports the /Os option, which directs the compiler to optimize for size.

■ **FACT:** *The /Os option directs CL to optimize for size rather than for speed.*

One of the obstacles the C compiler faces when it attempts to optimize your code is *aliasing*, a phenomenon that occurs when two names reference the same memory location. The following program (NOALIAS.C) aliases the variable *a* with the pointer **ptr*.

```
main()
{
    int a, *ptr;

    ptr = &a;  /* alias */
}
```

The C compiler dutifully keeps track of any aliasing that takes place (intentional or not) and stores this information in the resulting executable file. If you would like to prevent the compiler from doing this, use the /Oa option or include the *a* optimization argument with the /Ot, /Os, or /Ol option. Determining whether to disable alias checking can involve a range of factors, a full discussion of which is beyond the scope of this book. For more information on this subject, see the optimization section of your C compiler user's guide.

■ **TIP:** *If your program does not use aliasing, you can include the lowercase letter* a *in the /Ot, /Os, and /Ol switches to reduce the alias checking the compiler performs during optimization.*

The following program (LOOP.C) loops 1000 times; with each iteration, it displays the current value of the variables *i* and *j*.

```
main()
{
    int i, j;

    for (i = 0; i < 1000; ++i)
        {
        j = 5;
        printf("%d %d\n", i, j);
        }
}
```

Note that the program initializes *j* within the *for* loop; with each iteration *j* gets initialized to 5. This unnecessary processing can have a significant impact on performance.

■ **FACT:** *The /Ol option directs CL to optimize the code that appears within loops.*

Now compile LOOP.C with the following command line:

```
C> CL /Fa /Oal LOOP.C
```

Remember, the *a* in */Oal* simply reduces alias checking. If you examine the assembly language listing, LOOP.ASM, you find that the compiler has optimized the loop by moving the initialization of *j* outside the loop. In so doing, the compiler compensates for a programming mistake.

On occasion, you might prefer to compile without optimizing at all. You can use the /Od option to suppress the compiler's optimizing logic.

■ **FACT:** *The CL option /Od disables optimization.*

By disabling optimization during debugging operations, you can be sure the compiler generates code exactly as it is written. For example, the following command:

```
CL /Od /Zi DEBUG.C
```

directs the compiler to produce an unoptimized object file that contains debugging information for use with CodeView.

By default, the compiler stores floating point values in an 80-byte register. When the program accesses the value, the compiler moves the value from the register to a 32-bit (or 64-bit) memory location. As a result, the final 48 (or 16) bits are truncated. Because this truncation occurs each time the program references the value, a frequently referenced variable can exhibit inconsistency.

■ **FACT:** *The /Op option directs CL to store floating point values as variables in 64-bit (or 32-bit) memory locations rather than in an 80-bit register. In so doing, the compiler sacrifices precision to avoid truncation errors.*

If you have a program in which mathematical precision is paramount, experiment with the /Op directive and note its impact on your results.

Last, the CL command supports the /Ox option, which requests maximum optimization. The /Ox option is equivalent to the following combination of options: /Oailt /Gs.

■ **FACT:** *The /Ox option directs CL to maximize its optimization. In general, this switch directs the compiler to use intrinsic functions, to apply loop and speed optimization, to reduce alias checking, and to disable stack checking.*

After you fully test your application, you can get the best optimization by using /Ox.

USING THE *CL* ENVIRONMENT VARIABLE

Each time you invoke CL, it examines the environment for a *CL=* entry.

■ **FACT:** *The* CL= *environment entry lets you define the switches you want CL to use each time you compile a program.*

The following command line creates an entry in the environment that defines /W3, /Fs, and /Fa as default options for use with CL:

```
C> SET CL= /W3 /Fs /Fa
```

Once the environment entry exists, CL displays all warning messages and generates a source listing and an assembly language listing for each source file you compile.

■ **TIP:** *Once you determine the* CL= *setting that works best for you, place that entry in AUTOEXEC.BAT.*

USING *#pragma* COMPILER DIRECTIVES

Many of the capabilities we have examined with CL directives can also be requested with compiler directives. A compiler directive, or *pragma,* is a special instruction to the compiler. In this section we examine compiler directives that correspond to CL switches we have discussed. Note, however, that some of the following pragmas are not supported by the QuickC compiler or by versions of the Microsoft C Compiler prior to 5.0.

■ **TIP:** *Many capabilities are available both as CL options and as pragmas; whenever possible, use pragmas.*

Pragmas are generally preferable to comparable compiler options. You place pragmas in line, as part of your source code. Consequently, you can't omit a pragma when you recompile, although you might forget to include a CL option.

■ **FACT:** *The* check_stack *pragma enables or disables stack checking. For example, the directive* #pragma check_stack(on) *turns on stack checking.*

The following program (PRAGMA.C) uses the *check_stack* pragma to disable stack checking:

```
#pragma check_stack(off)   /* disables stack checking */
#include <math.h>          /* needed for sqrt */

main()
{
    int i;

    for (i = 0; i < 100; ++i)
        printf("%f %d\n", sqrt(i), i);
}
```

■ **FACT:** *The* intrinsic *pragma directs the compiler to generate in-line code for the specified functions. For example,* #pragma intrinsic(cos) *directs the compiler to generate in-line code for the* cos *function.*

The following program (PRAGMA2.C) uses the *intrinsic* pragma to govern compilation of the *sqrt* function:

```
#include <math.h>          /* needed for sqrt */
#pragma intrinsic(sqrt);   /* generates fast in-line code for sqrt */

main()
{
    int i;

    for (i = 0; i <= 100; ++i)
        printf("%f %d\n", sqrt(i), i);
}
```

■ **FACT:** *The* function *pragma ensures that the compiler uses function calls to the specified functions instead of generating in-line code.*

The following program (PRAGMA3.C) uses the *function* pragma to ensure that the compiler calls the functions *cos* and *tan*:

```
#include <math.h>              /* needed for cos and tan */

#pragma function(cos, tan)     /* forces function call to cos and tan */

main()
{
    /* remainder of code */
}
```

The next four pragmas—*title, subtitle, linesize,* and *pagesize*—deal with source listing format. They correspond to the compiler options /St, /Ss, /Sl, and /Sp.

■ **FACT:** *The* title *pragma directs the compiler to generate the specified title string in the source listing.*

■ **FACT:** *The* subtitle *pragma directs the compiler to generate the specified subtitle string in the source listing.*

■ **FACT:** *The* linesize *pragma directs the compiler to create a source listing with the specified number of columns. By default, the compiler uses 80.*

■ **FACT:** *The* pagesize *pragma directs the compiler to restrict each page in the source listing to the specified number of lines.*

The following program (PRAGMA4.C) uses the four pragmas that set the format of a source listing:

```
#pragma title("Square root program")  /* sets listing file title */
#pragma subtitle("SQRT.C")             /* sets listing file subtitle */
#pragma linesize(80)                   /* sets 80 columns per page */
#pragma pagesize(55)                   /* sets 55 lines per page */
#pragma check_stack(off)               /* disables stack checking */

#include <math.h>                       /* needed for sqrt */

main()
{
    int i;

    for (i = 0; i <= 100; ++i)
        printf("%f %d\n", sqrt(i), i);
}
```

When you compile the program with the /Fs option, CL produces a source listing that contains the following text:

```
Square root program                                         PAGE   1
SQRT.C                                                      05-01-89
                                                           12:00:00


 Line#  Source Line                         Microsoft C Compiler Version 5.10

     1  #pragma title("Square root program")  /* sets listing file title */
     2  #pragma subtitle("SQRT.C")            /* sets listing file subtitle */
     3  #pragma linesize(80)                  /* sets 80 columns per page */
     4  #pragma pagesize(55)                  /* sets 55 lines per page */
     5  #pragma check_stack(off)              /* disables stack checking */
     6
     7  #include <math.h>                     /* needed for sqrt */
     8
     9  main()
    10  {
    11      int i;
    12
    13      for (i = 0; i <= 100; ++i)
    14          printf("%f %d\n", sqrt(i), i);
    15  }

main  Local Symbols

Name                      Class   Type          Size    Offset   Register

i . . . . . . . . . . . . auto                          -0002

Global Symbols

Name                      Class   Type          Size    Offset

main. . . . . . . . . . . global  near function   ***    0000
printf. . . . . . . . . . extern  near function   ***    ***
sqrt. . . . . . . . . . . extern  near function   ***    ***

Code size = 0054 (84)
Data size = 0007 (7)
Bss size  = 0000 (0)

No errors detected
```

■ **FACT:** *The* pack *pragma directs the compiler to align structure members on the specified boundary. For example, the directive* #pragma pack(4) *directs the compiler to align structure members on 4-byte boundaries.*

■ **FACT:** *The* loop_opt *pragma directs the compiler to enable or disable loop optimization.*

The following program (PRAGMA5.C) uses the *loop_opt* pragma to enable loop optimization:

```
#pragma loop_opt(on)   /* enables loop optimization */

main()
{
    int i, j;

    for (i = 0; i < 1000; ++i)
        {
        j = 5;
        printf("%d %d\n", i, j);
        }
}
```

To achieve full loop optimization, compile the program with the /Oa option, which reduces alias checking by the compiler.

■ **FACT:** *The* message *pragma directs the compiler to display a message to stdout when it compiles the line containing the pragma.*

The following program (PMESSAGE.C) uses the *message* pragma before each function; the messages let you monitor the progress of compilation.

```
#pragma message("Starting compilation")  /* display during compile */
#include <math.h>                         /* needed for sqrt */

main()
{
    int i;

    for (i = 0; i <= 100; ++i)
        printf("%f %d\n", sqrt(i), i);
}

#pragma message("Compilation complete")  /* display during compile */
```

When you compile this program, your screen shows

```
Microsoft (R) C Optimizing Compiler Version 5.10
Copyright (c) Microsoft Corp 1984, 1985, 1986, 1987, 1988. All rights reserved.

PMESSAGE.C
Starting compilation
Compilation complete
```

SUMMARY

Looking at Preprocessor Directives

■ **FACT:** *The CL option /D lets you define a macro or constant in the CL command line for use in the program.*

■ **FACT:** *If you are using the Microsoft QuickC Compiler, you can compile programs from the command line with the QCL command.*

■ **FACT:** *The /U option directs CL to undefine one of the constants that are predefined by the Microsoft C Compiler.*

■ **FACT:** *The /u option directs CL to undefine each of its predefined constants.*

■ **FACT:** *The CL option /I changes the search order that the preprocessor uses to locate include files. The preprocessor first searches the specified directories and then searches the default location if the include files have not been found.*

■ **FACT:** *The /X option directs CL not to examine the default include directory.*

■ **FACT:** *The /E option directs CL to send the output of the preprocessor to the screen. CL does not compile and link the file; it generates only the preprocessor output.*

■ **FACT:** *The /P option directs CL to write the preprocessor output to a file with the extension I. CL does not compile and link the program; it generates only the pre-processor output.*

■ **FACT:** *The /EP option directs CL to write the preprocessor output to the screen but to suppress the #line information normally displayed with /E. CL does not compile and link the file; it generates only the preprocessor output.*

■ **FACT:** *The /C option directs CL to leave comments in the preprocessor output if the command line also contains the /E, /P, or /EP option. For example, the command line CL /EP /C MINMAX.C performs preprocessing on MINMAX.C and writes the output to the screen with comments but without #line information.*

Generating Various Output Files

■ **FACT:** *The /Fs option directs CL to produce a listing of the source file. By default, CL uses the basename of the source file and adds the extension LST.*

■ **FACT:** *The /Fa option directs CL to produce an assembly language listing of the program. By default, CL uses the basename of the source file and adds the extension ASM.*

■ **FACT:** *The /Fl option directs CL to create an object code listing of your source code. By default, CL uses the basename of the source file and adds the extension COD.*

■ **FACT:** *The /Fc option directs CL to create an object code listing that contains not only the assembly language output and equivalent hexadecimal machine code but also the C source code. By default, CL uses the basename of the source file and adds the extension COD.*

■ **FACT:** *The /Fm option directs CL to create a file containing the link map. By default, CL uses the basename of the source file and adds the extension MAP.*

Changing Object or Executable Filenames

■ **FACT:** *The CL option /Fo lets you specify the name of the object file.*

■ **FACT:** *The CL option /Fe lets you change the name of an executable file.*

Customizing Source Listings

■ **FACT:** *The /Sl option directs CL to use a specified number of columns when it creates the source listing. By default, CL creates an 80-column source listing.*

■ **FACT:** *The /Sp option directs CL to place only the specified number of lines on each page of the source listing. By default, CL places 65 lines on each page.*

■ **FACT:** *The CL option /St lets you assign a title that appears on each page of the source listing.*

■ **FACT:** *The CL option /Ss lets you assign a subtitle within the source listing. The subtitle appears below the main title on each page.*

Specifying the Memory Model

■ **FACT:** *The /AS, /AC, /AM, /AL, or /AH option directs CL to use the small, compact, medium, large, or huge memory model. The default memory model is the small model.*

Floating Point Processing

■ **FACT:** *The /FPc option directs CL to use calls to the floating point emulator. If the system has a math coprocessor, the library uses it.*

■ **FACT:** *The /FPi option directs CL to generate in-line code to support a math coprocessor if one exists. If the system has no math coprocessor, calls to the emulator library are used. This option specifies the default method for floating point processing.*

■ **TIP:** *A program compiled with the /FPc or /FPi option offers the advantage of running on a system with or without a math coprocessor.*

■ **FACT:** *The /FPc87 option directs CL to generate calls to the math coprocessor library. A computer must have a math coprocessor to execute programs compiled with /FPc87.*

■ **FACT:** *The /FPi87 option directs CL to generate in-line code that references the math coprocessor libraries.*

■ **FACT:** *The /FPa option directs CL to use the alternative math library, which trades precision for speed.*

Miscellaneous Options

■ **FACT:** *The /c option directs CL to compile the specified source file to create an object file but not to link the file.*

■ **FACT:** *The CL option /V lets you place a string in your object file that specifies the version number.*

■ **FACT:** *The /J option directs CL to treat the type* char *as* unsigned *and thus capable of storing the values 0 through 255.*

■ **FACT:** *The CL option /H lets you restrict the number of characters the compiler distinguishes in external names.*

■ **FACT:** *The /Tc option informs CL that the filename that follows identifies a C source file.*

■ **FACT:** *The CL options /W0, /W1, /W2, and /W3 indicate levels of warning messages the C compiler displays on your screen. Warning level 1, which you specify with /W1, is the default level.*

■ **TIP:** *Use /W3 for production programs. In so doing, you might catch errors during compilation that would be difficult to debug.*

Looking at Code Generation

■ **FACT:** *The /G0, /G1, or /G2 option directs CL to generate code for the 8086, 80186, or 80286 instruction set. The default compiler output is restricted to the 8086 instruction set, which you can specify explicitly with /G0.*

■ **FACT:** *The /Gc option directs CL to handle a function's arguments from left to right.*

■ **FACT:** *The /Gm option directs CL to place string constants in the constant segment.*

Looking at Language Specifics

■ **FACT:** *The /Ze option directs CL to enable extensions to the ANSI specification. The extensions are enabled by default.*

■ **FACT:** *The /Za option directs CL to disable extensions to the ANSI specification.*

■ **FACT:** *The /Zp option directs CL to align members of a structure on 1-byte, 2-byte, or 4-byte boundaries.*

■ **FACT:** *The /Zl option directs CL not to place the name of the default library into object files.*

■ **FACT:** *The /Zi option directs CL to include in the object file information used by the CodeView debugger, such as symbol tables and line numbers.*

■ **FACT:** *The /Zd option directs CL to include in the object file line number information used by the SYMDEB debugger.*

■ **FACT:** *The /Zg option directs CL to display the functions declared in the specified source file. You can redirect the list of function declarations to a file. CL does not compile the source file.*

■ **FACT:** *The /Zs option directs CL to examine the syntax of a file but not to generate an object file or invoke the linker.*

Looking at Linker Options

■ **FACT:** *The CL option /F directs the linker to allocate a specified number of bytes for the stack. The number of bytes must be expressed as a hexadecimal value.*

■ **FACT:** *The CL option /Lp directs the linker to produce a protected mode executable file.*

■ **FACT:** *The CL option /Lc directs the linker to produce a real mode executable file.*

■ **FACT:** *The /Fb option directs the CL command to execute the linker and the Bind utility to produce a bound dual mode executable program.*

■ **FACT:** *The LINK option /HELP directs the linker to display a summary of its command line switches.*

■ **FACT:** *The CL option /link lets you include linker options in the CL command line.*

Optimizing for Performance

■ **FACT:** *The /Gs option directs CL to disable stack checking.*

■ **TIP:** *After you finish testing your program, recompile it with stack checking disabled to improve its performance.*

■ **FACT:** *The /Oi option directs CL to generate in-line code for a set of run-time library functions. The in-line code executes faster than a function call.*

■ **FACT:** *The /Ot option directs CL to optimize for execution time. The /Ot option is exercised by default.*

■ **FACT:** *The /Os option directs CL to optimize for size rather than for speed.*

■ **TIP:** *If your program does not use aliasing, you can include the lowercase letter a in the /Ot, /Os, and /Ol switches to reduce the alias checking the compiler performs during optimization.*

■ **FACT:** *The /Ol option directs CL to optimize the code that appears within loops.*

■ **FACT:** *The CL option /Od disables optimization.*

■ **FACT:** *The /Op option directs CL to store floating point values as variables in 64-bit (or 32-bit) memory locations rather than in an 80-bit register. In so doing, the compiler sacrifices precision to avoid truncation errors.*

■ **FACT:** *The /Ox option directs CL to maximize its optimization. In general, this switch directs the compiler to use intrinsic functions, to apply loop and speed optimization, to reduce alias checking, and to disable stack checking.*

Using the *CL* Environment Variable

■ **FACT:** *The* CL= *environment entry lets you define the switches you want CL to use each time you compile a program.*

■ **TIP:** *Once you determine the* CL= *setting that works best for you, place that entry in AUTOEXEC.BAT.*

Using *#pragma* Compiler Directives

■ **TIP:** *Many capabilities are available both as CL options and as pragmas; whenever possible, use pragmas.*

■ **FACT:** *The* check_stack *pragma enables or disables stack checking. For example, the directive* #pragma check _stack(on) *turns on stack checking.*

■ **FACT:** *The* intrinsic *pragma directs the compiler to generate in-line code for the specified functions. For example,* #pragma intrinsic(cos) *directs the compiler to generate in-line code for the* cos *function.*

■ **FACT:** *The* function *pragma ensures that the compiler uses function calls to the specified functions instead of generating in-line code.*

■ **FACT:** *The* title *pragma directs the compiler to generate the specified title string in the source listing.*

■ **FACT:** *The* subtitle *pragma directs the compiler to generate the specified subtitle string in the source listing.*

■ **FACT:** *The* linesize *pragma directs the compiler to create a source listing with the specified number of columns. By default, the compiler uses 80.*

■ **FACT:** *The* pagesize *pragma directs the compiler to restrict each page in the source listing to the specified number of lines.*

■ **FACT:** *The* pack *pragma directs the compiler to align structure members on the specified boundary. For example, the directive* #pragma pack(4) *directs the compiler to align structure members on 4-byte boundaries.*

■ **FACT:** *The* loop_opt *pragma directs the compiler to enable or disable loop optimization.*

■ **FACT:** *The* message *pragma directs the compiler to display a message to stdout when it compiles the line containing the pragma.*

GLOSSARY

aliasing A phenomenon that occurs when two names reference the same memory location. Because C uses pointers extensively, a program commonly contains two names that reference the same location.

assembly language listing A file that contains the assembly language output generated by the compiler, grouped by the corresponding line numbers in the C source file. The CL option /Fa creates an assembly language listing.

compiler option A switch that you include in the CL command line that modifies or supplements the output of the CL command. For example, the compiler option /Fa directs CL to produce an assembly language listing of your file.

floating point emulator A collection of software routines that performs the same function as the 8087 math coprocessor chip. The floating point emulator lets systems that lack a math coprocessor perform complex math operations by using software instead.

object code listing A file that contains the assembly language and binary output of the compiler. The CL option /Fc creates an object code listing.

pragma A compiler option that you place in your source file. The C *#pragma* statement lets you place pragmas in your file. The statement *#pragma check_stack(off)*, for example, disables stack checking.

source listing A file containing the source code of your program, with line numbers, as well as a summary of the variables and functions used. The CL option /Fs creates a source listing.

## CHAPTER 27

Simplifying Program Development with LIB and MAKE

Earlier in this book you learned that you could build an executable file by combining separately compiled object files. This process reduces the amount of code that the compiler examines each time you invoke it, which in turn reduces your compilation time and program development time. In this chapter we take the process one step further—we use the LIB command, which lets you create and maintain your own run-time libraries. In addition, we examine the MAKE utility, a labor saver for program maintenance and development. Using MAKE, you can easily update an EXE file or library whenever a change occurs to a source file the program or library uses.

As the size and complexity of your programs increase, you'll find that tools such as LIB and MAKE can help you make more productive use of your development time.

GETTING STARTED WITH LIB

A run-time library is a collection of related precompiled object files. When you link a program, the linker searches for functions and external variables—first in the object code for the source file, and then in any other OBJ files specified in the CL command. If the linker does not locate the function or variable, it examines any LIB files you place on the command line, as well as the default library the C compiler provides for the memory model you are using.

The linker uses the *LIB=* environment entry to tell it where run-time libraries reside on disk. If you examine the files in your directory, you find several library files. Let's examine the library file that contains the run-time library for the small memory model, SLIBCE.LIB.

■ **FACT:** *The LIB command is a librarian that lets you create, change, or display a library file. By default, library files use the extension LIB.*

An object library is a collection of useful routines in object file format. The linker reads the library and copies the object code for routines referenced in the program. The LIB command lets you create and manipulate libraries. When you execute the LIB command, it prompts you for the library name:

```
Microsoft (R) Library Manager  Version 3.11
Copyright (C) Microsoft Corp 1983-1988.  All rights reserved.

Library name:
```

Type *SLIBCE.LIB* and press Enter. LIB prompts you next for the operations that you want to perform:

```
Library name:SLIBCE.LIB
Operations:
```

Later in this chapter you will learn how to add and delete object files in a library. We do not want to change SLIBCE.LIB, however, so simply press Enter. LIB then prompts you for the name of the list file. The list file created by LIB contains an entry for each object file in the library.

A library can contain hundreds of routines in object file format. If you type *CON* and press Enter, LIB displays the name of each routine in the library. If you type *PRN* or a filename, LIB writes the list to your printer or to the specified file. If you specify nothing (the default), no output will be generated. In this case simply type *CON* and press Enter:

```
Library name:SLIBCE.LIB
Operations:
List file:CON
```

LIB displays all the functions contained in the run-time library SLIBCE.LIB (the functions that appear in the Microsoft C run-time library documentation).

524

Now let's create a library from a series of object modules and then use the functions it contains. To begin, create the file STRLEN.C, which contains the following:

```
str_length(char *str)
{
    int i = 0;

    while (*str++)
        i++;

    return (i);
}
```

Compile STRLEN.C with the following command line:

```
C> CL /c STRLEN.C
```

As you recall from Chapter 26, the /c switch directs CL to compile the code to produce an object file, but not to link the file to produce executable code. Next, create the following file, STRCOPY.C, and compile it with /c to produce an object file.

```
void str_copy(char *source, char *target)
{
    while (*target++ = *source++)
        { ; }
}
```

Last, create the following file, STRDISP.C, and compile it with the /c option to produce STRDISP.OBJ.

```
#include <stdio.h>  /* needed for putchar */

void str_display(char *str)
{
    while (*str)
        putchar(*str++);
}
```

You now have three object files—STRLEN.OBJ, STRCOPY.OBJ, and STRDISP.OBJ. Using the LIB utility, let's create a library file called STRING.LIB that contains all three object files. First, enter the following command:

```
C> LIB STRING.LIB
```

Because STRING.LIB does not exist, LIB prompts you to see if you want to create the file. If you type *Y*, LIB creates the file. If you type *N*, LIB returns to the system prompt.

In this case type *Y* to create the file. LIB then prompts you for the operation you want to perform.

■ **FACT:** *The plus operator (+) directs LIB to add one or more object files to the library. LIB assumes that object files have the extension OBJ.*

To add the object files STRLEN.OBJ and STRCOPY.OBJ to the library, use the plus operator (+), as follows:

```
Microsoft (R) Library Manager  Version 3.11
Copyright (C) Microsoft Corp 1983-1988.  All rights reserved.

Library does not exist.  Create? (y/n) Y
Operations:+STRLEN+STRCOPY
```

When LIB prompts you for a list file, type *CON* to display the library contents. Your screen shows the following:

```
_str_copy........STRCOPY              _str_length........STRLEN

STRLEN              Offset: 00000010H  Code and data size: 26H
  _str_length

STRCOPY             Offset: 00000150H  Code and data size: 20H
  _str_copy
```

■ **FACT:** *You can specify the name of the library file and the file operations you want to perform in your LIB command line.*

Now enter the following command—notice that you can use the command line to provide the same information you would enter at the LIB prompts.

```
C> LIB STRING.LIB +STRDISP,CON
```

This command adds the object file STRDISP.OBJ to the library file STRING.LIB and directs LIB to display the list file to the screen. Before it displays the list file, LIB prompts you to specify an output library file. Whenever you change the contents of a library file, LIB lets you write the new library to a different file. Type *STRING.LIB* or simply press Enter. Your screen shows

```
Output library:
_str_copy........STRCOPY              _str_display........STRDISP
_str_length........STRLEN

STRLEN              Offset: 00000010H  Code and data size: 26H
  _str_length
```

(continued)

continued

```
STRCOPY              Offset: 00000150H   Code and data size: 20H
  _str_copy

STRDISP              Offset: 00000280H   Code and data size: 42H
  _str_display
```

To suppress the prompt for the new output library, simply include the library name in the command line, as follows:

```
C> LIB STRING.LIB +STRDISP,CON,STRING.LIB
```

Now that the file STRING.LIB exists, let's use it with a small test program. Create the following file (STRTEST.C), which references all three functions in the library:

```
main()
{
    char str[128];

    str_copy("TESTING LIB FILE", str);
    printf("%s contains %d characters\n", str, str_length(str));
    str_display(str);
}
```

Next, simply compile and link the source file using the following command:

```
C> CL STRTEST.C STRING.LIB
```

The CL command compiles the program STRTEST.C to produce STRTEST.OBJ, which the linker then combines with STRING.LIB and SLIBCE.LIB to generate the executable file STRTEST.EXE. Figure 27-1 depicts this process.

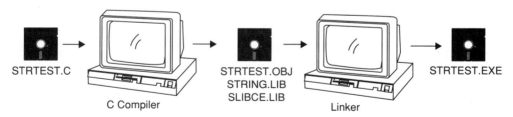

STRTEST.C   C Compiler   STRTEST.OBJ STRING.LIB SLIBCE.LIB   Linker   STRTEST.EXE

FIGURE 27-1.
References to your custom libraries, like those to the default library, are resolved at linktime.

The linker copies from the library only those object files used in the program. If the object file is not found, the linker displays an *unresolved external* error.

If you get an error message, double-check the spelling of the function and display the contents of the library to ensure that the function exists.

Adding functions to a library is simple and straightforward. Suppose you create another string-manipulating function, *str_append*, in a file named STRAPPD.C:

```
void str_append(char *source, char *target)
{
    while (*target++)                /* find end of target */
        { ; }

    while (*target++ = *source++) /* append source */
        { ; }
}
```

You can compile the file using /c on the command line, as follows:

C> CL /c STRAPPD.C

Then you can add the new object module to your existing library STRING.LIB with the following command:

C> LIB STRING.LIB +STRAPPD,CON,STRING.LIB

■ **TIP:** *To conserve disk space, you might want to use the /Zl option when you compile functions for a library.*

The /Zl option, discussed in Chapter 26, directs the compiler to omit the default library name from an object file. If you are creating a library from a great number of functions, the savings in disk space can become significant. You need to include the default library only once in an executable file.

If you discover a bug in one of your library functions, LIB lets you remove the code for the function from your library.

■ **FACT:** *The minus operator (−) directs LIB to remove the specified object module from the library file.*

The following LIB command line uses the minus operator (−) to remove the object module STRCOPY from the library file STRING.LIB.

C> LIB STRING.LIB -STRCOPY,CON,STRING.LIB

When LIB displays the list file on your screen, you can verify that it has removed STRCOPY.

LIB supports another operator that lets you replace an object module in the library with a newer version that resides as an OBJ file on disk. The newer version might be debugged or optimized, for example.

■ **FACT:** *The replacement operator (−+) directs LIB to replace a module in a library with a newer version.*

LIB uses the minus sign followed immediately by the plus sign as its replacement operator (−+). LIB locates the specified object file on disk and updates the library with the current version. The following LIB command line, for example, directs LIB to update the module STRLEN:

```
C> LIB STRING.LIB -+STRLEN,CON,STRING.LIB
```

To replace the specified module, LIB searches for the file STRLEN.OBJ in the current directory.

LIB also lets you copy a module from the library to a separate disk file.

■ **FACT:** *The copy operator (*) directs LIB to copy the specified module to disk as an object file.*

LIB uses the asterisk (*) as its copy operator. LIB locates the specified module and copies it to a disk file with the extension OBJ. Many programmers use the copy operator to save working copies of library modules in an object file before they update a library.

If the file STRDISP.OBJ exists on your disk, delete it or rename it. Then use the copy operator in the following LIB command to recreate the object file on disk:

```
C> LIB STRING.LIB *STRDISP,CON;
```

■ **TIP:** *If you place a semicolon on the command line after you specify the operations or after the list file, LIB uses defaults in the remaining fields.*

LIB lets you end a command with a semicolon (;) to choose the defaults for the remaining command line entries. In the following command, for example, LIB uses the default destination for the list file (NUL device) and the default name for the output file (STRING.LIB):

```
C> LIB STRING.LIB +STRLEN;
```

Last, LIB lets you save a module to disk and remove it from the library in one operation.

■ **FACT:** *A minus sign followed immediately by an asterisk (−*) directs LIB to copy the specified module to disk and then remove it from the library.*

In the following LIB command, the minus operator and the copy operator are combined:

```
C> LIB STRING.LIB -*STRDISP,CON,STRING.LIB
```

This command directs LIB to copy the module STRDISP from the library to disk; LIB creates STRDISP.OBJ and then removes the module STRDISP from the library.

■ **TIP:** *If you are performing several library operations at one time, use the ampersand (&)*
to continue your operations to the next line.

If you want to perform a series of operations on a library file, you can use the ampersand (&) to place each operation on a separate line. For example, you might add several modules to a library, as follows:

```
Operations: +STRLEN &
Operations: +STRCOPY &
Operations: +STRAPPD
```

The compilation process is time consuming. Whenever you reduce the amount of code the compiler must examine, you decrease your development time. Creating and using run-time libraries is one way of becoming a more productive C programmer.

USING THE /Zg DIRECTIVE

If you have a large source file containing functions you want to place in a library, don't forget about the /Zg compiler directive discussed in Chapter 26. When you include /Zg in the CL command line, CL writes the function declarations for each function in the file to stdout. By redirecting this output to a file, you can create an include file that defines the functions in the library.

To demonstrate this procedure on a small scale, let's use our series of string-manipulating functions. Type the following command to combine the files STRCOPY.C, STRLEN.C, and STRDISP.C into the file MYSTRING.C:

```
COPY STRCOPY.C +STRLEN.C +STRDISP.C MYSTRING.C
```

The combined source file contains the three functions, as follows:

```c
void str_copy(char *source, char *target)
{
    while (*target++ = *source++)
        { ; }
}
str_length(char *str)
{
    int size = 0;

    while (*str++)
        size++;

    return (size);
}
```

(continued)

continued

```
#include <stdio.h>  /* needed for putchar */

void str_display(char *str)
{
    while (*str)
        putchar(*str++);
}
```

Now type the following to compile MYSTRING.C with the /Zg option and redirect the output to MYSTRING.H:

```
CL /Zg MYSTRING.C > MYSTRING.H
```

The result is the following series of definitions:

```
extern  void str_copy(char *source,char *target);
extern  int str_length(char *str);
extern  void str_display(char *str);
```

After you create the include file, your programs can include it for function declarations. For example, you can include MYSTRING.H in the following modified version of our test program (STRTEST2.C):

```
#include "mystring.h"  /* needed for str_copy, str_length, */
                       /* and str_display */

main()
{
    char str[128];

    str_copy("TESTING INCLUDE FILE", str);
    printf("%s contains %d characters\n", str, str_length(str));
    str_display(str);
}
```

USING MAKE, THE PROGRAM MAINTENANCE UTILITY

As your programs increase in complexity, you may find them more complicated to modify and maintain. A single program might depend on several include files, several C source files, and several libraries. If one of these files changes, you might need to recompile several other files—perhaps you modify a function and need to update a library file so that you can create a new executable program based upon the most recent version of every file it uses.

The MAKE utility simplifies the process of applying changes to your programs. MAKE uses a description file that tells it which files a program uses and the specific relationships among those files. Most MAKE description files use the same name as the application but have no extension.

Let's look at a simple example. Suppose a program uses the user-defined include file DEFN.H, which contains the following definitions:

```
#define SIZE 255
#define MAX(a, b) ((a) > (b) ? (a) : (b))
```

The program, MAXVAL.C, generates the number of random numbers specified by the constant SIZE and then displays the maximum value it generates:

```
#include "defn.h"   /* needed for SIZE and MAX */

main()
{
    int i, max_val = 0;

    for (i = 0; i < SIZE; ++i)
        max_val = MAX(max_val, rand());

    printf("Max value generated %d\n", max_val);
}
```

Our MAKE description file in this case is named MAXVAL. Within this file we set up a list of file *dependencies*. A dependency is a relationship between files whereby modification of one file necessitates rebuilding of a second.

■ **FACT:** *In a MAKE description file, a dependent file is one from which the target file is created. For example, an object file is the target file for a dependent source file.*

MAXVAL contains the dependency shown here:

```
MAXVAL.EXE: DEFN.H MAXVAL.C
    CL MAXVAL.C
```

In this case the file MAXVAL.EXE is the target file. The dependent files are DEFN.H and MAXVAL.C. Suppose you invoke MAKE as follows:

```
C> MAKE MAXVAL
```

The MAKE utility examines the date and time stamps for MAXVAL.EXE. If either dependent file, DEFN.H or MAXVAL.C, has a more recent date and time stamp, MAKE executes the specified command.

■ **TIP:** *View the MAKE description file as a series of* if *statements: If the target file is older than any one of the dependent files, the specified command is executed.*

In this case the dependency directs MAKE to compile MAXVAL.C and create a new version of MAXVAL.EXE using any changes made to DEFN.H or MAXVAL.C. Because the file MAXVAL.EXE does not yet exist, MAKE creates it and displays the following:

```
Microsoft (R) Program Maintenance Utility  Version 4.07
Copyright (C) Microsoft Corp 1984-1988.  All rights reserved.

MAKE : warning U4000: 'MAXVAL.EXE' : target does not exist
  CL MAXVAL.C
Microsoft (R) C Optimizing Compiler Version 5.10
Copyright (c) Microsoft Corp 1984, 1985, 1986, 1987, 1988. All rights reserved.

MAXVAL.C

Microsoft (R) Overlay Linker  Version 3.65
Copyright (C) Microsoft Corp 1983-1988.  All rights reserved.

Object Modules [.OBJ]: MAXVAL.OBJ
Run File [MAXVAL.EXE]: MAXVAL.EXE /NOI
List File [NUL.MAP]: NUL
Libraries [.LIB]:
```

Reissue the command

```
C> MAKE MAXVAL
```

Because the newly created MAXVAL.EXE is now more recent than the other associated files, the compiler is not invoked.

Next, change the definition of the constant SIZE in DEFN.H from 255 to 300, and then reissue the command

```
C> MAKE MAXVAL
```

When MAKE compares file date and time stamps, it detects that DEFN.H is more recently revised than MAXVAL.EXE; consequently, it issues the CL command to recompile MAXVAL.C.

Earlier in this chapter we used the files STRCOPY.OBJ, STRLEN.OBJ, and STRDISP.OBJ to create the library file STRING.LIB. The MAKE file on the following page (STRING) examines each of the object files to ensure that the library is current.

```
STRCOPY.OBJ: STRCOPY.C
     CL /c STRCOPY.C

STRLEN.OBJ: STRLEN.C
     CL /c STRLEN.C

STRDISP.OBJ: STRDISP.C
     CL /c STRDISP.C

STRING.LIB: STRCOPY.OBJ STRLEN.OBJ STRDISP.OBJ
     LIB STRING.LIB -+STRCOPY-+STRLEN-+STRDISP;
```

If any of the source files changes, MAKE recompiles the source file and then updates the library with the new object module.

■ **FACT:** *MAKE ignores all text on the line following a pound sign (#). Comments can appear anywhere in a MAKE description file.*

In a MAKE description file, a comment is introduced by a pound sign (#). If a comment is the only text on a line, the pound sign must occur in the first column. Note the way in which comments improve the readability of the preceding description file (STRING):

```
# MAKE Descriptor file for the library STRING.LIB
# Written 01-18-89  KAJ

# Compile routines into OBJ modules using CL /c

# STRCOPY is a string copy routine
STRCOPY.OBJ: STRCOPY.C
     CL /c STRCOPY.C

# STRLEN returns the number of characters in a string
STRLEN.OBJ: STRLEN.C
     CL /c STRLEN.C

# STRDISP displays the characters in a string to stdout
STRDISP.OBJ: STRDISP.C
     CL /c STRDISP.C

# Add the updated modules to the library file STRING.LIB
STRING.LIB: STRCOPY.OBJ STRLEN.OBJ STRDISP.OBJ
     LIB STRING.LIB -+STRCOPY-+STRLEN-+STRDISP;
```

Many of your MAKE files will take the following general form:

```
filename.EXE: filename.C
     CL filename.C
```

MAKE supports the use of macros that allow a single MAKE description file to support multiple applications.

■ **FACT:** *MAKE lets you reference filenames in your description files with macros in the form* $(macro_name).

In the description file a macro is indicated by a dollar sign ($) followed by a macro name in parentheses. When you execute MAKE, you can specify a name for the macro; for example,

```
MAKE macro_name=STRING.C MAKEFILE
```

In Chapter 26 you learned that the /Zi option lets you include CodeView debugging information in the object file. You were also advised to disable optimization with /Od during debugging. Accordingly, you might create the following generic MAKE description file (DEBUG), which contains the macro $(FILE) for the basename of the file to be compiled:

```
$(FILE).EXE: $(FILE).C
    CL /Zi /Od $(FILE).C
```

After you create DEBUG, you can compile the program DISPLAY.C with the following command:

```
C> MAKE FILE=DISPLAY DEBUG
```

When MAKE examines the description file, it substitutes the name DISPLAY for each occurrence of the macro $(FILE).

In addition to specifying macros in the MAKE command line, you can define them at the start of the description file. Many programmers use this technique to define compiler or linker options. For example, suppose you create the following description file (DEBUG2):

```
compiler_option = /Zi /Od /Fs

$(FILE).EXE: $(FILE).C
    CL $(compiler_option) $(FILE).C
```

Now execute MAKE with this file and define the macro $(FILE) on the command line, as follows:

```
C> MAKE FILE=DISPLAY DEBUG2
```

MAKE expands the macros to specify both filenames and options:

```
DISPLAY.EXE: DISPLAY.C
    CL /Zi /Od /Fs DISPLAY.C
```

■ **FACT:** *MAKE predefines the macro $* as the basename of the target file.*

The following MAKE description block uses the $* macro, which is predefined by the MAKE utility as the basename of the target file:

```
STRCOPY.EXE: STRCOPY.C
    CL $*.C
```

In this case, when MAKE encounters the $* macro, it substitutes the basename STRCOPY.

■ **FACT:** *MAKE defines the $@ macro as the complete name of the target file, including the file extension.*

The following description file (CALC) uses another predefined macro, $@, which represents the entire target filename:

```
CALC.OBJ: CALC.C
    CL $*.C
    LINK PROG + $@
```

When you execute MAKE with CALC, the utility replaces the macros; the following expanded dependency is the result:

```
CALC.OBJ: CALC.C
    CL CALC.C
    LINK PROG + CALC.OBJ
```

Notice that CALC lists two commands. If MAKE needs to perform multiple commands to update a target file, simply list the commands one after another. MAKE continues to execute commands until it encounters another dependency.

■ **FACT:** *MAKE defines the macro $** as the complete list of dependent files.*

The following description file (EXPENSES) uses the $** macro to compile each of the dependent files. The $** macro is predefined to represent all the dependent files. The CL command is executed if any of the dependent files has a date and time stamp more recent than that of the target file.

```
EXPENSES.EXE: EXPENSES.C CALC.C PRINT.C
    CL $**
```

When you execute MAKE with EXPENSES, the utility expands the macro to produce the following:

```
EXPENSES.EXE: EXPENSES.C CALC.C PRINT.C
    CL EXPENSES.C CALC.C PRINT.C
```

By default, MAKE echoes each command to your screen as the command is executed. To suppress this information, use the /S option with MAKE.

■ **FACT:** *The /S option directs MAKE to suppress display of the commands it executes.*

The following command line directs MAKE to use the description file STRINGS, suppressing the display of the commands MAKE executes:

```
C> MAKE /S STRINGS
```

In some cases you might want to check the commands executed by MAKE before they run. The MAKE /N option lets you see the commands that would be activated by the dependencies.

■ **FACT:** *The /N option directs MAKE to display rather than execute the commands it would normally execute based on date and time stamps.*

The following command line, for example, directs MAKE to display each command in STRINGS that it would normally execute based on file date and time stamps:

```
C> MAKE /N STRINGS
```

Remember, MAKE doesn't actually execute the commands; it simply displays them so that you can verify the indicated processing.

■ **FACT:** *The /D option directs MAKE to display the date and time stamp of each target file and each dependent file as it scans them.*

One of the best ways to understand the processing of description files is to execute MAKE with the /D switch. MAKE displays the date and time information for each file so that you can see exactly why MAKE performs the sequence of commands it does.

Another feature of MAKE is that it lets you define inference rules that tell the utility how to convert dependent files with one extension to a target file with a different extension.

■ **FACT:** *Inference rules tell MAKE how to convert dependent files with one extension to a target file with a different extension.*

MAKE inference rules exist to reduce the number of entries you must place in the description file. For example, the following MAKE description file (INFER) uses two inference rules:

```
.C.OBJ:
    CL /c $*.C

.C.EXE:
    CL $*.C

STRCOPY.OBJ: STRCOPY.C
```

(continued)

continued

```
STRLEN.OBJ: STRLEN.C

DISPLAY.EXE: DISPLAY.C

CALC.EXE: CALC.C
```

The MAKE file does not contain specific commands for updating target files. Instead, MAKE uses inference rules. If MAKE is updating an object file, that is, converting a file with the extension C to one with the extension OBJ, it uses the following rule:

```
CL /c $*.C
```

If MAKE is updating an EXE file, it uses the command for converting a dependent file with the extension C to a target file with the extension EXE:

```
CL $*.C
```

By including inference rules, you simplify the creation of description files with multiple dependencies.

Admittedly, most programmers won't bother with MAKE files for smaller applications. However, if you are creating an application that uses many files, MAKE helps you ensure that you are using the latest versions of component files.

SUMMARY

Getting Started with LIB

■ **FACT:** *The LIB command is a librarian that lets you create, change, or display a library file. By default, library files use the extension LIB.*

■ **FACT:** *The plus operator (+) directs LIB to add one or more object files to the library. LIB assumes that object files have the extension OBJ.*

■ **FACT:** *You can specify the name of the library file and the file operations you want to perform in your LIB command line.*

■ **TIP:** *To conserve disk space, you might want to use the /Zl option when you compile functions for a library.*

■ **FACT:** *The minus operator (–) directs LIB to remove the specified object module from the library file.*

■ **FACT:** *The replacement operator (–+) directs LIB to replace a module in a library with a newer version.*

■ **FACT:** *The copy operator (*) directs LIB to copy the specified module to disk as an object file.*

■ **TIP:** *If you place a semicolon on the command line after you specify the operations or after the list file, LIB uses defaults in the remaining fields.*

■ **FACT:** *A minus sign followed immediately by an asterisk (–*) directs LIB to copy the specified module to disk and then remove it from the library.*

■ **TIP:** *If you are performing several library operations at one time, use the ampersand (&) to continue your operations to the next line.*

Using MAKE, the Program Maintenance Utility

■ **FACT:** *In a MAKE description file, a dependent file is one from which the target file is created. For example, an object file is the target file for a dependent source file.*

■ **TIP:** *View the MAKE description file as a series of* if *statements: If the target file is older than any one of the dependent files, the specified command is executed.*

■ **FACT:** *MAKE ignores all text on the line following a pound sign (#). Comments can appear anywhere in a MAKE description file.*

■ **FACT:** *MAKE lets you reference filenames in your description files with macros in the form* $(macro_name).

■ **FACT:** *MAKE predefines the macro $* as the basename of the target file.*

■ **FACT:** *MAKE defines the $@ macro as the complete name of the target file, including the file extension.*

■ **FACT:** *MAKE defines the macro $** as the complete list of dependent files.*

■ **FACT:** *The /S option directs MAKE to suppress display of the commands it executes.*

■ **FACT:** *The /N option directs MAKE to display rather than execute the commands it would normally execute based on date and time stamps.*

■ **FACT:** *The /D option directs MAKE to display the date and time stamp of each target file and each dependent file as it scans them.*

■ **FACT:** *Inference rules tell MAKE how to convert dependent files with one extension to a target file with a different extension.*

GLOSSARY

dependency A relationship between files whereby modification of one necessitates a change to the other. In this sense, a dependency exists between an object file and the source file or files from which it is compiled. The object file is considered the target file in this dependency, and the source file or files are dependent files.

librarian A software package that lets you add, delete, and update object modules. For DOS and OS/2, the object file librarian is called LIB.

object library A collection of functions in object file format that the linker can use when you create executable files.

## CHAPTER 28

Understanding Memory Models

Before we examine C's interface to assembly language and to other high-level languages, we need to discuss C memory models and the impact each model has on the code the C compiler generates. So far, we have used only the default small memory model. In this model the compiler uses one 64 KB code segment and one 64 KB data segment.

In this chapter we examine C's small, compact, medium, large, and huge memory models. We also discuss applications best suited to each model, and we look at the trade-offs each model presents.

SMALL MEMORY MODEL

By default, the C compiler uses the small memory model when it compiles your programs. In the small model the compiler creates one 64 KB code segment and one 64 KB data segment. Figure 28-1 on the following page illustrates this use of memory.

■ **FACT:** *The C small memory model uses one 64 KB code segment and one 64 KB data segment.*

The small memory model is appropriate for most small applications. Because all your code and data reside in 64 KB segments, the program can use near (16-bit) pointers to access the code and data.

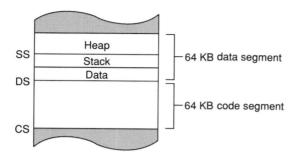

FIGURE 28-1.
Execution of a small model program requires one 64 KB code segment and one 64 KB data segment.

Remember, the PC divides memory into distinct segments of 64 KB each. An object in memory has both a segment address and an offset address, which together specify the particular segment and the location within that segment. In the small memory model all variables reside in the same data segment. Consequently, when a program passes the location of a variable to a function, the program can pass the offset address alone. The function knows the segment address of the variable because all the data for the program has the same segment address.

For our discussion of the C memory models, let's work with the following program, MODEL.C. The program declares three variables—*a*, *b*, and *c*—and passes them to the function *initialize*, which initializes them to the values 1, 2, and 3.

```
main()
{
    int a, b, c;
    void initialize(int *, int *, int *);

    initialize(&a, &b, &c);
    printf("%d %d %d\n", a, b, c);
}

void initialize(int *a, int *b, int *c)
{
    *a = 1;
    *b = 2;
    *c = 3;
}
```

Now compile the program with the /Fa option to generate the following assembly language listing (MODEL.ASM):

```
;       Static Name Aliases
;
        TITLE   MODEL.C
        NAME    MODEL

        .8087
_TEXT   SEGMENT  WORD PUBLIC 'CODE'
_TEXT   ENDS
_DATA   SEGMENT  WORD PUBLIC 'DATA'
_DATA   ENDS
CONST   SEGMENT  WORD PUBLIC 'CONST'
CONST   ENDS
_BSS    SEGMENT  WORD PUBLIC 'BSS'
_BSS    ENDS
DGROUP  GROUP    CONST, _BSS, _DATA
        ASSUME  CS: _TEXT, DS: DGROUP, SS: DGROUP
EXTRN   __acrtused:ABS
EXTRN   __chkstk:NEAR
EXTRN   _printf:NEAR
_DATA       SEGMENT
$SG107  DB       '%d %d %d',  0aH,   00H
_DATA       ENDS
_TEXT       SEGMENT
        ASSUME  CS: _TEXT
; Line 2
        PUBLIC  _main
_main   PROC NEAR
        push    bp
        mov     bp,sp
        mov     ax,6
        call    __chkstk ─────────────── near call to _chkstk function
;       a = -2
;       b = -4
;       c = -6
; Line 6
        lea     ax,WORD PTR [bp-6]      ;c
        push    ax
        lea     ax,WORD PTR [bp-4]      ;b
        push    ax
        lea     ax,WORD PTR [bp-2]      ;a
        push    ax
        call    _initialize
        add     sp,6
```

(continued)

continued

```
; Line 7
        push    WORD PTR [bp-6]         ;c
        push    WORD PTR [bp-4]         ;b
        push    WORD PTR [bp-2]         ;a
        mov     ax,OFFSET DGROUP:$SG107
        push    ax
        call    _printf ─────────────── near call to _printf function
; Line 8
        mov     sp,bp
        pop     bp
        ret
        nop

_main   ENDP
; Line 11
        PUBLIC  _initialize
_initialize     PROC NEAR ─────── initialize function
        push    bp
        mov     bp,sp
        xor     ax,ax
        call    __chkstk
;       a = 4
;       b = 6
;       c = 8
; Line 12
        mov     bx,WORD PTR [bp+4]      ;a
        mov     WORD PTR [bx],1
; Line 13
        mov     bx,WORD PTR [bp+6]      ;b ─────── near pointer arguments
        mov     WORD PTR [bx],2
; Line 14
        mov     bx,WORD PTR [bp+8]      ;c
        mov     WORD PTR [bx],3
; Line 15
        pop     bp
        ret
        nop

_initialize     ENDP
_TEXT   ENDS
END
```

In MODEL.ASM the references to WORD PTR within the *initialize* function tell you that the pointers are 16-bit, near pointers. A near pointer contains an offset only; a far pointer contains both a segment and an offset. Because the small memory model works only with offset addresses, it is the fastest memory model. The support for segment and offset addresses provided by other memory models does allow larger programs, but the increase in the amount of data comes at the cost of speed.

■ **TIP:** *For programs with less than 64 KB of code and less than 64 KB of data, the small memory model gives the best performance.*

MEDIUM MEMORY MODEL

For programs that are larger than 64 KB but that have less than 64 KB of data, the medium memory model is ideal. Its use of memory is depicted in Figure 28-2.

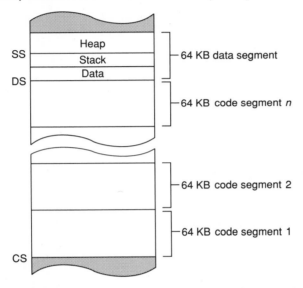

FIGURE 28-2.
Execution of a medium model program can occur in multiple code segments and one data segment.

■ **FACT:** *The C medium memory model supports multiple 64 KB code segments and one 64 KB data segment.*

Now recompile the program MODEL.C, again with the /Fa option, and this time with the /AM option to specify the medium memory model:

```
C> CL /Fa /AM MODEL.C
```

When you examine the file MODEL.ASM, you find that the calls to *_chkstk* and *_printf* are far calls. This means that both the instruction pointer and the code segment register change each time the function is called.

```
;        Static Name Aliases
;
        TITLE    MODEL.C
        NAME     MODEL

        .8087
MODEL_TEXT      SEGMENT  WORD PUBLIC 'CODE'
MODEL_TEXT      ENDS
_DATA   SEGMENT  WORD PUBLIC 'DATA'
_DATA   ENDS
CONST   SEGMENT  WORD PUBLIC 'CONST'
CONST   ENDS
_BSS    SEGMENT  WORD PUBLIC 'BSS'
_BSS    ENDS
DGROUP  GROUP    CONST, _BSS, _DATA
        ASSUME   CS: MODEL_TEXT, DS: DGROUP, SS: DGROUP
EXTRN   __acrtused:ABS
EXTRN   __chkstk:FAR
EXTRN   _printf:FAR
_DATA        SEGMENT
$SG107  DB       '%d %d %d',  0aH,  00H
_DATA        ENDS
MODEL_TEXT      SEGMENT
        ASSUME   CS: MODEL_TEXT
; Line 2
        PUBLIC   _main
_main   PROC FAR
        push     bp
        mov      bp,sp
        mov      ax,6
        call     FAR PTR __chkstk ———————— far call to _chkstk function
;        a = -2
;        b = -4
;        c = -6
; Line 6
        lea      ax,WORD PTR [bp-6]       ;c
        push     ax
        lea      ax,WORD PTR [bp-4]       ;b
        push     ax
        lea      ax,WORD PTR [bp-2]       ;a
        push     ax
        push     cs
        call     _initialize
        add      sp,6
; Line 7
        push     WORD PTR [bp-6]          ;c
        push     WORD PTR [bp-4]          ;b
        push     WORD PTR [bp-2]          ;a
        mov      ax,OFFSET DGROUP:$SG107
        push     ax
        call     FAR PTR _printf ———————— far call to _printf function
```

(continued)

continued

```
; Line 8
        mov     sp,bp
        pop     bp
        ret

_main   ENDP
; Line 11
        PUBLIC  _initialize
_initialize     PROC FAR ─────────── initialize function
        push    bp
        mov     bp,sp
        xor     ax,ax
        call    FAR PTR __chkstk
;       a = 6
;       b = 8
;       c = 10
; Line 12
        mov     bx,WORD PTR [bp+6]      ;a
        mov     WORD PTR [bx],1
; Line 13
        mov     bx,WORD PTR [bp+8]      ;b ────────  near pointer arguments
        mov     WORD PTR [bx],2
; Line 14
        mov     bx,WORD PTR [bp+10]     ;c
        mov     WORD PTR [bx],3
; Line 15
        pop     bp
        ret
        nop

_initialize     ENDP
MODEL_TEXT      ENDS
END
```

As you can see, *initialize* is also declared as a far procedure:

```
_initialize     PROC FAR
```

A call to *initialize* therefore requires the manipulation of both a segment address and an offset address. The overhead that accompanies each function call makes the program run slower.

Within *initialize*, however, each argument is a near pointer. Because the medium memory model has only one data segment, variables in the medium memory model can be accessed quickly with only offset addresses.

■ **TIP:** *The medium memory model is ideal for applications whose code exceeds 64 KB but whose data resides in less than 64 KB. By using near pointers to data, the medium memory model maintains fairly good speed.*

COMPACT MEMORY MODEL

The compact memory model is the reverse of the medium memory model. It restricts code to 64 KB but allows data to reside in multiple 64 KB data segments, as shown in Figure 28-3.

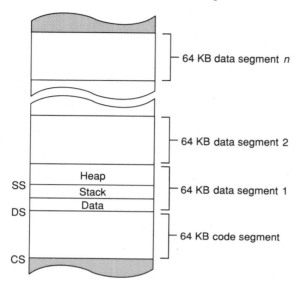

FIGURE 28-3.
Execution of a compact model program can occur in one code segment and multiple data segments.

■ **FACT:** *The C compact memory model supports one 64 KB code segment and multiple 64 KB data segments.*

Compile MODEL.C with the following command line, which contains the /AC option to specify the compact memory model:

```
C> CL /Fa /AC MODEL.C
```

The compiler creates the following assembly language listing in the file MODEL.ASM:

```
;       Static Name Aliases
;
        TITLE   MODEL.C
        NAME    MODEL

        .8087
_TEXT   SEGMENT  WORD PUBLIC 'CODE'
_TEXT   ENDS
```

(continued)

continued

```
_DATA    SEGMENT  WORD PUBLIC 'DATA'
_DATA    ENDS
CONST    SEGMENT  WORD PUBLIC 'CONST'
CONST    ENDS
_BSS     SEGMENT  WORD PUBLIC 'BSS'
_BSS     ENDS
DGROUP   GROUP    CONST, _BSS, _DATA
         ASSUME   CS: _TEXT, DS: DGROUP, SS: DGROUP
EXTRN    __acrtused:ABS
EXTRN    __chkstk:NEAR
EXTRN    _printf:NEAR
_DATA       SEGMENT
$SG107   DB      '%d %d %d',  0aH,   00H
_DATA       ENDS
_TEXT       SEGMENT
         ASSUME  CS: _TEXT
; Line 2
         PUBLIC  _main
_main    PROC NEAR
         push    bp
         mov     bp,sp
         mov     ax,6
         call    __chkstk———————— near call to _chkstk function
;        a = -2
;        b = -4
;        c = -6
; Line 6
         lea     ax,WORD PTR [bp-6]       ;c
         push    ss
         push    ax
         lea     ax,WORD PTR [bp-4]       ;b
         push    ss
         push    ax
         lea     ax,WORD PTR [bp-2]       ;a
         push    ss
         push    ax
         call    _initialize
         add     sp,12
; Line 7
         push    WORD PTR [bp-6]          ;c
         push    WORD PTR [bp-4]          ;b
         push    WORD PTR [bp-2]          ;a
         mov     ax,OFFSET DGROUP:$SG107
         push    ds
         push    ax
         call    _printf ———————— near call to _printf function
```

continued

```
; Line 8
        mov     sp,bp
        pop     bp
        ret
        nop

_main   ENDP
; Line 11
        PUBLIC  _initialize ──────── initialize function
_initialize     PROC NEAR
        push    bp
        mov     bp,sp
        xor     ax,ax
        call    __chkstk
;       a = 4
;       b = 8
;       c = 12
; Line 12
        les     bx,DWORD PTR [bp+4]      ;a ╲
        mov     WORD PTR es:[bx],1
; Line 13
        les     bx,DWORD PTR [bp+8]      ;b ──── ╲
        mov     WORD PTR es:[bx],2              ├── far pointer arguments
; Line 14                                        ╱
        les     bx,DWORD PTR [bp+12]     ;c ╱
        mov     WORD PTR es:[bx],3
; Line 15
        pop     bp
        ret

_initialize     ENDP
_TEXT   ENDS
END
```

As you can see, all the function invocations are near calls. Far calls are unnecessary because the compact model supports only one code segment. Within *initialize*, however, the DWORD pointers tell you that the function uses double word, or 32-bit, far addresses to each argument. Because variables can reside in one of several data segments, the compiler must pass the segment address as well as the offset.

■ **TIP:** *The compact memory model is ideal for applications that have less than 64 KB of code but large amounts of data. Although the compact model references data with far pointers, it accesses program code with near pointers and therefore reduces some of the overhead associated with the large and huge memory models.*

LARGE MEMORY MODEL

For large applications that have more than 64 KB of both code and data, the large memory model supports multiple code and data segments, as shown in Figure 28-4.

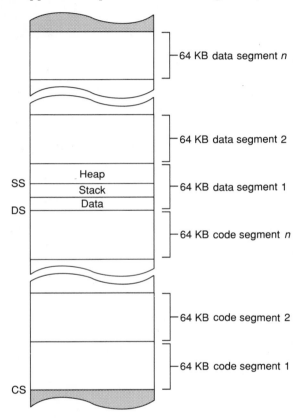

FIGURE 28-4.
Execution of large (and huge) model programs can occur in multiple code segments and multiple data segments.

■ **FACT:** *The C large memory model supports multiple 64 KB code and data segments.*

Compile MODEL.C with the /AL option, which specifies use of the large memory model library:

```
C> CL /Fa /AL MODEL.C
```

The compiler produces the following assembly language listing in the file MODEL.ASM:

```
;        Static Name Aliases
;
         TITLE    MODEL.C
         NAME     MODEL

         .8087
MODEL_TEXT        SEGMENT  WORD PUBLIC 'CODE'
MODEL_TEXT        ENDS
_DATA    SEGMENT  WORD PUBLIC 'DATA'
_DATA    ENDS
CONST    SEGMENT  WORD PUBLIC 'CONST'
CONST    ENDS
_BSS     SEGMENT  WORD PUBLIC 'BSS'
_BSS     ENDS
DGROUP   GROUP    CONST, _BSS, _DATA
         ASSUME   CS: MODEL_TEXT, DS: DGROUP, SS: DGROUP
EXTRN    __acrtused:ABS
EXTRN    __chkstk:FAR
EXTRN    _printf:FAR
_DATA       SEGMENT
$SG107   DB       '%d %d %d',  0aH,   00H
_DATA       ENDS
MODEL_TEXT        SEGMENT
         ASSUME   CS: MODEL_TEXT
; Line 2
         PUBLIC   _main
_main    PROC FAR
         push     bp
         mov      bp,sp
         mov      ax,6
         call     FAR PTR __chkstk ───────── far call to _chkstk function
;        a = -2
;        b = -4
;        c = -6
; Line 6
         lea      ax,WORD PTR [bp-6]      ;c
         push     ss
         push     ax
         lea      ax,WORD PTR [bp-4]      ;b
         push     ss
         push     ax
         lea      ax,WORD PTR [bp-2]      ;a
         push     ss
         push     ax
         push     cs
         call     _initialize
         add      sp,12
```

(continued)

continued

```
; Line 7
        push    WORD PTR [bp-6]         ;c
        push    WORD PTR [bp-4]         ;b
        push    WORD PTR [bp-2]         ;a
        mov     ax,OFFSET DGROUP:$SG107
        push    ds
        push    ax
        call    FAR PTR _printf ───────── far call to _printf function
; Line 8
        mov     sp,bp
        pop     bp
        ret

_main   ENDP
; Line 11
        PUBLIC  _initialize
_initialize     PROC FAR ──────────────── initialize function
        push    bp
        mov     bp,sp
        xor     ax,ax
        call    FAR PTR __chkstk
;       a = 6
;       b = 10
;       c = 14
; Line 12
        les     bx,DWORD PTR [bp+6]      ;a
        mov     WORD PTR es:[bx],1
; Line 13
        les     bx,DWORD PTR [bp+10]     ;b  ───┐─── far pointer arguments
        mov     WORD PTR es:[bx],2
; Line 14
        les     bx,DWORD PTR [bp+14]     ;c
        mov     WORD PTR es:[bx],3
; Line 15
        pop     bp
        ret

_initialize     ENDP
MODEL_TEXT      ENDS
END
```

When you compile with the large memory model, all the function calls are far calls, and arguments are accessed using 32-bit, far pointers.

■ **TIP:** *The large memory model supports large amounts of code and data; however, this flexibility also makes it the slowest memory model. If your program and its data requirements are both large, you have no choice but to trade size for speed.*

HUGE MEMORY MODEL

Like the large memory model (depicted in Figure 28-4), the C huge memory model supports multiple 64 KB code and data segments. In addition, the huge memory model supports the use of huge arrays, which can exceed 64 KB.

■ **FACT:** *The C huge memory model supports multiple 64 KB code and data segments. The huge memory model also removes the 64 KB size restriction for arrays.*

Compiling MODEL.C with the huge memory model produces the same assembly language output as the large memory model.

■ **TIP:** *The huge memory model lets your program use very large data structures. Like the large memory model, it uses far pointers to reference code and data, the result of which is slower performance.*

WHAT IS THE FAR HEAP?

In Chapter 25 you used the C run-time library routines to allocate memory dynamically from the heap. As you learned, the heap is the memory in the data segment that remains after variables are defined and the stack is allocated. In fact, as Figure 28-5 depicts, your programs actually have two heaps available—the near heap and the far heap.

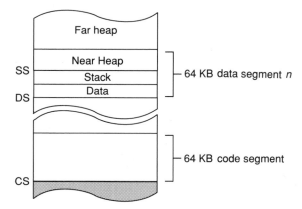

FIGURE 28-5.
The near heap lies within the data segment; the far heap occupies an area outside the current data segment.

The far heap exists outside the current data segment. A program that accesses the far heap must therefore use far pointers. The advantage the far heap provides is the extent of available memory. The disadvantage of using the far heap is the familiar one: loss of speed. Because the far heap requires the use of far pointers, manipulating its contents requires more time than manipulating the contents of the near heap.

The Microsoft C small and medium memory models always allocate memory from the near heap when they use *calloc* or *malloc*. The other memory models can allocate space from either heap.

To increase speed, some programs that use the large or compact memory models allocate memory from the near heap using *_nmalloc*. By allocating space from the near heap, the programs can access the memory using an offset address rather than the slower 32-bit segment-offset combination.

SUMMARY

Small Memory Model

■ **FACT:** *The C small memory model uses one 64 KB code segment and one 64 KB data segment.*

■ **TIP:** *For programs with less than 64 KB of code and less than 64 KB of data, the small memory model gives the best performance.*

Medium Memory Model

■ **FACT:** *The C medium memory model supports multiple 64 KB code segments and one 64 KB data segment.*

■ **TIP:** *The medium memory model is ideal for applications whose code exceeds 64 KB but whose data resides in less than 64 KB. By using near pointers to data, the medium memory model maintains fairly good speed.*

Compact Memory Model

■ **FACT:** *The C compact memory model supports one 64 KB code segment and multiple 64 KB data segments.*

■ **TIP:** *The compact memory model is ideal for applications that have less than 64 KB of code but large amounts of data. Although the compact model references data with far pointers, it accesses program code with near pointers and therefore reduces some of the overhead associated with the large and huge memory models.*

Large Memory Model

■ **FACT:** *The C large memory model supports multiple 64 KB code and data segments.*

■ **TIP:** *The large memory model supports large amounts of code and data; however, this flexibility also makes it the slowest memory model. If your program and its data requirements are both large, you have no choice but to trade size for speed.*

Huge Memory Model

■ **FACT:** *The C huge memory model supports multiple 64 KB code and data segments. The huge memory model also removes the 64 KB size restriction for arrays.*

■ **TIP:** *The huge memory model lets your program use very large data structures. Like the large memory model, it uses far pointers to reference code and data, the result of which is slower performance.*

GLOSSARY

memory model The basic way a program accesses its code and data. The C compiler supports the small, medium, compact, large, and huge memory models. In general, the models permit the use of different numbers of code and data segments, thereby trading speed for size.

CHAPTER 29

Getting the Most from Your Keyboard

So far, our programs have performed buffered input using *getchar*, *gets*, or *scanf*. As you have learned, the characters obtained with buffered input are not available to your program until the user presses Enter. The advantage of buffered input is that the user can make corrections to the input. The operating system relieves your program of the task of supporting this input-correction capability. Buffered input is not appropriate, however, for all programs. A word processor or text editor, for example, must respond to each key the user presses.

In this chapter we examine the keyboard functions provided by the run-time library. You learn how to test whether or not the user has pressed a key; how to perform direct input from the keyboard, which lets your program respond to each key as it is pressed; how to access and use the arrow keys; how to get information from the user, such as a password, without displaying the input on the screen; how to determine the current keyboard state, such as the status of Caps Lock, Num Lock, and so on; and how to obtain keyboard input when stdin has been redirected.

Keyboard control is critical to the success of a professional quality program. As you learn in this lesson, you can exercise extensive control of keyboard input with only four run-time library functions.

WAITING FOR THE USER TO PRESS A KEY

Many applications display instructions or status information to the user, concluding with the message *Press any key to continue*. In such cases the program doesn't care which key the user presses, only that the user has pressed a key. You can use the C run-time library function *kbhit* to determine that a key has been placed in the keyboard buffer.

■ **FACT:** *The* kbhit *function returns true (a nonzero value) when a key is available in the keyboard buffer; it returns false if the buffer is empty.*

The following program (PS.C) displays three lines with *printf* statements and then uses the *kbhit* function to pause the action before displaying the fourth *printf* statement:

```
#include <conio.h>   /* needed for kbhit */

main()
{
    printf("This is the first\n");
    printf("This is the second\n")

    printf("--press any key to continue--\n");
    while (!kbhit())
        { ; }

    printf("This is the third");
}
```

When you run PS.C, you get the following output:

```
This is the first
This is the second
--press any key to continue--
This is the third
```

The *while* loop after the third *printf* statement continues executing until the user loads a character into the keyboard buffer by pressing a key on the keyboard. When this occurs, the loop ends and the fourth *printf* statement is executed.

■ **FACT:** *The* kbhit *function does not remove the character from the keyboard buffer; it merely checks for the presence of a character in the buffer.*

If you use *kbhit* to test whether the user has pressed a key, remember that the keyboard value remains in the keyboard buffer.

The following program (SHOW99.C) demonstrates the relationship between the *kbhit* function and the keyboard buffer:

```
#include <conio.h>   /* needed for kbhit */

main()
{
    int i;

    for (i = 1; i < 100; ++i)
        {
        printf("\nLine %2d", i);
        if ((i % 24) == 0)   /* pause if i is a multiple of 24 */
            {
            printf("\nPress any key to continue...\n");
            while (!kbhit())
                { ; }
            }
        }
}
```

The aim of SHOW99 is to display 99 lines on the screen, waiting for a keypress after each set of 24 lines so that the user has time to read the information presented. When this version of SHOW99 is run, however, the program pauses only after line 24—not after lines 48, 72, and 96. The character entered into the keyboard buffer during the first *while* loop causes the remaining calls to the *kbhit* function to return a nonzero value until the character is removed from the keyboard buffer. To remove the character, you must use one of the C run-time library input routines we will discuss later in this chapter.

■ **TRAP:** *The* kbhit *function gets its input from stdin. If the user redirects input from the keyboard to a file, the return value of* kbhit *remains true as long as the file contains characters.*

The *kbhit* function obtains input from stdin, which can, of course, be redirected. To see an example of this, run the SHOW99 program using redirected input with the following command:

```
SHOW99 < SHOW99.C
```

SHOW99 runs to completion without pausing at all. Because stdin is redirected, *kbhit* finds a key waiting as long as a character remains in the SHOW99.C program.

Later in this chapter you learn to write programs that can access the keyboard for input even though stdin has been redirected.

PERFORMING DIRECT KEYBOARD INPUT

As we have noted, *getchar*, *gets*, and *scanf* perform buffered input. The characters the user types do not become available to the program until the user presses Enter.

■ **FACT:** *The* getche *function performs direct input from the keyboard and displays on the screen each character the user types.*

The run-time library function *getche* is similar to *getchar* in that it returns one input character. Unlike *getchar*, whose input is buffered, *getche* performs direct I/O to the keyboard.

■ **FACT:** *The* getche *function returns the letter that was typed. It does not convert the Enter key to the newline character, nor does it return EOF on end of file.*

The following program (READ.C) uses *getche* to read input from the keyboard until the user presses Enter or sends an end of file by typing Ctrl-Z:

```
#include <conio.h>   /* needed for getche */
#include <stdio.h>   /* needed for NULL */
#define CTRL_Z 26    /* Ctrl-Z is ASCII 26 */

main()
{
    int i = 0;
    char str[128], letter;

    while (((letter = getche()) != CTRL_Z) && (letter != '\r'))
        str[i++] = letter;

    str[i] = NULL;

    printf("\n%s", str);
}
```

The *getche* function does not convert the Enter key to the newline character. Instead, *getche* returns the ASCII value 13, which corresponds to the carriage return character, or the escape sequence \r.

■ **TRAP:** *Like the* kbhit *function*, getche *also gets input from stdin. The* getche *function can therefore read redirected input.*

Remember, unlike *getchar*, which returns EOF on end of file, *getche* returns the ASCII value 26 for the Ctrl-Z character. Unless *getche* specifically tests for Ctrl-Z, redirecting input to a program that uses *getche* can result in an infinite loop.

In some applications, you might want to examine the keystrokes the user enters without displaying them on the screen. For example, if a program requires the user to type a password before accessing specific data, the program should not display the password on the screen. Likewise, you might want to restrict a data entry program to working only with uppercase characters. The C run-time library routine *getch* lets you get a character from the user without echoing (displaying) the character on the screen.

■ **FACT:** *The* getch *function gets a character of input from the keyboard and returns it to the program. The function does not display on the screen the letter associated with the input value.*

The following program (CONVERT.C) uses *getch* to get a line of input from the user. The program lets the user enter only the letters a through z or A through Z; it ignores all other characters. If the user enters a lowercase letter, the program converts it to uppercase.

```c
#include <conio.h>   /* needed for getch */
#include <stdio.h>   /* needed for NULL and putchar */
#include <ctype.h>   /* needed for islower, isupper, and toupper */

#define CTRL_Z 26

main()
{
    int i = 0;
    char str[128], letter;

    while (((letter = getch()) != CTRL_Z) && (letter != '\r'))
        if (islower(letter))
            {
            str[i] = toupper(letter);
            putchar(str[i++]);
            }
        else if (isupper(letter))
            {
            str[i] = letter;
            putchar(str[i++]);
            }

    str[i] = NULL;

    printf("\nstring = %s\n", str);
}
```

When you execute this program, it ignores number keys, punctuation keys, and whitespace characters—it processes only the alphabetic keys.

In a similar manner, the following program (GETPASS.C) uses *getch* to get a password from the user. The program does not display the letters of the password as the user types them.

```c
#include <conio.h>   /* needed for getch */
#include <stdio.h>   /* needed for NULL */
#define CTRL_Z 26

main()
{
    char letter, password[128];
    int i = 0;

    printf("Enter password:  ");

    while (((letter = getch()) != CTRL_Z) && (letter != '\r'))
        password[i++] = letter;

    password[i] = NULL;

    printf("\nPassword entered:  %s\n", password);
}
```

■ **TRAP:** *The* getch *function uses stdin as its input source, so* getch *can read redirected input.*

Like *getche*, the *getch* function gets its input from stdin. To prevent I/O redirection from causing an infinite loop, be sure your program processes the Ctrl-Z end of file character.

USING *_bios_keybrd*

In addition to the input routines we have examined so far, the C run-time library provides direct access to the basic input/output services (BIOS) for the keyboard. The BIOS is a collection of routines built into your computer that perform input and output operations. Later in this book we examine the BIOS in detail. For now, simply note that the function *_bios_keybrd* is based upon these built-in services. Also note that programs that use the bios.h header file will not run in OS/2 protected mode.

■ **FACT:** *The* _bios_keybrd *function enables your program to test whether a character is available in the keyboard buffer, to read the next available character, or to return the current state of shift and lock keys. Redirected input does not affect* _bios_keybrd *because it does not use stdin for input.*

The _bios_keybrd function bases its processing on one of the following constants:

Value	Meaning
_KEYBRD_READ	Returns next character in the keyboard buffer; waits for a keyboard value if one is not available
_KEYBRD_READY	Returns a true value if a keyboard value exists in the keyboard buffer; returns 0 if the buffer is empty
_KEYBRD_SHIFTSTATUS	Returns the current keyboard status

■ **FACT:** *If you use _bios_keybrd with the constant _KEYBRD_READ, the function reads the next available key in the keyboard buffer. If a key is not available, _bios_keybrd waits for one. The function returns an* unsigned int *value that contains the ASCII value and the scan code for the key obtained.*

Every key on the PC keyboard has a unique identifier value called a *scan code*. Figure 29-1, for example, shows the scan codes for the keys on an IBM PC/AT keyboard.

FIGURE 29-1.
Scan codes for the IBM PC/AT keyboard, shown as hexadecimal values.

When you use _bios_keybrd to read characters from the keyboard, the function returns an *unsigned int* value. The low-order byte contains the ASCII code for the key pressed, and the high-order byte contains the scan code for the key. If, for example, the user presses Shift-A, the following value is returned:

1E	65
Scan code	ASCII code

A value of 0 in the low-order byte indicates that the user pressed a function key or an arrow key. The scan code reveals the specific key pressed. For example, if the user presses the F10 function key, the value returned by _bios_keybrd is the following:

68	0
Scan code	ASCII code

The following program (SHOWKEY.C) uses *_bios_keybrd* to read characters from the keyboard. The program uses bitwise operators to isolate the ASCII code and the scan code from the value returned by *_bios_keybrd*. SHOWKEY displays the ASCII character associated with standard characters, and it displays the scan code to identify special-purpose keys. The user presses F10 to end the program.

```c
#include <bios.h>   /* needed for _bios_keybrd */

main()
{
    unsigned int key_entry;
    int scancode, character;

    do
        {
        key_entry = _bios_keybrd(_KEYBRD_READ);
        character = key_entry & 0xFF;   /* low-order byte */
        scancode = key_entry >> 8;      /* high-order byte */

        printf("Scan code: %x Character: %c\n", scancode,
                (character) ? character : '0');
        }
    while (character != 0 || scancode != 68);   /* F10 ends program */
}
```

The following program (SHOWMORE.C) takes advantage of the fact that _bios_keybrd is not affected by I/O redirection. The program displays the next screenful of text when it detects a keypress.

```c
#include <bios.h>    /* needed for _bios_keybrd */
#include <stdio.h>   /* needed for fgets and fputs */

#define  PAGE_SIZE 23   /* number of lines to display before pause */

main()
{
    char buffer[128];     /* input buffer */

    int line_count = 0;   /* number of lines displayed */

    /* read data from stdin until end of file */
```

(continued)

continued

```
while (fgets(buffer, sizeof(buffer), stdin))
{
    fputs(buffer, stdout);

    /* if screenful has been displayed, pause */

    if ((++line_count % PAGE_SIZE) == 0)
        {
        fputs("Press any key to continue...\n", stderr);
        _bios_keybrd(_KEYBRD_READ);
        }
}
}
```

As you know, the DOS MORE command displays a screenful of redirected input and then pauses to display the prompt

```
-- More --
```

When the user presses a key to continue, MORE displays the next screenful of text. Notice that MORE gets input from two sources: text to display from a redirected source, and a continuation key from the keyboard. If we tried to use *getchar* or *getch* in our SHOWMORE program, the input routine would read the next redirected character as the keyboard input. The program must use a routine such as *_bios_keybrd*, which is unaffected by I/O redirection.

Most menu manipulation routines let the user make a selection by highlighting an option using the keyboard arrow keys. The program must be able to determine which arrow key was pressed. The following program (ARROW.C) contains the function *get_arrow*, which returns either 0, 1, 2, or 3, corresponding to the Up, Down, Left, and Right arrow keys. The *get_arrow* function ignores all keys except the arrow keys.

```
#include <bios.h>  /* needed for _bios_keybrd */

main()
{
    int get_arrow(void);
    int arrow;

    arrow = get_arrow();
```

(continued)

continued

```
    switch (arrow)
        {
        case 1: puts("Up arrow pressed");
                break;
        case 2: puts("Down arrow pressed");
                break;
        case 3: puts("Left arrow pressed");
                break;
        case 4: puts("Right arrow pressed");
                break;
        };
}

get_arrow(void)
{
    unsigned int key_entry;
    int character, scancode;
    int arrow = 0;                          /* arrow key returned */

    do
        {
        key_entry = _bios_keybrd(_KEYBRD_READ);
        character = key_entry & 0xFF;   /* low-order byte */
        scancode = key_entry >> 8;      /* high-order byte */

        if (character == 0)
            switch (scancode)
                {
                case 0x48: arrow = 1;  /* up arrow */
                           break;
                case 0x50: arrow = 2;  /* down arrow */
                           break;
                case 0x4B: arrow = 3;  /* left arrow */
                           break;
                case 0x4D: arrow = 4;  /* right arrow */
                           break;
                }
        }
    while (arrow == 0);

    return (arrow);
}
```

■ **FACT:** *If you use* _bios_keybrd *with the constant* _KEYBRD_READY, *the function returns the next character in the keyboard buffer if one exists, or 0 if the buffer is empty. The function does not remove the character from the buffer.*

The following program (TIMED.C) provides timed input. It contains a function *get_timed_char* that displays a delay message and then loops until either the user presses a key or the specified number of seconds elapses.

```
#include <time.h>  /* needed for time */
#include <bios.h>  /* needed for _bios_keybrd */

main()
{
    unsigned int get_timed_char();

    printf("Press a key before time runs out and see the scan code.\n\n");
    printf("\tScan code:  %x\n", get_timed_char("You have 8 seconds!", 8));
    printf("\tScan code:  %x\n", get_timed_char("You have 5 seconds!", 5));
    Printf("\tScan code:  %x\n, get_timed_char("You have 2 seconds!", 2));
}

unsigned int get_timed_char(char *prompt, int interval)
{
    long int start_time, current_time;

    printf("%s", prompt);

    time(&start_time);

    do
        time(&current_time);
    while ((current_time - start_time < interval)
            && !_bios_keybrd(_KEYBRD_READY));

    return (_bios_keybrd(_KEYBRD_READY) ? _bios_keybrd(_KEYBRD_READ) : 0);
}
```

The *get_timed_char* function returns an *unsigned int* value containing the ASCII code in the low-order byte and the scan code in the high-order byte. If the delay time elapses before a read operation, the function returns 0. Because the *get_timed_char* function uses *_bios_keybrd*, it is not affected by I/O redirection.

Last, your programs might need to determine the current keyboard state—the status of Num Lock, Caps Lock, and so on.

■ **FACT:** *If you use* _bios_keybrd *with the constant* _KEYBRD_SHIFTSTATUS, *it returns an* unsigned int *value whose low-order bits, if set, indicate the status of the various shift and lock keys.*

When you obtain the keyboard state with *_bios_keybrd*, it returns an unsigned integer that contains the following information in the low-order byte:

Bit	Significance (if set)
0	Right Shift key pressed
1	Left Shift key pressed
2	Ctrl key pressed
3	Alt key pressed
4	Scroll Lock on
5	Num Lock on
6	Caps Lock on
7	Insert mode on

The following program (KEYSTATE.C) displays the changes in keyboard state. It loops until the user presses F10 to end the program.

```
#include <bios.h>  /* needed for _bios_keybrd */

#define F10 (68 << 8)

main()
{
    unsigned int old_state, current_state;
    int done = 0;

    printf("Change keyboard states -- Press F10 to end\n");

    do
        {
        current_state = _bios_keybrd(_KEYBRD_SHIFTSTATUS);
        if (current_state != old_state)
            {
            if (current_state & 1)
                printf("Right Shift ");
            if (current_state & 2)
                printf("Left Shift ");
            if (current_state & 4)
                printf("Ctrl Key ");
            if (current_state & 8)
                printf("Alt Key ");
```

(continued)

continued

```
            if (current_state & 16)
                printf("Scroll Lock ");
            if (current_state & 32)
                printf("Num Lock ");
            if (current_state & 64)
                printf("Caps Lock ");
            if (current_state & 128)
                printf("Insert On ");

            printf("\n");
            old_state = current_state;
            }
        if (_bios_keybrd(_KEYBRD_READY))
            if (_bios_keybrd(_KEYBRD_READ) == F10)
                done = 1;
        }
    while (!done);
}
```

As you can see, by using a few run-time library functions in your programs, you increase control over the keyboard dramatically.

SUMMARY

Waiting for the User to Press a Key

■ **FACT:** *The* kbhit *function returns true (a nonzero value) when a key is available in the keyboard buffer; it returns false if the buffer is empty.*

■ **FACT:** *The* kbhit *function does not remove the character from the keyboard buffer; it merely checks for the presence of a character in the buffer.*

■ **TRAP:** *The* kbhit *function gets its input from stdin. If the user redirects input from the keyboard to a file, the return value of* kbhit *remains true as long as the file contains characters.*

Performing Direct Keyboard Input

■ **FACT:** *The* getche *function performs direct input from the keyboard and displays on the screen each character the user types.*

■ **FACT:** *The* getche *function returns the letter that was typed. It does not convert the Enter key to the newline character, nor does it return EOF on end of file.*

■ **TRAP:** *Like the* kbhit *function,* getche *also gets input from stdin. The* getche *function can therefore read redirected input.*

■ **FACT:** *The* getch *function gets a character of input from the keyboard and returns it to the program. The function does not display on the screen the letter associated with the input value.*

■ **TRAP:** *The* getch *function uses stdin as its input source, so* getch *can read redirected input.*

Using *_bios_keybrd*

■ **FACT:** *The* _bios_keybrd *function enables your program to test whether a character is available in the keyboard buffer, to read the next available character, or to return the current state of shift and lock keys. Redirected input does not affect* _bios_keybrd *because it does not use stdin for input.*

■ **FACT:** *If you use* _bios_keybrd *with the constant _KEYBRD_READ, the function reads the next available key in the keyboard buffer. If a key is not available,* _bios_keybrd *waits for one. The function returns an* unsigned int *value that contains the ASCII value and the scan code for the key obtained.*

■ **FACT:** *If you use* _bios_keybrd *with the constant* _KEYBRD_READY, *the function returns the next character in the keyboard buffer if one exists, or 0 if the buffer is empty. The function does not remove the character from the buffer.*

■ **FACT:** *If you use* _bios_keybrd *with the constant* _KEYBRD_SHIFTSTATUS, *it returns an* unsigned int *value whose low-order bits, if set, indicate the status of the various shift and lock keys.*

GLOSSARY

buffered input An input process by which the keys the user presses are not available to the program until the user presses Enter. The advantage of buffered input is that the user can edit the entry with the Backspace key.

echoing The process of displaying on the screen the letter that corresponds to each keystroke pressed by the user. The run-time library function *getche* echoes characters to the screen, but the *getch* function does not.

scan code The high-order byte of a keyboard value, which corresponds to the physical key on the keyboard. The scan code is critical for identifying special-purpose keys, such as arrow keys and function keys.

CHAPTER 30

Critical Error Handling

You are probably familiar with the DOS error message

```
Abort, Retry, Fail?
```

DOS displays this message whenever it cannot access a disk in the specified drive or cannot write to the printer. The message itself comes from the DOS critical error handler. Although the error message provides the user with an opportunity to correct the error and continue, the user is often confused by the message and unable to respond correctly. In this chapter you learn how to write your own critical error handlers. If the user forgets to insert a floppy disk or neglects to turn on the printer, for example, your program can display an appropriate error message.

UNDERSTANDING THE BASICS

When a critical error occurs, DOS invokes a critical error handler, which displays the *Abort, Retry, Fail?* message. If the user types *A*, DOS ends the program and returns control to the operating system. If the program has open files, the data in the files might be lost. If the user types *R*, DOS retries the operation that caused the error. This option lets the user place a disk in the drive or turn on the printer and then resume execution of the program. If the user types *F*, DOS returns a failing status value to the system service that encountered the error. This means that if a call to *fopen* caused the error, *fopen* returns the NULL pointer.

Unless a program defines its own replacement, DOS executes its built-in critical error handler. DOS locates this error handler (Int 0x24) by examining the program segment prefix, which is represented in Figure 22-1 on p. 393.

To help you implement your own critical error handling routines, C provides three runtime library functions: _harderr, _hardresume, and _hardretn.

WHAT ACTUALLY HAPPENS

When a critical error occurs in your system, DOS places information about the cause of the error in registers AX and DI. DOS also places in register BP:SI a pointer to the device driver header so that you can determine which device caused the error. Specifically, DOS sets the bits of AH (the high-order byte of the AX register) as follows:

Bit(s)	Significance
0	0 = Read error
	1 = Write error
1–2	Location of error
	00 DOS error
	01 FAT error
	10 Directory error
	11 File error
3	0 = Fail option not allowed
	1 = Fail option allowed
4	0 = Retry option not allowed
	1 = Retry option allowed
5	0 = Ignore option not allowed
	1 = Ignore option allowed
7	0 = Disk error
	1 = Other device error

For disk errors DOS places the drive number of the disk causing the error in AL—the low-order byte of the AX register. (Drive A = 0, B = 1, C = 2, and so on.) If the error is caused by a device other than a disk, the registers BP:SI point to the device driver header, which contains the information shown in Figure 30-1.

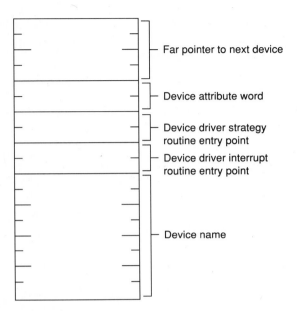

FIGURE 30-1.
If the value in AH indicates a non-disk error, BP:SI contains the address of the device driver header.

The value in the lower byte of the DI register contains information about disk drive errors, as follows:

Value	Meaning
00H	Write-protected disk
01H	Unknown drive unit
02H	Drive not ready
03H	Unknown command
04H	Data CRC error
05H	Bad request structure length
06H	Seek error
07H	Unknown medium type
08H	Sector not found
09H	Printer out of paper
OAH	Write fault
OBH	Read fault
OCH	General failure

By using this error information, a program can determine the cause of the critical error and prompt the user to take appropriate steps to resolve it. Once the error handler completes its task, it must return one of the following values to DOS:

Return Value	Meaning
00H	Ignore the error
01H	Retry the operation
02H	Abort (terminate) the program
03H	Fail the system call

Because the registers AX, DI, BP, and SI are available only through assembly language routines, the C run-time library contains routines that provide the necessary interface for your C program.

LOOKING AT A SIMPLE EXAMPLE

Let's look at a simple error handler that directs the user to verify that a disk is in the drive or that the printer is on line. The error handler does not determine whether the error is caused by a disk or by a printer. It displays the same message in either case.

To begin, we must create a C function that serves as the error handler.

■ **FACT:** *DOS passes three arguments to the critical error handler: an* unsigned int *variable that contains the value in AX, an* unsigned int *variable that contains the value in DI, and a far pointer to an* unsigned int *device handle.*

Our error handler defines the arguments *ax, di,* and *header,* which receive error information from DOS.

■ **FACT:** *Your error handler should be defined as a* void *function.*

The error-handling function does not actually return a value, so you can declare it *void.* The error handler uses one of two run-time library functions to return control to DOS.

■ **FACT:** *The* _hardretn *function returns control from your critical error handler to your program. If your handler determines that the program should continue, it can use* _hardretn *to return a status value to the program.*

The run-time library function *_hardretn* returns control to the location immediately following the point in your program at which the error occurred. By setting a global variable in its critical error handler, your program can test to see whether the critical error handler has run. If the variable is set, the program can handle the error accordingly.

If you would rather retry the failed operation, the run-time library function *_hardresume* lets your error handler return control to DOS.

■ **FACT:** *The* _hardresume *function returns control from your error handler to DOS. The call to* _hardresume *takes one argument, which indicates to DOS a response to the error.*

The following table lists the manifest constants that you can use as arguments with *_hardresume*. The constants indicate the action for DOS to take when it regains control from *_hardresume*.

Constant	*Meaning*
_HARDERR_IGNORE	Ignore error
_HARDERR_RETRY	Retry system call causing the error
_HARDERR_ABORT	Terminate the program
_HARDERR_FAIL	Fail system call causing the error

The following program (CRITERR.C) contains the function *error_handler*, which implements a basic critical error handler using the *_hardretn* function. The *error_handler* function sets the global variable *critical_error* to true, which notifies the program that a critical error has occurred.

```
#include <dos.h>    /* needed for _harderr and _hardretn */
#include <stdio.h>  /* needed for fopen, fclose, and puts */

unsigned int critical_error;  /* global critical error flag */

main()
{
    FILE *fp;
    void far error_handler(unsigned, unsigned, unsigned far *);

    _harderr(error_handler); /* install critical error handler */
    do
        {
        critical_error = 0;

        if (!(fp = fopen("A:TEST", "r")))
            {
            if (!critical_error)
                puts("Error opening TEST");
            }
        else
            {
            puts("TEST successfully opened");
            fclose(fp);
            }
        }
    while (critical_error != 0);
}
```

(continued)

continued

```
void far error_handler(unsigned int ax, unsigned int di,
    unsigned far *header)
{
    puts("DEVICE ERROR: Check disk drive or printer and press Enter");
    critical_error = 1;  /* set critical error flag to true */
    getchar();
    _hardretn(0);         /* return to program */
}
```

The CRITERR program uses the run-time library function *_harderr* to direct DOS to use your critical error handler.

■ **FACT:** *The* _harderr *function directs DOS to use the specified function to handle critical errors. When the program ends, DOS resumes use of its default handler.*

After the error handler is installed, the program attempts to open the file TEST on drive A. If drive A does not contain a disk, DOS passes control to *error_handler*, which uses *_hardretn* to return control to CRITERR. If the call to *fopen* fails, CRITERR checks the global variable *critical_error*. If the variable has been set to a nonzero value, the program tries again to open the file.

Execute CRITERR when you have no disk inserted in drive A. The program displays *Error opening TEST* until you insert a disk in drive A. Although this error handler is simplistic, it illustrates the steps you must take to create your own error handler:

- Create a *void* function that receives three arguments: two values of type *unsigned* and a far pointer to an *unsigned int* value.

- Include the error handling code within the function.

- Use *_hardresume* or *_hardretn* to return from the error handler.

- Use *_harderr* to install the error handler.

The following program (CRITERR2.C) changes *error_handler* to let the user type A, R, or F to abort, retry, or fail the operation:

```
#include <dos.h>    /* needed for _harderr and _hardretn */
#include <stdio.h>  /* needed for fopen, puts, and fclose */

unsigned int critical_error;  /* global critical error flag */

main()
{
    FILE *fp;
```

(continued)

continued

```
    void far error_handler(unsigned, unsigned, unsigned far *);

    _harderr(error_handler);  /* install critical error handler */

    do
        {
        critical_error = 0;

        if (!(fp = fopen("A:TEST", "r")))
            {
            if (!critical_error)
                puts("Error opening TEST");
            else
                {
                if (critical_error == _HARDERR_ABORT)
                    exit(3);
                else if (critical_error == _HARDERR_FAIL)
                    break;  /* continue without opening file */
                }
            }
        else
            {
            puts("TEST successfully opened");
            fclose(fp);
            }
        }
    while (critical_error != 0);
}

#include <bios.h>   /* needed for _bios_keybrd */
#include <ctype.h>  /* needed for _toupper */

void far error_handler(unsigned int ax, unsigned int di,
    unsigned far *header)
{
    int done = 0;
    char response;

    printf("\nDEVICE ERROR:  check disk drive or printer");
    critical_error = 1;  /* set critical error flag to true */

    while (!done)
        {
        printf("\nAbort, Retry, Fail? ");
        response = _bios_keybrd(_KEYBRD_READ);
```

(continued)

continued

```
        switch (_toupper(response))
            {
            case 'A': critical_error = _HARDERR_ABORT;
                      done = 1;
                      break;
            case 'R': critical_error = _HARDERR_RETRY;
                      done = 1;
                      break;
            case 'F': critical_error = _HARDERR_FAIL;
                      done = 1;
                      break;
            };
        }
    _hardretn(0);
}
```

The following program (CRITERR3.C) takes *error_handler* one step further. The function examines the disk error information in DI to determine the cause of a critical error and then displays useful instructions to the user.

```
#include <dos.h>    /* needed for _harderr and _hardretn */
#include <stdio.h>  /* needed for fopen, puts, and fclose */

unsigned int critical_error;  /* global critical error flag */

main()
{
    FILE *fp;
    void far error_handler(unsigned, unsigned, unsigned far *);

    _harderr(error_handler);  /* install critical error handler */

    do
        {
        critical_error = 0;

        if (!(fp = fopen("A:TEST", "r")))
            {
            if (!critical_error)
                puts("\nError opening TEST");
            else
                {
                if (critical_error == _HARDERR_ABORT)
                    exit(3);
```

(continued)

continued

```
                    else if (critical_error == _HARDERR_FAIL)
                        break;  /* continue without opening file */
                }
            }
        else
            {
            puts("\nTEST successfully opened");
            fclose(fp);
            }
        }
    while (critical_error != 0);
}

#include <bios.h>    /* needed for _bios_keybrd */
#include <ctype.h>   /* needed for _toupper */

void far error_handler(unsigned int ax, unsigned int di,
    unsigned far *header)
{
    int done = 0;
    char response;
    unsigned int di_low;        /* low-order byte in DI register */

    if ((ax & 0x8000) == 0)   /* high-order bit states disk error */
        {
        printf("\nError accessing disk in drive %c ", 'A' + (ax & 0xFF));
        di_low = di & 0xFF;  /* low-order byte */
        switch (di_low)
            {
            case 0:  printf ("-- write-protected disk\n");
                     printf("Cannot write to a disk containing");
                     printf(" a write protect tab\n");
                     break;
            case 1:  printf("-- unknown disk drive\n");
                     printf("Specify an existing drive\n");
                     break;
            case 2:  printf("-- disk drive not ready\n");
                     printf("Place a disk in the drive, or");
                     printf(" close the disk drive latch\n");
                     break;
            case 3:  printf("-- unknown command\n");
                     break;
            case 4:  printf("-- CRC data error\n");
                     printf("Back up disk contents immediately\n");
                     break;
            case 5:  printf("-- bad request structure length error\n");
                     break;
```

(continued)

continued

```
            case 6:  printf("-- seek error\n");
                     printf("Back up disk contents immediately\n");
                     break;
            case 7:  printf("-- unknown medium error\n");
                     printf("Make sure disk is formatted for DOS\n");
                     break;
            case 8:  printf("-- sector not found error\n");
                     printf("Back up disk contents immediately\n");
                     break;
            case 10: printf("-- write fault\n");
                     printf("Error writing to disk -- check space\n");
                     break;
            case 11: printf("-- read fault\n");
                     printf("Error reading the disk -- back up");
                     printf(" disk contents immediately\n");
                     break;
            case 12: printf("-- general failure\n");
                     printf("Make sure disk is formatted\n");
                     break;
            };
        }

    critical_error = 1;  /* set critical error flag to true */

    while (!done)
        {
        printf("\nAbort, Retry, Fail? ");
        response = _bios_keybrd(_KEYBRD_READ);
        switch (_toupper(response))
            {
            case 'A': critical_error = _HARDERR_ABORT;
                      done = 1;
                      break;
            case 'R': critical_error = _HARDERR_RETRY;
                      done = 1;
                      break;
            case 'F': critical_error = _HARDERR_FAIL;
                      done = 1;
                      break;
            };
        }

    _hardretn(0);
}
```

If the error code indicates that the drive is not ready, for example, the function displays the message

```
Error accessing disk in drive A -- disk drive not ready
Place a disk in the drive, or close the disk drive latch

Abort, Retry, Fail?
```

For a write protect error, the error handler displays the message

```
Error accessing disk in drive A -- write-protected disk
Cannot write to a disk containing a write protect tab

Abort, Retry, Fail?
```

As you can see, critical error handlers are easy to implement. Too many programs fail to handle critical errors in a way that makes the errors comprehensible. But once you become familiar with _harderr, _hardresume_, and _hardretn_, you can normally clarify the causes of errors by handling them in your own routines.

SUMMARY

Looking at a Simple Example

■ **FACT:** *DOS passes three arguments to the critical error handler: an* unsigned int *variable that contains the value in AX, an* unsigned int *variable that contains the value in DI, and a far pointer to an* unsigned int *device handle.*

■ **FACT:** *Your error handler should be defined as a* void *function.*

■ **FACT:** *The* _hardretn *function returns control from your critical error handler to your program. If your handler determines that the program should continue, it can use* _hardretn *to return a status value to the program.*

■ **FACT:** *The* _hardresume *function returns control from your error handler to DOS. The call to* _hardresume *takes one argument, which indicates to DOS a response to the error.*

■ **FACT:** *The* _harderr *function directs DOS to use the specified function to handle critical errors. When the program ends, DOS resumes use of its default handler.*

GLOSSARY

critical error An error that prevents the operating system from continuing until the user intervenes. The most common causes of critical errors are off-line printers and unready disk drives.

critical error handler A function designed to take over when a critical error occurs. The built-in DOS critical error handler displays the message *Abort, Retry, Fail?* when a critical error occurs.

## CHAPTER 31

Mixed Language Programming

Although C is rapidly becoming the most widely used microcomputer programming language, many programmers continue to use other programming languages, such as Pascal, FORTRAN, and assembly language. And even if you program almost exclusively in C, you will probably encounter situations in which you need to access a function written in either FORTRAN or Pascal, or situations that require you to write a hardware-dependent assembly language routine that you invoke from within your C program.

In this chapter you learn to write C functions that you can call from C or Pascal or FORTRAN, and you learn to access functions written in other high-level languages. We also create several simple assembly language routines that you can invoke from C. Once you learn a few secrets, accessing routines written in other programming languages is easy.

If you haven't read Chapter 28, "Understanding Memory Models," do so before you start this chapter. Chapter 28 provides necessary background for the further insights into C memory models in this chapter.

BACK TO BINARY

Before we actually begin to write C programs that access non-C routines, let's build a solid foundation for understanding code generation. At the lowest level, your executable file contains a binary representation of your program's instructions. As your program executes, the computer uses these 1s and 0s to perform specific operations. For example, the binary digits

1000100111011000

direct an Intel 8086 microprocessor to move the contents of the BX register into the AX register. Although these 1s and 0s work well for the computer, you would find it difficult, at best, to write a program using only binary digits. Debugging becomes almost impossible. To simplify the task of writing and debugging code, programmers developed assemblers which let you assign meaningful names to these binary digit combinations. The previous statement therefore becomes the following assembly language instruction:

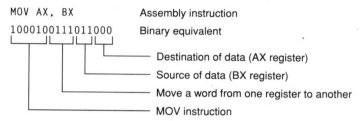

The assembler converts instructions from assembly language into the binary format that the computer executes. (These binary instructions are often displayed as hexadecimal numbers in program output so that they are easier to identify.) For many years, assembly language was the programmer's means to communicate with the computer.

To simplify program development to an even greater extent, programmers developed high-level programming languages, such as C, Pascal, and FORTRAN. These languages let you replace an assembly language loop, such as

```
     MOV WORD PTR [BP-2],0
     JMP SHORT TEST
LOOP:
     INC WORD PTR [BP-2]
TEST:
     CMP WORD PTR [BP-2],100
     JL LOOP
```

with statements, such as the following C loop:

```
for (i = 0; i < 100; ++i)
    { ; }
```

The compiler converts the C statements first to assembly language and then to executable instructions in binary code. Regardless of whether you use C, Pascal, or FORTRAN, your source file eventually becomes assembly language code and then binary code. Because the final output of each compiler is binary code, we can, as you might expect, connect routines written in different languages.

To review, let's use the /Fc option with CL to generate a program listing that contains your C source code, the compiler-generated assembly language, and the binary object code. Begin with the program on the following page (LOOP.C).

```
main()
{
    int i;

    for (i = 0; i < 100; ++i)
        printf("%d\n", i);
}
```

The following code is a portion of the resulting mixed listing, LOOP.COD, produced with the /Fc option:

```
;!*** main()
;!*** {
; Line 2
        PUBLIC_main                        ┌──── Machine code        ┌──── Assembly
_main   PROC NEAR                          │                         │     language
        *** 000000   55                    │      push   bp          │     code
        *** 000001   8b ec                 │      mov    bp,sp
        *** 000003   b8 02 00              │      mov    ax,2
        *** 000006   e8 00 00              │      call   __chkstk
;          i = -2                          │
;!***      int i;                          │
;!***                         ┌──── C source code
;!***      for (i = 0; i < 100; ++i)
; Line 5
        *** 000009   c7 46 fe 00 00        mov    WORD PTR [bp-2],0 ;i
                                    $FC104:
;!***   printf("%d\n", i);
; Line 6
        *** 00000e   ff 76 fe              push   WORD PTR [bp-2] ;i
        *** 000011   b8 00 00              mov    ax,OFFSET DGROUP:$SG107
        *** 000014   50                    push   ax
        *** 000015   e8 00 00              call   _printf
        *** 000018   83 c4 04              add    sp,4
        *** 00001b   ff 46 fe              inc    WORD PTR [bp-2] ;i
        *** 00001e   83 7e fe 64           cmp    WORD PTR [bp-2],100 ;i
        *** 000022   7c ea                 jl     $FC104
;!*** }
; Line 7
        *** 000024   8b e5                 mov    sp,bp
        *** 000026   5d                    pop    bp
        *** 000027   c3                    ret

_main   ENDP
_TEXT   ENDS
END
;!***
```

CALLING A FORTRAN SUBROUTINE

For years, scientists and analysts have been optimizing complex mathematical functions written in FORTRAN. If you can compile such subroutines with the Microsoft FORTRAN Compiler, you can access them from within your C programs. You don't have to rewrite the routines in C and risk introducing bugs in the conversion. And by using the FORTRAN subroutines, you have only the FORTRAN routines to maintain, not an additional set of C routines.

To demonstrate, let's use a simple FORTRAN subroutine (VIEW.FOR) that displays three *long int* values:

```
subroutine view (a, b, c)
integer a, b, c

write (6,*) a, b, c
return
end
```

Using the FORTRAN compiler, we can compile the subroutine to create the object file VIEW.OBJ. Next we can create a C program that calls *view* to display the values.

In Chapter 23 we briefly noted that when the C compiler passes arguments to a function, it places them onto the stack from right to left. A FORTRAN compiler, on the other hand, passes arguments from left to right. Unless you indicate to the C compiler that the function *view* is written in FORTRAN, the C compiler places the values onto the stack in the order opposite to the one the FORTRAN function requires.

■ **FACT:** *The C qualifier* fortran *directs the C compiler to call the specified function using the FORTRAN calling convention. When you place this keyword before a function name, the C compiler passes arguments to the function from left to right.*

To accommodate a call to *view*, the C program must make the following declarations:

```
void fortran view(long int *, long int *, long int *);
long int a = 1, b = 2, c = 3;
```

■ **FACT:** *FORTRAN always passes arguments by reference. The C compiler passes arguments by value unless you use pointers.*

By default, the C compiler passes arguments by value. To pass an argument by reference, you must pass its address. The C program on the following page (CALLVIEW.C) therefore passes the address of each variable to the FORTRAN routine.

```
main()
{
    void fortran view(long int *, long int *, long int *);
    long int a = 1, b = 2, c = 3;

    view(&a, &b, &c);  /* call by reference */
}
```

Compile and link these files with the following set of commands:

```
FL/c VIEW.FOR
CL /c /AL CALLVIEW.C
LINK CALLVIEW.OBJ VIEW.OBJ;
```

When you run this program, it displays the values 1, 2, and 3, in counting order. To verify that C and FORTRAN do in fact place arguments on the stack in opposite orders, remove the *fortran* qualifier from the declaration of *view* in CALLVIEW.C. When you recompile and run the program, it displays the values in the opposite order: 3, 2, 1.

■ **TRAP:** *By default, the FORTRAN compiler uses the large memory model. Be sure to compile your C program with a corresponding memory model.*

■ **FACT:** *The C qualifier* pascal *directs the C compiler to pass arguments to the specified function using the Pascal calling convention.*

Pascal, like FORTRAN, places arguments on the stack from left to right. To access these arguments in the correct order from a C program, use the *pascal* qualifier to declare a Pascal function.

TESTING MIXED LANGUAGE CONCEPTS FROM C

Not everyone has a FORTRAN or Pascal compiler. But by using the *fortran* or *pascal* keyword, you can test your interface entirely from C. You can write a C function that is equivalent to the FORTRAN function *view* (CVIEW.C) and that emulates the FORTRAN calling sequence:

```
void fortran view(long int *a, long int *b, long int *c)
{
    printf("%ld %ld %ld\n", *a, *b, *c);
}
```

When CALLVIEW calls *view*, the function displays the values 1, 2, and 3, in order. By using this C function, you can verify that your program calls the FORTRAN equivalent with the arguments in the correct order.

CREATING AND ACCESSING ASSEMBLY LANGUAGE ROUTINES

The C language simplifies the process of developing, changing, testing, and porting your programs: Write as much of your code as possible in C. Nevertheless, you cannot avoid assembly language when speed is critical or when hardware requirements demand its use. In this section we examine a simple assembly language routine that returns the major and minor version numbers of the operating system.

Chapter 32 discusses DOS system services in detail. For our immediate purposes, however, note that system services are a set of operating system routines that your programs can access. The following assembly language program, GETVER.ASM, calls DOS system service 0x30 to determine the current version of the operating system. The GETVER.ASM program is designed for DOS systems only and will not run in OS/2 protected mode.

```
        TITLE   GETVER.ASM
        NAME    GETVER

_TEXT   SEGMENT  WORD PUBLIC 'CODE'
_TEXT   ENDS

_DATA   SEGMENT  WORD PUBLIC 'DATA'
_DATA   ENDS
CONST   SEGMENT  WORD PUBLIC 'CONST'
CONST   ENDS
_BSS    SEGMENT  WORD PUBLIC 'BSS'
_BSS    ENDS

DGROUP  GROUP    CONST, _BSS, _DATA
        ASSUME   CS: _TEXT, DS: DGROUP, SS: DGROUP

_TEXT   SEGMENT
        ASSUME   CS: _TEXT
        PUBLIC   _getver

_getver PROC NEAR
        push    bp
        mov     bp,sp

        mov     ah, 30h                 ; get DOS version
        int     21h                     ; invoke the system service
```

(continued)

continued

```
        mov     bx, word ptr [bp+6]
        mov     word ptr [bx], ax       ; minor version number
        mov     cl, 8                   ; is in the high-order byte
        shr     word ptr [bx], cl       ; so shift left 8 bits

        mov     bx, word ptr [bp+4]     ; major version number
        mov     word ptr [bx], ax       ; is in the low-order
        and     word ptr [bx], 0ffh     ; byte

        pop     bp
        ret

_getver ENDP
_TEXT   ENDS

        END
```

GETVER assigns the major and minor components of the version number to the AL and AH registers, respectively. The routine is designed to be called by a high-level language program and returns the major and minor version arguments on the stack.

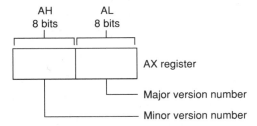

The GETVER routine has the same lines of header information as the other assembly language routines we have examined. The actual processing begins at the sixteenth line:

```
_getver PROC NEAR
```

The next two lines save the current contents of the *base pointer* and then set the base pointer to the value of the stack pointer. The base pointer is a register that points to the first argument on the stack. When GETVER is called from a C program, version number arguments and a return address to *main* are also on the stack, so the stack contains the elements shown on the following page.

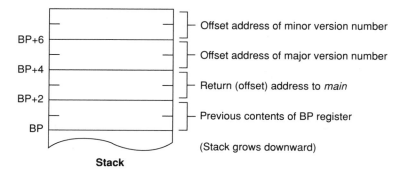

Stack

Next, the routine calls DOS service 30H, Get version Number, using Int 21H. The routine then assigns the major and minor version numbers to the arguments on the stack. Last, GETVER restores the previous contents of the base pointer and returns control to the calling program. Note that if the memory model of the calling program changes, the return address to *main* and the location of the arguments on the stack change.

Using the Microsoft Macro Assembler, you can assemble the routine (GETVER.ASM) as follows:

```
C> MASM GETVER.ASM;
```

The assembler creates an object file that you can later link to your C application. The following program (SHOWVER.C) uses the GETVER.OBJ object file:

```
main()
{
    void getver(int *, int *);
    int major, minor;

    getver(&major, &minor);
    printf("%DOS version is %d.%d\n", major, minor);
}
```

Compile and link SHOWVER.C as follows:

```
C> CL /c SHOWVER.C
C> LINK SHOWVER.OBJ GETVER.OBJ;
```

If you are using the medium memory model, you must change GETVER.ASM as follows (GETVER2.ASM) to reflect the fact that _getver_ becomes a far procedure:

```
        TITLE   GETVER.ASM
        NAME    GETVER

_TEXT   SEGMENT  WORD PUBLIC 'CODE'
_TEXT   ENDS
_DATA   SEGMENT  WORD PUBLIC 'DATA'
_DATA   ENDS
CONST   SEGMENT  WORD PUBLIC 'CONST'
CONST   ENDS
_BSS    SEGMENT  WORD PUBLIC 'BSS'
_BSS    ENDS


DGROUP  GROUP CONST, _BSS, _DATA
        ASSUME  CS: _TEXT, DS: DGROUP, SS: DGROUP

_TEXT   SEGMENT
        ASSUME CS: _TEXT
        PUBLIC _getver

_getver PROC FAR——————— Declared as a far procedure
        push    bp
        mov     bp,sp

        mov     ah, 30h                ; get DOS version
        int     21h                    ; invoke the system service

        mov     bx, word ptr [bp+8]——— Offsets reflect far pointer on stack
        mov     word ptr [bx], ax      ; minor version number
        mov     cl, 8                  ; is in the high-order byte
        shr     word ptr [bx], cl      ; so shift left 8 bits

        mov     bx, word ptr [bp+6]    ; major version number
        mov     word ptr [bx], ax      ; is in the low-order
        and     word ptr [bx], 0ffh    ; byte

        pop     bp
        ret

_getver ENDP
_TEXT   ENDS

        END
```

Not only do you have to define _getver_ as PROC FAR, but you also have to change the stack offsets for the arguments. (If you have version 5.0 or later of MASM, you can use the .MODEL directive to ensure that your procedures are defined properly.) For the medium memory model, the stack now contains four bytes for a far return to *main*:

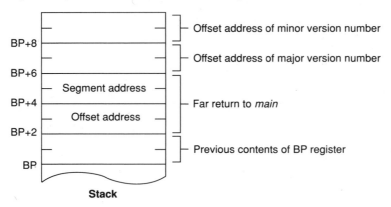

Figuring out the offsets for arguments for each memory model is simple. As a shortcut, create a program (SHORTCUT.C) that passes pointers to two variables to a function:

```
main()
{
    void init(int *, int *);
    int a, b;

    init(&a, &b);
}

void init(int *a, int *b)
{
    *a = 3;
    *b = 0;
}
```

Now compile SHORTCUT.C using the small memory model and create an assembly language listing:

`C> CL /Fa SHORTCUT.C`

When you do so, C creates the file SHORTCUT.ASM, which contains the code that follows.

```
;        Static Name Aliases
;
         TITLE    SHORTCUT.C
         NAME     SHORTCUT

         .8087
_TEXT    SEGMENT   WORD PUBLIC 'CODE'
_TEXT    ENDS
_DATA    SEGMENT   WORD PUBLIC 'DATA'
_DATA    ENDS
CONST    SEGMENT   WORD PUBLIC 'CONST'
CONST    ENDS
_BSS     SEGMENT   WORD PUBLIC 'BSS'
_BSS     ENDS
DGROUP   GROUP CONST, _BSS, _DATA
         ASSUME  CS: _TEXT, DS: DGROUP, SS: DGROUP
EXTRN    __acrtused:ABS
EXTRN    __chkstk:NEAR
_TEXT       SEGMENT
         ASSUME CS: _TEXT
; Line 2
         PUBLIC _main
_main    PROC NEAR ───────────── Near procedure
         push    bp
         mov     bp,sp
         mov     ax,4
         call    __chkstk
;        a = -2
;        b = -4
; Line 6
         lea     ax,WORD PTR [bp-4]      ;b
         push    ax
         lea     ax,WORD PTR [bp-2]      ;a
         push    ax
         call    _init
; Line 7
         mov     sp,bp
         pop     bp
         ret


_main    ENDP
; Line 10
         PUBLIC_init
_init    PROC NEAR
         push    bp
         mov     bp,sp
         xor     ax,ax
         call    __chkstk
```

(continued)

continued

```
;          a = 4
;          b = 6
; Line 11
          mov      bx,WORD PTR [bp+4]          ;a
          mov      WORD PTR [bx],3
; Line 12
          mov      bx,WORD PTR [bp+6]          ;b
          mov      WORD PTR [bx],0
; Line 13
          pop      bp
          ret

_init    ENDP
_TEXT    ENDS
END
```

Offsets reflect near pointers to arguments in small model compilation

Recompile the program using the large memory model, as follows:

```
C> CL /Fa /AL SHORTCUT.C
```

The offsets in SHORTCUT.ASM change to reflect the need for far pointers to arguments when the memory model permits multiple data segments. As you can see, the assembly language listings provide templates for you to use as you develop assembly language routines that you can call from your C programs.

```
;          Static Name Aliases
;
          TITLE    SHORTCUT.C
          NAME     SHORTCUT

          .8087
INIT_TEXT          SEGMENT  WORD PUBLIC 'CODE'
INIT_TEXT          ENDS
_DATA    SEGMENT  WORD PUBLIC 'DATA'
_DATA    ENDS
CONST    SEGMENT  WORD PUBLIC 'CONST'
CONST    ENDS
_BSS     SEGMENT  WORD PUBLIC 'BSS'
_BSS     ENDS
DGROUP   GROUP    CONST, _BSS, _DATA
          ASSUME   CS: SHORTCUT_TEXT, DS: DGROUP, SS: DGROUP
EXTRN    __acrtused:ABS
EXTRN    __chkstk:FAR
SHORTCUT_TEXT      SEGMENT
          ASSUME   CS: SHORTCUT_TEXT
```

(continued)

continued

```
; Line 2
        PUBLIC  _main
_main   PROC FAR ─────────────── Far procedure
        push    bp
        mov     bp,sp
        mov     ax,4
        call    FAR PTR __chkstk
;       a = -2
;       b = -4
; Line 6
        lea     ax,WORD PTR [bp-4]      ;b
        push    ss
        push    ax
        lea     ax,WORD PTR [bp-2]      ;a
        push    ss
        push    ax
        push    cs
        call    _init
; Line 7
        mov     sp,bp
        pop     bp
        ret
        nop

_main   ENDP
; Line 10
        PUBLIC_init
_init   PROC FAR
        push    bp
        mov     bp,sp
        xor     ax,ax
        call    FAR PTR __chkstk
;       a = 6
;       b = 10
; Line 11
        les     bx,DWORD PTR [bp+6]     ;a
        mov     WORD PTR es:[bx],3
; Line 12
        les     bx,DWORD PTR [bp+10]    ;b
        mov     WORD PTR es:[bx],0
; Line 13
        pop     bp
        ret

_init   ENDP
SHORTCUT_TEXT   ENDS
END
```

Offsets reflect far pointers to arguments in large model compilation

SUMMARY

Calling a FORTRAN Subroutine

■ **FACT:** *The C qualifier* fortran *directs the C compiler to call the specified function using the FORTRAN calling convention. When you place this keyword before a function name, the C compiler passes arguments to the function from left to right.*

■ **FACT:** *FORTRAN always passes arguments by reference. The C compiler passes arguments by value unless you use pointers.*

■ **TRAP:** *By default, the FORTRAN compiler uses the large memory model. Be sure to compile your C program with a corresponding memory model.*

■ **FACT:** *The C qualifier* pascal *directs the C compiler to pass arguments to the specified function using the Pascal calling convention.*

GLOSSARY

base pointer (BP) A register that contains the starting location of the arguments on the stack. Assembly language routines use offsets from the base pointer to access each argument.

## CHAPTER 32

Using DOS System Services

The tasks that DOS performs are accomplished by hundreds of small routines that are called within the operating system. These routines provide such services as file and directory manipulation, date and time information, process creation and termination, and screen and device I/O. Because the operating system makes constant use of these services, they must be readily available. The developers of DOS have implemented these routines in such a way that the services they provide are available to your programs as well.

In this chapter you learn how to access the DOS services, and you see the advantages of doing so. Like many of the chapters before it, this chapter is filled with information and short sample programs. Take time to execute the programs!

DOS SYSTEM SERVICES

As discussed, the DOS *system services* are a set of routines built into the operating system. A program obtains a service through a software interrupt. Assembly language programmers are already familiar with accessing the DOS system services. To invoke a system service, they place the number of the service in the AH register, load other arguments needed for the service in other registers, and then invoke the appropriate software interrupt, 21H (written 0x21 in C programs). In Chapter 31 we wrote an assembly language routine called GETVER that used this technique to obtain the DOS version number. When DOS returns control to the caller, it assigns values to the processor's general-purpose registers.

Because system services require direct manipulation of specific registers, they need an assembly language interface. But you need not develop an assembly language routine each time you want to access the operating system services—the C run-time library provides three functions for invoking system services.

Several DOS services associated with Interrupt 0x21 require only the number of the requested service and arguments in the AL and DX registers. When these system calls return, they place a status value in the AX register. You can call such services with the run-time library function *bdos.*

■ **FACT:** *The* bdos *function lets you invoke DOS system services that require arguments in only the AL and DX registers. After the service call is completed,* bdos *returns the value that the DOS service placed in the AX register.*

The general format of a call to *bdos* is the following:

```
result = bdos(service, dx, al);
```

where *service* is the number of the DOS service desired, *dx* contains the value to place in the DX register, and *al* contains the value to place in the AL register.

The *bdos* function is adequate for calling the DOS Character Output service.

■ **FACT:** *DOS service 0x2 writes the ASCII character identified in the DX register. It places the character at the current location of the cursor.*

The following program (OUTCHAR.C) uses DOS service 0x2 to write the message *DOS System Services* on your screen. The program uses the *bdos* run-time library routine as its interface to the system service.

```c
#include <dos.h>  /* needed for bdos */

main()
{
    char *message = "DOS System Services";

    while (*message)
        bdos(0x2, *message++, 0);
}
```

The call to *bdos* specifies the DOS service number, the character to write, and 0 for AL. (Generally, placing zeros in unused registers is a good practice.) If you simply change the service number to 0x5, *bdos* invokes the Printer Output service to send the character to the printer.

■ **FACT:** *DOS service 0x19 returns the drive number of the current disk drive in the AX register. The service does not use values for the DX and AL registers.*

The following program (GETDRIVE.C) uses DOS service 0x19 to display the current drive.

```
#include <dos.h>  /* needed for bdos */

main()
{
    printf("Current disk drive is %c\n", 'A' + bdos(0x19, 0, 0));
}
```

DOS service 0x19 returns an integer that corresponds to the drive letter for the current disk drive (0 for drive A, 1 for drive B, 2 for drive C, and so on). The *bdos* function, in turn, returns this value to *main*. By adding the value to the ASCII 'A', the program then displays the correct letter (A, B, C, and so on) for the current drive.

The following program (GETVER.C) uses *bdos* to display the current DOS version number. The GETVER program is functionally the same as the GETVER program we developed in Chapter 31.

```
#include <dos.h>  /* needed for bdos */

main()
{
    int version;

    version = bdos(0x30, 0, 0);
    printf("DOS version is %d.%d\n", version &0xFF, version >> 8);
}
```

To call many DOS services, *bdos* is inadequate. The services either require more arguments than simply AL and DX or return several values. The C run-time library routine *intdos* lets you pass a set of registers to such services.

If you examine the file dos.h, you find that it defines a union type REGS, as shown in Figure 32-1 on the following page. The members of the union correspond to the general-purpose registers for Intel 80x86 processors.

Within your program you assign values to the structure members that a given system service requires, and then you invoke the service with the run-time library routine *intdos*.

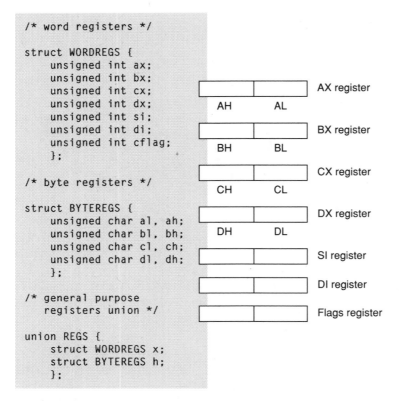

```
/* word registers */

struct WORDREGS {
    unsigned int ax;
    unsigned int bx;
    unsigned int cx;
    unsigned int dx;
    unsigned int si;
    unsigned int di;
    unsigned int cflag;
    };

/* byte registers */

struct BYTEREGS {
    unsigned char al, ah;
    unsigned char bl, bh;
    unsigned char cl, ch;
    unsigned char dl, dh;
    };

/* general purpose
   registers union */

union REGS {
    struct WORDREGS x;
    struct BYTEREGS h;
    };
```

FIGURE 32-1.
The structures that constitute a REGS union declare variables that correspond to the contents of general-purpose registers.

■ **FACT:** *The* intdos *function assigns the values in the REGS union to the appropriate general-purpose registers. Next the function calls Int 0x21 to access the requested system service. When the system call returns,* intdos *copies the new register contents back into the union members.*

To use the *intdos* function, your program must define two structures. The first contains the set of input register values, and the second receives the register values provided by the DOS service.

The REGS union lets you access the registers either as byte registers, by using *regs.h.al,* or as word registers, by using *regs.x.ax.* The way you access the members of the REGS union depends on the specific DOS service you need. Because register values in the two structures occupy the same memory locations, you can access members of both structures, as shown in Figure 32-2.

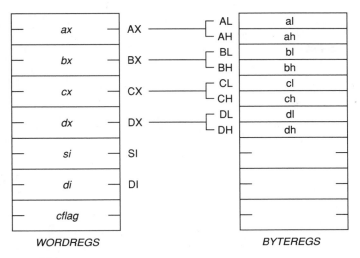

FIGURE 32-2.

In a REGS union, the two member structures are declared so that information for the same registers coincides in memory. This forethought lets you access word and byte values without conflict.

■ **FACT:** *DOS service 0x2C places the current system time in the CX and DX registers. The hours reside in CH, the minutes in CL. The seconds and hundredths of a second reside in DH and DL.*

The following program (SHOWTIME.C) uses *intdos* to access DOS service 0x2C, which returns the current system time. The Get Time service places the hours, minutes, seconds, and hundredths of a second into separate byte registers.

```
#include <dos.h>   /* needed for intdos and REGS */

main()
{
    union REGS inregs, outregs;

    inregs.h.ah = 0x2C;          /* service requested */
    intdos(&inregs, &outregs);   /* invoke Int 0x21 */

    printf("Current time %d:%d:%d.%d\n", outregs.h.ch, outregs.h.cl,
           outregs.h.dh, outregs.h.dl)
}
```

■ **FACT:** *DOS service 0x2A returns the current system date. The service places the day of the week in the AL register (Sunday = 0, Monday = 1, and so on), the year in CX, the month in DH, and the day in DL.*

The following program (SHOWDATE.C) uses *intdos* to access DOS service 0x2A, which returns the current system date:

```
#include <dos.h>  /* needed for intdos and REGS */

main()
{
    union REGS inregs, outregs;

    inregs.h.ah = 0x2A;          /* get date service */
    intdos(&inregs, &outregs);   /* invoke Int 0x21 */

    printf("Current date %d-%d-%d\n",
            outregs.h.dh, outregs.h.dl, outregs.x.cx);
}
```

To use some DOS system services, you need to specify both segment and offset addresses for variables. The run-time library function *segread* assigns the current values of the code segment register (CS), the data segment register (DS), the extra segment register (ES), and the stack segment register (SS) to the members of a structure of type SREGS.

The include file defines not only the REGS union, but also the SREGS structure, which contains the following members:

```
/* segment registers */

struct SREGS {
    unsigned int es;
    unsigned int cs;
    unsigned int ss;
    unsigned int ds;
    };
```

■ **FACT:** *The* segread *function reads the segment registers and assigns them to members of a structure of type SREGS.*

The following program (SHOWSEGS.C) uses *segread* to obtain the current values in the segment registers. It then displays the values *segread* places in members of an SREGS structure.

```
#include <dos.h>   /* needed for segread and SREGS */

main()
{
    struct SREGS segments;

    segread(&segments);
    printf("DS = %x CS = %x ES = %x SS = %x\n",
            segments.ds, segments.cs, segments.es, segments.ss);
}
```

When you run this program, your screen shows output similar to the following:

```
DS = 40ab CS = 3f39 ES = 40ab SS = 40ab
```

■ **FACT:** *DOS service 0x47 assigns a null-terminated string containing the current directory to a 64-byte buffer. The service uses the value in DL to determine the disk drive to which the request applies. The register DS contains the segment address of the 64-byte buffer, and SI contains the offset address of the buffer.*

The REGS union has no member that can pass the value in DS to *intdos*. Instead, you must use the run-time library function *intdosx* to pass the values in segment registers.

■ **FACT:** *Before it invokes Int 0x21, the* intdosx *function places values not only in the general-purpose registers but also in the segment registers.*

To call *intdosx*, you must not only pass pointers to REGS for input and output registers, but also pass a pointer to an SREGS structure that contains the current values for the segment registers. For example, the statement

```
intdosx(&inregs, &outregs, &segregs);
```

passes pointers to *inregs* and *outregs* for input and output of general-purpose registers and a pointer to the SREGS structure *segregs* for segment registers. The following program (SHOWDIR.C) uses *intdosx* to obtain the current directory from DOS service 0x47.

```
#include <dos.h>   /* needed for segread, REGS, and SREGS */

main()
{
    union REGS inregs, outregs;
    struct SREGS segments;
    char directory[64];
```

(continued)

continued

```
    segread(&segments);                        /* get segment registers */
    inregs.h.ah = 0x47;                        /* get directory service */
    inregs.h.dl = 0;                           /* current disk */
    inregs.x.si = directory;                   /* offset address */
    intdosx(&inregs, &outregs, &segments);     /* invoke Int 0x21 */

    printf("Current directory \\%s\n", directory);
}
```

Using the functions *bdos*, *intdos*, or *intdosx*, you can have access to all the DOS services available with Int 0x21.[†] In fact, you will find it easy to write a function such as *get_directory* or *remove_directory* that your programs can access. However, as the next section reveals, the C run-time library has done much of this work for you.

Because the run-time library routines are already written and are thoroughly tested, using them will save you considerable development time. But if you simply want to have fun mastering DOS, *bdos*, *intdos*, and *intdosx* should give you the tools you need.

USING RUN-TIME LIBRARY SERVICES FOR DOS

The C run-time library provides a collection of routines that call DOS system services. You have already used some of these routines, such as *_dos_findfirst* and *_dos_findnext*. Many other C run-time library routines duplicate DOS services. Where you find such duplication, use the C run-time library routine to improve your program's portability.

In previous chapters we looked extensively at file and directory manipulation from C. In this section we conclude our discussion of files by looking first at several functions that provide information about the current disk and then at several file manipulation functions.

■ **FACT:** *The _dos_getdrive function returns the drive number of the current disk drive, where A = 1, B = 2, C = 3, and so on. The function uses DOS service 0x1C.*

The following program (SHOWDRV.C) uses the run-time library function *_dos_getdrive* to display the current disk drive letter. Note that the program uses the expression *'A' + drive − 1* to determine the correct drive letter. By subtracting 1, we compensate for the fact that *_dos_getdrive* returns 1 for drive A, 2 for B, and so on.

[†]For a highly usable reference to DOS system services, see Ray Duncan's *MS-DOS Functions: Programmer's Quick Reference* (Microsoft Press, 1988).

```
#include <dos.h>  /* needed for _dos_getdrive */

main()
{
    unsigned int drive;

    _dos_getdrive(&drive);

    printf("The current drive is %c\n", 'A' + drive - 1);
}
```

■ **FACT:** *The _dos_setdrive function sets (changes) the current disk drive based on the specified drive number. The function also assigns the maximum number of available drives to the second argument. The function uses DOS service 0xE.*

The general format of a call to *_dos_setdrive* is as follows:

```
_dos_setdrive(drive_number, &max_drives);
```

The *drive_number* argument contains the drive number of the disk drive that you want to establish as the current drive. The function assigns to the argument *max_drives* the number of disk drives available in the system. The default number of drives configured by DOS is 5 (whether they exist or not). More drives can be added with the DOS LASTDRIVE configuration command.

The following program (SETDRIVE.C) uses *_dos_setdrive* to obtain the number of disk drives available in the system. Because we do not want *_dos_setdrive* to change the current drive, the program first calls *_dos_getdrive* to determine which drive to use in the call to *_dos_setdrive*.

```
#include <dos.h>  /* needed for _dos_getdrive and _dos_setdrive */

main()
{
    unsigned int drive, max_drives;

    _dos_getdrive(&drive);
    _dos_setdrive(drive, &max_drives);

    printf("The system is currently configured to support %d drives\n",
           max_drives);
}
```

■ **FACT:** *The* _dos_getdiskfree *function returns the number of free and used bytes on the specified disk. The function uses DOS service 0x36. If it obtains the requested information,* _dos_getdiskfree *returns 0; if* _dos_getdiskfree *is unable to get the information, it returns an error status.*

The run-time library function *_dos_getdiskfree* uses the *diskfree_t* structure, which is defined in dos.h as follows:

```
struct diskfree_t {
    unsigned total_clusters;
    unsigned avail_clusters;
    unsigned sectors_per_cluster;
    unsigned bytes_per_sector;
    };
```

Using the members of a *diskfree_t* structure, you can calculate the number of free bytes on your system as follows:

```
free = avail_clusters * sectors_per_cluster * bytes_per_sector
```

To determine the number of bytes in use, the calculation becomes

```
used = (total_clusters - avail_clusters) * sectors_per_cluster * bytes_per_sector
```

The following program (DISKFREE.C) uses the *_dos_getdiskdrive* function to display the current disk usage:

```
#include <dos.h>   /* needed for _dos_getdiskfree and diskfree_t */

main()
{
    long bytes_avail;
    long bytes_used;
    long total_bytes;

    struct diskfree_t disk;

    _dos_getdiskfree(0, &disk);

    total_bytes = (long) disk.total_clusters *
                  (long) disk.sectors_per_cluster *
                  (long) disk.bytes_per_sector;

    bytes_avail = (long) disk.avail_clusters *
                  (long) disk.sectors_per_cluster *
                  (long) disk.bytes_per_sector;
```

(continued)

continued

```
    bytes_used = total_bytes - bytes_avail;

    printf("Total disk space:\t%ld bytes\n", total_bytes);
    printf("Disk space used:\t%ld bytes\n", bytes_used);
    printf("Disk space available:\t%ld bytes\n", bytes_avail);
}
```

The C run-time library has another set of functions that use DOS system services to provide low-level file access.

■ **FACT:** *The _dos_open function opens the specified file. The function uses DOS service 0x3D to get a file handle for use by the other file manipulation services. If it obtains a handle, _dos_open returns 0; if an error occurs, _dos_open returns an error status.*

The general format of a call to *_dos_open* is as follows:

result = _dos_open(filename, mode, &handle);

The *filename* argument is the name of the file to open. It can contain a complete DOS pathname. The *mode* argument specifies the way you want to access the file. You can use the mode constants defined in the include file fcntl.h. The third argument is a pointer to a variable to which *_dos_open* assigns the file handle.

■ **FACT:** *The _dos_creat function creates a nonexisting file or truncates an existing file. The function uses DOS service 0x3C to get a file handle. If it obtains a file handle as requested, _dos_creat returns 0; if _dos_creat cannot provide a file handle, it returns an error status.*

The general format of a call to *_dos_creat* is as follows:

result = _dos_creat(filename, attribute, &handle);

The *filename* argument is the DOS pathname of the file to create. The *attribute* argument specifies one or more of the file types in the following list:

Value	Attribute
0	Normal file
1	Read-only file
2	Hidden file
3	System file
4	Volume ID
5	Subdirectory
6	Archive required

The third argument, *&handle*, is a pointer to a variable to which *_dos_creat* assigns the file handle.

■ **FACT:** *The* _dos_creatnew *function creates a file with the specified name. If a file exists on disk with the same name,* _dos_creatnew *returns an error status. If it creates the file as requested,* _dos_creatnew *returns 0. The function uses DOS service 0x5B.*

The calling sequence for a call to *_dos_creatnew* is the same as that for *_dos_creat*. The difference between the two functions is that *_dos_creat* truncates an existing file with the specified filename, whereas *_dos_creatnew* does not.

■ **FACT:** *The* _dos_read *function reads a specified number of bytes from a file into the specified buffer. If* _dos_read *gains access to the file, it returns 0; if an error occurs,* _dos_read *returns an error status. The function uses DOS service 0x3F.*

The general format of a call to *_dos_read* is as follows:

```
result = _dos_read(filehandle, buffer, size, &bytes_read);
```

The *filehandle* argument is the file handle returned by *_dos_open*, *_dos_creat*, or *_dos_creatnew*; *buffer* is a far pointer to the buffer to fill. The *size* argument specifies the number of bytes to read, and *bytes_read* is a pointer to a variable to which *_dos_read* assigns the actual number of bytes read.

■ **FACT:** *The* _dos_write *function writes the contents of the specified buffer to a file. The function uses DOS service 0x40. If it writes the buffer contents as requested,* _dos_write *returns 0; if an error occurs,* _dos_write *returns an error status.*

The general format of a call to *_dos_write* is as follows:

```
result = _dos_write(filehandle, buffer, size, &bytes_written);
```

The *filehandle* argument is the file handle returned by *_dos_open*, *_dos_creat*, or *dos_creatnew*. The *buffer* argument is a far pointer to the buffer whose contents are to be written to the file. The *size* argument specifies the number of bytes to write, and *&bytes_written* is a pointer to a variable to which *_dos_write* assigns the actual number of bytes written.

■ **FACT:** *The* _dos_close *function closes a file that is open for read or write operations. The function uses DOS service 0x3E.*

The following program (CPY.C) uses *_dos_open*, *_dos_read*, *_dos_write*, and *_dos_close* to copy the contents of the first file specified in the command line to the second file specified.

```
#include <dos.h>      /* needed for _dos functions */
#include <fcntl.h>    /* needed for _dos_open mode arguments */
#include <stdio.h>    /* needed for fputs */

main(int argc, char *argv[])
{
    char buffer[1024];

    int input, output;                /* file handles */
    int bytes_read, bytes_written;    /* actual number of bytes transferred */

    if (argc < 3)
        fputs("Must specify source and target file\n", stderr);
    else if (_dos_open (argv[1], O_RDONLY, &input))
        fputs("Error opening source file\n", stderr);
    else if (_dos_creat (argv[2], 0, &output))
        fputs("Error opening target file\n", stderr);
    else
        {
        while (!_dos_read(input, buffer, sizeof(buffer), &bytes_read))
            {
            if (bytes_read == 0)
                break;
            _dos_write(output, buffer, bytes_read, &bytes_written);
            }

        _dos_close(input);
        _dos_close(output);
        }
}
```

In addition to these low-level file manipulation functions, the C run-time library provides several functions that let you access the date and time stamps for a file.

■ **FACT:** *The* _dos_getftime *function uses a file handle to obtain a file's date and time stamps (the date and time a file was created or last modified). The function uses DOS service 0x57. If* _dos_getftime *gets the date and time information, it returns 0; if an error occurs,* _dos_getftime *returns an error status.*

The general form of a call to *_dos_getftime* is as follows:

result = _dos_getftime(*handle*, &*date*, &*time*);

The *handle* argument is the file handle returned by *_dos_open*, *_dos_creat*, or *_dos_creatnew*. The second and third arguments are pointers to structures of types *dosdate_t* and *dostime_t*. The *_dos_getftime* function assigns the date and time to specific bits of bitfield structures *date* and *time*, as shown in the illustrations on the following page.

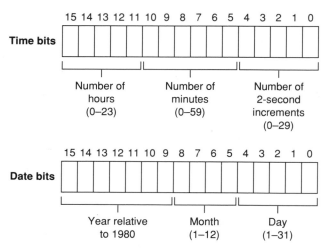

The following program (GETSTAMP.C) uses _dos_getftime_ to obtain the date and time stamps for the file specified in the command line. Note the way in which the program uses the different bitfields to access the date and time.

```c
#include <dos.h>      /* needed for _dos functions */
#include <stdio.h>    /* needed for fputs */
#include <fcntl.h>    /* needed for _dos_open mode arguments */

main (int argc, char *argv[])
{
    unsigned date, time;
    int handle;

    if (_dos_open(argv[1], O_RDONLY, &handle))
        fputs("Error opening source file\n", stderr);
    else
        {
        _dos_getftime(handle, &date, &time);

        printf("%s last modified %d-%d-%d %d:%d:%d\n", argv[1],
            (date & 0x1E0) >> 5,   /* month */
            (date & 0x1F),         /* day */
            (date >> 9) + 1980,    /* year */
            (time >> 11),          /* hours */
            (time & 0x7E0) >> 5,   /* minutes */
            (time & 0x1F) * 2);    /* seconds */
        _dos_close(handle);
        }
}
```

■ **FACT:** *The* _dos_setftime *function assigns new date and time stamps to the file associated with the specified handle. The function uses DOS service 0x57. If it alters the date and time stamps as requested, the function returns 0; if an error occurs,* _dos_setftime *returns an error status.*

The *_dos_setftime* function uses the same bit combinations to store date and time values as does *_dos_getftime*. The following program (SETSTAMP.C) uses the two functions to set the date and time stamp of the specified file to the current date and time. The program uses the *_dos_findfirst* and *_dos_findnext* functions to support DOS wildcard characters. SETSTAMP.C is functionally equivalent to the UNIX/XENIX TOUCH utility.

```c
#include <dos.h>     /* needed for _dos functions and structs */
#include <stdio.h>   /* needed for fprintf */
#include <fcntl.h>   /* needed for _dos_open mode arguments */

main(int argc, char *argv[])
{
    struct find_t file_info;  /* passed to _dos_findfirst/next */
    struct dosdate_t date;    /* for current date */
    struct dostime_t time;    /* for current time */
    int result;               /* result of _dos_findfirst/next */
    int handle;               /* file handle */
    unsigned fdate, ftime;    /* file date and time */
    unsigned int filedate, filetime;

    result = _dos_findfirst(argv[1], 0, &file_info);
    _dos_getdate(&date);
    _dos_gettime(&time);
    fdate = (date.year - 1980) << 9;
    fdate += date.month << 5;
    fdate += date.day;
    ftime = time.hour << 11;
    ftime += time.minute << 5;
    ftime += time.second / 2;

    while (!result)
        {
        if (_dos_open(file_info.name, 0, &handle))
            fprintf(stderr, "Error accessing %s\n", file_info.name);
        else
            {
            _dos_setftime(handle, fdate, ftime);
            _dos_close(handle);
            }

        result = _dos_findnext(&file_info);
        }
}
```

In Chapter 21 we examined the C run-time library function *chmod*, which lets you set a file to read or write access. In a similar manner the DOS service 0x43 sets a file's attributes using one or more of the following values:

Value	Attribute
0	Normal attribute
1	Read-only attribute
2	Hidden attribute
4	System attribute
32	Archive required attribute

■ **FACT:** *The* _dos_getfileattr *function returns the file attribute for the specified file. The function uses DOS service 0x43. If it obtains the attribute,* _dos_getfileattr *returns 0; if it is unable to get the attribute, it returns an error status.*

The following program (SHOWATTR.C) uses *_dos_getfileattr* to display the attribute of the specified file (wildcards are supported):

```
#include <dos.h>     /* needed for _dos functions and find_t struct */
#include <stdio.h>   /* needed for fprintf */

main(int argc, char *argv[])
{
    struct find_t file_info;  /* passed to _dos_findfirst/next */
    int result;               /* result of _dos_findfirst/next */
    int file_attr;            /* file attribute */

    unsigned match_attribute = 39;  /* all possible file attributes */

    result = _dos_findfirst(argv[1], match_attribute, &file_info);

    while (!result)
        {
        if (_dos_getfileattr(file_info.name, &file_attr))
            fprintf(stderr, "Error accessing %s\n", file_info.name);
        else
            printf("%s %d\n", file_info.name, file_attr);

        result = _dos_findnext(&file_info);
        }
}
```

■ **FACT:** *The* _dos_setfileattr *function sets the attribute of the specified file. The function uses DOS service 0x43. If it sets the attribute,* _dos_setfileattr *returns 0; if an error occurs,* _dos_setfileattr *returns an error status.*

The following program (SETFILE.C) uses *_dos_setfileattr* to hide or unhide the specified file (wildcards are supported). To hide files, run SETFILE as follows:

```
C> SETFILE H *.DAT
```

To unhide files, use the following command line:

```
C> SETFILE U *.DAT
```

Many programmers use the hidden attribute for key files to prevent a misguided DOS command from affecting the files.

After you hide a file, you can still type or print its contents (assuming you can remember the filename), but in most other respects DOS behaves as if the file does not exist (you cannot delete it, copy it, rename it, or view it in a directory listing). Remember, you can use the preceding program, SHOWATTR, to display all the filenames in the directory, regardless of their attributes.

```c
#include <dos.h>     /* needed for _dos functions and find_t struct */
#include <stdio.h>   /* needed for fprintf */
#include <ctype.h>   /* needed for toupper */

main(int argc, char *argv[])
{
    struct find_t file_info;    /* passed to _dos_findfirst/next */
    int result;                 /* result of _dos_findfirst/next */
    int file_attr;              /* file attribute */
    char option;

    unsigned match_attribute = 39;  /* all possible file attributes */

    if (argc < 3)
        fprintf(stderr, "SETFILE:  must specify U or H and filename\n");
    else
        {
        option = toupper(argv[1][0]);

        if (option != 'U' && option != 'H')
            fprintf(stderr, "SETFILE:  invalid option, use U or H\n");
        else
            {
            result = _dos_findfirst(argv[2], match_attribute, &file_info);
```

(continued)

continued

```
            while (!result)
                {
                if (_dos_getfileattr(file_info.name, &file_attr))
                    fprintf(stderr, "Error accessing %s\n", file_info.name);
                else
                    {
                    if (option == 'U')
                        file_attr &= ~2;
                    else
                        file_attr |= 2;

                    _dos_setfileattr(file_info.name, file_attr);
                    }

                result = _dos_findnext(&file_info);
                }
            }
        }
    }
```

In Chapter 15 we examined the C run-time library functions *_dos_getdate* and *_dos_gettime*. The run-time library provides two other functions, *dos_setdate* and *_dos_settime*, that let you set the current date and time.

■ **FACT:** *The* _dos_setdate *function sets the DOS system date to the date specified in a structure of type* dosdate_t. *The function uses DOS service 0x2B. If it sets the system date,* _dos_setdate *returns 0; if* _dos_setdate *cannot change the date as requested, it returns an error status.*

As discussed in Chapter 15, the structure *dosdate_t* contains the following members:

```
struct dosdate_t {
    unsigned char day;          /* 1-31 */
    unsigned char month;        /* 1-12 */
    unsigned int year;          /* 1980-2099 */
    unsigned char dayofweek;    /* 0-6, 0=Sunday */
    };
```

The following program (SETDATE.C) uses *_dos_setdate* to set the current date to December 25, 1989:

```
#include <dos.h>   /* needed for _dos_getdate, _dos_setdate, */
                   /* and dosdate_t struct */

main()
{
    struct dosdate_t date, save_date;

    _dos_getdate(&save_date);           /* save current date */
    date.month = 12;
    date.day = 25;
    date.year = 1989;

    if (_dos_setdate(&date))            /* change date to 12-25-89 */
        puts("Error setting system date");
    else
        puts("New system date 12-25-89");

    if (_dos_setdate(&save_date))       /* restore previous date */
        puts("Error resetting date");
    else
        puts("System date restored");
}
```

As you can see, the program uses the *_dos_getdate* function to save the current date so that it can later be restored. Next the program assigns the requested date to the structure *date* and then passes *date* to *_dos_setdate*. Before ending, the program restores the original system date.

■ **FACT:** *The* _dos_settime *function sets the current system time to the value specified in a structure of type* dostime_t. *The function uses DOS service 0x2D. If it sets the time,* _dos_settime *returns 0; if an error occurs,* _dos_settime *returns an error status.*

As discussed in Chapter 15, the structure *dostime_t* contains the following members:

```
struct dostime_t {
    unsigned char hour;     /* 0-23 */
    unsigned char minute;   /* 0-59 */
    unsigned char second;   /* 0-59 */
    unsigned char hsecond;  /* 0-99 */
    };
```

The following program (SETTIME.C) uses _dos_settime to set the current system time to 11:59:59.99 AM:

```
#include <dos.h>   /* needed for _dos_settime and dostime_t struct */

main()
{
    struct dostime_t time;

    time.hour = 11;
    time.minute = 59;
    time.second = 59;
    time.hsecond = 99;

    if (_dos_settime(&time))
        puts("Error setting time");
    else
        puts("Time set to 11:59:59.99");
}
```

Before you run this program, note that it does not save the original system time! Use the DOS or OS/2 TIME command to reset your system time.

The C run-time library provides access to several memory allocation routines that use DOS system services. Although the DOS services differ slightly in implementation from functions such as *calloc* and *malloc*, their net result is to allocate memory and return a pointer. In most cases you should use *calloc* or *malloc* to increase the portability of your program.

■ **FACT:** *The* _dos_allocmem *function uses DOS service 0x48 to allocate the requested number of 16-byte paragraphs. The function assigns the location of the memory to the second argument. If it succeeds, the function returns 0; if it cannot allocate the requested memory,* _dos_allocmem *returns an error status.*

The general format of a call to *_dos_allocmem* is as follows:

```
result = _dos_allocmem(num_paragraphs, &ptr);
```

The *num_paragraphs* argument specifies the number of 16-byte paragraphs to allocate, and *ptr* is a pointer to which the function assigns the memory location of the allocated space.

■ **FACT:** *The* _dos_setblock *function lets you change the size of memory previously allocated with* _dos_allocmem. *The function uses DOS service 0x4A. If it resizes the memory block,* _dos_setblock *returns 0; if an error occurs, the function returns an error status. If the available memory is not sufficient to meet the request, the third argument contains the size of the largest available block.*

The general format of a call to *_dos_setblock* is as follows:

```
result = _dos_setblock(new_size, ptr, &maxsize);
```

The *new_size* argument specifies the requested number of 16-byte paragraphs, *ptr* is a pointer to the current block of allocated memory, and *maxsize* is a buffer in which the function places the maximum available block size.

Just as you used the run-time library function *free* to release allocated memory in Chapter 25, you should use *_dos_freemem* to release memory allocated by the DOS services when you no longer need it.

■ **FACT:** *The* _dos_freemem *function releases the memory associated with the specified pointer. The function uses DOS service 0x49. If it releases the memory,* _dos_freemem *returns 0; if an error occurs, the function returns an error status.*

The general format of a call to *_dos_freemem* is as follows:

```
result = _dos_freemem(ptr);
```

The *ptr* argument is a pointer to the memory you want to release.

■ **TRAP:** *Although the* _dos_allocmem, _dos_setblock, *and* _dos_freemem *functions let you allocate and manipulate memory dynamically, they are less portable than* calloc *and* malloc.

As is true of other DOS services, the services that duplicate memory manipulation capabilities provided by other C functions diminish the portability of your program.

Each time you press Ctrl-Break, DOS invokes software Int 0x23. Using the run-time library function *_dos_setvect*, your program can specify its own interrupt handler.

■ **FACT:** *The* _dos_setvect *function sets the interrupt vector that points to the handler for the specified interrupt to the specified far pointer address. The function uses DOS service 0x25. If* _dos_setvect *registers the new handler, it returns 0; if an error occurs, the function returns an error status.*

The substituted interrupt handler must be a far function that returns the type *void*. DOS does not pass any arguments to the function. The following program (CTRL-C.C) uses *_dos_setvect* to install a new Ctrl-Break handler. The program then loops and prompts the user to press Ctrl-Break. Unlike the default Ctrl-Break handler, the *ctrlc_handler* function ignores Ctrl-Break. To end the program, press Ctrl-Z. When the program ends, DOS resumes use of its default Ctrl-Break handler.

```
#include <dos.h>     /* needed for _dos_setvect */
#include <stdio.h>   /* needed for getchar and EOF */

main()
{
    void far interrupt ctrlc_handler(void);

    if (_dos_setvect(0x23, ctrlc_handler))
        puts("Error setting handler");
    else
        {
        puts("Press Ctrl-Break to test interrupt handler\n");
        while (getchar() != EOF)
            { ; }
        }
}

void far interrupt ctrlc_handler(void)
{
    printf("Press Ctrl-Z and Enter to quit\n");
}
```

Note that the function *ctrlc_handler* uses a printf statement to display an error handling message. Because DOS is not reentrant (a DOS interrupt cannot be called from within
a DOS interrupt) you should not use any functions inside an interrupt handler that rely on Int
0x21 for their processing. Keep the processing in your interrupt handler short and simple.
Note that the function *ctrlc_handler* is declared with the *interrupt* qualifier.

■ **FACT:** *When you declare a function with the* interrupt *qualifier, the C compiler treats the
function as an interrupt handler, which entails saving the contents of the current registers
and using the IRET instruction to return from the function (as opposed to RET).*

In most cases your program should save the current interrupt vector before you use
_dos_setvect to change it. The run-time library function *_dos_getvect* lets you do so. Before
your program ends, it can then use *_dos_setvect* to restore the original contents of the interrupt vector.

■ **FACT:** *The* _dos_getvect *function returns a far pointer to the interrupt handler for the
specified interrupt. The function uses DOS service 0x35.*

The following program (CTRL-C2.C) changes CTRL-C.C slightly to save the current
Int 0x23 handler before changing it. Before the program ends, it restores the original contents of the vector.

```
#include <dos.h>     /* needed for _dos_getvect and _dos_setvect */
#include <stdio.h>  /* needed for getchar and EOF */

main()
{
    void far interrupt ctrlc_handler(void);
    void (far interrupt *save_vect) ();

    save_vect = _dos_getvect(0x23);

    if (_dos_setvect(0x23, ctrlc_handler))
        puts("Error setting handler");
    else
        {
        puts("Press Ctrl-Break to test interrupt handler");
        while (getchar() != EOF)
            { ; }
        _dos_setvect(0x23, save_vect);
        }
}

void far interrupt ctrlc_handler(void)
{
    printf("Press Ctrl-Z and Enter to quit\n");
}
```

■ **FACT:** *The* _dos_keep *function directs DOS to install the current program as a memory resident program (often called a* terminate and stay resident *program, or* TSR). *The routine uses DOS service 0x31.*

The general format of a call to *_dos_keep* is as follows:

```
_dos_keep(exit_status, memory_size);
```

The *exit_status* argument is the value the program returns to DOS, and *memory_size* is the number of 16-byte paragraphs the program needs to reserve for variables and stack space. (A brief discussion of memory resident programs would be dangerous. The topic requires book-length treatment.)

When a DOS service fails, it returns an error status. The C run-time library function *dosexterr* returns specific error information.

■ **FACT:** *The* dosexterr *function returns a structure containing specific information about the failure of a DOS system service. The function uses DOS service 0x59 to determine the source of the error.*

The include file dos.h defines the structure DOSERROR, which contains the following members:

```
struct DOSERROR {
    int exterror;
    char class;
    char action;
    char locus;
    };
```

The member *exterror* contains the DOS extended error code. Possible values for *exterror* include those described in the following table:

Value (Dec.)	Value (Hex.)	Meaning
0	0x00	Successful call
1	0x01	Invalid service number
2	0x02	File not found
3	0x03	Path not found
4	0x04	Too many files open
5	0x05	Access denied
6	0x06	Invalid file handle
7	0x07	Memory control blocks destroyed
8	0x08	Insufficient memory
9	0x09	Invalid memory-block address
10	0x0A	Invalid environment
11	0x0B	Invalid format
12	0x0C	Invalid access code
13	0x0D	Invalid data
14	0x0E	Reserved for future use
15	0x0F	Invalid drive
16	0x10	Attempt to remove current directory
17	0x11	Not same device
18	0x12	No more files
19	0x13	Disk is write protected
20	0x14	Unknown unit
21	0x15	Drive not ready
22	0x16	Unknown command
23	0x17	CRC data error
24	0x18	Bad request-structure length
25	0x19	Seek error
26	0x1A	Not a DOS disk

(continued)

continued

Value (Dec.)	Value (Hex.)	Meaning
27	0x1B	Sector not found
28	0x1C	Printer out of paper
29	0x1D	Write fault
30	0x1E	Read fault
31	0x1F	General failure
32	0x20	Sharing violation
33	0x21	Lock violation
34	0x22	Disk change invalid
35	0x23	File control block unavailable
36	0x24	Network busy
37	0x25	Reserved for future use
38	0x26	Handle end of file not completed
39–49	0x27–0x31	Reserved for future use
50	0x32	Network support unavailable
51	0x33	Remote computer down
52	0x34	Network name duplicated
53	0x35	Network name not found
54	0x36	Network busy
55	0x37	No such network device
56	0x38	Net BIOS limit exceeded
57	0x39	Network hardware error
58	0x3A	Incorrect network response
59	0x3B	Unexpected network error
60	0x3C	Remote adapter incompatible
61	0x3D	Print queue full
62	0x3E	Queue not full
63	0x3F	Print file deleted
64	0x40	Network name deleted
65	0x41	Access denied
66	0x42	Incorrect network device
67	0x43	Network name not found
68	0x44	Network name limit exceeded
69	0x45	Net BIOS limit exceeded
70	0x46	Temporarily paused
71	0x47	Network request not accepted
72	0x48	Printer and disk redirection paused

(continued)

continued

Value (Dec.)	Value (Hex.)	Meaning
73–79	0x49–0x4F	Reserved for future use
80	0x50	File already exists
81	0x51	Reserved for future use
82	0x52	Cannot make directory
83	0x53	Fail on Int 0x24
84	0x54	Too many redirections
85	0x55	Duplicate redirections
86	0x56	Invalid password
87	0x57	Invalid parameter
88	0x58	Network data fault
89	0x59	Function not supported on network
90	0x5A	Required system component not installed

The member *class* provides information about the type of error. Common values include the following:

Value (Dec.)	Value (Hex.)	Class
1	0x01	Out of resource
2	0x02	Temporary error—delay and try again
3	0x03	Authorization error
4	0x04	Internal system error
5	0x05	Hardware error
6	0x06	System failure
7	0x07	Application program error
8	0x08	Item not found
9	0x09	Bad format
10	0x0A	Item currently locked
11	0x0B	Medium failure
12	0x0C	Item already exists
13	0x0D	Unknown

The member *action* specifies recommended actions:

Value	Action
1	Retry operation
2	Delay and then retry
3	User reentry
4	Abort application after closing files
5	Abort immediately
6	Ignore error
7	Retry after user intervention

The member *locus* provides information to help you determine the specific location of the error. Common values include the following:

Value	Meaning
1	Unknown source
2	Disk error
3	Network error
4	Serial device error
5	Memory error

By using *dosexterr*, you can often determine the source of an error and respond accordingly.

The following program (GETERROR.C) tries to open a file on a nonexistent disk drive (drive G). The program then calls *dosexterr* to determine the cause of the error.

```
#include <dos.h>     /* needed for dosexterr and DOSERROR struct */
#include <stdio.h>   /* needed for fopen */

main()
{
    FILE *fp;
    char buffer[64];
    struct DOSERROR error;

    fp = fopen("g:test", "r");

    dosexterr(&error);
    printf("Extended error %d  Class %d  Locus %d  Action %d\n",
            error.exterror, error.class, error.locus, error.action);
}
```

When you run the program, your screen shows

`Extended error 3  Class 8  Locus 2  Action 3`

If you check the extended error in the table, you find the message "Path not found" corresponding to error value 3. The class reveals "Item not found." The locus indicates that the error is disk related, and the action tells you to specify a new drive.

SUMMARY

DOS System Services

■ **FACT:** *The* bdos *function lets you invoke DOS system services that require arguments in only the AL and DX registers. After the service call is completed,* bdos *returns the value that the DOS service placed in the AX register.*

■ **FACT:** *DOS service 0x2 writes the ASCII character identified in the DX register. It places the character at the current location of the cursor.*

■ **FACT:** *DOS service 0x19 returns the drive number of the current disk drive in the AX register. The service does not use values for the DX and AL registers.*

■ **FACT:** *The* intdos *function assigns the values in the REGS union to the appropriate general-purpose registers. Next the function calls Int 0x21 to access the requested system service. When the system call returns,* intdos *copies the new register contents back into the union members.*

■ **FACT:** *DOS service 0x2C places the current system time in the CX and DX registers. The hours reside in CH, the minutes in CL. The seconds and hundredths of a second reside in DH and DL.*

■ **FACT:** *DOS service 0x2A returns the current system date. The service places the day of the week in the AL register (Sunday = 0, Monday = 1, and so on), the year in CX, the month in DH, and the day in DL.*

■ **FACT:** *The* segread *function reads the segment registers and assigns them to members of a structure of type SREGS.*

■ **FACT:** *DOS service 0x47 assigns a null-terminated string containing the current directory to a 64-byte buffer. The service uses the value in DL to determine the disk drive to which the request applies. The register DS contains the segment address of the 64-byte buffer, and SI contains the offset address of the buffer.*

■ **FACT:** *Before it invokes Int 0x21, the* intdosx *function places values not only in the general-purpose registers but also in the segment registers.*

Using Run-Time Library Services for DOS

■ **FACT:** *The* _dos_getdrive *function returns the drive number of the current disk drive, where A = 1, B = 2, C = 3, and so on. The function uses DOS service 0x1C.*

■ **FACT:** *The* _dos_setdrive *function sets (changes) the current disk drive based on the specified drive number. The function also assigns the maximum number of available drives to the second argument. The function uses DOS service 0xE.*

■ **FACT:** *The* _dos_getdiskfree *function returns the number of free and used bytes on the specified disk. The function uses DOS service 0x36. If it obtains the requested information,* _dos_getdiskfree *returns 0; if* _dos_getdiskfree *is unable to get the information, it returns an error status.*

■ **FACT:** *The* _dos_open *function opens the specified file. The function uses DOS service 0x3D to get a file handle for use by the other file manipulation services. If it obtains a handle,* _dos_open *returns 0; if an error occurs,* _dos_open *returns an error status.*

■ **FACT:** *The* _dos_creat *function creates a nonexisting file or truncates an existing file. The function uses DOS service 0x3C to get a file handle. If it obtains a file handle as requested,* _dos_creat *returns 0; if* _dos_creat *cannot provide a file handle, it returns an error status.*

■ **FACT:** *The* _dos_creatnew *function creates a file with the specified name. If a file exists on disk with the same name,* _dos_creatnew *returns an error status. If it creates the file as requested,* _dos_creatnew *returns 0. The function uses DOS service 0x5B.*

■ **FACT:** *The* _dos_read *function reads a specified number of bytes from a file into the specified buffer. If* _dos_read *gains access to the file, it returns 0; if an error occurs,* _dos_read *returns an error status. The function uses DOS service 0x3F.*

■ **FACT:** *The* _dos_write *function writes the contents of the specified buffer to a file. The function uses DOS service 0x40. If it writes the buffer contents as requested,* _dos_write *returns 0; if an error occurs,* _dos_write *returns an error status.*

■ **FACT:** *The* _dos_close *function closes a file that is open for read or write operations. The function uses DOS service 0x3E.*

■ **FACT:** *The* _dos_getftime *function uses a file handle to obtain a file's date and time stamps (the date and time a file was created or last modified). The function uses DOS service 0x57. If* _dos_getftime *gets the date and time information, it returns 0; if an error occurs,* _dos_getftime *returns an error status.*

■ **FACT:** *The* _dos_setftime *function assigns new date and time stamps to the file associated with the specified handle. The function uses DOS service 0x57. If it alters the date and time stamps as requested, the function returns 0; if an error occurs,* _dos_setftime *returns an error status.*

■ **FACT:** *The* _dos_getfileattr *function returns the file attribute for the specified file. The function uses DOS service 0x43. If it obtains the attribute,* _dos_getfileattr *returns 0; if it is unable to get the attribute, it returns an error status.*

■ **FACT:** *The* _dos_setfileattr *function sets the attribute of the specified file. The function uses DOS service 0x43. If it sets the attribute,* _dos_setfileattr *returns 0; if an error occurs,* _dos_setfileattr *returns an error status.*

■ **FACT:** *The* _dos_setdate *function sets the DOS system date to the date specified in a structure of type* dosdate_t. *The function uses DOS service 0x2B. If it sets the system date,* _dos_setdate *returns 0; if* _dos_setdate *cannot change the date as requested, it returns an error status.*

■ **FACT:** *The* _dos_settime *function sets the current system time to the value specified in a structure of type* dostime_t. *The function uses DOS service 0x2D. If it sets the time,* _dos_settime *returns 0; if an error occurs,* _dos_settime *returns an error status.*

■ **FACT:** *The* _dos_allocmem *function uses DOS service 0x48 to allocate the requested number of 16-byte paragraphs. The function assigns the location of the memory to the second argument. If it succeeds, the function returns 0; if it cannot allocate the requested memory,* _dos_allocmem *returns an error status.*

■ **FACT:** *The* _dos_setblock *function lets you change the size of memory previously allocated with* _dos_allocmem. *The function uses DOS service 0x4A. If it resizes the memory block,* _dos_setblock *returns 0; if an error occurs, the function returns an error status. If the available memory is not sufficient to meet the request, the third argument contains the size of the largest available block.*

■ **FACT:** *The* _dos_freemem *function releases the memory associated with the specified pointer. The function uses DOS service 0x49. If it releases the memory,* _dos_freemem *returns 0; if an error occurs, the function returns an error status.*

■ **TRAP:** *Although the* _dos_allocmem, _dos_setblock, *and* _dos_freemem *functions let you allocate and manipulate memory dynamically, they are less portable than* calloc *and* malloc.

■ **FACT:** *The* _dos_setvect *function sets the interrupt vector that points to the handler for the specified interrupt to the specified far pointer address. The function uses DOS service 0x25. If* _dos_setvect *registers the new handler, it returns 0; if an error occurs, the function returns an error status.*

■ **FACT:** *When you declare a function with the* interrupt *qualifier, the C compiler treats the function as an interrupt handler, which entails saving the contents of the current registers and using the IRET instruction to return from the function (as opposed to RET).*

■ **FACT:** *The* _dos_getvect *function returns a far pointer to the interrupt handler for the specified interrupt. The function uses DOS service 0x35.*

■ **FACT:** *The* _dos_keep *function directs DOS to install the current program as a memory resident program (often called a* terminate and stay resident *program, or* TSR*). The function uses DOS service 0x31.*

■ **FACT:** *The* dosexterr *function returns a structure containing specific information about the failure of a DOS system service. The function uses DOS service 0x59 to determine the source of the error.*

GLOSSARY

general-purpose registers A collection of fast storage locations that are built into the CPU (Intel 80x86 family). These registers serve as your interface to the DOS system services. The general-purpose registers include AX, BX, CX, and DX. Programs can access these registers as 16-bit registers or as a series of (low-order and high-order) 8-bit registers, named AL, AH, BL, BH, CL, CH, DL, and DH.

system services A collection of routines built into the operating system and essential to its functioning. Because these routines are always present in memory, the DOS developers have made them available to your programs by means of a software interrupt, Int 0x21. Under OS/2, system services comprise the Application Program Interface and are available via far calls to named entry points.

## CHAPTER 33

Using the ROM BIOS

In Chapter 32 you learned that DOS contains a series of powerful services that you can access from your C programs. In a similar manner, the IBM PC (and compatibles) and IBM PS/2 models have a collection of routines built into read-only memory (ROM) that perform basic input and output services. This collection of routines is commonly referred to as the ROM BIOS services.

In this chapter you learn how to access these services from within your C programs. You'll find that accessing BIOS services is similar to calling the DOS system services, as shown in Chapter 32.

UNDERSTANDING THE INTERFACE

Just as the DOS services use Int 0x21 as their interface, the ROM BIOS services use unique interrupt numbers for specific services.[†] For example, the video services use Int 0x10, and the BIOS disk services use Int 0x13.

To access the BIOS system services, assembly language programmers assign arguments to specific general-purpose registers. Then they invoke the specific BIOS interrupt. To simplify your interface to the BIOS services, C provides the run-time library routines *int86* and *int86x*.

■ **FACT:** *The* int86 *function places the members of a REGS union in the general-purpose registers and then invokes the specified BIOS interrupt. When the service call returns,* int86 *assigns the ending values in the general-purpose registers to the members of another union.*

[†]As your guide to these services, I strongly recommend Ray Duncan's *IBM ROM BIOS: Programmer's Quick Reference* (Microsoft Press, 1988). The book discusses each of the available BIOS services.

The following program (BLUEBIO.C) uses *int86* to display the message *Video BIOS Call* in blue on your screen. The interrupt specified is 0x10 because this task requires the video BIOS.

```c
#include <bios.h>  /* needed for int86 and REGS */

main()
{
    char *str = "Video BIOS Call";
    int column = 20;
    union REGS inregs, outregs;

    /* set the cursor to row 10, column 20 */
    inregs.h.ah = 2;              /* service number */
    inregs.h.bh = 0;              /* display page */
    inregs.h.dh = 10;             /* row 10 */
    inregs.h.dl = column;         /* column 20 */
    int86(0x10, &inregs, &outregs);

    while (*str)
        {
        /* display the character and attribute */
        inregs.h.ah = 9;          /* service number */
        inregs.h.al = *str++;     /* character to display */
        inregs.h.bh = 0;          /* video display page */
        inregs.h.bl = 1;          /* color */
        inregs.x.cx = 1;          /* count of characters */
        int86(0x10, &inregs, &outregs);

        /* set the cursor to same row next column */
        inregs.h.ah = 2;          /* service number */
        inregs.h.bh = 0;          /* display page */
        inregs.h.dh = 10;         /* row 10 */
        inregs.h.dl = ++column;   /* next column */
        int86(0x10, &inregs, &outregs);
        }
}
```

To position and display text the program uses two video BIOS services: Set Cursor Position and Write Character and Attribute.

■ **FACT:** *The video BIOS service 0x2 directs the BIOS to set the cursor to the row and column position specified in the registers DH and DL. The service sets the cursor for the video display page specified in BH (usually 0).*

■ **FACT:** *The video BIOS service 0x9 writes the character and attribute specified in the AL and BL registers to the display page contained in BH. The CX register contains a count of the number of times you want the service to write the character.*

Several ROM BIOS disk services require both segment and offset addresses for input and output buffers. The C run-time library function *int86x* lets you pass an SREGS structure to the BIOS services. For example, the following statement,

```
int86x(0x14, &inregs, &outregs, &segregs);
```

loads general-purpose registers and segment registers with the values assigned to *inregs* and *segregs* and then calls Int 0x14. When the interrupt returns, *int86x* copies register values to *outregs* and *segregs*.

■ **FACT:** *The* int86x *function not only places values in the general-purpose registers before invoking a BIOS service, but it also places values in the segment registers.*

As you learned in Chapter 32 when you looked at *intdosx*, you can usually pass the segment register values returned by *segreads*. In most cases, the same technique works with calls to *int86x*.

USING PREDEFINED BIOS RUN-TIME LIBRARY ROUTINES

To simplify your interface to the ROM BIOS services, the C run-time library provides a collection of functions that access specific services. You used one such function, *_bios_keybrd*, in Chapter 29 to enhance your keyboard control. In this section we examine the other BIOS services available through the run-time library.

■ **FACT:** *The _bios_memsize function returns the total amount of conventional memory (memory under 640 KB) installed in your computer. The value returned is in 1024-byte (1 KB) units. The function uses BIOS interrupt 0x12.*

The following program (MEMSIZE.C) uses *_bios_memsize* to display the amount of conventional memory physically connected to the system:

```
#include <bios.h>   /* needed for _bios_memsize */

main()
{
    printf("Total conventional memory in system:  %u KB\n",
           _bios_memsize());
}
```

Much like _bios_memsize, the run-time library function _bios_equiplist lets you determine the hardware connected to the system.

■ **FACT:** *The* _bios_equiplist *function returns an unsigned integer whose bit settings indicate the equipment present in the system. The function uses BIOS interrupt 0x11.*

The following table describes the significance of specific bits in the value returned by _bios_equiplist:

Bit(s)	Meaning
0	1 = at least one floppy disk present
1	1 = math coprocessor present
2–3	System memory (original IBM PC only):
	00 = 16 KB
	01 = 32 KB
	10 = 48 KB
	11 = 64 KB
4–5	Initial video mode:
	01 = 40×25 color
	10 = 80×25 color
	11 = 80×25 mono
6–7	Number of floppy disks:
	00 = 1
	01 = 2
	10 = 3
	11 = 4
9–11	Number of serial ports
12	1 = game adapter present
14–15	Number of printers

In some cases programs need to make processing decisions based on available hardware. The _bios_equiplist function lets your programs access the computer's hardware checklist. The following program (HARDWARE.C) uses _bios_equiplist to display the current equipment list.

```
#include <bios.h>  /* needed for _bios_equiplist */

main()
{
    unsigned int equipment;

    equipment = _bios_equiplist();

    if (equipment & 2)
        printf("Math coprocessor present\n");

    printf("Initial video mode %d\n", (equipment & 0x30) >> 4);

    printf("Number of floppy disks %d\n", 1 + ((equipment & 0xC0) >> 6));

    printf("Number of serial ports %d\n", (equipment & 0x300) >> 9);

    if (equipment & 0x1000)
        printf("Game adapter present\n");

    printf("Number of parallel printers %d\n", (equipment & 0xC000) >> 14);
}
```

The BIOS services support I/O operations to your video display, disk, keyboard, serial port, and parallel printer. The C run-time library function _bios_printer provides your programs an interface to the parallel printer.

■ **FACT:** *The* _bios_printer *function uses BIOS interrupt 0x17 services to initialize, determine the status of, or write to the current printer.*

The general format of a call to _bios_printer is as follows:

status = _bios_printer(*service, printer, data*);

The *service* argument identifies one of the following printer constants:

Service	Meaning
_PRINTER_WRITE	Writes the character specified and returns status
_PRINTER_INIT	Initializes printer and returns status
_PRINTER_STATUS	Gets printer status

The *printer* argument specifies the parallel printer of interest (0 for LPT1, 1 for LPT2, and so on). The *data* argument contains the character to write when the function uses the _PRINTER_WRITE service.

The _bios_printer function returns an unsigned integer whose bits contain the current printer status, as shown on the following page.

Bit(s)	Meaning
0	Printer timed out
1–2	Reserved for future use
3	I/O error
4	Printer selected
5	Printer out of paper
6	Printer acknowledgment
7	Printer not busy

The following program (CHKPRN.C) checks the status of the printer until the user presses a key. Run the program and then turn the printer on and off, remove and replace the paper, and so on. The program displays status information on the screen when the printer status changes.

```
#include <bios.h>  /* needed for _bios_printer and _bios_keybrd */
#define F10 (68 << 8)

main()
{
    unsigned int old_state, current_state;
    int done = 0;

    printf("** Change printer states - Press F10 to end **\n");

    do
        {
        current_state = _bios_printer(_PRINTER_STATUS, 0, 0);

        if (current_state != old_state)
            {
            printf("Current states:  ");
            if (current_state & 1)
                printf("Printer timeout, ");
            if (current_state & 8)
                printf("Printer I/O errror, ");
            if (current_state & 16)
                printf("Printer selected, ");
            if (current_state & 32)
                printf("Printer out of paper, ");
            if (current_state & 64)
                printf("Printer ACK, ");
            if (current_state & 128)
                printf("Printer not busy, ");
            printf("\n");
```

(continued)

continued

```
            old_state = current_state;
            }
        if (_bios_keybrd(_KEYBRD_READY))
            if (_bios_keybrd(_KEYBRD_READ) == F10)
                done = 1;
        }
    while (!done);
}
```

The BIOS also provides services that support the serial port.

■ **FACT:** *The* _bios_serialcom *function uses BIOS interrupt 0x14 services to access the serial port.*

The general format of a call to *_bios_serialcom* is as follows:

status = _bios_serialcom(*service, port, data*);

The *service* argument specifies one of the services available through Int 0x14, as follows:

Service	*Meaning*
_COM_INIT	Initializes the serial port to the communications settings provided
_COM_SEND	Writes a character to the serial port
_COM_RECEIVE	Reads a character from the serial port
_COM_STATUS	Returns the current serial port status

The value of the *port* argument is 0 for COM1, 1 for COM2, and so on. The *data* argument contains the characters to write if the function specifies the _COM_SEND service, and the serial port communication settings if it specifies the _COM_INIT service.

The include file bios.h defines several communications arguments that you can use to initialize the serial port. The following program (INITCOM1.C) initializes the serial port COM1 to 9600 baud, 8 data bits, no parity, and 1 stop bit.

```
#include <bios.h>  /* needed for _bios_serialcom */

main()
{
    /* set the communications parameters */
    _bios_serialcom(_COM_INIT, 0 /* COM1 */, _COM_9600 : _COM_CHR8 :
                    _COM_NOPARITY : _COM_STOP1);

    /* remainder of program code */
}
```

For the _COM_INIT or _COM_STATUS services, _bios_serialcom_ returns a two-part value: The 8 low-order bits contain the modem status, whereas the 8 high-order bits contain the port status. The individual bits have the following specific meanings:

Bit	Meaning
0	Change in clear to send
1	Change in data set ready
2	Trailing edge ring indicator
3	Change in receiving line signal detect
4	Clear to send
5	Data set ready
6	Ring indicator
7	Receive line signal detect
8	Receive data ready
9	Data overrun error
10	Parity error
11	Framing error
12	Break detected
13	Transmit holding register empty
14	Transmit shift register empty
15	Timeout error

In addition to device control, the BIOS provides access to the system clock.

■ **FACT:** *The _bios_timeofday function uses BIOS interrupt 0x1A services to get or set the current clock count. For PC or PS/2 models, clock ticks occur 18.2 times per second.*

The general format of a call to _bios_timeofday_ is as follows:

```
status = _bios_timeofday(service, &count);
```

The *service* argument directs _bios_timeofday_ to get or set the clock ticks, as follows:

Service	Meaning
_TIME_GETCLOCK	Get clock ticks
_TIME_SETCLOCK	Set clock ticks

The *count* argument is a *long int* value. It receives the current clock ticks obtained by _bios_timeofday_, or it contains the number of clock ticks to which you want to set the clock. If you specify _TIME_GETCLOCK, you can test *status* to determine whether the clock has been reset to zero (has passed midnight) since the clock was last read.

The following program (BIOTIME.C) uses _bios_timeofday to implement a timed read function. The function get_timed_char returns the hexadecimal scan code and ASCII code of the key pressed by the user; it returns 0 if the specified time interval expires before the read operation occurs.

```
#include <bios.h>   /* needed for _bios_timeofday and _bios_keybrd */

main()
{
    unsigned int get_timed_char ();

    puts("Press a key in the allotted time and see its character value.");
    printf("value is %x\n", get_timed_char("You have 8 seconds...", 8));
    printf("value is %x\n", get_timed_char("You have 5 seconds...", 5));
    printf("value is %x\n", get_timed_char("You have 2 seconds...", 2));
}

unsigned int get_timed_char(char *prompt, int interval)
{
    long int start_time, current_time;

    printf("%s ", prompt);

    /* get current time in clock ticks */
    _bios_timeofday(_TIME_GETCLOCK, &start_time);

    interval *= 18.2;   /* 18.2 clock ticks per second */
    do
        _bios_timeofday(_TIME_GETCLOCK, &current_time);
    while ((current_time - start_time < interval)
            && !_bios_keybrd(_KEYBRD_READY));

    return (_bios_keybrd(_KEYBRD_READY) ? _bios_keybrd(_KEYBRD_READ) : 0);
}
```

The ROM BIOS also provides a set of services that support disk I/O operations.

■ **FACT:** *The* _bios_disk *function uses BIOS interrupt 0x13 services to access the disk; the function provides a set of diverse disk I/O services.*

The general format of a call to _bios_disk is as follows:

status = _bios_disk(*service*, *&diskstructure*);

The *service* argument specifies the BIOS disk service to request when the function calls Int 0x13. You can identify these services by using one of the constants listed in the table on the following page.

Service	Meaning
_DISK_RESET	Resets the disk controller
_DISK_STATUS	Gets disk status
_DISK_READ	Reads specific disk sectors
_DISK_WRITE	Writes specific disk sectors
_DISK_VERIFY	Verifies disk sectors
_DISK_FORMAT	Formats a track on the disk

The *disk_structure* argument is a structure of type *diskinfo_t*, which is defined in bios.h as follows:

```
struct diskinfo_t {
    unsigned drive;
    unsigned head;
    unsigned track;
    unsigned sector;
    unsigned nsectors;
    void far *buffer;
    };
```

If *_bios_disk* performs the requested service, it returns zero in the high-order byte. Otherwise, *_bios_disk* sets the high-order byte in the return value to one of the nonzero status values in the following table:

Error Code	Meaning	Disk Type
0	No error	Hard/floppy
1	Invalid command	Hard/floppy
2	Address mark not found	Hard/floppy
3	Disk write protected	Floppy
4	Sector not found	Hard/floppy
5	Reset failed	Hard
6	Disk removed	Floppy
7	Bad parameters table	Hard
8	DMA overrun	Floppy
9	DMA across 64 KB boundary	Hard/floppy
10	Bad sectors	Hard
11	Bad track	Hard
12	Medium type not found	Floppy
13	Invalid number of sectors	Hard
14	Control data address mark found	Hard

(continued)

continued

Error Code	Meaning	Disk Type
15	Bad DMA arbitration level	Hard
16	CRC or ECC error	Hard/floppy
17	Correctable ECC error	Hard
32	Disk controller failed	Hard/floppy
64	Seek failed	Hard/floppy
128	Disk time out	Hard/floppy
170	Drive not ready	Hard
187	Undefined error	Hard
204	Write fault	Hard
224	Status register error	Hard
255	Sense operation failure	Hard

The following program (DCOPY.C) uses the _bios_disk function to copy the contents of one 360 KB floppy disk in drive A to a disk in drive B. The program does not provide any error checking nor does it format the target disk. A 360 KB disk uses tracks 0 through 39 and sectors 1 through 9.

```
#include <bios.h>   /* needed for _bios_disk and diskinfo_t struct */

main()
{
    char buffer[1024];

    struct diskinfo_t input, output;
    int head, track, sector;

    input.drive = 0;    /* drive A */
    output.drive = 1;   /* drive B */
    input.buffer = (void far *) buffer;
    output.buffer = (void far *) buffer;
    input.nsectors = 1;
    output.nsectors = 1;

    for (head = 0; head <= 1; head++)
        {
        input.head = head;
        output.head = head;
```

(continued)

continued

```
        for (track = 0; track <= 39; track++)
            {
            input.track = track;
            output.track = track;

            for (sector = 1; sector <= 9; sector++)
                {
                input.sector = sector;
                output.sector = sector;
                _bios_disk (_DISK_READ, &input);
                _bios_disk (_DISK_WRITE, &output);
                }
            }
        }
    }
```

At one time, programmers who wanted to take advantage of the BIOS services had to use assembly language routines. As you can see, the C run-time library makes the BIOS services more easily accessible.

SUMMARY

Understanding the Interface

■ **FACT:** *The* int86 *function places the members of a REGS union in the general-purpose registers and then invokes the specified BIOS interrupt. When the service call returns,* int86 *assigns the ending values in the general-purpose registers to the members of another union.*

■ **FACT:** *The video BIOS service 0x2 directs the BIOS to set the cursor to the row and column position specified in the registers DH and DL. The service sets the cursor for the video display page specified in BH (usually 0).*

■ **FACT:** *The video BIOS service 0x9 writes the character and attribute specified in the AL and BL registers to the display page contained in BH. The CX register contains a count of the number of times you want the service to write the character.*

■ **FACT:** *The* int86x *function not only places values in the general-purpose registers before invoking a BIOS service, but it also places values in the segment registers.*

Using Predefined BIOS Run-Time Library Routines

■ **FACT:** *The* _bios_getmem *function returns the total amount of conventional memory (memory under 640 KB) installed in your computer. The value returned is in 1024-byte (1 KB) units. The function uses BIOS interrupt 0x12.*

■ **FACT:** *The* _bios_equiplist *function returns an unsigned integer whose bit settings indicate the equipment present in the system. The function uses BIOS interrupt 0x11.*

■ **FACT:** *The* _bios_printer *function uses BIOS interrupt 0x17 services to initialize, determine the status of, or write to the current printer.*

■ **FACT:** *The* _bios_serialcom *function uses BIOS interrupt 0x14 services to access the serial port.*

■ **FACT:** *The* _bios_timeofday *function uses BIOS interrupt 0x1A services to get or set the current clock count. For PC or PS/2 models, clock ticks occur 18.2 times per second.*

■ **FACT:** *The* _bios_disk *function uses BIOS interrupt 0x13 services to access the disk; the function provides a set of diverse disk I/O services.*

GLOSSARY

BIOS services A collection of routines built into the read-only memory (ROM) of IBM PCs (and compatibles) and PS/2 models. These services perform basic input/output services for video, keyboard, disk, printer, and serial port I/O.

clock tick A time increment that occurs 18.2 times per second in the CPU of the IBM PC (and compatibles) and PS/2 models.

## CHAPTER 34

Getting the Most from Text Display

With the exception of one or two ROM BIOS routines in Chapter 33, our program output to the video display has all been produced with *putchar, puts,* or *printf.* Although this has proven quite functional, the output lacks the flair you expect from professional programs. In this lesson we take a look at several ways to enhance the output of your programs with C run-time library routines.

Specifically, you learn how to set the background colors on your screen, use video pages for fast I/O, restrict your program's output to a specific window, and write your output using any of 16 available colors.

All these capabilities exist within the C run-time library. Unlike the programs in Chapter 2, which use the ANSI driver to obtain video capabilities, the programs in this chapter rely only on the C run-time library. As you will quickly find, color gives your programs a professional flair.

DETERMINING A MACHINE'S VIDEO CAPABILITIES

Not all machines are equal. Some PCs have monochrome monitors, whereas others have color graphics monitors using CGA, EGA, MDPA, MCGA, or VGA *video adapters.* If you develop an application that uses the video capabilities discussed in this chapter, the application must first find out the video capabilities of the computer on which it is running and then use color and graphics accordingly. To obtain video information, use the C run-time library function _getvideoconfig, which places information about the computer's video capabilities in a structure of type *videoconfig*.

■ **FACT:** *The* _getvideoconfig *function assigns values to a structure containing the maximum number of picture elements (pixels), the number of rows and columns for text display, the number of video display pages, the display adapter type, and the amount of video memory the adapter provides.*

The include file defines the *videoconfig* structure, which contains the following members:

```
struct videoconfig {
        short numxpixels;        /* number of pixels on x-axis */
        short numypixels;        /* number of pixels on y-axis */
        short numtextcols;       /* number of text columns available */
        short numtextrows;       /* number of text rows available */
        short numcolors;         /* number of actual colors */
        short bitsperpixel;      /* number of bits per pixel */
        short numvideopages;     /* number of available video pages */
        short mode;              /* current video mode */
        short adapter;           /* active display adapter */
        short monitor;           /* active display monitor */
        short memory;            /* adapter video memory in kilobytes */
};
```

In graphics mode, your computer draws images and lines by lighting sets of small screen locations, called *pixels* (picture elements). The first two members of the *videoconfig* structure are related to screen *resolution*: The first gives the number of pixels on the x-axis (horizontally) followed by the number of pixels along the y-axis (vertically). The density of pixels depends on the particular monitor you own. The more pixels per square inch, the sharper the image.

The next two members, *numtextcols* and *numtextrows*, contain the number of columns and rows the screen makes available for text display. In most cases these values are 80 columns and 25 rows. The *numcolors* member contains the number of distinct colors available to your program. The *bitsperpixel* member tells the number of bits used to represent each pixel displayed on the screen. The greater the number of bits, the more colors the video configuration can support.

Many adapters have multiple video pages available; your program can write to one video page while displaying another. When the user is ready for the next screenful of information, the program can simply make the new page visible. Because the program has already written the information to the *video display page*, output appears instantaneously. Your choice of video adapter determines the number of display pages available.

The *mode* member specifies the current *video mode*, and the next two arguments, *adapter* and *monitor*, identify the video adapter and type of monitor installed. The last member, *memory*, specifies the amount of memory, in kilobytes, that the adapter supplies.

The following program (VIDEOCFG.C) uses the *_getvideoconfig* function and the *videoconfig* structure to display the current video configuration:

```c
#include <graph.h>  /* needed for _getvideoconfig and videoconfig struct */

main()
{
    struct videoconfig video;

    _getvideoconfig(&video);

    printf("X axis pixels:  %d\nY axis pixels:  %d\n",
            video.numxpixels, video.numypixels);
    printf("Text rows:  %d\nText columns:  %d\n",
            video.numtextrows, video.numtextcols);
    printf("Number of colors supported:  %d\n",
            video.numcolors);
    printf("Number of bits per pixel:  %d\n",
            video.bitsperpixel);
    printf("Number of video display pages:  %d\n",
            video.numvideopages);
    printf("Current video mode:  %d\n", video.mode);

    switch (video.adapter)
        {
        case _CGA:  printf("CGA adapter\n");
                    break;
        case _EGA:  printf("EGA adapter\n");
                    break;
        case _MDPA: printf("MDPA adapter\n");
                    break;
        case _MCGA: printf("MCGA adapter\n");
                    break;
        case _VGA:  printf("VGA adapter\n");
                    break;
        };

    switch (video.monitor)
        {
        case _ANALOG:   printf("Analog monitor\n");
                        break;
        case _COLOR:    printf("Color monitor\n");
                        break;
```

(continued)

continued

```
        case _ENHCOLOR: printf("Enhanced color monitor\n");
                        break;
        case _MONO:     printf("Monochrome monitor\n");
                        break;
        };

    printf("Video memory present:  %d KB\n", video.memory);
}
```

To compile this program, direct CL to link to the GRAPHICS.LIB run-time library. By default, the compiler does not use the file GRAPHICS.LIB. To direct CL to link with GRAPHICS.LIB, you must specify the library file in the CL command line. If this library resides in the directory \LIB, for example, your CL command line becomes

```
C> CL VIDEOCFG.C \LIB\GRAPHICS.LIB
```

The information supplied by calling *_getvideoconfig* is often essential for subsequent processing. After you determine the system's video configuration, you can invoke the run-time library video routines appropriately.

CLEARING THE SCREEN

In Chapter 2 you learned how to clear your screen with the ANSI escape sequence *Esc[2J*. If your program is linked with the GRAPHICS.LIB library file, you can use the run-time library function *_clearscreen* to clear your screen.

■ **FACT:** *The* _clearscreen *function clears your screen in both text and graphics modes.*

The *_clearscreen* function lets you clear your screen display in either text mode or graphics mode. As you learn later in this chapter, the C run-time library allows you to create a window on your screen. Using the *_clearscreen* function with one of the following constants, you can clear the entire screen, the graphics viewport, or the text window:

Parameter	Meaning
_GCLEARSCREEN	Clears the entire screen display
_GVIEWPORT	Clears the graphics viewport
_GWINDOW	Clears the text window

The following program (CLRTEST.C) clears the screen and displays the letters of the alphabet five times.

```
#include <graph.h>  /* needed for _clearscreen */
#include <stdio.h>  /* needed for putchar */

main()
{
    char letter;
    int i;

    _clearscreen(_GCLEARSCREEN);

    for (i = 0; i < 5; ++i)
        {
        for (letter = 'A'; letter <= 'Z'; ++letter)
            putchar(letter);
        putchar('\n');
        }
}
```

DISPLAYING TEXT IN COLOR WITH _outtext

Later in this chapter you learn techniques for setting the screen background color and the foreground color (the color of your characters). Keep in mind, however, that these techniques do not work for routines such as *putchar, puts,* and *printf.* Instead, you must use a routine, such as the run-time library function *_outtext,* that specifically supports color output and text windows.

■ **FACT:** *The _outtext function displays a null-terminated ASCII string at the current text position. The function displays the characters of the string in the current foreground color.*

The *_outtext* function writes a string of characters to the screen. If your program needs to write numbers to the screen, first use the *sprintf* function to create a character string, and then use *_outtext* to display the string, as the following program (CLRPRINT.C) demonstrates:

```
#include <graph.h>  /* needed for _outtext */
#include <stdio.h>  /* needed for sprintf */

main()
{
    char str[164];

    sprintf(str, "This is Chapter %d\n", 34);
    _outtext(str);
}
```

By using *sprintf* in this way, your programs maintain the same output capabilities with *_outtext* that they normally possess with *printf.*

■ **FACT:** *The _settextcolor function sets the text foreground color that _outtext uses. The function returns the previous color value.*

The run-time library function *_settextcolor* lets you select one of 16 text foreground colors. Subsequent output by *_outtext* uses that color. Remember, routines such as *printf, putchar,* and *puts* don't use the color capabilities.

The following program (COLORS.C) loops through the 16 support colors and displays the following message using the specified color value in place of *n*:

```
The current color value is n
```

The COLORS program also displays a message with *printf* to show that *printf* does not use the text foreground color *_settextcolor* selects. Note that one of the lines will be invisible to you because the foreground color matches the background color.

```c
#include <graph.h>   /* needed for _clearscreen, _settextcolor, */
                     /* and _outtext */
#include <stdio.h>   /* needed for sprintf */

main()
{
    int i;
    char str[128];

    _clearscreen(_GCLEARSCREEN);

    for (i = 0; i < 16; i++)
        {
        _settextcolor(i);
        sprintf(str, "Current color value is %d\n", i);
        _outtext(str);
        }

    printf("Text displayed by printf unaffected by foreground color\n");
}
```

■ **FACT:** *In addition to the color values 0 through 15,* _settextcolor *lets you use the values 16 through 31 to specify the same colors but with the blinking attribute.*

The following program (COLORS2.C) uses *_settextcolor* with *_outtext* to display the nonblinking colors (values 0 through 15) and the blinking colors (values 16 through 31). Figure 34-1 summarizes the color values *_settextcolor* uses.

```
#include <graph.h>  /* needed for graphics functions */
#include <stdio.h>  /* needed for sprintf */

main()
{
    int i;
    char str[128];

    _clearscreen(_GCLEARSCREEN);

    for (i = 0; i < 32; i++)
        {
        _settextcolor(i);
        sprintf(str, "Current color value is %d\n", i);
        _outtext(str);
        }

    printf("Text displayed by printf unaffected by foreground color\n");
}
```

Color	Value	Color	Value
Black	0	Gray	8
Blue	1	Light blue	9
Green	2	Light green	10
Cyan	3	Light cyan	11
Red	4	Light red	12
Magenta	5	Light magenta	13
Brown	6	Light yellow	14
White	7	Bright white	15

FIGURE 34-1.
With _settextcolor, you can set the foreground to one of 16 colors, each of which has an associated color value.

■ **TRAP:** *Monochrome systems do not support color values. Instead, many of the color values map to monochrome display attributes.*

If you experiment with the color values on a monochrome system, you can discover a range of display attributes, such as reverse video, in which the foreground and background are swapped.

The C run-time library function _ *gettextcolor* returns the current foreground color.

■ **FACT:** *The* _gettextcolor *function returns the value for the current foreground color.*

Many user-defined functions call *_gettextcolor* to save the current color value before they change the foreground color. By saving the color value, a function can later restore the color to its original value. You can, however, often avoid a call to *_gettextcolor* by saving the value returned by *_settextcolor*. For example, the following pair of statements

```
save_color = _gettextcolor();
_settextcolor(BLUE);
```

accomplishes no more than a single call to *_settextcolor*, as follows:

```
save_color = _settextcolor(BLUE);
```

■ **TIP:** *Keep in mind that* _settextcolor *returns the previous foreground color. If you assign the return value to a variable, you can avoid a separate call to* _gettextcolor *to save the initial color value.*

USING BACKGROUND COLORS

With the C run-time library, you can set not only the text foreground color but also the background color.

■ **FACT:** *The* _setbkcolor *function sets the background color to 1 of 16 colors in text mode. The function returns the previous background color.*

The following program (RWB.C) uses the run-time library function *_setbkcolor* to display the words *RED WHITE BLUE* in corresponding background colors:

```
#include <graph.h>  /* needed for graphics functions */

main()
{
    int row, count, save_color;

    save_color = _settextcolor(15);  /* bright white text */

    for (row = 0; row < 10; row++)
        {
        for (count = 0; count < 4; count++)
            {
            _setbkcolor(4L);           /* red background */
            _outtext(" RED ");
            _setbkcolor(7L);           /* white background */
```

(continued)

continued

```
        _outtext(" WHITE ");
        _setbkcolor(1L);        /* blue background */
        _outtext(" BLUE ");
        _setbkcolor(0L);        /* black background */
        }
    _outtext("\n");
    }

_settextcolor(save_color);
}
```

RWB first sets the text foreground color to bright white so that the word *WHITE* appears in the white background. The program then simply loops, setting the background color as required.

■ **FACT:** *The _getbkcolor function returns the value for the current background color.*

Most programs save the current background color before they change it. The run-time library function _*getbkcolor* lets your programs do that. Remember, however, that saving the value returned by _*setbkcolor* also gives you a way to restore the original background color.

■ **TIP:** *The _setbkcolor function returns the previous background color. If you assign the return value to a variable, you can avoid a separate call to _getbkcolor to save the initial background color value.*

USING VIDEO DISPLAY PAGES

By default, your programs normally use video display page 0. This display page remains visible, even when your programs are writing output to it. Depending on the video mode, some adapters have as many as eight display pages. By writing to a display page other than the one currently visible, an application can format the data on the page as it requires and then make the page active. To the end user, the output appears instantaneous! To determine the number of video pages your adapter has, run the VIDEOCFG program at the beginning of this chapter.

The C run-time library provides two functions that support video page switching. The first of these functions, _*setactivepage*, defines the video page to which _*outtext* writes. The second, _*setvisualpage*, selects the video page that actually appears on your screen.

■ **FACT:** *The* _setactivepage *function selects the video display page to which* _outtext *writes its output. If* _setactivepage *selects the requested page, it returns the number of the previous page; if an error occurs, the function returns −1.*

If your program selects an active page other than the visible page, *_outtext* writes all its output to the active page. To view that page, you must use *_setvisualpage.*

■ **FACT:** *The* _setvisualpage *function selects the video display page that appears on your screen. If* _setvisualpage *selects the requested page, it returns the page number of the previous video page. If an error occurs, the function returns −1.*

The following program (PAGE.C) uses *_setactivepage* and *_setvisualpage* to demonstrate the use of display pages. The program first calls *_getvideoconfig* to determine the number of available display pages. The program then fills each display page with its page number and allows the user to step through the pages.

```
#include <graph.h>   /* needed for paging and text functions */
#include <bios.h>    /* needed for _bios_keybrd */
#include <stdlib.h>  /* needed for itoa */

main()
{
    struct videoconfig video;

    int active_page, visual_page, i;
    int row, column;
    char buffer[64];

    _getvideoconfig(&video);  /* get number of video pages */

    if (video.numvideopages <= 1)
        printf("Video pages not supported\n");
    else
        {
        _outtext("Writing to video pages - please wait\n");

        /* fill each video page with its corresponding number and color */

        for (i = 1; i < video.numvideopages; i++)
            {
            itoa(i, buffer, 10);   /* convert page number to string */
            _setactivepage(i);     /* select page as active */
            _settextcolor(i);      /* color corresponds to page number */
```

(continued)

continued

```
            for (row = 0; row < 25; row++)
                for (column = 0; column < 80; column++)
                    _outtext(buffer);
            }

        _setactivepage(0);
        _outtext("Press any key to toggle through display pages\n");
        _bios_keybrd(_KEYBRD_READ);

        /* display each video page */

        for (i = 1; i < video.numvideopages; i++)
            {
            _setvisualpage(i);
            _bios_keybrd(_KEYBRD_READ);
            }

        _setvisualpage(0);   /* reset visual page to default page 0 */
        }
    }
```

Earlier in this book we wrote our own version of the DOS MORE command, which displays information a screenful at a time. The following program (MOREVP.C) uses video pages to display the contents of a file a screenful at a time. Rather than scrolling information past you on the screen, MOREVP.C first fills all of the available video display pages. After the program fills the video pages, you can rapidly display each page by pressing any key. The program then repeats this process; it refills the display pages as often as necessary to display redirected input. For monochrome systems, the program uses only page 0. If your system has a CGA, the program uses the values 0 through 3. If your system has an EGA or a VGA, it uses 0 through 7.

```
#include <graph.h>      /* needed for graphics functions */
#include <bios.h>       /* needed for _bios_keybrd */
#include <stdio.h>      /* needed for fgets */

#define PAGE_SIZE 24   /* number of lines to display before pause */

main()
{
    char buffer[128];          /* input buffer */
    int current_page;          /* active video display page */
    int line_count = 0;        /* line number on a specific page */
```

(continued)

continued

```
    int pages_used;              /* number of pages containing information */
    int old_page;                /* previous visual page */

    struct videoconfig video;

    _getvideoconfig(&video);   /* get number of video pages */

    /* read data from stdin until end of file */
    while (fgets(buffer, sizeof(buffer), stdin))
        {
        _clearscreen(_GCLEARSCREEN);
        current_page = 0;      /* page 0 is default */
        pages_used = 0;        /* haven't used any pages yet */
        old_page = 1;          /* don't want old_page to
                                  equal current_page to start */

        /* while video pages are available, fill them */

        while (current_page < video.numvideopages)
            {
            if (old_page != current_page)
                {
                _setactivepage(current_page);  /* select new page */
                _clearscreen(_GCLEARSCREEN);
                old_page = current_page;
                }

            _outtext(buffer);                      /* write to active page */

            /* if screenful has been displayed, start new page */

            if ((++line_count % PAGE_SIZE) == 0)
                {
                _outtext ("[Press any key to continue]");
                current_page++;
                pages_used++;
                }

            /* if end of input, display partial page */

            if (fgets(buffer, sizeof(buffer), stdin) == NULL)
                {
                _outtext ("[Press any key to continue]");
                break;
                }
            }
```

(continued)

continued

```
/* cycle through display pages one at a time displaying
   the information we have just written to them */

for (current_page = 0; current_page <= pages_used; current_page++)
    {
    if (_setvisualpage(current_page) != -1)
        _bios_keybrd(_KEYBRD_READ);
    }
}

_setactivepage(0);
_clearscreen(_GCLEARSCREEN);
_setvisualpage(0);   /* always reset to 0 when program ends */
}
```

Before the program ends, it calls _*setactivepage* and _*setvisualpage* to make page 0 the active, visible page once again. Many applications write their output only to page 0. If this page is not active, the program does not appear to work. The program is writing its output to page 0, but a different page is visible. By resetting the video page to 0 before your program ends, you eliminate this potential error.

DEFINING A TEXT MODE WINDOW

By default, the _*outtext* function can write its output to the entire screen. In some cases, however, you might want _*outtext* to place its output only in a specific region of the screen, or window.

■ **FACT:** *The* _settextwindow *function lets you define the region on the screen to which* _outtext *must restrict its output. The function uses the row and column coordinates of the upper left and lower right corners of the window to define the text window.*

Many programmers use the run-time library function _*settextwindow* to create a screen window similar to a popup menu. The following program (WINDOW.C) creates a window in the center of your screen and writes the letters of the alphabet to the window 10 times, changing the color of the letters each time. Because _*outtext* works only with strings, the program assigns the letters to the character string *outstr*.

```
#include <graph.h>   /* needed for _settextwindow, _settextcolor, */
                     /* and _outtext */

main()
{
    int i;
    char letter, outstr[2];

    outstr[1] = '\0';
    _settextwindow(10, 25, 20, 55);

    for (i = 0; i < 10; i++)
        {
        _settextcolor(i);

        /* _outtext uses character strings. Assign the letter
           to outstr[0] and display the string using _outtext */

        for (letter = 'A'; (outstr[0] = letter) <= 'Z'; letter++)
            _outtext(outstr);
        _outtext("\n");
        }
}
```

Now change the program slightly to display the letters of the alphabet 100 times, rather than 10. As you will see, the program scrolls the text in the window.

■ **TIP:** *By passing the constant _GWINDOW to the _clearscreen function, your program can direct _clearscreen to clear only the contents of the window; the rest of the screen remains intact.*

Next, reduce the width of the window in the preceding program:

```
_settextwindow(10, 25, 20, 40);
```

When you run the new version you find that _outtext wraps its output within the window. The run-time library function _wrapon lets you specify whether you want _outtext to wrap text in this manner.

■ **FACT:** *The _wrapon function enables and disables text wrapping within a window. If you call _wrapon with the constant _GWRAPOFF, the function disables wrapping and truncates text at the window border. If you call _wrapon with _GWRAPON (the default condition), the function enables _outtext to wrap text.*

If you change WINALPHA.C once again to include the statement

```
_wrapon(_GWRAPOFF);
```

immediately after the call to _settextwindow, the program disables wrapping.

SETTING TEXT POSITION WITHIN A WINDOW

We have used _settextwindow_ to select a specific location on the screen for text output. Within a window, you can use the C run-time library function _settextposition_ to select a specific location for output.

■ **FACT:** _The_ _settextposition _function lets your program select the row and column position within a window at which output is to begin. All row and column positions are relative to the upper left corner of the window. The function places information in a structure of type_ rccoord _that specifies the previous text position._

The include file graph.h defines the structure _rccoord_, which contains the following members:

```
/* structure for text position */
struct rccoord {
        short row;
        short col;
};
```

■ **FACT:** _The_ _gettextposition _function places values in a structure of type_ rccoord _that contains the current text position. The coordinates are relative to the upper left corner of the window._

The following program (RANDWIN.C) uses three functions, each of which creates its own text window. The program invokes each routine with a random time slice in seconds (not to exceed 5). Each routine displays the letters of the alphabet within its window for as long as its time slice permits. To end the program, press any key.

```
#include <graph.h>    /* needed for graphics functions */
#include <bios.h>     /* needed for _bios_timeofday */
#include <conio.h>    /* needed for kbhit */

main()
{
    int time_slice;
    void first(int), second(int), third(int);

    _clearscreen(_GCLEARSCREEN);

    while (!kbhit())
        {
        time_slice = (rand() % 5) * 18.2;
        first(time_slice);
        time_slice = (rand() % 5) * 18.2;
```

(continued)

continued

```
            second(time_slice);
            time_slice = (rand() % 5) * 18.2;
            third(time_slice);
            }
}

void first(int time_slice)
{
    long start_time, current_time;
    char str[2], letter = 'A';

    str[1] = '\0';
    _settextwindow(1, 1, 10, 20);
    _settextposition(1, 1);
    _settextcolor(1);

    _bios_timeofday(_TIME_GETCLOCK, &start_time);
    _bios_timeofday(_TIME_GETCLOCK, &current_time);

    while ((current_time - start_time) < time_slice)
        {
        str[0] = letter++;
        _outtext(str);
        if (letter > 'Z')
            letter = 'A';
        _bios_timeofday(_TIME_GETCLOCK, &current_time);
        }
}

void second(int time_slice)
{
    long start_time, current_time;
    char str[2], letter = 'A';

    str[1] = '\0';
    _settextwindow(1, 25, 10, 45);
    _settextposition(1, 1);
    _settextcolor(2);

    _bios_timeofday(_TIME_GETCLOCK, &start_time);
    _bios_timeofday(_TIME_GETCLOCK, &current_time);

    while ((current_time - start_time) < time_slice)
        {
        str[0] = letter++;
        _outtext(str);
        if (letter > 'Z')
            letter = 'A';
```

(continued)

continued

```
        _bios_timeofday(_TIME_GETCLOCK, &current_time);
        }
}

void third(int time_slice)
{
    long start_time, current_time;
    char str[2], letter = 'A';

    str[1] = '\0';
    _settextwindow(1, 50, 10, 70);
    _settextposition(1, 1);
    _settextcolor(3);

    _bios_timeofday(_TIME_GETCLOCK, &start_time);
    _bios_timeofday(_TIME_GETCLOCK, &current_time);

    while ((current_time - start_time) < time_slice)
        {
        str[0] = letter++;
        _outtext(str);
        if (letter > 'Z')
            letter = 'A';
        _bios_timeofday(_TIME_GETCLOCK, &current_time);
        }
}
```

If you examine the include file graph.h, you will find that the C run-time library provides a complete set of graphics routines in addition to the text mode routines we have examined. The graphics routines, however, are a subject for an entire book.

SUMMARY

Determining a Machine's Video Capabilities

■ **FACT:** *The* _getvideoconfig *function assigns values to a structure containing the maximum number of picture elements (pixels), the number of rows and columns for text display, the number of video display pages, the display adapter type, and the amount of video memory the adapter provides.*

Clearing the Screen

■ **FACT:** *The* _clearscreen *function clears your screen in both text and graphics modes.*

Displaying Text in Color with _outtext

■ **FACT:** *The* _outtext *function displays a null-terminated ASCII string at the current text position. The function displays the characters of the string in the current foreground color.*

■ **FACT:** *The* _settextcolor *function sets the text foreground color that* _outtext *uses. The function returns the previous color value.*

■ **FACT:** *In addition to the color values 0 through 15,* _settextcolor *lets you use the values 16 through 31 to specify the same colors but with the blinking attribute.*

■ **TRAP:** *Monochrome systems do not support color values. Instead, many of the color values map to monochrome display attributes.*

■ **FACT:** *The* _gettextcolor *function returns the value for the current foreground color.*

■ **TIP:** *Keep in mind that* _settextcolor *returns the previous foreground color. If you assign the return value to a variable, you can avoid a separate call to* _gettextcolor *to save the initial color value.*

Using Background Colors

■ **FACT:** *The* _setbkcolor *function sets the background color to 1 of 16 colors in text mode. The function returns the previous background color.*

■ **FACT:** *The* _getbkcolor *function returns the value for the current background color.*

■ **TIP:** *The* _setbkcolor *function returns the previous background color. If you assign the return value to a variable, you can avoid a separate call to* _getbkcolor *to save the initial background color value.*

Using Video Display Pages

■ **FACT:** *The* _setactivepage *function selects the video display page to which* _outtext *writes its output. If* _setactivepage *selects the requested page, it returns the number of the previous page; if an error occurs, the function returns* −1.

■ **FACT:** *The* _setvisualpage *function selects the video display page that appears on your screen. If* _setvisualpage *selects the requested page, it returns the page number of the previous video page. If an error occurs, the function returns* −1.

Defining a Text Mode Window

■ **FACT:** *The* _settextwindow *function lets you define the region on the screen to which* _outtext *must restrict its output. The function uses the row and column coordinates of the upper left and lower right corners of the window to define the text window.*

■ **TIP:** *By passing the constant* _GWINDOW *to the* _clearscreen *function, your program can direct* _clearscreen *to clear only the contents of the window; the rest of the screen remains intact.*

■ **FACT:** *The* _wrapon *function enables and disables text wrapping within a window. If you call* _wrapon *with the constant* _GWRAPOFF, *the function disables wrapping and truncates text at the window border. If you call* _wrapon *with* _GWRAPON *(the default condition), the function enables* _outtext *to wrap text.*

Setting Text Position Within a Window

■ **FACT:** *The* _settextposition *function lets your program select the row and column position within a window at which output is to begin. All row and column positions are relative to the upper left corner of the window. The function places information in a structure of type* rccoord *that contains the previous text position.*

■ **FACT:** *The* _gettextposition *function places values in a structure of type* rccoord *that specifies the current text position. The coordinates are relative to the upper left corner of the window.*

GLOSSARY

pixel The smallest addressable unit on a computer screen. A combination of the words *picture* and *element*.

resolution The density of pixels (picture elements) on the screen. The more pixels per square inch, the sharper the images.

video adapter The printed circuit board or built-in video chips in your computer that provide an interface between your computer and the screen display.

video display page A region of adapter memory that holds a full screen image. Many display adapters support multiple display pages. By using display pages, your program can display one page on the screen (the visual page) while writing a second page (the active page). By switching between display pages, the program makes the output appear to be instantaneous.

video mode The screen's current state of operation. Widely used video modes include color graphics mode, black-and-white graphics mode, color or black-and-white text mode with 25 rows of 80 columns, and color or black-and-white text mode with 25 rows of 40 columns.

CHAPTER 35

Process Control and Signal Handling

As the complexity of your applications increases, you might need to access DOS commands, such as PRINT, BACKUP, or RESTORE, from within your programs. You might even want to let the user exit your application temporarily to issue commands at the DOS prompt. When the user wants to return to your application, he or she can use the DOS EXIT command.

In this chapter we examine several ways to access DOS commands from within your program. In addition, we look at several exceptions, such as Ctrl-Break, that can occur during the execution of your program and how you can install functions that handle them. In this chapter, as in all those that have preceded, the programs are short. Experiment with them, and begin your own list of C secrets!

INVOKING DOS COMMANDS FROM WITHIN YOUR PROGRAMS

In this section we examine several ways to invoke DOS commands from within your program. The easiest method is to use the C run-time library function *system*.

■ **FACT:** *The* system *function executes the specified DOS command, after which DOS returns control to your program. The function uses the DOS environment entry* COMSPEC= *to locate* COMMAND.COM *and the* PATH= *entry to locate external commands. If* system *executes the specified command, it returns 0; if an error occurs,* system *returns an error status.*

The following program (DOSDIR.C) uses the *system* function to execute the DOS DIR command:

```
#include <process.h>   /* needed for system */

main()
{
    system("DIR");
}
```

The DOS DIR command is an internal DOS command. Had the program invoked an external DOS command instead, such as DISKCOPY or BACKUP, DOS would first search the location specified in the function argument, then the current directory, and following that, the locations identified in the *PATH=* environment entry.

The *system* function is helpful in other ways. Most users like the convenience of working with familiar applications. By using *system*, your programs can satisfy this preference by executing the end user's word processor, spreadsheet, or other application. Likewise, *system* provides a way for users to exit an application temporarily to look up files or to perform other DOS commands.

■ **TIP:** *Calling* system *with the argument "COMMAND" enables the user to issue DOS commands as needed and then return to your program by typing* EXIT.

The following program (SYS.C) uses *system* to exit the application temporarily so that the user can issue DOS commands. When the user finishes executing commands at the DOS prompt, he or she can type *EXIT* and press Enter to return to the program.

```
#include <process.h>   /* needed for system */
#include <stdio.h>      /* needed for getchar */

main()
{
    printf("Type EXIT to continue");
    system("COMMAND");
    printf("Back in application - press Enter\n");
    getchar();
}
```

The *system* function is the easiest way to issue DOS commands from your programs. To give you greater control, the run-time library also provides two series of routines that access DOS commands: *exec* functions and *spawn* functions.

■ **FACT:** *The* exec *functions execute the specified DOS commands. The specified DOS command replaces your program in memory. The various* exec *functions differ in their treatment of command line arguments and environment entries.*

The *exec* functions invoke a DOS command without returning control to the program when the command completes. The C run-time library provides eight forms of the *exec* function—*execl, execle, execlp, execlpe, execv, execve, execvp,* and *execvpe*. In general, the differences among them are the ways the calling program passes command line arguments and environment entries to the command and the directories DOS searches to locate a command. The letters in the function name suffix have the meanings described in the following table:

Letter	Meaning
l	Passes a variable number of command line arguments, the last being NULL
v	Passes an array of pointers to command line arguments
p	Supports the *PATH* environment variable
e	Passes an array of pointers to environment entries

■ **FACT:** *The* execl *function executes the specified DOS command and passes a variable number of command line arguments. The last command line argument must be NULL. The* execl *function does not support the* PATH *environment variable.*

To demonstrate the way various *exec* functions work, let's create a program that you can invoke with them. Enter and compile the following program (SHOW.C), which displays its command line arguments and environment entries:

```
main(int argc, char *argv[], char *env[])
{
    while (*argv)  /* display command line arguments */
        puts(*argv++);

    while (*env)   /* display environment entries */
        puts(*env++);
}
```

The following program (RUNSHOW.C) uses the *execl* function to execute SHOW.EXE. The output of SHOW reveals that it receives the arguments specified in RUNSHOW and a copy of the RUNSHOW environment entries.

```
#include <process.h>  /* needed for execl */
#include <stdio.h>     /* needed for NULL */

main()
{
    execl("SHOW.EXE", "SHOW", "A", "B", "C", NULL);
    printf("This line will never be executed\n");
}
```

Let's look at the arguments for *execl*. The first argument is a character string that identifies the program to execute. If the program does not reside in the current directory, specify a complete pathname. Remember, *execl* does not support the *PATH* environment variable. The remaining string arguments represent entries on the DOS command line, *argv[0]* through *argv[3]*. The NULL pointer terminates the argument list. Note that the *printf* statement never executes: When you use an *exec* function, your program does not resume control.

■ **FACT:** *The* execlp *function performs the same processing as* execl, *but* execlp *also supports the* PATH *environment variable.*

You might modify RUNSHOW.C slightly by replacing *execl* with *execlp*. The new version would support the *PATH* environment entry.

■ **FACT:** *The* execle *function executes the specified command and supports a variable number of command line arguments. The* execle *function lets you pass an array of pointers to strings that serves as the program environment.*

The following program (RUNSHOW2.C) uses the C run-time library function *execle* to execute SHOW.EXE. RUNSHOW2.C defines a new environment and passes it to SHOW.EXE:

```
#include <process.h>  /* needed for execle */
#include <stdio.h>     /* needed for NULL */

main()
{
    char static *new_env[4] = { "BOOK=C SSS",
                                "CHAPTER=35",
                                "COMPILER=MSC" };

    execle("SHOW.EXE", "SHOW", "A", "B", "C", NULL, new_env);
}
```

When you run this program, your screen shows

```
SHOW.EXE
A
B
C
BOOK=C SSS
CHAPTER=35
COMPILER=MSC
```

■ **FACT:** *The* execlpe *function is identical to* execle *except that* execlpe *supports the* PATH *environment variable, whereas* execle *does not.*

Each of the preceding *exec* functions passes the command line entries as a variable number of arguments. The next set of *exec* functions passes the command line as an array of pointers to character strings.

■ **FACT:** *The* execv *function executes the specified command and passes the command line arguments as an array of pointers to character strings. The function does not support the* PATH *environment variable.*

The following program (RUNSHOW3.C) defines an array of pointers to character strings that serve as the command line arguments for SHOW.EXE. The program uses the *execv* function to invoke SHOW.

```
#include <process.h>   /* needed for execv */

main()
{
    static char *args[4] = { "SHOW",
                             "A",
                             "B" };

    execv("SHOW.EXE", args);
}
```

■ **FACT:** *The* execvp *function performs the same processing as* execv *except that* execvp *does support the* PATH *environment variable.*

Try substituting *execvp* for *execv* in RUNSHOW3.C. Then experiment with different locations of SHOW.EXE. As long as the new location is identified in your *PATH=* entry, *execvp* is able to run SHOW.

■ **FACT:** *The* execve *function executes the specified command; it passes an array of pointers to the command line and an array of pointers to the environment entries.*

The following program (RUNSHOW4.C) defines an array of pointers to the command line and an array of pointers to environment entries. The program calls *execve*, which uses these arrays to execute SHOW.EXE.

```
#include <process.h>   /* needed for execve */

main()
{
    static char *args[4] = { "SHOW",
                             "A",
                             "B" };

    static char *new_env[4] = { "BOOK=C SSS",
                                "CHAPTER=35",
                                "COMPILER=MSC" };

    execve("SHOW.EXE", args, new_env);
}
```

■ **FACT:** *The* execvpe *function performs the same processing as* execve *except that it does support the* PATH *environment variable.*

The *exec* functions are useful when you do not want control to return to your program. But if your program needs to regain control when the command is complete, the program must use one of the *spawn* functions.

■ **FACT:** *The* spawn *functions temporarily suspend the current program to execute a specified DOS command. When the command is complete, DOS returns control to the program.*

The C run-time library provides eight varieties of *spawn* functions, just as it does for *exec*. In this section let's examine the two primary *spawn* routines, *spawnlpe* and *spawnvpe*.

■ **FACT:** *The C run-time library uses the same naming convention for* spawn *functions as it uses for* exec *functions. A function whose suffix contains the letter* p *supports the* PATH *environment variable. A function whose suffix contains the letter* e *lets you pass environment entries. The letter* l *appears in the suffix of functions that pass a variable-length, NULL-terminated list of command line arguments, and the letter* v *in a suffix means that the function passes command line entries as an array of pointers.*

The various suffix letters have the same meanings for *spawn* functions as they do for the *exec* set of functions. Figure 35-1 contains a table that summarizes the *spawn* functions.

Function Name	PATH= Support	Environment Entries	Command Line Entries
spawnl	No	Copies current	NULL-terminated list
spawnle	No	Array argument	NULL-terminated list
spawnlp	Yes	Copies current	NULL-terminated list
spawnlpe	Yes	Array argument	NULL-terminated list
spawnv	No	Copies current	Array argument
spawnve	No	Array argument	Array argument
spawnvp	Yes	Copies current	Array argument
spawnvpe	Yes	Array argument	Array argument

FIGURE 35-1.
The spawn *functions behave as their suffixed letters specify.*

■ **FACT:** *Each* spawn *function uses a mode flag defined in the include file process.h. If you call the function with the mode flag P_WAIT, the program stops temporarily to execute the DOS command. When the command is completed, the program resumes operation. If you call the function with the mode flag P_OVERLAY, a* spawn *function behaves like an* exec *function: It executes the command but does not return control to the program.*

The *spawn* functions are convenient in that they let an application execute a second program and then—if the mode flag is set to P_WAIT—regain control when the program is complete. Consequently, most applications use the P_WAIT flag when they call *spawn* functions. If an application does not need to regain control after it executes a command, it can use an *exec* function.

■ **FACT:** *The* spawnlpe *function executes the specified DOS command; it passes command line arguments as a NULL-terminated list. The function passes a list of environment entries to the command as an array of pointers to strings.*

The following program (RUNSHOW5.C) uses *spawnlpe* to execute SHOW.EXE. The program creates an array of pointers to environment entries and passes them to *spawnlpe*. When SHOW.EXE is complete, DOS returns control to RUNSHOW5, which displays a message to verify the return of execution.

```
#include <process.h>  /* needed for spawnlpe */
#include <stdio.h>    /* needed for NULL */

main()
{
    static char *new_env[4] = { "BOOK=C SSS",
                                "CHAPTER=35",
                                "COMPILER=MSC" };

    spawnlpe(P_WAIT, "SHOW.EXE", "A", "B", NULL, new_env);

    printf("Back from spawn\n");
}
```

■ **FACT:** *Each* spawn *function returns a value. This value is the exit status of the spawned program.*

In Chapter 19 you learned that programs can return an exit status when they end. If you spawn a program, the *spawn* function returns the exit status of the program.

■ **FACT:** *The* spawnvpe *function executes the specified program; it passes both the command line arguments and the environment entries as arrays of pointers to character strings.*

The following program (RUNSHOW6.C) uses *spawnvpe* to execute SHOW.EXE. When DOS returns control to RUNSHOW6, the program displays SHOW's exit status.

```
#include <process.h>  /* needed for spawnvpe */

main()
{
    static char *new_env[4] = { "BOOK=C SSS",
                                "CHAPTER=35",
                                "COMPILER=MSC" };

    static char *args[4] = { "SHOW",
                             "A",
                             "B" };

    int result;

    result = spawnvpe(P_WAIT, "SHOW.EXE", args, new_env);

    printf("Back from spawn - Exit value is %d\n", result);
}
```

SIGNAL HANDLING

As operating systems offer a richer set of services, we will find that the operating system treats more and more events in the system as *signals*. A signal can be viewed as an alarm the operating system rings when a specific event occurs. Each unique signal has its own alarm. Under DOS, the three signals your programs can receive are SIGINT, which occurs when a user presses Ctrl-Break; SIGFPE, which occurs when a floating point error (such as division by zero) is detected; and SIGABRT, which occurs when a program aborts with an exit status of 3.

The C run-time library function *signal*, defined in the include file signal.h, lets you install a function that executes when a specific signal occurs. The signal.h file should not be used under OS/2.

■ **FACT:** *The* signal *function lets your program install a function that serves as a signal handler. Each time the specified signal occurs, the handler is executed.*

The following program (CBREAK.C) defines the function *ctrl_break* and installs it to handle the SIGINT signal, which occurs when the user presses Ctrl-Break. Our handler ignores the signal until the user has pressed Ctrl-Break five times. On the fifth occurrence of Ctrl-Break, the program ends.

```c
#include <signal.h>    /* needed for signal */
#include <stdio.h>     /* needed for getchar */
#include <process.h>   /* needed for exit */

main()
{
    int ctrl_break();

    signal(SIGINT, ctrl_break);
    printf("Press Ctrl-Break 5 times to terminate program\n");
    getchar();
}

ctrl_break()
{
    static int count = 1;

    signal(SIGINT, SIG_IGN);
    if (count++ == 5)
        {
        printf("Program terminated by Ctrl-Break\n");
        exit();
        }

    signal(SIGINT, ctrl_break);
}
```

The function *ctrl_break* is the signal handler. It directs DOS to ignore Ctrl-Break signals that occur while the handler is executing. The routine then increments a count of the number of Ctrl-Break signals that have occurred. Last, the function reinstalls itself as the Ctrl-Break handler.

■ **FACT:** *The signal function lets you pass one of three values as the second argument. If the argument is an address,* signal *installs the address as the signal handler. If the argument is the constant SIG_IGN,* signal *directs DOS to ignore future signals of the type specified. And if the argument is the constant SIG_DFL,* signal *directs DOS to use its default signal handler.*

Our *ctrl_break* function calls *signal* with SIG_IGN, which directs DOS to ignore incoming signals of the same type while the handler executes. After the handler performs its processing, it uses *signal* to reinstall itself as the Ctrl-Break handler.

As you begin to write signal handlers, you will find that testing a handler is, in some cases, quite difficult. To assist you, the C run-time library provides the *raise* function.

■ **FACT:** *The* raise *function lets your program generate one of the exceptions specified in the include file signal.h.*

The following program (RAISE.C) defines the function *abort_handler* and installs it as the SIGABRT handler. Next the program raises the signal so that you can test your handler.

```
#include <signal.h> /* needed for signal, raise, and constants */
#include <stdio.h>  /* needed for fcloseall */

main()
{
    int abort_handler();

    signal(SIGABRT, abort_handler);
    raise(SIGABRT);
}

abort_handler()
{
    signal(SIGABRT, SIG_IGN);
    printf("In abort handler -- closing all open files\n");
    fcloseall();
}
```

By using *raise* in this manner, your program can test your handler and verify that it responds to SIGABRT. You might then replace the call to *raise* with a call to the run-time library function *abort* and so verify that DOS raises the SIGABRT signal when the program aborts.

Signal processing is still in its infancy. With the advent of OS/2, you will see its use grow, as signals become an important tool for interprocess communication.

SUMMARY

Invoking DOS Commands from Within Your Programs

■ **FACT:** *The* system *function executes the specified DOS command, after which DOS returns control to your program. The function uses the DOS environment entry* COMSPEC= *to locate COMMAND.COM and the* PATH= *entry to locate external commands. If* system *executes the specified command, it returns 0; if an error occurs,* system *returns an error status.*

■ **TIP:** *Calling* system *with the argument "COMMAND" enables the user to issue DOS commands as needed and then return to your program by typing* EXIT.

■ **FACT:** *The* exec *functions execute the specified DOS command. The specified DOS command replaces your program in memory. The various* exec *functions differ in their treatment of command line arguments and environment entries.*

■ **FACT:** *The* execl *function executes the specified DOS command and passes a variable number of command line arguments. The last command line argument must be* NULL. *The* execl *function does not support the* PATH *environment variable.*

■ **FACT:** *The* execlp *function performs the same processing as* execl, *but* execlp *also supports the* PATH *environment variable.*

■ **FACT:** *The* execle *function executes the specified command and supports a variable number of command line arguments. The* execle *function lets you pass an array of pointers to strings that serves as the program environment.*

■ **FACT:** *The* execlpe *function is identical to* execle *except that* execlpe *supports the* PATH *environment variable, whereas* execle *does not.*

■ **FACT:** *The* execv *function executes the specified command and passes the command line arguments as an array of pointers to character strings. The function does not support the* PATH *environment variable.*

■ **FACT:** *The* execvp *function performs the same processing as* execv *except that* execvp *does support the* PATH *environment variable.*

■ **FACT:** *The* execve *function executes the specified command; it passes an array of pointers to the command line and an array of pointers to the environment entries.*

■ **FACT:** *The* execvpe *function performs the same processing as* execve *except that it does support the* PATH *environment variable.*

■ **FACT:** *The* spawn *functions temporarily suspend the current program to execute a specified DOS command. When the command is complete, DOS returns control to the program.*

■ **FACT:** *The C run-time library uses the same naming convention for* spawn *functions as it follows for* exec *functions. A function whose suffix contains the letter* p *supports the PATH environment variable. A function whose suffix contains the letter* e *lets you pass environment entries. The letter* l *appears in the suffix of functions that pass a variable-length, NULL-terminated list of command line arguments, and the letter* v *in a suffix means that the function passes command line entries as an array of pointers.*

■ **FACT:** *Each* spawn *function uses a mode flag 'defined in the include file process.h. If you call the function with the mode flag P_WAIT, the program stops temporarily to execute the DOS command. When the command is completed, the program resumes operation. If you call the function with the mode flag P_OVERLAY, a* spawn *function behaves like an* exec *function: It executes the command but does not return control to the program.*

■ **FACT:** *The* spawnlpe *function executes the specified DOS command; it passes command line arguments as a NULL-terminated list. The function passes a list of environment entries to the command as an array of pointers to strings.*

■ **FACT:** *Each* spawn *function returns a value. This value is the exit status of the spawned program.*

■ **FACT:** *The* spawnvpe *function executes the specified program; it passes both the command line arguments and the environment entries as arrays of pointers to character strings.*

Signal Handling

■ **FACT:** *The* signal *function lets your program install a function that serves as a signal handler. Each time the specified signal occurs, the handler is executed.*

■ **FACT:** *The* signal *function lets you pass one of three values as the second argument. If the argument is an address,* signal *installs the address as the signal handler. If the argument is the constant SIG_IGN,* signal *directs DOS to ignore future signals of the type specified. And if the argument is the constant SIG_DFL,* signal *directs DOS to use its default signal handler.*

■ **FACT:** *The* raise *function lets your program generate one of the exceptions specified in the include file signal.h.*

GLOSSARY

child process A program invoked by another program using *system*, an *exec* function, or a *spawn* function. When DOS loads a program invoked by *system* or by an *exec* function, DOS overwrites the calling program. When DOS loads a program invoked by a *spawn* function, it suspends execution of the calling program until the second program is complete. DOS can then allow the caller to regain control.

signal A mechanism for communication between processes. DOS raises three signals that your programs can receive: SIGINT, which occurs when the user presses Ctrl-Break; SIGFPE, which occurs when a floating point error is detected; and SIGABRT, which occurs when a program aborts with an error status of 3.

ASCII Character Set

Char †	Dec	Oct	Hex	Control	Description
	0	000	00	NUL	Null
☺	1	001	01	SOH	Start of heading
☻	2	002	02	STX	Start of text
♥	3	003	03	ETX	End of text
♦	4	004	04	EOT	End of transmission
♣	5	005	05	ENQ	Enquiry
♠	6	006	06	ACK	Acknowledge
•	7	007	07	BEL	Bell
◘	8	010	08	BS	Backspace
○	9	011	09	HT	Horizontal tab
◎	10	012	0A	LF	Linefeed
♂	11	013	0B	VT	Vertical tab
♀	12	014	0C	FF	Formfeed
♪	13	015	0D	CR	Carriage return
♫	14	016	0E	SO	Shift out
☼	15	017	0F	SI	Shift in
►	16	020	10	DLE	Data link escape
◄	17	021	11	DC1	Device control 1
↕	18	022	12	DC2	Device control 2
‼	19	023	13	DC3	Device control 3
¶	20	024	14	DC4	Device control 4
§	21	025	15	NAK	Negative acknowledge
▬	22	026	16	SYN	Synchronous idle
↨	23	027	17	ETB	End transmission block
↑	24	030	18	CAN	Cancel
↓	25	031	19	EM	End of medium
→	26	032	1A	SUB	Substitute
←	27	033	1B	ESC	Escape
∟	28	034	1C	FS	File separator
↔	29	035	1D	GS	Group separator
▲	30	036	1E	RS	Record separator
▼	31	037	1F	US	Unit separator
<space>	32	040	20		

†For control characters, the accompanying graphics characters are defined by IBM.

(continued)

ASCII Character Set *continued*

Char	*Dec*	*Oct*	*Hex*	*Control*	*Description*
!	33	041	21		
"	34	042	22		
#	35	043	23		
$	36	044	24		
%	37	045	25		
&	38	046	26		
'	39	047	27		
(	40	050	28		
)	41	051	29		
*	42	052	2A		
+	43	053	2B		
,	44	054	2C		
−	45	055	2D		
.	46	056	2E		
/	47	057	2F		
0	48	060	30		
1	49	061	31		
2	50	062	32		
3	51	063	33		
4	52	064	34		
5	53	065	35		
6	54	066	36		
7	55	067	37		
8	56	070	38		
9	57	071	39		
:	58	072	3A		
;	59	073	3B		
<	60	074	3C		
=	61	075	3D		
>	62	076	3E		
?	63	077	3F		
@	64	100	40		
A	65	101	41		
B	66	102	42		
C	67	103	43		
D	68	104	44		
E	69	105	45		
F	70	106	46		
G	71	107	47		
H	72	110	48		
I	73	111	49		
J	74	112	4A		
K	75	113	4B		
L	76	114	4C		
M	77	115	4D		
N	78	116	4E		
O	79	117	4F		

(continued)

ASCII Character Set *continued*

Char	Dec	Oct	Hex	Control	Description
P	80	120	50		
Q	81	121	51		
R	82	122	52		
S	83	123	53		
T	84	124	54		
U	85	125	55		
V	86	126	56		
W	87	127	57		
X	88	130	58		
Y	89	131	59		
Z	90	132	5A		
[	91	133	5B		
\	92	134	5C		
]	93	135	5D		
^	94	136	5E		
_	95	137	5F		
`	96	140	60		
a	97	141	61		
b	98	142	62		
c	99	143	63		
d	100	144	64		
e	101	145	65		
f	102	146	66		
g	103	147	67		
h	104	150	68		
i	105	151	69		
j	106	152	6A		
k	107	153	6B		
l	108	154	6C		
m	109	155	6D		
n	110	156	6E		
o	111	157	6F		
p	112	160	70		
q	113	161	71		
r	114	162	72		
s	115	163	73		
t	116	164	74		
u	117	165	75		
v	118	166	76		
w	119	167	77		
x	120	170	78		
y	121	171	79		
z	122	172	7A		
{	123	173	7B		
¦	124	174	7C		
}	125	175	7D		
~	126	176	7E		
Δ	127	177	7F	DEL	Delete

Compiled Glossary

access mode An argument that specifies the way in which a program can access a file. C supports read, write, append, and read/write modes. Your program must specify an access mode when it opens a file using *fopen*.

address operator An operator that returns the memory location of a variable. Its symbol is the ampersand (&).

aliasing A phenomenon that occurs when two names reference the same memory location. Because C uses pointers extensively, a program commonly contains two names that reference the same location.

ANSI C The standards for implementing C in compliance with the specifications written by the American National Standards Institute (ANSI). By conforming to ANSI standards, programs written in C under one compiler or operating system will compile and run using another compliant compiler or operating system.

argument A value passed to a function. The C compiler passes arguments by value, which means that functions receive a copy of the value stored in a variable rather than accessing the value itself.

array A compound data type that lets you group logically related values of the same type in a single variable.

array index The means of accessing a specific element in an array. Using an index value of 0, *sales[0]* accesses the first element in the *sales* array. Similarly, with an index value of 1, *sales[1]* accesses the second element.

assembly language listing A file that contains the assembly language output generated by the compiler, grouped by the corresponding line numbers in the C source file. The CL option /Fa creates an assembly language listing.

base pointer (BP) A register that contains the starting location of the arguments on the stack. Assembly language routines use offsets from the base pointer to access each argument.

binary mode A file access mode in which C file manipulation functions do not translate the file contents when they read or write information. In binary mode, the file manipulation functions locate the end of file using the file size specified in the directory entry for the file.

BIOS services A collection of routines built into the read-only memory (ROM) of IBM PCs (and compatibles) and PS/2 models. These services perform basic input/output services for video, keyboard, disk, printer, and serial port I/O.

bit field structure A structure in which each member resides in a specific number of bits. Each member is declared as an *unsigned int*, and a value that follows the name of the member specifies the number of bits allotted to that member.

bitwise operator A C operator that lets you manipulate values in their binary representations.

buffered input An input process in which the keys the user presses are not available to the program until the user presses Enter. The advantage of buffered input is that the user can edit the entry with the Backspace key.

call by reference A method of passing function arguments. The function receives the address of a variable and thereby the ability to manipulate the value of the variable itself.

call by value The default method of passing an argument to a function. The function receives a copy of the argument's value but no means of manipulating the argument itself.

cast operator Directs the compiler to convert an expression of one type to the type contained in parentheses before the expression. For example: $a = (float)\ b;$

C compiler A software program that examines your C program for syntax errors and, if successful, creates an object (OBJ) file.

character string A collection of one or more related characters. C programmers also call character strings ASCII zero strings or null-terminated strings.

child process A program invoked by another program using *system*, an *exec* function, or a *spawn* function. When DOS loads a program invoked by *system* or by an *exec* function, DOS overwrites the calling program. When DOS loads a program invoked by a *spawn* function, it suspends execution of the calling program until the second program is complete. DOS can then allow the caller to regain control.

clock tick A time increment that occurs 18.2 times per second in the CPU of the IBM PC (and compatibles) and PS/2 models.

command line The characters you enter at the system prompt. Command line processing is the use of information contained in the command line within a program.

compiler option A switch that you include in the CL command line that modifies or supplements the output of the CL command. For example, the compiler option /Fa directs CL to produce an assembly language listing of your file.

compound statement A series of instructions enclosed by a pair of grouping symbols, the left and right braces *{* and *}*.

conditional preprocessor directive A preprocessor directive that controls the inclusion of subsequent instructions, depending on the truth value of the condition it presents. For example, *#ifdef NAME* includes the instructions that follow if the identifier NAME is defined.

conditional statement A statement that executes only when a given condition is true. The *if* statement provides conditional processing.

constant A value that does not change during the execution of a program. The C *#define* directive lets you assign meaningful names to constants.

control string The series of characters in double quotation marks that follows the *printf* function name. The control string includes literal characters to write as well as characters that tell the function how to format your output. The characters "Find the sum of %d and %6f\n" are an example of a *printf* control sequence.

critical error An error that prevents the operating system from continuing until the user intervenes. The most common causes of critical errors are off-line printers and unready disk drives.

critical error handler A function designed to take over when a critical error occurs. The built-in DOS critical error handler displays the message *Abort, Retry, Fail?* when a critical error occurs.

debug write statement An output statement that displays an intermediate result or a message that you can use to track down logic errors in your program.

dependency A relationship between files whereby modification of one necessitates a change to the other. In this sense, a dependency exists between an object file and the source file or files from which it is compiled. The object file is considered the target file in this dependency, and the source file or files are dependent files.

device driver A program that the operating system uses to communicate with a device. The ANSI.SYS device driver expands the capabilities of your screen and keyboard.

echoing The process of displaying on the screen the letter that corresponds to each keystroke pressed by the user. The run-time library function *getche* echoes characters to the screen, but the *getch* function does not.

editor A program that allows you to create or change a file.

enumerated type A user-defined type that identifies the specific values a variable of that type can store. The declaration *enum suits { spades, hearts, diamonds, clubs };*, for example, creates a type called *suits*, which can store one of four possible values.

environment A region in memory that DOS and OS/2 set aside each time your system starts. The environment is used to store information such as the system prompt, command path, and other information your programs can access, such as the location of specific files.

environment variables Names defined system-wide that specify often-used values or directory locations.

escape sequence A series of characters, beginning with the ASCII escape character (decimal 27), used to manipulate the display or keyboard. The *printf* function uses the escape sequence \t to indicate a tab. The ANSI.SYS device driver uses *Esc*[2J to clear your screen.

exit list A list of functions that a program executes when your program terminates. The C run-time library routine *atexit* lets you define the functions contained in the exit list.

exit status A value that a terminating program returns to the operating system. The DOS batch command IF ERRORLEVEL lets you test a program's exit status.

external variable A global variable defined in a different object file. To access an external variable, you must precede the variable declarations with the *extern* specifier.

far pointer A 32-bit pointer that contains a 16-bit segment and a 16-bit offset value. Far pointers let your programs access memory locations outside the 64 KB data segment.

file pointer A variable that points to a memory location containing information specific to an open file. To declare a file pointer, your program must include the file stdio.h and then declare the pointer in the form *FILE *fp;*.

floating point emulator A collection of software routines that performs the same function as the 8087 math coprocessor chip. The floating point emulator lets systems that lack a math coprocessor perform complex math operations by using software instead.

floating point value A value that contains a decimal point. In C, the type *float* defines a floating point value.

function A block of code with a unique name that is called from within a program to carry out a specific task.

general-purpose registers A collection of fast storage locations that are built into the CPU (Intel 80x86 family). These registers serve as your interface to the DOS system services. The general-purpose registers include AX, BX, CX, and DX. Programs can access these registers as 16-bit registers or as a series of (low-order and high-order) 8-bit registers, named AL, AH, BL, BH, CL, CH, DL, and DH.

Greenwich mean time (GMT) The time in Greenwich, England, through which the prime meridian (0° longitude) passes. The C run-time library provides several functions based on Greenwich mean time.

grouping symbols The characters { and } that let you group a related set of instructions.

handle An integer value used by the C low-level file I/O routines to access a file or device. The run-time library routines *open* and *creat* return a file handle. Some C programmers refer to file handles as file descriptors.

heap The unused portion of the data segment that is available for dynamic memory allocation. The C run-time library routines *calloc* and *malloc* allocate memory from the heap.

huge array An array that exceeds 64 KB. The compiler lets you create a huge array by specifying the keyword *huge* in your array declaration.

indirection operator An operator that lets you access the value in the memory location referenced by a pointer. Its symbol is the asterisk (*). For example: *value = *ptr;*

integer value A whole number. In C, the type *int* defines an integer value.

I/O redirection The process of using either the system input redirection operator or the system output redirection operator to route input to a command from a source other than the keyboard, or to write output from a command to a destination other than the screen.

iterative process A series of one or more instructions that repeat until an ending condition is met. The three iterative constructs in C are the *while, for,* and *do-while* statements.

keyword A word that has special meaning within the C language. The compiler does not allow you to use keywords as variable names in your programs.

librarian A software package that lets you add, delete, and update object modules. For DOS and OS/2, the object file librarian is called LIB.

linked list A storage facility that contains a list of entries connected by pointers. In a singly linked list, each entry contains a single pointer to the next entry. A doubly linked list contains two pointers per entry—one to the previous entry and one to the next entry.

linker A software program that combines object (OBJ) and library (LIB) files to create an executable program that has the extension EXE.

logical error An error that occurs when your program doesn't perform as you intended. Logical errors are also known as bugs.

logical operator Any of a set of C operators (&&, ¦¦, !) that yield a true or false (nonzero or zero) result. The result depends on the truth or falsity of the expression or expressions to which the operator is applied.

low-level I/O File input or output that relies on a set of run-time library functions that bypass the buffering capacities of the operating system. Low-level functions use integer file handles rather than file pointers to identify files.

macro A shorthand notation for an expression or a group of instructions. The *#define* directive lets you define a C macro.

member One of the entries in a structure. To refer to a structure member, use the dot operator between the variable name and the name of the member.

memory model The basic way a program accesses its code and data. The C compiler supports the small, medium, compact, large, and huge memory models. In general, the models permit the use of different numbers of code and data segments, thereby trading speed for size.

modulus operator A mathematical operator that returns the remainder of an integer division. The modulus operator in C is the percent sign (%). Read the expression *15 % 4* as "the remainder of 15 divided by four."

multidimensional array An array that specifies columns of values as well as rows. The declaration *int box[3][5];* creates an integer array named *box* with 3 rows of 5 columns each.

near pointer A 16-bit pointer that can reference values contained in the 64 KB data segment. Unless a pointer declaration contains the keyword *far*, the variable is a near pointer.

nested loop A loop that is embedded within another loop.

newline character A combination of a carriage return and a linefeed that causes subsequent output to begin on the next line. The escape sequence for a newline character in the C programming language is \n.

null character An undisplayed character with ASCII code 0. The compiler terminates character strings with the null character. To represent the null character, type the sequence '\0'.

object code listing A file that contains the assembly language and binary output of the compiler. The CL option /Fc creates an object code listing.

object file A machine code file produced by compilation of source code.

object library A collection of functions in object file format that the linker can use when you create executable files.

operator precedence The order in which C evaluates the operations that constitute an expression. Because multiplication has a higher operator precedence than addition, C finds the product of 2 and 3 before it adds 4 in the expression *a = 4 + 2 * 3*.

parse To examine the contents of a string and break the string into distinct fields. For example, the C run-time library function *_splitpath* parses a pathname into its components: disk drive, path, filename, and extension.

pixel The smallest addressable unit on a computer screen. A combination of the words *picture* and *element*.

pointer A variable type that contains a memory address. To declare a pointer in C, specify a type and immediately precede the variable name with an asterisk. For example, the statement *int *ptr;* declares the pointer *ptr*, which references an *int* value.

pragma A compiler option that you place in your source file. The C *#pragma* statement lets you place pragmas in your file. The statement *#pragma check_stack(off)*, for example, disables stack checking.

preprocessor A program that runs before C compiles your program. The C preprocessor replaces the constants and macros with their corresponding values and inserts any include files you specify with *#include*.

program A list of instructions for the computer to perform. C programmers refer to these instructions as source code. Programs are also known as software.

program segment prefix (PSP) A 256-byte data block that contains information, such as the program's environment entries and its Ctrl-Break handling routine. DOS places this information at the beginning of your program at run time.

protected mode Execution mode supported under OS/2 that lets you execute several programs at the same time, sharing files and other information among them.

read-only file A file whose contents a program can read but cannot modify. When you set the mode of a file to read-only, the system lets you read the file with commands such as TYPE and PRINT. However, the system does not let you modify the file or delete it from disk. The C run-time library function *chmod* lets you set a file to read-only access.

real mode Execution mode in which DOS programs run. Under OS/2 real mode, only one program can execute in real mode at any given time. Real mode is often called DOS mode.

recursion The process by which a function calls itself successively until an ending condition is met.

relational operator Any of a set of C operators (>, <, ==, >=, <=, !=) that let you compare two values. The result is either true or false (nonzero or zero).

resolution The density of pixels (picture elements) on the screen. The more pixels per square inch, the sharper the images.

run-time library A collection of existing routines that your programs can access. The run-time library contains functions and macros that perform memory allocation, string manipulation, math functions, and file and screen I/O. The run-time library is the C programmer's tool set. The Microsoft C run-time library is the collection of functions and macros supplied with the Microsoft C Compiler.

scan code The high-order byte of a keyboard value, which corresponds to the physical key on the keyboard. The scan code is critical for identifying special-purpose keys, such as arrow keys and function keys.

signal A mechanism for communication between processes. DOS raises three signals that your programs can receive: SIGINT, which occurs when the user presses Ctrl-Break; SIGFPE, which occurs when a floating point error is detected; and SIGABRT, which occurs when a program aborts with an error status of 3.

source code The processing instructions that are written in a given computer language and that collectively constitute a source file.

source file A text file that contains a program. C source files have the extension C—for example, FILENAME.C.

source listing A file containing the source code of your program, with line numbers, as well as a summary of the variables and functions used. The CL option /Fs creates a source listing.

stack A region of memory that the compiler uses for temporary storage of arguments passed to a function. When the function ends, the compiler removes the arguments from the stack.

static variable A variable that retains its value from one invocation of a function to the next. To create a static variable, include the *static* specifier in the declaration.

stdaux The location of the standard auxiliary device. By default, DOS and OS/2 associate stdaux with COM1.

stderr The standard error destination for programs. Stderr always points to the screen. The DOS and OS/2 redirection operators cannot redirect error messages written to stderr away from the screen.

stdin The standard input source for programs. By default, DOS and OS/2 associate stdin with the keyboard. By using the input redirection operator, <, you can redirect stdin from the keyboard to an existing file.

stdout The standard output destination for programs. By default, DOS and OS/2 associate stdout with the screen. By using the output (>) or append (>>) redirection operator, you can redirect stdout from the screen to a file or a different device.

stdprn The location of the standard printer device. By default, DOS and OS/2 associate stdprn with LPT1.

stream I/O Character-based input or output in which the input or output is handled one character at a time in a continuous stream until the end of file occurs. The C functions *fopen*, *fgets*, *fputs*, and so forth are commonly used stream I/O routines.

structure A user-defined C type that lets programs group variables of different types into one named type. The C keyword *struct* declares a C structure.

syntax error An error that occurs when you violate one of the rules of C, such as forgetting a semicolon or a grouping symbol.

system services A collection of routines built into the operating system and essential to its functioning. Because these routines are always present in memory, the DOS developers have made them available to your programs by means of a software interrupt, Int 0x21. Under OS/2, system services comprise the Application Program Interface and are available via far calls to named entry points.

tag The optional name of a structure type. After you define a structure and assign it a tag, you can use the tag when you declare structure variables of the defined type.

text mode The default file access mode. C file manipulation functions translate carriage return–linefeed characters and interpret Ctrl-Z as an end of file indicator.

type A C keyword that defines the kind of values a variable can store, as well as the set of operations that can be performed on the variable. C provides the basic types *int, float, char,* and *double.*

type qualifier A C keyword that modifies the way C stores values within a specific type. C supports the type qualifiers *signed, unsigned, short,* and *long.*

union A data type that lets you store one of several types of values. Unlike a structure, which can contain many values at the same time, a union can store only one value at any time.

variable A name that C assigns to a memory location. Rather than referring directly to memory locations when they store and retrieve values, your C programs can instead refer to variable names.

video adapter The printed circuit board or built-in video chips in your computer that provide an interface between your computer and the screen display.

video display page A region of adapter memory that holds a full screen image. Many display adapters support multiple display pages. By using display pages, your program can display one page on the screen (the visual page) while writing a second page (the active page). By switching between display pages, the program makes the output appear to be instantaneous.

video mode The screen's current state of operation. Widely used video modes include color graphics mode, black-and-white graphics mode, color or black-and-white text mode with 25 rows of 80 columns, and color or black-and-white text mode with 25 rows of 40 columns.

whitespace Unprinted characters such as blank spaces, tabs, or formfeeds.

wildcard expansion The process of converting DOS wildcard characters to the corresponding filenames. Microsoft C provides a routine in the object file SETARGV.OBJ that performs wildcard expansion of your command line and assigns the corresponding files to *argv.*

INDEX

Special Characters

! (logical NOT operator) 69–70

!= (not equal to operator) 66

" (double quotation marks) 19, 23–24, 40, 106–7, 122

(preprocessor directive). *See* preprocessor directives

% (percent sign)

   as modulus operator 45, 63, 72–73

   as prefix to format specifier 27, 31

& (ampersand)

   as address operator 163–64, 168, 192

   as bitwise AND operator 56, 57

   in LIB commands 530

&& (logical AND operator) 69–70

( ) (parentheses) 5, 55, 103, 126

* (asterisk)

   as indirection operator 165, 166–67, 168, 192

   as LIB copy operator 529

   as multiplication operator 44

/ / (comment symbols) 49–50, 312

*= (multiplication assignment operator) 53

+ (addition operator) 44

+ (LIB plus operator) 526

++ (increment operator) 51–53

+= (addition assignment operator) 53

, (comma operator) 76

– (minus sign/hyphen)

   as LIB minus operator 528

   as subtraction operator 44

–+ (LIB replacement operator) 529

–– (decrement operator) 51–53

–= (subtraction assignment operator) 53

. (dot operator) 286, 288

/ (forward slash)

   in character strings 148

   in comments 49–50, 312

   as division operator 44

/= (division assignment operator) 53

; (semicolon) 6, 67, 70, 75, 102–3, 529

< (less than sign)

   as input redirection operator 352–53

   as less than operator 66

<< (left shift operator) 56

<= (less than or equal to operator) 66

<> (angle brackets)

   for include files 106–7

= (equal sign)

   as assignment operator 42, 45, 51, 53–54

== (equal to operator) 66

> (greater than sign)

   as greater than operator 66

   as output redirection operator 351–52

>= (greater than or equal to operator) 66

>> (double greater than signs)

   as append redirection operator 353–54

   as right shift operator 56

[] (square brackets) 116, 136

   in multidimensional arrays 203, 204

\ (backslash) 23, 92, 104–5

^ (bitwise exclusive OR operator) 56

¦ (vertical line)

   as bitwise OR operator 56, 57

   as pipe redirection operator 354, 355

¦ ¦ (logical OR operator) 69–70

{} (left and right braces) 5

   for compound statements 5

   in multidimensional arrays 205

~ (bitwise complement operator) 56

Kris Jamsa

Kris Jamsa graduated from the United States Air Force Academy with a degree in computer science in 1983. Upon graduation he moved to Las Vegas, Nevada, where he began work as a VAX/VMS system manager for the U.S. Air Force. In 1986 Jamsa received a master's in computer science with an emphasis in operating systems, from the University of Nevada, Las Vegas. He then taught computer science at the National University in San Diego, California, for one year before leaving the Air Force in 1988 to begin writing full-time. He is the author of more than a dozen books on DOS, OS/2, Windows, hard disk management, and Pascal and C programming languages. Jamsa currently resides in Las Vegas with his wife and their two daughters.

Special Offer

Companion Disks for
Microsoft C: Secrets, Shortcuts, and Solutions

All the programs and functions presented in gray, tinted boxes throughout this book are readily available on two 360 KB disks from Kris Jamsa Software, Inc. The code matches the programs and functions exactly as they appear in the book. The cost of the disk package is minor when compared to the time you would spend typing the code and debugging your typing errors.

ORDERING INFORMATION

Domestic Orders:

To order, send $24.95 per disk set (includes shipping and handling) to the address below. For fastest delivery, please send cashier's check or money order.

All Foreign Orders:

To order, send $29.95 (USD) per disk set (includes air mail shipping) to the address below. For fastest delivery, please send an international postal money order.

(Credit card orders not accepted.)

- -

Order Today!

Please send me _____ copies of the Companion Disk set for *Microsoft C: Secrets, Shortcuts, and Solutions.*

Enclosed is my check or money order for $ _____

Name _____

Address _____

City _____ State _____ Zip _____

Please send your order with payment to:
Kris Jamsa Software, Inc.
P.O. Box 26031
Las Vegas, Nevada 89216

The manuscript for this book was prepared and submitted to Microsoft Press in electronic form. Text files were processed and formatted using Microsoft Word.

Cover design by Thomas A. Draper
Interior text design by Darcie S. Furlan
Illustrations by Becky Geisler-Johnson
Principal typography by Ruth Pettis
Color separations by Wescan Color Corporation

Text composition by Microsoft Press in Garamond with display in Helvetica Black, using the Magna composition system and the Linotronic 300 laser imagesetter.

Printed on recycled paper stock.